Judith K [illegible]

COMPLETE COURSE

Third Edition

CENTURY 21® TYPEWRITING

To Dr. D. D. Lessenberry, the original author, we give special recognition. For fifty years, his learning materials and teaching methods set the pattern and pace of typewriting instruction throughout the United States.

T. James Crawford
Chairman
Department of Administrative Systems and Business Education
Graduate School of Business
Indiana University

Lawrence W. Erickson
Assistant Dean
Graduate School of Education
University of California, Los Angeles

Lee R. Beaumont
Professor of Business, Emeritus
Indiana University of Pennsylvania

Jerry W. Robinson
Senior Editor
South-Western Publishing Co.

Arnola C. Ownby
Coordinator of Graduate Studies
Department of Business Education
Oklahoma State University

ISBN: 0-538-20500-8

Library of Congress Catalog Card Number: 80-52709

2 3 4 5 6 7 8 9 10 11 12 13 14 H 9 8 7 6 5 4 3 2

Printed in U.S.A.

T50

Published by

SOUTH-WESTERN PUBLISHING CO.

CINCINNATI   WEST CHICAGO, ILL   DALLAS   PELHAM MANOR, N.Y.   PALO ALTO, CALIF.

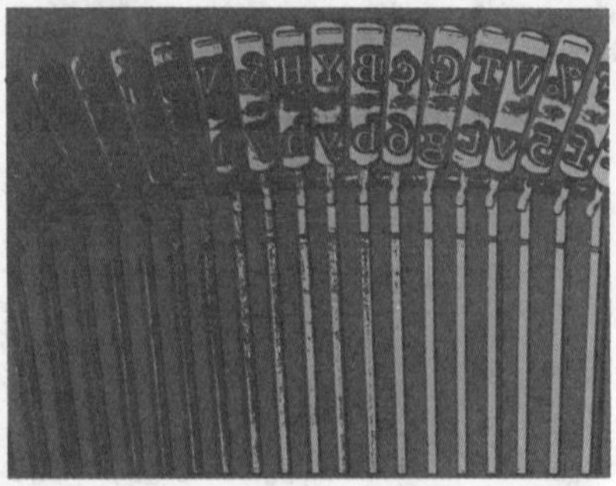

Contents

Cycle 1 Lessons 1-75
Learn to Operate the Typewriter

Cycle 2 Lessons 76-150
Build Personal/ Professional Typing Skills

Cycle 3 Lessons 151-225
Develop Typewriting Production Power

Cycle 4 Lessons 226-300
Simulated Office Typing

Preface

Two of the ways we "talk" with one another are writing and reading. This 2-way process is called *written* communication. Typewriting has become the major means of written communication in business and is becoming increasingly so in our personal and professional lives. Once the almost exclusive province of clerks and secretaries, typing skill is now put to profitable use by doctors, lawyers, engineers, and other professionals as well as by office support personnel, supervisors, managers, and executives.

The typewriter has thus become an almost universal tool of personal, professional, and business communication. Those who can use this "writing machine" with knowledge and skill have an advantage over those who have not learned to type. It is sometimes said that "typewriting is a key to communication literacy." The growing use of electronic communicating and calculating devices—including information processing equipment and microcomputers—makes keyboarding skill a virtual necessity in a growing number of careers.

The reasons students give for wanting to learn to type vary widely. The amount of time individual students are willing or able to devote to building the skill varies, also. Further, various job classifications require different levels of typing competence for successful job performance. Therefore, a program designed to accommodate these variable objectives, time limits, and competency levels must first emphasize those knowledges and skills common to all uses of the typewriter. Thereafter, in a series of expanding cycles, these basic knowledges and skills should be improved, broadened, and applied to achieve the competencies required at the various levels of the job hierarchy in professional and business occupations.

Century 21 Typewriting, Complete Course, Third Edition, is organized as 4 progressively expanded cycles to fulfill these variable learning/training needs.

Cycle 1
Learn to operate the typewriter

Cycle 1 (Lessons 1-75) emphasizes the knowledges and skills common to all uses of the typewriter. It is organized as three 25-lesson phases, each with specific purposes.

Phase 1 (Lessons 1-25) focuses on alphabetic keyboard learning, technique development, and keyboarding fluency and speed. Scientifically designed materials and classroom-tested procedures are used to assure keyboard mastery and maximize skill.

Phase 2 (Lessons 26-50) presents the top-row keys and develops skill on straight copy and copy containing figures and frequently used symbols. In addition, it presents basic/personal applications with emphasis on copy layout and the procedures required to arrange and type centered announcements, personal notes, short unfootnoted reports, and personal-business letters.

Phase 3 (Lessons 51-75), in addition to improving basic skills, emphasizes layout features and procedures required in arranging/typing business letters in modified block style, unbound reports with as well as without footnotes, and short tables of 2 and 3 columns with main and secondary headings.

Thus, a student who successfully completes Cycle 1 can use the typewriter as a tool of personal communication, can continue the typing program on a solid foundation, and can use the typewriter to a limited extent in part-time work.

Cycle 2
Personal/professional typing

Cycle 2 (Lessons 76-150) serves 4 main functions: (1) recalls/extends the basic and applied knowledges and skills acquired in Cycle 1; (2) recalls/improves related communication skills; (3) develops production skill on letters, tables, and reports; (4) adapts basic/production knowledge and skill to special office applications in an "on-the-job" or simulated office work setting.

Basic keyboarding skills on straight copy, script, rough draft, and statistical copy are assessed at the beginning of the cycle. Thereafter, these skills are improved through a series of progressive difficulty activities strategically placed in each of the three 25-lesson phases.

After early recall of the basic typing operations (centering, letters, tables, and reports), separate units develop production skill on each one individually. A 4-step production skill-building plan is used to develop production competency to job-entry levels.

Related English (language arts) knowledge and skill are recalled and improved by special at-the-typewriter activities that begin in Lesson 81. These activities are arranged in a learn/apply/recall sequence to assure learning and minimize forgetting.

The last 25 lessons recycle the student through the basic typing operations: first, through a series of skill-extension activities; next, by a set of integrated job assignments in a simulated work-experience setting. In the last unit, all major skills and applications are measured.

Students are thus led in graded steps from skill-building activities to simulated office activities that require them to think, to make decisions, and to adapt what they have learned to new situations.

Cycle 3
Develop typewriting production power

Cycle 3 (Lessons 151-225) begins the second-year program which is devoted specifically to the development of vocational typewriting competencies.

Because students usually enter the advanced typing program after a substantial period of little or no practice, the first 25-lesson phase checks and improves basic keyboarding skill; assesses, recalls, and improves production knowledge and skill on letters, reports, and tables; and continues the language arts development begun during the first-year program.

The next 25 lessons develop production power on correspondence typed on special-size stationery, letters with special features, and communications of special kinds (memos, message/reply forms, news releases, and telegraphic messages). All these require students to adapt previously acquired knowledge and skill to job tasks that have new or modified layout, placement, and spacing features.

The third 25-lesson phase builds production power on more complex tables and on business forms. Then the student "goes to work" in an information processing center in which a variety of jobs are typed under realistic work conditions. Most jobs are presented in script or rough-draft form. The student is held responsible for the acceptability of all work completed.

Cycle 4
Simulated office typing

Cycle 4 (Lessons 226-300) has a twofold purpose: (1) to provide a final drive toward basic skill/production proficiency and (2) to integrate all knowledge and skills in simulated office typing situations.

The first 25-lesson phase achieves the first goal through high-intensity practice to improve basic skills and by production skill-building activities under time-pressure conditions.

The next 25-lesson phase places the student in a series of specialized office simulations that mirror the work in administrative, finance, sales/purchasing, and executive offices. The final unit involves employment communications and testing.

The last 25 lessons provide work experience in simulated legal, medical, information processing, reprographics, and government offices.

Students often work from script and rough-draft copy; assimilate data from various sources to complete jobs; verify numerical data; and edit, proofread, and correct all typed documents.

The final unit measures and assesses competency levels of both basic and production skills.

TJC ■ LWE ■ LRB ■ JWR ■ ACO

Alphabetic sentences [1]

Figure sentences [2]

Figure/Symbol sentences [3]

Fluency (speed) sentences [4]

[1] An alphabetic sentence appears in every Conditioning practice, beginning on page 30.

[2] A figure sentence appears in most of the Conditioning practices, beginning on page 45.

[3] A figure/symbol sentence appears in many of the Conditioning practices, beginning on page 58.

[4] Beginning on page 27, an easy sentence, designed for speed building or fluency practice, appears in every Conditioning practice in the book.

Concentration drills

Guided writing copy

Metric activities

Preapplication manipulative activities

Problems in rough draft and script

Related communication activities

Skill-transfer timed writings

Straight-copy timed writings

Technique drills

Keystroking:

Machine parts:

Response patterns:

Index

1 Changing a typewriter ribbon

The technique for changing a typewriter ribbon is not the same for all machines. In no case, however, is it a difficult operation; but the following suggestions may be helpful.

If you are working with a fabric ribbon, wind it onto one spool (usually the one containing the less ribbon) before beginning the procedure.

Observe carefully the winding path of the ribbon in the machine before you remove it. Make pencil notes if necessary. Reverse the procedure to install the new ribbon.

Consult the machine manufacturer's manual for their recommendations for changing ribbons.

In case of unusual difficulty, consult with the manufacturer's representative or the retailer from whom the typewriter was purchased.

2 Correcting errors

Rubber eraser

Move the carriage or carrier to the right or left to prevent bits of rubber from damaging the type mechanism.

To avoid disturbing the alignment of the typed copy, turn the cylinder forward if the erasure is to be made on the upper ⅔ of the paper; backward, on the lower ⅓ of the paper.

To erase on the original sheet, lift the paper bail out of the way, place a 5″ x 3″ card or other heavy paper in front of the first carbon sheet. Use an eraser shield to protect the typing that is not to be erased. Use a special typing eraser. Brush eraser bits away from the type mechanism.

If more than one copy is involved, move the protective card in front of the second sheet of carbon paper. Erase errors on carbon copies with a soft (pencil) eraser; then, if necessary, use the hard typing eraser used to erase original copies.

When the error has been erased on all copies, remove the protective card, position the carriage or carrier to the proper point, and type the necessary correction.

Correction paper/lift-off film

Backspace to the error. Place the correction paper or film in front of the error, coated side toward the paper.

Special correction paper is available for use in correcting carbon copies. Turn the cylinder forward if the correction is to be made on the upper ⅔ of the paper; backward, on the lower ⅓ of the paper. Place a piece of the special correction paper between the carbon and the copy, coated side toward the copy. Then place the correction paper or film in front of the error on the original.

Retype the error. The substance on the correction paper or film will cover or remove the error.

Correction fluid

Be sure the color of the fluid matches the color of the paper.

Turn the paper forward or backward to ease the correction procedure.

Brush the fluid on sparingly. Cover only the error—and it lightly—on the original and all carbon copies.

Wait a few seconds for the fluid to dry. Return to typing position and type the correction.

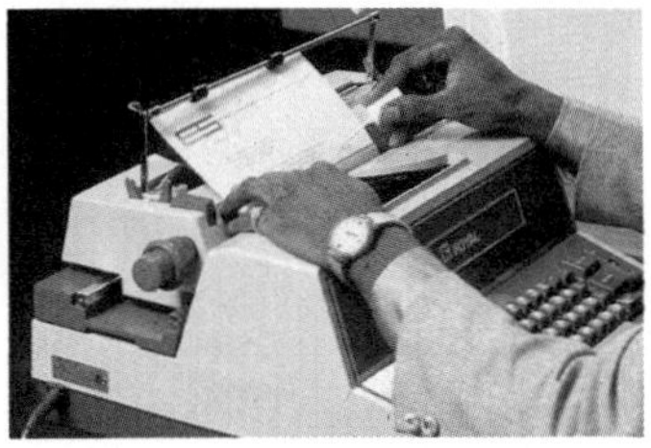

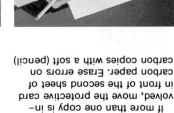

3 Squeezing/spreading of letters

In correcting errors, it is often possible to "squeeze" omitted letters into half spaces or to "spread" letters to fill out spaces.

Error
an omitte letter

an omitted letter
Correction

1 An omitted letter at the beginning or end of a word

Corrective steps

a Move carriage to the letter *e*.

b Depress and hold down the space bar; strike the letter *d*.

Note: On an electric typewriter, it may be necessary to hold the carriage by hand at the half-space point, or to use the half-space mechanism.

Error
a leter within

a letter within
Correction

2 An omitted letter within a word

Corrective steps

a Erase the incorrect word.

b Position the carriage at the space after the letter *a*.

c Press down and hold the space bar; strike the letter *l*.

d Release the space bar, then press it down again and hold it; strike the next letter.

e Repeat the process for any additional letters.

Note: On single-element and some other electrics, use the half-space mechanism.

Error
a lettter within

a letter within
Correction

3 Addition of a letter within a word

Corrective steps

a Erase the incorrect word.

b Position the carriage as if you were going to type the letter *l* in its regular position following the space.

c Press down and hold the space bar; strike the letter *l*.

d Release the space bar; then repeat the process for each remaining letter.

Note: On single-element and some other electrics, use the half-space mechanism.

1 Desk-top assembly method

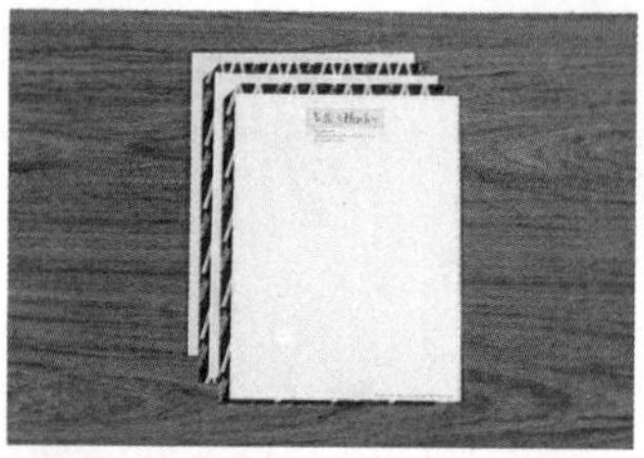

1 Assemble letterhead, carbon sheets (uncarboned side up), and second sheets as illustrated above. *Use one carbon and one second sheet for each copy desired.*

2 Grasp the carbon pack at the sides, turn it so that the *letterhead faces away from you, the carbon side of the carbon paper is toward you, and the top edge of the pack is face down.* Tap the sheets gently on the desk to straighten.

3 Hold the sheets firmly to prevent slipping; insert pack into type-writer. Hold pack with one hand; turn platen with the other.

Tips for wrinkle-free assembly

Start pack into typewriter with paper-release lever forward; then reset the paper-release lever and turn pack into the machine.

2 Inserting the pack with a trough

To keep the carbon pack straight when feeding it into the typewriter, place the pack in the fold of a plain sheet of paper (paper trough) or under the flap of an envelope. Remove the trough or envelope when the pack is in place.

3 Removing carbon sheets

Hold the left edge of the letterhead and second sheets; remove all carbons at one time with the right hand.

4 Machine assembly method

1 Assemble paper for insertion (original on top; second sheets beneath). Turn the "pack" so *original faces away from you* and *the top edge faces down.*

2 Insert sheets until the tops are gripped by the feed rolls; then pull the bottom of all sheets except the last over the top (front) of the typewriter.

3 Place carbon paper between sheets, *carboned side toward you.* Flip each sheet back (away from you) as you add each carbon sheet.

4 Roll pack into typing position.

5 Slotted drawer assembly method

1 With sheets correctly arranged in slotted drawer, pick up a letterhead with left hand, a sheet of carbon paper with right hand; pull sheets slightly forward; grasp both sheets with left hand as right hand reaches and pulls second sheet into position.

2 Pull sheets from slots. Straighten pack by tapping gently on desk as the sides of the sheets are held loosely by both hands.

3 Add extra sheets (a second sheet and a carbon) for any additional copies that may be needed.

4 Insert into typewriter as with desk-top assembly method.

Front feeding small cards and labels

Prepare

1. Insert and align paper.

2. Clear margin stops by moving them to extreme ends of the scale.

3. Clear all tab stops.

4. Move carriage (carrier) to center of paper.

5. Decide the number of spaces to be left between columns (for intercolumns)—preferably an even number (4, 6, 8, 10, etc.).

1 Plan vertical placement

Follow either of the vertical centering methods explained on page ix.

Spacing headings. Double–space (count 1 blank line space) between main and secondary headings, when both are used. Triple–space (count 2 blank line spaces) between the last table heading (either main or secondary) and the first horizontal line of column items or column headings. Double–space between column headings (when used) and the first line of the columns.

2 Plan horizontal placement

Backspace from center of paper 1 space for each 2 letters, figures, symbols, and spaces in *longest item* of each column and for each 2 spaces to be left between columns. Set left margin stop at this point. If an extra space occurs at the end of the longest item when backspacing, carry it forward to the next column. Ignore an extra space at the end of the last column. (See illustration below.)

An easy alternate method is to backspace for the longest item in each column first, *then* for the spaces to the left between columns.

Note. If a column heading is longer than the longest item in the column, it may be treated as the longest item in determining placement. The longest column item must then be centered under the heading, and the tab stop set accordingly.

Set tab stops. From the left margin stop, space forward 1 space for each letter, figure, symbol, and space in the longest item in the first column and for each space to be left in the first intercolumn. Set a tab stop at this point for the second column. Follow this procedure for each additional column to be typed.

3 To center column headings

Backspace-from-column-center method

From point at which column begins (tab or margin stop), space forward (→) once for each 2 letters, figures, or spaces in the longest item in the column. This leads to the column center point; from it, backspace (←) once for each 2 spaces in column heading. Ignore an odd or leftover space. Type the heading at this point; it will be centered over the column.

Mathematical methods

1. To the number on the cylinder (platen) or line–of–writing scale immediately under the first letter, figure, or symbol of the longest item of the column, add the number shown under the space following the last stroke of the item. Divide this sum by 2; the result will be the center point of the column. From this point on the scale, backspace (1 for 2) to center the column heading.

2. From the number of spaces in the longest item, subtract the number of spaces in the heading. Divide this number by 2; ignore fractions. Space forward this number from the tab or margin stop and type the heading.

4 To type horizontal lines

Depress shift lock; strike underline key.

5 To draw vertical lines

Operate the automatic line finder. Place a pencil or pen point through the cardholder (or the type bar guide above the ribbon or carrier). Roll the paper up until you have a line of the desired length. Remove the pencil or pen and reset the line finder.

MAIN HEADING

Secondary Heading

These	Are	Column	Heads
xxxxxx	*longest*	xxxx	xxxxx
xxxx	*item*	*longest*	xxx
xxxxx	xxxxx	*item*	*longest*
longest	xxxxxx	xxxxx	*item*
item	xxxx	xxx	xxx

lo|ng|es|t1|23|41|on|ge|st|12|34|lo|ng|es|t1|23|41|on|ge|st

- Capitalize
- Close up
- Delete
- Insert
- Insert comma
- Insert space
- Insert apostrophe
- Insert quotation marks
- Move right
- Move left
- Move down; lower
- Move up; raise
- Set in lowercase
- Paragraph
- No new paragraph
- Set flush; align type
- Spell out
- Let it stand; ignore correction
- Transpose
- Underline or Italics

Proofreader's marks

Sometimes typed or printed copy may be corrected with proofreader's marks. The typist must be able to interpret correctly these marks in retyping the corrected copy or *rough draft* as it may be called. The most commonly used proofreader's marks are shown above.

1 Horizontal centering

1 Move margin stops to extreme ends of scale.

2 Clear tab stops; then set a tab stop at center of paper.

3 Tabulate to center of paper.

4 From center, backspace *once* for each 2 letters, spaces, figures, or punctuation marks in the line.

5 Do not backspace for an odd or leftover stroke at the end of the line.

6 Begin to type where backspacing ends.

Formula for finding horizontal center of paper

	Example
Scale reading at left edge of paper	0
+Scale reading at right edge of paper	102
Total ÷ 2 = Center Point	102 ÷ 2 = 51

2 Spread headings

1 Backspace from center once for each letter, character, and space *except the last letter or character* in the heading. Begin to type where the backspacing ends.

2 In typing a spread heading, space once after each letter or character and 3 times between words.

3 Vertical centering

Backspace-from-center method
Basic rule

From vertical center of paper, roll platen (cylinder) back once for each 2 lines, 2 blank line spaces, or line and blank line space. Ignore odd or leftover line.

Steps to follow:

1 To move paper to vertical center, start spacing down from top edge of paper.

a half sheet
down 6 TS (triple spaces)
− 1 SS (Line 17)

b full sheet
down 11 TS
+ 1 SS (Line 34)

2 From vertical center

a half sheet, SS or DS: follow basic rule, back 1 for 2.

b full sheet, SS or DS: follow basic rule, back 1 for 2; then back 2 SS for *reading position*.

Mathematical method

1 Count lines and blank line spaces needed to type problem.

2 Subtract *lines to be used* from *lines available* (66 for full sheet and 33 for half sheet).

3 Divide by 2 to get top and bottom margins. If fraction results, disregard it. Space down from top edge of paper *1 more than number of lines to be left in top margin.*

For *reading position*, which is above exact vertical center, subtract 2 from exact top margin.

Formula for vertical mathematical placement

$$\frac{\text{Lines available} - \text{lines used}}{2} = \text{top margin}$$

5 Leftbound, contents page

1½″ pica; 2″ elite

CONTENTS

DS

Section 1: Employment Conditions

DS

DS

Page

I.	COMPENSATION	1
	A. Payday Schedule	1
	B. Overtime Hours	2
	C. Overtime Rate of Pay	2
	D. Separation Pay	3
II.	PROMOTIONS	4
III.	BREAKS	4
IV.	EXIGENCIES	5
	A. Tardiness	5
	B. Absences	5
	C. Leaving the Premises	6
V.	HIRING POLICIES	6
	A. Probationary Period	6
	B. Temporary Help	6
	C. Relatives	6
	D. Retired Workers	7

TS

Section 2: Employee Time-Off Benefits

DS

I.	MILITARY SERVICE	8
II.	MATERNITY LEAVE	8
III.	JURY DUTY	8
IV.	ILLNESS	9
V.	FUNERALS	9

1½″ 1″

6 Leftbound, bibliography

1½″ pica; 2″ elite

REFERENCES

TS

Indent 5

American Psychological Association. Publication Manual. 2d ed. Washington, D.C.: American Psychological Association, 1974.

Bates, Jefferson D. Writing with Precision. Washington, D.C.: Acropolis Books, Ltd., 1978.

Committee on Writing Standards, The National Council of Teachers of English. "Standards for Basic Skills Writing Programs." College English, October 1979, pp. 220-222.

Cross, Donna W. Word Abuse. New York: Coward, McCann & Geoghegan, Inc., 1979.

Graves, Robert, and Alan Hodge. The Reader Over Your Shoulder. New York: Random House, 1979.

Lanham, Richard. UCLA Writing Project Lecture, 1979.

Stone, Marvin. "Due Dismay About Our Language." U.S. News & World Report, April 23, 1979, p. 102.

Strunk, Jr., William, and E. B. White. The Elements of Style. 3d ed. New York: Macmillan Publishing Co., Inc., 1979.

Tibbetts, Arn, and Charlene Tibbetts. What's Happening to American English. New York: Charles Scribner's Sons, 1978.

"'80s-Babble: Untidy Treasure." Time, January 28, 1980, p. 90.

Walshe, R. D. "What's Basic to Teaching English?" The English Journal, December 1979, pp. 51-56.

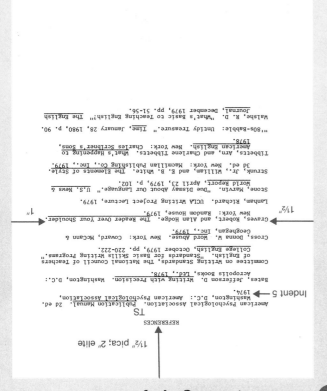

1½″ 1″

7 Topbound, page 1

2″ pica; 2½″ elite

Section 1

DS

EMPLOYMENT CONDITIONS

TS

The guidelines provided in this manual do not mean that policies are fixed rules. Policies are simply major guides to help us all follow the same practices under similar circumstances. Individual decisions will have to be made, and many of these are not covered by policies. If we all follow standard practices, however, there will be fewer misunderstandings; and our customers and employees will be happier.

1″ 1″

Side head: Compensation

¶ head: Payday schedule. Employees who are not exempt from the overtime provisions of the Fair Labor Standards Act (clerical, shipping, and assembly room personnel) are paid by check every Friday for all time worked for the week ending the previous Saturday.

Employees who are exempt from the overtime provisions of the Fair Labor Standards Act (supervisors, managers, and executives) are paid by check semimonthly on the 15th and the last day of the month unless these days fall on a weekend, in which case payment is made on the preceding Friday, or if Friday is a holiday, on the last workday of the pay period.

Compensation for clerical employees is calculated on a monthly basis, and each week's pay is approximately 4.333 divided into the monthly rate. Exempt employees receive half the monthly rate each

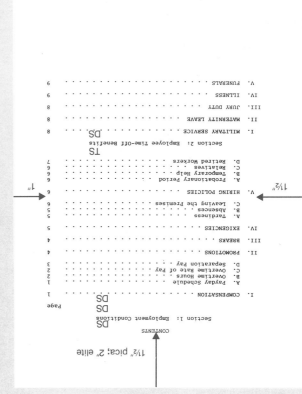

1″ (approx.)

1

8 Interoffice memorandum

Contemporary Office Associates INTEROFFICE COMMUNICATION

TO: All Typists

FROM: Richard Buchanan

DATE: April 26, 19--

SUBJECT: Care of Typewriters

TS

Because of our increasing typewriter repair costs, we are requesting that you follow these care-of-typewriter steps:

1″ 1″

1. End of each day. At the end of each day, please follow these procedures:
   a. Use a stiff brush to clean the typeface. If you use an element-type machine, remove the element to clean it.
   b. Brush away any eraser crumbs, etc., that have fallen into the typebar segment. (May I remind typists who use typebar machines to move the carriage to the extreme right or left before erasing an error.)
   c. Dust your desk beneath your machine with a dustcloth.
   d. Pull the paper release lever forward and leave it in this position overnight.
   e. Finally, center the carriage (typebar machine) and cover the typewriter.
2. End of each week. At the end of each week, do the following:
   a. With a soft, lintfree cloth with a corner moistened slightly with typewriter oil, wipe the carriage rails of the typebar machine; then wipe them again with the unmoistened portion of the cloth.
   b. Clean the platen with another soft, lintfree cloth moistened with alcohol.
3. Know your operator's manual. Review, as needed, the care and maintenance steps given in the operating instructions manual for your typewriter.

1½″ pica; 2″ elite

Main head

MANUSCRIPT OR REPORT FORM

TS

The guides presented here represent one acceptable form of typing manuscripts or reports.

TS

Side head

Spacing and Margins

Manuscripts or reports may be either single- or double-spaced. The form that is followed is dependent upon the type of report that is prepared. School reports, formal reports, and manuscripts to be submitted for publication should be typed in double-spaced form. Reports that are prepared for use in the business office often are typed in single-spaced form.

1″ 1″

Maintain an approximate 1-inch bottom margin. Leave 1-inch top and side margins on all pages with these exceptions:

1. Leave a 1 1/2-inch (pica) or 2-inch (elite) top margin on the first page of an unbound or leftbound manuscript; a 2- or 2 1/2-inch top margin on the first page of a topbound manuscript.
2. Leave a 1 1/2-inch top margin on the second and succeeding pages of a topbound manuscript.
3. Leave a 1 1/2-inch left margin on all pages of a leftbound manuscript.

Indent numbered items 5 spaces from left and right margins

The first line of a paragraph may be indented either 5, 7, or 10 spaces. Quoted material of 4 lines or more is single-spaced and indented 5 spaces from the left and right margins. It is preceded and followed by 1 blank line space.

Headings and Subheadings

¶ head

Main heading. A main heading is centered over the line of writing in all capitals and is followed by 2 blank line spaces.

1″ (approx.)

1

½″

1 Unbound, page 1

4th line space

2

Line 7

Side headings. Side headings are typed even with the left margin and underlined; main words are started with a capital letter. These headings are preceded by 2 blank line spaces and followed by 1 blank line space. Side headings serve as guideposts to the reader of a report.

Paragraph headings. You have just typed a paragraph heading. It is indented and underlined. Usually, only the first word is capitalized. Paragraph headings, also, are an aid to the reader.

TS

Page Numbers

The first page may or may not be numbered. The number, if used, is centered and typed a half inch from the bottom edge. As a general rule, other page numbers are typed on the fourth line in the upper right corner approximately even with the right margin; however, if the manuscript or report is to be bound at the top, the page numbers are typed in first-page position (centered and typed a half inch from the bottom edge).

1″ 1″

Other General Guides

Avoid ending a page with 1 line of a new paragraph or carrying 1 line of a paragraph to a new page. This general rule, however, is no longer strictly observed, even in formal writing.

The general word division rules govern the division of words at the ends of lines. Avoid dividing words at the ends of more than 2 consecutive lines or at the end of a page.

2 Unbound, page 2

1½″ pica; 2″ elite

Main head

THE TRADITIONAL VS. THE "SIMPLIFIED" KEYBOARD

TS

The first practical American typewriter was patented in 1868 by Sholes, Glidden, and Soule. It was produced and sold, after many improvements, by Remington & Sons in 1874. The location of the keys on the Remington typewriter soon became the standard arrangement for keyboards for nearly all other makes. This keyboard, with minor changes and additions, is almost the same as that of the millions of typewriters used in offices, schools, and homes even today.[1]

1½″ 1″

Keyboard "reform"--efforts to make the keyboard more efficient and easier to operate--has a long history. Hammond, for example, in 1881 marketed a typewriter with an "improved" keyboard. Hoke in 1924 was issued a patent for a keyboard arranged according to frequency of letter use and facility of the various fingers. In 1932, Dvorak and Dealey received a patent for still another keyboard arrangement called the "Simplified" keyboard (quotation marks theirs).[2] Not one of these attempts to improve the arrangement of the letter keys received more than passing interest.

From time to time, a new spark of interest in simplifying the traditional keyboard is ignited, flames for awhile, then dies. This may be true today regarding the Dvorak-Dealey

SS

DS

[1]Bruce Bliven, Jr., The Wonderful Writing Machine (New York: Random House, 1954), p. 114.

DS

[2]Jerry W. Robinson, "An Idea Whose Time Has Come...Again?" Century 21 Reporter (Spring 1975), p. 2.

1″ (approx.)

1

½″

3 Leftbound, page 1

4th line space

2

Line 7

keyboard. It is generally agreed that the Hoke and the Dvorak keyboards are more scientific in design than is the "Universal" keyboard and should be more efficient to operate. Just how much more efficient either is, however, remains a moot question. Many claims are made, but there is little proof that is based on valid, reliable research.

In 1956, Strong reported on the basis of his data that to retrain a typist skilled on the traditional keyboard to use a "Simplified" keyboard with equal facility required about one hundred hours! Further, he reported that "traditional" typists outgained "simplified" typists during a period of further training to improve skill. He concluded that "A recommendation for the adoption of the Simplified Keyboard for use by the Federal Government cannot be justified based on the findings of this experiment."[3]

1½″ 1″

It is unfortunate that Dvorak and later proponents of his keyboard did not provide dependable comparative data from which viable conclusions can be drawn. Until such data are available--and no carefully controlled experiments appear to be under way to provide them--the currently rekindled interest in keyboard "reform" is likely to remain in the heads of a limited group of Dvorak devotees.[4]

DS

[3]Earl P. Strong, A Comparative Experiment in Simplified Keyboard Retraining (Washington: General Services Administration, 1956), p. 114.

DS

[4]Shirley Boes Neill, "Dvorak vs. Querty: Will Tradition Win Again?" Phi Delta Kappan (June 1980), pp. 671-73.

1″ (approx.)

4 Leftbound, page 2

1 Addressing procedure

Envelope address

Set a tab stop (or margin stop if a number of envelopes are to be addressed) 10 spaces left of center for a small envelope or 5 spaces for a large envelope. Start the address here on Line 12 from the top edge of a small envelope and on Line 14 of a large one.

Style

Type the address in *block style*, single–spaced. Type the city name, state name or abbreviation, and ZIP Code on the last address line. The ZIP Code is typed 2 spaces after the state name abbreviation.

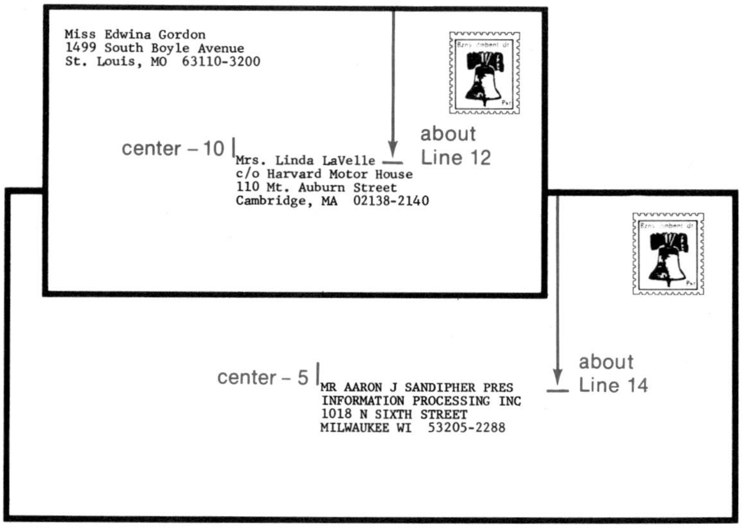

Addressee notations

Type addressee notations, such as *Hold for Arrival, Please Forward, Personal,* etc., a triple space below the return address and about 3 spaces from the left edge of the envelope. Type these notations in all capitals.

If an *attention line* is used, type it immediately below the company name in the address line.

Mailing notations

Type mailing notations, such as SPECIAL DELIVERY and REGISTERED, below the stamp and at least 3 line spaces above the envelope address. Type these notations in all capital letters.

2 Folding and inserting procedure

Small envelopes (No. 6¾, 6¼)

Step 1 With letter face up, fold bottom up to ½ inch from top.

Step 2 Fold right third to left.

Step 3 Fold left third to ½ inch from last crease.

Step 4 Insert last creased edge first.

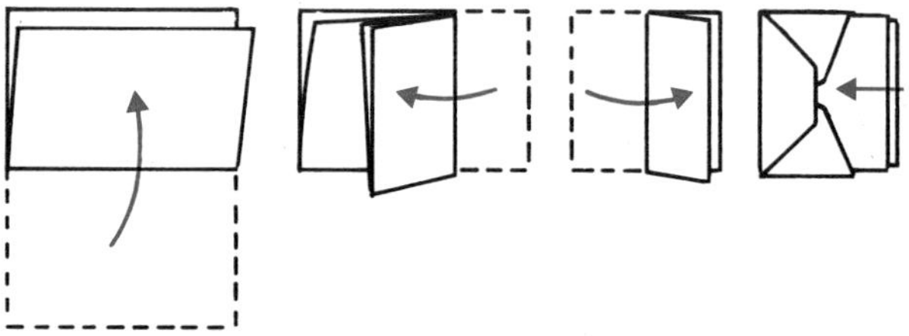

Large envelopes (No. 10, 9, 7¾)

Step 1 With letter face up, fold slightly less than ⅓ of sheet up toward top.

Step 2 Fold down top of sheet to within ½ inch of bottom fold.

Step 3 Insert letter into envelope with last crease toward bottom of envelope.

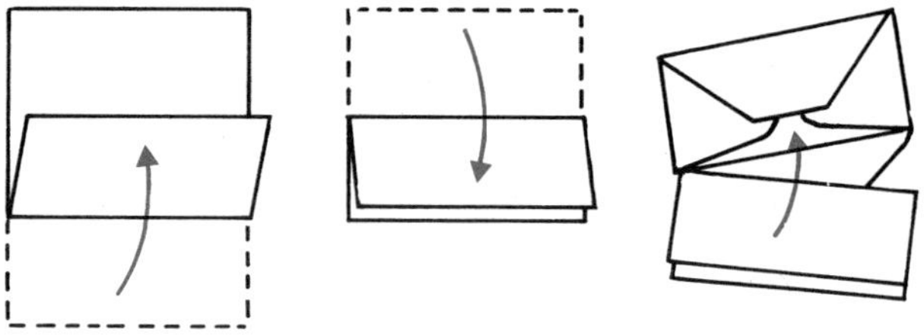

Window envelopes (letter)

Step 1 With sheet face down, top toward you, fold upper third down.

Step 2 Fold lower third up so address is showing.

Step 3 Insert sheet into envelope with last crease at bottom.

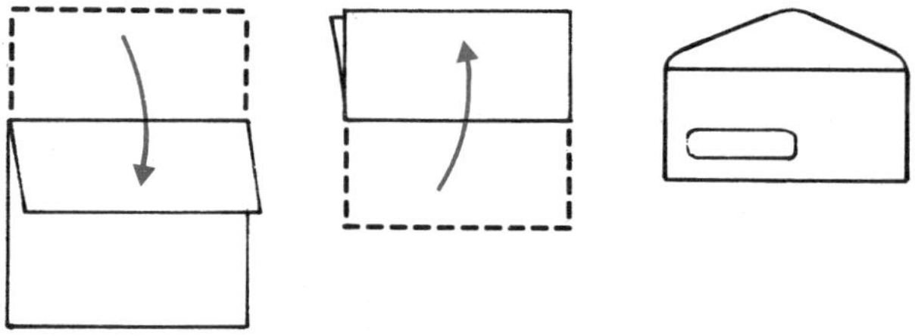

Window envelopes (invoices and other forms)

Step 1 Place sheet face down, top toward you.

Step 2 Fold back top so address shows.

Step 3 Insert into envelope with crease at bottom.

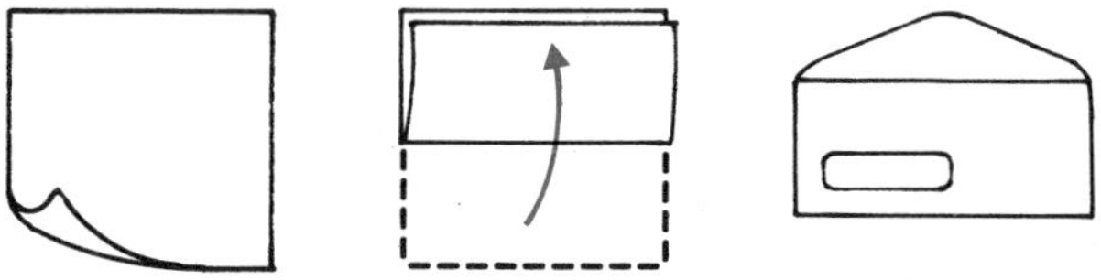

oei

OFFICE EFFICIENCY, INC.
EXPERTS IN OFFICE RESEARCH
1300 VAN NESS AVENUE, SUITE 1101 • SAN FRANCISCO, CA 94109-4305
TEL (415) 823-4500

January 15, 19--

Tri-State Corporation
Attention Office Manager
501 Liberty Avenue
Pittsburgh, PA 15222-3140

Ladies and Gentlemen

Today many business firms use the block style letter for their correspondence. This letter is an example of that style. Note that all lines start at the left margin. The advantage of this style is that the mechanical process of indenting the dateline, paragraphs, and closing lines is eliminated. This practice saves valuable typing time as well as space.

Open punctuation is used in this letter. Punctuation is omitted after the salutation and the complimentary close. Elimination of these punctuation marks helps to increase letter production rates. Another recommended timesaving feature is to type only the typist's initials for reference when the author's or originator's name is typed in the closing lines.

As you see, the block style gives good placement appearance. Because many extra typing strokes and motions are eliminated, the use of this style does help to increase letter production rates. I recommend the use of block style for letters prepared in the business office.

Sincerely yours

Dolores Verdugo

Miss Dolores Verdugo
Communications Consultant

tjc

Our new <u>Communications Guide</u> will be sent to you as soon as it comes from the press.

1 Block, open

oei

OFFICE EFFICIENCY, INC.
EXPERTS IN OFFICE RESEARCH
1300 VAN NESS AVENUE, SUITE 1101 • SAN FRANCISCO, CA 94109-4305
TEL (415) 823-4500

January 20, 19--

Mr. Joshua P. Abramson
President, Apex Corporation
One Independent Drive
Jacksonville, FL 32202-5136

Dear Mr. Abramson

MODIFIED BLOCK STYLE LETTER

This letter is an example of the modified block style, one of the most popular personal and business letter styles in use today. As you see, it differs from the block style in that the dateline and the closing lines (the complimentary close and the typed name and title) are blocked at horizontal center. Although open punctuation is used in this letter, mixed punctuation is often used with modified block style: a colon after the salutation and a comma after the complimentary close.

When modified block style is used, production efficiency dictates that the dateline, the complimentary close, and the typed name and title be started at the same horizontal point. Actual practice in the business office varies widely, however. For example, the dateline may be centered, typed to end at the right margin, or placed in relation to some feature of the letterhead. Similarly, the closing lines may be started five spaces left of center or may be typed to end approximately at the right margin.

Although the modified block style gives attractive placement, its popular appeal is difficult to understand because, as compared with the block style, additional typing motions are involved in the placement of the various parts. The reason may be that the user has not seriously considered the effect of the letter style used on letter production efficiency.

Cordially yours

Elsa Willis

Mrs. Elsa Willis, Director

lwe

cc Ms. Luella Lutmer

2 Modified block, open

oei

OFFICE EFFICIENCY, INC.
EXPERTS IN OFFICE RESEARCH
1300 VAN NESS AVENUE, SUITE 1101 • SAN FRANCISCO, CA 94109-4305
TEL (415) 823-4500

February 18, 19--

CERTIFIED MAIL

Mrs. Cynthia Staun, Manager
Trans-America Industries
1011 San Jacinto Boulevard
Austin, TX 78701-2288

Dear Mrs. Staun:

MODIFIED BLOCK STYLE/INDENTED PARAGRAPHS

Thanks for your inquiry about letter styles. This letter is arranged in modified block style with 5-space paragraph indentions. Business letters are usually typed on 8 1/2- by 11-inch letterhead stationery which has the name of the company sending the letter and other identifying information printed at the top of the sheet.

The position of the dateline is varied according to the length of the letter. More space is left above the dateline of short letters than of long letters. The address is typed on the fourth line (3 blank lines) below the date. Some business offices use standard margins (a set line length) for all letters; others adjust the margins according to the length of the letter.

Other questions about letter placement are covered in the letter style booklet which is enclosed with this letter. Don't hesitate to write to us if there is any other information you need. Good luck in your efforts to improve letter production rates in your office.

Sincerely,

Kermit L. Johnson

Kermit L. Johnson
Communications Consultant

jwr

Enclosure

pc Mr. Evan T. Hollis

3 Modified block, indented ¶s, mixed

oei

OFFICE EFFICIENCY, INC.
EXPERTS IN OFFICE RESEARCH
1300 VAN NESS AVENUE, SUITE 1101 • SAN FRANCISCO, CA 94109-4305
TEL (415) 823-4500

March 12, 19--

Word Processing Supervisor
The Diamond Corporation
909 Broadway Plaza
Tacoma, WA 98402-1485

AMS SIMPLIFIED LETTER STYLE

The unique Simplified letter style for business correspondence is sensible, streamlined, and effective. It is a simplified "block style" with all lines beginning at the left margin. Some of its other features are listed below.

1. The address is typed 3 or more lines below the date.

2. The salutation and the complimentary close are omitted.

3. A subject heading in all capitals is typed a triple space below the address.

4. Unnumbered listed items are indented 5 spaces, but numbered items are typed flush with the left margin.

5. The author's name and title are typed in all capitals 4 line spaces (3 blank lines) below the body of the letter.

6. Reference initials consist of the typist's initials only.

7. Copy notations are typed a double space below the reference line.

Because of the timesaving features of this AMS Simplified letter style, its use will reduce your letter-writing costs and give your letters a distinctive "eye appeal." Try it. You will like it.

Kevin Cushing

KEVIN CUSHING, ADMINISTRATIVE ASSISTANT

lrb

Copy to Miss Amanda Jefferson

4 AMS Simplified

Word-division guides

1 Divide words between syllables only; therefore, do not divide one-syllable words. **Note:** When in doubt, consult a dictionary or a word division manual.

through-out pref-er-ence em-ploy-ees
reached toward thought

2 Do not divide words of five or fewer letters even if they have two or more syllables.

into also about union radio ideas

3 Do not separate a one-letter syllable at the beginning of a word or a one- or two-letter syllable at the end of a word.

across enough steady highly ended

4 You may usually divide a word between double consonants; but, when adding a syllable to a word that ends in double letters, divide after the double letters of the root word.

writ-ten sum-mer expres-sion excel-lence
will-ing win-ner process-ing fulfill-ment

5 When the final consonant is doubled in adding a suffix, divide between the double letters.

run-ning begin-ning fit-ting submit-ted

6 Divide after a one-letter syllable within a word; but when two single-letter syllables occur together, divide between them.

sepa-rate regu-late gradu-ation evalu-ation

7 When the single-letter syllable *a*, *i*, or *u* is followed by the ending *ly*, *ble*, *bly*, *cle*, or *cal*, divide before the single-letter syllable.

stead-ily siz-able vis-ible mir-acle
cler-ical but musi-cal practi-cal

8 Divide only between the two words that make up a hyphenated word.

self-contained well-developed

9 Do not divide a contraction or a single group of figures; try to avoid dividing proper names and dates.

doesn't $350,000 Policy F238975

Letter-placement points

Paper-guide placement

Check the placement of the paper guide for accurate horizontal centering of the letter.

Margins and date placement

Use the following guide:

5-Stroke Words in Letter Body	Side Margins	Date-line
Up to 125	2"	19
126–225	1½"	16*
Over 225	1"	13

* Dateline is moved up 2 line spaces for each additional 25 words.

Horizontal placement of date varies according to the letter style.

Address

The address is typed on the fourth line (3 blank line spaces) below the date. A personal title, such as Mr., Mrs., Miss, or Ms., should precede the name of an individual. An official title, when used, may be typed on the first or the second line of the address, whichever gives better balance.

Two-page letters

If a letter is too long for one page, at least 2 lines of the body of the letter should be carried to the second page. The second page of a letter, or any additional pages, requires a proper heading. Either the block or the horizontal form may be used for the heading; each is followed by a triple space.

Second-page headings (begin on line 7)

Block form

```
Mr. J. W. Smith
Page 2
June 5, 19--
```

Horizontal form

```
Mr. J. W. Smith        2        June 5, 19--
```

Attention line

An attention line, when used, is typed on the second line of the letter address.

Subject line

A subject line is typed on the second line (a double space) below the salutation. It may be either centered or typed at the left margin.

Company name

Occasionally the company name is typed in the closing lines. When this is done, it is typed in *all capital letters* 2 lines (a double space) below the complimentary close. The modern practice is to omit the company name in the closing lines if a letterhead is used.

Typewritten name/official title

The name of the person who dictated the letter and his/her official title are typed 4 lines (3 blank line spaces) below the complimentary close, or 4 lines below the typed company name when it is used. When both the name and official title are used, they may be typed on the same line or the official title may be typed on the next line below the typed name.

Unusual features

Letters having unusual features, such as tabulated material, long quotations, or an unusual number of lines in the address or the closing lines, may require changes in the settings normally used for letters of that length.

ZIP Code abbreviations

Alabama, AL
Alaska, AK
Arizona, AZ
Arkansas, AR
California, CA
Colorado, CO
Connecticut, CT
Delaware, DE
District of Columbia, DC
Florida, FL
Georgia, GA
Guam, GU
Hawaii, HI
Idaho, ID
Illinois, IL
Indiana, IN
Iowa, IA
Kansas, KS
Kentucky, KY
Louisiana, LA
Maine, ME
Maryland, MD
Massachusetts, MA
Michigan, MI
Minnesota, MN
Mississippi, MS
Missouri, MO
Montana, MT
Nebraska, NE
Nevada, NV
New Hampshire, NH
New Jersey, NJ
New Mexico, NM
New York, NY
North Carolina, NC
North Dakota, ND
Ohio, OH
Oklahoma, OK
Oregon, OR
Pennsylvania, PA
Puerto Rico, PR
Rhode Island, RI
South Carolina, SC
South Dakota, SD
Tennessee, TN
Texas, TX
Utah, UT
Vermont, VT
Virgin Islands, VI
Virginia, VA
Washington, WA
West Virginia, WV
Wisconsin, WI
Wyoming, WY

▶Use an exclamation mark

1 After emphatic interjections.

Wow! Hey there! What a day!

2 After sentences that are clearly exclamatory.

"I won't go!" she said with determination.
How good it was to see you in New Orleans last week!

▶Use a hyphen

1 To join compound numbers from twenty-one to ninety-nine that are typed as words.

forty-six fifty-eight over seventy-six

2 To join compound adjectives before a noun which they modify as a unit.

well-laid plans five-year period two-thirds majority

3 After each word or figure in a series of words or figures that modify the same noun (suspended hyphenation).

first-, second-, and third-class reservations

4 To spell out a word or name.

s-e-p-a-r-a-t-e G-a-e-l-i-c

5 To form certain compound nouns.

WLW-TV teacher-counselor AFL-CIO

▶Use the parentheses

1 To enclose parenthetical or explanatory matter and added information.

The amendments (Exhibit A) are enclosed.

2 To enclose identifying letters or figures in lists.

Check these factors: (1) period of time, (2) rate of pay, and (3) nature of duties.

3 To enclose figures that follow spelled-out amounts to give added clarity or emphasis.

The total contract was for six hundred dollars ($600).

▶Use a question mark

At the end of a sentence that is a direct question; however, use a period after a request in the form of a question.

What day do you plan to leave for Honolulu?
Will you mail this letter for me, please.

▶Use quotation marks

1 To enclose direct quotations.

He said, "I'll be there at eight o'clock."

2 To enclose titles of articles and other parts of complete publications, short poems, song titles, television programs, and unpublished works like theses and dissertations.

"Sesame Street" "The Next Twenty Years"
"Out Where the West Begins" "Living"

3 To enclose special words or phrases, or coined words.

"limited resources" "Murphy's Law"

▶Use a semicolon

1 To separate two or more independent clauses in a compound sentence when the conjunction is omitted.

To err is human; to forgive, divine.
It is easy to be critical; it is not so easy to be constructive.

2 To separate independent clauses when they are joined by a conjunctive adverb (*however*, *consequently*, etc.).

I can go; however, I must get excused.

3 To separate a series of phrases or clauses (especially if they contain commas) that are introduced by a colon.

These officers were elected: Lu Ming, President; Lisa Stein, vice president; Juan Ramos, secretary.

4 To precede an abbreviation or word that introduces an explanatory statement.

She organized her work; for example, by putting work to be done in folders of different colors to indicate degrees of urgency.

▶Use an underline

1 With titles of complete works such as books, magazines, and newspapers. (Such titles may also be typed in ALL CAPS without the underline.)

Century 21 Shorthand New York Times TV Guide

2 To call attention to special words or phrases (or you may use quotation marks).
Note: Use a continuous underline unless each word is to be considered separately.

Stop typing when time is called.
Spell these words: steel, occur, separate.

▶Use an apostrophe

1 As a symbol for *feet* in billings or tabulations or as a symbol for *minutes*. (The quotation mark may be used as a symbol for *seconds* and *inches*.)

12′ × 16′   3′54″   8′6″ × 10′8″

2 As a symbol to indicate the omission of letters or figures (as in contractions or figures).

can't   wouldn't   Spirit of '76

3 Add *s* to form the plural of most figures, letters, and words. In market quotations, form the plural of figures by the addition of *s* only.

6's   A's   five's   ABC's   Century Fund 4s

4 To show possession: Add the *apostrophe and s* to (a) a singular noun and (b) a plural noun which does not end in *s*.

a man's watch   women's shoes   boy's bicycle

Add the *apostrophe and s* to a proper name of one syllable which ends in *s*.

Bess's Cafeteria   Jones's bill

Add the *apostrophe only* after (a) plural nouns ending in *s* and (b) a proper name of more than one syllable which ends in *s* or *z*.

boys' camp   Adams' home   Melendez' report

Add the *apostrophe* after the last noun in a series to indicate joint or common possession of two or more persons; however, separate possession of two or more persons is indicated by adding the possessive to each of the nouns.

Lewis and Clark's expedition
the manager's and the treasurer's reports

▶Use a colon

1 To introduce an enumeration or a listing.

These are my favorite poets: Shelley, Keats, and Frost.

2 To introduce a question or a long direct quotation.

This is the question: Did you study for the test?

3 Between hours and minutes expressed in figures.

10:15 a.m.   4:30 p.m.

▶Use a comma (or commas)

1 After (a) introductory words, phrases, or clauses and (b) words in a series.

If you can, try to visit Chicago, St. Louis, and Dallas.

2 To set off short direct quotations.

She said, "If you try, you can reach your goal."

3 Before and after (a) words which come together and refer to the same person, thing, or idea and (b) words of direct address.

Clarissa, our class president, will give the report.
It was good to see you, Terrence, at the meeting.

4 To set off nonrestrictive clauses (not necessary to the meaning of the sentence), but not restrictive clauses (necessary to meaning).

Your report, which deals with the issue, is great.
The girl who just left is my sister.

5 To separate the day from the year and the city from the state.

July 4, 1982   New Haven, Connecticut

6 To separate two or more parallel adjectives (adjectives that could be separated by the word "and" instead of the comma).

a group of young, old, and middle-aged persons

Do not use commas to separate adjectives so closely related that they appear to form a single element with the noun they modify.

a dozen large red roses   a small square box

7 To separate (a) unrelated groups of figures which come together and (b) whole numbers into groups of three digits each (however, *policy*, *year*, *page*, *room*, *telephone*, and most *serial numbers* are typed without commas).

During 1982, 1,750 cars were insured under Policy 806423.
page 1042   room 1184   (213) 825-2626

▶Use a dash

1 For emphasis.

The icy road--slippery as a fish--was a hazard.

2 To indicate a change of thought.

We may tour the Orient--but I'm getting ahead of my story.

3 To introduce the name of an author when it follows a direct quotation.

"Hitting the wrong key is like hitting me."--Armour

4 For certain special purposes.

"Well--er--ah," he stammered.
"Jay, don't get too close to the --." It was too late.

Reference guide

▶ Capitalize

1 The first word of every sentence and the first word of every complete direct quotation. Do not capitalize (a) fragments of quotations or (b) a quotation resumed within a sentence.

She said, "Hard work is necessary for success."
He stressed the importance of "a sense of values."
"When all else fails," he said, "follow directions."

2 The first word after a colon if that word begins a complete sentence.

Remember this: Type with good techniques.
We carry these sizes: small, medium, and large.

3 First, last, and all other words in titles of books, articles, periodicals, headings, and plays, except words of four letters or less used as articles, conjunctions, or prepositions.

Century 21 Typewriting   "How to Buy a House"
Saturday Review   "The Sound of Music"

4 An official title when it precedes a name or when used elsewhere if it is a title of distinction.

President Lincoln   He is the Prime Minister.
The doctor is in.   She is the treasurer.

5 All proper nouns and their derivatives.

Canada   Canadian Festival   France   French food

6 Days of the week, months of the year, holidays, periods of history, and historic events.

Sunday   Labor Day   New Year's Day
June   Middle Ages   Civil War

7 Seasons of the year only when they are personified.

icy fingers of Winter   the soft kiss of Spring

8 Geographic regions, localities, and names.

the North   Upstate New York   Mississippi River

9 Street, avenue, company, etc., when used with a proper noun.

Fifth Avenue   Avenue of the Stars   Armour & Co.

10 Names of organizations, clubs, and buildings.

Girl Scouts   Commercial Club   Trade Center

11 A noun preceding a figure except for common nouns such as *line*, *page*, and *sentence*, which may be typed with or without a capital.

Style 143   Catalog 6   page 247   line 10

▶ Type as words

1 Numbers from one to ten except when used with numbers above ten, which are typed as figures.
Note: It is common business practice to use figures for all numbers except those which begin a sentence.

Was the order for four or eight books?
Order 8 shorthand books and 15 English books.

2 A number beginning a sentence.

Fifteen persons are here; 12 are at home sick.

3 The shorter of two numbers used together.

ten 50-gallon drums   350 five-gallon drums

4 Isolated fractions or indefinite amounts in a sentence.

Nearly two thirds of the students are here.
About twenty-five people came to the meeting.

5 Names of small-numbered streets and avenues (ten and under).

1020 Sixth Street   Tenth Avenue

▶ Type as figures

1 Dates and time, except in very formal writing.

May 9, 1982   10:15 a.m.
Ninth of May   four o'clock

2 A series of fractions.

Type 1/2, 1/4, 5/6, and 7 3/4.

3 Numbers preceded by nouns.

Rule 12   page 179   Room 1208   Chapter 15

4 Measures, weights, and dimensions.

6 ft. 9 in. tall   5 lbs. 4 oz.   8 1/2" × 11"

5 Definite numbers used with the percent sign (%); but type *percent* (spelled) with approximations in formal writing.

The rate is 15 1/2%.
About 50 percent of the work is done.

6 House numbers except house number One.

1915 - 42d Street   One Jefferson Avenue

7 Sums of money except when spelled for extra emphasis. Even sums may be typed without the decimal.

$10.75   25 cents $300
seven hundred dollars ($700)

136d-144b, continued

Assignment 11, continued

Remainder of assignment is in semiproblem form. Follow page 1 style except for a 1" top margin and page number on Line 4 at the right margin.

Executive Board Dinner Meeting

Mr. Garvey suggested that an invitation be extended to Mr. Cousins and his party to join the members of the Executive Board at its Executive Board Dinner Meeting, June 25, at 7:00 p.m. in the Garden Room of the Beverly Hills Hotel. After discussion, it was the consensus that the suggestion be implemented. Ms. Cruz will extend the invitation to Mr. Cousins to join the Board at its Dinner Meeting.

Scholarship Committee Report

Next, President Cey called on Thomas Hawkins for the report of the Scholarship Committee. Mr. Hawkins reported that two outstanding students had been selected to receive the POCA National Scholarships for advanced studies in the field of business education. The first recipient is Miss Alice Sheng, who will graduate from University High School in Los Angeles in June. The second recipient is Mr. Chris Fisher, who will graduate from Rye High School, Rye, New York, also in June. President Cey announced that the recipients will be invited, all expenses paid, to our National Convention where they will be honored and awarded the four-year scholarships to a college or university of their choice.

Mr. Hawkins suggested that the scholarship recipients be invited to the Executive Board dinner honoring Norman Cousins, and that board members be appointed to host Alice and Chris and to introduce them to board members attending the dinner. It was the consensus that the suggestion be implemented.

Hospitality Committee Report

President Cey called on Doris Porter for the report of the Hospitality Committee. Mrs. Porter announced that the Blue Room at the Palmer House Hotel had been reserved for the May 15 membership meeting.

Next Board Meeting

President Cey announced October 20 as the date of the next meeting of the Executive Board. The meeting is again scheduled for the Conference Board Room of Office Future Associates and will begin with a special luncheon at 12 noon.

There being no further business, a motion for adjournment was made, seconded, and passed. The meeting was adjourned at 9:15 p.m.

2DS

____

Iris Aponte, Recording Secretary

Assignment 12
Type an itinerary

Type the initerary shown on p. 232 as follows: 1cc; 1" top and side margins. Type the itinerary as illustrated. SS items, but DS between them.

Note: Before starting to type a column of figures, check alignment of figures in the column. Some figures will need to be indented to keep them in alignment.

An itinerary (a travel schedule) usually includes a chronological listing of departure and arrival times; mode of travel and accommodations; and often a list of scheduled activities.

136d-144b, continued

Assignment 11
Type minutes of meeting

Page 1: Type as shown here.

Page 2: 1" top margin; page number on Line 4 at right margin.

Note: Shown here is one form that may be used for typing minutes of a meeting. The side headings are used for easy identification of meeting actions and as an aid to indexing.

Several officers of POCA are members of the firm OFFICE FUTURE ASSOCIATES. They have asked you to type the minutes in final form.

1 ½" top margin (pica type) (elite type, 2")

MINUTES OF MEETING
EXECUTIVE BOARD
PROFESSIONAL OFFICE CONSULTANTS ASSOCIATION

TS

Place of Meeting

DS

Indent 5 → The semiannual meeting of the Executive Board of the Professional Office Consultants Association (POCA) was held in the Conference Board Room of Office Future Associates, 742 S. Michigan Avenue, Chicago, on April 10, 19--.

TS

Call to Order

1" side margins

The meeting was called to order at 7:00 p.m. by Merle Cey, President; Iris Aponte was the recording secretary.

Officers and Members Present

Officers and members present were:

Indent 10 →
Merle Cey, President
C. K. Garvey, Vice President
Josephine Cruz, Professional Development Chairperson
Thomas Hawkins, Scholarship Chairperson
Doris Porter, Hospitality Chairperson
Iris Aponte, Recording Secretary
Robert Eaton, Member at Large
Diana Crowley, Member at Large
Charles Trumbull, Member at Large

Approval of Minutes

The minutes of the meeting of October 15 were distributed and approved as distributed.

Professional Development Committee Report

President Cey called on Josephine Cruz for the report of the Professional Development Committee. Ms. Cruz reported that the committee had been successful in obtaining Norman Cousins, former editor of the Saturday Review and currently Professor-in-Residence in the UCLA School of Medicine, as the keynote speaker for the National Convention to be held in Los Angeles, June 24-27, 19--. Mr. Cousins' topic will be "The Humanized Office: A Saner, Healthier, and More Productive Environment."

Approximately 1"

(continued, page 231)

ITINERARY OF ARA JACKSON

DS

May 2 to May 5

Seattle, Vancouver (Canada)

TS

<u>MONDAY, MAY 2: CHICAGO TO SEATTLE</u>

DS

10:15 a.m.	Leave O'Hare International Airport on United 143 (tickets in travel folder). Lunch on board. DS
12:15 p.m.	Arrive Seattle/Tacoma International Airport. Avery Porter of Seattle office will meet you and drive you to Plaza Hotel. (Confirmed reservations in travel folder.)
3:00 p.m.	Interview Senior Office Consultant applicants at Seattle office. (Resumes in marked folder.)

DS

<u>TUESDAY, MAY 3: SEATTLE AND VANCOUVER, CANADA</u>

7:00 a.m.	Breakfast at hotel with Avery Porter before drive to Washington State offices in Olympia to discuss state office efficiency study with Governor.
12:30 p.m.	Lunch with Seattle office staff. Discuss Washington State study with them.
5:30 p.m.	Leave Seattle/Tacoma International Airport on Pacific Western 359.
6:05 p.m.	Arrive Vancouver International Airport. (Confirmed reservations at Bayshore Hotel in travel folder. Take airport limo to hotel.)

<u>WEDNESDAY, MAY 4: VANCOUVER</u>

9:00 a.m.	Meet Leslie White of Vancouver office at hotel. Make inspection tour of Sunshine Industries headquarters. (Study Progress Report in marked folder.)
12:30 p.m.	Lunch with Vancouver office staff. Discuss new office technology studies with them. (See marked folders.)

<u>THURSDAY, MAY 5: VANCOUVER TO CHICAGO</u>

7:40 a.m.	Leave Vancouver International Airport on United 224, breakfast flight to Chicago.
1:30 p.m.	Arrive O'Hare International Airport.

136d-144b, continued

Assignment 10
Type an interoffice memo: simplified style

[LM p. 107] or plain full sheet

1" side margins; 1cc; correct errors

Date may be placed on Lines 10–12, depending on memo length.

Office Future Associates

742 S. Michigan Avenue
Chicago, IL 60605-7904

phone (312) 825-2020

Current date   Line 12
TS

All Typists
TS

CARE OF TYPEWRITERS
TS

Because of our increasing typewriter repair costs, we are requesting that you follow these care-of-typewriter steps:

1. End of each day. At the end of each day, please follow these procedures:

    a. Use a stiff brush to clean the typeface. If you use an element-type machine, remove the element to clean it.

    b. Brush away any dust or dirt that may have fallen into the typebar segment.

    c. Dust your desk beneath your machine with a dustcloth.

    d. Pull the paper release forward and leave it in this position overnight.

    e. Finally, center the carriage (typebar machine) and cover the typewriter.

2. End of each week. At the end of each week, do the following:

    a. With a soft, lintfree cloth with a corner moistened slightly with typewriter oil, wipe the carriage rails of the typebar machine; then wipe them again with the unmoistened portion of the cloth.

    b. Clean the platen with another soft, lintfree cloth moistened with alcohol.

3. Know your operator's manual. Review, as needed, the care and maintenance steps given in the operating instructions manual for your typewriter.
TS

JOAN RICHARDS, OFFICE MANAGER

xx

136d-144b, continued

Assignment 13
Type a speech

Ms. Magellan has given you a handwritten copy of a talk she is to give at a conference (see copy at right and pp. 234, 235). She needs the entire speech typed in final form.

Because a typed copy of a speech must be easy to read and follow, do this:

Leave

- 1½" top margin, p. 1
- 1½" side margins
- 1" bottom margin (approx.)
- 1" top margin on second and other pages

DS the ¶s with 2DS between them. Indent ¶s 5 spaces. Number pages (after page 1) on Line 4 at right margin.

¶1 As a member of this panel, my task is to discuss briefly "Work Measurement in the Office." Perhaps, at the outset, a definition of work measurement is in order.

WORK MEASUREMENT IN THE OFFICE

¶3 Most of you are aware that cost of labor is the major expense of the office. Time-related work measurement techniques are needed, therefore, to gather information vital for effective planning and control in the office. Information which relates the accomplishment of a particular task or set of duties to the time it takes normally to perform that task may be called a "standard." Work measurement provides the information necessary to set standards. Later I shall demonstrate how a standard is set for a common office task.

¶4 Actually, the ability to measure the amount of work required to perform a specific task or job ^is essential for anyone concerned with improving working conditions and having job tasks completed in the most effective and satisfying manner. The measurement of work provides the means for making evaluations and decisions concerning a task which would otherwise be made subjectively.

¶2 Work measurement involves the study of HOW and WHY the job is performed, analysis to determine whether the work is being performed in the prescribed manner with the proper level of quality control, and analysis to determine whether the work itself is necessary or whether the methods of performing it can be improved.

¶5 Today, several basic work measurement techniques are being used--each has its own unique place and value when

136d-144b, continued

Assignment 8
Type invoices
[LM pp. 99–106]

1. Type invoices (1cc) from the data in the illustration to the first four companies on your **Index Card List** (Assignment 4, p. 223). For each new invoice, change the last digit of the *Order Nos.* to the next number.

The other items on the invoice will remain the same. If forms are unavailable, type only the typewritten copy, arranged in the same style as shown on the form.

Set tab stops for typed items. Type across the line, using tab key or bar. In the total column, type last amount; underline; DS; type total.

2. Fold each invoice for a window envelope (see RG, p. vi).

Office Future Associates

742 S. Michigan Avenue
Chicago, IL 60605-7904
phone (312) 825-2020

Invoice

Margin ↓

Continental Oil Co.
30 Rockefeller Plaza
New York, NY 10020-2465

Tab ↓

Date Current date

Our Order No. OFA-4310

Cust. Order No. CI-14782

Terms 2/10, n/30 Tab ↓ Tab ↓ Tab ↓

Quantity	Description	Unit Price	Total
10 days	On-site systems analysis	250.00 da.	2,500.00
1	Study presentation and report	500.00	500.00
			3,000.00

Assignment 9
Type an appointment schedule

Ms. Lois Magellan asks you to prepare her appointment schedule.

1. Arrange schedule attractively on a full sheet; 1" top and side margins.

2. Center heading lines:

APPOINTMENT SCHEDULE
DS
LOIS MAGELLAN
DS
June 10, 19--
TS

3. SS appointment listings; DS below each item.

11:00 a.m. Conference call. Ester Guzman (Los Angeles office), James van Dyke (New Orleans office), and Valery Ambroise (Philadelphia office) regarding consulting team--Crown Zellerback Study.

11:15 a.m. Interview Norman Matsuda for Word Processing Specialist position. Resume in work folder.

2:30 p.m. Meet at Field Research Institute with Daro Van Zyl, Director of Productivity Research.

Special Reminders:

1. Call ARROWHEAD Conference Center regarding September meeting.
2. Approve final draft of speech for June 20 meeting.
3. Review report for Castle & Cooke--report due June 15.

136d-144b, continued
Assignment 13, continued

used correctly. Briefly, these techniques are: estimates, historical records, time studies, micromotion studies, work sampling, and predetermined time ^systems ~~standards~~. Predetermined time systems, a term used to include about five or six major systems, are generally considered the most accurate and objective of the tech-niques available. The basic data have been developed by highly qualified persons; these data are consistent; and, in some instances, they may be used easily and quickly by a person with limited technical knowledge ^for the purposes of introduction to work measurement. However, it is important to understand that to use ^standards of predetermined time ^systems ~~standards~~ correctly, highly specialized training is required.

Predetermined time systems describe in precise detail well-defined tasks. They were developed, for the most part, when time study specialists ask^ed themselves why the same basic movements were studied and restudied when the work remained the same. After all, the human body can (only) (perform) so many motions. ^For example, To (lc) insert a sheet of paper into a typewriter in New York requires no more effort than it does in Chicago, or here in Los Angeles, and the time requirements should be the same. In other words, why not classify certain repetitive activities and measure them ONCE AND FOR ALL? As a result, predetermined time systems have been established for many types of work, including many office tasks. They have been established by thorough study of the minute movements a person uses in performing a repetitive task.

The method of application is the same for all predetermined time systems. To illustrate, let's take a simple but repetitive and representative task, such as the typing of an average-length

136d-144b, continued

Assignment 7
Evaluation

full sheets; 1" top and side margins; approx. 1" bottom margin

You are to participate in a special evaluation program to test employee knowledge of proper forms to use with special letter parts. You may use the *Office Manual* sheets you prepared as Assignment 6 for reference.

Type *Drill* and number, then DS. Read the directions for the drill; then type the letter information as directed, using proper spacing between parts. TS below each drill item.

Drill 1: Type two forms that may be used for typing the following attention line: Attention Miss Jacqueline Brown. Use the letter address below:

White Construction Company, Inc.
3402 High Point Road
Greensboro, NC 27404-6369

Drill 2: Type the address of Drill 1, including the attention line as the second line of the address, with the following subject line: NEW CONSTRUCTION CONTRACTS. Use an appropriate salutation.

Drill 3: Type the address shown below twice. The first time, use as the official title, Superintendent; the second, Superintendent of Public Instruction.

Dr. Lorraine Bock
State Department of Education
Sacramento, CA 95814-3011

Drill 4: Type the following long address line in a 2-line form along with the street and city address:

The North American Banking and Savings Association
520 Beechmont Avenue
Cincinnati, OH 45230-8712

Drill 5: Type DART INDUSTRIES, INC. as the company name in the following closing lines: Sincerely yours Michael Miner, President

Drill 6: Type the closing lines of Drill 5, but change President to Chairman of the Board.

Drill 7: Type the dictator/typist initials as a reference notation assuming that **J. W. Richmond** is the dictator and you are the typist.

Drill 8: Type the following items as the listed enclosures of the letter: Invoice No. 312; Check for $325.

Drill 9: Type the correct copy notation for a photocopy of a letter to be sent to Mrs. Betty Caine.

Letter typed in block style, open punctuation.

Drill 10: On a new sheet, type the second-page heading (horizontal style) along with the second-page letter copy and postscript lines. The letter is addressed to Mrs. Sylvia Porter. Use the current date. Repeat drill on another new sheet, using the block heading for the second page.

Letter copy for second page

Unless we can be of service to your organization, there will be no cost or obligation. Please contact us soon--you won't regret this decision. Sincerely yours OFFICE FUTURE ASSOCIATES Kevin Mulcahy, Senior Partner Enclosure

Postscript lines

Enclosed is a list of firms in your area for whom we have done office productivity studies. They have given us permission for you to contact them. Satisfied clients are the best recommendation for our services.

one-page letter, and apply a predetermined time system to get a standard time for the task of typing a letter. The completed example is projected on the screen to aid you in following the steps I shall list:

<u>Step 1</u>. Closely observe the basic movements required to accomplish the task.

<u>Step 2</u>. Briefly describe these movements or elements in proper sequence of their performance.

<u>Step 3</u>. Determine through observation the frequency with which each element occurs in relation to the final task output (in the case of this illustration--the one-page letter), which is used as a consistent and measurable unit.

<u>Step 4</u>. Look up in Predetermined Time Systems Tables the standard time required for each element.

<u>Step 5</u>. Calculate, based on the frequency with which the element occurs in relation to the final production unit, the total time for the unit.

<u>Step 6</u>. Total elemental times and appropriate personal allowances.

You can see in the example projected on the screen that, by applying predetermined time standards to a repetitive typing task, a standard time of 8.177 minutes has been established for producing an average-length letter. Also note that over 40 percent of the time required to produce the letter involves nontyping activity. This information suggests that close attention to methods is required for the most effective performance, and it highlights the importance of methods as one of the valuable uses of quantitative work measurement.

That in a nutshell, Ladies and Gentlemen, is what work measurement in the office is all about. In conclusion, I'm tempted to paraphrase a somewhat shopworn joke and say, "Time specialists never die--they continue to measure away."

12

REFERENCE NOTATION

The initials of only the typist may be used in the reference notation; or, the initials of the dictator and those of the typist may be used.

Typist initials only:	Dictator/typist initials:
jb	LE:JB

ENCLOSURE NOTATION

If only one enclosure is mentioned in a letter, type the word "Enclosure" a double space below the reference initials; however, if several enclosures are mentioned, they may be listed.

One enclosure:	Several enclosures:
Enclosure	Enclosures: Check for $50 Copy of contract

COPY NOTATIONS

Use "cc" for carbon copy and "pc" for photocopy.

cc Mr. Henry Jackson

pc Dr. Marilyn Crawford

POSTSCRIPT

The postscript is an added thought or statement typed a double space below the closing parts of the letter. Its placement makes it unnecessary to use the abbreviation "P.S." with the postscript lines, although it is permissible to use P.S.

HEADING FOR SECOND PAGE OF A LETTER

The heading for a second page of a letter is started 1 inch from the top edge of the second or other additional pages. A triple space is left below the heading before typing the letter material.

Horizontal style:

Mrs. Karen Beddow	2	June 15, 19--

Block style:

Mrs. Karen Beddow
Page 2
June 15, 19--

136d-144b, continued

Assignment 14
Type a short unbound report

Report to be circulated among key executives of firm.

SS report and table data; use standard spacing above and below table parts. Number second page in upper right corner. Report will be duplicated by photocopy process.

PRINCIPAL OFFICE USES
OF THE TYPEWRITER

Many persons, with different office job titles, use the typewriter in accomplishing office tasks assigned to them. It would be difficult to think of an office in which the typewriter does not play an important role.

Typewriting Tasks

A recent study of a random sample of business firms in the United States reveals that the typewriter is used in the preparation of a variety of business papers that are an important part of business activity. The table below shows the percentage of total time of typewriter use that is devoted to various typewriting tasks (whatever the job classification):

TYPEWRITING TASKS

(Percent of Total Typing Time)

Letters	30%
Reports, Manuscripts	20
Memoranda	19
Business forms	13
Tables	10
Other typing tasks	8
Total	100%

As is evident from the table, the typewriter is used most often for producing either business letters (30%) or reports (20%). The typing of memoranda (internal correspondence) is another important activity involving typewriter time (19%).

The "other" category of typewriting tasks included such typing activities as the typing of messages, index card items, envelope addresses, itineraries, rough-draft copy, contracts, minutes of meetings, and press releases, as well as other items.

Sources of Typewriting Tasks

Nearly one half (49%) of all typewriting tasks originate in handwriting. It is difficult to imagine in this age of sophisticated dictating equipment that handwriting is still the predominant input source of materials for the typewriter. Rough-draft materials (typed material with handwritten revisions) are also another important input source for the typewriter. Fifteen percent of all materials coming to the typewriter operator are in rough-draft form. Shorthand notes (10%), dictation tapes or discs (10%), and self-composition (14%) are other important input sources for the final typed product whether this be letters, reports, memoranda, business forms, tables, or other typed materials.

Stay alert!

LONG LINES IN LETTER ADDRESSES

When one of the lines in the letter address is extremely long, double it back to the second line as illustrated below:

The San Francisco Auto Supply
   and Accessory Company
536 Market Street
San Francisco, CA 94101-4272

COMPANY NAME IN CLOSING LINES

When the company name is included in the closing lines, type it in ALL CAPS a double space below the complimentary close. Four line spaces (3 blank lines) are left below the company name in the closing lines.

Sincerely yours

OFFICE FUTURE ASSOCIATES

Lee O'Brien, Vice President

OFFICIAL TITLE IN CLOSING LINES

In the closing lines, the official title may be typed on the same line as the typed name or on the line immediately below the typed name. Choose a placement that will give good balance to the lines.

On same line:

Sincerely yours

Eric Johnson, Manager

On line below typed name:

Sincerely yours

Henry R. Jamison
Assistant Vice President

Personal titles of women usually are used in the closing lines, and the personal title is typed on the same line as the typed name. The use of the personal title in the closing lines is helpful to others who address correspondence to a woman.

Sincerely yours

Ms. Janice King
Executive Vice President

Enrichment activity

Two-page form letter
[LM pp. 109–110] or plain full sheet

1cc; plain second sheet; address large envelope with attention line typed as 2d line of address

block style, open punctuation; type attention line a DS below letter address; type subject line in ALL CAPS at left margin a DS below salutation

Type page 2 heading in horizontal style.

Note: Before typing any long letter, make a pencil mark at the right edge of the sheet about 1½" from the bottom of the page, and another at the 1" mark. You can then judge where to end page 1.

As time permits, type the letter to the second addressee on your Index Card List (Assignment 4, p. 223). For the attention line use:
Attention Office Manager

Special Note: Some business firms place the *attention line* as the second line of the address lines and the *subject line* a double space below the address lines as shown below:

Continental Oil Co.
Attention Mrs. Trudy Kelly, Office Manager
30 Rockefeller Plaza
New York, NY 10020-2465

PRODUCTIVE OFFICE ENVIRONMENTS

Ladies and Gentlemen

words

April 13, 19-- Continental Oil Co. 30 Rockefeller Plaza New York, NY 10020- 15
2465 Attention Mrs. Trudy Kelly, Office Manager Ladies and Gentlemen 29
PRODUCTIVE OFFICE ENVIRONMENTS 35
¶ 1) You are aware that today's office is the most labor-intensive sector of our 50
society. Few organizations can afford to neglect ways to improve productivity 66
in the office. It is in this area of work that we can help you. 79
¶ 2) Our firm has earned an international reputation for solving office work 94
problems. We have broad experience in ways to increase office efficiency and 109
office productivity. Our staff of highly trained consultants specializes in the 126
design of office environments and the implementation of office work measure- 141
ment systems as strategies for improving office productivity. 153
¶ 3) We are experts in the application of predetermined time systems to office 168
work measurement. Close attention is given to work methods required for most 184
effective performance. Through predetermined time systems, we can provide 199
an excellent and readily available resource for appraising and evaluating job 214
performance in the office. Time is the common denominator for establishing 230
office job performance standards. These systems provide the means to make 245
equitable and consistent comparisons of the productivity of workers perform- 260
ing diverse tasks. 264
¶ 4) We are leaders, too, in the design and implementation of landscaped offices 279
that are cost efficient and flexible. Our total planning approach to the open- 295
landscaped office includes streamlined workflow and work organization, 309
energy-efficient lighting suited to the tasks and workers involved, and the re- 325
duction of noise levels as well as sight lines--all of which lead to more produc- 341
tive use of time. 345
¶ 5) Attractively designed movable office partitions enable you to change of- 359
fice space as your needs change. This flexibility is an important consideration 375
in planning any office layout. Couple this with an appropriate use of color and 392
the office arrangement can have an impact on how we feel in a work environ- 407
ment and how well we work in that environment. When we have redesigned 421
office work space for business organizations with whom we have consulted, the 437
first comment we usually get from persons assigned to the redesigned office 452
space goes somewhat as follows: "This is now an exciting place in which to 467
work." 469
¶ 6) And the best part of all is the fact that the cost of our service is nominal. A 485
qualified member of our staff will be pleased to discuss your special problems 501
with you at your convenience. We shall then present a written proposal which 516
will realistically define the scope and cost of the assignment. 529
¶ 7) Don't hesitate to call me collect (312/825-2626) about any questions you 544
may have; or, just return the enclosed card and we will take the next steps. Until 561
you decide that we can provide a valuable service to your organization, there 576
will be no cost or obligation. Please contact us soon--you won't regret this 592
decision. Sincerely yours OFFICE FUTURE ASSOCIATES Kevin Mulcahy, 605
Senior Partner Enclosures 610
Enclosed is a list of firms in your area for whom we have done office produc- 626
tivity studies. They have given us permission for you to contact them. Satisfied 642
clients are the best recommendation for our services. 653/**675**

136d-144b, continued

Assignment 6
Type pages for *Office Manual*

You have been asked to type the copy given here and on pp. 225–226 as pages 10, 11, and 12 of the *Office Manual* (a reference source for office workers).

Center heading over the line of writing 1" from top edge of page 10, then TS and type side heading. DS above illustrations; TS above each side heading.

Number pages in upper right corner.

Since copy is to be inserted into the *Office Manual*, use these margins:

top: 1"
left: 1½"
right: 1"
bottom: approx. 1"

Start 2d column, when used, as follows:

pica: center + 5
elite: center + 10

Set a tab stop for this point. Type all the first column material; then turn platen back to proper point and tab to second column. It is not necessary to make a complete return when typing 2d column lines; when carriage or element reaches center of line, tab to move quickly to proper point.

Give attention to the material as you type it.

Save copy for reference.

PLACEMENT OF SPECIAL LETTER PARTS
TS

ATTENTION LINE
DS

The attention line may be typed as the second line of the letter address, or it may be typed a double space below the letter address. The guide to use is the preference of the dictator of the letter.
DS

Typed as second line:

Brown & Jordan Company
Attention Mr. Ralph Barnes
1142 East 42d Street
New York, NY 10017-2991
DS
Ladies and Gentlemen

Typed below address:

Brown & Jordan Company
1142 East 42d Street
New York, NY 10017-2991

Attention Mr. Ralph Barnes

Ladies and Gentlemen
TS

SUBJECT LINE

The subject line is usually typed in ALL CAPS a double space below the salutation. It may be typed flush with the left margin, indented to the paragraph point if the letter paragraphs are indented, or it may be centered. It is not necessary to use the word "Subject," since the placement of the line indicates that it is the subject of the letter.

Brown & Jordan Company
Attention Mr. Ralph Barnes
1142 East 42d Street
New York, NY 10017-2991

Ladies and Gentlemen

PRICE LIST CHANGES

OFFICIAL TITLE IN LETTER ADDRESS

In the letter address, the official title usually is typed on the same line as the personal name. A long official title may be typed on the second line of the letter address to give balance to the lines.

Title on same line:

Mr. Donald W. Dorsey, Manager
The Superior Dairy Company
St. Cloud, MN 56301-3104

Title on second line:

Mrs. Agnes Williamson
Vice President and Secretary
Athens Publishing Company
674 Washington Avenue
Waterloo, IA 50701-5576

unit **26** lessons 145-146

Improve speed/accuracy

Learning goals

1. To refine techniques.

2. To increase speed and/or improve accuracy.

Machine adjustments

Make the usual machine adjustments as required for the various activities.

145

145a ▶ 5 Conditioning practice

each line 3 times (slowly, faster, in-between rate); as time permits, retype selected lines for extra credit

alphabet	1	Even for box numbers, just show the ZIP Codes to get a quick delivery.
fig/sym	2	Your Future Is Now was published in 1974, list price $26.85, less 30%.
space bar	3	If they do the work for us, Jenny may help them clean up the map room.
fluency	4	Type with your fingers curved and upright and with the wrists relaxed.

| 1 | 2 | 3 | 4 | 5 | 6 | 7 | 8 | 9 | 10 | 11 | 12 | 13 | 14 |

145b ▶ 25 Improve basic skill: speed-forcing drill

1. In each set, try to complete each sentence on the call of the 15", 12", or 10" timing as directed. Force speed to higher levels as you move from line to line.

2. Move from Set 1 to Set 2 to Set 3 as you are able to complete the lines in the time allowed. As the lines become more difficult, try to maintain speed.

3. Type two 1' speed-forcing timings on Lines 1e, 2e, and 3e. Compare rates.

4. Type additional 1' timings on the sentence or sentences on which you made your lowest rates.

Set 1: Balanced-hand word emphasis

		gwam 15"	12"	10"
1a	She may go with them to do the work for the widow.	40	50	60
1b	Jan may go with them to the city to do the work for me.	44	55	66
1c	If they do the work for us, he may make them sign the forms.	48	60	72
1d	Kale may go down to the lake to fish and to dig the clams for me.	52	65	78
1e	I may make them sign the right audit form if they wish to do the work.	56	70	84

| 1 | 2 | 3 | 4 | 5 | 6 | 7 | 8 | 9 | 10 | 11 | 12 | 13 | 14 |

Set 2: Combination-response emphasis

		15"	12"	10"
2a	Send a copy of the statement to me with the check.	40	50	60
2b	Will your price list be the same for your special sale?	44	55	66
2c	If she pays the price we ask, please send this check to her.	48	60	72
2d	Should she send the statement to the firm on or before that date?	52	65	78
2e	On or before the end of this month, she must be sure to read the case.	56	70	84

| 1 | 2 | 3 | 4 | 5 | 6 | 7 | 8 | 9 | 10 | 11 | 12 | 13 | 14 |

Set 3: One-hand word emphasis

		15"	12"	10"
3a	You were to get my opinion only on the estate tax.	40	50	60
3b	In his opinion, the average minimum reserve is too low.	44	55	66
3c	Did Greta quote a minimum rate on these water reserve cases?	48	60	72
3d	Refer only the extra estate tax case to me for a written opinion.	52	65	78
3e	Was Polly aware of his stated opinion in the oil minimum reserve case?	56	70	84

| 1 | 2 | 3 | 4 | 5 | 6 | 7 | 8 | 9 | 10 | 11 | 12 | 13 | 14 |

136d-144b, continued

Assignment 2
Type an address list in table form

half sheet, long side up; DS data of columns; use **ADDRESS LIST** as table heading

				words
			heading	3
Continental Oil Co.	30 Rockefeller Plaza	New York, NY	10020-2465	16
Ford Motor Co.	The American Road	Dearborn, MI	48121-8664	27
General Mills, Inc.	9200 Wayzata Blvd.	Minneapolis, MN	55426-3803	41
H. J. Heinz Co.	1062 Progress St.	Pittsburgh, PA	15230-6970	53
Inland Steel Co.	30 W. Monroe Avenue	Chicago, IL	60603-7775	65
Lockheed Corp.	2555 Hollywood Way	Burbank, CA	91503-4039	77
RCA Corporation	30 Rockefeller Plaza	New York, NY	10020-2469	89
Shell Oil Company	One Shell Plaza	Houston, TX	77001-5287	101

Assignment 3
Address large envelopes
[LM pp. 87–94]

Type 8 large envelopes from the address list given above. First line of each address:

Office of the President

Note: Beginning office typists should be able to type about 2 envelope addresses a minute. Try to meet this standard.

Position envelopes for easy pickup: Stack at left, *flaps down and away from you* (face up).

Learn quick placement: Start address on Line 14, about 5 spaces left of horizontal center of envelope. Observe and learn to judge by eye measurement the proper starting point.

Assignment 4
Prepare an index-card list
[LM pp. 95–98]

1. Using the illustration as a model, type a 5″ × 3″ index card, or paper cut to size, for each firm listed in Assignment 2 above.

2. Fasten the cards together by paper clip and save for later use.

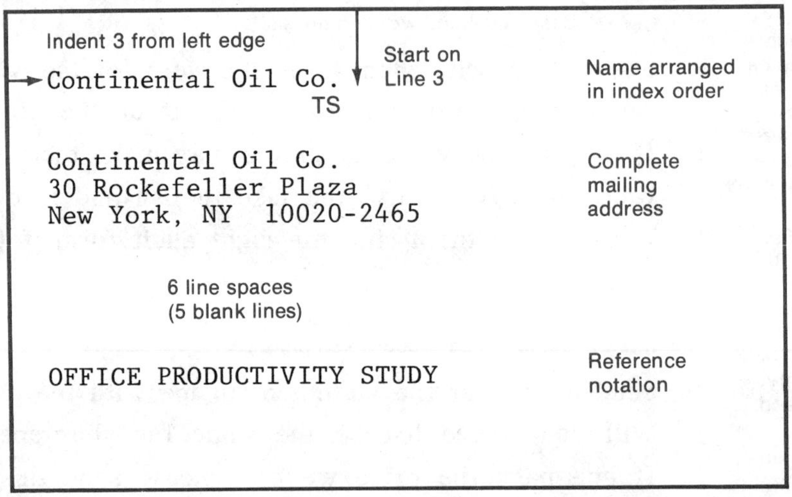

Assignment 5
Type a meeting agenda

DS items of agenda; arrange attractively on a half sheet, long side up

PROFESSIONAL OFFICE CONSULTANTS ASSOCIATION
DS
Executive Board
DS
Agenda for Meeting, April 10, 19--
TS

1. Call to Order
2. Minutes of March Meeting
3. Report of Professional Development Committee
4. Report of Scholarship Committee
5. Report of Hospitality Committee
6. Announcement of Next Meeting
7. Adjournment

145c ▶ 20
Transfer improved speed to paragraphs

1. Type 15" timings on each ¶. Try to maintain your ¶1 rate as you type ¶2 and ¶3.

2. Type 30" timings on each ¶. Again try to maintain your ¶1 rate on ¶s 2 and 3.

3. Type two 1' writings for speed on each ¶. Compare rates.

4. Type additional 1' writings on the ¶ on which you made your lowest rate.

5. Using your lowest rate as a guide, type 1' guided writings on each ¶ at a control rate—try to limit your errors to not more than 1 error on each writing. Type with continuity and control.

6. Increase your rate by 4 *gwam* and repeat Step 5.

7. As time permits, type additional 1' timings on the ¶ on which you made the greatest number of errors.

Practice goal: Fingers curved and upright with speedy finger key-stroking action. Wrists low and relaxed.

Paragraph 1: Balanced-hand word emphasis

They may go with me to the city to do the work. While I am in the city, I may visit with the auditor about the problem of the forms. The auditor may help me prepare the forms so that they can be filed with the city civic center. When the forms are filed with the city, this work will then be done.

Paragraph 2: Combination-response emphasis

Often, when writing a letter to another person, it is necessary to check for the correct address of that person. Using the correct address will help insure that a letter is delivered without undue delay. It is important, too, to use the correct ZIP Code. Mail is now sorted by the ZIP Code number.

Paragraph 3: One-hand word emphasis

You and I were the only extra persons whose tax cases were reviewed by the judge. Acting with great reserve, his opinion, stated only after careful study, was well received. It covers an area of tax rates which affect us all. After he stated and reviewed the facts, he gave his considered opinion.

146

146a ▶ 5
Conditioning practice

Follow standard directions, p. 238.

alphabet 1 Brave mice make journeys through perplexing mazes in quest of rewards.

fig/sym 2 Pay Jay & Co.'s bill for $137.56 before you pay Ed & Al's for $248.90.

long words 3 Systems engineers had complete responsibility in space communications.

fluency 4 Elena and a neighbor may go to the city to work for that big oil firm.

| 1 | 2 | 3 | 4 | 5 | 6 | 7 | 8 | 9 | 10 | 11 | 12 | 13 | 14 |

136c ▶ 5
Proofreading evaluation

half sheet, long side up; 70-space line; vertical center

Correct the typing and spelling errors in the copy at the right as you type it. The copy contains many errors.

PROOFREADER WANTED

Donn't you hate it when copy that you prepair has typping and spelling errors? Well, you can do soemthing about it by learning to be a good prufreader with are Company. We need peeple who can find ty-ping and spelling errors to insore that their our no misteaks in hte copy that is sent out on are letterhead stationary. If you can fine all the misteaks in thsi copy, this couldd be youre big chance. Wed like to have you work for us.

136d ▶ 25
137b-144b ▶ 45

Assignment 1
Interoffice memo
[LM p. 85] or plain full sheet

1" side margins; TS below last heading line

TO: (Your name)

FROM: (Your teacher's name)

DATE: (Current date)

SUBJECT: YOUR OFFICE ASSIGNMENT

In Lessons 136-144, you are to assume the role of special office assistant employed by Office Future Associates, a Chicago-based consulting firm with offices in key cities of the United States.

At Office Future Associates, you will work in the central office. As an employee, you will type the variety of assignments presented in these lessons. At times, you will be given only minimum directions; in some cases, as in an office, you will be asked to use your judgment in placing material on the page.

All your typed work will be judged for acceptability for office use. This statement means that you must proofread your work, correcting neatly all errors, and that you must judge whether your work is acceptable before submitting it for final evaluation.

Your daily schedule will be as follows:

Lessons 136-144	
Conditioning practice	5'
Lesson 136	
Assignments	25'
Lessons 137-144	
Assignments	45'

Some of the assignments you will type will be in the nature of skill building or new learning activities; others will represent officelike typing activities.

xx

146b ▶ 20
Increase speed/ improve control

Repeat 145c, p. 239.

Practice goal: Refine your techniques (finger position, keystroking, spacing, response patterns, etc.) as you work to increase your speed and/or improve your control.

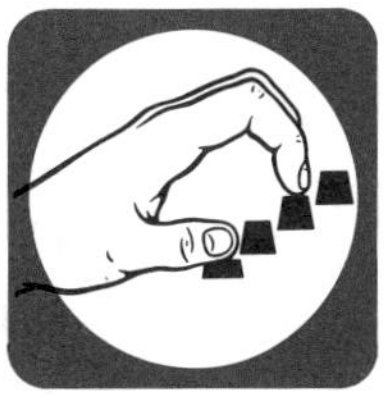

Fingers curved

Finger-action keystroking

Down-and-in thumb motion

146c ▶ 25
Improve basic skill: straight copy

1. Type a 5′ writing. Work for increased speed or improved control as needed, based on your performance in 146b above. Determine *gwam*; circle errors.

2. Add 4 words to your *gwam* of Step 1.

3. Type two 1′ guided writings on ¶1 at your goal rate.

4. Type two 1′ guided writings on ¶2 at your goal rate.

5. Type a 2′ writing on ¶1; then a 2′ writing on ¶2.

Goal: To maintain Steps 3 and 4 rates.

6. Type two 3′ writings on both ¶s. **Goal:** To increase your speed and/or to improve your control, based on your performance in Step 1.

all letters used | A | 1.5 si | 5.7 awl | 80% hfw |

	gwam 3′	5′	
Over the years, the eraser has been the principal method or proce-	4	3	51
dure used to correct typewriting errors. The eraser is still used to	9	5	53
a limited extent; however, other ways or methods used to correct errors	14	8	56
are taking its place. For example, in many typewriting classrooms,	18	11	59
correction tape or paper is often used as the chief method to correct	23	14	62
errors. In using the tape, the typist backspaces to the point of the	28	17	65
error. The tape is placed behind the ribbon, and then he or she types	32	19	67
the error again as it was made, with chalk from the tape covering the	37	22	70
error. The tape is then taken out, and the typist backspaces and types	42	25	73
the needed changes.	43	26	74
In the business office, many typewriters now have a special lift-off	48	29	77
tape. When an error is made, a special key is used to backspace to the	53	32	80
point of the error. The incorrect letter or figure is taken off the	57	34	82
paper by again striking that particular letter or figure. The correc-	62	37	85
tion can then be typed immediately. This entire process is simple and	67	40	88
may take just a few seconds. With specialized typing equipment, errors	72	43	91
can be corrected simply by backspacing. Using this procedure, an error	76	46	94
is corrected at once. The procedure is quick and easy.	80	48	96

gwam 3′ | 1 | 2 | 3 | 4 | 5 |
5′ | 1 | 2 | 3 |

unit **25** lessons 136-144

Learn special office applications

Learning goals

1. To develop knowledge and skill in typing a variety of office-like applications.

2. To maintain basic skill.

Machine adjustments

Make the usual machine adjustments as required for various activities.

Procedures

The 9 lessons of this unit are comprised, primarily, of a series of assignments which include skill building, new learning, evaluation, and job-like assignments. In typing the various assignments, you are to proofread carefully your typed work and to correct all errors (using eraser, tape, or fluid). At the start of each class period after the first, type the *conditioning practice* in 136a; then continue your work on the assignments.

136-144

136a-144a ▶ 5
Conditioning practice

each line 3 times (slowly, faster, in-between rate); as time permits, retype selected lines for extra credit

alphabet 1 Most companies emphasize extra valuable jobs for good quality workers.

fig/sym 2 Type these figures and symbols: $44, 5%, 6, (90), 3#, 2", 1', 8*, 7&.

fingers 3, 4 3 Aza Waxman sold all six of the popular old quill pens in Oslo, Norway.

fluency 4 Jane may meet many men and women and then go to the map room to study.

| 1 | 2 | 3 | 4 | 5 | 6 | 7 | 8 | 9 | 10 | 11 | 12 | 13 | 14 |

136b ▶ 15
Measure basic skill: straight copy

two 5′ writings; determine *gwam*; proofread, circle errors; record better rate

all letters used | A | 1.5 si | 5.7 awl | 80% hfw |

	gwam 3′	5′
In the word-processing area of work, there is now an increasing	4	3
demand for persons who can type with speed. Typing errors are not as	9	5
important as they were in the past because of the ease of correction	14	8
of such errors with the modern electronic typewriting equipment now in	18	11
use. Along with speed of typing, the next most important factor is	23	14
good proofreading skill. A typist must be able to proofread the copy	27	16
that he or she prepares and to find and correct any errors that were	32	19
made. There are no shortcuts in the development of proofreading skill.	37	22
Proofreading is learned through zealous effort and much practice.	41	25
An individual can become a speedy typist through concentrated prac-	46	28
tice. The most important element in building speed is to learn to type	51	30
with the requisite technique or good form patterns. Good form means that	56	33
the fingers are kept curved over the keys and the keystroking action is	60	36
limited to the fingers. The hands and arms must be kept in a relatively	65	39
quiet position. A good typist also has to learn to space quickly after	70	42
every word and to begin the next word without a stop. To do this, the	75	45
typist makes a reading adjustment and learns to read slightly ahead in	80	48
the copy to be typed so as to anticipate keystroking or response patterns.	84	51

gwam 3′ | 1 | 2 | 3 | 4 | 5 |
5′ | 1 | 2 | 3 |

unit **27** lessons 147-150

Evaluate typewriting competence

Evaluation/learning goals

1. To measure and evaluate your overall typing skill.

2. To help you develop skill in typing a letter of application and a personal data sheet.

3. To acquaint you with some of the testing procedures which may be used in evaluating your qualifications for office employment.

Machine adjustments

Make the usual machine adjustments as required for the various activities.

147

147a ▶ 5 Conditioning practice

each line 3 times (slowly, faster, in-between rate); as time permits, retype selected lines for extra credit

alphabet	1	Just by typing with improved techniques, final skill can be maximized.
fig/sym	2	I borrowed $125,800 at 9 3/4% in 1980 under an FHA mortgage (560-770).
long reaches	3	Cedric may bring many bright nylon flags to the civic center ceremony.
fluency	4	Try to type with a fluent, flowing rhythm to reach your maximum speed.

| 1 | 2 | 3 | 4 | 5 | 6 | 7 | 8 | 9 | 10 | 11 | 12 | 13 | 14 |

147b ▶ 45 Apply for employment

plain full sheets

Assignment 1
Type a letter of application

personal business style; modified block, mixed; 1½" side margins; start return address on Line 10

Assignment 2
Type a personal data sheet

Type the data sheet shown on p. 242 to enclose with the letter of application (Assignment 1). The illustration shows one acceptable style.

Assignment 3
Compose a letter of application and prepare a personal data sheet

As time permits, assume that you are applying for the job in the advertisement. Prepare in rough form (x-out errors) a letter of application and a data sheet that are appropriate for you. Type final copies from your corrected rough draft.

The advertisement shown at the right appeared in the Help Wanted section of a newspaper.

OFFICE ADMINISTRATIVE ASSISTANT
Must have good typing skill. Send letter of application and data sheet to: Ms. Julie Bauserman, Personnel Director, Continental Industries, Inc., 611 Wilshire Blvd., Los Angeles, CA 90017-4286

360 S. Roxbury Drive Beverly Hills, CA 90212-4997 June 8, 19-- Ms. Julie Bauserman Personnel Director Continental Industries, Inc. 611 Wilshire Boulevard Los Angeles, CA 90017-4286 Dear Ms. Bauserman: (¶ 1) Are you interested in a person who is willing to work hard and who has a background of education for the business office? At Beverly Hills High School, I have majored in business education and have studied such subjects as records management, typewriting, accounting, and office procedures. I believe I am the type of employee you are looking for to fill the office administration position you advertised in today's <u>Los Angeles Times.</u>

(¶ 2) I shall be graduated from Beverly Hills High School next week. In addition to the subjects I have listed, my program has included courses in general business, business law, and economics. I can type over 70 words a minute on straight-copy materials, and I have developed good typing production skills. In school, I have been active in several organizations. Last year I was president of the Junior Achievement Club. This year I was elected student body treasurer. During summer employment, I received an award for a work simplification suggestion.

(¶ 3) The enclosed data sheet will give you additional information about me. My success in my high school subjects, my work experience, and my participation in school activities are an indication that I can succeed in the position for which I am applying. May I come for an interview at a time that is convenient to you. I can be reached by mail at the address above or by telephone at 658-8911.

Sincerely yours, Fulton Weathers Enclosure

135

135a ▶ 5
Conditioning practice

Follow standard directions, p. 207.

alphabet 1 The Aztec jewelry makes an exquisite gift of which everybody is proud.
fig/sym 2 The prime rate rose from 8 2/9% to 17 3/4% before dropping to 10 5/6%.
shift key 3 Recently, Dr. T. James Crawford was given the John Robert Gregg Award.
fluency 4 Keep the stroking action in the fingers to increase your typing skill.

| 1 | 2 | 3 | 4 | 5 | 6 | 7 | 8 | 9 | 10 | 11 | 12 | 13 | 14 |

135b ▶ 15
Improve basic skill: straight copy

two 5′ writings of 130b, p. 213.

1. In the first 5′ writing, try to type at your best rate.
Goal: Not more than 10 errors.

2. In the second 5′ writing, increase your speed if you made the Step 1 goal; if not, decrease speed slightly and try to type with greater control.

135c ▶ 30
Measure letter production skill: review of letter styles

plain full sheets; correct errors

Time schedule

Planning and preparing .... 4′
Production timing .... 20′
Proofreading; computing *n*-pram .... 6′

Type as many of the style letters as you can in the time allowed. Make pencil notations of the page numbers and general directions so that you will not need to refer to this page.

Style letter 4, p. 153
Style letter 3, p. 145
Style letter 2, p. 83
Style letter 1, p. 71

As you type each letter, evaluate its acceptability: An acceptable letter is attractively placed on the page, is typed with uniform (even) keystroking, has proper word division at ends of lines, and has all errors neatly corrected.

Enrichment activities

Build high speed

1. Type each sentence three times, each time trying to increase typing speed.
2. Type the paragraph three times, again trying to increase speed with each repetition.
3. Type three 1′ writings on the paragraph. Build speed by keeping the keystroking action in your fingers—hands quiet.
4. Type a 2′ writing during which you try to maintain your best 1′ rate.

Union staff members referred a minimum number of cases for my opinion.
The maps may aid them when they do the work for the town and city.

| 1 | 2 | 3 | 4 | 5 | 6 | 7 | 8 | 9 | 10 | 11 | 12 | 13 | 14 |

The primary element of high speed typewriting is knowing that you are typing with good technique or form patterns. An individual who can perform at high proficiency levels will be in demand in the world of work. In the busy world of work, personality is another important element of success. If there is one thing of which we can be sure in the world of work, it is the tremendous importance of both of these elements, the element of proficiency and the element of personality.

heading centered 1" from top; 1" side margins; use judgment in arranging data

PERSONAL DATA SHEET

Fulton Weathers
360 S. Roxbury Drive
Beverly Hills, CA 90212-4997
(213) 658-8911

Age: 18
Single
6'2" 175 pounds
Health: Excellent

EDUCATION

Senior at Beverly Hills High School
High school diploma, pending graduation
Major: Business education
Grade average: B+ (upper 15% of graduating class)

SCHOOL ACTIVITIES

Student body treasurer, senior year. Receive and disburse student body funds; keep records; prepare purchase requisitions.

Member of varsity basketball team, junior and senior years.

President of Junior Achievement Club, junior year. Organized Beverly High Products Company which designed and sold personalized T-shirts.

WORK EXPERIENCE

Clerk/typist at NBC Television Studios for two summers. Typed forms and letters; sorted and distributed mail; operated Xerox duplicating equipment; acted as studio guide. Received Idea of the Month Award for a work simplification suggestion which resulted in a reduction of errors.

Newspaper route, one year. Delivered 120 papers daily, made monthly collections, and solicited new subscriptions. Was instrumental in increasing circulation on route by 25 percent.

PERSONAL BACKGROUND

Lived first twelve years and attended public schools in Huron, South Dakota. Interests include model building and reading. Enjoy backpacking, tennis, basketball, and swimming.

REFERENCES (by permission)

Mr. Sol Levine, Principal, Beverly Hills High School, 241 S. Moreno Drive, Beverly Hills, CA 90212-4906.

Mrs. Leonor Sandoval, Business Instructor, Beverly Hills High School, 241 S. Moreno Drive, Beverly Hills, CA 90212-4906.

Mr. Paul Guyer, Office Manager, NBC Television Studios, 3000 W. Alameda Ave., Burbank, CA 91505-5823.

134b ▶ 15
Improve tabulation skill

full sheet; reading position; DS columnar data; use judgment as to spacing between columns; correct errors

Goal: To complete typing of table in 15′ or less.

Each figure is used a minimum of 9 times.

			words
FORUM SPEAKERS BUREAU			4
Name	Telephone	Topic	12
Amato, Julius (D/E) *	387-9450	Taxes	19
Barouk, Phyllis (D)	490-8645	Contracts	27
Calvert, John (E)	275-1931	Zoning	34
Damonte, Stacy (E)	693-1582	Physical Fitness	43
Engel, Peter (D/E)	746-0836	Home Safety	51
Gertler, Gale (D)	592-1637	Investments	57
Hee, Patricia (D/E)	480-9542	Insurance	67
Ingram, George (E)	218-7064	Health Care	75
Kado, Stephen (E)	589-0273	Real Estate	82
LaVigne, Ara (D/E)	415-6321	Nutrition	90
McGahan, Kathleen (D)	790-8045	Investments	99
Morande, Reuben (D/E)	362-3181	Personal Defense	108
Ramsey, Deborah (E)	949-5720	Foreign Affairs	117
Tiano, Loren (E)	361-8726	Auto Repair	125
________________			129
*The letter D indicates available days; E, evenings.			139

134c ▶ 30
Type index cards

[LM pp. 71–78]

1. From the illustration at the right, type a 5″ × 3″ index classification card. Follow the spacing directions shown in color.

If cards are not available, use slips of paper cut to size.

2. Guided by this card, type a card for each additional name on the list of 134b, above. Arrange the items in correct order.

3. Sort cards alphabetically according to the topic (for example, **TAXES** in the illustration).

4. Type an identification card using the heading **FORUM SPEAKERS BUREAU** and the current date. Center lines vertically and horizontally DS on the card. Fasten cards with rubber band or paper clip.

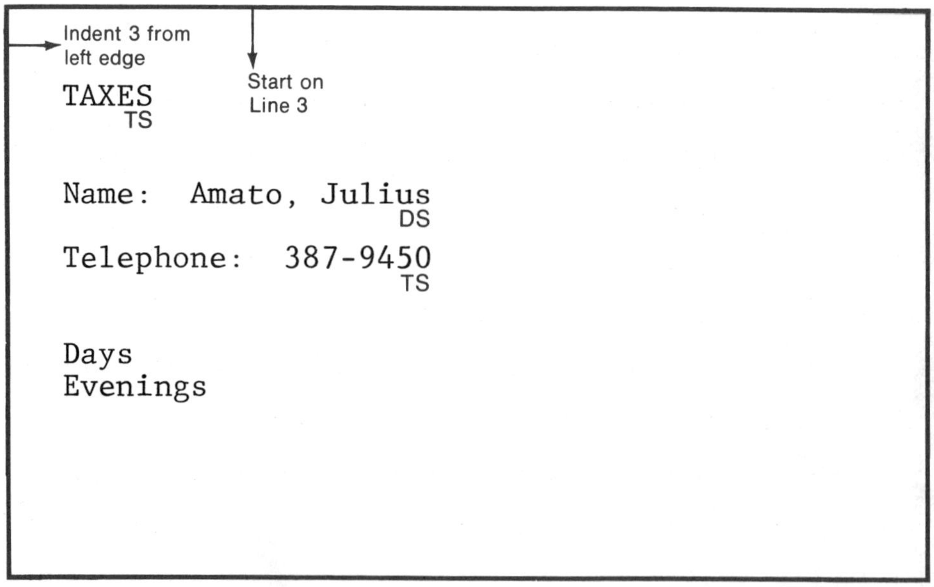

148

148a ▶ 5
Conditioning practice

Follow standard directions, p. 241.

alphabet 1 The big majority of black voters quietly expressed many zealous views.
fig/sym 2 The home located at 12345 Strawberry Drive sold for $98,670 last year.
fingers 3, 4 3 Wally, Quin, and Raul used a zax to trim the polo cottage roof slates.
fluency 4 Did he send a statement to the firm at their new address on that date?

| 1 | 2 | 3 | 4 | 5 | 6 | 7 | 8 | 9 | 10 | 11 | 12 | 13 | 14 |

148b ▶ 45
Measure skill: Preemployment testing

Although practice varies, many personnel departments of business firms require an applicant to come for a preliminary interview and to take certain tests as an initial screening device. If the applicant passes these tests, he or she is then considered for the position and may take other employment tests required by the company.

Test 1
Measure straight-copy skill (15′)

two 5′ writings; circle errors; determine *gwam*; record better rate

all letters used | A | 1.5 si | 5.7 awl | 80% hfw |

gwam 3′ | 5′

To hunt for a job is a bit of an art. Be sure to organize your 4 3
attack with care. At the outset, get all cogent or pertinent personal 9 5
data, such as your social security number, the names and addresses of 14 8
persons whom you can use for reference, and the dates of your schooling 18 11
and work experiences. Next, prepare a data sheet that lists or sums up 23 14
your personal characteristics, education, and work experiences. If you 28 17
have any useful skills, such as typing or shorthand, be sure to list 33 20
them. Finally, list the names of two or three individuals other than 37 22
relatives who know something about you. 40 24

Now you are ready to hunt for job leads. Inquire among friends, 44 27
relatives, and others who may be in a position to help you. Your school 49 30
may have a placement bureau--be sure to utilize it. Examine the "Help 54 32
Wanted" advertisements in your newspaper. When you locate a promising 59 35
job opportunity, ask by letter or telephone for an interview, unless 63 38
you know that you are to go at once for an interview. If you write a 68 41
letter of application, it should be neatly and correctly typed. When 73 44
you are invited for an interview, dress simply and in good taste; exhibit 78 47
an interest in the company and the job; sell yourself, your skills, and 82 49
your abilities; and you will increase your chances of getting the job. 87 52

gwam 3′ | 1 | 2 | 3 | 4 | 5 |
5′ | 1 | 2 | 3 |

133b, continued

words

storage. This problem, of course, will be greatly reduced or alleviated 575
if economical methods can be found to convert salt water to fresh water. 590
6. Climate. Concentrations of carbon dioxide and ozone-depleting chem- 606
icals are expected to increase, especially if coal burning becomes an alternate 622
source of energy, at rates that would warm the world's climate with a possible 637
ultimate melting of the polar ice caps. In addition, acid rains currently are de- 654
stroying fish and other aquatic life in our freshwater lakes. 666
7. Plant and animal species. Plant and animal species may decrease 685
dramatically with 20 percent of all species on earth made extinct by the year 701
2000. Even humankind may become an endangered species unless dramatic 715
population control steps are taken along with reductions in pollutions. 729
The GLOBAL 2000 REPORT concludes with this summary: 740

> The available evidence leaves no doubt that the world . . . 752
> faces enormous, urgent, and complex problems in the decades 764
> immediately ahead. Prompt and vigorous changes in public policy 777
> around the world are needed . . . . If decisions are delayed until 791
> the problems become worse, options for effective action will be 803
> severely reduced. 807

Commenting on the GLOBAL 2000 REPORT, an editorial in The Christian 823
Science Monitor (July 29, 1980) had this to say: "With the new U.S. Report 842
added to several other global studies . . . humanity can't say it has not been 857
warned." If the REPORT startles the world into constructive and creative so- 873
lutions to these and other problems, it will have accomplished its purpose. We 889
will need to help solve the urgent problems of this planet Earth--we can do it if 905
we plan together. The world can become a better place to live for everyone. 919

Prepare the references shown at the right as page 4 of your report.

REFERENCES 2

Global 2000 Report. U.S. Government Printing Office, 1980, 766 pages. 20

"2000 A.D.--It's Up to Us." The Christian Science Monitor, July 29, 1980, p. 24. 42

134

134a ▶ 5 Conditioning practice

Follow standard directions, p. 207.

alphabet 1 This quick quiz will cover exceedingly important factors of job skill.
fig/sym 2 Type # next to the figure with which it is used: #5, 6#, #38, 2,970#.
shift key 3 Mrs. Gregory B. McCrary, Jr. lives on Madison Avenue in New York City.
fluency 4 It is easier to make the figure-key reaches if the fingers are curved.
| 1 | 2 | 3 | 4 | 5 | 6 | 7 | 8 | 9 | 10 | 11 | 12 | 13 | 14 |

148b, continued

Test 2
Measure rough-draft skill (15′)

two 5′ writings; circle errors; determine *gwam* and % of transfer; record better rate and % of transfer

all letters used | A | 1.5 si | 5.7 awl | 80% hfw

gwam 3′ | 5′

workers list
In a national study, office ~~employees~~ were asked to ~~highlight~~ 4 | 2

#
some of the things that they wished hadbeen a part of their educa- 8 | 5

By far lc workers need for
tion. The largest number of ~~respondents~~ mentioned the ~~importance~~ 13 | 8

skills, things
~~of~~ language arts, which includes such ~~elements~~ as grammar, spell- 17 | 10

write.
ing, punctuation, vocabulary, and hte abiltiy to ~~compose~~ ~~This~~ 21 | 13

The workers said
~~group of employees believed~~ that better preparation in language 24 | 15

skills enabled to do a better
arts could have ~~helped~~ them ~~improve their~~ job. ~~performance~~ Many 29 | 17

workers w routine
of the ~~respondents~~ said that they were not expected to compose 33 | 20

and had a very real writing skills.
letters and reprots, thus theyneed for ~~improved language arts~~ 38 | 23

office workers who were part of the study also said
The ~~respondents, also, mentioned~~ that shorthand skill would 44 | 26

very lc amazing
have been help ful to them in their jobs. DEspite the growth of 49 | 29

a very tool taking
word processing installations, shorthand is useful for ~~recording~~ 54 | 32

telephone messages, ~~taking~~ notes, ~~recording~~ minutes of meetings, 57 | 34

items. workers
and ~~taking~~ confidential ~~correspondence~~ The ~~respondents~~ felt a 60 | 36

and decision-making it would be well for
need for management skills. They suggested that our schools ~~to~~ 67 | 40

and
~~should~~ teach students how to be versatile, resourceful, and how to 71 | 43

quickly from one task to another may that
switch ~~tasks~~ as more urgent needs arise. In addition, they said 78 | 47

and adjust to the
students must be sure to learn to work under pressure of time. 83 | 50

Test 3
Measure letter skill (15′)

plain full sheets; block style, open; proofread, circle errors; determine *gwam*

Using standard margins, type a 10′ writing on the letter arranged in proper form.

words

June 10, 19-- Dr. Daniel Wunsch Business Education Department De Kalb 14
High School De Kalb, IL 60115-7136 Dear Dr. Wunsch 24
(¶ 1) To make the transition from school to work easier for young persons, 38
many schools are making experience-based career education, executive- 52
internship, cross-age tutoring, work-study, cooperative education, and similar 68
programs a part of the overall educational program of the school. In the 83
classroom, typing programs are incorporating office simulation into the 97
learning activities of students as a way to give students officelike experi- 112
ences. 114
(¶ 2) We are planning a conference for educators and students on the school- 128
to-work problem. To help us in the planning, we need input from you and 142
your students. Please take a few minutes to complete the Teacher Question- 157
naire and have two students that you select complete the Student Question- 172
naires that are enclosed. When the questionnaires are completed, return 187
them to us in the enclosed postage-paid envelope. 197
(¶ 3) May we hear from you soon. We need your help. 207
Sincerely yours CONTEMPORARY RESEARCH INSTITUTE Ms. Donna Brown, 220
Conference Planner xx Enclosures (182) 226

133b ▶ 45
Type a report with a table and paragraph headings

DS report; TS below main heading; DS above and below table; DS columnar items

Margins

top: 2″ elite
1½″ pica
side: 1″
bottom: approx. 1″

Note: If you do not have a page line gauge, make a light pencil mark about 1″ from the bottom edge of the page, and another mark about ½″ above that to alert you to the page ending.

Goal: To complete report in time provided.

words

THE GLOBAL 2000 REPORT 5

In 1980, the U.S. Government released its three-year study, the GLOBAL 19
2000 REPORT, the first full-scale demographic and ecological model in history 34
released by a government. The massive report highlighted the growing 48
awareness of the interdependence of population, resources, and environment. 64
The report depicts conditions that are likely to develop by the year 2000 if 79
there are no changes in public policies, institutions, and rates of technologi- 95
cal growth and development. 101

The GLOBAL 2000 REPORT presents findings that are similar to those of 115
other global studies, such as those published by the World Bank, various 129
United Nations commissions, the Club of Rome, and the World Future Soci- 144
ety. The principal findings of the REPORT are these: 155

1. Population. The rapid growth of world population at a rate of ap- 171
proximately 100 million annually will continue until the year 2000. The esti- 186
mated population growth is shown in the table below: 197

WORLD POPULATION GROWTH 202

(In Billions) 205

1980	4.4	207
1990	5.3	208
2000	6.3	210

Where there are two people today, there will be three by the year 2000. 224
Nearly 90 percent of the growth will occur in the poorest countries of the 239
world, countries least able to support such population growth. 252

2. Wealth. The economic gap between rich and poor nations will con- 267
tinue to widen, all of which will lead to serious problems of unrest and a vola- 283
tile and unsettled world political situation. 292

3. Arable land. The arable land in cultivation is being both reduced 309
and increased, with a net expected increase of only 4 percent by the year 324
2000. Rain forests of the Amazon and other regions are being denuded and 339
destroyed by the inroads of population growth. This fact, some predict, may 354
change the climate of the world and increase the probability of serious 368
droughts. With a population increase of about 50 percent by the year 2000, 384
the future outlook for food is indeed bleak. Presently, faulty methods are 399
turning grassland and cropland into a "barren wasteland" at an alarming 413
rate. As a consequence, hunger and starvation will greatly increase in the 428
future. 430

4. Energy. With world oil production approaching its limits, there will 446
be a serious energy crisis by the year 2000 with many countries having dif- 461
ficulties meeting even a minimum of energy needs. The only hope will be in 476
the rapid development of alternate energy resources, such as hydrogen, 490
liquified coal, solar, thermal, and wind energies. 501

5. Water. Water will become an increasingly scarce resource as popu- 516
lation growth doubles the demand for water. With the world's forests dis- 531
appearing at the rate of an area about half the size of California each year, 546
the problem of the future will become one of adequate sources of water 560

(continued, p. 218)

149a ▶ 5
Conditioning practice

Follow standard directions, p. 241.

alphabet	1	By frequent but zany adjustments, these executives kept your goodwill.
fig/sym	2	H78-15 radial tires (whitewall) were priced at $42.39, plus $2.60 FET.
shift key	3	They read the articles "Fatigue," "How to Relax," and "Saving Energy."
fluency	4	He may sign a contract by the end of the week so we can test the case.
		| 1 | 2 | 3 | 4 | 5 | 6 | 7 | 8 | 9 | 10 | 11 | 12 | 13 | 14 |

149b ▶ 15
Measure basic skill: statistical copy

two 5′ writings; circle errors; determine *gwam* and % of transfer; record better rate and % of transfer score

all letters used | A | 1.5 si | 5.7 awl | 80% hfw |

	gwam 3′	5′	
In an analysis of a random sample of the business letters produced	4	3	46
by firms in the United States, it was revealed that a majority of the	9	5	49
letters (57%) were in the shorter classification (125 words or less).	14	8	51
Average-length letters (126-225) made up the next largest category of	18	11	54
letters produced (26%). Long letters (226-325) were found in only 9% of	23	14	57
the random sample of letters. Two-page letters were even less frequently	28	17	60
used as they made up only 8% of the random sample.	32	19	62
A majority of the letters (54%) in the random sample were typewrit-	36	22	65
ten with a standard 6-inch line. The 2-letter state ZIP Code abbrevia-	41	25	68
tion was used with 30% of the letters. An additional 11% of the letters	46	27	71
incorporated tables as a part of the body of the letter. Standard let-	51	30	73
terhead stationery (8 1/2″ × 11″) was used with 97% of the letters.	55	33	76
That the block style letter is increasing in popularity is indicated	60	36	79
by the finding that 45% of the letters were typed in the block style.	64	39	82
The name of the signer of the letter was typed in the closing lines in	69	41	85
95% of the letters in the random sample.	72	43	86

gwam 3′ | 1 | 2 | 3 | 4 | 5 |
5′ | 1 | 2 | 3 |

149c ▶ 8
Measure spelling skill from dictation

half sheet, short side up; DS columnar items; center heading on Line 11

Left margin setting
elite: 16
pica: 10

Tab stop setting
elite: 38
pica: 32

Arrange words in a 2-column table as they are dictated to you by your teacher.

1. Center and type heading.
2. Close book and type words from dictation.
3. Check your spelling with that shown in book.
4. Score spelling skill by deducting 3½ points for each misspelled word from a possible perfect score of 100.

WORDS FREQUENTLY MISSPELLED

argument	mileage	attendance	miscellaneous
beginning	misspell	belief	ninety
believe	occasion	brief	occurred
calendar	planned	campaign	privilege
conferring	proceed	copying	quantity
definite	receipt	desirable	recommend
enough	separate	familiar	similar

132

132a ▶ 5 Conditioning practice

Follow standard directions, p. 207.

alphabet	1	Just strive for maximum progress by quickly organizing the daily work.
fig/sym	2	May I order the 16-, 20-, and 24-foot beams (5 7/8" × 9 3/4") for you?
long reaches	3	Many union officials brought bright nylon flags to the union ceremony.
fluency	4	Please send a tax statement to them at their old civic center address.

| 1 | 2 | 3 | 4 | 5 | 6 | 7 | 8 | 9 | 10 | 11 | 12 | 13 | 14 |

132b ▶ 45 Build production skill: form letters

plain full sheets; block style, open; 1 cc; correct errors

1. In the time available, type personalized form letters to as many as possible of the names and addresses given on the cc of the 131c memo. Because you are writing for a *local* branch of Union Federal Savings & Loan, use your school's city and ZIP Code for each letter address.

2. Proofread each letter before removing it from your typewriter to be sure all errors are corrected.

Note: No job or task is always exciting; make this activity challenging by trying to type each new letter in less time. Good luck!

words

May 12, 19-- (Provide address lines and salutation) (¶ 1) Your Money Market 14
Certificate, No. (show account number), will mature on (show maturity date). Your 26
account will automatically renew at the current Union Federal rate in effect on 42
the maturity date unless we hear from you. (¶ 2) You have a seven-day grace 56
period following the maturity date to make whatever changes you would like, 71
such as (1) changing your interest rate to a higher Union Federal rate; 85
(2) adding to or reinvesting your funds; or, (3) changing the time and manner in 102
which interest is to be paid to you. (¶ 3) Please mail us your passbook in the 116
enclosed envelope, so that it can be updated to reflect the current interest rate 133
and new maturity date; or better still, come in and visit your Union Federal 148
office. We want to give you any personal assistance we can with the various 164
options available to you. You are a special saver, (title/last name), and we'd like 179
to treat you as a special person. Sincerely yours Xavier Thomas Branch Man- 195
ager xx Enclosure (176) * 198

* The word count is based on the average number of words in the insertions.

133

133a ▶ 5 Conditioning practice

Follow standard directions, p. 207.

alphabet	1	Jack Lowfax made amazing progress by using improved typing techniques.
fig/sym	2	Is the total charge on Order No. 7832, dated May 10, $45.69 or $54.96?
space bar	3	May Jenny go with them when they go to the city to sign the pay forms?
fluency	4	Try to let the fingers do the typing and your skill will grow rapidly.

| 1 | 2 | 3 | 4 | 5 | 6 | 7 | 8 | 9 | 10 | 11 | 12 | 13 | 14 |

149d ▶ 7
Check related learning skill

1" top margin; 70-space line; DS sentences

1. Type the sentence number and the period; space twice; then type the sentences, making any needed corrections or insertions at the points of the color underlines.

2. Mark your errors as your teacher reads the corrections. Record your name and number of errors.

1. the basic colors are red_ yellow_ and blue_
2. i shall meet senator bradley at the olympic club_
3. 9 visitors are here_ twelve or 13 more will arrive soon.
4. The letter _Exhibit A_ and the report _Exhibit B_ are needed.
5. The boys hat, the mens shirts, and the girls sweaters are lost.
6. Read the articles: _running,_ diet right,_ and healthful hints._
7. _Will he go_ she asked, _this week or next_
8. Everyone (is, are) here.
9. Each of the students (is, are) ready to go.
10. Two thirds of the work (is, are) done.
11. Jan and Jill have lost (her, their) books.

149e ▶ 15
Check table typing skill

full sheet; reading position; DS data of columns; correct errors

To give you the experience of working under the pressure of time, you are asked to type the table as directed in 15' or less.

As time permits, retype the table on a half sheet, long side up.

TYPING TASKS PERFORMED
ACCORDING TO JOB CLASSIFICATIONS

(Percent of Typing Time)

	Typist	Steno.	Secretary	W.P.O.*	Other**
Letters	21%	27%	32%	32%	23%
Reports	16	20	19	24	21
Memos	12	19	22	14	13
Forms	29	11	11	7	24
Tables	9	13	9	15	8
Other typing	13	10	7	8	11
Totals	100%	100%	100%	100%	100%

*Word Processing Operators.

**Workers with titles other than those listed.

131

131a ▶ 5
Conditioning practice
Follow standard directions, p. 207.

alphabet	1	Liza picked several exquisite flowers which grew by the jungle swamps.
fig/sym	2	Is USAir 25, a 747 jet, scheduled to arrive at 8:36 p.m. or 9:01 p.m.?
long reaches	3	A minimum number of units were needed by my new special service group.
fluency	4	Keep the right thumb close to the space bar in order to space quickly.

| 1 | 2 | 3 | 4 | 5 | 6 | 7 | 8 | 9 | 10 | 11 | 12 | 13 | 14 |

131b ▶ 20
Measure tabulation skill
two 5′ writings; proofread; determine *gwam*

full sheet; reading position; 4 spaces between columns; DS data in columns

Each figure is used a minimum of 17 times.

Arrange table in proper form. You will have 3′ to 4′ to determine left margin stop and tab stops for columns. Also, determine points at which main heading and column headings start. Make notations of these points.

Main heading: MONEY MARKET ACCOUNTS — words 4

Name	Address	Acct. No.	Amount	words
Column headings				16
Wayne Albertson	1314 Marion Circle	6-573-205	$14,598	26
Dr. Lily Beck	249 S. Palm Drive	7-458-629	$27,360	36
Ms. Dale DiNatale	747 17th St., S.E.	6-920-783	$13,546	47
Mrs. Janet Kehl	880 Hilldale Avenue	6-038-359	$11,247	57
Francis Muller	30527 Cutlass Lane	3-674-204	$38,596	68
Ms. Yvette Parks	288 Barrington Court	6-729-427	$15,380	79
Monty Raintree	803 Oletha Lane	5-809-956	$27,436	88
Victor Sanchez	13 Royal Avenue	5-981-367	$10,924	98
Norman Takeda	647 St. Alban Plaza	4-008-276	$29,351	108
Miss Betty Unger	904 Oberlin Blvd.	1-738-946	$17,250	118
Zack von Daalen	795 West 34th Street	2-830-565	$46,197	129
David Zeitman	314 Old Ranch Road	6-288-107	$14,935	139

131c ▶ 25
Type a memo
plain full sheet; 1″ side margins, 1½″ top margin; 1 cc; correct errors; SS table

Save carbon copy for use in 132b, p. 216.

Indent 5→ TO: Mr. Xavier Thomas, Branch Manager

Indent 3→ FROM: Jean Cey, Savings Accounting

Indent 3→ DATE: May 10, 19--

Left margin→ SUBJECT: June 20, Money Market Maturities

Money Market Certificates that will mature on June 20 are shown below. These names are being sent to you so that the regular form letter for maturing accounts can be sent to them.

(¶) Triple-space and type the entire table given in 131b above. Center the table horizontally as directed. SS columnar items.

150

150a ▶ 5 Conditioning practice

Follow standard directions, p. 241.

alphabet	1	Jack Wolfram quickly realized that excellent typing skill is valuable.
fig/sym	2	The Oriental rug (12′ × 15′) was $7,680, but it is on sale for $4,934.
space bar	3	Ann said she may pay us to do the job for her if we can do it by noon.
fluency	4	If we are to do the work, she may help us with the audit of the firms.

| 1 | 2 | 3 | 4 | 5 | 6 | 7 | 8 | 9 | 10 | 11 | 12 | 13 | 14 |

150b ▶ 15 Measure basic skill: straight copy

two 5′ writings; circle errors; determine *gwam*; record better rate

Keystroking: manual or electric

* Strike each key with a quick, snappy stroke.
* Use a quick, down-and-in motion of the finger.
* Release key quickly.
* Keep wrists low and relaxed; hands quiet.
* Use finger-reach action.

Correct finger curvature

Correct finger alignment

Quick snap stroke

all letters used | A | 1.5 si | 5.7 awl | 80% hfw |

	gwam 3′	5′
A fundamental approach in the improvement of your writing competency	5	3
is to utilize the technique of oral writing or dictation. It may be less	10	6
difficult to begin your campaign of writing development if you first	14	8
record what you want to write; then, as you listen to the playback, you	19	11
can determine if what you have dictated is clear, concise, and complete.	24	14
The objective of all good writing should be to talk to the reader in	28	17
words of everyday good English. As you dictate, try to visualize and	33	20
adapt your dictation to your reader. Your target in writing, or in the	38	23
dictation of what you wish to write, should be to make personal contact	43	25
with your reader.	44	26
The initial step in preparation for dictation is to gather any	48	29
needed reference materials. In the business office, the needed reference	53	32
materials may be the letter or the memorandum to which you are respond-	58	35
ing. If such is the case, it may be useful to underline the primary	62	37
points in these documents. Another step that is often urged is the	67	40
preparation of a brief outline in which you list in priority order the	72	43
exact points you wish to cover. Sometimes, all that is necessary is to	77	46
jot down a few brief notes of the items you plan to include in your	81	49
letter, report, or paper. Lastly, the language of good writing should	86	51
be natural, just as though you were talking to your reader.	90	54

gwam 3′ | 1 | 2 | 3 | 4 | 5 |
5′ | 1 | 2 | 3 |

130c ▶ 30 Measure production skill: letters

[LM pp. 67-70] or plain full sheets

Time schedule

Planning and preparing . 4′
Production and timing .. 20′
Proofreading; computing *n-pram* .... 6′

Problem 1

block style, open; 1″ side margins

Note: If pica type is used, start date on Line 12; elite, Line 13. Indent enumerated items 5 spaces from either margin.

words

Current date Mrs. Rose Gard Business Education Department Middletown High 15
School Middletown, NY 10940-2237 Dear Mrs. Gard (¶ 1) I am glad to respond 29
to your request to describe some of the things we expect from our beginning 45
office typists. In all departments, our typists are expected to be able to type 61
letters, reports, forms, and other copy from handwriting, rough draft, or other 77
source materials. Before they begin the typing task, they are expected to get any 93
special reference materials that may be needed in typing the final copy. (¶ 2) The 109
materials needed to complete typing tasks may originate in a variety of ways: 125

1. They may be given to the typist by the supervisor. 136

2. The typist may be asked to refer to the files for needed mate- 149
rials. 151

3. The typist may need to go to other offices to secure the source 164
materials or other data. 170

(¶ 3) To perform effectively in an office situation, the typists must have 183
learned to listen to, understand, and follow directions without asking unneces- 199
sary questions. They must also have learned to make critical judgments relat- 215
ing to the acceptability of the copy they have typed. We expect our typists to 231
proofread their completed work and to find and correct all typing errors. (¶ 4) 246
Please let me know if you or your students have other questions or problems 261
with which I might help you. I hope the comments I have made in this letter 276
will be of value to you. Sincerely yours CONTINENTAL ENTERPRISES, INC. 291
John Lambert, President xx (269) **296/315**

Problem 2

block style, open

Note: Because of the table, use 1½″ side margins and start the date on Line 16. Use your judgment in setting up the table.

Current date Mr. John Gonzales San Diego Mesa College 7250 Artillery Drive 16
San Diego, CA 92111-6474 Dear Mr. Gonzales (¶ 1) A recent study of the margin 30
settings used for business letters shows the following practices: 44
DS

MARGINS FOR LETTERS 48
TS

Variable margins	68%	52
	DS	
Fixed margins*	32	55

________________ SS DS 59

*Most typists use the standard 65
6-inch line. 68
DS

(¶ 2) When variable margins are used, the typist adjusts the margin stops accord- 83
ing to the length of the letter being typed. Fixed margins means that the same 99
margins are used for all letters, irrespective of the length. (¶ 3) The study also 114
revealed that the block style letter is rapidly gaining in popularity. Sincerely 131
yours Ms. Janet Scribner Communications Consultant xx (104) **141/159**

150c ▶ 30
Check report typing skill

Type report in unbound manuscript form; DS; number second page in upper right corner; DS data of table; correct errors.

Keep a record of the time it takes you to type the report. Your goal is to type it in 30′ or less.

words

HOW OFFICE WORKERS USING THE TYPEWRITER 8
SPEND THEIR TYPING TIME 13

A recent study of a random sample of business firms in the United 26
States reveals that the typewriter is used for a variety of typing activities by 42
workers in various job classifications. 50
When typewriting tasks were analyzed according to job classifications, 65
the differing roles of office workers in terms of the kinds of materials typed 80
are as shown in the following table: 88

TYPING TASKS PERFORMED 93
ACCORDING TO JOB CLASSIFICATIONS 99

(Percent of Typing Time) 104

	Typist	Steno.	Secretary	W.P.O.*	Other**	
Letters	21%	27%	32%	32%	23%	125
Reports	16	20	19	24	21	129
Memos	12	19	22	14	13	134
Forms	29	11	11	7	24	138
Tables	9	13	9	15	8	142
Other typing	13	10	7	8	11	152
Totals	100%	100%	100%	100%	100%	159

(header row: 119)

──────── 163
* Word Processing Operators. 169
** Workers with titles other than those listed. 178

Typists, usually the least experienced and lowest paid of the office cler- 193
ical staff, typed more business forms (29 percent) than any other kind of typ- 209
ing activity. The typing of letters was second in importance with this group 224
of workers. 227
Among stenographers, 27 percent of their typing time was spent in typ- 241
ing letters. Reports (20 percent) and memos (19 percent) ranked a close sec- 256
ond and third. As would be expected, secretaries spend much of their time 271
(32 percent) typing business letters. Next in importance for secretaries, in 287
terms of typing time, was the typing of memos or interoffice correspondence 302
(22 percent). 305
It would be expected that word processing operators, who usually oper- 319
ate highly sophisticated electronic typewriting equipment, would spend most 334
of their time (32 percent) typing letters. The typing of reports occupied 349
another 24 percent of their typing time. The analysis revealed, too, that word 365
processing operators spend more of their typing time typing tables (15 per- 380
cent) when compared with workers in other job classifications; however, 395
stenographers spend nearly as much time typing tables (13 percent). 409
Workers classified as "Other" were comparable to typists in the per- 422
cent of typing time devoted to typing various kinds of materials. As is true 438
with workers in traditional job classifications, these "Other" workers also 453
spend much time typing letters (23 percent) and reports (21 percent). 467
"Other typing" included such typing activities as the typing of mes- 481
sages, index card items, envelope addresses, itineraries, rough-draft copy, 496
contracts, minutes of meetings, press releases, and miscellaneous other 510
items. 512

130

130a ▶ 5 Conditioning practice

Follow standard directions, p. 207.

alphabet	1	Just take what belongs to Paula; exit quickly from the velodrome zone.
fig/sym	2	McNeil & DeWeise, 13478 Quin Blvd., paid Invoice No. 256 ($90), May 1.
adj key/ long reaches	3	In perfect formation, four porpoises jumped over many of the pontoons.
fluency	4	They had moved to a new address when the statement was mailed to them.

| 1 | 2 | 3 | 4 | 5 | 6 | 7 | 8 | 9 | 10 | 11 | 12 | 13 | 14 |

130b ▶ 15 Measure basic skill: straight copy

two 5′ writings; determine *gwam*; proofread and circle errors; record better rate.

Goal: To improve your straight-copy rate. Do this by typing with continuity and without "a sense of hurry."

all letters used | A | 1.5 si | 5.7 awl | 80% hfw |

	gwam 3′	5′	
The office of the future will continue to generate enormous amounts	5	3	49
of paperwork, ranging all the way from letters to entire books. Whether	9	6	52
the copy is originally submitted by way of or with the aid of dictating	14	9	55
devices, shorthand notes, or handwritten pages is not the issue. Regard-	19	11	58
less of the format or the form, a written communication is generally	24	14	61
typed as the final step in its production cycle, and only one person, a	28	17	64
typist, or however that person is named, is the one who is responsible	33	20	67
for the final product. That person will continue to do a most important	38	23	69
and exciting job in the office of the future.	41	25	71
In addition, typing in the future will become an integral part of	46	27	74
many jobs, and not just the job of the so-called typist. Typewriters	50	30	77
are used now to communicate with computers, for calling up materials	55	33	80
from electronic files, and as a general timesaver in other writing.	59	36	82
Probably in the future, the typewriter will be used in the home as an	64	38	85
interaction mechanism with educational television. To be able to type	69	41	88
is recognized as one of the most valuable skills we can acquire. It	73	44	91
is important, therefore, that we learn to type and to type well.	78	47	93

gwam 3′ | 1 | 2 | 3 | 4 | 5 |
5′ | 1 | 2 | 3 |

phase 7 lessons 151-175

Recall /improve performance skills

Phase 7 begins with a unit designed to check and improve your skill on straight, script, rough-draft, and statistical copy. It is followed by units which will review and improve your skill in typing letters, tables, and reports.

The last two units measure basic skills and production typing.

The 25 lessons in Phase 7 will give you many opportunities to:

1. Improve your speed and accuracy on straight, script, rough-draft, and statistical copy.

2. Improve your transfer skill from straight copy to script, rough-draft, and statistical copy.

3. Improve your skill in typing letters, tables, and reports.

4. Improve various language arts skills.

5. Improve techniques that contribute to typewriting power.

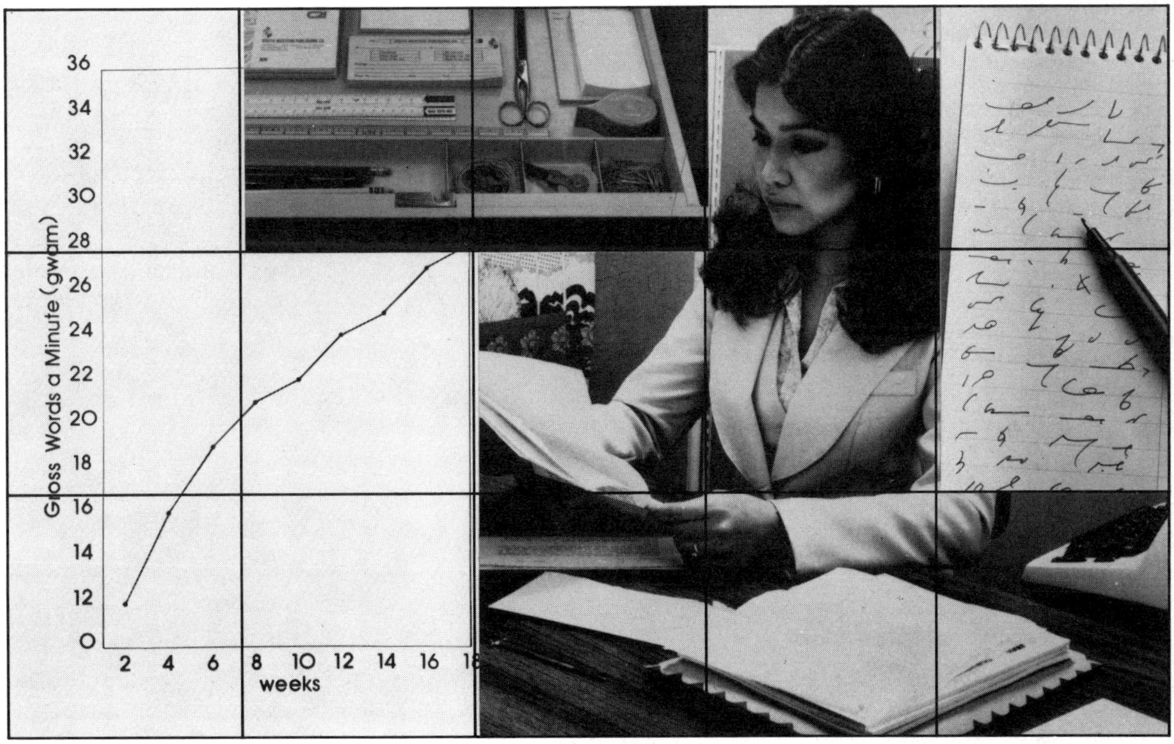

unit 28 lessons 151-155

Check/improve basic skills

Learning goals

1. To improve your straight-copy speed and accuracy.

2. To improve your transfer skill to at least 90% on script, 80% on rough-draft, and 75% on statistical copy from straight copy.

3. To improve word-division skills.

4. To improve keystroking skill.

Machine adjustments

1. Paper guide at *0*.

2. Ribbon control to type on top half of ribbon.

3. Margin sets: 70-space line for drills and timed writings; as directed for language arts and tabulating drills.

4. Spacing: SS sentence drills; DS ¶s; as directed for language arts and tabulating drills.

129c ▶ 20
Build letter production skill

plain full sheets; block style, open; 2" side margins; date on Line 19

1. A 3′ writing on the letter to establish a base rate. If you finish before time is called, start over.

2. Determine *gwam*. Add 8 to this rate. Divide new goal rate by 4; note ¼′ checkpoints for guided writings.

3. Reset margins for a standard 6–inch line. Beginning with the date, type three 1′ guided writings on the opening parts of the letter and ¶1. Leave proper spacing between letter parts, but begin letter (dateline) on Line 7. Start second and third writings a DS below last line of previous writing.

4. Repeat Step 3, but use ¶2 and the closing lines of the letter.

5. Type another 3′ writing on the letter. Use standard 6–inch line. Try to maintain your new goal rate. Do this by using good techniques (fingers curved; quick, snappy keystroking) and by typing with continuity. Determine *gwam* and compare it with the rate attained in Step 1.

	words in parts	gwam 3′
May 7, 19-- Mr. Henry Jimenez 4138 N. Central Avenue Phoenix,	12	4
AZ 85012-8543 Dear Mr. Jimenez	19	6
(¶ 1) There are many ways to improve letter production skills.	11	10
One way, but not always the most efficient way, is to type many	24	14
letters. This approach works well if the typist makes an	36	18
earnest effort to improve.	41	20
(¶ 2) Often, a more effective way to improve letter production	53	24
skills is to type letters within some time frame, such as a	65	28
timed production writing. When this is done, the typist can	77	32
give a specific purpose to the practice activities so as to	89	36
improve.	91	37
Sincerely Ms. Lynn Oaks Communications Consultant xx	10	40

gwam 3′ | 1 | 2 | 3 | 4 |

129d ▶ 15
Improve letter production skill

plain full sheets; modified block style, indented ¶s, mixed; 2" side margins; 1cc; correct errors; use your initials as reference; address large envelopes or paper cut to envelope size (see Reference Guide, p. vi)

Type letter of 129c, above, to as many of the addresses given here as time permits. Proofread by typing each letter from the preceding one.

Dr. Susan Hess Records Office Ohio University Athens, OH 45701-8816

Ms. Carmen Delatorre 424 N. Roxbury Drive Beverly Hills, CA 90210-7202

Dr. David Schrier 402 N. Michigan Avenue Chicago, IL 60611-9320

Dr. Gordon Berry 1502 S. Prairie Avenue Sioux Falls, SD 57101-8740

Mrs. Larry Stern 605 Cooper Landing Road Cherry Hill, NJ 08002-3303

Miss Melinda Pierson 156 South Swan Street Albany, NY 12210-6215

151a ▶ 5 Conditioning practice

each line twice SS (slowly, then faster); DS between 2-line groups; if time permits, retype selected lines

alphabet	1	Gomez jokes expertly with a friend but can be very shy and very quiet.
figures	2	The following pages need some corrections: 8, 25, 36, 47, 50, and 91.
fig/sym	3	Jones & Co. paid $1,287.49 for a Model #65302 copier for their office.
fluency	4	The auditors may work with the problems of the six firms if they wish.
		| 1 | 2 | 3 | 4 | 5 | 6 | 7 | 8 | 9 | 10 | 11 | 12 | 13 | 14 |

151b ▶ 15 Check straight-copy skill

1. Two 1′ writings on each of the 3¶s; determine *gwam* and number of errors on each writing.

2. A 3′ writing on ¶s 1–3 combined; determine *gwam* and number of errors.

all letters used | A | 1.5 si | 5.7 awl | 80% hfw |

	gwam 1′	3′
People who work in what is now being called word processing need	13	4
more than manipulative power. To be effective, they must have good	27	9
knowledge of language, also. It is more often a lack of command of	40	13
language, instead of a lack of manipulative ability, that causes many	54	18
a word processing worker to fail. Is spelling important in an office?	68	23
Of course it is. Is the ability to use good grammar needed? Yes, it	84	27
is, too. These are two major communication skills in an office.	96	32
It is reliably estimated that for the next several years there	13	36
will be between three and four hundred thousand jobs a year available	27	41
to those trained as secretaries and typists in this country. Some of	40	45
these will be new positions; others will be existing jobs that are	54	50
being vacated by people who will retire, by those who have been pro-	67	54
moted, and by others who have quit to take other positions or for some	82	59
other reason.	85	60
Many of these jobs will be open to high school graduates, particu-	13	64
larly to individuals who have top skills in typing, in related English,	28	69
in shorthand or machine transcription, and in related modern office	41	74
procedures. The prize jobs will go to those people who, through at	55	78
least part-time work, have demonstrated that they can work harmoniously	69	83
with others as well as build their job skills to a very high level.	83	88
Skills help us to get the job; human relations help us to keep it.	97	92

gwam 1′ | 1 | 2 | 3 | 4 | 5 | 6 | 7 | 8 | 9 | 10 | 11 | 12 | 13 | 14 |
3′ | 1 | 2 | 3 | 4 | 5 |

151c ▶ 15 Improve straight-copy skill

1. Determine a goal of speed or of control according to your needs based on performance on 151b above. Work for *control* if you exceeded 2 errors a minute in the 1′ writings; otherwise, work for *speed*.

2. Two 1′ writings on each ¶ of 151b above.

3. A 3′ writing on ¶s 1–3 combined; determine *gwam* and number of errors. Compare scores with first 3′ scores.

4. Record your 3′ *gwam* for use in Lessons 152–154.

128b, continued

Problem 3 Average length letter — words

Current date **Mrs. Corinna Andrade 11045 Dug Gap Road Dalton, GA 30720-2146** (¶ 1) **The language of investing can be confusing to the layperson. Often the confusion arises when the same term is used to describe different processes. The term depreciation is a case in point. Real estate brokers and tax advisers often use the term to describe an accounting deduction provided by our tax laws. In this context, depreciation does not necessarily reflect an actual decrease in value of property.** (¶ 2) **On the other hand, real estate appraisers often use the terms depreciation and obsolescence interchangeably when analyzing the physical, functional, and economic factors of property. So there you have it. The term depreciation is used both to describe an accounting tax deduction and to describe a process that can result in an actual decrease in value. Dale Schumm Investment Counselor**

Line ends	words
…30720-	15
…Often	29
…pro-	44
…and tax	60
…provided by	75
…an actual	92
…appraisers	108
…when	122
…So there	138
…tax	154
…decrease in	169
…Counselor	177/190

129

129a ▶ 5 Conditioning practice

Follow standard directions, p. 207.

alphabet	1	**Xavier Whipple quickly recognized justice as a basic tenet of freedom.**
fig/sym	2	**Discount terms on Order No. 47-5603 (June 28; $9,500) were 2/10, n/30.**
adj key	3	**Web decided to weigh the poodle, but it darted quickly under the cart.**
fluency	4	**Please sign the contract by the end of the day so I can test the case.**

| 1 | 2 | 3 | 4 | 5 | 6 | 7 | 8 | 9 | 10 | 11 | 12 | 13 | 14 |

129b ▶ 10 Type copy with right margin justified

2 half sheets, short side up; 32-space line; SS; indent ¶s 3 spaces

You are to type the 2 ¶s in Column 1 with the right margin even; SS between ¶s.

1. Type ¶s 1 and 2 of the **WORK COPY** with the / to show needed extra spacing for each line.

2. Center and retype the copy, making the line endings even. Center the heading, **COPY WITH EVEN RIGHT MARGIN,** above the column. Correct all errors.

Paragraph 1 of the **WORK COPY** and the final copy is in completed form. To get right margin even, use your judgment and distribute the spaces so that they are least noticeable.

```
WORK COPY

////////////////////////////////
   Copy is justified (typed with
the right margin even) by adding
extra spaces between words to///
fill out short lines and using//
half spaces between words when//
it may be necessary to squeeze an
extra letter on a line.
   School newspapers which may
be produced with the typewriter
are often typed in this manner
so that the duplicated copies
have the appearance of a printed
page.  First a stencil or spirit
master is typed from the work
copy, and then the desired number
of copies is duplicated.
```

```
COPY WITH EVEN RIGHT MARGIN

   Copy is justified (typed with
the right margin even) by adding
extra  spaces between  words  to
fill out  short lines and  using
half spaces  between words  when
it may be necessary to squeeze an
extra letter on a line.
```

151d ▶ 15
Improve language arts: word division

1. Study word-division guides, Reference Guide, p. iv.
2. Set tab stops according to the key.
3. Center the heading on Line 11 and type the first line of tabulated copy as shown.
4. Type remaining lines in same way, showing in Column 2 all syllable breaks and in Column 3 all acceptable points of word division. If a word should not be divided, type it without hyphens in Column 3.

WORD DIVISION

TS

DS

typewriter	type-writ-er	type-writer
minimal		
increasing		
any		
concentrate		
attention		
everything		
hesitate		
message		
final		
great		
keyboarding		
higher		

key | 11 | 8 | 13 | 8 | 13 |

152

152a ▶ 5
Conditioning practice

each line twice SS (slowly, then faster); DS between 2-line groups; if time permits, retype selected lines

alphabet 1 Beth gave soft drinks and played exotic jazz music to win quick favor.
figures 2 The 1934 coupe and the 1927 roadster were bought by Carmen for $8,065.
fig/sym 3 John's fee for Policy No. 8284519 (underwritten by Centro) was $76.30.
fluency 4 Lane is the man they got to fix their bicycle for the big city social.

| 1 | 2 | 3 | 4 | 5 | 6 | 7 | 8 | 9 | 10 | 11 | 12 | 13 | 14 |

152b ▶ 15
Improve technique: keystroking

each line twice SS; DS between 2-line groups; retype difficult lines as time permits

Response patterns

letter 1 as my in be at mop you sat are tax him were bare loop care only street
word 2 to so go me and wit did cow lap big torn girl with firm held name down
combination 3 in to us up no for ace end few may hand jump them area they form serve

letter 4 are you | were my | in feat | loop on | as my feet | few facts | get him | as stated
word 5 to go | of the | if he | with it | by an | pay it | the box | when he | to wish | for it
combination 6 worn bare | are right | their cases | great city | my name | big area | best world

letter 7 Johnny, were you aware my tax rebate was based only on a minimum rate?
word 8 Is it their duty to fight for the amendment and risk their own profit?
combination 9 When you go to see him, get the right facts so we may handle the case.

| 1 | 2 | 3 | 4 | 5 | 6 | 7 | 8 | 9 | 10 | 11 | 12 | 13 | 14 |

128

128a ▶ 5 Conditioning practice

Follow standard directions, p. 207.

alphabet	1	Huck Bagani quietly expressed the view and zeal of the majority party.
fig/sym	2	Write checks for these amounts: $37.50, $62.94, $8.10, and $1,385.95.
underline	3	<u>Education for the World View</u> is the title of the book by Jean Jackson.
fluency	4	Send a draft of the statement to the union at the address on the card.

| 1 | 2 | 3 | 4 | 5 | 6 | 7 | 8 | 9 | 10 | 11 | 12 | 13 | 14 |

128b ▶ 45 Build letter production skill: short/average/long letters

[LM pp. 63-66] or plain full sheets; modified block style, block paragraphs, mixed punctuation; adjust margins according to letter length

Type letters, supplying appropriate parts as needed. Correct errors. **Goal:** To complete all letters.

Note: In Problem 1, because of the inclusion of a table, start the date on Line 12. Also, leave only a DS after the table heading, an exception that is made when a letter must fit on one page.

Problem 1 Long letter with table — words

April 23, 19-- Dr. Ellis Jones Department of Business Education Gustavus 15
Adolphus College St. Peter, MN 56082-6791 (¶ 1) The "Land of the Midnight 28
Sun" will be the destination of the International Society for Business Education 45
annual group travel program this year. (¶ 2) Scandinavia is a land of con- 58
trasts--spectacular fjords, sparkling waters, placid farmlands, medieval cities 74
shouldering modern bustling cities. Whether your tastes are for gloom in 89
Hamlet's Castle or fun in Tivoli Gardens; shopping for world-famous crystal, 105
silverware, pewter, or textiles; dining on ocean-fresh delicacies piled high 120
in smorgasbords; sightseeing; or simply relaxing in a totally different atmos- 136
phere; the choice is yours. The travel itinerary is shown below: 149
DS

SCANDINAVIAN ADVENTURE 154
DS

City	Dates	Hotel	
Stockholm	Aug. 16-19	Stockholm Hotel SS	167
Oslo	Aug. 20-23	Hotel Scandinavia	174
Copenhagen	Aug. 24-27	Hotel Scandinavia	182

(header row: 160)

DS

(¶ 3) We shall leave the Minneapolis/St. Paul International Airport on August 15 197
and return on August 28. If you have been on an ISBE-sponsored trip before, 212
you know that it is travel with a maximum of convenience, a minimum of 227
annoyances, and a fine group of traveling companions. The enclosed folder 242
describes the "Scandinavian Adventure" in more detail. If you have any ques- 257
tions that are not answered, please call Roy DeSoto at 555-4181. Adrian Stanley 273
Executive Director 277/**297**

Note: In Problem 2, use your best judgment in arranging the listed items.

Problem 2 Short personal business letter with listed items

Your home address; current date Consumer Information Center Pueblo, CO 8
81009-2002 Ladies and Gentlemen: (¶ 1) Enclosed is my check for $4.30. Please 23
send me the publications listed below: 31

A Dollars and Cents Guide to Energy Saving		39
Home Improvements (956G)	$1.70	45
Firewood for Your Fireplace (047G)	.60	53
The Energy-Wise Home Buyer (109G)	<u>2.00</u>	61
	$4.30	62

(¶ 2) Please send these publications to me soon. Sincerely yours, Your name 74
Enclosure 76

Problem 3 is on p. 211.

152c ▶ 15 Check script-copy skill

1. Two 1′ writings on each ¶; determine *gwam* and number of errors on each writing.

2. A 3′ writing on ¶s 1–3 combined; determine *gwam* and number of errors.

all letters used | A | 1.5 si | 5.7 awl | 80% hfw

gwam 1′ 3′

A vital aim of all your typewriting effort now 9 3
should be to develop the highest skill possible. It 20 7
makes little difference whether you plan to apply 30 10
the skill at home, at school, or in industry; the 40 13
basic intent of all your practice is to attain top 50 17
skill. The greatest assurance of eventual success 60 20
is to build typing power now. 66 22

There is no magic plan or simple system by 9 25
which you can obtain maximum typing power. To 18 28
attain a high skill, you must expend extra energy, 28 31
devote many hours to building proper technique on 38 35
copy that includes ideas for growth, and use the 48 38
best and most effective work habits in each prac- 58 41
tice. Top skill is built; it is not presented. 67 44

Students who try for the top rung of the skill 9 48
ladder must be able to adjust to various practice 19 51
routines. No single skill-building activity can supply 31 55
the variety of experiences that will bring maximum 41 58
progress and skill. Sometimes the object of practice 52 62
is to reach out for speed; at other times, the intent 62 65
may be to practice at a slower rate to lower the 72 68
number of errors. Learn now to apply every kind 82 72
of practice procedure with equal zest. 90 74

152d ▶ 15 Improve script-copy skill

1. Determine goal of speed or of control according to your needs based on performance on 152c above. Work for *control* if you exceeded 2 errors a minute on the 1′ writings; otherwise, work for *speed*.

2. Two 1′ writings on each ¶ of 152c above.

3. A 3′ writing on ¶ 1–3 combined; determine *gwam* and number of errors. Compare scores with first 3′ scores.

4. Determine % of transfer: 3′ *gwam* on ¶s above ÷ 3′ *gwam* on ¶s of 151b.

127c, continued

Company name in closing lines

Sincerely yours
DS

WESTWIND COMPANY
2 DS

Mrs. Christy Seligman
Real Estate Consultant
DS

xx
DS

Enclosures

Stay alert! Remember to supply missing parts.

Problem 2 words

Ms. Leslie Flores 15933 Rambla Pacifico Road Malibu, CA 90265-2489 (¶ 1) 14
Enclosed is the residential sales survey you requested. You will find the sur- 29
vey informative and, I think, interesting. (¶ 2) If you would like a more 43
detailed analysis of the figures as they apply to your property, please give me 59
a call at 550-7871; or, if you prefer, just mail the enclosed postage-paid card 75
and we will send you the information. WESTWIND COMPANY Mrs. Christy 89
Seligman Real Estate Consultant Enclosures 97

Problem 3

Dr. Martin Bodine Training Director City Center Hospital 625 Euclid 14
Avenue Kansas City, MO 64124-8813 (¶ 1) Enclosed is the literature you 27
requested on the products of AUDIO GRAPHICS, INC. We are a full-line 41
audiovisual equipment dealer. (¶ 2) We have a complete service department 55
staffed by highly trained technicians to support our clients' equipment care 70
needs. (¶ 3) Why not let one of our representatives arrange a demonstration 84
visit for you soon. Just call 825-0961 for an appointment. AUDIO GRAPHICS, 100
INC. Michael Portney Industrial Sales Division 109

Problem 4

May 10, 19-- Miss Pam Pagetti 2150 South Thurston Avenue Los Angeles, CA 15
90049-4345 (¶ 1) Come join us for a complimentary afternoon in our STEP 28
Program Series for Teenage Success. 35

ROBINSON'S 38
Saturday, June 7 41
Fifth Floor Auditorium 46
Modern Etiquette--1:00-2:00 p.m. 52
Personal Grooming Tips--2:00-3:00 p.m. 60

(¶ 2) An informal discussion session with refreshments will follow im- 73
mediately after the program. Space is limited, so return the enclosed card 88
today to confirm your reservation. Jerry Brophe Teen-World Coordinator 102

Problem 5

Mr. Tracy Connors 11438 Vista Lane Sunriver, OR 97701-4742 (¶ 1) Won't 13
you take a few minutes to read the enclosed booklet about your health insur- 28
ance plan. This new booklet tells you about your benefits and how they work. 44
(¶ 2) Keep the booklet in a handy place with your other benefit papers in case 59
there is a need to file a claim. If you have specific questions about your in- 75
surance, just write or call the Benefits Representative. Miss Anice Ahmad 90
Benefits Manager 93

153

153a ▶ 5 Conditioning practice

each line twice SS (slowly, then faster); DS between 2-line groups; if time permits, retype selected lines

alphabet 1 Zack did fly quite a way by private plane just for the extra meetings.
figures 2 What is the sum of 12 and 39 and 1 and 43 and 75 and 48 and 93 and 60?
fig/sym 3 The store clerk replied, "The cost of 10 dozen #74529 pens is $63.80."
fluency 4 They may wish to pay their own dues for fuel when they visit the firm.

| 1 | 2 | 3 | 4 | 5 | 6 | 7 | 8 | 9 | 10 | 11 | 12 | 13 | 14 |

153b ▶ 15 Check rough-draft skill

1. Two 1′ writings on each ¶; determine *gwam* and number of errors on each writing.
2. A 3′ writing on ¶s 1–3 combined; determine *gwam* and number of errors.

all letters used | A | 1.5 si | 5.7 awl | 80% hfw |

	gwam 1′	3′
A manager is one who acheives a goal or objective by	11	4
guidingother poeple. We my think a manager is required to	23	8
work in a business;but home makers, teachers and leaders of	35	12
youth ~~groups,~~ are examples of managers too as they seek to	48	16
obtain reuslts throught others.	54	18
It is very probably that you wil be ~~selected,~~ to perform the	12	22
job of a manager of some kind If so, you will be expected	24	26
ot set long-,intermediate-, and short-term goals. Therefore,	36	30
you must organize ~~several~~ resources that may involve people,	49	35
equipment and materials to help	59	38
as a manager, you will also play the parts of controller	11	42
and leader. ~~In order,~~ to control, you will analyze effort to	22	45
make sure thet goals are ~~accomplished,~~ quickly. As a leader,	33	49
you will get people to want to expeditethe stated objectives.	46	53
Actuating is and other work some times used to mean lead.	57	57

153c ▶ 15 Improve rough-draft skill

1. Determine goal of speed or control according to your needs based on performance on 153b above. Work for *control* if you exceeded 2 errors a minute on the 1′ writings; otherwise, work for *speed*.

2. Two 1′ writings on each ¶ of 153b above.

3. A 3′ writing on ¶s 1–3 combined; determine *gwam* and number of errors. Compare scores with first 3′ scores.

4. Determine % of transfer: 3′ *gwam* on ¶s above ÷ 3′ *gwam* on the ¶s of 151b.

126c ▶ 30
Improve letter production skill

plain full sheets; block style, open punctuation; standard 6" line; current date on Line 16; supply appropriate opening and closing lines

Use your name as dictator with title, **Communications Consultant,** and with **R-1: (your initials)** as reference.

Type letters to as many of the addresses given here as time permits. Make 1 carbon copy. As ¶1, use the paragraph shown at the right; then use ¶s 2 and 3 of 126b, p. 207. Type each letter, after the first, from the previous copy. (Disregard color underlines.)

(¶1) Your questions about how personal titles are used in letters are frequently asked. The guides given here represent some of the accepted ways to use a personal title with a name.

Addresses

			gwam 3'
Miss Beth Ingram	619 Chapel Drive	Gary, IN 46410-8391	4
Dr. Lloyd Sobel	165 Cedar Lane	Ogden, UT 84403-5668	7
Ms. Keri Clark	607 Midland Road	Fairfax, VA 22031-4034	11
Mr. James Deitz	10 Acela Drive	Tiburon, CA 94920-2875	15
Mrs. Glenda Jett	812 Ross Avenue	Newport, KY 41073-7681	18
Dr. Jack Nagai	712 Spiral Court	Tampa, FL 33610-6295	22

127

127a ▶ 5
Conditioning practice

Follow standard directions, p. 207.

alphabet	1	Vague new exploratory uses of helium amazed quaint, judicious brokers.
fig/sym	2	The purchase price is $24,517.90 plus 6% sales tax and 38% excise tax.
adj key	3	A porter pushed sulky carts across a weed field opposite the new fort.
fluency	4	The auditor will send a statement to the firm by the end of the month.

| 1 | 2 | 3 | 4 | 5 | 6 | 7 | 8 | 9 | 10 | 11 | 12 | 13 | 14 |

127b ▶ 10
Improve tabulation skill

full sheet

Two 3' writings on addresses only in 126c, above, arranged as SS tables. Arrange the addresses in 3 columns: Col. 1, name; Col. 2, street; and Col. 3, city, state, ZIP. Leave 4 spaces between columns (longest line is color underlined); leave about a 1" top margin. If you complete list, DS and start over. Determine *gwam* and % of transfer.

Goal: To try to reach 50% of your straight copy rate of 123b, p. 202.

127c ▶ 35
Build letter production skill: short letters

5 plain full sheets; block style, open; standard 6" line

Type letters, here and on next page, supplying appropriate parts as needed. Correct errors.

Goal: To complete all letters in 35' or less.

Problem 1 — words

Mr. Matthew E. Miner Rabbit Track Farm Chelsea, VT 05308-6371 (¶1) The 12
enclosed booklet illustrates 17 reasons why Fidelity is now America's leading 28
mutual fund group. But YOU are one of the 450,000 reasons why Fidelity has 43
been able to achieve this position of leadership. (¶ 2) We'd like to thank you for 59
being a part of the Fidelity family and for helping us to grow. Our continuing 75
goal is to serve you and your investment needs. Walter L. Tate President 90
Enclosure 91

153d ▶ 15
Improve language arts: word division

60-space line

1. Review word-division guides if necessary.

2. Set tab stops according to the key.

3. Center the heading on Line 11 and type the first line of tabulated copy as shown.

4. Type remaining lines in same way, showing in Column 2 all syllable breaks and in Column 3 all acceptable points of word division. If a word should not be divided, type it without hyphens in Column 3.

WORD DIVISION

TS

comparable	com-pa-ra-ble	com-pa-ra-ble
DS situation		
area		
in-depth		
foundation		
initial		
favorable		
doing		
application		
alight		
success		
questionnaire		
procedure		

key | 13 | 8 | 15 | 8 | 15 |

154

154a ▶ 5
Conditioning practice

each line twice SS (slowly, then faster); DS between 2-line groups; if time permits, retype selected lines

alphabet 1 Mac Gregory planned to review the book and relax just before the quiz.
figures 2 The 8,527 full-time and 90 part-time workers recorded 1,346 sick days.
fig/sym 3 If you mail an order for 284 ties by May 26, 10% (or $37.59) is saved.
fluency 4 The formal amendment is a penalty and not an aid to the downtown firm.

| 1 | 2 | 3 | 4 | 5 | 6 | 7 | 8 | 9 | 10 | 11 | 12 | 13 | 14 |

154b ▶ 10
Improve technique: keystroking

each line twice SS; DS between 2-line groups; retype difficult lines as time permits

balanced-hand 1 Dorma paid the six firms for the bodywork they did on the eight autos.
one-hand 2 In my opinion, fastest car racers are at ease in minimum garage areas.
combination 3 Steve may go to town for the car tags and abstracts after we get paid.

home-row 4 Jake said he is glad of his deal; he will sell half his old odd jades.
third-row 5 Tye wrote that he will equip our property with the proper water tiles.
bottom-row 6 If given much extra time, Sam and Alma can bake a fancy cake for Zane.

double letters 7 Sammie feels she will soon make a passing letter grade with your help.
adjacent key 8 There are twelve green trucks we may want to stop operating for today.
direct-reach 9 Any debts assumed must produce mutual trust between debtor and lender.

| 1 | 2 | 3 | 4 | 5 | 6 | 7 | 8 | 9 | 10 | 11 | 12 | 13 | 14 |

126

126a ▶ 5 Conditioning practice

each line 3 times (slowly, faster, in-between rate); as time permits, retype selected lines for extra credit

alphabet	1	Jo and Pat quickly calm the big, excited zoo animals for new visitors.
fig/shift lock	2	The address is AUDIO VISUAL, INC., Dept. 846, Chicago, IL 60945-1237.
adj key/ long reaches	3	As we were passing the national monument, a union official stopped us.
fluency	4	I may sign the contract and take title to the eight acres by the lake.

| 1 | 2 | 3 | 4 | 5 | 6 | 7 | 8 | 9 | 10 | 11 | 12 | 13 | 14 |

126b ▶ 15 Type a short report from script copy

full sheet; DS copy

1. Center the heading: PERSONAL AND PROFESSIONAL TITLES on Line 13 (elite type); or Line 10 (pica type). TS below heading.

2. Indent 5 for ¶ s.

3. Use 1" side margins.

4. Correct errors (eraser, tape, or liquid) as directed by your teacher.

Goal: To complete report with all errors corrected as you are timed for 10 minutes. If you finish before time is called, start over on a new sheet. Compute *n–pram*.

words

heading 7

If you are employed as a typist, you will frequently 17
be called on to choose the appropriate personal title to 29
use with someone's name. Of course, there are also 39
occasions when the use of any title is inappropriate, 50
and you will need to recognize them. A few simple guides 61
are given below and represent some of the accepted 72
usages. 73

A personal title (Mr., Mrs., or Miss) should precede 84
the name of an individual in a letter address or in a 95
salutation that includes a surname. When you do not 105
know the marital status of a woman or when she herself 116
has used the title, use "Ms." Some professional title 127
(for example, Dr., Professor, or Dean) may replace the 138
personal title in these lines. 145

In the closing lines of a letter, a personal or 154
professional title is never used with a man's name 165
and needn't be used with a woman's name. A woman 175
writer, however, can show consideration for the reader 186
just by typing a title before her typed name or by 196
writing it (in parentheses) before her script signature. 207

154c ▶ 15
Check statistical-copy skill

1. Two 1′ writings on each ¶; determine *gwam* and number of errors.

2. A 3′ writing on ¶s 1–3 combined; determine *gwam* and number of errors.

all letters used | A | 1.5 si | 5.7 awl | 80% hfw

gwam 1′ | 3′

The Grand Canyon National Park, which is located in Arizona, was 13 | 4
established as a national park on February 26, 1919. However, additional 28 | 9
land was absorbed by the park as late as 1975, making a total acreage 42 | 14
of just over 1.2 million. This unique exposure of rock is 217 miles long 57 | 19
and from 4 to 18 miles wide. During recent years, it has been seen by 71 | 24
about 2,840,000 people each year. 78 | 26

Another beautiful national park is the Great Smoky Mountains Na- 13 | 30
tional Park. It has an acreage of about 273,550 in North Carolina and 27 | 35
about 241,206 in Tennessee, for a total of over 500,000. It was ap- 41 | 39
proved on May 22, 1926, and established for full development in 1934. 55 | 44
The diverse plant life is quite beautiful and is seen by over 11 million 69 | 49
persons each year. 73 | 50

Fascinating in even a different way and older and larger than any 13 | 55
of the other national parks, Yellowstone was established in 1872. Its 27 | 59
more than 2,219,000 acres cover parts of three states. It has over 41 | 64
10,000 geysers, dozens of majestic falls, canyons, and quiet wildlife 55 | 69
areas. People from all over the world come to it in numbers that exceed 70 | 73
2,487,000 each year. 74 | 75

gwam 1′ | 1 | 2 | 3 | 4 | 5 | 6 | 7 | 8 | 9 | 10 | 11 | 12 | 13 | 14 |
3′ | 1 | 2 | 3 | 4 | 5 |

154d ▶ 15
Improve statistical-copy skill

1. Determine goal of speed or of control according to your needs based on performance on 154c above.

2. Two 1′ writings on each ¶ of 154c above.

3. A 3′ writing on ¶s 1–3 combined; determine *gwam* and number of errors. Compare with 154c.

4. Determine % of transfer: 3′ *gwam* on ¶s above ÷ 3′ *gwam* on ¶s of 151b.

154e ▶ 5
Learn to proofread statistical copy

1. Study guides below for reading numbers.

16	sixteen
1978	nineteen seventy-eight
2,384	two comma three eighty-four
7.62	seven point sixty-two
238,641,000	two thirty-eight comma six forty-one comma oh oh oh

2. Read horizontally the table at the right applying the guides above.

1979	273,550	2,840,000	1.2
1975	241,206	2,219,000	13.6
1982	500,000	2,487,000	4.8
1995	28,531	5,874,590	8.4
1948	9,403	8,930,450	18.2
1980	850,304	9,405,309	3.9

phase 6 lessons 126-150

Master professional typing skills

The 25 lessons of Phase 6 further refine the *planned program* to improve your typing skills (see p. 125). The lessons are designed to help you:

1. Extend and improve your letter, report, and table typing skills.

2. Apply your improved skills in an office work simulation.

3. Improve your proofreading skills.

4. Increase your speed and improve your accuracy.

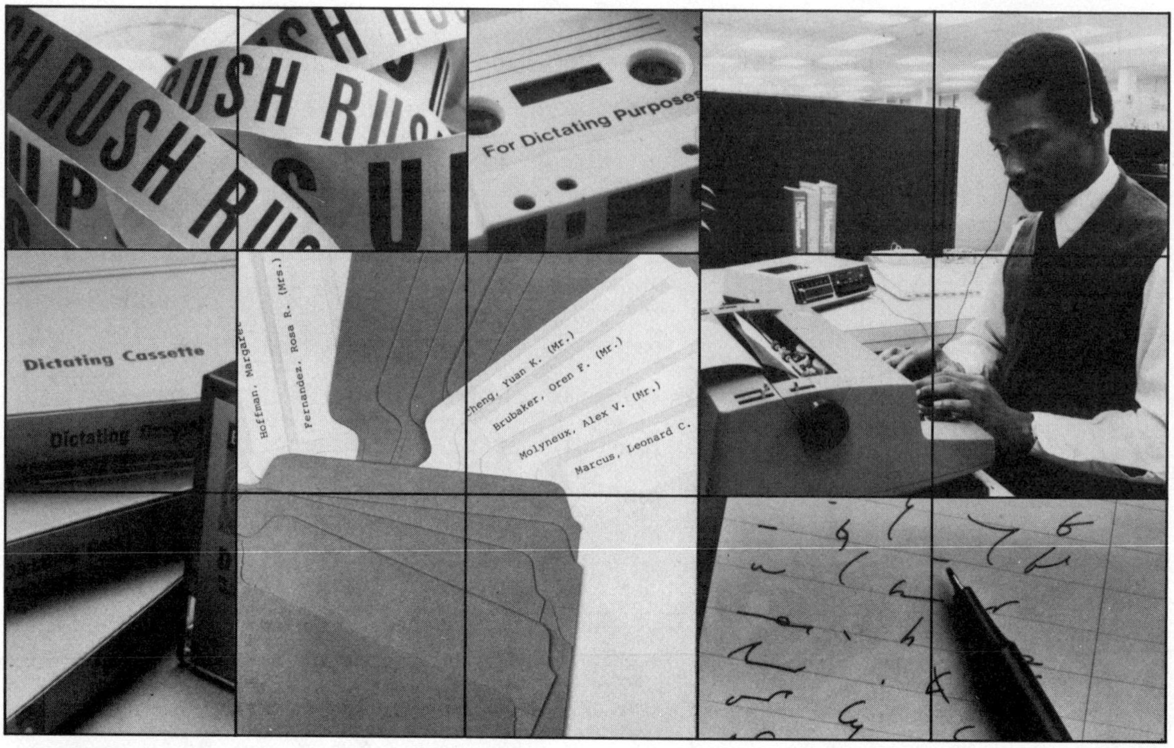

unit 24 lessons 126-135

Extend letter/report/table typing skills

Learning goals

1. To enlarge and extend your typing production skills on letters of varying length and letters with tables, and on memos, tables, reports, etc.

2. To develop added competency in making error corrections.

3. To learn techniques for justifying the right margin (making it even).

4. To review basic letter styles.

5. To maintain your straight- and script-copy typing skills.

Machine adjustments

1. Paper guide at *0*.

2. 70-space line and SS or as directed.

3. Line space selector on *1* or as directed.

4. Ribbon control to type on upper portion of ribbon (on black; *R* on Selectric).

155

155a ▶ 5 Conditioning practice

each line twice SS (slowly, then faster); DS between 2-line groups; if time permits, retype selected lines

alphabet 1 Even a lax child can make fine quiz scores by applying just two rules.

figures 2 Hugo's test scores were 80, 73, 94, 62, 91, and 85 for a total of 485.

fig/sym 3 Over <u>any</u> 3- to 6-year period between now and 1998, I expect a <u>7% gain</u>.

fluency 4 Henry laid eight bushels of corn on the sod by the dock for the ducks.

| 1 | 2 | 3 | 4 | 5 | 6 | 7 | 8 | 9 | 10 | 11 | 12 | 13 | 14 |

155b ▶ 15 Measure straight-copy skill

1. Two 5′ writings on ¶s 1–3 combined.

2. Determine *gwam* and number of errors.

3. Record the better score for comparison in Lesson 172.

all letters used | A | 1.5 si | 5.7 awl | 80% hfw |

	gwam 3′	5′
The administrative manager deals in setting goals and in employee	4	3
development. Goals must be set so that jobs are done with quality and	9	5
on time. Employee development means having a concern for workers as	14	8
people and knowing that all people have worth as individuals. The best	18	11
administrative managers try to help other people grow and develop so	23	14
that they realize their full potential. Many managers feel that one of	28	17
the best ways to teach others is to be an example of the point they are	33	20
trying to teach.	34	21
Just as all leaders need to excel in communicating, so must the	38	23
administrative manager. In fact, good communication skill is needed in	43	26
all types of business. There must be a clear awareness of goals by	47	29
those workers who are expected to help attain the goals set by a company.	52	32
Open communication is regarded as a prerequisite to high employee morale	57	34
and strong motivation, that is, to a strong desire on the part of the	62	37
workers to want to do their best. The administrative manager is not apt	67	40
to be effective if he or she does not have good skills in communicating.	72	43
One who expects to become an administrative manager must recognize	76	46
the need for good interpersonal relationships. Even though the techni-	81	49
cal phase of the job is important, the human aspect is critical in the	86	51
minds of most who hold this kind of position. Since the duty requires	91	54
one to get results through people, it is easy to see the need for good	95	57
skill in human relations. This kind of skill can evolve through formal	100	60
education as well as self-study.	102	61

gwam 3′ | 1 | 2 | 3 | 4 | 5 |

5′ | 1 | 2 | 3 |

125b, continued

words

The merger of ZIP and OCR occurred in 1967 when the Optical Charac- 269
ter Reader began full-time operation in the Detroit Post Office. Since then, 285
the OCR has been installed in other major cities, and current plans call for at 301
least 200 installations by 1986. 308

The OCR has peculiar reading habits. For example, it first scans from 322
right to left to find the beginning of the address lines on the envelope; then it 341
reads from left to right, starting with the bottom line and reading toward the 359
top. Thus, addresses on envelopes must appear within a specified "read 374
zone"; otherwise, the envelopes will be rejected and will have to be manually 389
sorted. 391

Addressing guides supplied by the U.S. Postal Service are recom- 404
mended for both personal and business mail. 413

Although the OCR can read speedily and accurately state names spelled 427
in full or abbreviated in dictionary style, the U.S. Postal Service prefers the 443
use of 2-letter (without periods and spaces) ZIP abbreviations--but only if ZIP 459
Codes are used with them. The names and standard 2-letter ZIP abbrevia- 473
tions of ten of the most populous states are given below as examples: 487

SS data of table; 12 spaces between columns; DS above and below table

California	CA	490
New York	NY	493
Pennsylvania	PA	496
Texas	TX	498
Illinois	IL	500
Ohio	OH	502
Michigan	MI	504
New Jersey	NJ	507
Florida	FL	509
Massachusetts	MA	512

The 2-letter abbreviations for all states are available from the local post 528
office in USPS Notice 85. Furthermore, because businesses so often use 542
mechanical addressing devices which limit the number of spaces that can be 557
typed per line, USPS Publication 59 provides standard abbreviations for city 572
and street names. 576

If time permits, retype manuscript for extra credit.

155c ▶ 18
Improve language arts: word division

60-space line

1. Set tab stops according to the key.

2. Center the heading on Line 8 and type the first line of tabulated copy as shown.

3. Type remaining lines in same way, showing in Column 2 all syllable breaks and in Column 3 all acceptable points of word division. If a word should not be divided, type it without hyphens in Column 3.

WORD DIVISION

TS

location	lo-ca-tion	lo-ca-tion

DS

operation
letter
professional
appearance
beginning
impression
information
leader
after
traits
position
value
described
natural
stopping
self-inventory
continuation
beautiful
yourself
recognize
able

key | 14 | 8 | 17 | 8 | 14 |

155d ▶ 12
Check proofreading skill on statistical copy

1. Set margin and tab stops according to the key.

2. Type the columns at the right, reading the numbers as directed in 154e, p. 255.

3. Proofread; correct errors.

4. Exchange papers with a classmate; read aloud from text while classmate checks your paper. Check classmate's paper while he/she reads.

8,704	22,409	358,274	35.99
788	3,204	363,789	7.04
3	7,496	121	82.16
26	1,583	374,903	317.08

DS

key | 5 | 8 | 6 | 8 | 7 | 8 | 6 |

124b, continued

Problem 4

half sheet, long side up; 4 spaces between column headings

If time permits, retype as many problems as possible for extra credit.

words

HIGHER EDUCATION ENROLLMENT 6

(Millions) 8

Year	Total Enrollment	Percent Increase	words
1965	5.9	–	26
1975	11.2	89.8	29
1985	13.4	19.6	32

(Header line: 23; rule: 35)

Source: Department of Health, Education, and 44
Welfare. 46

125

125a ▶ 5 Conditioning practice

Follow standard directions, p. 203.

alphabet 1 Famous barrio painter Juan Vazquez gave Wade the key to mixing colors.

fig/sym 2 Haro & Sons, 132 West 85th Street, just paid $4,679,000 for a Picasso.

shift key 3 Statistician Rita St. James works for McGill, McAfee, Lyons, & McNair.

fluency 4 They may name the burley blend for their neighbor if I sign the forms.

| 1 | 2 | 3 | 4 | 5 | 6 | 7 | 8 | 9 | 10 | 11 | 12 | 13 | 14 |

125b ▶ 45 Type an unbound manuscript with a table

Type copy in unbound manuscript form; DS; number page 2 in upper right corner; correct errors.

words

ELECTRONIC MAIL SORTING 5

The ZIP Code system of sorting mail was begun in 1963. ZIP (Zoning 18
Improvement Plan) divides the country into delivery units, each given a 33
5-digit number. The first digit represents one of ten geographic areas; the 48
second, a certain part of a geographic area; the third, one of the sectional 64
center areas for sorting mail; the last two, a zone number for internally 78
zoned cities or the delivery station for smaller ones. 90

Recently, the U.S. Postal Service announced an Expanded ZIP Code to 103
consist of the present 5-digit ZIP Code plus a new 4-digit add-on preceded by 119
a hyphen. An example of an expanded ZIP Code is the following: 45227-1035. 134
The first two add-on digits (10 in the example) divide the Zone (27) into <u>sec-</u> 150
<u>tors</u> for refining the sorting of the mail. The last two add-on digits (35 in the 168
example) represent a still further refinement which permits fine sorting of 183
the mail to a designated carrier's assigned route. 193

ZIP Coding was only one step in a massive program designed to bring 207
efficiency to the chaotic condition of mail handling. This system foresaw the 223
eventual use of the Optical Character Reader, an electronic mail sorter that 238
depends upon a numeric language (the ZIP Code) for maximum efficiency in 253
handling mail. 256

(continued, p. 205)

unit **29** lessons 156-160

Recall/improve letter typing skills

Learning goals

1. To review letter and punctuation styles.

2. To improve skills in typing business letters.

3. To review selected spelling, punctuation, and capitalization rules.

Machine adjustments

1. Paper guide at *0*.

2. Ribbon control to type on top half of ribbon.

3. Margin sets: 70-space line for conditioning practices and language arts activities; as directed for reports and letters.

4. Spacing: DS language arts; as directed for reports and letters.

156

156a ▶ 5 Conditioning practice

each line twice SS (slowly, then faster); DS between 2-line groups; if time permits, retype selected lines

alphabet 1 Income tax itemizing is a vexing job and requires plenty of hard work.

figures 2 My group sold 560 chili dogs, 487 hamburgers, 915 drinks, and 32 pies.

shifting 3 Sue and Joe studied with Jane and Steve for the American history test.

fluency 4 To own land with a big lake full of fish is their goal for the future.

| 1 | 2 | 3 | 4 | 5 | 6 | 7 | 8 | 9 | 10 | 11 | 12 | 13 | 14 |

156b ▶ 45 Unbound report on letter styles

Margins

page 1 top: 2" elite; 1½" pica

page 2 top: 1" for pica and elite

side and bottom: 1" for both pages

Type the report with 5-space ¶ indentions; DS ¶s; SS listed items, DS between them. Type the second page number ½" from the top at the right margin.

Study the report before proceeding to the next lesson; keep the report for future use.

words

LETTER PLACEMENT AND PUNCTUATION 6

TS

The placement of some letter parts is standardized while that of others 20
varies depending upon the letter style selected. Punctuation style is usually a 36
matter of personal preference. 42

TS

<u>Guide for All Letters</u> 46

DS

Apply the following rules for all letter styles typed: 57

DS

1. The line on which the date is placed varies with the length of the 71
letter. The date is followed by 3 blank line spaces (operate the 84
return 4 times). 87

DS

2. When a letter is addressed to a company, it is sometimes directed 101
to the attention of an individual. If so, type the word "Attention" 114
followed by the person's name with a personal title as the second 127
line of the address. 131

3. When a letter is addressed to an individual, the salutation should 145
include that person's name. When a letter is addressed to a com- 157
pany, even if an attention line is included, use "Ladies and Gen- 169
tlemen" as the salutation. When a letter is addressed to an un- 181
identified person such as "Office Manager," the salutation "Dear 194
Sir or Madam" may be used. Double-space above and below the 206
salutation. 208

(continued, p. 259)

unit **23** lessons 124-125

Evaluate performance

Measurement goals

1. To evaluate your table typing skill.

2. To evaluate your report typing skill.

Machine adjustments

Make the usual machine adjustments as required for various activities.

124

124a ▶ 5

Conditioning practice

each line 3 times, (slowly, faster, in-between rate); as time permits, retype selected lines for extra credit

alphabet	1	With quick jabs and deft parries, a young boxer amazed several people.
fig/sym	2	Total employment rose by 9,583,420 (11%) to 96.7 million in two years.
space bar	3	Many men and women may be needed to help restore the museum paintings.
fluency	4	Their problem is to fix the torn fur rug or risk a big penalty for it.

| 1 | 2 | 3 | 4 | 5 | 6 | 7 | 8 | 9 | 10 | 11 | 12 | 13 | 14 |

124b ▶ 45

Evaluate table typing skill

In this activity, you will be evaluated on your ability to arrange and type tables. Only minimum directions are given. Correct errors.

Problem 1

half sheet, long side up; 20 spaces between column headings

		words: parts	total
HIGH SCHOOL GRADUATES AS PERCENT		7	7
OF TOTAL 18-YEAR-OLD POPULATION		13	13
<u>Year</u>	<u>Percent</u>	18	18
1965	73.9	2	10
1975	74.3	4	22
1985	76.0	6	24
______		4	28
Source: <u>The Condition of Educa-</u>		15	38
<u>tion</u>, 1979, p. 184.		19	43

Problem 2

full sheet; reading position; 6 spaces between column headings

Note: If your typewriter does not have the + symbol, type the hyphen, backspace and type the diagonal (/).

Problem 3

Retype Problem 2 on half sheet, short side up; 6 spaces between column headings.

			words: parts	total
SCHOOL ENROLLMENT: GRADES 9-12			6	6
	Enrollment	Percent	10	10
<u>Year</u>	<u>(Millions)</u>	<u>Change</u>	19	19
1940	7.1	–	3	22
1950	6.5	– 8.5	6	25
1960	9.6	+ 47.7	9	28
1965	13.0	+ 35.4	13	31
1975	15.7	+ 20.8	16	35
1985	13.3	– 15.3	19	38
______			4	42
Source: Department of Health,			10	48
Education, and Welfare.			15	52

Problem 4 is on p. 204.

156b, continued

Block style;
open punctuation

LANDFORM, INC.
4851 South Overland Drive Oklahoma City, OK 73115-7480
(405) 487-3848

September 10, 19--

Ms. Juanita Mesa, Attorney
Mesa and Smith
321 West 11th Street
Stillwater, OK 74074-7590

Dear Ms. Mesa

Subject: New Office Design

As we discussed on the telephone yesterday, I should like to visit the site selected for your new office building before construction begins. It would be helpful if you or another member of your firm could be present to answer questions concerning your needs and desires.

Would you please indicate on the enclosed card if you can meet me at the location of the new building at 2:30 p.m. on September 27.

Sincerely

LANDFORM, INC.

Mrs. Nicole Lincoln
Principal

xx

Enclosure

Modified block;
open punctuation

Idaho Education Association
University of Idaho
Moscow, ID 52760-6424
(509) 361-6624

July 15, 19--

Executive Vice President
AC Publishing Co.
1499 South Boyle Avenue
St. Louis, MO 63110-3200

Dear Sir or Madam

The Idaho Education Association will hold its annual convention in Boise on October 22 and 23, and we request your assistance in sponsoring a speaker for one of the business education meetings.

We need a person to present a three-hour workshop concerning teaching techniques which are especially effective in advanced typewriting. Some of the time might be devoted to methods for developing basic skills, but we would like to have the majority of the time spent on methods for improving production typing skill. Can you suggest an appropriate person for this assignment?

The enclosed program is tentative, but it will give you some idea of the overall theme for this year's convention.

Cordially

Ms. Sue Sheid, President
Idaho Education Association

xx

Enclosure

Modified block,
indented ¶s; mixed
punctuation

AC Publishing Co.
1499 South Boyle Avenue
St. Louis, MO 63110-3200
(314) 782-8994

July 20, 19--

Dr. Danjiro Nishamura
Department of Business Education
North Texas State University
Denton, TX 76201-7660

Dear Dan:

Thank you for agreeing to conduct the workshop on advanced typewriting at the Idaho Education Association Convention. Your three-hour session is tentatively scheduled to begin at 1:30 p.m. on October 23.

Ms. Sue Sheid, IEA President, will contact you with details soon.

Sincerely,

AC PUBLISHING CO.

R. D. Lee
Executive Vice President

xx

words

4. The subject line, when used, is typed below the salutation with a 222
double space above and below it. Type the word "Subject" fol- 234
lowed by a colon and 2 spaces. 240

5. Type the complimentary close a double space below the last line 254
of the body of the letter. 259

6. When a company name is used in the closing lines, type it in ALL 273
CAPS a double space below the complimentary close. 283

7. Type the signer's name on the fourth line space below the com- 296
plimentary close (or company name, if used). 304

8. Type the official title of the signer either on the line with the 318
name, preceded by a comma, or on the next line, without a 330
comma. If the signer is writing as an officer of an association, 343
type in capital and lowercase letters the association's name on the 357
next line below the signer's name and title. 365

9. Type reference initials a double space below the signer's name 378
and/or title at the left margin. Only the typist's initials are needed 392
for reference when the signer's name is typed. 401

10. Type an enclosure notation (when used) a double space below the 415
reference initials. 419

TS

Block Style Letters 423

The block style letter is simple and efficient to use. In the block style 438
letter, all lines begin at the left margin. These lines include all opening lines, 455
message lines, and closing lines. 461

Modified Block Style Letters 467

The modified block style differs from the block style in that the date, 482
complimentary close, and signer's name and title begin at the center point of the 498
paper. Set a tab stop at the center point to speed alignment. 510

Modified Block Style with Indented Paragraphs 519

The modified block style with indented paragraphs differs from the 532
modified block style only with respect to the indention of paragraphs. Indent 548
the first line of each paragraph, usually 5 spaces; however, some companies 563
prefer a 10-space indention. 568

Punctuation Styles 571

Either open or mixed punctuation may be used with any of these letter 585
styles. However, most typists prefer to use open punctuation with block style, 601
which is in keeping with the simplicity and efficiency of the block style letter. 618
In open punctuation, no punctuation follows the salutation or the com- 632
plimentary close. In mixed punctuation, a colon follows the salutation and a 648
comma follows the complimentary close. 655

123

123a ▶ 5
Conditioning practice

Follow standard directions, p. 197.

alphabet	1	Barbara Gonzales' quick move helped prevent an injury to Frank Wilcox.
fig/sym	2	Is the discount rate on the Jaye & Co. invoice (79-486-53) 2/10, n/30?
space bar	3	Jan or Bob may go with them to the city to do the field box form work.
fluency	4	Rick may wish to go downtown by bus to pay a visit to a busy rug firm.

| 1 | 2 | 3 | 4 | 5 | 6 | 7 | 8 | 9 | 10 | 11 | 12 | 13 | 14 |

123b ▶ 15
Measure basic skill: straight copy

two 5′ writings; determine *gwam*; circle errors; record better rate

all letters used | A | 1.5 si | 5.7 awl | 80% hfw |

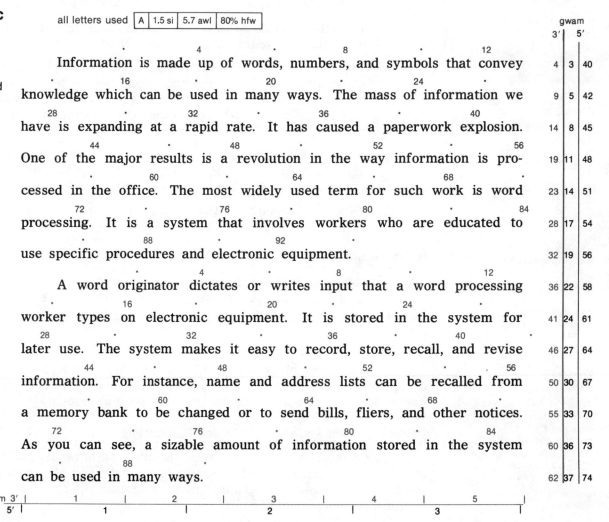

	gwam 3′	5′	
Information is made up of words, numbers, and symbols that convey	4	3	40
knowledge which can be used in many ways. The mass of information we	9	5	42
have is expanding at a rapid rate. It has caused a paperwork explosion.	14	8	45
One of the major results is a revolution in the way information is pro-	19	11	48
cessed in the office. The most widely used term for such work is word	23	14	51
processing. It is a system that involves workers who are educated to	28	17	54
use specific procedures and electronic equipment.	32	19	56
A word originator dictates or writes input that a word processing	36	22	58
worker types on electronic equipment. It is stored in the system for	41	24	61
later use. The system makes it easy to record, store, recall, and revise	46	27	64
information. For instance, name and address lists can be recalled from	50	30	67
a memory bank to be changed or to send bills, fliers, and other notices.	55	33	70
As you can see, a sizable amount of information stored in the system	60	36	73
can be used in many ways.	62	37	74

gwam 3′ | 1 | 2 | 3 | 4 | 5 |
5′ | 1 | 2 | 3 |

123c ▶ 15
Improve basic skill: straight copy

1. Add 4 to 8 words to your 123b rate. **Goal:** Increased speed.

2. Two 1′ guided writings on ¶ 1 of 123b at your new goal rate as the ¼′ guides are called.

3. A 2′ guided writing on ¶ 1. **Goal:** To maintain 1′ rate.

4. Repeat Step 2, using ¶ 2.

5. Repeat Step 3, using ¶ 2.

6. A 3′ timed writing using both ¶ s. **Goal:** To maintain your new speed rate for 3′.

123d ▶ 15
Increase speed

1. A 1′ writing on each sentence of 122c, p. 201. Try to reach a new speed level.

2. Additional 1′ writings on sentences on which lowest rates were made.

157

157a ▶ 5 Conditioning practice

each line twice SS (slowly, then faster); DS between 2-line groups; if time permits, retype selected lines

alphabet 1 The fawns jumped over the box hedge, then quickly zipped away from us.

figures 2 Flight 294 will leave 30 minutes before Flight 156 arrives at Gate 78.

shifting 3 A sign said "Vote for Judge J. K. G. Vick for a Fifth Term in Office."

fluency 4 The right way to handle the city problem is the goal of the amendment.

| 1 | 2 | 3 | 4 | 5 | 6 | 7 | 8 | 9 | 10 | 11 | 12 | 13 | 14 |

157b ▶ 40 Type business letters

Review report in 156b and type the letters; proofread and circle errors.

Problem 1
Short letter

plain full sheet

block style, open punctuation; date on Line 19; 2" side margins

	words parts	total
September 10, 19-- Ms. Juanita Mesa, Attorney Mesa and Smith 321 West 11th	15	15
Street Stillwater, OK 74074-7590 Dear Ms. Mesa Subject: New Office Design	30	30
(¶ 1) As we discussed on the telephone yesterday, I should like to visit the site	15	45
selected for your new office building before construction begins. It would be	30	60
helpful if you or another member of your firm could be present to answer	44	74
questions concerning your needs and desires.	52	82
(¶ 2) Would you please indicate on the enclosed card if you can meet me at the	14	96
location of the new building at 2:30 p.m. on September 27.	25	107
Sincerely LANDFORM, INC. Mrs. Nicole Lincoln Principal xx Enclosure	14	121

Problem 2
Average-length letter

plain full sheet

modified block style, mixed punctuation; date on Line 16; 1½" side margins

Problem 3

plain full sheet

Type Problem 1 in modified block style, open punctuation. Address the letter to:

Mr. Dan C. Port, Attorney
Port and Duncan, Inc.
403 South Boulder
Tulsa, OK 74103-7663

Supply an appropriate salutation.

	words parts	total
September 14, 19-- Mrs. Nicole Lincoln, Principal Landform, Inc. 4831	14	14
South Overland Drive Oklahoma City, OK 73115-7480 Dear Mrs. Lincoln:	28	28
(¶ 1) Because I will be out of town the week of September 27, Mr. Samuel Blair,	15	43
an attorney in our firm, will meet you at our new building site at 2:30 p.m.	30	58
on the 27th. He is well informed concerning our needs and preferences and	45	73
should be able to answer all of your questions.	54	82
(¶ 2) It may be helpful to you to review the enclosed Site Analysis for the block	15	97
on which our land is located. This report was prepared last year and is up to	31	113
date with respect to the present buildings in the area. We should have the	46	128
details concerning building restrictions and protective covenants for the area	62	144
as well as a list of building space allocations for you to take back with you on	78	160
the 27th.	79	161
Sincerely yours, Ms. Juanita Mesa Attorney-at-Law xx Enclosure	13	174

157c ▶ 5 Language arts

Type the ¶, correcting spelling, punctuation, and capitalization errors as you type. Do not correct your typographical errors. Check solution with 158b, Problem 2, ¶2.

The enclosed booklets describe, in detail, the functions that can ve performed on each of these machines; and I have listed the currant price on the front of each Booklet. I have, also, enclosed an information request Card which is stamped and addressed to your area representative for your convience in arrangeing for a demonstration and try-out.

122

122a ▶ 5 Conditioning practice

Follow standard directions, p. 197.

alphabet 1 Jeb Wily recognized and fixed his mind on techniques to improve skill.

fig/sym 2 These are the order numbers and prices: 16791, $28.30; 14593, $75.95.

shift key 3 Jan Nesen and Cathy Ridley wrote "The McNeil & McNair Survey Reports."

fluency 4 A busy visitor may work with usual vigor to form the key social panel.

| 1 | 2 | 3 | 4 | 5 | 6 | 7 | 8 | 9 | 10 | 11 | 12 | 13 | 14 |

122b ▶ 12 Improve basic skill: statistical rough-draft

Type a 3′ and a 5′ writing on ¶s of 121b, p. 200; determine *gwam*; compare rates; circle errors.

122c ▶ 25 Select-a-goal practice: progressive difficulty sentences

1. Beat-the-clock speed spurt: Try to type Sentence 1 as you are timed for 20″, 15″, and 12″. Repeat for other sentences.

2. Accuracy emphasis: Repeat Step 1, but with emphasis on reducing errors.

3. Check rates: Type a 1′ writing on each sentence.

Figures give 1′ rate in terms of guide call.

guide	gwam													
20″	3	6	9	12	15	18	21	24	27	30	33	36	39	42
15″	4	8	12	16	20	24	28	32	36	40	44	48	52	56
12″	5	10	15	20	25	30	35	40	45	50	55	60	65	70

balanced hand 1 They may lend us a map of the ancient city and the ancient land forms.

space bar 2 The man and the girl may go with them to the city if it is their wish.

variable rhythm 3 Were a number of these cases referred to the city auditors for review?

long words 4 Zale received national recognition for his impressive accomplishments.

long reaches 5 Briny brown broth was served to a number of us by the eccentric cooks.

fig/sym 6 Order #83 of May 25 for 7 files, 9 desks, and 6 chairs totaled $1,470.

shift key 7 Sy O'Brien, Don McNeil, and Mei-Ling Liu may visit St. Paul and Fargo.

one hand 8 You were taxed on minimum oil reserves only after I stated my opinion.

| 1 | 2 | 3 | 4 | 5 | 6 | 7 | 8 | 9 | 10 | 11 | 12 | 13 | 14 |

122d ▶ 8 Improve accuracy: common errors

each line 3 times (slowly, faster, in-between rate)

Goal: Not over 1 error in each line. As time permits, retype any line on which you made more than 1 error.

Emphasize quiet hands and curved, upright fingers

adjacent-key and long-reach errors

1 A number of economic reports predict a bright outlook for the economy.

2 In my opinion, few errors of the covert type were made by the officer.

Emphasize concentration on copy and continuity of typing

vowel-confusion errors

3 A thief stole a pie from my neighbor during the weird but quiet storm.

4 I tried to seize the foreign piece before it was weighed by the chief.

Emphasize down-and-in spacing with thumb curved and close to space bar

spacing errors

5 If he is to do the work for us, she may not be able to work with them.

6 Many men and women may share my interest in an exhibit of pop artists.

158

158a ▶ 5
Conditioning practice

each line twice SS (slowly, then faster); DS between 2-line groups; if time permits, retype selected lines

alphabet 1 Hap and J. V. went quickly by taxi to get four dozen eggs at a market.
figures 2 What are the locations for these area codes: 918, 405, 267, 202, 813?
shifting 3 Lee took Cory, Sean, Jackie, Kay, and Jo to see the Walt Disney movie.
fluency 4 Both of the girls will go to the downtown movie if they wish to do so.

| 1 | 2 | 3 | 4 | 5 | 6 | 7 | 8 | 9 | 10 | 11 | 12 | 13 | 14 |

158b ▶ 40
Type business letters

Review report in 156b. See RG p. iv for letter placement points; proofread and circle errors.

Problem 1
Short letter

plain full sheet

modified block style, indented ¶s, mixed punctuation

	words parts	total
Current date Cannon Equipment & Supplies Attention Mr. Joe Ang 5206	15	15
North Linwood Street Detroit, MI 48208-4421 Ladies and Gentlemen:	28	28
(¶ 1) In the near future, I plan to purchase an electronic printing/display	14	42
calculator. I need one that has the capacity for at least six decimal places and	30	58
for holding the multiplier in memory while calculating percentages.	43	71
(¶ 2) Would you please send brochures describing your models which fit my	14	85
needs, along with a current price list.	22	93
Sincerely yours, James B. Anthony Secretary xx	9	102

Problem 2
Average-length letter

plain full sheet

modified block style, open punctuation

Problem 3

plain full sheet

Type Problem 1 in block style, open punctuation. Address the letter to:

Sales Manager
Walker Electronics Co.
481 South Amboy Street
Dearborn, MI 48127-2401

Supply an appropriate salutation.

	words parts	total
Current date Mr. James B. Anthony, Secretary Luna & Company 1864 East	15	15
Atherton Road Flint, MI 48507-3317 Dear Mr. Anthony	25	25
(¶ 1) Your inquiry about an electronic printing/display calculator is very timely,	15	40
as we have just accepted the dealership for CALTRON. This is a new line of	30	55
calculators offering several special features at a reasonable price. We	45	70
are especially excited about Models CL-4426 and CL-4428, both of which have	60	85
the features you need plus several additional ones.	70	95
(¶ 2) The enclosed booklets describe in detail the functions that can be per-	14	109
formed on each of these machines, and I have listed the current price on the	29	124
front of each booklet. I have also enclosed an information-request card, which	45	140
is stamped and addressed to your area representative, for your convenience	60	155
in arranging for a demonstration and tryout.	68	163
Cordially CANNON EQUIPMENT & SUPPLIES Joe Ang, Sales Manager xx	13	176
Enclosures	15	191

158c ▶ 5
Language arts

Type the ¶, correcting spelling, punctuation, and capitalization errors as you type. Do not correct your typographical errors. Check solution with 157b, Problem 2, ¶1.

Because I will be out-of-town the week of september 27 mr. samuel blair an attourney in our firm will meet you at our new building cite at 2:30 P.M. on the 27th. He is well-informed conserning our needs and preferences, and should be able to anser all of your questions.

121b ▶ 15

Type a short report from statistical rough-draft copy

full sheet; DS copy

1. On Line 13, center the heading:
TIME NEEDED TO TYPE A LETTER

2. Indent 5 for ¶s.

3. Use 1½" side margins.

4. Correct errors.

all letters used | A | 1.5 si | 5.7 awl | 80% hfw |

		gwam 3'	5'	
Typing letters or similar items, as one would		3	2	47
expect, is the most frequent job task of the		6	3	49
office typist.		7	4	50
who types about 40 words a minute, / Why does it take the ordinary typist, so long to type an		13	8	53
Standard time / average letter of approximately 176 words? Studies show that		18	11	56
just / k / it takes such a typist approximately 18.3 seconds to pic up,		23	14	59
(At a rate of 40 words a minute, / insert, and align a sheet of paper in the typewriter. The		29	17	63
typist makes about 3.3 key strokes a second, so another 4.4		33	20	65
minutes are needed in typing a letter of 176 words, assuming		37	22	68
that no errors are made.		39	23	69
What other things consumer time? Every error that has		42	25	71
to correct / to be corrected may take from 30 to 98 seconds, depending on		47	28	74
the number of carbon copies that are made of the letter. To		57	34	79
proof read a letter of 176 words takes 1.87 minutes of time.		61	36	82
(pauses, looking up, finding place in copy, checking typing) / Waste time as the letter is typed consumes yet anotehr 1.05		69	41	87
minutes. The average typist, then, uses 8.17 minutes, or		73	44	89
even more, just to type a letter of 176 words. Do you		76	45	91
realize that the average typist uses 1.32 seconds				
just to make the return?				

121c ▶ 15

Improve basic skill: statistical rough-draft

Two 3' writings on ¶s of 121b above; then one 5' writing.

Goal: To maintain 3' rate for 5'. Proofread; circle errors; record better 3' rate and 5' rate.

121d ▶ 15

Compose at the typewriter

full sheet; 1" top and side margins; DS copy; indent 5 for ¶s

Compose a complete paragraph answer to each of the questions at the right. X–out or strikeover any errors you make as you compose.

1. What is your favorite typing activity? Why?
2. What is your least favorite typing activity? Why?
3. What do you think you need to do to improve your typing skill still more?

159

159a ▶ 5

Conditioning practice

each line twice SS (slowly, then faster); DS between 2–line groups; if time permits, retype selected lines

alphabet	1	Some extremely strange flavors jeopardized the swanky company banquet.
figures	2	The Literary Club read 154 plays, 163 books, and 207 articles in 1982.
shifting	3	Use the Shift-Lock Key when typing such items as: CPA, CPS, and NBEA.
fluency	4	The risks taken by the eight city firms held their usual profits down.

| 1 | 2 | 3 | 4 | 5 | 6 | 7 | 8 | 9 | 10 | 11 | 12 | 13 | 14 |

159b ▶ 45

Build sustained production skill: letters

Net production rate a minute (*n-pram*) = **(total words typed − penalty*) ÷ 30′**

* Penalty is 15 words for each uncorrected error.

Study addressing procedures (RG p. vi) and correcting errors (RG p. xii)

Time schedule

Preparation .... 5′
Timed production ..... 30′
Final check:
compute *n–pram* ... 10′

proofread; correct errors; address envelope for each letter

Problem 1
Long letter [LM p. 9]
block style, open punctuation

words	parts	total
May 4, 19-- Personnel Director Foshee Insurance Agency 3597 Almeda Road	15	15
Houston, TX 77004-1404 Dear Sir or Madam Subject: Recommendation of	29	29
Miss Sally Greenfield	33	33
(¶ 1) Miss Sally Greenfield has shown a keen interest in the insurance business	15	48
this last year in my Advanced General Business class. She has expressed an	30	63
interest in pursuing a career in that field. I recommended that she apply for a	46	79
secretarial position in your summer employment program to gain some practi-	61	94
cal experience in business.	66	99
(¶ 2) Sally's academic success in a wide variety of business education courses	15	114
during the past four years indicates that she is well qualified for a secretarial	31	130
job. The skills she gained in typewriting, shorthand, records management, and	47	146
business English were put to good use during her senior year when she worked	62	161
four hours a day in the principal's office. Perhaps of even greater value,	77	176
though, was the experience she gained in human relations as she assumed a	92	191
great deal of responsibility in handling both faculty and student problems.	107	206
(¶ 3) I am enclosing (with her permission) a copy of the term paper she prepared	15	221
in my class this year. It provides evidence of the insight she possesses concern-	31	237
ing the role of insurance in our economic system.	41	247
(¶ 4) I believe that Sally will be an asset to your agency even for a few summer	15	262
months.	16	263
Cordially Henry Uhlich Business Education Instructor xx Enclosure	13	277
		290

Problem 2
Short letter [LM p. 11]
Type the letter below right in modified block style, mixed punctuation.

Problem 3
[LM p. 13]
Type Problem 2 in modified block style with indented ¶s, open punctuation, making the following changes:
Send to **Mrs. Sidney Hitt**, same title and address; supply salutation; change **Sally Greenfield** to **Mr. Salvador Moya** and use appropriate pronoun references.

Problem 4
Retype Problem 1 on plain full sheet if you finish all 3 letters before time is called.

	parts	total
June 10, 19-- Mr. Henry Uhlich Business Education Instructor South High	15	15
School 3807 South 80 Street Houston, TX 77012-3384 Dear Mr. Uhlich	29	29
(¶ 1) Thank you for recommending Miss Sally Greenfield for a secretarial job in	15	44
our summer employment program. She began working for us on Monday of this	30	59
week, and we are already quite pleased with her performance.	42	71
(¶ 2) Your interest in our summer employment program is appreciated.	12	83
Sincerely FOSHEE INSURANCE AGENCY Ms. Susan Bell Personnel Director	14	97
xx	15	98
		120

120c ▶ 15
Refine techniques and improve control

each line twice (slowly, faster); as time permits, retype selected lines

Goal: To refine techniques and to type with control.

Emphasize quick, down–and–in spacing motion; no pauses

space bar
1 Pay the men and the women and then go with them when they do the work.
2 Both of them may go with me to the city to do civic work for the firm.
3 Jamey may pay the mentor and me to do the work for the city amendment.

Emphasize curved, upright fingers; finger–action keystroking

3d and 4th fingers
4 Paul saw many zebra eating waxy poppy pods down by the old plaza pool.
5 Polly was appalled by the losses suffered by Sally in the gold market.
6 Lea and Aza saw Walt as he rode a plump polo pony across a waxy floor.

Emphasize quick reach with little finger, other fingers in typing position

shift key 7 Smith & Co. published my article "The Power to Choose the Work We Do."
shift lock 8 Jan, Zeb, and Sue read the book TYPEWRITING--LEARNING AND INSTRUCTION.*
underline 9 Thomas C. Wheeler wrote the new book <u>The Great American Writing Block</u>.*

* Book titles may be typed in all caps or with the underline.

Emphasize finger–reach action keystroking; quiet hands

long reaches
10 Many concerned nylon experts went to a number of economic conferences.
11 Cecil lost an umber-colored nylon umbrella at a unique union ceremony.
12 The brusque union umpires referred to Cecily as being quite eccentric.

120d ▶ 15
Transfer refined techniques and improved control

1. Two 1′ timed writings; determine *gwam*; circle errors.
2. Deduct 4 words from better rate; determine ¼′ goals.
3. Two 15″ writings; try to reach goal and to type without error.
4. Two 30″ writings; try to reach goal and to type without error.
5. Four 1′ guided writings at goal rate. **Goal:** To type with not more than 2 errors.

all letters used

Cecil lived for many years in New York City. At Shea Stadium, he loved to watch zany pitchers throw curve balls by eccentric batters. Later in life, after appalling losses in the wool market, he decided to move to Phoenix. It was in Phoenix that he got the inspiration to write QUEST FOR THE JUST.

121

121a ▶ 5
Conditioning practice

Follow standard directions, p. 197.

alphabet 1 Jack Perez will quiz the six children before giving them the big toys.
fig/sym 2 My number in Woodland Hills, CA, after March 5 will be (213) 468-9700.
long words 3 Achievement of higher production was made without sacrificing quality.
fluency 4 The fury of the storm kept a visitor to the city in an ancient chapel.

| 1 | 2 | 3 | 4 | 5 | 6 | 7 | 8 | 9 | 10 | 11 | 12 | 13 | 14 |

160

160a ▶ 5
Conditioning practice

each line twice SS (slowly, then faster); DS between 2-line groups; if time permits, retype selected lines

alphabet	1	Fifty big jets climbed into a hazy sky at exactly quarter past twelve.
figures	2	Purchase Order 75416, mailed July 23, was sent to 890 West Elm Street.
shifting	3	Mrs. Kathryn Lyn Jones joined the American Tax Workers Society (ATWS).
fluency	4	The social problems of the world may shape the civic work of the town.

| 1 | 2 | 3 | 4 | 5 | 6 | 7 | 8 | 9 | 10 | 11 | 12 | 13 | 14 |

160b ▶ 45
Measure production skill: letters

Time schedule
Preparation .... 5′
Timed production ... 30′
Final check; compute *n–pram* .. 10′
proofread; correct errors; address envelope for each letter

Problem 1
Average-length letter [LM p. 17]
block style, open punctuation

	words: parts	total
July 15, 19-- Executive Vice President AC Publishing Co. 1499 South Boyle	15	15
Avenue St. Louis, MO 63110-3200 Dear Sir or Madam	25	25
(¶ 1) The Idaho Education Association will hold its annual convention in Boise on	15	40
October 22 and 23, and we request your assistance in sponsoring a speaker for	31	56
one of the business education meetings.	39	64
(¶ 2) We need a person to present a three-hour workshop concerning teaching	14	78
techniques which are especially effective in advanced typewriting. Some of the	30	94
time might be devoted to methods for developing basic skills, but we would like	46	110
to have the majority of the time spent on methods for improving production	61	125
typing skill. Can you suggest an appropriate person for this assignment?	76	140
(¶ 3) The enclosed program is tentative, but it will give you some idea of the	15	155
overall theme for this year's convention.	23	163
Cordially Ms. Sue Sheid, President Idaho Education Association xx Enclo-	15	178
sure	16	179
		199

Problem 2
Short letter [LM p. 19]
modified block style, mixed punctuation

	parts	total
July 20, 19-- Ms. Sue Sheid, President Idaho Education Association University	16	16
of Idaho Moscow, ID 52760-6424 Dear Ms. Sheid Subject: Convention	30	30
Speaker	31	31
(¶ 1) Dr. Danjiro Nishamura of North Texas State University has agreed to	14	45
conduct the typewriting workshop for your annual meeting. He is a dynamic,	29	60
knowledgeable speaker; and we are pleased to sponsor his appearance for the	44	75
benefit of the business educators of Idaho.	52	83
(¶ 2) If I may assist your group in any other way, please let me know.	12	95
Sincerely AC PUBLISHING CO. R. D. Lee Executive Vice President xx	13	108
		127

Problem 3
Short letter [LM p. 21]
modified block style with indented ¶s, mixed punctuation

	parts	total
July 20, 19-- Dr. Danjiro Nishamura Department of Business Education North	15	15
Texas State University Denton, TX 76201-7660 Dear Dan	26	26
(¶ 1) Thank you for agreeing to conduct the workshop on advanced typewriting	14	40
at the Idaho Education Association Convention. Your three-hour session is ten-	30	56
tatively scheduled to begin at 1:30 p.m. on October 23.	41	67
(¶ 2) Ms. Sue Sheid, IEA President, will contact you with details soon.	13	80
Sincerely AC PUBLISHING CO. R. D. Lee Executive Vice President xx	13	93
		114

Problem 4
Retype Problem 1 on plain full sheet if you finish all 3 letters before time is called.

119d ▶ 15
Improve basic skill: straight copy

two 3′ writings; then one 5′ writing

Goal: To maintain 3′ rate for 5′.

Proofread; circle errors; record better 3′ and 5′ rates.

all letters used

Text	gwam 3′		5′
Selecting a career or an area of employment that is right for you	4	3	47
is not a simple task. Choosing a career is one of the most important	9	5	50
decisions you will make; however, you may want to get a variety of job	14	8	53
experiences before you make your career selection. Do this when you	18	11	55
are young and before you accumulate family and home responsibilities.	23	14	58
In choosing a career, you should try to match that career with your	28	17	61
aptitudes, interests, and goals. If you consider such factors when	32	19	64
you make a career choice, it may help you find a large share of the	37	22	66
pleasures and satisfactions of life in your work.	40	24	68
Perhaps you have been thinking about a career in office work. The	45	27	71
job of typist offers many opportunities for the beginning worker. As	49	30	74
a rule, a high school diploma is needed for this job along with skill	54	32	77
in typing. The work of typist requires attention to detail and good	59	35	79
proofreading skill. Typists who can do a variety of office tasks will	63	38	82
maximize their chances for work and for promotion on the job. The op-	68	41	85
portunities for full- and part-time work in the typewriting field are	73	43	88
almost unlimited.	74	44	89

gwam 3′ | 1 | 2 | 3 | 4 | 5 |
5′ | 1 | 2 | 3 |

120

120a ▶ 5
Conditioning practice

Follow standard directions, p. 197.

alphabet 1 Jane Badge has willingly agreed to check five or six parts of my quiz.

fig/sym 2 On March 19, we'll be at the Burlinge Hotel, telephone 1-612-854-7320.

3d and 4th fingers 3 Aza and Poa like the aqua-blue color of the waxy poppy plant blossoms.

fluency 4 The visitor may make an oak workbox to end the skepticism of the girl.

| 1 | 2 | 3 | 4 | 5 | 6 | 7 | 8 | 9 | 10 | 11 | 12 | 13 | 14 |

120b ▶ 15
Improve basic skill: straight copy

1. Add 4 to 8 words to your 119d *gwam* rate. **Goal:** To try to reach a new speed level.

2. Two 1′ writings on ¶1, 119d above. Try to reach your goal rate.

3. A 2′ writing on ¶1. Try to maintain your 1′ goal rate. (2′ *gwam* = total words ÷ 2.)

4. Repeat Step 2, using ¶2.

5. Repeat Step 3, using ¶2.

6. A 3′ timed writing using both ¶s. **Goal:** To maintain your new speed rate for 3′.

unit **30** lessons 161-165

Recall/improve table typing skills

Learning goals

1. To review vertical and horizontal centering.
2. To continue learning to proofread numbers.
3. To improve table typing skill.

Machine adjustments

1. Paper guide at *0*.
2. Ribbon control to type on top half of ribbon.
3. Margin sets: 70-space line for conditioning practices and ¶s; as directed for problems.
4. Spacing: DS ¶s; as directed for problems.

161

161a ▶ 5 Conditioning practice

each line twice SS (slowly, then faster); DS between 2-line groups; if time permits, retype selected lines

alphabet 1 Jobe watched the foxy old goat quickly zip over those mountain ledges.

figures 2 On May 28, Dan paid for 30 hats and 45 scarves with Check Number 9761.

fig/sym 3 My firm (Acme & Co.) charges 12% interest on loans of $35,900 or more.

fluency 4 All of them did sign the amendment to give the city title to the land.

| 1 | 2 | 3 | 4 | 5 | 6 | 7 | 8 | 9 | 10 | 11 | 12 | 13 | 14 |

161b ▶ 15 Topbound report on table typing

Margins

top: 2" pica; 2½" elite

sides: 1"

¶ indention: 5; numbered item indention: 5 from each margin; DS ¶s; SS numbered items with a DS between them. Proofread and make corrections in pencil. Keep report for future use.

words

VERTICAL AND HORIZONTAL CENTERING OF TABLES 9

To arrange data in a table format so they can be conveniently and clearly read, you must know how to center vertically and horizontally. Basic guides to vertical centering and spacing are given below. 49

1. Exact center--count total lines used, including blank lines; subtract from total lines available; divide remainder by 2 (ignore fraction if one occurs). That figure represents the top margin; space down one additional line from the top of the page to type the first line. 105

2. Reading position--subtract 2 from exact center. 116

To plan the horizontal placement of a table to be centered, follow the guides below: 133

1. Clear all margin and tab stops. 140

2. Find exact horizontal center of any size paper by adding the typewriter scale readings at the left and right edges of the paper and dividing the total by 2. 173

3. Backspace from center once for each 2 strokes in the longest line of each column, then for each 2 spaces between columns. Set left margin stop. 203

4. Space forward once for each stroke in the longest line in the first column and once for each space to be left between Columns 1 and 2--set tab. Continue in this manner to set tab stops for remaining columns. 246

unit **22** lessons 119-123

Improve speed/accuracy

Learning goals

1. To refine and improve your basic typing techniques.
2. To increase your speed and improve your accuracy on basic skill copy.
3. To improve composing skill.

Machine adjustments

1. Paper guide at *0*.
2. 70–space line and SS unless otherwise directed.
3. Line space selector on *2* (DS) for all timed writings of more than 1′.

119

119a ▶ 5 Conditioning practice

each line 3 times (slowly, faster, in-between rate); as time permits, retype selected lines for extra credit

alphabet	1	Jackie Zeno will give a small quaint box to those five happy children.
fig/sym	2	She ordered 95 (2″ × 8″ × 6′) and 30 (1″ × 4″ × 7′) s4s prime redwood.
long words	3	These correspondents and cinematographers are dedicated to excellence.
fluency	4	The firms may make a big profit if the city pays for half of the fuel.

| 1 | 2 | 3 | 4 | 5 | 6 | 7 | 8 | 9 | 10 | 11 | 12 | 13 | 14 |

119b ▶ 20 Refine techniques and increase speed

1. Lines 1-3: Each line twice at top speed; move from Line 1 to Line 2 to Line 3 without pausing.
Goal: To force speed as lines increase in difficulty.
2. Repeat Step 1 using Lines 4–6.
3. Lines 1-3: Two 1′ writings on each line; compare rates.
4. Repeat Step 3 using Lines 4–6.

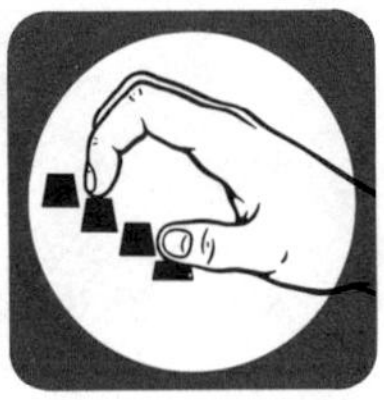
Fingers curved

Fingers upright

Finger–action keystroking

Emphasize fast finger reaches with quiet hands; wrists low, relaxed

balanced	1	I may go with them to the city to make the right form for the big box.
variable	2	I may go with them to the address given on the statement and the card.
one–hand	3	In my opinion, you exaggerated a tax case on average minimum reserves.
balanced	4	She may visit the city and sign the eight forms for their usual audit.
variable	5	She may go to that address to sign the statement and the address form.
one–hand	6	John acted on a case only after I gave my opinion on minimum reserves.

| 1 | 2 | 3 | 4 | 5 | 6 | 7 | 8 | 9 | 10 | 11 | 12 | 13 | 14 |

119c ▶ 10 Transfer refined techniques and increased speed: guided writing

1. Two 1′ writings; determine *gwam*.
2. Add 4 words to better rate; determine ¼′ goals.
3. Two 15″ writings; try to equal or exceed ¼′ goal.
4. Two 30″ writings; try to equal or exceed ½′ goal.
5. Two 1′ guided writings at goal rate.

· 4 · 8 · 12
I recognize that the primary element of high-speed typing is to try
· 16 · 20 · 24 ·
to type with good form and refined technique patterns. In each of the
28 · 32 · 36 · 40
lessons of this unit, my goal will be to fix my mind on the principal
· 44 · 48 · 52 · 56
elements of keystroking, quick spacing, and a fast return with a quick
· 60
start of a new line.

161c ▶ 30
Type 2-column tables

each table as directed; proofread; circle errors

Problem 1
half sheet, long side up

Type the table in exact vertical center; DS body; 10 spaces between columns.

		words parts	total
SPACING MEASUREMENT FOR TYPEWRITING		7	7
(Horizontal and Vertical Summary)		14	14
Pica spaces to a horizontal inch	10	7	21
Elite spaces to a horizontal inch	12	15	29
Pica spaces to an 8 1/2″ line	85	21	35
Elite spaces to an 8 1/2″ line	102	28	42
Vertical lines to an 11″ sheet	66	35	49
Vertical lines to a 5 1/2″ (half) sheet	33	44	58

Problem 2
full sheet

Type the table in reading position; DS body; 12 spaces between columns.

Problem 3
half sheet, short side up

If time permits, retype Problem 1; reading position; decide spacing between columns.

		parts	total
SOME NOTED CONTEMPORARY BLACK AMERICANS		8	8
(Athletes and Entertainers Excluded)		15	15
James Baldwin	Author/playwright	6	22
Alex Haley	Author	10	25
Patricia Harris	U.S. cabinet member	17	33
Jesse Jackson	Civil rights leader	24	39
Barbara Jordan	Congresswoman	30	45
Thurgood Marshall	Supreme court justice	38	53
Donald McHenry	U.S. ambassador	44	59

162

162a ▶ 5
Conditioning practice

each line twice SS (slowly, then faster); DS between 2-line groups; if time permits, retype selected lines

alphabet 1 Gustov expected to jump quickly from the frozen car into a warm cabin.
figures 2 Place Contract 75280 and Invoice 1463 in Drawer 9 of the current file.
fig/sym 3 Call Judy's house (634-8579) before 12:30 p.m., Thursday, December 27.
fluency 4 Do they wish to go to the city to visit with the man who laid the rug?

| 1 | 2 | 3 | 4 | 5 | 6 | 7 | 8 | 9 | 10 | 11 | 12 | 13 | 14 |

162b ▶ 5
Learn to proofread figures

Type the copy at the right; proofread as directed in the ¶; circle errors.

When it is possible for you to verify statistical copy by reading to a co-worker, you should read each punctuation mark and special symbol individually. However, figures should be read in groups, as follows: Read 3891 as <u>thirty-eight-ninety-one</u>; read 2,845 as <u>two-comma-eight-forty-five</u>. Read the number 0 (zero) as <u>oh</u> and the decimal point as <u>point</u>. Read .0071 as <u>point-oh-oh-seventy-one</u>. Type and proofread the following figures: 8592; 86,486; .00098; 35.86; 6.08; 7.36; 8750; .07; 50.38.

117, 118

117a, 118a ▶ 5
Conditioning practice

Follow standard directions, p. 183.

alphabet	1	Peg Jackson may start to move old boxes of zinc to a quaint warehouse.
fig/sym	2	A trade discount of 10%, 5%, and 2% on $24,398.76 totals to $3,955.21.
shift key	3	Ann, Roy, Donna, and Raul will visit McNeil, MacArthur, Jellicoe & Co.
fluency	4	An auditor may codify a civic amendment of the ancient Malaysian city.

| 1 | 2 | 3 | 4 | 5 | 6 | 7 | 8 | 9 | 10 | 11 | 12 | 13 | 14 |

117b ▶ 45
Learn to type leftbound manuscripts with textual citations

Continue 114c, pp. 191–195.

118b ▶ 45
Learn to type leftbound manuscripts with textual citations

Complete the manuscript report, 114c, pp. 191–195.

Problem 1
Type a reference list or bibliography

top margin same as p. 1; other margins as in report; center heading over line of writing; start first line of each entry at left margin; indent additional lines 5 spaces; SS each entry; DS between entries

(See illustration in lower right corner of this page.)

REFERENCES
TS

American Psychological Association. Publication Manual. 2d ed. Washington, D.C.: American Psychological Association, 1974.

Bates, Jefferson D. Writing with Precision. Washington, D.C.: Acropolis Books, Ltd., 1978.

Committee on Writing Standards, The National Council of Teachers of English. "Standards for Basic Skills Writing Programs." College English, October 1979, pp. 220-222.

Cross, Donna W. Word Abuse. New York: Coward, McCann & Geoghegan, Inc., 1979.

Graves, Robert, and Alan Hodge. The Reader Over Your Shoulder. New York: Random House, 1979.

Lanham, Richard. UCLA Writing Project Lecture, 1979.

Stone, Marvin. "Due Dismay About Our Language." U.S. News & World Report, April 23, 1979, p. 102.

Strunk, Jr., William, and E. B. White. The Elements of Style. 3d ed. New York: Macmillan Publishing Co., Inc., 1979.

Tibbetts, Arn, and Charlene Tibbetts. What's Happening to American English. New York: Charles Scribner's Sons, 1978.

"'80s-Babble: Untidy Treasure." Time, January 28, 1980, p. 90.

Walshe, R. D. "What's Basic to Teaching Writing?" The English Journal, December 1979, pp. 51-56.

Problem 2
Type a title page

1. Center title over line of writing used in report, 2½" from top edge.

2. Center and type your name 2½" below title; DS; center and type name of school.

3. Center and type current date 2½" below name of school.

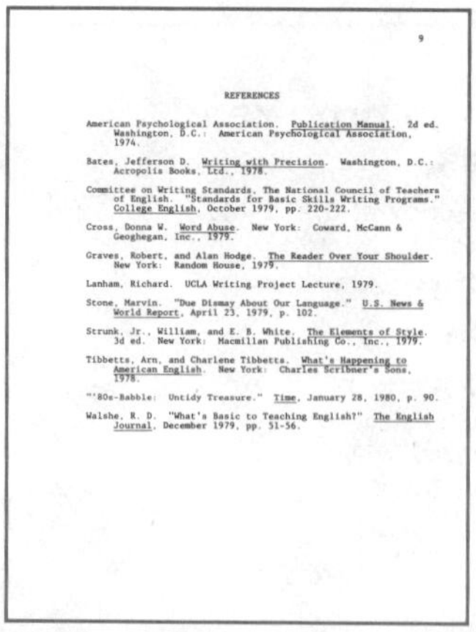

162c ▶ 10 Improve table typing

Drill 1: Begin on Line 7; 8 spaces between columns; make adjustments and type as quickly as possible.

Drill 2: Repeat Drill 1 with 10 spaces between columns.

CURRENT CROP FORECAST

(Based on Conditions as of August 1)

			words parts	total
CURRENT CROP FORECAST			4	4
(Based on Conditions as of August 1)			12	12
Corn	5.85 billion bushels	26% increase	8	20
Cotton	9.40 million bushels	18% increase	16	27
Soybeans	1.46 billion bushels	18% increase	24	36

162d ▶ 30 Type 3-column tables

each table as directed; proofread; circle errors

Problem 1

half sheet, long side up

Type the table in exact vertical center; SS body; 6 spaces between columns.

For tables with fractions appearing in the final column, consider fractions as part of the column when planning table placement.

			words parts	total
FRESHWATER FISHING RECORDS FOR 1980			7	7
(By Pounds and Length)			12	12
Whiterock Bass	20#	30″	5	16
Bigmouth Buffalo	56#	44 3/4″	10	22
Blue Catfish	97#	57″	15	26
Black Crappie	5#	19 1/4″	20	31
Gar Alligator	279#	93″	24	36
Chinook Salmon	93#	50″	29	40

Problem 2

half sheet, short side up

Type the table in reading position; DS body; decide spacing between columns; type heading in 2 lines SS as shown.

Problem 3

full sheet

If time permits, retype Problem 1; DS body; decide spacing between columns.

			words parts	total
SELECTED INVENTIONS AND INVENTORS			7	7
FROM 1642 to 1885			10	10
(Listed Alphabetically)			15	15
Adding machine	1642	Blaise Pascal	7	22
Calculating machine	1823	Charles Babbage	15	30
Dictating machine	1885	Charles S. Taintor	24	39
Telephone	1876	Alexander G. Bell	30	47
Typewriter	1714	Henry Mill	35	52

163

163a ▶ 5 Conditioning practice

each line twice SS (slowly, then faster); DS between 2-line groups; if time permits, retype selected lines

alphabet 1 Janis Box left my TV quiz show and gave back three prizes she had won.

figures 2 I did Exercises 20, 18, 93, 46, and 57 yesterday at the training camp.

fig/sym 3 Key indicators: cost index 249.5 (up 27.6%), profits 187.2 (up 8.3%).

fluency 4 Their theory is to form the right social goals to handle key problems.

| 1 | 2 | 3 | 4 | 5 | 6 | 7 | 8 | 9 | 10 | 11 | 12 | 13 | 14 |

114c, continued

Summary Statement

Now what about your writing style? The basic requirement of writing style is to follow the elementary rules of grammar and good usage. Other than that, writing style is unique with each of us. Words arranged in one manner in a sentence are capable of stirring the reader deeply. The same words only slightly rearranged may be impotent. Lincoln's Gettysburg Address is one example of words arranged effectively. And so is Thomas Paine's now famous line, "These are the times that try men's souls." Arranged in any other way, the Gettysburg Address or Paine's oft-quoted sentence would not be nearly so effective.

The question of writing style, then, has no single answer. Each of us must develop a writing style that is unique to us. But we must start somewhere, and that somewhere is to start by writing.

116

116a ▶ 5 Conditioning practice

Follow standard directions, p. 183.

alphabet	1	Julie must quickly help Rowen fix that monkey cave in the big old zoo.
fig/sym	2	Please add these amounts: $123.75, $46.90, $85.72, $1.75, and $18.75.
space bar	3	Did she go with them to do the work for the firm down by the big lake?
fluency	4	Orlando paid the civic firm for the authentic ancient chapel ornament.

| 1 | 2 | 3 | 4 | 5 | 6 | 7 | 8 | 9 | 10 | 11 | 12 | 13 | 14 |

116b ▶ 20 Check number expression and capitalization skills

full sheet; DS; 1" top margin; 70-space line

1. Type each sentence in enumerated form making the corrections needed as the line is typed.

2. As the corrections for each sentence are read to you, circle the number of any sentence in which you have an error.

3. Reinsert your paper, align it, then retype correctly any sentence in which you made an error of number expression or capitalization in the blank space below that sentence.

1. 6 typing books, four english books, and 15 math books are needed.
2. Did Sue order fifteen 10-gallon cans, or 10 fifteen-gallon cans?
3. Nearly 1/2 of the work is still to be completed.
4. How do you type one half, three fourths, and one and seven eights?
5. check guide six, Page eighty-five, in volume ten.
6. He weighs one hundred sixty-five pounds and is six feet two inches tall.
7. Approximately 35% of the loans were made at the 15 1/4 percent rate.
8. did she say, "you learn to write by writing?"
9. Gail's basic theme concerned "Decreasing productivity."
10. "you learn new words", she said, "By reading difficult materials".
11. Do this for tomorrow: try to complete activity 114c, Pages 190-194.
12. i read the book by bates, "writing with precision".
13. They asked professor crawford to speak at the meeting.
14. The Doctor will see you soon.
15. We studied greco-roman wrestling.
16. In the Spring, we usually have our vacation during easter week.
17. The jones company moved from fifth avenue to the federated building.

116c ▶ 25 Learn to type leftbound manuscript with textual citations

Continue 114c, pp. 191–195.

163b ▶ 10
Drill on column headings

Review centering and tabulation in RG p. x. Then type the drills as directed.

Drill 1
Center by column entries.

Drill 2
Center by column headings.

Drill 3
Center by longest item in each column, whether heading or entry. **Note:** This procedure should be used in future problems unless otherwise specified.

Drill 1

Tags	Income	State
324,128	$38,502,947	California

Drill 2

Page Number	Average Tax per Annum	Mean Rate
489	36.5%	$25.36

Drill 3

Due Dates	Total Revenue	Average Cost per Person
April 3-April 31	$2.6M	$2.78

163c ▶ 35
3-column tables with column headings

each table as directed; proofread; correct errors

Problem 1
half sheet, long side up
Type the table in exact vertical center; SS body; center by longest item in each column; align decimals as shown in Column 3. Allow 8 spaces between columns.

			words parts	total
UNIT CONVERSIONS TO			4	4
METRIC MEASUREMENTS			8	8
To Convert	Into	Multiply by	18	18
BTU/hr.	watts	0.2931	4	23
Feet	centimeters	30.48	9	27
Gallons	liters	3.785	13	31
Inches	centimeters	2.54	18	36
Miles (statute)	kilometers	1.609	24	43

Problem 2
full sheet
Type the table in reading position; DS body; center by column entries. Allow 10 spaces between Columns 1 and 2, 6 spaces between Columns 2 and 3.

Problem 3
If time permits, retype Problem 1 on a full sheet in reading position; DS body; decide spacing between columns.

			parts	total
SALES BY DIVISIONS			4	4
(June 30 Report)			7	7
Division	1st Quarter	2d Quarter	20	20
Division 1	$263,478	$246,563	6	26
Division 2	78,136	101,486	11	31
Division 3	111,186	99,878	19	39
Total (Indent 3 spaces)	$452,800	$447,927	23	44

164

164a ▶ 5
Conditioning practice

each line twice SS (slowly, then faster); DS between 2-line groups; if time permits, retype selected lines

alphabet 1 Davis froze the fermented mixtures in the deep brown jugs too quickly.
figures 2 On Wednesday, August 2, take Flight 959 at 7:46 or Flight 123 at 8:00.
fig/sym 3 His Model D-394 sander sold for $16.75 at the garage sale on 12/13/81.
fluency 4 Diane may lend an auto to the downtown firm if they wish her to do so.

| 1 | 2 | 3 | 4 | 5 | 6 | 7 | 8 | 9 | 10 | 11 | 12 | 13 | 14 |

Going to school gives you many opportunities to develop your writing skills. Some students have improved their writing by using the technique of "oral writing." In oral writing, you tape-record what you want to write and then play back what you have said to see how it sounds before you write it.

Plan carefully what you want to say in a paper before writing it. "No one," as Tibbetts and Tibbetts (1978, p. 167) have indicated, "can write a first draft without an outline or plan." Much of the hard work of writing is in the planning, but it must be done if you are to write well. As you make your plan, you can write key ideas and their supporting evidence or statements on 6" by 4" or 8" by 5" cards. You can then give a topic to each card, arrange the cards in a logical order of presentation, and write your paper from the cards.

If you plan what you want to write, writing then becomes what it is--a process. And this writing process involves your successive efforts to clarify your thinking so that what you write is clear, concise, and direct. Walshe (1979, pp. 54-56) lists these steps as a part of the writing process:

* Selection of a topic
* Pre-writing preparation, including planning
* Draft writing
* Editing, rewriting, with feedback and evaluation from your peer group
* Final writing, publication, or sharing

Be sure to type your first draft; the typewriter is the most effective writing tool we have. Double-space your paper to make it easier to proofread, edit, and revise. Writing the first draft is the most difficult job of all. But Bates (1978, p. 3) offers some basic guides to good, clear writing:

* Be concise. Keep sentences and paragraphs short.
* State your purpose clearly.
* Get straight to the point.
* Be specific; avoid abstractions.
* Know your audience.
* Write to be understood, not to impress.
* Prefer the active voice. Put action in your verbs.
* Weed out unnecessary words, phrases, and ideas.

3. Edit, revise, and prepare the final draft. All writing needs careful editing and revision. Hemingway is said to have made thirty-nine revisions of the ending to his best seller, FAREWELL TO ARMS. Mario Puzo, author of the top-selling novel of the 1970's, THE GODFATHER, states categorically that "rewriting is the whole secret to writing" (Walshe, 1979, p. 55).

When you edit your work, it is helpful to have your classmates, or others, evaluate your writing. Some teachers have students work in small groups to read and review the writing of other students. In the editing and the revision of writing, Professor Richard Lanham of UCLA suggests the use of the "CBS Style," CBS standing for Clarity, Brevity, and Sincerity. In writing, he warns us to avoid the "Official or Bureaucratic Style" which often characterizes government publications. We have only to read this statement that the Chairman of the Nuclear Regulatory Commission wrote after the Three Mile Island accident to agree with Professor Lanham: "It would be prudent to consider expeditiously the provision of instrumentation that would provide an unambiguous indication of the level of fluid in the reactor vessel." If we translated this statement from the "Bureaucratic Style," it would probably read something like: We need accurate measuring devices.

When you edit your writing, check for errors of spelling, grammar, and punctuation. Check for incomplete as well as long and involved sentences. A long sentence can be shortened and improved by removing nonfunctional words and by restoring a logical order. If necessary, a long sentence can be divided into two shorter sentences. Make sure all words are used correctly in a sentence; avoid the pitfalls of misplaced modifiers, incorrect verbs, and run-on sentences. Stay away from the kind of "confusing writing" we often see in the signs on office building doors, such as: EMERGENCY EXIT ONLY--NOT TO BE USED UNDER ANY CIRCUMSTANCES. If the door cannot be used under any circumstances, it cannot be used at all!

Your writing should deal with particulars. Strunk and White (1979, p. 21) have this to say: "The greatest writers--Homer, Dante, Shakespeare--are effective largely because they deal in particulars and report the details that matter. Their words call up pictures." Do yours?

164b ▶ 45
Sustained production: tables

Time schedule

Preparation .... 5′
Timed production .... 30′
Final check;
compute *n-pram* .... 10′

each table as directed; proofread; correct errors

Problem 1
full sheet

Type the table in reading position; DS body; 10 spaces between columns.

LEADING TV ADVERTISERS IN 1979
(Rounded to Nearest Million)

Company	Amount	words parts	total
LEADING TV ADVERTISERS IN 1979		6	6
(Rounded to Nearest Million)		12	12
Company	Amount	18	18
Procter & Gamble Co.	$ 463	6	23
General Foods Corp.	297	10	28
American Home Products Corp.	165	17	35
General Mills, Inc.	157	22	39
General Motors Corp.	147	27	44
Bristol-Myers Co.	141	33	50
Total	$1,370	35	53

Problem 2
half sheet, long side up

Type the table in exact center; SS body; 6 spaces between columns.

Date	Holiday	State Celebrating	parts	total
HOLIDAYS IN AUGUST			4	4
Date	Holiday	State Celebrating	16	16
August 5	American Family Day	Arizona	7	23
August 13	Victory Day	Rhode Island	14	30
August 16	Bennington Battle Day	Vermont	22	38
August 18	Admission Day	Hawaii	29	44
August 27	Lyndon B. Johnson's Birthday	Texas	38	53
August 30	Huey P. Long Day	Louisiana	45	61

Problem 3
full sheet

Type the table in exact center; DS body; decide spacing between columns.

Problem 4

Retype Problem 1 if you finish all 3 problems before time is called.

		parts	total
EMPLOYMENT OUTLOOK		4	4
(Average Annual Openings, 1976-1985)		11	11
Accountants	51,500	4	15
Bookkeeping workers	95,000	9	20
Computer operating personnel	8,500	16	27
Office machines operators	7,700	23	34
Programmers	9,700	26	37
Secretaries and stenographers	295,000	34	45
Typists	63,000	37	48

Note: The ellipsis, indicating omission of words from a quotation, is typed by alternating 3 periods and spaces (. . .) or 4 (. . . .) if the end of a sentence is included in the quotation.

> . . . there are everywhere obvious differences between written and spoken English. A speaker reinforces his meaning with gestures and vocal inflections, and if people he addresses still do not understand, they can ask for further explanations; whereas a writer, not enjoying either of these advantages, must formulate and observe certain literary principles if he wishes to be completely understood.

This statement means that written English, unlike spoken English, often has only one shot at getting the reader's interest and attention. And so, we have to give it our best shot!

Why Is Writing Important?

Writing helps us review and revise our ideas as we think through what it is we want to write. As Professor Carlos Baker, the Chairman of English at Princeton University, has said, "Learning to write is learning to think" (Cross, 1979, p. 226). And Dr. S. I. Hayakawa, a semanticist and therefore deeply concerned with the meaning of language, says much the same thing when he tells us, "You just don't know anything until you can write it" (Cross, 1979, p. 226).

Writing leads to the kind of human development that Henry David Thoreau called "being alive." But writing also helps us to remember things and so makes us better learners, and that's a very practical goal in our culture. Being able to write well contributes to success in school, too. And good writing is just as important to success in a job or a career, especially those careers where good written communication skills are required.

Also, as pointed out by the Committee on Writing Standards (1979, p. 220), "Writing can be a deeply personal act of shaping our perceptions of the world and our relationships to people and things in that world." Writing can be an important means of self-discovery, of finding out what we believe and know. And so our writing is our personal representative in the eyes of those who read it. It should represent us well.

Some Suggestions to Help You Improve Your Writing

1. Read, read, read. As Cross (1979, p. 226) has noted, "It is words that give coherence to the billion bits of information that fill our brains . . . ." In order to write, you must use words and you can't use words you don't have in your vocabulary. Reading can help develop your vocabulary, and having a large vocabulary increases your potential as a writer. So you should plan to read a lot, especially things that challenge your intellect. If you come across words you don't know, and that happens to all of us at one time or another, look up the words in the dictionary; then add them to your vocabulary. The dictionary also helps you to pick the right word to express your thoughts. By picking the right word and using it properly, you can avoid the kind of misuse of words that happened recently in an advertisement in a Lafayette, Indiana, newspaper: "Lafayette's Most Unique Restaurant Is Now Even More Unique." Now if a restaurant is "unique," it can't be "most unique" or even "more unique!" Some words have many meanings, but some like "unique" are absolutes and cannot be qualified by such words as "most" or "more."

When we use words we should stay away from jargon. In the past decade, as highlighted in a Time essay (January 28, 1980, p. 90), "Americans have exhausted 'uptight' and 'far out,' 'situationwise' and the 'bottom line,' 'charisma' and 'stonewalling' . . . ." As the essay indicates, however, "Good buddy and 10-4" may have become a part of the lingo of "CBers."

The same essay expresses a concern about our vocabularies: "Take the American language. It is more than a million words wide, and new terms are constantly added to its infinite variety. Yet as the decade starts, the U.S. vocabulary seems to have shrunk to child size." As Stone (1979, p. 102) has said, our limited vocabularies present "the danger that language will become a collection of vague grunts, y'knows, and other whatchamacallits." You only have to listen to the people around you to recognize the truth of this statement.

You can increase your vocabulary by making notes of new words in your study materials. And you should learn how to use your library since it contains the best written works of our culture. As you study and learn the meaning of words, singulars and plurals of nouns, tenses and modes of verbs, the right places to put punctuation, and ways to arrange sentences to show what goes with what, your writing will improve.

2. Write, write, write. We learn to write by writing. This statement is supported by Walshe (1979, p. 52) when he suggests that "A steady quantity of writing is the necessary precondition of quality." Writing is hard work, but it is like any other skill--practice leads to improvement.

165a ▶ 5 Conditioning practice

each line twice SS (slowly, then faster); DS between 2-line groups; if time permits, retype selected lines

alphabet 1 Quincy Baker owns five or six huge stores adjacent to the Plaza Motel.
figures 2 Order 175 reams of bond, 403 erasers, 69 rulers, and 28 dozen pencils.
fig/sym 3 He said, "Ship 20 #84 posts, listed at $37.96 less 15% cash discount."
fluency 4 All eight firms may fight with vigor the amendment to the profit rule.

| 1 | 2 | 3 | 4 | 5 | 6 | 7 | 8 | 9 | 10 | 11 | 12 | 13 | 14 |

165b ▶ 45 Measure production skill: tables

Time schedule

Preparation .... 5′
Timed production .... 30′
Final check;
compute *n-pram* .... 10′

each table as directed; proofread; correct errors

Problem 1

full sheet

Type the table in reading position; DS body; 10 spaces between columns.

		words
HIGHEST PER PUPIL COST OF EDUCATION		7
(By State/District)		11
Alaska	$3,710	14
New York	2,580	17
Wyoming	2,142	20
District of Columbia	2,125	25
New Jersey	2,122	29

Problem 2

half sheet, long side up

Type the table in exact center; SS body; 8 spaces between columns.

MILEAGE REPORT			3
(September)			5
Date	Miles	Cost (20 cents/mi.)	18
September 3	156	$ 31.20	23
September 10	238	47.60	27
September 13	88	17.60	32
September 21	116	23.20	37
September 26	94	18.80	44
Total	692	$138.40	48

Problem 3

full sheet

Type the table in exact center; DS body; decide spacing between columns.

Problem 4

Retype Problem 1 if you finish all 3 problems before time is called.

AMERICAN WOMEN WRITERS		5
(Listed Alphabetically)		9
Name	Classification	17
Elizabeth Bishop	poet	21
Gwendolyn Brooks	poet	26
Rosalyn Drexler	dramatist	31
Ellen Glasgow	novelist	35
Ada Louise Huxtable	journalist	41

1½" top margin (pica type)
(1" on all other pages)

IMPROVE YOUR WRITING

All of us write from time to time. Writing well is a problem that has become a national concern.

What Is Writing?

The National Council of Teachers of English formed a Committee on Writing Standards to try to find out what good writing is all about. The Committee (1979, p. 220) has given us a useful definition of writing: "Writing is the process of selecting, combining, arranging, and developing ideas in effective sentences, paragraphs, and often longer units of discourse." "Good writing," according to the American Psychological Association (1967, p. 15), "is clear, precise, unambiguous, and economical."

1½" 1"

When you or I sit down to write, we tend to follow the writing process that the Committee on Writing Standards spoke about. Thoughts and ideas flow from the words we use, with the words forming sentences and the sentences growing into paragraphs. The words we use show our stream of thought and should carry the readers on an easy and pleasurable cruise through our report or other communication. What we write should have no hidden navigational hazards which might throw readers off course, or completely "out of the boat," so that they stop reading.

Our written English differs greatly from our spoken English. Graves and Hodge (1979, p. 17) support this point:

Approximately 1"

unit 31 lessons 166-169

Recall/improve report typing skills

Learning goals

1. To develop skill at composing in rough-draft form at the typewriter.
2. To gain skill in typing a report, table of contents, and title page.

Machine adjustments

1. Paper guide at *0*.
2. Ribbon control to type on top half of ribbon.
3. Margin sets: 70-space line for conditioning practices and language arts activities; as directed for problems.
4. Spacing: DS language arts; as directed for problems.

166

166a ▶ 5
Conditioning practice

each line twice SS (slowly, then faster); DS between 2-line groups; if time permits, retype selected lines

alphabet 1 Jacki Zorba moved from her extra quiet place in the Wyoming mountains.

figures 2 Stephen is sure Questions 1, 5, 7, 19, 24, and 30 are from Chapter 68.

superior figures 3 Articles supporting his new theory were written by Brown ^{1} and Morris.^{2}

fluency 4 This panel is the height to show key elements of the dials and wiring.

| 1 | 2 | 3 | 4 | 5 | 6 | 7 | 8 | 9 | 10 | 11 | 12 | 13 | 14 |

166b ▶ 15
Review how to type footnotes

1. Set margins for an unbound report (see RG p. vii).
2. Note placement of footnotes (RG p. vii). Read footnote placement information in report on p. 274.
3. Using a page line gauge [LM p. 6] as a guide for placing footnotes at bottom of page, type the copy in report form beginning on Line 45.
4. Use 1 as page number.
5. Proofread and mark errors.

According to Connell, the leader in the Office of the Future "must be a manager of technology, a manager of information, and, most importantly, a manager of people." ^{3}

____________________ SS
DS

^{1} Michele Simmons, "Office Productivity Needed for the 80s," The Secretary (April 1980) p. 8.

^{2} H. T. Smith and W. H. Baker, The Administrative Manager (Chicago: Science Research Associates, Inc., 1978), pp. 535-549.

^{3} John J. Connell, "The 'People Factor' in the Office of the Future," Administrative Management (January 1980) p. 76.

166c-169c ▶ 30
Type a leftbound report

Keep report for future use.

1. Begin typing the report on pages 272-275. Use leftbound format (see RG p. vii).
2. Proofread each completed page and correct each error before removing the paper from the typewriter.
3. When time is called to end a class period, complete any line you have begun. Continue typing from this point during the next production period.

167

167a ▶ 5
Conditioning practice

Use standard directions given in 166a.

alphabet 1 Mrs. Johansen and her six friends quickly zipped by the two villagers.

figures 2 We drove 153 miles on Highway 240, then 87 miles on Route 69 to Tulsa.

subscripts 3 The symbols H_2O and CO_2 are the formulas for water and carbon dioxide.

fluency 4 The firm spent six busy days and got the right title for the key land.

| 1 | 2 | 3 | 4 | 5 | 6 | 7 | 8 | 9 | 10 | 11 | 12 | 13 | 14 |

114c ▶ 37
Learn to type leftbound manuscripts with textual citations

full sheets; center heading over line of writing; DS the ¶s; indent 5 spaces

Correct errors as directed by your teacher.

Margins

top, page 1: pica 1½"
elite 2"
left margin: 1½"
right margin: 1"
bottom (approx.): 1"
top, page 2: 1"

Type page numbers on second, and additional pages, in upper right corner (see 111b, p. 185).

Note: You are not expected to complete the manuscript in this lesson; additional time is provided in Lessons 115–118.

The first page of the manuscript (in pica type) is shown in arranged form on p. 192.

The textual citation form of reference notation is illustrated in the manuscript. This is the preferred form in manuscripts prepared for publication in various magazines.

Guide: Make a light pencil mark at the right edge of the sheet 1" from the bottom, and another ½" above the 1" mark, as a page-end reminder as you type the manuscript; or, use the page line guage provided in LM, p. 7.

115

115a ▶ 5
Conditioning practice

Follow standard directions, p. 183.

alphabet 1 As Yuki watched, six blazing jets zipped skyward from that quay cover.
fig/sym 2 These 2-drawer oak filing cabinets (15" × 26" × 30") sell for $148.79.
double letters 3 A bookkeeping committee will meet to discuss current and fixed assets.
fluency 4 Their handiwork may entitle them to make a profit if they do the work.

| 1 | 2 | 3 | 4 | 5 | 6 | 7 | 8 | 9 | 10 | 11 | 12 | 13 | 14 |

115b ▶ 8
Improve capitalization skill: related learning

full sheet; 1" top margin; 70-space line

Follow standard directions, p. 135.

CAPITALIZATION GUIDES, continued

11. Capitalize geographic regions, localities, and names. Do not capitalize points of the compass when used to indicate directions or in a descriptive sense.

12. Capitalize such words as street, avenue, company, etc., when used with a proper noun.

13. Capitalize names of organizations, clubs, and buildings.

14. Capitalize a noun preceding a figure, except for common words such as line, page, and sentence, which may be typed with or without a capital.

learn 11. Rosa lives in Southern California, not southern Indiana.
learn My home is four blocks east and five blocks north of our school.

apply Beth lived in the south for a brief period.
apply The storm came roaring out of the Northwest.

learn 12. Use the Madison Avenue address for the Smith-Jones Company.
apply Walk up Fifth avenue toward Central Park.

learn 13. We recently joined the Future Business Leaders of America (FBLA).
apply The key club is planning a trip to the empire state building.

learn 14. Refer to Lesson 81b, Unit 16, on page 134 of your textbook.
apply Order style 34 (see Page 110, catalog 3).

115c ▶ 37
Learn to type leftbound manuscripts with textual citations

Continue 114c, pp. 191–195.

167b ▶ 15
Improve language arts: composing

1. Read the ¶ at the right.

2. Compose one or two double-spaced ¶s in rough-draft form to answer one of the two questions at the end of the ¶.

3. Revise your copy; then type it in final form with errors corrected.

You are standing in line waiting to purchase a ticket to the biggest basketball game of the year. You know that there is a good chance that all of the available tickets will be sold before you reach the ticket counter. You notice that the person just ahead of you allows a friend to crowd into the line, and you overhear their conversation to the effect that the friend wants to purchase six tickets. Will you express your objection to the two people in front of you? If so, why; and what will you say? If not, why not?

167c ▶ 30
Type a leftbound report

Continue typing the leftbound report where you stopped at the end of Lesson 166.

168

168a ▶ 5
Conditioning practice

Use standard directions as found in 166a.

alphabet	1	Packing the strawberry jam in dozens of boxes was quite a lively task.
figures	2	Gymnasium Lockers 48 and 27 have the same combination: R39, L16, R50.
superior figures	3	Support for his theory can be found in Ray,[1] Ames,[2] Byrd,[3] and Jones.[4]
fluency	4	They got the right quantity of eight bushels of corn for the busy men.

| 1 | 2 | 3 | 4 | 5 | 6 | 7 | 8 | 9 | 10 | 11 | 12 | 13 | 14 |

168b ▶ 15
Review how to type a bibliography

1. Arrange the bibliography at the right in alphabetical order and type it using the format shown on RG p. viii.

2. Set margins for leftbound report.

3. Use 5 as the page number.

4. Proofread and mark errors.

BIBLIOGRAPHY

Smith, Harold T., and William H. Baker. <u>The Administrative Manager</u>. Chicago: Science Research Associates, Inc., 1978.

Connell, John J. "The 'People Factor' in the Office of the Future." <u>Administrative Management</u>, January 1980, pp. 36-37, 74, 76.

Quible, Zane K. <u>Introduction to Administrative Office Management</u>. Cambridge: Winthrop Publishers, Inc., 1980.

Simmons, Michele. "Office Productivity Needed for the 80s." <u>The Secretary</u>, April 1980, pp. 8-9.

Ranftl, Robert M. "Productivity--A Critical Challenge of the 1980s." <u>Infosystems</u>, October 1979, pp. 55, 59, 62, 66.

168c ▶ 30
Type a leftbound report

Continue typing the leftbound report where you stopped at the end of Lesson 167.

113c, continued

however, that economists do not always agree on the reasons for nor the effects of inflation.

In recent years, as Parker[4] has noted, overall inflation has hit hardest in the four key sectors of the economy that hurt all of us--housing, health, food, and energy. Isn't it time then, as Parker has asked, that we stop the political debate about inflation and begin constructive measures to reduce it? As a start, Parker suggests that these steps be taken:

1. Put a lid on selected prices, from hospital costs to oil and gas to basic foods.

2. Expand the supply of basics such as housing through selected mortgage support; push conservation over synfuels; introduce consumer co-ops, family farm aid, and more direct marketing of goods.

3. Institute new public--public, not government--institutions, from energy corporations to health-maintenance organizations, to force the huge corporations to compete both openly and more efficiently.[5]

We can stop inflation but it will take a concerted effort; it is an effort that must enlist all of us in the war against inflation, and it is an effort that must be concerned with our total welfare--indeed our very survival as a nation.

---

[4] Richard Parker, "Inflation and Recession: Our Demoniac Duo," Los Angeles Times (August 12, 1979), Part V, p. 1.

[5] Parker, p. 1.

114

114a ▶ 5
Conditioning practice
Follow standard directions, p. 183.

alphabet	1	Jack Foz marveled at the big waxy pods in the pond in the town square.
fig/sym	2	Order the roll-top desks (57" × 26" × 48") from Glabman's for $193.50.
3d and 4th fingers	3	Sally, Aza, Paula, and Zax saw six plump polo ponies down by the quay.
fluency	4	The girls got the bicycle, bugle, and burlap from an Orlando neighbor.

| 1 | 2 | 3 | 4 | 5 | 6 | 7 | 8 | 9 | 10 | 11 | 12 | 13 | 14 |

114b ▶ 8
Improve capitalization skill: related learning
full sheet; 1" top margin; 70-space line

Follow standard directions, p. 135.

CAPITALIZATION GUIDES, continued

7. Do not capitalize business or professional titles used without the name of the person.

8. Capitalize all proper nouns and their derivatives.

9. Capitalize the names of the days of the week, months of the year, holidays, periods of history, and historic events.

10. Capitalize the seasons of the year only when they are personified.

learn	7.	The professor is unable to give the lecture.
learn		Will you ask Professor Jones if she can take the class.
apply		The Dean is not in. Is dean Goodlad in Europe?
learn	8.	The Canadians and the Americans will join in the Commemoration.
apply		I participated in the scottish Folk Dance Festival.
learn	9.	Capitalize these words: Friday, July Fourth, Civil War Period.
apply		On monday, october 10, the test will be on the hellenic period.
learn	10.	The soft breath of Spring awakened the hibernating bear.
learn		Will the Festival be held in the fall, winter, spring, or summer?
apply		We plan to tour New England this Fall.
apply		You can almost feel the icy fingers of winter approaching.

169

169a ▶ 5
Conditioning practice

Use standard directions given in 166a, p. 270.

alphabet 1 The bold zebra quickly jumped over the sixth wagon at the county fair.

figures 2 Our warehouse stored 205 tables, 183 chairs, 69 lamps, and 47 mirrors.

subscripts 3 Q_1, Q_2, Q_3, and K_3 are some of the terms needed to type many formulas.

fluency 4 Kaye may vote by proxy if she wishes to do so when the voting is held.

| 1 | 2 | 3 | 4 | 5 | 6 | 7 | 8 | 9 | 10 | 11 | 12 | 13 | 14 |

169b ▶ 15
Improving language arts: composing

1. Read the ¶s at the right.
2. Compose one or two double-spaced ¶s expressing your feelings concerning the statements. Answer the questions in the last ¶.
3. Correct your copy; then type in final form on a full sheet.

John Donne wrote that "no man is an island," that is, that no one can live totally independent of others. We are dependent upon others for both emotional and physical needs from time to time in our lives.

Anne Morrow Lindbergh wrote that we are all islands, that is, we are all alone in reality. We have no choice about this state of solitude, and we are much better off to realize this fact.

Do you agree with either or both of these points of view? Why or why not? Can you give examples which represent each of these views?

169c ▶ 30
Type a leftbound report

Continue typing the leftbound report where you stopped at the end of Lesson 168.

166c-169c
Type a leftbound report

words

MANUSCRIPT AND REPORT WRITING [TS] 6

This report [describes] ~~represents~~ one acceptable form for typing 17

manuscripts and reports. [Follow these guides carefully.] [TS] 28

Spacing and Margins 36

[DS]

The form selected depends on the use of the [document] ~~report~~. 47

Reports prepared [for] ~~to~~ use in the business ofice [f] as a means 59

of internal [communication] ~~reporting~~ are often typed single-spaced like 71

inter-office memoranduns. Manuscirpts, school reports, and 83

formal reports to be submitted for publication should be 94

double-spaced. 97

the margins to be used vary depending upon where and if 109

the manuscript or report is to be bound. The correct mar- 120

gins follow: 123

(continued, p. 273)

1½" top margin (pica type)
(1" on all other pages)

INFLATION

During the past decade, an awesome enemy has engulfed us. That enemy is not some foreign power; it is inflation. In economic terms, inflation can be defined as a sustained increase in the general price level with a corresponding decrease in the purchasing power of the dollar.[1] The basic ingredient of inflation is suggested by this statement:

1" 1"

Indent 5 spaces from left and right margins; SS

> Classic inflation has just one element: too much money chasing too few products, thus pushing up prices. To concoct the witches' brew of modern inflation, you start with that basic recipe. A liberal dash of budget deficits, plus a pinch of presidential and congressional politics, will help supply excessive money. Then you finish off with whatever unexpected nasty seasoning comes to hand--such as oil price increases.[2]

Inflation affects everyone; however, some individuals or groups fare better than others. Debtors, stockholders, and business firms are among those likely to benefit by inflation. On the other hand, creditors and savers, retired people, the poor, and people on fixed incomes are those apt to be hurt most by inflation. If this is the case, should not certain groups be in favor of inflation? Not necessarily, as Poindexter explains: "Most individuals are both creditors and debtors. The real value of the wealth they hold in the form of dollar claims is eroded as prices rise."[3] It should be noted,

---

[1]Laurence H. Meyer, <u>Macroeconomics: A Model Building Approach</u> (Cincinnati: South-Western Publishing Co., 1980), p. 4.

[2]"Inflation's Ingredients," <u>Money</u> (June 1979), p. 42.

[3]J. Carl Poindexter, <u>Macroeconomics</u> (Hinsdale, IL: The Dryden Press, 1976), p. 351.

Approximately 1"

166c-169c, continued

words

Unbound 124

First page Top: 1 1/2" pica, 2" elite 132

Bottom: about 1" 135

Sides: 1" 137

Other pages Top: 1" 141

Bottom and side margins are same as 149

on the first page 151

Topbound Same as unbound except increase 160

the top margin 1/2" 164

Leftbound Same as unbound except increase 174

the left margin 1/2" 178

The first line of a paragraph is usually indeted 5 spaces 190
but a 7 or 10 space indention is also acceptable Direct 202
quotations of 4 or more lines is single-spaced and indented 214
5 spaces from the left and right margin. A single blank 224
line space (DS) is left above and below direct long quotes. 237

Heading and Subheadings 246

Main headings. The Main heading is typed in all CAPS and 260
centered over a line of writing followed with 1 blank line 272
space (DS) if a secondary heading is used or 2 blank line 284
spaces (TS) if no secondary heading is used. The secondary 296
heading (if used) is typed a double space below the main head- 309
ing with main words capitalized, followed by 2 blank lines (TS). 324

Side headings. The main words of side headings begin with 338
a capitol letter. These are typed underlined even with the 350
left margin with no terminal punctuation. A triple space is 363
left and above a double space is left below a side heading. 375

Paragraph headings. A paragraph heding is indented 390
underlined, and followed by a peroid. Usually on ly the first 403
words and proper nouns are capitalized. 411

Page Numbers 416

A page number is not needed on the first page of a report. 429
If a page number is used, however, it iscentered and typed one 441
half inch from the bottom edge. The second and remaining pages 454
are numbered on line 4 at the right margin of a left bound and 466
unbound manuscripts or reports. The page numbers on topbound 478
reports are centered a half inch from the bottom on all pages. 491

(continued, p. 274)

113

113a ▶ 5 Conditioning practice

Follow standard directions, p. 183.

alphabet 1 Jan was very quick to fix many broken zippers for the bright children.

fig/sym 2 The bookcase (36″ × 59″ × 14 1/2″) is on sale at the Mart for $178.50.

shift key 3 F. T. McNeil and A. Z. O'Brien are employed by Brown & Yamaguchi, Inc.

fluency 4 A neighbor may do the work for them when they audit the ancient firms.

| 1 | 2 | 3 | 4 | 5 | 6 | 7 | 8 | 9 | 10 | 11 | 12 | 13 | 14 |

113b ▶ 10 Improve capitalization skill: related learning

full sheet; 1″ top margin; 70-space line

Follow carefully the Study/Learn/Apply/Correct procedures given on p. 135.

CAPITALIZATION GUIDES

1. Capitalize the first word of every sentence and the first word of every complete direct quotation.
2. Do not capitalize fragments of quotations.
3. Do not capitalize a quotation resumed within a sentence. Type the comma or period before the ending quotation mark.
4. Capitalize the first word after a colon if that word begins a complete sentence. Space twice after the colon.
5. Capitalize first and last words and all other words in titles of books, articles, periodicals, headings, and plays, except words of four or fewer letters used as articles, conjunctions, or prepositions.
6. Capitalize an official title when it immediately precedes a name. When used elsewhere, type the title without the capital unless it is a title of high distinction or the title is used in place of the name.

learn 1. Did he say, "The chief aim of the writer is to be understood"?
apply she said, "i can teach you how to write but not how to create."

learn 2. She stressed the importance of "doing as well as knowing."
apply Carol denied that she was "A neurotic editor."

learn 3. "It was Zapata," she said, "who led the fight for justice."
apply "I have learned silence," Gibran said, "From the talkative".

learn 4. Do this daily: Make all needed machine adjustments.
apply Here is a reminder: be sure to type with good technique.

learn 5. Alice read the book Catcher in the Rye.
apply She also read the article "the purpose of the Nobel Prize."

learn 6. President Reagan will give the State of the Union Message.
learn The Senator from Ohio will introduce the President.

apply She is the Executive Assistant to the vice president.

113c ▶ 35 Type an unbound manuscript with footnotes

full sheets; DS the ¶s; indent 5 for ¶s; SS enumerated items

Correct errors as directed by your teacher.

Follow standard directions for typing an unbound manuscript as given on p. 183.

The first page of the manuscript (in pica type) is shown in arranged form on p. 189; the second page is typeset.

Number footnotes as shown in the report.

Guide: To leave space for the footnotes and a 1″ bottom margin, do this:

Make a light pencil mark at the right edge of the sheet 1″ from the bottom. As you type each *footnote reference number*, add another pencil mark ½″ above the previous one. in this way, you will reserve about 3 line spaces for typing each footnote. Erase marks when you have completed the page.

If you have a page line gauge [LM p. 7], use it.

words

Manuscript and Report Documentation 505

When material is cited that did not originate with the writer, the source 520
of the information must be acknowledged. This process, called documenta- 534
tion, is usually accomplished by using footnotes or endnotes. In addition to 550
documentation, footnotes and endnotes may be used to: 562

1. support arguments; 566
2. provide the reader with additional information; 577
3. refer the reader to other parts of the text. 586

Placement of Footnote and Endnote Reference Figures 607

Footnotes are indicated by typing a reference figure as a superior figure 621
in the text of the report. Endnotes may also be indicated in the same way. 637
Reference figures may be placed as follows: 645

1. at the end of material that is directly or indirectly paraphrased 659
   or quoted; 662
2. at the end of the statement that introduces directly quoted material; 676
3. following the side or paragraph heading if most or all of the material 691
   following the heading is based on source material; 702
4. after the name of the author of the cited work. 712

Placement of Footnotes, Endnotes, and Explanatory Notes 734

Footnotes. The preferred placement of footnotes is in numerical order 750
ending about 1 inch from the bottom of the page. Separating the footnotes from 766
the body of the report is a single space and a 1 1/2 inch divider line. Footnotes 782
are single-spaced with a double space between them. On a partially filled page, 799
footnotes may be typed at the bottom of the page or immediately below the last 814
line of the body of the report. 821

Endnotes. Endnotes are placed at the end of the report or manuscript. 837
They are usually listed in alphabetic order. If, however, the references are 852
numbered in the text, the endnotes must be listed numerically to correspond 867
with the order in which they are referenced in the body of the report. 881

Explanatory notes. When the writer feels that a statement needs to be 899
clarified, an explanatory note is used, placed as a footnote would be. If more 915
than one explanatory note is used, the notes are referenced in numerical order 931
throughout the body of the report.[1] 938

________________ 941

[1] When only one explanatory note is needed, it is referenced with an 954
asterisk (*). 957

(continued, p. 275)

correction was made on the original, then retype the correction so that it will be recorded on the carbon copy. An eraser, correction fluid, or correction tape may be used to make corrections on carbon copies when lift-off tape is used for error correction on the original.

Correction Fluid

On typewriters not equipped with lift-off tape, correction fluid may be used to correct errors. Correction fluid is packaged in a small bottle with an applicator brush attached on the inside of the cap. Follow these steps when using the correction fluid for the correction of errors:

1. Turn the cylinder forward or up a few spaces.
2. Shake the bottle containing the correction fluid; remove the applicator from the bottle; daub excess fluid on inside of the bottle opening.
3. Apply fluid sparingly to the error by a touching action over the error with the tip of the brush. The fluid covers the error.
4. Return applicator to the bottle and tighten cap. The latter step is important to prevent evaporation of the fluid. Blow on the correction to speed the drying of the fluid.
5. When fluid is dry, type the correction.

Correction Paper

Use of correction tape or paper is another way to correct errors. Correction paper covers (masks) the error with a powderlike substance. It is easy to use. Here are the steps to follow:

1. Backspace to the beginning of the error.
2. Insert the correction tape or paper strip behind the typewriter ribbon and in front of the error.
3. Retype the error exactly as you made it. In this step, powder from the correction paper masks the error.
4. Remove the correction paper; backspace to the point where the correction is to begin and then type the correction.

If carbon copies are to be corrected, insert special correction paper behind the carbon and in front of the error to be corrected; then follow the steps outlined above.

Correction paper comes in colors to match the colors of paper commonly used in the business office--white, blue, pink, and yellow.

Rubber Typewriter Eraser

Before the newer procedures for error correction were available, the typewriter eraser was used to correct errors. It is now used less frequently in the business office for error correction. When using the eraser, care must be taken not to smudge the paper with your fingers, and the eraser crumbs must be brushed away from the paper so they do not fall into the typewriter.

Follow these steps when using the eraser for error correction:

1. Turn the platen or cylinder forward a few spaces; then move the carriage or element to the extreme right or left so that it is easy to get at the error. In this way, too, you can keep the eraser crumbs from falling into the operating parts of the machine.
2. Lift the paper bail out of the way. Pull the original sheet forward and place a card (5 by 3 inches, or slightly larger) in front of, not behind, the first carbon. The card protects the carbon copy from smudges as the erasure is made and helps prolong the life of the carbon paper.
3. Flip the original sheet back and make the erasure. Brush or blow the eraser crumbs from the paper.
4. Move the protective card to a position in front of the second carbon if more than one copy is being made. Erase the error (use a soft eraser) on the first carbon copy. Correct errors on other copies in a like manner.
5. Remove the card and type the correction.

166c-169c, continued

words

Bibliography 962

A bibliography, if used, is the final part of a report and is typed using 977
the same margins as the first page of the report. It is arranged alphabetically 993
with the page(s) numbered appropriately.[2] 1001

Title Page 1005

The arrangement of a title page varies depending upon the amount of 1019
information needed. It usually contains the name of the report on the top half of 1036
the page, the name of the person preparing the report and other identifying 1051
information in approximate center of the page, and the date on the lower half of 1067
the page. 1069

Table of Contents 1076

The table of contents is typed after the report is finished because accurate 1092
page numbers must be inserted into the table. The margins are the same as 1107
those for the first page of the report. Leaders, typed by alternating periods and 1123
spaces, separate the headings from the page numbers. Leaders are properly 1137
aligned by noting whether the first period of the first leader begins on an odd or 1155
even space on the typewriter scale. Subsequent rows of leaders are typed to 1170
align under the first row. 1175

____________________ 1178

[2] A model of a bibliography page is shown in the reference guide on 1192
page viii. 1193

166c-169c, continued

Prepare table of contents and title page

Study the models and prepare the table of contents and title page for the report you have just completed. Insert the appropriate page numbers in the table of contents.

Insert leaders by alternating periods and spaces, noting whether you start the periods on an odd or even space.

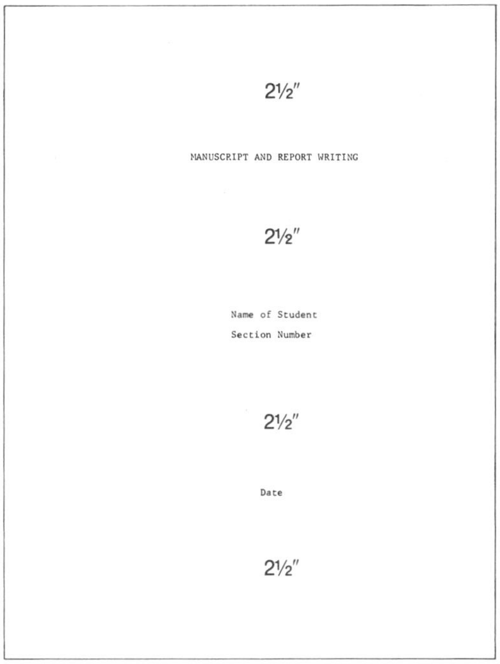

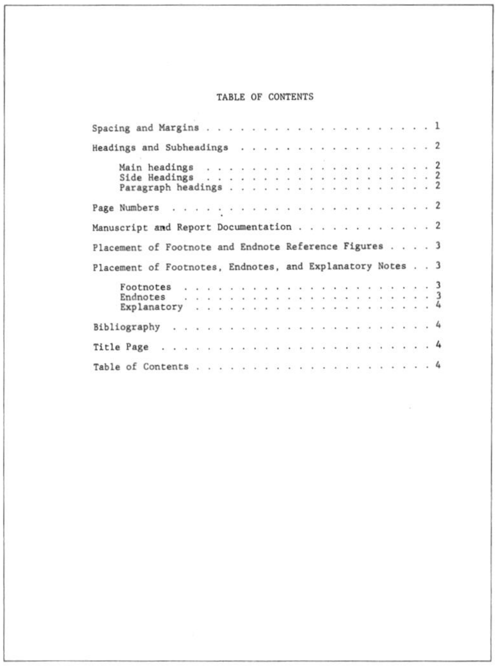
TABLE OF CONTENTS

Spacing and Margins	1
Headings and Subheadings	2
Main headings	2
Side Headings	2
Paragraph headings	2
Page Numbers	2
Manuscript and Report Documentation	2
Placement of Footnote and Endnote Reference Figures	3
Placement of Footnotes, Endnotes, and Explanatory Notes . .	3
Footnotes	3
Endnotes	3
Explanatory	4
Bibliography	4
Title Page	4
Table of Contents	4

112b ▶ 45
Type an unbound manuscript from rough draft, script, and straight copy

full sheets; DS the ¶s; 5-space ¶ indention; SS enumerated items; correct errors

Follow standard directions for typing an unbound manuscript as given on p. 183.

Correcting Typing Errors ← Center and type in ALL CAPS

TS

Before an error can be corrected in type written work, it must be detected. When employers the business person comlains about the about the accuracy of typists, what they he usually are is complaining about is the proofreading skill of typists. Some error-correction of these procedures are discussed in this short report. Once an error is found, it can be corrected by any of several error-correction procedures.

Lift-Off tape

One of The most common error correction procedures inuse in the business office is the error lift-off procedure. All modern Typewriters are equipped with a special lift-off tape which is used in correcting errors on the original copy. making the correction.

The procedure is relatively simple: When an error is made, a special key, or similar device, is used to back space to the error; the incorrect character is lifted off the paper bay again striking the incorrect character. The typing element stays in place, and the corroet character is typed.

If a carbon copy is to be corrected, another error-correction procedure must be used on it. Before backspacing to the error position, insert a piece of correction paper in front of the error on the carbon copy. Next, correct the error on the original as directed; then turn the platen forward and remove the correction paper. Turn the platen back, return to the point where the

(continued, p. 187)

unit **32** lessons 170-172

Improve/measure basic skills

Learning goals

1. To improve straight–copy skill.

2. To prepare for measurement of letter, table, and report typing skill.

Machine adjustments

1. Paper guide at *0*.

2. Ribbon control to type on top half of ribbon.

3. Margin sets: 70–space line for ¶ copy; as directed for problems.

4. Spacing: DS ¶ copy; as directed for problems.

170

170a ▶ 5
Conditioning practice

each line twice SS (slowly, then faster); DS between 2-line groups; if time permits, retype selected lines

alphabet 1 Ray Pizlo became quite sick Friday from jogging over to the next town.

figures 2 The 46 workers typed 309 letters, 225 reports, and 187 invoices today.

adjacent keys 3 The progress report discussed his participation in the weekly meeting.

fluency 4 Analena may visit eight foreign towns when she goes to audit the firm.

| 1 | 2 | 3 | 4 | 5 | 6 | 7 | 8 | 9 | 10 | 11 | 12 | 13 | 14 |

170b ▶ 20
Guided writings on paragraphs

1. A 3′ writing on ¶s 1–2 combined; determine *gwam*.

2. A 1′ writing on ¶ 1; determine *gwam* to establish base rate.

3. Add 2–6 words to Step 2 *gwam*; use this as your *goal* rate.

4. From the table below, find quarter–minute checkpoints; note these figures in ¶ 1.

5. Type three 1′ speed writings on the ¶, trying to reach your quarter–minute checkpoints as the guides (1/4, 1/2, 3/4, time) are called.

6. Follow Steps 2–5 for ¶ 2.

7. Repeat Step 1. Compare *gwam* rates.

gwam	1/4′	1/2′	3/4′	1′
32	8	16	24	32
36	9	18	27	36
40	10	20	30	40
44	11	22	33	44
48	12	24	36	48
52	13	26	39	52
56	14	28	42	56
60	15	30	45	60
64	16	32	48	64
68	17	34	51	68
72	18	36	54	72
76	19	38	57	76
80	20	40	60	80

all letters used | A | 1.5 si | 5.7 awl | 80% hfw |

	gwam 3′	
Our society has acquired a desire for instant, effortless living.	4	69
With instant meals and automatic machines, we have moved away from an	9	73
active society to one in which much of our personal and job time is	14	78
spent in a sitting position. We read dials and push buttons while	18	82
things do the work for us. Even our free time is spent in sedentary	23	87
activities such as reading, seeing movies, and just watching TV. Such	27	92
activity makes the body weak and the mind sluggish.	31	95
There is no objection to the fast and easy way of doing essential,	35	100
routine things, of course; but doctors tell us that the increasing time	40	104
spent in sedentary activity is impairing our physical and mental health.	45	109
They tell us to use more of our leisure time for active things. For ex-	50	114
ample, walk more, ride less; take a zestful swim instead of a sunbath;	55	119
take part in athletic activities instead of merely sit and view them.	60	124
They ask us to get a better balance between sitting and acting.	64	128

gwam 3′ | 1 | 2 | 3 | 4 | 5 |

Note: See illustration on p. 183 for format.

space (2 blank line spaces). Note: When a 1 1/2-inch left margin is used, the center of the line of writing is different from the horizontal center of a sheet. To find center, add the figures at the left and right margins and divide by 2.

Side headings. Side headings are typed even with the left margin and underlined; main words are capitalized. These headings are preceded by a triple space (2 blank line spaces) and followed by a double space (1 blank line space).

Paragraph headings. The paragraph heading which you have just typed is indented and underlined. Paragraph headings help to highlight the important parts of a report.

Reference Notations

Footnotes. Reference citations in a report or manuscript may be made by means of footnotes, which are typed at the foot of the page on which the quoted reference appears. Footnotes are indented to the paragraph point, are preceded (without spacing) by a reference figure raised 1/2 line space, and are single-spaced with double spacing between footnotes. Footnotes are separated from the manuscript copy by a dividing line 1 1/2 inches long (18 elite or 15 pica spaces). The dividing line is typed a single space below the last line of the page and is followed by a double space.

Footnotes are numbered consecutively throughout a report, and "superior figures" (Arabic numbers typed about 1/2 space above the line) are used to refer the reader to the footnotes. In the planning for the footnotes, allowance must be made for a bottom margin of approximately 1 inch below the footnotes on all pages except the last. Footnotes must be typed in an accepted and consistent form throughout a report. Various style manuals show acceptable forms for typing footnotes.

Textual citations. Reference citations also may be typed as a part of the text of a report or manuscript. When this is done, footnotes are not used; the references are cited by enclosing the author's surname and the year of publication in parentheses in the textual copy. Example: (Beaumont, 1982) When the name of the author is used in the report, the reference citation need be only the year of publication. Example: (1982) If a reference has no author, the first two or three words of the title and the year of publication are used. Example: (Webster's Dictionary, 1982) Enough words of the title should be used so the reader can locate the reference in the reference list included at the end of the report. Textual citations usually follow the format recommended by the American Psychological Association in its Publication Manual.

Footnotes are used in the manuscript copy of 113c, page 188, and textual citations are used in 114c, page 191.

Page Numbers

The first page may or may not be numbered. The number, if used, is centered and typed a half inch from the bottom edge of the sheet. As a general rule, other page numbers are typed on the fourth line in the upper right corner of the sheet approximately even with the right margin; however, if the manuscript or report is to be bound at the top, the page numbers are typed in the first-page position (centered and typed a half inch from the bottom edge).

112

112a ▶ 5 Conditioning practice

Follow standard directions, p. 183.

alphabet	1	Jackie saw a covey of prime quail and a big fox down by that zoo lake.
fig/sym	2	The building located at 14750 O'Farrell Street sold for $6,382,975.00.
variable rhythm	3	Did he send a statement to the firm at the address listed on the card?
fluency	4	It is their wish to visit the ancient field box down by the city lake.

| 1 | 2 | 3 | 4 | 5 | 6 | 7 | 8 | 9 | 10 | 11 | 12 | 13 | 14 |

170c ▶ 25
Prepare for measurement: letters

Problem 1
Short letter

plain full sheets; modified block style, mixed punctuation

1. Three 1′ writings in letter form on the opening lines (date through subject line). Try to type at least 1 or 2 more words each time you repeat the drill.

2. Three 1′ writings in letter form on the closing lines (complimentary close through enclosure notation). Try to type at least 1 or 2 more words each time you repeat the drill.

3. On another full sheet, type a 5′ writing in letter form on the entire letter; determine *gwam*; circle errors.

	words parts	total
October 3, 19-- Masud Oil Company Attention Miss Johanna Colson 684 17th	15	15
Street Rockford, IL 61108-7541 Ladies and Gentlemen: Subject: Time	29	29
Management Seminar	32	32
(¶ 1) At the request of Ms. Klara Teter, I am recommending to you a person	13	45
who could conduct an exciting and informative seminar on time management.	28	60
He is Dr. D. L. Pate.	32	64
(¶ 2) Dr. Pate has conducted numerous workshops and seminars on this sub-	45	77
ject, as you can see from his enclosed data sheet. In addition, he has written	61	93
extensively in this area. He is well prepared to handle the kinds of sessions	77	109
Ms. Teter indicated you need.	82	114
(¶ 3) I hope that you will be successful in arranging this program with	95	127
Dr. Pate.	97	129
Sincerely yours, T & D CONSULTANTS, INC. Mrs. Francesca Draper	13	142
President xx Enclosure	17	146

Problem 2
Average-length letter

2 plain full sheets; block style, open punctuation

1. A 5′ writing in letter form on entire letter, typing with control. Determine *gwam*; circle errors.

2. If time permits, type another 5′ writing, trying to improve rate. Determine *gwam*; circle errors. Compare *gwam* of the 2 writings.

	gwam 5′
October 8, 19-- Dr. D. L. Pate 6394 North Washburn Avenue Minneapolis,	3
MN 55430-6678 Dear Dr. Pate Subject: Time Management Seminar	6
(¶ 1) Mrs. Francesca Draper has indicated to us that you are experienced	9
in conducting seminars and workshops on the subject of time management.	12
After reviewing your data sheet, which she sent us, we are sure that you are	15
just the person who can present the kind of program we need.	17
(¶ 2) We feel that it is important for both the office personnel and their	20
immediate supervisors to participate in this seminar; therefore, the times	23
available are somewhat limited. Would it be possible for you to meet with	26
us on either November 2 and 3, November 9 and 10, or December 7 and 8?	29
(¶ 3) In addition to your travel expenses, we are prepared to pay a $1,000	32
honorarium for your services. We shall arrange for hotel accommodations,	35
but we suggest that you make your own travel arrangements.	37
(¶ 4) If you can assist us with this program, please let us know as soon as	40
possible so we can notify those who are interested in attending.	43
Cordially MASUD OIL COMPANY Miss Johanna G. Colson, Training Director	46
xx	47

1½" top margin (pica type)
(1" on all other pages)

Main heading

MANUSCRIPT OR REPORT FORM Line 10
TS

The guides presented here represent one acceptable form of typing manuscripts or reports.
TS

Side heading

Spacing and Margins
DS

Manuscripts or reports may be either single- or double-spaced. The form that is followed is dependent upon the type of report. School reports, formal reports, and manuscripts to be submitted for publication should be typed in double-spaced form. Reports that are prepared for use in the business office in single-spaced form.

1" 1"

More needed

Maintain an approximate 1-inch bottom marg top and side margins on all pages with these ex

2 spaces

1. Leave a 1 1/2-inch (pica) or 2-inch (e gin on the first page of an unbound or manuscript; a 2- or 2 1/2-inch top mar first page of a topbound manuscript.
DS
2. Leave a 1 1/2-inch top margin on the s ceeding pages of a topbound manuscript
3. Leave a 1 1/2-inch left margin on all pages leftbound manuscript.

Indent numbered items 5 spaces from left and right margins

The first line of a paragraph usually is indented 5 spaces. Quoted material of 4 lines or more is single-spaced and indented 5 spaces from the left and right margins. It is preceded and followed by a double space (1 blank line space).

Headings and Subheadings

¶ heading

Main headings. A main heading is centered over the line of writing and is typed in ALL CAPITALS. It is followed by a triple

Approximately 1"

171

171a ▶ 5
Conditioning practice

Use standard procedure given in 170a, page 276.

alphabet	1	Peggy and Franz will back the council vote on the major tax questions.
figures	2	Over 4,750 people attended the 236 exhibits at the 1982 New Arts Fair.
adjacent keys	3	He agreed to start building his store on a street north of the region.
fluency	4	If the firms make a big profit, he is eligible for the usual dividend.

| 1 | 2 | 3 | 4 | 5 | 6 | 7 | 8 | 9 | 10 | 11 | 12 | 13 | 14 |

171b ▶ 10
Improve techniques: response patterns

1. Each set of 3 lines twice SS (slowly, then faster); DS between 6-line groups.

2. A 1′ writing on each of Lines 3, 6, and 9; determine *gwam* on each writing. Compare rates.

word response	1	bug but when also work pair lake forms visit right sight vigor problem
	2	aid us | to rush | key goal | if he did | both coal and clay | also handy for me
	3	A box firm spent the profit for eighty big signs for the island docks.
letter response	4	in oil bad ate you milk care state taxes union faced cedar polio trade
	5	my dad | we were | get upon | in my joy | at my age | tax on gas | only base rates
	6	In my opinion, only test case data were stated in rare rate decreases.
combination response	7	both read hand upon than reserve sick only rich refer soap wages sight
	8	was best | an end | in fact | to do so | for the town | get my facts | may go with
	9	It was up to you to get all the facts and to base the opinion on them.

| 1 | 2 | 3 | 4 | 5 | 6 | 7 | 8 | 9 | 10 | 11 | 12 | 13 | 14 |

171c ▶ 20
Prepare for measurement: tables

1 full sheet, 1 half sheet

1. Center and type the table DS in reading position on a full sheet, leaving 8 spaces between columns. Proofread and circle errors.

2. If time permits, retype the table on a half sheet, short side up with these changes: omit secondary heading; type main heading in two lines (SS), as **ANALYSIS OF THE USES OF WORKING CAPITAL** omit Column 3; leave 4 spaces between Columns 1 and 2.
Total words: 77

words

ANALYSES OF THE USES OF WORKING CAPITLE (I; AL) 8

(Rate Based on Percentage of Total Workni̇g Capital) 18

Account	Amount	Rate	words
Capitle (al) Expenditures	$730,000	80.7	33
Cash Dividemt (d) Payments	73,651	8.1	39
Increase in Investments	28,210	~~21.1~~ 3.1	46
Intangable (i) Assets Acquired	7,129	0.8	54
Net Increase in Long-Term Receivables	3,780	0.4	63
Other Uses	10,700	1.2	68
Perpayment of Pension Costs	8,410	0.9	75
Purchase of Companys Own Stock	2,212	0.2	84
Reduction of Prior Borrowings	40,482	4.5	95
Total	$904,574	99.9	99

unit **21** lessons 111-118

Increase report typing skill

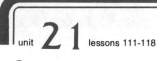

Learning goals

1. To improve your manuscript- and report-typing skill.
2. To learn basic guides for capitalization.
3. To learn basic steps to follow in correcting errors.

Machine adjustments

1. Paper guide at *0*.
2. 70-space line and SS, unless otherwise directed.
3. Line space selector on *1*, or as directed for various activities.
4. Ribbon indicator on black (*R* on Selectric).

111

111a ▶ 5
Conditioning practice

each line 3 times (slowly, faster, in-between rate); as time permits, retype selected lines for extra credit

alphabet 1 Many big jackdaws quickly zipped over the fox pen near your new house.
fig/sym 2 The rates varied from 15 1/2% to 17 1/4% on loans from $98 to $36,500.
shift lock 3 The pamphlet is printed in FOUR COLORS on Smith #20 BRISTOL PKG paper.
fluency 4 Is it right to make them do the work for both the town and city firms?

| 1 | 2 | 3 | 4 | 5 | 6 | 7 | 8 | 9 | 10 | 11 | 12 | 13 | 14 |

111b ▶ 45
Learn to type an unbound manuscript without footnotes

full sheets; DS the ¶s; SS enumerated items; correct errors

Margins
top, page 1: pica 1½″
elite 2″
bottom (approx.): 1″
top, page 2: 1″
side: 1″

Number pages in upper right corner; do not number page 1.

Note: Make a light pencil mark at the right edge of the paper about 1″ from the bottom edge (and again at 1½″) or use a backing sheet to alert you to leave a 1″ bottom margin.

A page line gauge (backing sheet) is provided on LM p. 7. This sheet indicates the number of line spaces above and below your line of typing.

1. Study the illustration and the paragraphs on manuscript or report form, pp. 184–185.

2. Type the unbound manuscript as directed. Indent the enumerated items 5 spaces from the left and right margins; space them as illustrated.

Note: Page 1 is shown in model form on p. 184; a miniature model of page 2 is shown at the right.

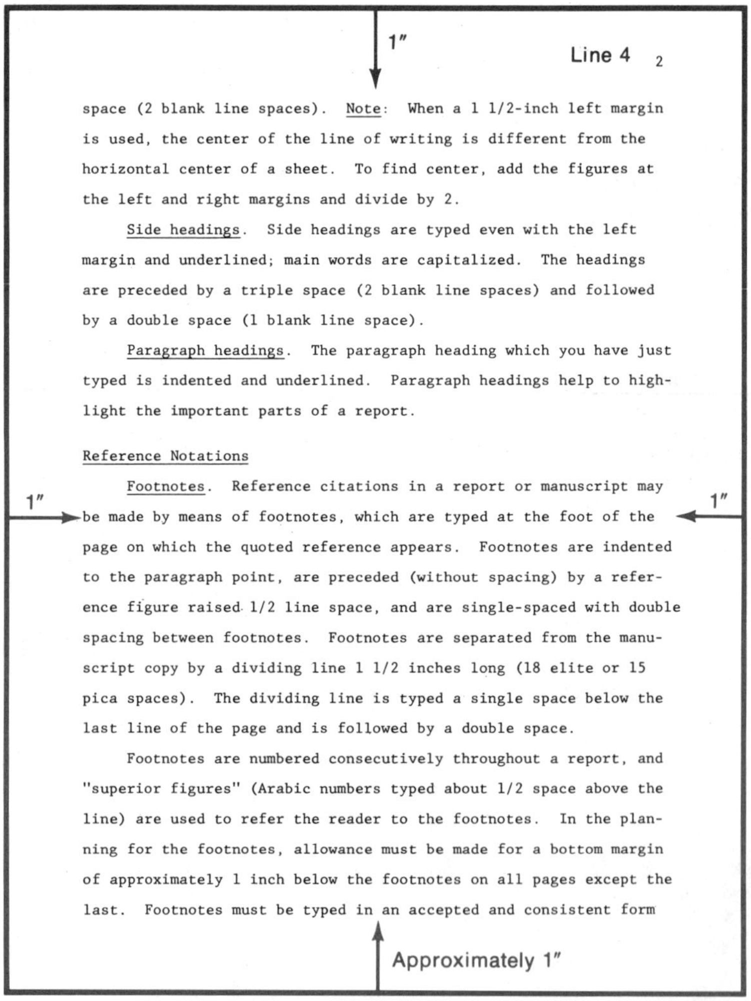

2

space (2 blank line spaces). Note: When a 1 1/2-inch left margin is used, the center of the line of writing is different from the horizontal center of a sheet. To find center, add the figures at the left and right margins and divide by 2.

Side headings. Side headings are typed even with the left margin and underlined; main words are capitalized. The headings are preceded by a triple space (2 blank line spaces) and followed by a double space (1 blank line space).

Paragraph headings. The paragraph heading which you have just typed is indented and underlined. Paragraph headings help to highlight the important parts of a report.

Reference Notations

Footnotes. Reference citations in a report or manuscript may be made by means of footnotes, which are typed at the foot of the page on which the quoted reference appears. Footnotes are indented to the paragraph point, are preceded (without spacing) by a reference figure raised 1/2 line space, and are single-spaced with double spacing between footnotes. Footnotes are separated from the manuscript copy by a dividing line 1 1/2 inches long (18 elite or 15 pica spaces). The dividing line is typed a single space below the last line of the page and is followed by a double space.

Footnotes are numbered consecutively throughout a report, and "superior figures" (Arabic numbers typed about 1/2 space above the line) are used to refer the reader to the footnotes. In the planning for the footnotes, allowance must be made for a bottom margin of approximately 1 inch below the footnotes on all pages except the last. Footnotes must be typed in an accepted and consistent form

171d ▶ 15 Guided writing: paragraphs

1. A 1′ writing on ¶1; determine *gwam* to establish base rate.

2. Add 2–6 words to Step 1 *gwam* for a new *goal* rate.

3. From table below, find quarter-minute checkpoints; note these figures in ¶ 1.

4. Three 1′ writings on the ¶, trying to reach your quarter-minute checkpoints as the guides (1/4′, 1/2′, 3/4′, time) are called.

5. Follow Steps 1–4 for ¶2.

6. A 3′ writing on ¶s 1–2 combined; determine *gwam*.

gwam	1/4′	1/2′	3/4′	1′
32	8	16	24	32
36	9	18	27	36
40	10	20	31	40
44	11	22	33	44
48	12	24	36	48
52	13	26	39	52
56	14	28	42	56
60	15	30	45	60
64	16	32	48	64
68	17	34	51	68
72	18	36	54	72
76	19	38	57	76
80	20	40	60	80

all letters used | A | 1.5 si | 5.7 awl | 80% hfw — gwam 3′

We all use a vocabulary. We all possess the power of recognition. 5 59
The greater our recognition, the greater the usefulness of our vocabu- 9 64
lary. Most of us can recognize about ten times the number of words we 14 68
actually use in speaking and writing. We can use a word only when we 19 73
know it exists, and we must know its exact definition to convey just 23 78
the meaning required to communicate our true thoughts. 27 81

You can enhance your word power in numerous ways. First, join a 31 86
book club. An avid reader is invariably an avid word lover. Second, 36 90
become a student of words. Develop an interest in words, in their mean- 41 95
ings, in their origins. Most important, acquire the dictionary habit. 46 100
It's one you will never want to neglect. Words are like people--after 50 105
you know them, they can bring you a great deal of pleasure. 54 109

gwam 3′ | 1 | 2 | 3 | 4 | 5 |

172

172a ▶ 5 Conditioning practice

Use standard procedure given in 170a, page 276.

alphabet 1 Jim quickly fixed five ground wires that jeopardized Jeb when he fell.
figures 2 We ordered 209 keys, 148 locks, 73 doors, and 65 files for a building.
adjacent keys 3 Her sincere interest in the correspondence was present in her answers.
fluency 4 He may go with us to the big lake south of the city to fish for trout.

| 1 | 2 | 3 | 4 | 5 | 6 | 7 | 8 | 9 | 10 | 11 | 12 | 13 | 14 |

172b ▶ 10 Check language arts

Type the ¶, correcting spelling, punctuation, and capitalization as you type.

See ¶2, Problem 2, page 277 to check the accuracy of your copy.

we feel that it is improtant for both the office personel and thier imediate supervisers to partricipate in this seminar Therefore the times availabel are somewhat limited. Would it be possible for you to meet with us on ether november 2 and 3 november 9 and 10 or december 7 and 8.

110

110a ▶ 5 Conditioning practice

Follow standard directions, p. 169.

alphabet	1	Quinten Zaxen and Wilbur Fojec may go to the markets in old Liverpool.
fig/sym	2	The "Bar X" Ranch, located at 17846 Red River Road, sold for $235,950.
3d & 4th fingers	3	Paula and Lorenzo waxed eloquently while reciting Shakespearean plays.
fluency	4	Janel may go by autobus to the city to pay for the authentic ornament.

| 1 | 2 | 3 | 4 | 5 | 6 | 7 | 8 | 9 | 10 | 11 | 12 | 13 | 14 |

110b ▶ 15 Improve basic skill: statistical rough draft

Repeat 109b, p. 181.

Goal: Increased speed or accuracy.

110c ▶ 30 Measure production skill: tabulation

Time schedule

Planning and preparing .... 6′
Production timing .... 20′
Proofreading; computing *n–pram* .... 4′

Correct all errors. If you complete the problems before time is called, start over on a new sheet.

Proofread your work. Determine *n–pram*. (Deduct 15 words from total words for each uncorrected error; divide by 20.)

Problem 1

full sheet; DS data; reading position; 8 spaces between column headings

			words
CIVILIAN LABOR FORCE GROWTH, 1930-1990			8
(Persons 16 Years Old and Over)			14
Year	Millions	Increase	23
1930	47.4	–	26
1940	53.0	11.8%	29
1950	59.2	11.7	32
1960	69.2	16.9	35
1970	82.7	19.5	38
1980	101.7	23.0	41
1990	113.8	11.9	45
______________			48
Source: Bureau of Labor Statistics.			56

Problem 2

full sheet; DS data; reading position; 8 spaces between column headings

			words
LABOR FORCE GROWTH, 1900-1985			6
(Stenographers, Typists, and Secretaries)			14
Year	Millions	Increase	23
1900	0.1	–	26
1910	0.4	300.0%	29
1920	0.8	100.0	32
1930	1.1	38.0	35
1940	1.2	9.1	38
1950	1.7	41.7	41
1960	2.3	35.3	43
1970	3.9	69.6	46
1985	6.3	61.5	49
______________			53
Source: Bureau of Labor Statistics.			60

172c ▶ 15 Measure straight-copy skill

1. Two 5′ writings; determine *gwam* and number of errors.

2. Compare the better rate with the 5′ rate recorded in Lesson 155.

all letters used | A | 1.5 si | 5.7 awl | 80% hfw |

	gwam 3′	5′
In the early years of American history, most firms were set up and	4	3
run in an informal manner. The owner of a business was, in many cases,	9	6
the only executive; he or she was able to keep in close touch with all	14	8
phases of the day-to-day operations of the firm. Few records were main-	19	11
tained, and most of the decisions were based on past experiences. How-	23	14
ever, changes in technology and shifts in the buying habits of consumers	28	17
created a heavy impact on business. Much of this impact was reflected	33	20
in a greater increase in the kinds of office work required. Soon it	38	23
became evident that the informal business practices of the past were	42	25
no longer meeting the needs of our swiftly changing and ever-expanding	47	28
economy.	48	29
Management has become increasingly dependent on the information	52	31
that it can retrieve from data systems with greater speed and ease than	57	34
it had been able to do at any time in the past. Today, the office acts	62	37
as the memory unit of the firm through the records it keeps. Gathering,	66	40
analyzing, and storing these data require an efficient and well-trained	71	43
staff. As a result, many good jobs exist in the field at the present	76	46
time. Not only are the numbers of jobs increasing rapidly, but the	80	48
values placed by employers on these kinds of duties are increasing as	85	51
well. The future is bright for competent workers who can add to the	90	54
success of their employers.	91	55

gwam 3′ | 1 | 2 | 3 | 4 | 5 |
5′ | 1 | 2 | 3 |

172d ▶ 20 Prepare for measurement: reports

2 plain full sheets; leftbound report style; DS ¶s; proofread and circle errors

1. Center the main heading over the line of writing; then type the introductory ¶ beneath it.

2. Type **Side heading 1** as given at the right, followed by ¶1 of 172c above.

3. Type **Side heading 2** as given at the right, followed by ¶2 of 172c above.

4. Type the closing ¶ and the footnote.

5. Repeat in unbound style if time permits.

Main heading: RECORDS MANAGEMENT YESTERDAY AND TODAY

Introductory ¶: Many opportunities exist in the field of records management today. The complexity of the modern office demands an efficient system for storing and retrieving data.

Side heading 1: Informal Record Keeping

Side heading 2: Modern Record Keeping

Closing ¶: Those interested in records management will find the demand great for their services.*

Footnote: * Summary of speech given at 1982 Records Management Society Convention.

109

109a ▶ 5 Conditioning practice

Follow standard directions, p. 169.

alphabet	1	Next week Quig Juget may paint the safety zones and the curb for Livy.
fig/sym	2	The 7 reams of 8 1/2″ × 11″ paper (20#) on Order 569 will cost $34.00.
3d & 4th fingers	3	Paul, Quin, and Sally may play old alto saxhorns at a plaza bandstand.
fluency	4	Vivian and a visitor may go with them to the city to pay for the maps.

| 1 | 2 | 3 | 4 | 5 | 6 | 7 | 8 | 9 | 10 | 11 | 12 | 13 | 14 |

109b ▶ 15 Improve basic skill: statistical rough draft

two 3′ writings; then one 5′ writing; proofread; circle errors; record better 3′ and 5′ rates

Goal: To maintain 3′ rate for 5′.

all letters and figures used

Text	gwam 3′	5′	
Costs [to produce a] ~~of producing~~ business letters [keep going up.] ~~have continued to in-~~	3	2	47
~~crease~~. During the 1930's, a business letter could be produced	7	4	49
for about 29 cents. During the 1970's, [as] ~~according to~~ a study by	11	6	51
the Dartnell Corporation [shows,] costs to produce [a] ~~the average~~ business	15	9	54
letter varied from $3.19 to $5.59. The costs were [made up of these items:] ~~broken down~~	20	12	57
~~as follows:~~ [time of dictator,] ~~dictator's time~~ $1.45; [time of secretary,] ~~secretary's time~~ $1.59;	23	14	59
[time which is of a variety] nonproductive ~~time~~ (waiting, illness, etc.), 46 cents; fixed or	29	17	62
overhead costs, $1.58; [paper and other such] ~~material~~ costs, 19 cents; and mailing	34	20	65
and filing costs, 32 cents.	36	21	66
Just a part of the problem of [the amazing cost rise] ~~increasing costs~~ to produce	40	24	69
various types of business [papers] ~~communications~~ is the increased cost	44	26	71
of the sophisticated equipment ~~used~~ now used to produce such	47	28	73
communications. For [example,] ~~instance~~ text-editing and [other] electronic type-	52	31	76
writers may vary in cost from about $3,750 to $14,000 [or more.] Salaries	57	34	79
of [office] workers, too[,] have been in an up ward spiral. Despite these	61	37	82
factors, productivity has not increased a graet deal over the	66	39	84
years. [a secretary] ~~It~~ still [may require] ~~takes a secretary~~ 6, 7, 8, 9, or even as much	70	42	87
as 15 minutes to type a let ter varying in length from 126 to	74	44	89
225 words.	75	45	90

109c ▶ 30 Build sustained production skill: tabulation

Time schedule

Planning and preparing	6′
Production timing	20′
Proofreading; computing *g-pram*	4′

Type a 20′ sustained production writing on these problems:

106c, Problem 1, p. 177
106c, Problem 3, p. 178
107c, Problem 1, p. 179

If you complete the problems before time is called, start over. Plan and prepare for each problem with a minimum of waste time.

unit **33** lessons 173-175

Measure production skills

Measurement goals

1. To produce mailable letters at an acceptable rate.

2. To arrange and type tables and reports at an acceptable rate.

Machine adjustments

1. Paper guide at *0*.

2. Ribbon control to type on top half of ribbon.

3. Margin sets: 70-space line for conditioning practices; as directed for problems.

4. Spacing: SS drills; DS ¶s; as directed for problems

173-175

173a-175a ▶ 5 Conditioning practice

each line twice SS (slowly, then faster); DS between 2-line groups; if time permits, retype selected lines

alphabet	1	The judge kept quizzing Mr. Voyles, executor of the will, about dates.
figures	2	These 96 buildings house 1,420 offices, 387 apartments, and 51 stores.
direct reaches	3	Bring annually any offers received to serve on my arbitration council.
fluency	4	The man got rich when he sold a big quantity of land for a big profit.

| 1 | 2 | 3 | 4 | 5 | 6 | 7 | 8 | 9 | 10 | 11 | 12 | 13 | 14 |

173b ▶ 45 Evaluate production skill: letters

Time schedule

Preparation .... 5′
Timed production .... 30′
Final check; compute *n-pram* ... 10′

3 letterheads [LM pp. 23–28]; type an envelope for each letter; correct errors

Problem 1
Average-length letter

block style, open punctuation

	words parts	total
October 21, 19-- Flores Realty Company Attention Mrs. Kathryn Seaton 100	15	15
Techwood Drive, NW Atlanta, GA 30303-5775 Ladies and Gentlemen Subject:	30	30
Home Location	33	33
(¶ 1) On January 1 of next year, Carol and Cecil Ledinski will be moving to	14	47
Atlanta, where Mrs. Ledinski will manage our regional office. They will be in	30	63
Atlanta during the Thanksgiving break to look for housing.	42	75
(¶ 2) The Ledinskis would like a home in the northwest area, as that is the	56	89
location of our regional office. They would like a four-bedroom home with	71	104
three baths. A formal dining room is a high priority; and they prefer a home	86	119
with a formal living area as well as a family room, although two specific living	102	135
areas are not required.	109	142
(¶ 3) It would be especially helpful if you could locate several homes for the	123	156
Ledinskis to look at on Friday and Saturday after Thanksgiving.	136	169
Sincerely yours T & M ASSOCIATES, INC. Franz B. Kline Manager xx	13	182
		202

Problem 2
Short letter

modified block style, mixed punctuation

	words parts	total
October 25, 19-- Mr. Franz B. Kline, Manager T & M Associates, Inc. 535 Com-	16	16
mercial Street Waterloo, IA 50701-3321 Dear Mr. Kline Subject: Home for	31	31
the Ledinskis	34	34
(¶ 1) There are several homes in the northwest area of Atlanta that I believe	14	48
would meet the requirements of Mr. and Mrs. Ledinski. One of our sales as-	29	63
sociates will be happy to show these homes at the Ledinskis' convenience. May	45	79
we set up a specific appointment for Friday morning?	55	89
(¶ 2) The enclosed list describes the homes in detail. Mr. and Mrs. Ledinski may	70	104
wish to note those they would like to see first.	80	114
Cordially yours Mrs. Kathryn Seaton, Agent xx Enclosure	12	126
		145

Problem 3 is on next page.

108

108a ▶ 5 Conditioning practice

Follow standard directions, p. 169.

alphabet 1 Jake Ganz said he will move from Quincy to Nova Scotia next September.

fig/sym 2 Zane & Borne Company sold the home at 18374 Ocean Avenue for $256,900.

long words 3 A physician's diagnosis of autotoxicosis frightened the older patient.

fluency 4 Their prodigy may go with me to an ancient city for an authentic bowl.

| 1 | 2 | 3 | 4 | 5 | 6 | 7 | 8 | 9 | 10 | 11 | 12 | 13 | 14 |

108b ▶ 45 Improve tabulating skill: applications

Problem 1

full sheet; DS data; reading position; 4 spaces between column headings

Cue: After typing second heading line, space down 4 times. Determine placement of and type column headings. Turn platen back 1 space; center **Years** over 3 age-group headings; center **Percent** over **of Total**. Space down to proper point and type data of table. Remember to reset tab stops for column entries.

Problem 2

Retype Problem 1 on half sheet, long side up; DS data; vertical center; 4 spaces between column headings.

words

YOUTH AGE GROUPS AS PERCENT 6
OF TOTAL U.S. POPULATION 11

	Years			Percent	words
Year	14-17	18-21	22-24	of Total	18 / 30
1950	5.5	5.8	4.7	16.0	34
1960	6.2	5.3	3.7	15.2	39
1970	7.8	7.2	4.9	19.9	43
1980	7.1	7.7	5.6	20.4	47
1990	5.3	6.0	4.4	15.7	52
2000	6.1	5.8	3.7	15.6	56

60

Source: U.S. Bureau of the Census. 67

Problem 3

full sheet; DS data; reading position; 4 spaces between column headings

Cue: Remember to reset tab stops as necessary.

U.S. POPULATION BY TOTAL AND AGE GROUPS 8

(Millions) 10

		Years				Median	words
Year	Total	14-17	18-21	22-24	25-Up	Age	19 / 34
1930	123.2	–	–	–	–	–	40
1940	132.6	–	–	–	–	–	46
1950	152.3	8.4	8.9	7.1	127.9	30.2	54
1960	180.7	11.2	9.6	6.6	153.3	29.4	61
1970	204.9	15.9	14.7	10.0	164.3	27.9	69
1980	222.2	15.8	17.1	12.3	177.0	30.2	76
1990	243.5	12.8	14.5	10.6	205.6	32.8	83
2000	260.4	16.0	15.0	9.7	219.7	35.5	91

95

Source: U.S. Bureau of the Census. 102

173b, continued

Problem 3
Short letter

modified block style, indented ¶s; open punctuation

	words: parts	total
October 30, 19-- Mrs. Kathryn Seaton, Agent Flores Realty Company 100	15	15
Techwood Drive, NW Atlanta, GA 30303-5775 Dear Mrs. Seaton	27	27
(¶ 1) The list of homes that you sent appears to be quite adequate, and we	14	41
appreciate your efforts to locate ones which meet our specific needs. The	29	56
enclosed list indicates those that interest us most. However, I might mention	45	72
that we enjoy living in a wooded area; and we would like to see first any of	60	87
those on the list that have wooded lots.	68	95
(¶ 2) We shall be in your office at 8:30 a.m. on the Friday after Thanksgiving, and	84	111
we can spend all day Friday and Saturday looking.	94	121
Sincerely yours T & M ASSOCIATES, INC. Mrs. Carol Ledinski Administrative	15	136
Manager xx Enclosure	19	140
		159

174b ▶ 45
Evaluate production skill: tables

Time schedule
Preparation .... 5′
Timed production .... 30′
Final check;
compute *n–pram* .... 10′

Problem 1
half sheet, short side up; reading position; DS body; 10 spaces between columns; correct errors

AIR DISTANCES 3
FROM SAN FRANCISCO 7

Anchorage	2,005	10
Chicago	1,860	13
Denver	953	15
Houston	1,648	18
New York City	2,574	22
Seattle	679	24
St. Louis	1,744	28

Problem 2
half sheet, long side up; exact center; SS body; 12 spaces between columns; correct errors

Problem 3
Retype Problem 2 on a full sheet in reading position; DS body; correct errors.

COMMERCIAL PASSENGER PLANES 6
(United States) 9

Company and Type	Capacity	Speed	21
Boeing 707-120	181	600	26
Boeing 720	167	600	29
Boeing 747	500	640	33
Fairchild Hiller FH-227	52	300	39
General Dynamics Convair 990	130	600	47
Lockheed TriStar L-1011	400	620	53
McDonnell Douglas DC-9 Super 80	172	576	61

107c ▶ 35
Improve tabulating skill: applications

Problem 1

full sheet; DS data; reading position; 12 spaces between column entries (see note)

Note: In arranging some tables horizontally on a sheet, it may be necessary to use judgment to avoid an off-center appearance of the data. In this table, use the longest column entry in each column to determine horizontal placement. The Column 3 heading is then centered over the longest entry in that column.

Problem 2

Retype Problem 1 on half sheet, short side up; DS data; vertical center; 8 spaces between column entries.

words: parts | total

PRINCIPAL PARTS OF TROUBLESOME 6 | 6
IRREGULAR VERBS 9 | 9

Present	Past	Past Participle	parts	total
			20	20
see	saw	seen	3	23
do	did	done	5	25
go	went	gone	8	28
break	broke	broken	11	32
choose	chose	chosen	15	36
drink	drank	drunk	19	39
eat	ate	eaten	22	42
freeze	froze	frozen	26	46
give	gave	given	29	49
know	knew	known	32	53
ring	rang	rung	35	56
run	ran	run	38	58
speak	spoke	spoken	41	62
swim	swam	swum	44	65
take	took	taken	48	68
write	wrote	written	51	72

Problem 3

full sheet; DS data; reading position; 6 spaces between column headings

Cue: Remember to reset tab stops as necessary.

EFFECT OF INFLATION AND POPULATION GROWTH 8 | 8
ON HOME PRICES 11 | 11

Average New Home 15 | 15

Year	Southern California	United States	parts	total
			30	30
1970	$ 30,400	$29,200	5	35
1971	31,700	31,100	9	39
1972	33,200	32,700	13	42
1973	35,800	36,900	16	46
1974	40,700	39,500	20	50
1975	46,900	43,000	24	54
1976	57,200	47,000	28	58
1977	74,700	52,500	32	61
1978	91,500	60,900	35	65
1979	111,400	69,000	39	69

4 | 73

Sources: So. Calif. Real Estate Research Council; 14 | 83
Bureau of the Census. 18 | 88

175b ▶ 45
Evaluate production skill: reports

Time schedule

Preparation .... 5′
Timed production .... 30′
Final check;
compute *n-pram* .... 10′

2 full sheets

Type in leftbound report style. If time permits, retype in unbound style.

words

ADDRESSING FOR EFFICIENT MAIL HANDLING 8

All who depend upon the U.S. Postal Service to process, sort, and deliver 23
their mail to proper destinations seek two benefits: speed and low cost. From 39
Pony Express to modern jet planes, the speed of transporting mail from "here" 54
to "there" has been drastically increased. But, at the same time, so has postage 71
cost to the mailer. 75

During the past twenty-five years, major attempts have been made to 89
match the internal speed and efficiency of processing mail with the external 104
speed of moving mail from place to place once it has been processed and sorted. 120
These efforts include the use of expanded ZIP Codes, bar coding devices, OCR's, 136
and a variety of other sorting devices. 144

It is difficult to tell, however, just how efficient the new systems are 159
because of the steadily increasing volume of mail that must be handled. Accord- 175
ing to the Postmaster General's Office, over 89.7 million pieces of mail are now 191
being processed annually.[1] Further, it is estimated that as much as 90 percent 207
of the mail must be sorted by less efficient equipment than the OCR or must be 223
sorted by hand.[2] 226

To increase the percentage of mail processable by OCR and other mechan- 241
ical equipment, and thus reduce the cost, the U.S. Postal Service suggests, but 256
does not demand, the following addressing practices: 267

1. Use block-style format, all lines having a uniform left margin. 281
2. Use uppercase letters without punctuation. 291
3. Type attention lines (when used) on the next line below the com- 304
   pany name. 307
4. Type the street address or box number on the second line from 320
   the bottom. 323
5. Type apartment numbers (when used) immediately after the 335
   street address on the same line. 342
6. Type the city name, the two-letter state abbreviation, and the ZIP 356
   Code on the last line. (The ZIP Code should not be typed on a line 369
   by itself.) 372

OCR equipment can read ALL-CAP, unpunctuated addresses more effi- 385
ciently than those typed in cap-and-lowercase letters with punctuation. 400
Human sorters, however, read the latter more efficiently when hand sorting or 415
precoding for subsequent mechanical processing. It is therefore likely that 431
cap-and-lowercase addresses will be acceptable by the U.S. Postal Service for 446
several years to come. 451

____________________ 454

[1] Letter from Mrs. Rita Moroney, Research Administration/Historian, 467
Office of the Postmaster General, 1979. 476

[2] W. Timothy DeRoche, Jr., "Addressing Mail for the Eighties," The 490
Balance Sheet (February 1981), pp. 219-222. 501

106c, continued

Problem 3
Unarranged table

full sheet; DS data; reading position; 20 spaces between columns

Column 1 heading: **Year**

Column 2 heading: **Population**

Cue: When typing the table, remember to space twice from left margin for first entry of Column 1, and twice from tab stop for first five entries of Column 2.

Problem 4

Retype Problem 3 on half sheet, short side up; SS data; vertical center; 12 spaces between columns.

		words parts	total
WORLD POPULATION, 30-2000 A.D.		6	6
(In Millions)		9	9
	column headings	15	15
30	250	2	17
1650	545	4	19
1700	623	7	22
1750	728	9	24
1800	906	11	26
1850	1,171	13	28
1900	1,608	15	30
1940	2,170	18	33
1950	2,501	20	35
1960	2,986	22	37
1970	3,610	24	39
1980	4,374	26	41
1990	5,280	29	44
2000	6,254	31	46
______________		4	50
Sources:	Wyotinsky & Wyotinsky;	10	56
	United Nations Popula-	15	61
	tion Studies.	17	63

107

107a ▶ 5 Conditioning practice

Follow standard directions, p. 169.

alphabet 1 Jack Bevquid may ask Gina to work with zeal so as to pay the food tax.

fig/sym 2 The #329 item is sold by Jaynes & Co. for $875.46 (less 10% for cash).

adjacent key 3 In our opinion, Rowert really made a great try to save the new treaty.

fluency 4 It is right to pay them when they go to a papaya field to do the work.

| 1 | 2 | 3 | 4 | 5 | 6 | 7 | 8 | 9 | 10 | 11 | 12 | 13 | 14 |

107b ▶ 10 Improve number expression: related learning

full sheet; 1" top margin; 70-space line

Follow learning procedures given on p. 135.

Note: When extensive use is made of both approximations and definite percentages in typed materials, the "rule of consistency" applies. As a rule, the percentage symbol (%) is used for emphasis (see Guide 7).

NUMBER GUIDES, continued

5. Numbers preceded by nouns are usually expressed in figures.

6. Express measures, weights, and dimensions in figures without commas.

7. Use the percent sign (%) with definite numbers typed in figures. Percent (spelled) is preferred with approximations and in formal writing.

8. Spell names of small-numbered avenues and streets (ten and under). Type house numbers in figures except for house number One.

learn 5. Type Rule 5 on page 136 in Monograph 121.
apply Guide five is given in Activity 102b, page one hundred thirty-six.

learn 6. Darren Daye is 6 ft. 7 in. tall. The package weighs 3 lbs. 7 oz.
apply He is nearly seven ft. two in. in height. The box is four ft. by 6 ft.

learn 7. The interest rate is 15 1/2%. Nearly 50 percent of the class is ill.
apply Approximately 40% of the loans are due. The rate is 12 1/2 percent.

learn 8. Our store is at 784 Fifth Avenue; our office, at 15 W. 42d Street.
apply They will move from 1 Lexington Avenue to 718 6th Street.

phase 8 lessons 176-200

Build skill in office communications

Anyone planning to use keyboarding skills in an office must be prepared to type business communications of many kinds with skill and efficiency. The purpose of Phase 8, therefore, is to:

1. Build skill in planning, organizing, and producing office communications.

2. Increase basic keystroking skill through increased rates and reduced errors on straight, script, rough-draft, and statistical copy.

3. Develop skill in typing correspondence on special-size stationery.

4. Develop skill in typing special business communications such as interoffice and intraoffice memos, message/reply communications, and telegraphic messages.

5. Build skill in typing letters that contain special features such as the attention line, subject line, mailing notation, and carbon copy notation.

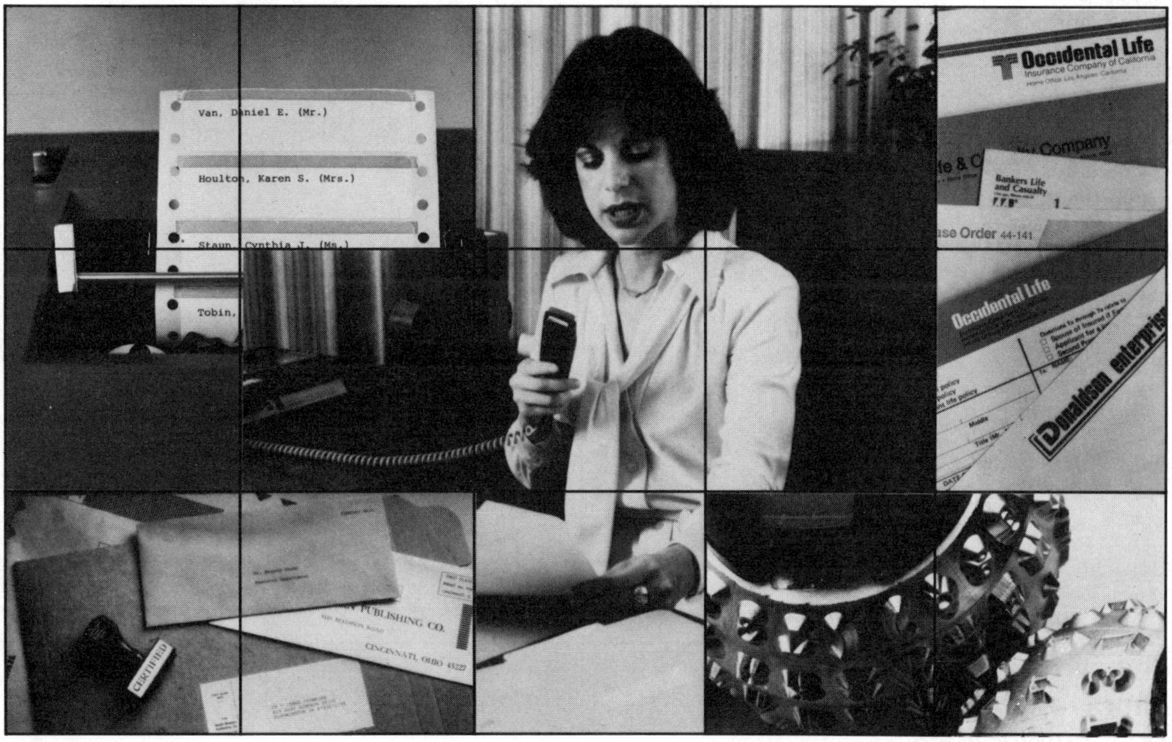

unit 34 lessons 176-180

Correspondence on special-size stationery

Learning goals

1. To learn how to type letters on executive-size and half-size stationery.

2. To learn how to type message/reply forms.

3. To increase skill in typing on special-size stationery.

Machine adjustments

1. Paper guide at *0*.

2. Ribbon control to type on top half of ribbon.

3. Line length: 70 for drills and timed writings; as required for production work.

4. Spacing: SS sentence drills with a DS between sentence groups; space problems as directed or required.

106

106a ▶ 5
Conditioning practice

Follow standard directions, p. 169.

alphabet	1	Zeno Zack, a Bay World executive, requested the fig price adjustments.
fig/sym	2	Make finger reaches (hands quiet) to type 303#, $1,475.98, and 126.9%.
space bar	3	Try to do the work for her and then go to the city with me for a week.
fluency	4	Jan may pay for an authentic ornament and then go with me to the lake.

| 1 | 2 | 3 | 4 | 5 | 6 | 7 | 8 | 9 | 10 | 11 | 12 | 13 | 14 |

106b ▶ 10
Improve number expression: related learning

full sheet; 1" top margin; 70-space line

Follow carefully the Study/Learn/Apply/Correct procedures given on p. 135.

Note: A common practice in business is to use figures for all numbers except those which begin a sentence.

In these concise guides, not every acceptable alternative is included—to do so would lead to confusion. The guides given, however, may be used with confidence; they represent basic guides to good usage.

NUMBER GUIDES

1. Spell numbers from one to ten except when used with numbers above ten (see note).
2. Always spell a number beginning a sentence even though figures are used later in the sentence.
3. As a general rule, spell the shorter of two numbers used together.
4. Spell isolated fractions in a sentence, but type a series of fractions in figures. Use the diagonal (/) for "made" fractions.

learn 1. Our teacher ordered <u>6</u> typing books and <u>20</u> English books.
apply Although 48 students had registered, only seven attended the class.

learn 2. <u>Nine</u> persons said they would attend; <u>15</u> declined.
apply 18 workers were hired today; 25 more will be hired next week.

learn 3. Please order <u>six</u> 50-gallon drums and 150 <u>ten</u>-gallon cans.
apply We need 275 5-pound boxes and 10 100-gallon drums.

learn 4. Approximately <u>one half</u> of the order was filled.
learn Type <u>1/2</u>, <u>1/4</u>, <u>3/4</u>, <u>5/6</u>, and <u>3 7/8</u>.

apply Nearly 1/3 of the work is completed.
apply Add these figures: one half, one 2/3, three fourths, and 1 7/8.

106c ▶ 35
Improve tabulating skill: applications

Problem 1

half sheet, long side up; DS data; vertical center; 6 spaces between columns

Note: In Column 2, center 2d item under first item, then reset tab stop.

Problem 2

Retype Problem 1 on full sheet; DS data; reading position; 10 spaces between columns.

Problems 3 and 4 are on p. 178.

SEVEN WONDERS OF ANCIENT WORLD		words
		6
Pyramids of Egypt	3000-1800 B.C.	13
Hanging Gardens of Babylon	600 B.C.	20
Statue of Zeus at Olympia	432 B.C.	27
Mausoleum at Halicarnassus	325 B.C.	34
Temple of Artemis	315 B.C.	40
Colossus of Rhodes	292 B.C.	45
Pharos of Alexandria	280 B.C.	51

176a ▶ 5
Conditioning practice

each line twice SS (slowly, then faster); DS between 2-line groups; if time permits, retype selected lines

alphabet 1 Bev was amazed when Rex told her to report quickly for the grand jury.
figures 2 The population of the city rose from 3,095 in 1882 to 264,775 in 1982.
fig/sym 3 We made payments of $14, $25.60, $37.91, $187.24, $356.90, and $1,865.
fluency 4 If they audit the eight auto firms, they may hand down a firm penalty.

| 1 | 2 | 3 | 4 | 5 | 6 | 7 | 8 | 9 | 10 | 11 | 12 | 13 | 14 |

176b ▶ 45
Learn to type letters on executive-size stationery

3 letterheads/envelopes [LM pp. 35-40]; circle errors

Study the illustration below and the material given in Problem 1.

Problem 1

modified block style, mixed punctuation; leave 4 spaces between columns; save letter for future reference

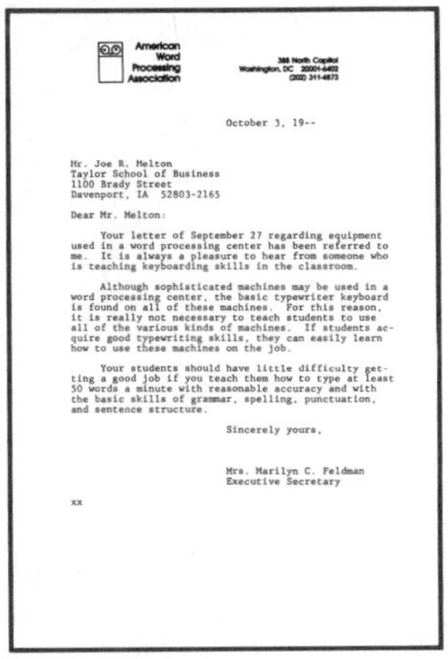

American Word Processing Association
388 North Capitol
Washington, DC 20001-6402
(202) 311-4873

October 3, 19--

Mr. Joe R. Melton
Taylor School of Business
1100 Brady Street
Davenport, IA 52803-2165

Dear Mr. Melton:

Your letter of September 27 regarding equipment used in a word processing center has been referred to me. It is always a pleasure to hear from someone who is teaching keyboarding skills in the classroom.

Although sophisticated machines may be used in a word processing center, the basic typewriter keyboard is found on all of these machines. For this reason, it is really not necessary to teach students to use all of the various kinds of machines. If students acquire good typewriting skills, they can easily learn how to use these machines on the job.

Your students should have little difficulty getting a good job if you teach them how to type at least 50 words a minute with reasonable accuracy and with the basic skills of grammar, spelling, punctuation, and sentence structure.

Sincerely yours,

Mrs. Marilyn C. Feldman
Executive Secretary

xx

Executive-size
7¼″ × 10½″

words

October 3, 19-- Ms. Sandra C. Brendon 5230 Hillside Avenue Indianapolis, 15
IN 46220-1569 Dear Ms. Brendon: (¶ 1) In your letter of September 24, you 29
questioned a statement in the June issue of Data Processing World regarding 48
the use of special-size stationery in business offices. Although 8 1/2″ × 11″ 63
paper is the most commonly used size for correspondence, other sizes are 78
used. Chief among these sizes are executive-size stationery, which is 7 1/4″ × 94
10 1/2″; half-size stationery, which is 5 1/2″ × 8 1/2″; and message/reply form, 110
which is often 8 1/2″ × 9 1/4″. When using these special sizes, the following 126
guide may be helpful: 131

Stationery	Margins	Date Placement	words
			143
Half-size	3/4″	Line 9	148
Executive-size	1″	Line 11	153
Message/Reply	3/4″	In space provided	160

(¶ 2) The correspondence on half-size and executive-size stationery can be 174
typed in any style, and the format is the same as that for letters on regular- 190
size stationery. (¶ 3) We hope that this information will help answer your 204
questions. Sincerely yours, Mrs. Marilyn C. Feldman Executive Secretary xx 219
233

Problem 2

modified block style, mixed punctuation; indent ¶s

Problem 3

If time permits, retype Problem 2, but address the letter to:

Mrs. Viola C. Scott, President
Federal Insurance Association
1329 K Street NW
Washington, DC 20005-0317

Provide an appropriate salutation.

October 3, 19-- Mr. Joe R. Melton Taylor School of Business 1100 Brady 14
Street Davenport, IA 52803-2165 Dear Mr. Melton: (¶ 1) Your letter of Sep- 28
tember 27 regarding equipment used in a word processing center has been 43
referred to me. It is always a pleasure to hear from someone who is teaching 58
keyboarding skills in the classroom. (¶ 2) Although sophisticated machines 72
may be used in a word processing center, the basic typewriter keyboard is 87
found on all of these machines. For this reason, it is really not necessary to 103
teach students to use all of the various kinds of machines. If students ac- 118
quire good typewriting skills, they can easily learn how to use these 132
machines on the job. (¶ 3) Your students should have little difficulty getting a 147
good job if you teach them how to type at least 50 words a minute with rea- 162
sonable accuracy and with the basic skills of grammar, spelling, punctuation, 178
and sentence structure. Sincerely yours, Mrs. Marilyn C. Feldman Executive 193
Secretary xx **196/213**

105

105a ▶ 5 Conditioning practice

Follow standard directions, p. 169.

alphabet	1	Jack G. Zemsky will box and ship five fresh quail to Paula J. Andrews.
fig/sym	2	Order No. 19503 for 8 desks ($467.25 ea.) will be shipped November 23.
3d & 4th fingers	3	Carlota saw the popular ape eat an apple under a tall old poplar tree.
fluency	4	It is their duty to dismantle the dirigible down by the downtown lake.

| 1 | 2 | 3 | 4 | 5 | 6 | 7 | 8 | 9 | 10 | 11 | 12 | 13 | 14 |

105b ▶ 15 Improve basic skill: straight copy

Repeat 104b, p. 174.

Goal: Increased speed or improved accuracy.

105c ▶ 30 Measure production skill: tabulation

Time schedule

Planning and preparing .... 6′
Production timing .... 20′
Proofreading; computing *n–pram* .... 4′

Correct all errors. If you complete the problems before time is called, start over on a new sheet.

Proofread your work. Determine *n–pram*. (Deduct 15 words from total words for each uncorrected error; divide remainder by 20.)

Problem 1

full sheet; DS data; reading position; 12 spaces between columns

Problem 2

Retype Problem 1 with these changes: half sheet, short side up; exact vertical center; 8 spaces between columns.

WORK PLANS OF HIGH SCHOOL SENIORS

		words
WORK PLANS OF HIGH SCHOOL SENIORS		7
Professional	44.7%	11
Clerical	14.7	14
Artisan	7.7	17
Technical	6.6	20
Service	4.1	22
Manager, Administrator	3.0	28
Homemaker	3.0	31
Sales	3.0	33
Laborer	2.5	35
Military	2.4	37
Operative	2.3	40

Problem 3

half sheet, long side up; DS data; vertical center; 4 spaces between columns

Note: Longest entry in each column is color underlined for easy identification.

NEW REPRESENTATIVES 4

Name	Street	City, State, ZIP Code	17
Mr. Mark Albert	232 S. Park Drive	Greensboro, NC 27401-5662	29
Ms. Marjan Azimi	15 Charles Street	Portland, ME 04102-3424	41
Mr. Farshid Khodiefar	1232 River Front Plaza	Louisville, KY 40202-7091	56
Mr. David Schrier	402 Hudson Avenue	Albany, NY 12203-4427	67
Miss Trudie Shribman	52 Camino de la Reina	San Diego, CA 92108-4528	81
Mrs. Angia Tapia	950 Dakota Avenue	Huron, SD 57350-8603	92

177a ▶ 5
Conditioning practice

Use standard procedure given in 176a, p. 285.

alphabet 1 Extra technique emphasis helped Jeff Weyganz boost speed very quickly.
figures 2 Report to 7896 Oak Street at 12:45 p.m. on May 13 or 20 for a checkup.
fig/sym 3 Interest on my $15,000 note at 8% was $1,200 annually or $100 monthly.
fluency 4 The big goal of eight auto firms is to cut spending and make a profit.

| 1 | 2 | 3 | 4 | 5 | 6 | 7 | 8 | 9 | 10 | 11 | 12 | 13 | 14 |

177b ▶ 45
Learn to type letters on half-size stationery

4 letterheads/envelopes [LM pp. 41-44]; circle errors

Study the illustration below and the material given in Problem 1, page 285.

Problem 1

block style, open punctuation; leave 4 spaces between columns in table

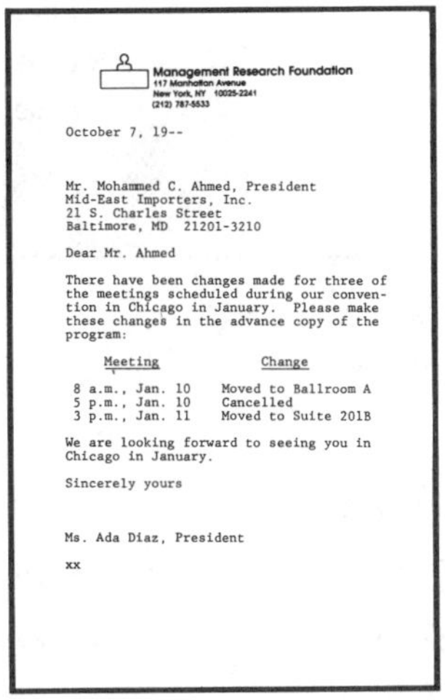
Management Research Foundation
117 Manhattan Avenue
New York, NY 10025-2241
(212) 787-5533

October 7, 19--

Mr. Mohammed C. Ahmed, President
Mid-East Importers, Inc.
21 S. Charles Street
Baltimore, MD 21201-3210

Dear Mr. Ahmed

There have been changes made for three of the meetings scheduled during our convention in Chicago in January. Please make these changes in the advance copy of the program:

Meeting	Change
8 a.m., Jan. 10	Moved to Ballroom A
5 p.m., Jan. 10	Cancelled
3 p.m., Jan. 11	Moved to Suite 201B

We are looking forward to seeing you in Chicago in January.

Sincerely yours

Ms. Ada Diaz, President

xx

Half-size
5½" × 8½"

words

October 7, 19-- Mr. Mohammed C. Ahmed, President Mid-East Importers, 14
Inc. 21 S. Charles Street Baltimore, MD 21201-3210 Dear Mr. Ahmed There 28
have been changes made for three of the meetings scheduled during our con- 43
vention in Chicago in January. Please make these changes in the advance 58
copy of the program: 62

Meeting	Change	
8 a.m., Jan. 10	Moved to Ballroom A	75
5 p.m., Jan. 10	Cancelled	80
3 p.m., Jan. 11	Moved to Suite 201B	87

(header row: 68)

We are looking forward to seeing you in Chicago in January. Sincerely yours 103
Ms. Ada Diaz, President xx 108/**129**

Problem 2

modified block style, mixed punctuation

October 7, 19-- Mr. B. C. Ames, President Ames-Warner, Inc. 401 South 14
Tryon Street Charlotte, NC 28285-4376 Dear Mr. Ames: (¶ 1) The American 28
Word Processing Association will hold its Fifth Annual Convention at the 42
Conrad Hotel in Chicago on January 10-11. I know that the members of the 57
Association would be interested in your views on word processing. Would 72
you, therefore, agree to join us for a panel discussion, "Implementing a Word 87
Processing System," on January 10 from 1 to 3 p.m.? All of your expenses 102
will be paid by the Association. (¶ 2) Will you please let us know no later than 117
November 1 if you can join us at that time. Sincerely yours, Ms. Ada Diaz 132
President xx 135/**153**

Problem 3

modified block style, mixed punctuation; indent ¶s

October 14, 19-- Miss Marian Duval Reservations Manager Conrad Hotel 14
150 East Wacker Drive Chicago, IL 60601-2819 Dear Miss Duval: (¶ 1) Mr. 27
B. C. Ames, President of Ames-Warner, Inc., will be a member of one of the 42
panel discussions at the American Word Processing Association convention to 58
be held at your hotel on January 10-11. He will arrive in Chicago on January 73
10 and depart late in the evening of January 11. (¶ 2) Will you please reserve 88
a single room for Mr. Ames for the evenings of January 10 and 11 and charge 103
his expenses to our convention account. Sincerely yours, Ms. Ada Diaz 117
President xx 120/**139**

Problem 4

If time permits, retype Problem 1, but address the letter to:

Mrs. Anna M. Knight
Oxford Junior College
100 Newbury Street
Boston, MA 02116-3261

Provide an appropriate salutation.

104c, continued

Problem 1

full sheet; DS data; reading position; 12 spaces between columns

Alertness cue: Reset tab stop for Column 2 as needed.

Problem 2

Retype Problem 1 with these changes: half sheet, short side up; exact vertical center; 6 spaces between columns.

		words parts	total
REASONS OF FRESHMEN FOR ATTENDING COLLEGE	DS	8	8
(Percent of Total Responding)	TS	14	14
Get a better job	77.0%	5	19
Learn more about things	69.5	10	25
Make more money	68.8	15	29
Gain general education	64.1	20	35
Meet new and interesting people	54.9	28	42
Prepare for graduate school	48.1	34	49
Improve reading/study skills	31.9	41	55
Become a more cultured person	28.4	48	62
Parental pressure	26.2	53	67
Get away from home	9.4	57	72
Could not find a job	2.9	63	77
Nothing better to do	1.8	68	82
Underline 1 1/2" ______________ SS DS		4	86
Source: UCLA and American Council on Education		13	96
Freshmen Survey.		17	99

Type the source note the width of the table.

Problem 3

full sheet; DS data; reading position; 10 spaces between columns

		words parts	total
GROSS NATIONAL PRODUCT OF LEADING NATIONS		8	8
(In Millions)		11	11
United States	$1,899,500	6	17
U.S.S.R.	780,930	9	20
Japan	642,200	12	23
West Germany	500,930	15	27
France	387,060	19	30
People's Republic of China	346,350	26	37
United Kingdom	247,170	31	42
Canada	196,990	34	45
Italy	194,520	36	48
Brazil	157,700	39	51
Spain	115,460	42	53
Poland	109,460	45	56
Australia	103,240	49	60
Netherlands	99,130	53	64
India	97,370	55	67

178

178a ▶ 5
Conditioning practice

Use standard procedures given in 176a, p. 285.

alphabet 1 Vick Goffman relaxed when the jazz quintet played the ballads quietly.

figures 2 On August 15, he purchased 3,648 shares; on September 2, 4,790 shares.

word division 3 Correct division points are: bev-er-age, pos-si-bly, and ex-cep-tion.

fluency 4 A big problem for the firm is to shape a plan to cut the cost of fuel.

| 1 | 2 | 3 | 4 | 5 | 6 | 7 | 8 | 9 | 10 | 11 | 12 | 13 | 14 |

178b ▶ 15
Learn to type message/reply memos

message/reply form
[LM p. 45]

Read the information about the message/reply form on page 288. Then, on a message/reply form, type an original of the model memo shown on page 288. Make 1 cc on a plain sheet.

Circle errors and address an envelope marked **COMPANY MAIL.** Save the message/reply memo for later reference.

Note: Although most message/reply forms come in sets of three to provide the necessary two carbon copies, students are to make the specified number of copies on plain sheets.

178c ▶ 30
Type message/reply memos

message/reply forms
[LM pp. 47-50]

Type the message and the reply for each of the message/reply memos at the right.

Problem 1

1 cc on plain sheet; circle errors; address an envelope marked **COMPANY MAIL**

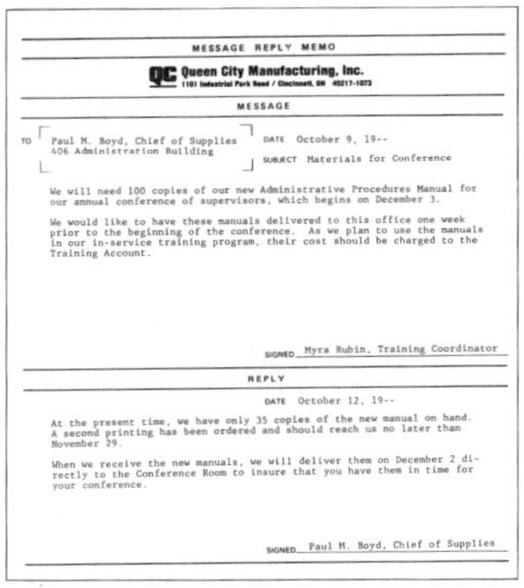
MESSAGE REPLY MEMO

QC Queen City Manufacturing, Inc.
1101 Industrial Park Road / Cincinnati, OH 45217-1073

MESSAGE

TO Paul M. Boyd, Chief of Supplies
406 Administration Building

DATE October 9, 19--

SUBJECT Materials for Conference

We will need 100 copies of our new Administrative Procedures Manual for our annual conference of supervisors, which begins on December 3.

We would like to have these manuals delivered to this office one week prior to the beginning of the conference. As we plan to use the manuals in our in-service training program, their cost should be charged to the Training Account.

SIGNED Myra Rubin, Training Coordinator

REPLY

DATE October 12, 19--

At the present time, we have only 35 copies of the new manual on hand. A second printing has been ordered and should reach us no later than November 29.

When we receive the new manuals, we will deliver them on December 2 directly to the Conference Room to insure that you have them in time for your conference.

SIGNED Paul M. Boyd, Chief of Supplies

Message/reply memo
8½″ × 9¼″

words

TO: Paul M. Boyd, Chief of Supplies 406 Administration Building DATE: 12
October 9, 19-- SUBJECT: Materials for Conference (¶ 1) We will need 100 24
copies of our new Administrative Procedures Manual for our annual con- 38
ference of supervisors, which begins on December 3. (¶ 2) We would like to 52
have these manuals delivered to this office one week prior to the beginning 67
of the conference. As we plan to use the manuals in our in-service training 82
program, their cost should be charged to the Training Account. SIGNED: 95
Myra Rubin, Training Coordinator 101

(Reply) DATE: October 12, 19-- (¶ 1) At the present time, we have only 35 112
copies of the new manual on hand. A second printing has been ordered and 127
should reach us no later than November 29. (¶ 2) When we receive the new 140
manuals, we will deliver them on December 2 directly to the Conference 154
Room to insure that you have them in time for your conference. SIGNED: 167
Paul M. Boyd, Chief of Supplies 173/**187**

Problem 2

1 cc on plain sheet; circle errors; address an envelope marked **COMPANY MAIL**

TO: Myra Rubin, Training Coordinator 220 Services Building DATE: October 13
27, 19-- SUBJECT: Conference Materials Requested (¶ 1) The printer has just 25
notified us that the second printing of our new Administrative Procedures 40
Manual will not be finished until December 3. If the shipment is sent to us 55
by special express, we will have the manuals by noon on December 4. (¶ 2) 69
We have on hand 30 copies of the manual, which we can deliver to you on 83
December 3; the remaining copies can be delivered the following day. We 98
are sorry that the manuals will not be available as you requested. SIGNED: 111
Paul M. Boyd, Chief of Supplies 117

(Reply) DATE: October 31, 19-- (¶) Please earmark the 30 copies on hand for 130
our use. We can change our conference schedule so that the remaining 143
copies will not be required until the afternoon of December 4. Will you 157
please have the manuals delivered to the Conference Room on that date. 171
SIGNED: Myra Rubin, Training Coordinator 178/**191**

104

104a ▶ 5 Conditioning practice

Follow standard directions, p. 169.

alphabet 1 Zack visited Quincy, Sioux Falls, St. Paul, Fargo, and Omaha with Jeb.
fig/sym 2 The Dow & Son check, dated May 12, should be $45.39 instead of $67.80.
long words 3 Tax cuts without corresponding spending reductions result in deficits.
fluency 4 Kay may make an authentic map of the ancient city for the title firms.

| 1 | 2 | 3 | 4 | 5 | 6 | 7 | 8 | 9 | 10 | 11 | 12 | 13 | 14 |

104b ▶ 15 Improve basic skill: straight copy

two 3′ writings; then one 5′ writing

Goal: To maintain 3′ rate for 5′.

proofread; circle errors; record better 3′ and 5′ rates

all letters used

Text	gwam 3′	gwam 5′	
The placement of the dateline of a business letter varies according	5	3	48
to the length of the body of the letter. Long letters require a higher	9	6	51
placement of the date than do short letters. Once the placement of the	14	8	54
dateline is determined, the spacing between the other parts of a letter	19	11	57
is standardized. For example, four line spaces, or just three blank	24	14	59
spaces, separate the date and the letter address, and four line spaces	28	17	62
separate the complimentary close and the typed name or the title in the	33	20	65
closing lines. In all other cases, a double space separates letter	37	22	67
parts.	38	23	68
A completed business letter should present a balanced appearance	42	25	71
on the letterhead page. It should look much like a picture in a frame.	47	28	74
It is not difficult to place letters properly on the letterhead page	52	31	76
once the approximate number of words in the body of the letter is deter-	57	34	79
mined. The dateline placement is quite easy to remember. When a long	61	37	82
letter is typed, the dateline is usually placed on the thirteenth line	66	40	85
from the top edge of the sheet. With average-length letters, type the	71	43	88
dateline on line sixteen; and with short letters, on line nineteen.	75	45	90

gwam 3′ | 1 | 2 | 3 | 4 | 5 |
5′ | 1 | 2 | 3 |

104c ▶ 30 Build sustained production skill: tabulation

Time schedule

Planning and preparing	6′
Production timing	20′
Proofreading; computing *g-pram*	4′

Type a 20′ sustained production writing on the problems given on p. 175. If you complete the problems before time is called, start over.

Plan and prepare for each problem with a minimum of waste time. Have needed materials ready so you can move quickly from one problem to the next.

3/4" MESSAGE REPLY MEMO 3/4"

QC Queen City Manufacturing, Inc.
1101 Industrial Park Road / Cincinnati, OH 45217-1073

MESSAGE

TO Mark C. Horvath
Director of Administration
980A, Administration Building

DATE September 2, 19--

SUBJECT Test of Message/Reply Form

For a period of three months beginning October 1, we will test the use of the message/reply form in the Administration Division to determine whether it is feasible to use the form throughout the organization.

This form is used when brief messages are exchanged among offices within a company. Both the message and the reply are typed on the original (white) copy of the multiple-copy form. The sender types the message in the top part, keeps the second (yellow) copy, and forwards the others (white and pink) to the addressee. The addressee types the reply in the lower part, keeps the third (pink) copy, and returns the original (white) copy to the sender. The signatures of both parties may be handwritten or typed and initialed.

SIGNED P. A. Wong, Forms Control

REPLY

DATE September 6, 19--

This looks like a good idea. Be sure to keep detailed records, however, so that we can compare the cost of using message/reply forms with the cost of using a standard interoffice memorandum form. Only if there is a reduction in cost can we justify the adoption of another form.

Please let me have a monthly progress report on this test.

SIGNED Mark C. Horvath

Model of a message/reply memo.

103b, continued

Drill 2
Column headings longer than column entries

1. If column headings are longer than column entries, first center and type the column headings horizontally (in this drill leave 4 spaces between headings).

2. Then DS, center, and type the longest column entry under the heading. Use forward-space, backspace method. Check your solution by the mathematical method. (See 85e, p. 142.)

(1)

Study Each Word	Pronounce by Syllables	Capitalize Trouble Spots
mathematics	math-e-mat-ics	mathEmatics

(2)

Endangered Mammals	Known Distribution
Manatee	Florida

(3)

Endangered Birds	Known Distribution
Whooping Crane	Canada, USA

103c ▶ 30
Apply skill

Problem 1

full sheet; DS data; reading position; 8 spaces between columns

ENDANGERED SPECIES

Common Name	Location	words parts	total
ENDANGERED SPECIES		4	4
Common Name	Location	12	12
Grizzly Bear	USA	4	15
Black-Footed Ferret	Western USA	10	22
Condor	California	14	25
Bald Eagle	USA	17	28
Peregrine Falcon	Canada, USA	22	34
Brown Pelican	USA	26	38
Ivory-Billed Woodpecker	USA	31	43

Problem 2

full sheet; DS data; reading position; 4 spaces between column headings

Problem 3

As time permits, retype Problem 1 on half sheet, short side up; DS data; vertical center; 4 spaces between columns.

IMPROVE YOUR SPELLING

Study Each Word	Pronounce by Syllables	Capitalize Trouble Spots	words parts	total
IMPROVE YOUR SPELLING			4	4
Study Each Word	Pronounce by Syllables	Capitalize Trouble Spots	29	29
address	ad-dress	ADdress	5	34
believe	be-lieve	belIEve	10	39
courtesy	cour-te-sy	COURteSY	16	45
disease	dis-ease	dISease	21	50
eligible	el-i-gi-ble	eligIBLE	27	56
unforgettable	un-for-get-ta-ble	unforgetTABLE	36	65

179

179a ▶ 5 Conditioning practice

Use standard procedure given in 176a, p. 285.

alphabet 1 Major Jack Sterling watched five zealous boys build aquatic expertise.

figures 2 They found 629 stamps, 174 records, 50 puzzles, and 83 decks of cards.

fig/sym 3 I bought the #40879 pens at a total cost of $36.14 (26 at $1.39 each).

fluency 4 He may go to town and pay for an oak handle and eight bushels of corn.

| 1 | 2 | 3 | 4 | 5 | 6 | 7 | 8 | 9 | 10 | 11 | 12 | 13 | 14 |

179b ▶ 5 Carbon-pack assembly and erasing tips

Desk-top method

1. Turn the noncarboned side of the carbon paper toward you as you assemble the carbon pack.

2. Insert the pack into the typewriter with the heading down and facing the back of the machine.

Machine method

1. Insert the letterhead and second sheets until they are barely gripped by the feed rolls.

2. Insert the carbon paper between the gripped sheets, being sure that the carboned side of each carbon sheet is facing you. Then roll the pack into typing position.

Notes

1. To straighten the pack in the typewriter, hold the pack firmly, operate the paper-release lever, move the pack until it is aligned properly, then reset the paper-release lever.

2. Both methods of assembling a carbon pack are fully illustrated on RG page xi.

Erasing

Before erasing on the original sheet, place a 5″ × 3″ card *in front of* the first carbon sheet. To erase the first carbon copy, move the card to the same position in front of the second carbon sheet, etc. (See RG page xii).

179c ▶ 40 Build sustained production skills: correspondence on special-size stationery

Time schedule

Preparation .... 3′
Timed production .... 30′
Final check; compute *n–pram* .... 7′

plain full sheets
letterheads and forms [LM pp. 51–56]
carbon sheet

1. Make a list of problems to be typed:

page 285, 176b, Problem 1
page 286, 177b, Problem 1
page 287, 178c, Problem 1

2. Arrange letterheads and plain sheets for rapid handling. Make 1 cc of each problem on plain sheet; address envelopes.

3. When directed to begin, type for 30′. Follow directions given for each problem; correct errors neatly. Proofread each sheet carefully before removing it from the machine. If you finish all problems before time is called, retype the first problem on a plain full sheet as an average-length letter.

4. After computing *n–pram*, turn in all problems arranged in the order in which they are given in Step 1.

180

180a ▶ 5 Conditioning practice

Use standard procedure given in 176a, p. 285.

alphabet 1 Joyce Clarke won six clubs and other golf equipment at Hazlewood Cove.

figures 2 I need 120 pints of No. 853679 liquid masking compound and 48 brushes.

fig/sym 3 Belth & Wise bought 1,825# of finished fiber for $6,743.90 last month.

fluency 4 She may pay for the pair of big fish that lay by the prow of the dory.

| 1 | 2 | 3 | 4 | 5 | 6 | 7 | 8 | 9 | 10 | 11 | 12 | 13 | 14 |

180b ▶ 45 Measure production skills: correspondence on special-size stationery

Time schedule

Preparation .... 5′
Timed production .... 30′
Final check; compute *n–pram* .... 10′

plain full sheets
letterheads and forms [LM pp. 57–62]
carbon sheet

1. Arrange stationery and supplies for easy handling.

2. Type the problems on page 290 for 30′.

3. Correct errors neatly; circle uncorrected errors found in final check.

4. Compute *n–pram*.

102c, continued

Problem 3
2-column table

full sheet; DS data; reading position; 10 spaces between columns

Learning cue: Reset tab stop for Column 2 after typing Item 1.

Problem 4
Build skill

Retype Problem 3 on half sheet, short side up; DS data; vertical center; 6 spaces between columns.

CALORIES CONSUMED PER HOUR		words
		5
Walking up stairs	1,080	11
Jogging	920	13
Racquetball	600	16
Skin diving	600	19
Swimming (crawl)	510	24
Tennis (singles)	450	28
Disco dancing	450	31
Skating	450	34
Chopping wood	380	37
Basketball	350	40
Bowling	145	43
Office work	75	46

103

103a ▶ 5 Conditioning practice

Follow standard directions, p. 169.

alphabet	1	These quaint weavers fixed the black zoo pads for Hugh and James Yahl.
figures	2	She lives at 1695 Strawberry Drive, and her telephone is 213-783-8401.
space bar	3	Emi Eto may question a man or a woman about your work in the map room.
fluency	4	Sue and a neighbor may do the handiwork if they pay them for the work.

| 1 | 2 | 3 | 4 | 5 | 6 | 7 | 8 | 9 | 10 | 11 | 12 | 13 | 14 |

103b ▶ 15 Learn skill applications

full sheet; start drill on Line 10

Drill 1
Column headings shorter than column entries

Problem solving steps

1. Recall: Center and type column entries horizontally; 6 spaces between columns.

2. Tryout: Center, type, and underline the headings on the second and third line spaces above the column entries.

3. Check: Check your work with suggested procedure at right.

4. Redo: Space down 7 line spaces and retype drill following steps of forward-space, backspace method.

Drill 2 is on p. 173.

Study Each Word	Pronounce by Syllables	Capitalize Trouble Spots
environmental	en-vi-ron-men-tal	enviRONmenTAL

Forward-space, backspace method

Space forward (→) 1 space for each 2 strokes in the longest column entry (or heading, when it is the longest line), ignoring any odd or leftover stroke. This point will be the center of the column (or heading); note point on scale.

Forward space →

1 2 3 4 5 6 spaces
en | vi | ro | nm | en | ta |

From this point, backspace (←) once for each 2 strokes in heading line to be centered (or longest column entry if it is to be centered under a column heading), ignoring any leftover stroke.

← Backspace

1 2 3 4 spaces
Ea | ch | #W | or

At this point, type and underline second heading line. It will be centered over the column. Next, center and type the first heading line in the same way.

180b, continued

Problem 1
Letter on half-size stationery
block style, open punctuation; 1 cc on plain sheet; address envelope

	words
November 3, 19-- Miss Mildred Starman Executive Vice President Urban	14
Manufacturing Company 220 S. Main Street Rockford, IL 61101-2435 Dear	28
Miss Starman (¶ 1) Hundreds of companies interested in more effective	41
administrative procedures have benefited from our expert advice. They have	56
saved time and money through our suggestions. (¶ 2) To help small com-	69
panies establish and maintain more efficient office operations, we have	83
planned a series of workshops that will offer practical solutions to adminis-	99
trative problems. (¶ 3) Our workshop in Rockford will be held at the Talcott	113
Hotel on March 5-7. We cordially invite you and the key members of your	128
staff to attend. Sincerely yours Gorge Jiminez Workshop Director xx	142/**165**

Problem 2
Letter on executive-size stationery
modified block style, mixed punctuation; type table, indenting 5 spaces from each margin; 1 cc on plain sheet; address envelope

November 3, 19-- Miss Kathryn Warren Vice President, Administration Uni-	14
versal Chemicals, Inc. 780 Broad Street Newark, NJ 07102-1628 Dear Miss	29
Warren: (¶ 1) We shall offer a timely one-day seminar for top executives in	43
Philadelphia next January 7; meetings will be held in the William Penn Room	58
of the International Inn. The following sessions have been scheduled:	73

Time	Topic	
8-10 a.m.	Analyzing Data Needs	83
10-12 a.m.	Technology and Data Systems	91
1- 3 p.m.	Personnel and Data Systems	98
3- 5 p.m.	Financing a Systems Network	105

(The header row "Time Topic" counts 77 words.)

(¶ 2) This seminar will be repeated in the Rodney Room of the new Concord	119
Hotel in Wilmington, Delaware, on January 9 and in the Petite Ballroom of	134
the Chatham Hotel in Baltimore, Maryland, on January 11. (¶ 3) I should like	148
to have you join us for the Philadelphia seminar and share your expertise and	164
experience in the discussions. I know seminar participants will profit from	179
your contributions. Please consent to be with us in Philadelphia, will you?	195
Sincerely yours, Mrs. Marilyn C. Feldman Executive Secretary xx	207/**230**

Problem 3
Message/Reply memo
1 cc on plain sheet; address **COMPANY MAIL** envelope

TO: Brenda Wayne Chief of Personnel 101A Administration Building DATE:	12
November 3, 19-- SUBJECT: Temporary Clerical Assistance (¶ 1) In the very	24
near future, we must begin to review all records on file for the last fiscal	39
year. It will take one of our experienced employees approximately six weeks	55
to complete this task. (¶ 2) At this time, we have vacancies for a clerk-typist	70
and a file clerk. Because of this shortage of personnel, it will not be possible	86
for us to review last year's records unless we receive additional help. (¶ 3)	101
Would it be possible for us to have at least one junior typist to help us during	117
the period that the records are being reviewed? SIGNED: Lila J. Walls,	130
Records Manager	133
(Reply) DATE: November 5, 19-- (¶) Mr. Shiska of the Reprographic Section	144
has agreed to let you have the services of Miss Emi Nitobe, a clerk-typist,	159
beginning on March 1. Miss Nitobe will remain with you for a six-week	173
period or until we are able to fill one of your vacancies. SIGNED: Brenda	187
Wayne, Chief of Personnel	192/**207**

Problem 4
Letter on half-size stationery
Type the letter in Problem 1 in modified block style with mixed punctuation and indented ¶s. Make 1 cc on a plain sheet and address an envelope. Send to:

Miss Margaret DeRiggi
Administrative Manager
Crestline Corporation
101 North Church Street
Rockford, IL 61101-2437

Provide an appropriate salutation.

102

102a ▶ 5
Conditioning practice

Follow standard directions, p. 169.

alphabet	1	Betty may ask the five zealous experts to judge the French Yquem wine.
fig/sym	2	Use the / to type these fractions: 1/2, 3/4, 1/6, 7/8, 9/10, and 1/5.
3d & 4th fingers	3	Sara, Wassel, and Paul were enthralled by the work of Edgar Allan Poe.
fluency	4	They may do the problems for us and then go with me to visit the town.

| 1 | 2 | 3 | 4 | 5 | 6 | 7 | 8 | 9 | 10 | 11 | 12 | 13 | 14 |

102b ▶ 5
Improve figure- and tab-key control

four 1′ writings; 74-space line; tab stops at 10-space intervals; last 2 digits of each group give word count; each figure used a minimum of 12 times

Emphasize finger-reaches; quiet hands; quick tab spacing

9101	3902	4803	5804	6305	7306	8407	9508
4609	3710	2911	9212	8513	6814	7415	5916
6417	7518	8419	9520	6021	7522	4823	6924
3925	6726	4527	7828	3729	4730	5931	6832

102c ▶ 40
Apply learning: table typing

Problem 1
3-column table

half sheet, long side up; DS data; vertical center; 6 spaces between columns

Check your solution with placement cues at bottom of this page.

Problem 2
Build skill

Retype Problem 1 on half sheet, short side up; DS data; vertical center; 4 spaces between columns.

Problems 3 and 4 are on p. 172.

lines used				words
1	WORDS FREQUENTLY MISSPELLED			6
2				
3				
4	accommodate	library	scissors	11
5				
6	answer	license	separate	16
7				
8	changeable	miniature	sergeant	22
9				
10	equipped	misspell	supersede	28
11				
12	familiar	mortgage	synonym	33
13				
14	laboratory	occurred	vengeance	39

Placement cues for Problem 1

Vertical placement

Formula: $\frac{\text{lines available} - \text{lines used}}{2}$ = top margin

$\frac{33 - 14}{2}$ = 9 blank line spaces in top margin (extra line space left at bottom)

Proof: 9 + 14 + 10 = 33 (lines available for use)

Horizontal placement

Backspace from center of paper 1 space for each 2 strokes in longest item of each column and for spaces between columns:

ac | co | mm | od | at | el | 23 | 45 | 6m | in | ia | tu | re | 12 | 34 | 56 | ve | ng | ea | nc |

Set left margin stop; then space forward to determine tab stops for Columns 2 and 3.

unit 35 lessons 181-187

Letters with special features

Learning goals

1. To learn to type business letters with special features.

2. To learn to type letters in the AMS simplified style.

3. To learn to type informal government letters.

4. To improve skill in composing at the typewriter.

5. To reinforce selected language arts skills.

Machine adjustments

1. Paper guide at *0*.

2. Ribbon control to type on top half of ribbon.

3. Margin sets: 70-space line for drills (sentence, ¶, and preview); as required for problems.

4. Spacing: SS sentence drills; DS ¶ activities; as directed for problems.

181

181a ▶ 5 Conditioning practice

each line twice SS (slowly, then faster); DS between 2-line groups; if time permits, retype selected lines

alphabet	1	Jacques Moreau blazed new ski trails exactly five miles from Huge Gap.
figures	2	The dealers handled 203 cars, 185 trucks, 49 vans, and 67 motor homes.
punctuation marks	3	The bank director said, "There may be more money available for loans."
fluency	4	The busy visitor held the pen and paper in both hands for the auditor.

| 1 | 2 | 3 | 4 | 5 | 6 | 7 | 8 | 9 | 10 | 11 | 12 | 13 | 14 |

181b ▶ 10 Review/learn placement of special features in letters

2 plain full sheets; 1½" side margins

Drill 1: Attention and subject lines

1. Begin typing on Line 13 from top.

2. Type in modified block style the opening lines shown.

Drill 2: Company name in closing lines

1. On same sheet, space down 15 lines.

2. Type in modified block style the closing lines shown.

Drill 3: Mailing notation

1. Insert a new sheet for Drill 3. Begin typing on Line 13 from top.

2. Type the opening lines in block style. Follow directions given for typing the mailing notation.

Drill 4: Listed enclosures

1. On the same sheet, space down 15 lines.

2. Type the closing lines shown in block style. Indent the listed enclosures 3 spaces from the left margin.

Review the spacing and typing of these special features with your teacher.

Drill 1: Attention and subject lines

Current date

Piedmont Developers, Inc.
Attention Mrs. Ruth Fushel, Treasurer
3105 Spring Grove Avenue
Greensboro, NC 27401-1325

Ladies and Gentlemen

Subject: Rural Project Approval

We are pleased to learn that the . . .

Drill 2: Company name in closing lines

Sincerely yours

HAMILTON & D'ONOFRIO, INC.

Herbert M. Hamilton
Project Engineer

xx

Enclosures

Drill 3: Mailing notation in letter

If a special mailing notation (**REGISTERED, CERTIFIED, SPECIAL DELIVERY**, etc.) is used in a letter, type it a double space below the dateline at the left margin of the letter in ALL-CAPS.

Current date

REGISTERED

Rendleman Motor Works, Inc.
Attention Ms. Ana Cruz, Manager
5652 Clio Road
Flint, MI 48504-8332

Ladies and Gentlemen

Subject: Environmental Protection

It has been brought to our . . .

Drill 4: Listed enclosures

Type **Enclosures** at left margin a DS below reference initials. Type listed items on succeeding lines, indented 3 spaces from left margin.

Sincerely yours

MORRIS AUTO SUPPLIES, INC.

Edward A. McGee
Sales Manager

xx

Enclosures
   Parts Catalogue
   Discounts

101b, continued

Note: Remainder of copy is in unarranged form. Indent and space copy properly as you type it. Stay alert!

3. Set the left margin stop at point where back-spacing ends.
4. From the left margin stop, space forward once for each stroke in the longest line in the first column and once for each space to be left between the first and the second columns. Set a tab stop at this point for the start of the second column. Continue procedure for any additional columns.

B. Spacing Between Columns
1. As a general rule, leave an even number of spaces between columns (4, 6, 8, 10, or more).
2. The number of spaces to be left between columns is governed by the space available, the number of columns, and ease of reading the table.

C. Column Headings
1. Column headings (if used) usually are centered over the columns.
2. If a table contains single-line column headings and also some headings of two or more lines, type the bottom line of each heading on the same line as the single-line headings.

Save sheets for use as a reference in typing tables.

101c ▶ 15
Check learning: composition

full sheet; 1″ top, side, and bottom margins

Using the **TABLE PLACEMENT GUIDE** you just typed for reference, **type complete sentence answers to the questions** listed here. Number and type your answers in enumerated form. SS the lines of each answer; DS between answers. X-out or strike over any typing errors as you compose.

1. How many line spaces are available on a full sheet (8 1/2″ × 11″)?
2. How many line spaces are available on a half sheet with long side up (8 1/2″ × 5 1/2″)?
3. How many line spaces are available on a half sheet with short side up?
4. How many line spaces are available on a full sheet with long side up?
5. When only a MAIN HEADING is used, how many blank line spaces are left below it?
6. How many blank line spaces separate the MAIN HEADING from a Secondary Heading?
7. If a secondary heading is used, how many blank line spaces are left below it?
8. What is meant by typing a table in reading position?
9. What governs the number of spaces to be left between columns?
10. In your own words, give the steps to follow to determine the vertical placement of a table.
11. In your own words, give the steps to follow in using the Backspace-from-Center Method to determine the horizontal placement of columns.

181c ▶ 30
Learn to type letters with special features

6 plain full sheets; arrange paper and carbon paper

For all letters: Use 1½" side margins; to allow for special features, type date on Line 13; modified block style, open punctuation; 1 cc; circle errors.

Note: See Reference Guide pp. xi–xii for carbon pack assembly and error correction clues.

Problem 1

See 181b, page 291, for placement of special features.

words

October 21, 19-- CERTIFIED Southern Products Company, Inc. Attention Mr. R. 15
J. Grimes, Building Manager 1802 Lincoln Avenue Evansville, IN 47714-2187 30
Ladies and Gentlemen Subject: Company Security Programs 41
(¶ 1) Security within an industry is a matter of urgent concern to all forward- 56
looking managers. I'm sure that you, too, are interested in effective security 72
for your company. (¶ 2) Good security systems must be tailored to specific 86
company needs; they must provide maximum protection from the major risks 101
involved. We specialize in helping companies design complete security pro- 116
grams. (¶ 3) Please review the enclosed reports. Then, may I have the pleas- 130
ure of discussing possible security installations for your company? Sincerely 147
yours DENBY SECURITY SYSTEMS Ms. Ruth A. Cann, Manager xx Enclosures 160
Defining High Risk Areas Security Estimates Company Protection Plans 173

Problem 2

See 181b, page 291, for placement of special features.

Problem 3

If time permits, retype Problem 2 with these changes:

1. Address the letter to **Mrs. Linda Fowler** instead of the company; revise the salutation.

2. Omit the subject line.

3. Omit the listed enclosures. Since the subject line and the listed enclosures have been omitted, type the letter as a short letter.

Total words: 147

October 21, 19-- CERTIFIED Bluegrass Implement Company Attention Mrs. 14
Linda Fowler, Controller 1906 Harrodsburg Road Lexington, KY 40503-1037 29
Ladies and Gentlemen Subject: Office Security 38
(¶ 1) Are your offices a security risk? This fact may amaze you: Many office 52
buildings lack an adequate security system even though highly sensitive and 68
expensive security hardware has been installed. Particularly vulnerable to in- 83
trusion are open-plan offices such as those found in your organization. Statis- 99
tics show that losses from open work environments are becoming alarmingly 114
high. (¶ 2) I am enclosing some security literature for your perusal. May we 129
talk about some ideas for improving the security in your offices? 142
Sincerely yours DENBY SECURITY SYSTEMS Ms. Ruth A. Cann, Manager xx 155
Enclosures Invest in Security Protect Your Offices Integrated Protection 170
Plans 171

181d ▶ 5
Learn to arrange completed work

1. As you complete a letter and its envelope, place the letter under the envelope flap.

2. Lay the letter face down on the desk.

3. If work is to be turned in or evaluated, turn the stack of completed work face up so that your work will be in correct sequence.

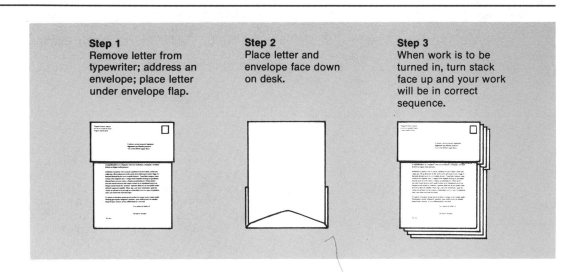

Step 1
Remove letter from typewriter; address an envelope; place letter under envelope flap.

Step 2
Place letter and envelope face down on desk.

Step 3
When work is to be turned in, turn stack face up and your work will be in correct sequence.

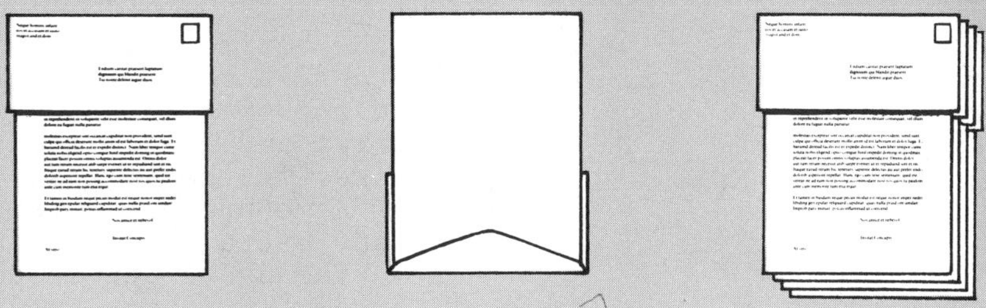

101

101a ▶ 5 Conditioning practice

each line 3 times (slowly, faster, in-between rate); as time permits, retype selected lines for extra credit

alphabet 1 Hamp Cox will get five dozen quarts of the bakery jam for Celia Brown.

figures 2 Please ship today 32 files, 48 desks, 790 chairs, and 156 typewriters.

space bar 3 Day by day typing skill may grow rapidly if you really try to improve.

fluency 4 They may do the work for me when he pays them for their big field box.

| 1 | 2 | 3 | 4 | 5 | 6 | 7 | 8 | 9 | 10 | 11 | 12 | 13 | 14 |

101b ▶ 30 Learn table placement

full sheets; correct errors

Margins

side and bottom: 1"
top, page 1: 1 1/2"
top, page 2: 1"

Number page 2 in upper right corner at right margin, 1/2" from top edge.

Vertical spacing

Space copy properly as you type it.

As a page-end reminder, use a line gauge backing sheet [LM, p. 7], or make a light pencil mark at the right edge of the sheet 1" from the bottom and another mark about 1/2" above the 1" mark to alert you to be ready to end the page. Erase marks when page is completed.

Second page reminder

Remember to indent to proper point before typing copy.

Reminder: Use margin release to move outside left margin stop.

TABLE PLACEMENT GUIDE
TS

I. VERTICAL PLACEMENT
DS

A. How to Determine Placement
   1. Count all lines to be used in table (including all blank line spaces).
   2. Subtract this figure from total lines available on sheet.
      Note: Most typewriters have six line spaces to the vertical inch; therefore, paper 8 1/2" x 11" has 66 line spaces (11 x 6 = 66).
   3. Divide the remainder by 2. Ignore any fraction. This figure will indicate the number of blank lines to be left in the top margin. Start typing on the next line.

B. Spacing Below Heading Lines
   1. Leave a double space (1 blank line space) between the MAIN HEADING and the Secondary Heading (when used).
   2. Leave a triple space (2 blank line spaces) below a main heading if a secondary heading is not used, or below a secondary heading when both a main heading and a secondary heading are used.
   3. Leave a double space (1 blank line space) below column headings (when used).

C. Reading Position
   1. Reading position (visual center) is a point approximately 2 line spaces above the exact vertical center of the sheet.
   2. To center copy in reading position, determine the top margin as usual; then subtract 2 from the number of lines to be left in the top margin.

II. HORIZONTAL PLACEMENT OF COLUMNS IN TABLES

A. Backspace-from-Center Method
   1. Move margin stops to ends of scale and clear all tab stops.
   2. From the horizontal center of the sheet, backspace once for each 2 strokes in the longest line in the first column and once for each 2 spaces to be left between the first and the second columns; then once for each 2 strokes in the longest line of the second column. Follow same procedure for any additional columns. Ignore any extra space at the end of the last column.
      Note: The usual center point for pica type is 42; for elite, 51.

(continued, p. 170)

182

182a ▶ 5

Conditioning practice

Use standard directions given in 181a, page 291.

alphabet 1 Maria Gonzalez of Peoria required six heavy stitches for a broken jaw.

figures 2 They shipped 184 tires, 305 batteries, 72 springs, and 96 heavy jacks.

punctuation marks 3 Joan said, "We want to read the article 'Reducing Home Expenditures.' "

fluency 4 She may pay them for their work on the six maps of the downtown firms.

| 1 | 2 | 3 | 4 | 5 | 6 | 7 | 8 | 9 | 10 | 11 | 12 | 13 | 14 |

182b ▶ 5

Improve language arts

full sheet; 70-space line

Type the ¶ shown at the right, making necessary corrections as you type. Verify your corrected copy with your teacher.

	words
mister huffmans check for one hundred fifty dollars, in full	8
payment of invoice number one three six two zero, was	14
(maled; mailed) on (febuary; february) sixteen. (fourty; forty) six	21
other customers (delaid; delayed) paying (there; their) accounts	30
and were billed for an additional eighteen percent (penulty;	39
penalty) charge.	42

182c ▶ 10

Learn placement of special features in letters

2 plain full sheets; 1" side margins

Before beginning to type, study comments at the right and illustrations below.

Drill 1: Foreign mail

Type the date and opening lines shown in Column 1. Type dateline at center point on Line 11 from top; type the rest of Drill 1 in correct sequence and correctly spaced.

Drill 2: Carbon copy notation

On the same sheet, space down 23 lines and type in modified block style the closing lines with carbon copy notations shown in Column 2.

Drill 3: Postscript

1. On a second sheet, retype Drill 1 through the salutation, omitting the subject line; then space down 18 lines.

2. Type in modified block style, properly spaced, the closing lines shown in Column 3.

3. DS; type the postscript notation single-spaced.

Note: Block or indent postscripts to agree with the letter style.

Foreign mail: Type **AIRMAIL** in ALL CAPS at the left margin a DS below the dateline and a DS above the address. In letter and envelope addresses, type the name of a foreign city and country in ALL CAPS.

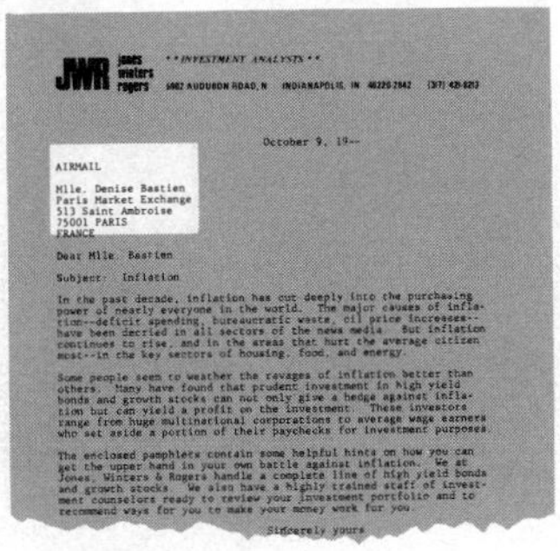

October 9, 19-- DS

AIRMAIL DS

Mlle. Denise Bastien
Paris Market Exchange
513 Saint Ambroise
75001 PARIS
FRANCE DS

Dear Mlle. Bastien DS

Subject: Inflation

Carbon copy notation: Type a carbon copy notation a DS below the reference initials or enclosure notation (if any). When there is more than one cc notation, list them on succeeding lines indented 3 spaces from the left margin. **Note:** When photo copies are made, use the letters "pc."

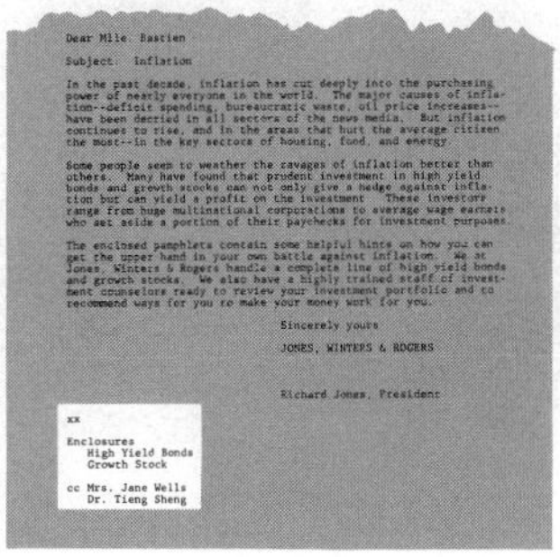

Sincerely yours DS

JONES, WINTERS & ROGERS

QS

Richard Jones, President DS

xx DS

Enclosures
   High Yield Bonds
   Growth Stock DS

cc Mrs. Jane Wells
   Dr. Tieng Sheng

Postscript: Type the postscript at the left margin a DS below the last item at the end of the letter. Omit the letters P.S. at the beginning of the postscript.

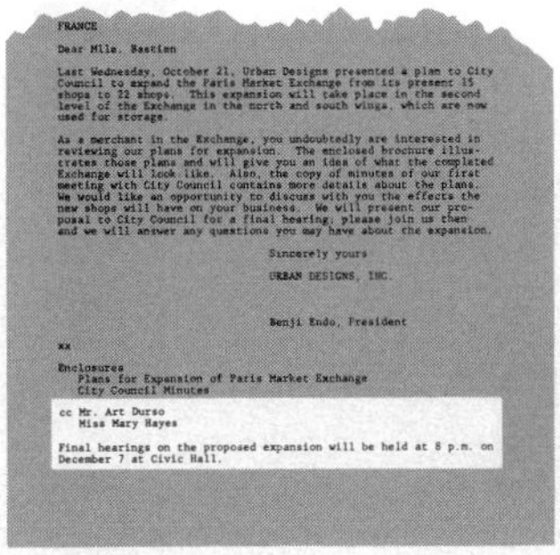

Sincerely yours DS

URBAN DESIGNS, INC.

QS

Benji Endo, President DS

xx DS

Enclosures
   Plans for expansion of
   Paris Market Exchange
   City Council Minutes DS

cc Mr. Art Durso
   Miss Mary Hayes DS

Final hearings on the proposed expansion will be held at 8 p.m. on December 7 at Civic Hall.

phase 5 lessons 101-125

Improve personal/professional typing skills

The 25 lessons of Phase 5 continue the *planned program* to improve your typing skills (see p. 125). The lessons are designed to help you:

1. Improve and extend your tabulation skills.

2. Learn basic guides for (a) typing numbers and (b) capitalization.

3. Improve your manuscript- and report-typing skills.

4. Increase your speed and improve your accuracy.

5. Refine still more your basic typing techniques.

unit 20 lessons 101-110

Increase table typing skill

Learning goals

1. To improve skill in arranging material in table (tabulated) form.

2. To improve spelling and word-use skills.

3. To increase straight-copy and statistical rough-draft copy skills.

4. To learn basic guides for typing numbers.

Machine adjustments

1. Paper guide at *0*.

2. Ribbon control to type on upper portion of ribbon (black; *R* on Selectric).

3. Line space selector on *1* or as directed.

4. 70-space line and SS or as directed.

182d ▶ 30 Learn to type letters with special features

6 plain full sheets; arrange paper and carbon paper

For all letters, use 1" side margins; type date on Line 13; modified block style, open punctuation; 1 cc; circle errors.

Note: See Reference Guide xi and xii for carbon pack assembly and error correction clues.

Problem 1

See 182c, page 293, for placement of special features.

words

October 25, 19-- AIRMAIL Frau Rita Wehrmann, President Bavarian Manu- 14
facturing Company Marien Gasse 291 8000 MUNICH WEST GERMANY Dear 27
Frau Wehrmann Subject: Consortium Research Study 37
(¶ 1) Members of the International Consortium are committed to industrial 50
progress. In the spirit of that commitment, we try to assist internationally 66
oriented firms in planning for the future. (¶ 2) We are now conducting an 80
in-depth study of selected countries to determine significant changes, both 95
economic and social, that might take place between now and the end of the 110
century. We welcome your participation in the study and ask that you review 125
the enclosed materials carefully before distributing copies to those working 141
with you. Sincerely yours INTERNATIONAL BUSINESS CONSORTIUM Michael 154
J. D'Ambrosio Director of Research xx Enclosures Data Instruments Ros- 168
ter of Companies cc Ms. Dorothy Adams, Executive Director (PS) Each 181
participating firm will receive six copies of the final research report. 195

Problem 2

See 182c, page 293, for placement of special features.

Problem 3

If time permits, retype Problem 2, but address it to:

Mlle. Yvonne D. Moreau
Executive Director
Paris Market Exchange
513 Saint Ambroise
75001 PARIS
FRANCE

Use salutation:
Dear Mlle. Moreau

October 25, 19-- AIRMAIL Mrs. Isabel Nieves, President Continental Insur- 15
ance Company Rue de Chantilly 5 1170 BRUSSELS BELGIUM Dear Mrs. 28
Nieves Subject: Executive Leadership Seminar 37
(¶ 1) Executives like to consult one another on critical management problems; 51
candid discussion generally produces new and innovative ideas. (¶ 2) Our 65
Seminar for Executive Leadership, which will be held next May 1-15, will 79
provide a timely forum for top management discussion. Why not reserve a 94
place in this forthcoming seminar by returning a reservation form with reg- 109
istration fee before March 15? Sincerely yours INTERNATIONAL BUSINESS 123
CONSORTIUM Mrs. June H. McKinzie Director of Conference Bureau xx 136
Enclosures Reservation Forms Seminar Program cc Ms. Dorothy Adams, 150
Executive Director (PS) Published proceedings of all discussion sessions will 164
be available shortly after July 1. 171

183

183a ▶ 5 Conditioning practice

Use standard directions given in 181a, page 291.

alphabet 1 Maxine Bouvier worked quickly to sew the zippers on four golf jackets.

figures 2 I stored 402 sleds, 65 toboggans, 318 ice skates, and 79 hockey pucks.

punctuation marks 3 The speaker asked pointedly, "How well are you able to accept change?"

fluency 4 An amendment to the old document is providing aid for eight bus firms.

| 1 | 2 | 3 | 4 | 5 | 6 | 7 | 8 | 9 | 10 | 11 | 12 | 13 | 14 |

183b ▶ 30 Learn to type the AMS Simplified letter

3 plain full sheets; carbon paper

1. Study the AMS letter on page 295; then type it with date on Line 13 and 1½" side margins.

2. Proofread; circle errors; check copy for correct style.

3. Review AMS features; then retype the AMS letter, addressing the letter to:

Miss Sharon Bell
Badger Utilities, Inc.
839 N. Broadway
Milwaukee, WI 53202-1358

Make 1 cc; correct errors.

Enrichment activities

Increase your speed and/or improve your control

The paragraphs progress in length by 10–word increments from 40 words to 80 words.

Type each paragraph until you can type it in a 1′ period. Then move to the next paragraph, and so on until you can type the 80–word paragraph.

If your teacher so directs, type each paragraph at the guided rate indicated by the copy, on the call of each 1/4′ interval.

In a similar way, build, control (improve accuracy) on each paragraph.

Quarter-Minute Checkpoints

gwam	¼′	½′	¾′	1′
24	6	12	18	24
28	7	14	21	28
32	8	16	24	32
36	9	18	27	36
40	10	20	30	40
44	11	22	33	44
48	12	24	36	48
52	13	26	39	52
56	14	28	42	56
60	15	30	45	60
64	16	32	48	64
68	17	34	51	68
72	18	36	54	72
76	19	38	57	76
80	20	40	60	80

40–word paragraph

If you try to type without a sense of hurry, typing at a rate of forty words a minute is not too difficult. Just type with continuity by keeping the carriage or element moving at a steady, even pace.

50–word paragraph

As you learn to type with the keystroking action in your fingers and with quiet hands, you will begin to make amazing skill growth. You may recall the importance of having a purpose or a goal for all your typing work. In this way, your skill grows.

60–word paragraph

Another way to gain typing skill is to type drill lines or other copy at alternating levels of typing speed. The line may be typed slowly as you give attention to typing with good techniques; then it is typed at a faster rate as you maintain the good techniques and push your speed to higher levels.

70–word paragraph

There is only a slight difference between sixty and seventy words a minute. At sixty words a minute, you are making five keystrokes or keystrokes and spaces every second. You only have to increase this stroking rate to about six keystrokes every second to type at a rate of seventy words a minute. Avoid breaks or pauses as you push to a new rate.

80–word paragraph

All the copy that you type is composed of words which are either balanced hand, one hand, or a combination of balanced-hand and one-hand sequences. A good typist is able to recognize the words which can be typed at high speed and the words which, because of the mixture of letter sequences, require an adjustment in the keystroking pattern. The good typist soon learns to type with variable rhythm.

Office Administration Specialists, Inc.

225 N. Michigan Avenue
Chicago, IL 60601-3950
(312) 922-2326

words

Begin all major lines at left margin

October 27, 19-- 4

Begin address 3 blank line spaces below date

Miss Karen E. Lentz 8
Director of Personnel 12
Modern Electronic Systems 17
5107 Lindell Boulevard 22
St. Louis, MO 63108-2137 27

Omit salutation

Subject line in all capital letters; triple-space above and below it

AMS SIMPLIFIED LETTER STYLE 33

We are using the simplified letter style recommended by 44
the Administrative Management Society; it is typed as 55
follows: 57

Begin enumerated items at left margin; indent unnumbered items 5 spaces

1. Use block format. 61

2. Type the address on the fourth line below the date. 73

3. Omit the salutation and complimentary close. 83

4. Always use a subject heading, typed in ALL CAPS, a 94
   triple space below the address; triple-space from the 104
   subject line to start the body of the letter. 114

5. Type enumerated items at the left margin; indent 124
   unnumbered items five spaces. 131

6. Type the writer's name and title in ALL CAPS on the 142
   fourth line space below the body of the letter. 152

7. Type reference initials (typist's only) in lowercase 163
   a double space below the writer's name. Separate 173
   enclosure notations, carbon copy references, and 183
   postscripts (if used) by one blank line. 191

We like this letter style. Enclosed are brochures giving 203
further information on AMS correspondence preferences. 214

Omit complimentary close

Writer's name and title in ALL CAPS at least 3 blank line spaces below letter body

GABRIEL J. SEIDEL, OFFICE MANAGER 221

xx 222

Enclosures 223/**246**

Style letter 5: AMS Simplified

100

100a ▶ 5
Conditioning practice

Follow standard directions, p. 164.

alphabet 1 Jack Fox said he would help me plan five parts of my big quiz exhibit.

figures 2 What is the sum of 510 and 748 and 936 and 205 and 13,295 and 414,875?

shift lock 3 He read the latest publication titled THE TEAM APPROACH TO MANAGEMENT.

fluency 4 He may do the eight proxy problems right if he works with proficiency.

| 1 | 2 | 3 | 4 | 5 | 6 | 7 | 8 | 9 | 10 | 11 | 12 | 13 | 14 |

100b ▶ 8
Measure basic skill: statistical rough draft

Type a 5′ writing on 99c, p. 165; determine *gwam*; circle errors; record rate.

100c ▶ 37
Measure production skill: letters

Time schedule

Planning and preparing .. 2′
Production timing .... 20′
Proofreading; computing *n–pram* .... 5′
Follow–up practice ...... 10′

1. Use separate letterheads [LM pp. 45–48] or plain full sheets; adjust margins according to letter length (see Placement Table); block style; open punctuation; correct all errors.

2. When time is called, proofread your completed work; mark any uncorrected errors; deduct 15 words from total words for each uncorrected error. Compute *n–pram*.

3. In the time that remains, make any needed corrections in your letters; if necessary, retype letters that are unacceptable or complete the letter you were typing when time was called.

Letter 1 words

March 27, 19-- | Mr. C. A. Adams, President | Office Efficiency, Inc. | 1300 14
Van Ness Avenue, Suite 1101 | San Francisco, CA 94109-4305 | Dear Mr. 28
Adams (¶ 1) You were right. Our entire management team found the recent 41
seminar which your staff offered to be of great value to us. (¶ 2) Now we 55
have a special problem. Has the research of your organization uncovered 69
any managerial approach that seems to work best in motivating employees to 84
increase productivity? (¶ 3) I'll look forward to hearing from you. Sincerely 99
yours | Ms. Betty Ashland | President | xx (68) 106/**129**

Letter 2

March 30, 19-- | Ms. Betty Ashland, President | Reynolds International | 2500 14
South Harbor Boulevard | Anaheim, CA 92802-4526 | Dear Ms. Ashland 27
(¶ 1) There has been much research, including research which we have done, 41
devoted to the problem of best ways to manage so as to improve motivation 56
and increase productivity of employees. As you are well aware, managers 70
come in all sizes, shapes, and philosophies. Some managers are "gung ho" 85
for production with little concern for the worker. Others concentrate on 100
being the "nice guy" at the expense of accomplishment. Still others seem to 115
take their cues from the head of the organization; they always play it safe, 131
and they never create much controversy. Although the latter group may get 146
the work done, they do not bring out the best in each employee, nor do they 161
spark much creativity. (¶ 2) Our research indicates that the managers who 175
can motivate others and, as a result, increase productivity are the managers 190
who use the "team approach" to building organizational effectiveness. We 205
have learned that productivity, creativity, and personal satisfaction of em- 220
ployees are best served when managers and their subordinates work as a 234
team to achieve objectives. The team approach to good management operates 249
on principles of trust and respect. It encourages goal setting, openness in in- 265
teractions, and resolution of disagreements and conflict based on mutual 280
understanding and agreement. (¶ 3) I am asking Mr. Bohnert of our Publica- 293
tions Department to send you our latest research publication titled THE 308
TEAM APPROACH TO MANAGEMENT IMPROVEMENT. If you have any ques- 321
tions after reviewing this publication, don't hesitate to write to me. Sincerely 337
yours | C. A. Adams, President | xx (308) 343/**364**

183c ▶ 15 Compose at the typewriter

full sheet; 70-space line

1. Type the ¶ shown at right.
2. Compose another ¶ as directed at the end of the copy.
3. Using proofreader's marks, edit your composition for clarity of thought and accuracy of typing.

	words
In this lesson, you have become familiar with the distinctive	12
features of the AMS letter style. You now have typed letters in	25
four basic letter styles: block, modified block, modified block	38
with indented paragraphs, and AMS. Now compose a short para-	50
graph indicating which letter style you would select for use in	63
your office were you responsible for deciding the style to be used	76
for all typists.	79

184

184a ▶ 5 Conditioning practice

Use standard directions given in 181a, page 291.

alphabet	1	Jack Ramirez bought sixty exquisite lamps for the camp at Nordic View.
figures	2	The four teams sold 258, 197, 46, and 30 boxes of grapes respectively.
punctuation marks	3	Did the coach ask, "Will he be ready to play in the next league game"?
fluency	4	He may wish to mend the rug, fix the chair, and cut the panel in half.

| 1 | 2 | 3 | 4 | 5 | 6 | 7 | 8 | 9 | 10 | 11 | 12 | 13 | 14 |

184b ▶ 15 Preview typing informal government letter

arrange government letterhead [LM p. 63], carbon sheet, second sheet

1. Assemble and insert carbon pack (RG p. xi).
2. Type opening lines shown in Column 1.
3. Space down 15 lines.
4. Study the directions given in Column 2 for typing on the carbon copy only; then type at the left margin the last line of the letter and the closing lines shown in Column 3.

DATE: October 29, 19--
DS

REPLY TO ATTN OF: AFAS
DS

SUBJECT: Budget Preparation
TS

TO: Director of Training
Federal Power Agency
105 Nashua Street
Boston, MA 02114-1763

Note: Start body of an informal government letter a DS below last line of address. When a window envelope is used, start the body at least 6 lines below the *To* caption. All informal government letters use 1" side margins.

To type on carbon copy only:

1. Position carriage to point where typing is to start.
2. Insert slip of paper (not flimsy) between the ribbon and the original copy.
3. Type notation and remove the slip of paper.

Note: For making blind carbon copies of letters, follow Steps 1 & 2 above; then, at the left margin, type "bcc," followed by the name of the one to receive the blind copy; for example,
bcc Robert Vidano

Last line of letter . . .

be reported by April 1.

QS (3 blank line spaces)

CHARLES E. RAY
Chief Budget Officer
DS

2 Enclosures:
Budget Guidelines
Line Estimates
DS

* ARAS:CERay:xx 10-29--

* typed on carbon copy only

184c ▶ 30 Learn to type the informal government letter

2 letterheads [LM pp. 65-68]; arrange letterheads, carbon sheet, second sheets

1. Study Style letter 6 shown on page 297; review features with your teacher.
2. Type the letter on a letterhead (1 cc), following cues shown in the illustration.
3. Circle errors; check copy for correct style.
4. Retype the style letter as directed in Steps 2 & 3, but address the letter to:
Ms. Virginia Jackson
Director of Personnel
Census Bureau
103 Federal Building
Dallas, TX 75209-1364

Note: Letters typed on the government agency form shown are mailed in window envelopes. Folding procedures for such letters are described and illustrated on RG p. vi.

99c ▶ 15
Type a short report from statistical rough-draft copy

full sheet; DS; 1 1/2" side margins

1. On Line 13, center the heading: OUR AGING POPULATION
2. Indent 5 for ¶s.
3. Correct errors as you type.
4. Proofread copy before you remove it from the machine; correct any additional errors you may find.
5. Evaluate and grade your work in terms of neatness of typing and correct division of words at ends of lines.

all figures and letters used | A | 1.5 si | 5.7 awl | 80% hfw |

	gwam 3'	5'	
"As long as you are alive, youare making an old person."	4	2	43
With that ^bit ~~kind~~ of logic, comedian Bill cosby once ^recalled ~~said~~, his	8	5	45
dad explained why there is no real difference between young~~er~~	12	7	48
and old~~er~~ persons. ^Demographic data show how successful we have been in	17	10	51
"making" older people. At the turn of hte century, the ^average life	21	13	53
expectancy was 49 years; today, the average ^life expectacy has ^increased ~~grown~~	26	16	56
to 69.9 years for males ^and to 77.0 years for females.	30	18	58
As a nation, too, we are growing older. In 1970, the me dian	34	21	61
age of our population was 27.9 years; by 1990, it willbe 32.8	38	23	63
years; and by the year 2000, the ^estimated median age will ^increase to approximately ~~be~~ 35.5 years.	45	27	67
This "graying of America" ^as it has been called, would indicate that the proportion of	51	30	71
our populaiton 65 years and over will in crease from 32 million	55	33	73
in the year 2005 to 55 million in 2030. As we grow older, we	59	35	76
will just have to discover new methods to utilize the	63	38	78
unique talent and wisdom that are characteristic of	66	40	80
the older person.	67	41	81

99d ▶ 15
Evaluate technique

70-space line; tab stop at center; each line twice; repeat if time permits

Make a self-evaluation of your typing techniques; compare with your teacher's evaluation of you as you type.

key-stroking 1
I may wish to make the usual audit and then bid for title to the firm.
Send these forms and the statement to them at the address on the card.
A number of the workers were certified by the popular union organizer.

space bar 2
When it is right for me to do so, I may go with them to the big field.
When they sign the right form for us, she may pay them for their work.
If they do the work for us, then I may pay them if they sign the form.

shift keys 3
James H. Forgie and Ramon Torres will visit Salt Lake City and Newark.
Jan McNeil and Amy Presley will meet Lana Roberts in Sioux City, Iowa.
Mrs. Epley, President of Epley Industries, Inc., lives in Dover, Mass.

tab and return 4
↓ tab set
——— tab to center ———→ Without looking, make a quick return
and start the new line. ——tab——→ (repeat twice)

continuity 5
Read slightly ahead in the copy to anticipate the keystroking pattern.
Just keep your eyes on this copy as you type without breaks or pauses.
If you just concentrate on this copy, you can avoid breaks and pauses.

PUBLIC SERVICE AGENCY

WASHINGTON, DC 20406-1322

words

DATE: October 30, 19-- 3
DS

REPLY TO ATTN OF: DSMA 4
DS

symbol for originating office

SUBJECT: Format for the Informal Government Letter 13
TS

TO: Director, Petroleum Supply Division 20
Federal Supply Agency 24
813 Federal Office Building 30
Houston, TX 77002-1365 35

Set left margin 2 spaces to right of headings.

1″ side margin

Start body on 6th line below *To*:

This letter shows the format for preparing letters for agencies 47
of the United States Government. This format expedites the prepa- 61
ration of correspondence and saves effort, time, and materials. 74
The following features of the format should please typists. 86

a. All elements except the first line of lettered items are 98
blocked at the left margin. This block style minimizes the use of 111
the space bar, the tabulator set, and the tabulator bar or key. 124

b. Salutations and complimentary closes are omitted in in- 136
formal government letters. They may be used, however, in formal 149
government letters to any individual on a personal or private mat- 162
ter (notices of serious illness, letters of condolence, where warm 176
and personal feeling is paramount, etc.), or where protocol or tra- 189
dition dictates. 193

c. The address is positioned to be visible after insertion 205
into a window envelope, eliminating the need for typing an envelope. 218

3 blank line spaces

MISS NANCY J. CRAWFORD 223
Director of Communications 228
DS

2 Enclosures: 231
Revised Style Manual 235
Tips for Effective Writing 241
DS

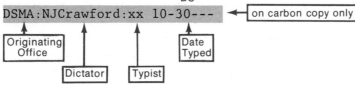

DSMA:NJCrawford:xx 10-30--- 246

on carbon copy only

Originating Office | Dictator | Typist | Date Typed

Style letter 6: informal government letter

unit **19** lessons 99-100

Evaluate Performance

Evaluation goals

1. To measure and help you evaluate your overall typing skill.

2. To help you identify areas of needed improvement.

Machine adjustments

1. Paper guide at *0*.

2. 70-space line, SS, unless otherwise directed.

3. Line space selector on *1* or as directed.

4. Ribbon control on black (*R* on selectric).

99

99a ▶ 5 Conditioning practice

each line twice (slowly, faster); as time permits, retype selected lines for extra credit

alphabet	1	Jack quickly recognized the problems as he fixed the five power boats.
fig/sym	2	All records numbered 47-215B, 87-735A, 92-041C, and 64-8010 were sold.
3d & 4th fingers	3	Sal saw six zebras as she and Paul ate apples and lollipops in a park.
fluency	4	Orlando may handle a quantity of the ancient land forms for the firms.

| 1 | 2 | 3 | 4 | 5 | 6 | 7 | 8 | 9 | 10 | 11 | 12 | 13 | 14 |

99b ▶ 15 Check grammar/punctuation skill

full sheet; DS; 1" top margin; 70-space line

1. Type each sentence in enumerated form, choosing the correct word in the parentheses or inserting correct punctuation as you type the line.

2. As your teacher reads the corrected sentences to you, circle the number of any sentence in which you have made an error.

3. Reinsert your paper, align it, then retype correctly any sentence in which you made an error of grammar or punctuation in the blank space below that sentence.

Awareness cue: Remember to reset margin when you reach the figure 10.

1. One of the workers (is, are) here to interview for the new clerical job.
2. Jan and Donna (is, are) going to the show with me tonight.
3. Jan, as well as Donna, (is, are) going to the show with me tonight.
4. Neither of my friends (is, are) with me.
5. Each of the girls (is, are) doing (her, their) work.
6. Some of the students (is, are) at the assembly in the campus auditorium.
7. He (don't, doesn't) like the food served in the new school cafeteria.
8. They (don't, doesn't) like the food served in the new school cafeteria.
9. Neither John nor Robert (has, have) written (his, their) report.
10. (Fewer, Less) students (is, are) enrolled in our typing program this semester.
11. I feel (bad, badly) today.
12. Fifty percent of the work (is, are) completed on the new classroom.
13. He said Techniques rhythm and continuity are very important.
14. Ms. Tanaka our new teacher knows how to teach typewriting.
15. A dozen large red white and pink carnations were sent to Carol.
16. I was in Stockholm Sweden on July 4 1982.
17. We have 2350 books stored in Room 1,358.
18. Will you please cover the typewriter when you leave?
19. Current assets see attached statement (is, are) incorrectly listed.
20. Sues report is 1 unclear, 2 imprecise, and 3 wordy.
21. I read the article The Year 2000 and Beyond.
22. I read the book Running which was reviewed in The Daily Reporter.
23. To type with speed is easy to type without error, difficult.
24. The boys hockey team will play the mens hockey team this month.

185a ▶ 5
Conditioning practice

Use standard directions given in 181a, page 291.

alphabet 1 Vera Paxton judged a sizable group of weekly workers at McQueen Hills.

figures 2 Quotas of 390, 275, 84, and 61 were given to the four new sales teams.

punctuation marks 3 "Please write," she said, "about your experiences with our equipment."

fluency 4 The issue they wish the formal panel to handle is the problem of fuel.

| 1 | 2 | 3 | 4 | 5 | 6 | 7 | 8 | 9 | 10 | 11 | 12 | 13 | 14 |

185b ▶ 10
Compose at the typewriter

full sheet; 70-space line

1. Compose three sentences illustrating the use of the quotation marks as shown in Line 3, 185a.

2. Verify the accuracy of your work with your teacher.

185c ▶ 35
Building skill on AMS and informal government letters

3 letterheads [LM pp. 69-74]; arrange letterheads, carbon sheet, second sheets; make 1 cc for each letter; correct errors

Problem 1
AMS Simplified letter

Type date on Line 13; use 1½" side margins; address envelope.

words

October 31, 19-- Miss Audra Roberts Director of Planning Industrial Land- 15
scaping, Inc. 219 S. Dearborn Street Chicago, IL 60604-2517 27

REPORT ON INTERIOR LANDSCAPING (¶ 1) For the next meeting of our Board 40
of Directors, we shall need some specific information relating to the comple- 55
tion of the Executive Suite of our new building. Specifically, I am requesting 71
the following information: 1. An inventory of all equipment recommended 86
for the administrative area. 2. A prospectus detailing the colors, lighting, and 103
other decorative features proposed for the offices. 3. Cost estimates of the 118
complete landscaping proposal. (¶ 2) We are looking forward to receiving 132
your report and to studying its contents. Enclosed is the copy of the minutes 148
of our last planning session that I promised you. 158

PAUL R. LEVITT, EXECUTIVE VICE PRESIDENT xx Enclosure 168/**191**

Problem 2
Informal government letter

window envelope

Date: October 31, 19-- Reply to Attn of: DSMA Subject: Staff Training Pro- 8
gram To: Mr. Peter Zilkowski Personnel Administrator Federal Building 22
Charleston, SC 29401-0371 27

(¶ 1) We are scheduling a one-week training program for government work- 40
ers to prepare them for participation in the federal government's new dis- 55
tributed data-processing system. Training sessions will be held March 11-15 70
from 9 a.m. to 3 p.m. daily. Three topics will be covered: a. Learning about 86
distributed data processing--using computer resources across locations and 101
across functions. b. Utilizing host and in-house computers--integrating com- 117
puting services for greater productivity. c. Training for specialized 132
services--seminars for supervisors, operators, and programmers. (¶ 2) I hope 146
you will be able to adjust your employees' work schedules so that they will 161
be free to attend these sessions. Program reservation materials are 175
enclosed. 177

MRS. AMALIA M. ESPINO Director, Information Processing 2 Enclosures: 191
Conference Program Reservation Forms DSMA:AMEspino:xx 10-31-- 203

Problem 3 is on page 299.

98b ▶ 10
Improve technique: keystroking

each line 3 times (slowly, faster, top speed)

Emphasize: Finger reaches; quiet hands; continuity. (Keep fingers curved and upright.)

long reaches	1	Many musical numbers, played at a branch ceremony, were well received.
	2	The eccentric umpire received a number of bronze plaques from a union.
difficult reaches	3	Today you may improve yesterday's typing rate if you just keep trying.
	4	The bright baby boys babbled with joy as the abbey cobbler hurried by.
3d and 4th fingers	5	Quai and Polly zigzagged around a buzzing bazaar with a quizzical lad.
	6	Cool cottons, in a popular azure color, are on sale at Pax and Popper.

98c ▶ 15
Measure basic skill: straight copy

two 5′ writings; determine *gwam*; circle errors; record better rate

all letters used | A | 1.5 si | 5.7 awl | 80% hfw |

	gwam 3′	5′	
As you read copy for typewriting, try to read at least a word or,	4	3	44
better still, a word group ahead of your actual typing. In this way,	9	5	47
you should be able to recognize the keystroking pattern needed as you	14	8	50
learn to type balanced-hand, one-hand, or combination word sequences.	18	11	53
The adjustments you make in your typing speed will result in the variable	23	14	56
rhythm pattern needed for expert typing. It is easy to read copy cor-	28	17	59
rectly for typewriting if you concentrate on the material being read.	33	20	61
When you first try to read copy properly for typewriting, you may	37	22	64
make more typing errors; but as you learn to concentrate on the copy	42	25	67
being read and begin to anticipate the keystroking pattern needed, your	47	28	70
errors will go down and your typewriting speed will grow. If you want	51	31	72
to increase your typewriting speed and reduce your errors, you must make	56	34	75
the effort to improve during each and every practice session. If you	61	37	78
will work to refine your techniques and to give a specific purpose to	66	39	81
all your practice activities, you can make the improvement.	69	42	83

gwam 3′ | 1 | 2 | 3 | 4 | 5
5′ | 1 | 2 | 3

98d ▶ 20
Improve speed/accuracy: straight copy

1. Add 4 words to your *gwam* rate of 98c. Type 1′ guided writings at this new goal rate on the ¶s of 98c. Start each new writing at the ending point of the previous writing.

2. Type another 5′ writing on 98c. Proofread; determine *gwam*. Compare the 5′ rates. Did you improve speed? or accuracy?

185c, continued

Problem 3
Informal government letter
window envelope

words

Date: **October 31, 19--** Reply to Attn. of: **AFEA** Subject: **Fuel Conservation** To: 8
Ms. Florene Watson Operations Officer Department of Interior 1961 Stout 22
Street Denver, CO 80202-3648 28

(¶ 1) **It is imperative that all government agencies take immediate steps to** 42
reduce vehicle fuel consumption. To achieve the urgent goal of greater fuel 58
economy, all units must follow these procedures: a. Reduce the number of 73
vehicles operating daily out of the agency motor pool. b. Consolidate trips 88
requiring the use of agency motor vehicles. c. Restrict the use of agency 104
vehicles to hours only in the regular work day. d. Adhere strictly to mainte- 119
nance regulations prescribed for all vehicles. (¶ 2) **We need to reduce fuel** 134
consumption drastically in the next few weeks, and we need the support of 148
all employees. The enclosed pamphlets may be used to inform all personnel 163
of our new policies. 167

VINCENTE J. RUIZ Energy Administrator 2 Enclosures: Plans for Fuel Con- 182
sumption Your Role in Fuel Conservation AFEA:VJRuiz:xx 10-31-- 194

186

186a ▶ 5 Conditioning practice

Use standard directions given in 181a, page 291.

alphabet 1 Wayne Prinz gave us exciting talks about techniques for broad jumping.
figures 2 The meeting rooms will seat conveniently 240, 167, 93, and 85 persons.
punctuation marks 3 The new manager, considered to be quite youthful, made wise decisions.
fluency 4 Turn to the right at the big sign; then, go eight blocks to the quays.

| 1 | 2 | 3 | 4 | 5 | 6 | 7 | 8 | 9 | 10 | 11 | 12 | 13 | 14 |

186b ▶ 45 Build sustained production: letters with special features

Time schedule
Preparation .... 5′
Timed production .... 30′
Final check; compute *n-pram* .... 10′

1. Make a list of problems to be typed:
p. 292, 181c, Problem 2
p. 294, 182d, Problem 2
p. 298, 185c, Problem 1
p. 298, 185c, Problem 2

2. Arrange plain sheets or letterheads [LM pp. 75–82]; second sheets; carbon paper. Make 1 cc for each problem; address envelopes where necessary.

3. Type for 30′ when directed to begin; follow directions given for each problem; correct all errors neatly, proofreading carefully before removing a letter from the typewriter.

4. Compute *n-pram*; then turn in completed work, arranged in the order listed in Step 1 (see 181d for arranging work).

187

187a ▶ 5 Conditioning practice

Use standard directions given in 181a, page 291.

alphabet 1 Roxanne Mazur just bought five quarts of yellow candy for Kevin Roper.
figures 2 The jeweler sold 963 coins, 84 bracelets, 120 pins, and 57 new clocks.
punctuation marks 3 Carol Young plans to write an article titled "Be Your Own Tax Expert."
fluency 4 It may take some time for the city to pay the auditors for their work.

| 1 | 2 | 3 | 4 | 5 | 6 | 7 | 8 | 9 | 10 | 11 | 12 | 13 | 14 |

97

97a ▶ 5 Conditioning practice

Follow standard directions, p. 160.

alphabet 1 Fritz requests extra guava jelly and peanut butter to make a sandwich.
figures 2 Please ship Order 741250 for 149 desks, 138 lamps, and 36 typewriters.
long words 3 Work for typing perfection through thoughtful and purposeful practice.
fluency 4 The proficient but haughty field hand may do their handiwork for them.

| 1 | 2 | 3 | 4 | 5 | 6 | 7 | 8 | 9 | 10 | 11 | 12 | 13 | 14 |

97b ▶ 15 Improve accuracy: progressive difficulty sentences

Retype 96b, p. 160, but with emphasis on control. Try to type each sentence with not more than 1 error.

97c ▶ 15 Transfer improved control: guided writing

1. A 2′ writing (at a controlled pace with fingers curved, quiet hands).

2. Determine *gwam*. Subtract 4 from your *gwam* rate. Determine ¼′ goals for 1′ writings at new goal rate.

3. Three 1′ writings at goal rate as the ¼′ guide is called.

Goal: not more than 1 error in each writing.

4. Another 2′ writing for control. Maintain goal rate; type for control.

all letters used — gwam 2′

The fear of making an error often causes you to make typing errors. 7
Poor techniques are another contributing factor. You can reduce your 14
typing errors if you keep your fingers in proper typing position with 21
your hands quiet. Just start a timing at a lazy, well-controlled pace, 28
and gradually vary or increase your speed as you begin to relax. As 35
your confidence increases, your typing errors will decrease. 41

gwam 2′ | 1 | 2 | 3 | 4 | 5 | 6 | 7 |

97d ▶ 15 Improve basic skill: straight copy

Repeat 96d, p. 161. **Goal:** To improve control; try to type with not more than 10 errors on each writing.

98

98a ▶ 5 Conditioning practice

Follow standard directions, p. 160.

alphabet 1 Quincy just gave six bushels of fine wheat to the old Pamkezak market.
fig/sym 2 Call Ocher & O'Brien, 62 St. Louis Drive, toll free at 1-800-574-9365.
long words 3 Proposed constitutional amendments require formal membership approval.
fluency 4 The maps of the Malayan land forms may aid them when they do the work.

| 1 | 2 | 3 | 4 | 5 | 6 | 7 | 8 | 9 | 10 | 11 | 12 | 13 | 14 |

187b ▶ 45
Measure production skill: letters with special features

Time schedule

Preparation .... 5′
Timed production ...... 30′
Final check; compute *n-pram* .... 10′

4 letterheads [LM pp. 85–92]

1. Arrange letterheads, second sheets, carbon paper, and envelopes. Make 1 cc of each problem.

2. Type for 30′ when directed to begin; correct errors neatly; proofread carefully before removing each letter from the typewriter.

3. Compute *n-pram*; turn in completed work arranged in sequence given below.

Problem 1
Letter with special features

Type date on Line 13; use 1½″ side margins; modified block style, open punctuation; address envelope.

words

November 1, 19-- CERTIFIED Tri-States Equipment Company Attention Mrs. 14
Diane Baker, Treasurer 1203 Elmwood Avenue Charleston, WV 25301-1640 28
Ladies and Gentlemen Subject: Photo Identification 38
(¶ 1) The magic key to your company's internal security problems could very 52
well be found in photo identification. With photo I.D.'s, personnel assigned to 68
designated areas can be monitored effectively, and unauthorized persons on 83
company premises can be detected quickly. Photo I.D.'s may also be used for 99
after-hours building access, parking lot control, equipment loans, cashing 114
checks, and a number of other uses involving personal identification. (¶ 2) 128
Enclosed are two publications dealing with photo identification. Please read 144
them; then let us help you design and install a system suited to your special 159
needs. Sincerely yours DENBY SECURITY SYSTEMS Ms. Ruth A. Cann, Man- 173
ager xx Enclosures Security Management Costs and Security Systems cc 187
Ernst Busch, Sales Representative (PS) For the period required to install one 202
of our security systems, we provide, free of charge, 24-hour surveillance. 216/**241**

Problem 2
AMS Simplified letter

Type date on Line 13; use 1½″ side margins; address envelope.

November 1, 19-- Miss Ayako Nozaki, Controller Technology Systems, Inc. 14
165 N. Main Street Memphis, TN 38103-1457 TIME MANAGEMENT (¶ 1) At- 27
tempts by top management to increase worker productivity have revealed 41
constantly the importance of time management. The following activities 55
have been found to detract from profitable use of time: 1. Ineffective 70
delegation of responsibility--inability to assign work. 2. Telephone 84
interruptions--poor channeling of incoming calls. 3. Ill-defined work 99
priorities--inability to determine relative importance of work to be done. 114
4. Vague and indefinite communications--inability to convey clear, concise 129
messages to workers. (¶ 2) Other factors relating to time management are 143
discussed in the enclosed documents. I hope this information proves helpful 158
to you. MS. CHARLEASE S. THOMAS, VICE PRESIDENT xx Enclosures 171/**190**

Problem 3
Informal government letter

window envelope

Date: November 1, 19-- Reply to Attn. of: ABAC Subject: On-site Facilities Study 9
To: Mr. Ricardo J. Perreira Director, Field Projects Bureau of Mines Fed- 23
eral Office Building Minneapolis, MN 55401-1362 33
(¶ 1) To enable us to provide adequate support for your proposed on-site facil- 47
ity utilization project, you must send us the following items: a. A roster of all 64
official personnel to be involved. b. An inventory of the number and type of 80
official vehicles required. c. Requisitions for items of special equipment 95
needed. d. A detailed estimate of personnel expenses and other project costs 111
for which special budget allocations must be requested. (¶ 2) We must have 125
the above-listed items before December 15 if the paperwork involved is to be 140
completed by the April 1 deadline. 147
JOHN A. RICH Project Coordinator 2 Enclosures: Project Report Forms 161
Equipment Requisitions ABAC:JARich:xx 11-1-- 170

Problem 4

Retype Problem 1, making these changes:
1. Type the date on Line 16; use 1½″ side margins.
2. Address the letter to Mrs. Baker.
3. Adjust salutation.
4. Omit the subject line.
5. Omit the cc notation.
6. Omit the postscript notation.
Total words: 201

96c ▶ 15
Transfer improved speed: guided writing

1. A 2′ writing for speed with fast finger-action keystroking and quick spacing.

2. Determine *gwam*. Add 4–8 words to your *gwam* rate. Set ¼′ goals for 1′ writings at your new goal rate.

3. Three 1′ writings at your goal rate as the ¼′ guides are called.

4. A 2′ guided writing; try to maintain your goal rate for 2′.

5. A 2′ writing for speed. Try to exceed your goal rate.

all letters used

	gwam 2′
When building typewriting speed, it is important to type with the	7
keystroking action in the fingers and with quiet hands. Just try to	14
keep the fingers in a curved and upright position over the home keys.	21
The wrists should be low and relaxed, but the base of the hands should	28
not touch the frame of the typewriter. If you practice with these goals	35
in mind, you will be amazed with your speed gains.	40

gwam 2′ | 1 | 2 | 3 | 4 | 5 | 6 | 7 |

96d ▶ 15
Improve basic skill: straight copy

two 5′ writings; determine *gwam*; record better rate.

Goal: Try to force your speed to a new level.

Fingers curved

Keystroke

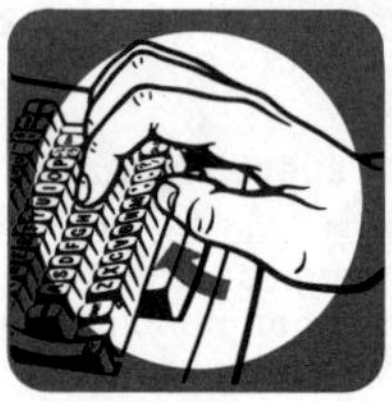
Spacing stroke

all letters used

	gwam 3′	gwam 5′	
If you have developed the typing techniques and various other ele-	4	3	47
ments suggested in this book, you really should be on your way toward	9	5	50
becoming an expert typist. In the remainder of the lessons of this cycle,	14	8	53
just make the effort to refine your typing form and response patterns	19	11	56
even more. You will be amazed at the difference that even a slight	23	14	59
refinement in this area can make in your typewriting skill. Always	28	17	61
be sure that your fingers are in the proper position and that they are	33	20	64
really curved and upright. Keep your wrists low and relaxed, with the	37	22	67
base of each hand nearly touching the frame of the typewriter.	42	25	70
Fast keystroking is very important on both the manual and the elec-	46	28	72
tric typewriters. Reaches to the keys should be made with the action	51	30	75
in the fingers and with the hands in a quiet and relaxed position. When	56	33	78
not in use, the fingers should be touching their home keys. Fast down-	60	36	81
and-in spacing with the right thumb after every word is another element	65	39	84
contributing to the growth of good typing skill. It is important, too,	70	42	87
to use proper motions in making capital letters or in making the return.	75	45	90

gwam 3′ | 1 | 2 | 3 | 4 | 5 |
5′ | 1 | 2 | 3 |

unit 36 lessons 188-193

Communications of special types

Learning goals

1. To improve skill in typing interoffice communications in standard and simplified styles.

2. To learn to arrange and type news releases.

3. To learn to arrange and type telegraphic messages.

4. To improve skill in composing at the typewriter.

5. To reinforce selected language arts skills.

Machine adjustments

1. Paper guide at *0*.

2. Ribbon control to type on top half of ribbon.

3. Margin sets: 70-space line for sentence and paragraph activities; as required for problems.

4. Spacing: SS sentence drills; DS¶ activities; as directed for problems.

5. Tab sets: for 5-space ¶ indention; as needed for problems.

188

188a ▶ 5

Conditioning practice

each line twice SS (slowly, then faster); DS between 2-line groups; if time permits, retype selected lines

alphabet 1 Jennie Wexford marked crazy bridle paths through quiet virgin forests.

figures 2 Sarah paid the travel invoice dated May 28, for $9,564.73, on June 10.

re/er 3 real peer more jeer mere here were cover three lower press never where

fluency 4 He may wish to make them pay for the six bushels of corn that he owns.

| 1 | 2 | 3 | 4 | 5 | 6 | 7 | 8 | 9 | 10 | 11 | 12 | 13 | 14 |

188b ▶ 20

Type a report about interoffice communications

margins: top, 1½"; side, 1"; DS the ¶; SS enumerated items; DS between them

1. Type the report.

2. Proofread and circle errors.

3. As time permits, study the content of the report and the form of the model; discuss procedures with your teacher.

4. Keep your copy for reference in 188c.

Model of full-sheet memo

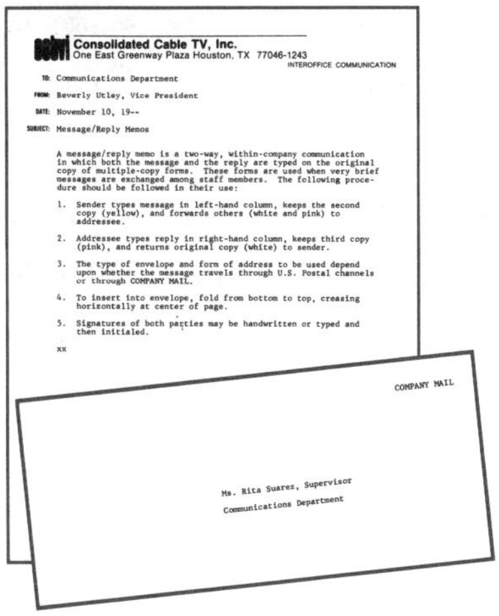

Consolidated Cable TV, Inc.
One East Greenway Plaza Houston, TX 77046-1243
INTEROFFICE COMMUNICATION

TO: Communications Department

FROM: Beverly Utley, Vice President

DATE: November 10, 19--

SUBJECT: Message/Reply Memos

A message/reply memo is a two-way, within-company communication in which both the message and the reply are typed on the original copy of multiple-copy forms. These forms are used when very brief messages are exchanged among staff members. The following procedure should be followed in their use:

1. Sender types message in left-hand column, keeps the second copy (yellow), and forwards others (white and pink) to addressee.
2. Addressee types reply in right-hand column, keeps third copy (pink), and returns original copy (white) to sender.
3. The type of envelope and form of address to be used depend upon whether the message travels through U.S. Postal channels or through COMPANY MAIL.
4. To insert into envelope, fold from bottom to top, creasing horizontally at center of page.
5. Signatures of both parties may be handwritten or typed and then initialed.

xx

COMPANY MAIL

Ms. Rita Suarez, Supervisor
Communications Department

words

INTEROFFICE COMMUNICATIONS 5

Interoffice memorandums are used for in-house messages. They have a number of special features as described below. 29

1. A form with printed headings is generally used for memo messages; the memo may be typed on half sheet or full sheet. 53
2. Memos are typed in block style (all lines beginning at the left margin) with 1-inch side margins. 74
3. Heading lines are printed in the 1-inch left margin so that the lines of the heading data and the message can begin 2 spaces to the right of the headings (at the margin stop set for the 1-inch left margin). 116
4. Omit personal titles (Miss, Mr., Ms., Dr., etc.) when typing the heading; however, type the titles when addressing the envelope. 143
5. No salutation or complimentary close is used. 153
6. Triple-space (TS) between last heading and the message; single-space (SS) the paragraphs, but double-space (DS) between them; double-space (DS) above and below a table or a numbered list when one is included in the message. 199
7. Reference initials are typed a DS below the message at the left margin. 215
8. Special colored envelopes are often used. However, if plain unmarked envelopes are used, type COMPANY MAIL in all capitals in the postage location. The address includes the addressee's personal title, name, and business title or name of department. 266

unit **18** lessons 96-98

Improve speed/accuracy

Learning goals

1. To improve and refine your typing techniques.

2. To increase your speed and improve your accuracy.

3. To increase your straight-copy rate.

Machine adjustments

1. Paper guide at *0*.

2. 70-space line and single spacing (SS) unless otherwise directed.

3. Line space selector on *2* (DS) for all timed writings of more than 1′.

4. Ribbon control on black (*R* on Selectric).

96

96a ▶ 5 Conditioning practice

each line twice (slowly, faster); as time permits, retype selected lines for extra credit

alphabet	1	Jon Wolfe maximized his skill just by improving his typing techniques.
fig/sym	2	You will need to change Item 1005, page 736, from $41.95 to $4,195.28.
long reaches	3	The unusual aluminum bridge is decorated with many bright nylon flags.
fluency	4	The big problem with their theory is the authenticity of the ornament.

| 1 | 2 | 3 | 4 | 5 | 6 | 7 | 8 | 9 | 10 | 11 | 12 | 13 | 14 |

96b ▶ 15 Improve speed: progressive difficulty sentences

1. Starting with Sentence 1, Set 1, gradually try to force your speed on the sentences as the 15″, 12″, or 10″ guide is called.

Move from one sentence to the next when the "return" is called. Try to maintain your speed as the sentences in each set progress in difficulty.

Emphasize: fast finger-action keystroking; quick down-and-in spacing.

2. Type two 1′ writings on each sentence in Set 5. On Sentences 14 and 15, try to equal the rate made on Sentence 13.

		gwam 15″	12″	10″
	Set 1			
1	Jan may go with them to do the work for the firms.	40	50	60
2	Did she send a statement to the firm on that date?	40	50	60
3	Was he to quote a minimum rate on the reserve oil?	40	50	60
	Set 2			
4	It is right to make them sign for the right audit form.	44	55	66
5	On or before this date, they should read the tax cases.	44	55	66
6	Were they aware of his opinion in the oil embargo case?	44	55	66
	Set 3			
7	He may sign the amendment form if they do work for the city.	48	60	72
8	She may refer a minimum number of union cases to the courts.	48	60	72
9	She was to get my opinion only on the estate tax settlement.	48	60	72
	Set 4			
10	If they do the work for the big firm, he may spend a day with me.	52	65	78
11	Was he aware that the statement was delivered to the old address?	52	65	78
12	The average reserve tax rate is greater than the minimum you set.	52	65	78
	Set 5			
13	To their dismay, the big city firms kept us busy with the audit forms.	56	70	84
14	A delegate from the union may have a statement to make about the case.	56	70	84
15	Only a few nylon monopoly cases were greatly exaggerated on our tests.	56	70	84

| 1 | 2 | 3 | 4 | 5 | 6 | 7 | 8 | 9 | 10 | 11 | 12 | 13 | 14 |

188c ▶ 25
Learn to type standard interoffice memos

[LM p. 93]
1″ side margins; proofread, circle errors; address envelope marked **COMPANY MAIL**

Problem 1
Half-page memo
Type the memo shown at the right.

Problem 2
Memo with changes
Retype Problem 1, making the following changes:

1. Address the memo to **David Goldberg, Controller.**

2. For ¶3, substitute the ¶ given below the illustration.

Standard half-page memorandum

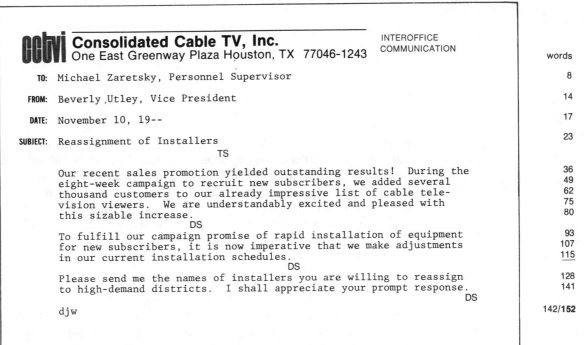

cctvi **Consolidated Cable TV, Inc.**
One East Greenway Plaza Houston, TX 77046-1243
INTEROFFICE COMMUNICATION

words

TO: Michael Zaretsky, Personnel Supervisor 8

FROM: Beverly Utley, Vice President 14

DATE: November 10, 19-- 17

SUBJECT: Reassignment of Installers 23

TS

Our recent sales promotion yielded outstanding results! During the 36
eight-week campaign to recruit new subscribers, we added several 49
thousand customers to our already impressive list of cable tele- 62
vision viewers. We are understandably excited and pleased with 75
this sizable increase. 80

DS

To fulfill our campaign promise of rapid installation of equipment 93
for new subscribers, it is now imperative that we make adjustments 107
in our current installation schedules. 115

DS

Please send me the names of installers you are willing to reassign 128
to high-demand districts. I shall appreciate your prompt response. 141

DS

djw 142/**152**

Please let me know the amount budgeted this quarter for overtime pay for our 128
installers. Thank you. djw 135/**142**

189

189a ▶ 5
Conditioning practice

Use standard directions given in 188a, page 301.

alphabet 1 Mixed groups were invited by Hazel Quinick to exhibit junior fashions.
figures 2 The classes tried to type 364, 501, 27, and 89 as rapidly as possible.
op/po 3 open port opals pours opera pound option report oppose exposed adopted
fluency 4 Eight tight turns of the handle may open the panels on the box for us.

| 1 | 2 | 3 | 4 | 5 | 6 | 7 | 8 | 9 | 10 | 11 | 12 | 13 | 14 |

189b ▶ 15
Learn about simplified interoffice memorandums

70-space line; DS; type the ¶; as time permits, study the content of the ¶ and the form of the model; discuss the features with your teacher

words

The simplified office memorandum is typed in block style on plain paper. 15
Side and top margins of one inch are used. The heading consists of the date, the 31
addressee's name and title, and the subject line--the three lines separated by 47
triple spacing. The paragraphs of the message are single-spaced, the first one 63
beginning a triple space below the subject line. The sender's name and title are 79
typed on a single line a triple space below the message. The reference initials 95
are typed a triple space below the sender's name and title. The simplified 110
memo is both easy to type and quite attractive. 119

| 1 | 2 | 3 | 4 | 5 | 6 | 7 | 8 | 9 | 10 | 11 | 12 | 13 | 14 |

Model of simplified memo

November 12, 19--

Eva Mendoza, Vice President

Membership in the Executives Club

The challenge of finding new members to insure our Club's future strength and vitality is an ever-present one. To attract new members, we need a membership committee that is aware of our unusual services and sensitive to our special needs.

I should like you to chair our membership committee for this next year. Your major concern will be to help develop a forceful membership drive and to assist with its implementation. I hope you will agree to chair this prime committee. Please accept.

Bella Herrera, M.D., President

njc

95c, continued

block style; open punctuation; standard 6-inch line; use Placement Table, p. 143, for letter placement

Stay alert!

Problem 1

words

April 28, 19-- | Mrs. Rosalyn Kalmar, Manager | United California Bank | 9460 14
Wilshire Boulevard | Beverly Hills, CA 90212-4467 | Dear Mrs. Kalmar 28
(¶ 1) Women in Business (WIB) is an organization created to serve business 41
women. WIB's goals are (1) to assist in meeting the changing needs of busi- 57
ness women; (2) to function as a resource through which members can learn 71
from each other's experiences; and (3) to collect and share career informa- 86
tion through a career support network. (¶ 2) WIB membership is limited to 100
women in business. If you would like to know how you can become a 114
member, just return the enclosed coupon. Complete information will be sent 129
to you by return mail. (¶ 3) When you receive the information about WIB and 143
learn what it can mean to you, I know you will want to join the growing le- 158
gion of women who hold WIB membership. Sincerely yours | Barbara Weise, 172
Ph.D. | Executive Director | xx | Enclosure (138) 180/**201**

Problem 2

May 18, 19-- | Ms. Cheryl Berry, Manager | Wilshire Comstock Hotel | 875 13
Comstock Avenue | Los Angeles, CA 90024-4818 | Dear Ms. Berry 25
(¶ 1) On Saturday, June 25, WIB (Women in Business) is sponsoring a Finan- 39
cial Management Conference for Women. The conference will be held in the 54
new Bonaventure Hotel in Los Angeles. The conference topics are listed and 69
described in the attached registration booklet. (¶ 2) Take a moment now to 83
complete the registration form. Just put it in the enclosed postpaid envelope 99
and return it to WIB. You won't regret taking this first step toward a better 114
understanding of financial management. Sincerely yours | Barbara Weise, 129
Ph.D. | Executive Director | xx | Enclosure (97) 136/**156**

Problem 3

August 13, 19-- | Dr. Lyn Clark, Editor | Enterprise Publishing Company | 1103 15
Avenue of the Stars | Century City, CA 90067-4702 | Dear Dr. Clark (¶ 1) 27
During October, WIB (Women in Business) is sponsoring two Breakfast Pro- 42
grams for Women. On Wednesday, October 8, the topic for the breakfast 56
program will be "Career Strategy." On Wednesday, October 22, the topic will 71
be "When the Boss is a Woman." (¶ 2) The breakfast programs will be held in 86
the Vista Room of the Boniventure Hotel. Breakfast will be served at 7:15 101
a.m. The program will start at 7:45 a.m. and will conclude by 8:30 a.m. All 116
members of WIB are eligible to attend these breakfast meetings. We only ask 132
that you make your reservations not later than the Monday preceding the 146
Wednesday breakfast. A phone call to my office will do. (¶ 3) At this time, 160
too, I'd like to alert you to another of WIB's Saturday Conferences for 175
Women. On Saturday, November 14, the conference will be concerned with 189
the topic "Stress Management." The program is described in the enclosed 204
brochure. (¶ 4) Plan now to be with your colleagues in WIB for the October 218
Breakfast Programs and the November Conference. These meetings are de- 232
signed for your professional growth and development. They represent 246
another in the series of WIB services to women in business. Sincerely yours | 261
Barbara Weise, Ph.D. | Executive Director | xx | Enclosure (231) 272/**293**

189c ▶ 30
Learn to type interoffice memos in simplified style

1″ top and side margins; proofread, circle errors

Problem 1
plain half sheet

Type the memo shown at the right.

Problem 2
plain half sheet

Retype Problem 1, making these changes:

1. Address the memo to **Jane Rankin, Past President.**

2. In ¶ 2, substitute "serve on" for the word "chair."

Half-page simplified memo

words

November 12, 19-- 4
TS

Eva Mendoza, Vice President 9
TS

Membership in the Executives Club 16
TS

The challenge of finding new members to insure our Club's future 29
strength and vitality is an ever-present one. To attract new mem- 42
bers, we need a membership committee that is aware of our unusual 55
services and sensitive to our special needs. 65
DS

I should like you to chair our membership committee for this next 78
year. Your major concern will be to help develop a forceful mem- 91
bership drive and to assist with its implementation. I hope you 104
will agree to chair this prime committee. Please accept. 117
TS

Bella Herrera, M.D., President 123
TS

njc 124

Problem 3
plain full sheet

Type page 2 of the memo shown in the model at the right; allow 8 spaces between columns of table.

Problem 4
plain full sheet

If time permits, retype Problem 2, but address the memo to **Michael Fulton, Publicity Department.**

Page 2 of simplified memo

1″ (begin on Line 7)

Eva Mendoza, Vice President 6
Page 2 7
November 14, 19-- 11
SS TS

To help you in organizing the membership committee, I suggest that 24
you ask the following Club members to accept responsibility for 37
recruiting persons in the designated areas: 46
DS

Jaye Bozurich	Legal professions	52
Tomas Borges	Health professions	59
Howard Green	Industrial organizations	66
Chigasu Wakui	Financial institutions	74

DS

Each of these people is interested in the growth of the Club and 87
should be of great assistance to you in the membership drive. 99
Please let me know the results of your contacts with them. 111
TS

Bella Herrera, M.D., President 117
TS

njc 118

94c ▶ 30
Build sustained production skill: letters

Time Schedule

Planning and preparing .... 4′
Production timing .... 20′
Proofreading; computing *g–pram* .... 6′

Type each letter problem in 92c, page 155, as directed there. Use a separate letterhead [LM pp. 29–34] or plain full sheet for each letter. Make notes of needed directions. If you complete all letters before time is called, start over on plain sheets. When time is called, proofread your letters; circle all errors; determine *g–pram* (total words ÷ 20). Compare *g–pram* with your letter–copy rate of 94b. Try to determine reasons for rate difference, if any.

95

95a ▶ 5
Conditioning practice

Follow standard directions, p. 143.

alphabet	1	Jeff Page may make them move the quaint old zinc box to the warehouse.
fig/sym	2	Your order (No. 413-9570) was received May 26 and was shipped June 18.
shift lock/ long reaches	3	Bring a minimum number of NYLON flags to the hymn dedication ceremony.
fluency	4	In the fury of the fight, she made the eight quick field goals for us.

| 1 | 2 | 3 | 4 | 5 | 6 | 7 | 8 | 9 | 10 | 11 | 12 | 13 | 14 |

95b ▶ 5
Improve punctuation skill: related learning

full sheet; 1″ top margin; 70-space line

Type as directed in 81c, p. 135.

PUNCTUATION GUIDES, concluded

35. Apostrophe: To show possession, add the *apostrophe and s* to (a) a singular noun and (b) a plural noun which does not end in *s*.

36. Apostrophe: To show possession, add the *apostrophe and s* to a proper name of one syllable which ends in *s*.

37. Apostrophe: To show possession, add *only the apostrophe* after (a) plural nouns ending in *s* and (b) a proper name of more than one syllable which ends in *s* or *z*.

38. Apostrophe: To indicate *joint or common possession* by two or more persons, *add the apostrophe* after the last noun in the series. *Note:* Separate possession by two or more persons is indicated by adding the possessive to each of the nouns; as, the *manager's* and the *treasurer's* reports.

learn 35. The boy's bicycle was found, but the women's shoes are missing.
apply Childrens toys are on sale; buy the girls bicycle.

learn 36. Please pay Jones's bill for $575 today.
apply Was it Bess' hat, Ross' shoes, or Chris' watch that was lost?

learn 37. The girls' counselor will visit the Adams' home.
apply Anthony Kalaus home is near the Retired Veterans Society Building.

learn 38. I read about Lewis and Clark's expedition.
apply Phils and Jeans bicycles were left at my aunt's and uncle's home.
(separate possession) (common possession)

95c ▶ 40
Measure production skill: letters

Time Schedule

Planning and preparing .... 4′
Production timing .... 20′
Proofreading; computing *n–pram* .... 6′
Follow–up practice .... 10′

Type the letter problems on page 159 on separate letterheads [LM pp. 35–40] or plain full sheets. Correct all errors. Proofread with care. Deduct 15 words from total words typed for each uncorrected error; divide remainder by 20 to determine *n–pram* (net production rate a minute.) In time that remains, make corrections needed to make letters acceptable; if necessary, retype any letters which are unacceptable on plain sheets.

190

190a ▶ 5 Conditioning practice

Use standard directions given in 188a, page 301.

alphabet 1 Jack Bingham and Wanda Overly fixed spicy pizzas for the racquet club.
figures 2 Jane typed the figures 648, 209, 75, and 31 very quickly on all tests.
sa/as 3 say ask sale pass same mask sack mast essay least sails assign passage
fluency 4 The city may pay us a small profit for six of the worn maps and signs.

| 1 | 2 | 3 | 4 | 5 | 6 | 7 | 8 | 9 | 10 | 11 | 12 | 13 | 14 |

190b ▶ 13 Compose at the typewriter

plain sheet; 70-space line

1. Type the ¶ as shown.
2. Compose a ¶ as directed in the copy at the right.
3. Edit your copy for accuracy and clarity using proofreader's marks.

words

In your typewriting classes, you have had experience with several types 14
of correspondence--letters on regular stationery, letters having special fea- 29
tures, and interoffice memos. While typing these various styles, you doubtless 45
developed a preference for typing one form rather than another. You are to 60
compose a short paragraph setting forth the features of the form of corre- 75
spondence you PREFER typing. Indicate as part of your composition the reasons 91
behind your preference. If there is a form you would NOT use in your office, 107
explain why. 109

190c ▶ 12 Type a memo about news releases

half-page standard interoffice memo [LM p. 95]

1. Type the memo.
2. Proofread, circle errors.
3. As time permits, study the content of the memo and the form of the model below; discuss procedures with your teacher.
4. Keep your copy for reference in 190d.

words

TO: ALL OFFICE PERSONNEL 4

FROM: Sharon Demetsky, Communications Specialist 12

DATE: November 21, 19-- 15

SUBJECT: Preparation of News Releases 21

News releases announce items of special interest. They should 34
always designate a place and time for release of the news. Use the 47
following guides for typing news releases: 55

1. Begin the message 2" from the top of the page (or a TS below the 69
last line of the printed heading). 76

2. Use 1-inch side margins; indent 5 spaces and start the first para- 90
graph with the city and date of release; DS the body. 101

3. Type the writer's name a TS below the message. 111

4. Type the reference initials, when used, a DS below the name. 124

jsm 125

Model of news release

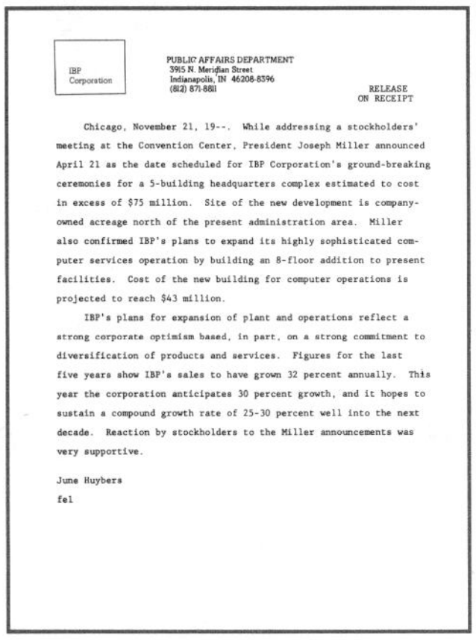

IBP Corporation

PUBLIC AFFAIRS DEPARTMENT
3915 N. Meridian Street
Indianapolis, IN 46208-8396
(812) 871-8811

RELEASE
ON RECEIPT

Chicago, November 21, 19--. While addressing a stockholders' meeting at the Convention Center, President Joseph Miller announced April 21 as the date scheduled for IBP Corporation's ground-breaking ceremonies for a 5-building headquarters complex estimated to cost in excess of $75 million. Site of the new development is company-owned acreage north of the present administration area. Miller also confirmed IBP's plans to expand its highly sophisticated computer services operation by building an 8-floor addition to present facilities. Cost of the new building for computer operations is projected to reach $43 million.

IBP's plans for expansion of plant and operations reflect a strong corporate optimism based, in part, on a strong commitment to diversification of products and services. Figures for the last five years show IBP's sales to have grown 32 percent annually. This year the corporation anticipates 30 percent growth, and it hopes to sustain a compound growth rate of 25-30 percent well into the next decade. Reaction by stockholders to the Miller announcements was very supportive.

June Huybers

fel

93c ▶ 30 Build production skill: letters

plain full sheets; block style; standard 6-inch line; date on Line 19

1. Type a 3′ writing on the letter to establish a base rate. If you finish before time is called, start over.

2. Determine *gwam*; to this rate add 8 *gwam* to set a new goal. Divide the goal rate by 4 and note the ¼′ checkpoints for guided writings.

3. On another plain sheet, type three 1′ guided writings on the opening parts of the letter and ¶1 at your goal rate. Type the dateline near the top of the sheet; leave proper spacing between letter parts. DS after each writing.

4. Repeat Step 3, using ¶2 and the closing lines of the letter.

5. Type another 3′ writing on the complete letter. Try to maintain or exceed your new goal rate for this writing. Determine *gwam* and compare it with the rate you attained in Step 1.

6. If time permits, type this letter from your teacher's dictation. Type the date on Line 19.

	words in parts	gwam 3′
June 17, 19-- | Ms. Jan Patterson | 1834 Constitution Place	11	4
Columbus, OH 43085-7724 | Dear Ms. Patterson	20	7
(¶ 1) We want to be sure to give you credit, but not the kind	11	10
of credit which is usually given by a credit manager. We	23	14
mean the kind of credit which is defined by Webster as "praise	35	18
or approval to which a person is entitled."	44	21
(¶ 2) The way you have handled your account with us during the	11	25
past year certainly merits our praise. We appreciate the	23	29
promptness with which you pay your account. So we want to	35	33
say thank you and "give credit where credit is due." It is	47	37
a pleasure to be of service to you.	54	40
Sincerely yours | Michael Poston, Credit Manager | 1we	10	43

94

94a ▶ 5 Conditioning practice

Follow standard directions, p. 143.

alphabet	1	Polly Fazzio bought six jacquard weaving looms at the market in Paris.
figures	2	Please reserve rooms 210, 563, and 987 for the September 4 conference.
shift keys	3	R. H. Smith, of McNeil, Paine, and Winn Company, is visiting in Akron.
fluency	4	The endowment may entitle them to the eighty ancient enamel ornaments.

| 1 | 2 | 3 | 4 | 5 | 6 | 7 | 8 | 9 | 10 | 11 | 12 | 13 | 14 |

94b ▶ 15 Build production skill: letters

plain full sheets

1. Type a 10′ writing on Style letter 4, p. 153. If you complete the letter before time is called, start over on a new plain sheet.

2. Proofread your copy and circle all errors; determine *g-pram* (total words typed ÷ minutes typed). Record your letter-copy rate.

190d ▶ 20

Learn to type news releases

Problem 1

Type the news release shown at the right DS on a plain sheet with 1" side margins. Type the RELEASE notation at the right margin, beginning on Line 9. Proofread your copy, using proofreaders marks to indicate corrections.

Problem 2

[LM p. 97]

Type a final copy from your own rough draft on a news release form; correct errors.

IBP Corporation

PUBLIC AFFAIRS DEPARTMENT
3915 N. Meridian Street
Indianapolis, IN 46208-8396
(812) 871-8811

words

RELEASE 2
ON RECEIPT 4

Chicago, Nobember ~~15~~ [21], 19--. [While] ~~A~~ddressing stock holders 16
~~convention~~ [meeting] in the Convention Center, ~~Chairman~~ [President] Joseph Miller 27
announced April 21 as the scheduled date for IBP Corporations 40
ground-breaking ceremony [ies] for a 5-building headquarter [s complex] esti- 54
mated to cost [in excess of] $75 million. Cite of the new developement is 68
[company-owned] acreage north of the present [administration] area. Miller also confirmed 86
IBP's plans to expand ~~their~~ [its] highly sophisticated computer 97
services [operation] by ~~erecting~~ [building] an 8 floor additon to ~~current~~ [present] facilities. 112
Cost of the [new] building for computer operations is ~~expected~~ [projected] to 125
reach $43 million. 129

IPB's plans for expansion of plant and operations 139
reflects a strong ~~corporation~~ [corporate] optimism based in part on a 150
strong committment to diversification of products and ser- 162
vices. Figures for the five last years show IBP's sales 173
to have ~~risen~~ [grown] 32 per cent annualy. This year the corporation 186
anticipates 20 [3] percent [growth,] and it hopes to sustain a compound 199
growth rate of 25-30 percent [well] into the next decade. Stock- 212
holder reactions to the Miller announcements was ~~highly~~ [very] 222
supportive. 225

[TS]

Ms. June Huybers [DS] 228
fel 229

191

191a ▶ 5

Conditioning practice

Use standard directions given in 188a, page 103.

alphabet 1 Bev Paquette and Jack Foley wrote exams on cases dealing with zoology.
figures 2 Sales reached $1,287,469.30, an increase of 34% for the third quarter.
op/po 3 top pot rope port open post opus poor cope pool copper reports copiers
fluency 4 They may risk half of their profit when they bid on the downtown firm.

| 1 | 2 | 3 | 4 | 5 | 6 | 7 | 8 | 9 | 10 | 11 | 12 | 13 | 14 |

93

93a ▶ 5
Conditioning practice

Follow standard directions, p. 143.

alphabet 1 Six famous major game plays were quarterback dives into the end zones.
figures 2 Nearly 1,651 girls and 738 boys are enrolled in typing Sections 29-40.
fingers 3, 4 3 Polly saw Paula and Zoa jump on the yellow polo pony down by the quay.
fluency 4 They may make a big profit when they dismantle the old dory for Dixie.

| 1 | 2 | 3 | 4 | 5 | 6 | 7 | 8 | 9 | 10 | 11 | 12 | 13 | 14 |

93b ▶ 15
Improve punctuation skill: related learning

full sheet; 1″ top margin; 70-space line

Type as directed in 81c, p. 135.

PUNCTUATION GUIDES, continued

27. Quotation marks: Use single quotation marks (the apostrophe) *to indicate* a quotation within a quotation.

28. Semicolon: Use a semicolon *to separate* two or more independent clauses in a compound sentence when the conjunction is omitted.

29. Semicolon: Use a semicolon *to separate* independent clauses when they are joined by a conjunctive adverb (*however, consequently*, etc.).

30. Semicolon: Use a semicolon *to separate* a series of phrases or clauses (especially if they contain commas) that are introduced by a colon.

31. Semicolon: Place the semicolon *outside* a closing quotation mark; the period, *inside* the quotation mark.

32. Apostrophe: Use the apostrophe as a *symbol* for *feet* in billings or tabulations or as a *symbol* for *minutes*. (The quotation mark may be used as a *symbol* for *inches* or *seconds*.)

33. Apostrophe: Use the apostrophe as a symbol to indicate the omission of letters or figures (as in contractions).

34. Apostrophe: Use the *apostrophe and s* to form the plural of most figures, letters, and words (6's, A's, five's). In market quotations, form the plural of figures by the addition of *s* only.

learn 27. He said, "We must take, as Frost suggests, the 'different road.'"
apply She wrote, "We must have, as Tillich said, the courage to be."

learn 28. To be critical is easy; to be constructive is not so easy.
apply We cannot live on past glory we must strive to improve.

learn 29. They did not follow directions; consequently, they got lost.
apply I cannot help you however, I know someone who can.

learn 30. Our sales were: 1982, $3,450,289; 1983, $4,129,386.
apply The new officers are: Dee O'Brien, President Jay Ford, Secretary.

learn 31. Mrs. Zane spoke on "Building Speed"; Mr. Paul, on "Accuracy."
apply He said, "Don't use sarcasm;" she said, "I try to be constructive".

learn 32. Please deliver ten 2″ × 4″ × 10′ unfinished fir to my address.
apply He ran the mile in 3 min. 54 sec. The room is 12 ft. 6 in. × 18 ft. 10 in.

learn 33. Each July 4th, we try to renew the "Spirit of '76."
apply Use the apostrophe in these contractions: isnt, cant, youll.

learn 34. Your f's look like 7's. Boston Fund 4s are due in 1996.
apply Cross your ts and dot your is. Sell United 6's this week.

191b ▶ 20
Type a memo about telegraphic messages

full-page memo form [LM p. 99]

1. Type the memo; proofread, circle errors.

2. As time permits, study the content of the memo and the form of the model below; discuss procedures with your teacher.

3. Keep your copy for reference in 191c.

Model of phoned telegram

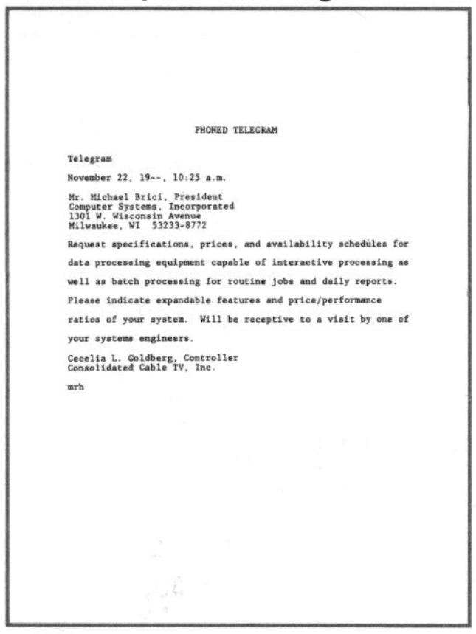

PHONED TELEGRAM

Telegram

November 22, 19--, 10:25 a.m.

Mr. Michael Brici, President
Computer Systems, Incorporated
1301 W. Wisconsin Avenue
Milwaukee, WI 53233-8772

Request specifications, prices, and availability schedules for data processing equipment capable of interactive processing as well as batch processing for routine jobs and daily reports. Please indicate expandable features and price/performance ratios of your system. Will be receptive to a visit by one of your systems engineers.

Cecelia L. Goldberg, Controller
Consolidated Cable TV, Inc.

mrh

words

TO: Communications Personnel 5
FROM: Tonda Gainey, Supervisor 10
DATE: November 22, 19-- 13
SUBJECT: Telegraphic Messages 17

Many messages are telephoned to Western Union for transmission. 30
When a message is to be phoned, it is typed on plain paper using a 43
60-space line. Follow these guides for typing messages to be phoned 57
to Western Union: 60

1. Center heading (PHONED TELEGRAM) 2 inches from top of sheet. 73
2. Type class of service (Telegram, Night Letter, Mailgram, 85
   Phone-A-Gram) at left margin a TS below heading. 95
3. Type name of account to be charged (if not that of sender) at left 109
   margin a DS below class of service. (omitted in illustration) 116
4. A DS below class of service (or name of account charged, when 129
   used), type date and time message was filed. 138
5. A DS below date, type complete address of addressee (including 151
   phone number if known) in block form SS. 159
6. DS; type message in block style DS. 167
7. DS below message and type name and title of sender, followed on 181
   next line by company name. 186
8. Type your initials for reference at left margin a DS below com- 199
   pany name. 201

Prepare one carbon copy for Accounting Department records and 213
additional copies as required for other uses. 222

mos 223

191c ▶ 15
Learn to type telegraphic messages

2 plain full sheets

Problem 1

Type the phoned telegram shown at the right; proofread, circle errors.

Problem 2

Retype Problem 1 as directed, but change the time to **10:40 a.m.** and address the message to:

Mr. Steven Ellis, President
Kirkwood Data Equipment, Inc.
3801 N. Lindell Boulevard
St. Louis, MO 63108-4047

PHONED TELEGRAM 3
TS

Telegram 5
DS
November 22, 19--, 10:25 a.m. 11
DS
Mr. Michael Brici, President 17
Computer Systems, Incorporated 23
1301 W. Wisconsin Avenue 28
Milwaukee, WI 53233-8772 33
DS
Request specifications, prices, and availability schedules for informa- 47
tion processing equipment capable of interactive processing as well as 61
batch processing for routine jobs and daily reports. Please indicate 75
expandable features and price/performance ratios of your system. Will 89
be receptive to a visit by one of your systems engineers. 100
DS
Cecelia L. Goldberg, Controller 106
Consolidated Cable TV, Inc. 111
DS
mrh 112

92c ▶ 30
Build production skill: letters

[LM pp. 23-28] or plain full sheets; block style; open punctuation; standard 6-inch line; use Placement Table, p. 143

Problem 1

words
April 25, 19--| Mr. Thomas Lasally, President| Lasally Enterprises, Inc.| 230 15
E. 16th Avenue| Denver, CO 80203-5291| Dear Mr. Lasally 26
(¶ 1) This letter is typed with a standard 6-inch line. An increasing number of 41
business firms are beginning to use the standard line for all letters whether 57
they be short, average, or long. (¶ 2) As you can see, the standard line gives 71
good placement appearance. Its use results in increased letter production 86
rates because the typist does not have to spend time resetting margins for 101
letters of varying lengths. (¶ 3) We recommend that all letters be typed with 116
the standard line. It is still another way to reduce the high cost of producing 132
business letters. Sincerely yours | Ms. Mercedes Hernandez | Com- 145
munications Consultant| xx (110) 150/**170**

Problem 2

April 30, 19--| Ms. Mercedes Hernandez| Communications Consultant| Office 14
Efficiency, Inc. | 1300 Van Ness Avenue, Suite 1101 | San Francisco, 27
CA 94109-4305| Dear Ms. Hernandez 34
(¶ 1) Your recent letter convinced us to try the standard 6-inch line for busi- 49
ness letters. During the next month, all our letters will be typed with this 64
standard line length. We'll measure production rates and compare them with 79
our past performance. (¶ 2) We'd like to contract with your company to do a 94
study of our letter production costs. It may be that we have overlooked some 109
important ways to reduce the cost of producing the letters we write. (¶ 3) 123
Will you please give me some idea of the cost of a study of the type I am 138
proposing. Sincerely yours| Thomas Lasally, President| xx (106) 149/**176**

Problem 3

Note: Job titles in letter address and closing lines may be typed on the line with the name or on the line immediately below the name. Usually, the job title is placed to give good balance to the lines.

May 3, 19--| Mr. Thomas Lasally, President| Lasally Enterprises, Inc.| 230 E. 15
16th Avenue| Denver, CO 80203-5291| Dear Mr. Lasally 25
(¶ 1) A study of your typewritten communications activities will require on- 39
site study involving about four days. (¶ 2) During the four days we are with 54
you, our staff becomes aware of the kind and volume of your typing activi- 69
ties. We observe and study work procedures used as the typewriter is oper- 84
ated. We look at production in terms of the acceptability of the copy pro- 99
duced as well as the rates at which it is produced. Both are important fac- 114
tors of production costs. As a final step, we spend two days retraining your 129
typists. We use standard time data for each typing operation. At the end of 145
the two-day period, each typist will have a good idea as to improvement 159
needed and steps to take in order to make the improvement we suggest. (¶ 3) 174
Upon our return to San Francisco, we'll prepare a detailed written report of 189
our study for you. It will include step-by-step procedures to follow to attain 205
the production-cost savings that our study reveals can be made. Then, after 220
a 30-day period, one of our staff will revisit your office to be sure the 235
suggestions we make are being put into practice. (¶ 4) Our guarantee is that 250
within six months your savings in letter production costs will more than 264
cover the cost of our study. I'll telephone you next week to discuss costs and, 280
if you agree to the study, to arrange a suitable starting time. Sincerely yours 297
| Ms. Mercedes Hernandez| Communications Consultant| xx (267) 307/**327**

191d ▶ 10
Improve language arts
plain sheet; 70-space line

Type the ¶s shown at right. As you type, select the correct word from the words in parentheses. If time permits, proofread your copy, mark errors for correction, and type the ¶s from your corrected copy. Correct errors you make as you type.

words

At the (resent; recent) meeting of the school (bored; board), 9
the (absence; abcense) of the high school (principal; principle) was 18
noticed. It was also noticed that (fewer; less) parents than usual 30
attended. The (affect; effect) of the new tax bill was the (principle; 42
principal) topic of discussion. 46

One of the members asked, "Why (don't; doesn't) the bank 56
lend us the money?" The (precedent; president) replied: "(Its; 66
It's) officers are considering (there; their; they're) position at a 75
meeting tonight, but we must consider the possibility of a federal 88
(lone; loan), (to; too; two). As a matter of (principal; principle), some 96
(board; bored) members want to avoid a federal (loan; lone)." 105

192

192a ▶ 5
Conditioning practice
Use standard directions given in 188a, page 301.

alphabet 1 Victor Klubman played squash on the new courts with famous Jinx Gonzo.
figures 2 Invoices 10579 and 29384, covering recent purchases, were sent by Pam.
tr/rt 3 trek cart true part tried party extra alert entry short trends departs
fluency 4 A firm for which she works paid for title to all the land by the lake.

| 1 | 2 | 3 | 4 | 5 | 6 | 7 | 8 | 9 | 10 | 11 | 12 | 13 | 14 |

192b ▶ 45
Build sustained production: memos, news releases, telegrams

Time schedule

Preparation .... 5′
Timed production .... 30′
Final check; compute *n-pram* .... 10′

1. Make a list of problems to be typed:
p. 302, 188c, Problem 1
p. 303, 189c, Problem 2
p. 305, 190d, Problem 1
p. 306, 191c, Problem 1

2. Arrange memo form [LM p. 101], plain sheets, and carbon paper (for 1 cc of each problem).

3. Type for 30′ when directed to begin; follow directions given for each problem; correct all errors neatly, proofreading carefully before removing a problem from the typewriter.

4. Compute *n-pram*; then turn in completed work, arranged as listed in Step 1.

193

193a ▶ 5
Conditioning practice
Use standard directions given in 188a, page 301.

alphabet 1 David Quigley has won six big prizes at the Jackson Creek summer fair.
figures 2 Checks were written for $985.63 and $742.10 for our business expenses.
oi/io 3 oils ions foil lion coils scion coins radio avoid unions voices onions
fluency 4 He may go into the city by auto to sign a statement for their auditor.

| 1 | 2 | 3 | 4 | 5 | 6 | 7 | 8 | 9 | 10 | 11 | 12 | 13 | 14 |

92

92a ▶ 5 Conditioning practice

Follow standard directions, p. 143.

alphabet 1 Jack Meier brought a dozen quarts of oxtail soup to the preview party.
figures 2 By 9:45 a.m., only 203 of the 1,678 students could get to the college.
adjacent keys 3 Rewards received for services rendered are related to effort expended.
fluency 4 She may cycle to the city to go to the ancient chapel by the big lake.

| 1 | 2 | 3 | 4 | 5 | 6 | 7 | 8 | 9 | 10 | 11 | 12 | 13 | 14 |

92b ▶ 15 Improve punctuation skill: related learning

full sheet; 1" top margin; 70-space line

Type as directed in 81c, p. 135.

PUNCTUATION GUIDES, continued

20. Parentheses: Use parentheses *to enclose* figures that follow spelled-out amounts when added clarity or emphasis is needed.

21. Parentheses: Use parentheses *to enclose* a name and date used as a reference.

22. Underline: Use the underline *to indicate* titles of books and names of magazines and newspapers. (Titles may be typed in ALL CAPS without the underline.)

23. Underline: Use the underline (or use quotation marks) to *call attention* to special words or phrases. *Note:* Use a continuous underline unless each word is to be considered separately.

24. Quotation marks: Use quotation marks *to enclose* direct quotations. *Note:* When a question mark applies to the entire sentence, it is typed outside the quotation marks.

25. Quotation marks: Use quotation marks *to enclose* titles of articles, poems, songs, television programs, and unpublished works like dissertations and theses.

26. Quotation marks: Use quotation marks *to enclose* special words or phrases used for emphasis or coined words (words not in dictionary usage).

learn 20. The note was for the sum of five hundred dollars ($500).
apply The balance in your account is one hundred fifty-two dollars $152.

learn 21. Purposeful repetition helps build skill (Robinson et al., 1979).
apply The speed and error scores are shown in Table 4 Crawford, 1982.

learn 22. The book Learning How to Learn was reviewed in Harper's.
apply I read the book review of Alternative Futures in the New York Times.

learn 23. She asked us to spell separate, privilege, and stationery.
apply He misspelled steel, occur, and weird.

learn 24. Jane asked, "When did you do this work?"
learn Was it Emerson who said, "To have a friend is to be one"?

apply He quoted the statement, The electorate is the jury writ large.
apply Did Shakespeare say, All the world is a stage?

learn 25. The musical "The Next Fifty Years" got rave reviews.
learn I read the poem "The Road Not Taken" by Robert Frost.

apply The children enjoyed watching the TV series Star Trek.
apply Bing Crosby was famous for his rendition of White Christmas.

learn 26. My problem is that I have "limited resources" and "unlimited wants."
apply His speech was liberally sprinkled with you know's.

193b ▶ 45
Measure production skill: memos, news releases, telegrams

[LM pp. 101–104]

Time schedule

Preparation .... 5'
Timed production ...... 30'
Final check; compute *n-pram* .... 10'

1. Arrange supplies (forms, plain paper, and carbon paper).
2. Make 1 cc of each problem; address envelopes marked **COMPANY MAIL** where appropriate.
3. Type for 30' when directed to begin; correct all errors neatly.
4. Compute *n-pram*; then turn in completed work arranged as listed.

Problem 1
Standard memo on half sheet

words

TO: Joseph Chi, Maintenance Engineer FROM: Norman Scholtze, President 12
DATE: November 26, 19-- SUBJECT: Building Maintenance 19

(¶ 1) At its last meeting, the Board of Directors decided that a vigorous program 34
of building maintenance should be launched immediately in our Central Area. 49
A strong case was made for the belief that timely maintenance can reduce both 65
monthly operating expenses and eventual replacement costs. 77

(¶ 2) Because any increase in maintenance activity will affect the workers and 93
the materials under your control, please report to me at once the number of 108
salaried and hourly employees now in our maintenance service. 120

jcr 121/**130**

Problem 2
News release on company form

RELEASE 1
ON RECEIPT 3

(¶ 1) Chicago, November 26, 19--. A new district office to be located in the 17
Southwest Metroplex of Dallas/Fort Worth will open early in the first quarter of 33
next year according to an announcement by Joseph Miller, President and Chief 48
Operations Officer of IBP Corporation. Speaking before the Metroplex 62
Chamber of Commerce, President Miller said the decision to locate in the 77
Dallas/Forth Worth area was based upon a combination of very favorable 91
factors. 93

(¶ 2) A highly strategic geographic location, extremely advanced com- 105
munications facilities, and an abundance of resources--both physical and 120
human--were significant considerations in reaching a corporate decision favor- 135
ing this location. Particularly impressive, too, said President Miller, was a 151
positive community attitude toward corporate enterprises. Company surveys 166
revealed a supportive local government, a favorable tax structure, and a vigor- 182
ous work force--all combining to create a local climate extremely desirable for 198
corporate investment. 202

(¶ 3) IBP has high expectations for rapid growth of its business through this new 217
district office. Marva Katona mab 224

Problem 3
Phoned telegram on plain sheet

Problem 4
Simplified memo on half sheet

If time permits, retype Problem 1 as a simplified memo on a plain half sheet.

PHONED TELEGRAM Telegram November 26, 19--, 11:15 a.m. Miss Joni Lewis, 15
President Space Management, Inc. 206 Smithfield Avenue Pittsburgh, 29
PA 15222-0376 32

Interested in having you submit proposals for major office renovations built 47
around the open plan concept. Would like to have offices landscaped for 61
maximum flexibility, productivity, and economy with accoustical panels and 76
movable partitions used wherever possible. Request you send facilities consul- 92
tant to discuss our project and to provide estimates. 103

Brenda Guerra, Office Manager Consolidated Cable TV, Inc. erg 116

oei

OFFICE EFFICIENCY, INC.
EXPERTS IN OFFICE RESEARCH

1300 VAN NESS AVENUE, SUITE 1101 • SAN FRANCISCO, CA 94109-4305
TEL: (415) 823-4500

	All lines started at left margin	words: parts	total
Dateline	April 25, 19-- Line 16 4 line spaces (3 blank lines)	3	3
Letter address	Mrs. June Roth, General Manager	9	9
	Southern California Citrus Assn.	17	17
	1842 El Cajon Boulevard	22	22
	San Diego, CA 92103-4261	27	27
Salutation	Dear Mrs. Roth	30	30
Body of letter	This letter is typed in the block style. All lines start at		
	the left margin. The block style is rapidly becoming the most	12	42
	frequently used business letter style. Its advantage is that	25	55
	the mechanical process of indenting opening lines, paragraphs,	37	67
	and closing lines is eliminated. This practice saves typing	50	80
	time as well as space.	62	92
		67	97
	Note, too, that open punctuation is used. The colon is omit-	79	109
	ted after the salutation, and the comma is omitted after the	91	121
	complimentary close. Another time-saving feature we recommend	104	134
	is to type only the initials of the typist for reference when	116	146
	the dictator's name is typed in the closing lines.	127	157
	As you can see, the block style letter gives good placement	139	169
	appearance. Because many extra typing strokes and motions are	151	181
	eliminated, the use of this letter style does help to increase	164	194
	letter production rates. It is the letter style we recommend	176	206
	for use in the business office. Try it. I'm sure you will	188	218
	like it.	190	220
Complimentary close	Sincerely yours	3	224
Signature	*Mercedes Hernandez*		
Typed name	Ms. Mercedes Hernandez	8	228
Official title	Communications Consultant	13	233
Reference initials	eh	14	234

Style letter 4: block style with open punctuation and standard 6″ line

unit **37** lessons 194-197

Improve/measure basic skills

Learning goals

1. To improve keystroking skill in typing special reaches.
2. To improve straight-copy typing on comparison writings.
3. To improve keystroking skill on straight-copy paragraphs.
4. To prepare for measurement on office communications—letters, memos, news releases, and telegrams.

Machine adjustments

1. Paper guide at *0*.
2. Ribbon control to type on top half of ribbon.
3. Margin sets: 70-space line for sentence and ¶ activities; as required for problems.
4. Spacing: SS sentence drills; DS ¶ activities; as directed for problems.
5. Tab sets: for 5-space ¶ indention; as needed for problems.

194

194a ▶ 5 Conditioning practice

each line twice SS (slowly, then faster); DS between 2-line groups; if time permits, retype selected lines

alphabet 1 Jayne Vazilio had to quote fixed prices for the bulk goods we sampled.
figures 2 The sheep ranch was divided into tracts of 290, 385, 74, and 61 acres.
long words 3 Our executive committee will have exceptionally difficult assignments.
fluency 4 The workers for a coal firm in town own the dory and dock at the lake.

| 1 | 2 | 3 | 4 | 5 | 6 | 7 | 8 | 9 | 10 | 11 | 12 | 13 | 14 |

194b ▶ 15 Improve technique: keystroking

each line twice SS (slowly, then faster); DS between drill groups; as time permits, select lines for added drill practice

Technique cues

- quiet hands
- finger-reach action
- wrists low, relaxed
- quick, sharp keystrokes
- down-and-in thumb motion on space bar
- keep carriage or element moving

Rows

3d 1 rope pipe trip your were upper power erupt tripe porter totter rewrote
1st 2 vex numb cave zany many zinc vicar brazen vacant banana boxcar bonanza
all 3 Your brazen porter rewrote our vacation plans for a bonanza cave trip.

Fingers

1st 4 gun hung brunt bunny ghost humble rubber throng hungry grumble nurture
2d 5 kids deed deck cede kind died idea creed kicked decide credit decisive
3d/4th 6 pop was lap sax pool saws plow soap allow lasso assess opposed swallow

Adjacent keys

op/tr 7 opera option optimum oppress optimist travel trust trial tropics treat
io/re 8 prior folio violin biology pious pioneer record revolt remorse retrace
ui/we 9 ruin bruise cruise suite quickly weary power welcome answer grower wed

Long reaches

ce/my 10 once celery deceive censor secede roomy army mystery mythical mystique
rv/un 11 carver marvel harvest curvacious lung tune under sundry bundle plunder
br/ny 12 break umbrella ambrosia breeze sobriety nylon homonym symphony harmony

Sentences

1st row 13 Branch Zabo maximized his time by coaching nine community music clubs.
3d row 14 Polly Powers worked part time at three theaters owned by young actors.
double letters 15 Annette Boon was successful all week in meeting assorted office needs.

| 1 | 2 | 3 | 4 | 5 | 6 | 7 | 8 | 9 | 10 | 11 | 12 | 13 | 14 |

91

91a ▶ 5 Conditioning practice

Follow standard directions, p. 143.

alphabet 1 A big Japanese yawl's mizzenmast quivered and fell at the dock's exit.
figures 2 Jane typed 51 letters, 84 envelopes, 37 tags, 92 labels, and 60 cards.
space bar 3 If I do the work, she may spend a day with me and then go to the city.
fluency 4 The busy men may blend the buckeye with the big bush by the city lake.

| 1 | 2 | 3 | 4 | 5 | 6 | 7 | 8 | 9 | 10 | 11 | 12 | 13 | 14 |

91b ▶ 10 Improve punctuation skill: related learning

full sheet; 1" top margin
70–space line

Type as directed in 81c, p. 135.

PUNCTUATION GUIDES, continued

15. Hyphen: Use the hyphen *to join* compound adjectives preceding a noun they modify as a unit.

16. Hyphen: Use a hyphen *after* each word or figure in a series of words or figures that modify the same noun (suspended hyphenation).

17. Hyphen: Use the hyphen, when necessary *to divide* words at ends of lines or to show the syllables of a word.

18. Parentheses: Use parentheses *to enclose* parenthetical or explanatory matter and added information. (Commas or dashes may also be used.) *Note:* When parentheses apply to the entire sentence, the closing parenthesis is placed outside the closing punctuation, as above.

19. Parentheses: Use parentheses *to enclose* identifying letters or figures in lists.

learn 15. The good-natured teacher read books on the best-seller list.
apply The out of bounds catch stopped our first down drive.

learn 16. Please check the rates on first-, second-, and third-class mail.
apply All 6, 7, and 8 foot boards were used during the 10 day period.

learn 17. The syllables of hallucination are hal-lu-ci-na-tion.
apply Divide these words into syllables: penmanship, separate.

learn 18. Enclosed are the contracts (Exhibits A and B).
apply Nichols' memoirs published by Delta Pi Epsilon are interesting.

learn 19. She stressed these two factors: (1) speed and (2) control.
apply Check these techniques: 1 keystroking and 2 spacing.

91c ▶ 35 Learn skill applications: block style letter

Step 1
Learn letter style
plain full sheet

Type Style letter 4, p. 153, in block style with open punctuation as shown (words in body: 190).

Use the standard 6" line (see Placement Table, p. 143). Type the letter at rough-draft speed; x-out or strike over any errors.

Step 2
Proofread and make rough-draft corrections

Proofread the letter you typed in Step 1. Indicate by handwritten corrections any changes that you need to make in the copy. Use standard proofreader's marks to indicate the needed corrections.

Step 3
Build skill [LM pp. 21, 22]

Using your corrected rough-draft copy, retype the letter in block style. As you type, make the corrections indicated in your copy.

Correct any other errors you make as you retype the letter. Compare your copy with the style letter.

194c ▶ 10
Check language arts

1. Type each sentence, including the number. Select correct words from those given in parentheses; check results with your teacher.

2. Retype the sentences from your corrected copy.

1. Some project money was used to (rite, write) basic (lessens, lessons).
2. One (cite, site) was selected for reporting the (senses, census) data.
3. A (sealing, ceiling) for the price of farm goods is at (steak, stake).
4. We issued shares of new stock to (raise, raze) new (capitol, capital).
5. (Currant, current) plane fares are (to, too) high for extensive trips.
6. We (was, were) allowed to (hear, here) reports of the special meeting.

194d ▶ 20
Skill comparison: progressive straight copy

1. A 2′ writing on each ¶; compare *gwam*.

2. A 2′ writing on the slower ¶; determine *gwam*. **Goal:** To increase speed on the more difficult ¶.

3. Two 3′ writings on both ¶s combined; determine *gwam*; circle errors.

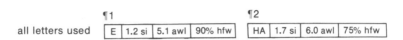

all letters used ¶1 | E | 1.2 si | 5.1 awl | 90% hfw | ¶2 | HA | 1.7 si | 6.0 awl | 75% hfw |

	gwam 2′	3′
Young people who have a keen liking for the world of business are	7	4
asked at times to choose at least one area or name one field in business	14	9
for which they can state a clear goal. This is often quite hard to do,	21	13
since very few young people have had enough contact with business courses	29	18
to make a sound choice. To be able to judge well all types of options,	36	22
it is good to talk to an astute business teacher or to a fine business	43	27
leader who can share some ideas about your future.	48	32
Those who counsel our young people in career planning declare some	7	36
amazement at the fact that so little is known by the aspiring business	14	41
leaders about the numerous facets of business. It is quite typical to	21	45
have students express an awareness of law, marketing, and accounting; but	28	50
few explore the vast fields of finance, utilities, economic forecasting,	35	55
or other very well-known fields in business. For anyone thinking about a	42	59
career in business, there are many exciting areas to be pursued.	49	64

gwam 2′ | 1 | 2 | 3 | 4 | 5 | 6 | 7 |
3′ | 1 | 2 | 3 | 4 | 5 |

195

195a ▶ 5
Conditioning practice

Use standard procedure given in 194a, page 309.

alphabet 1 Max and Zoe amazed a raucous crowd by jumping over the fences quickly.

figures 2 Yvonne lectured to groups numbering 59, 38, 206, and 147 respectively.

one-hand 3 limp ease loin mink nymph carves opinion swerve minimum regard retreat

fluency 4 The vivid theme given in the big play is a key theory for this author.

| 1 | 2 | 3 | 4 | 5 | 6 | 7 | 8 | 9 | 10 | 11 | 12 | 13 | 14 |

195b ▶ 20
Skill comparison: progressive straight copy

Retype 194d, above, as directed. **Goal:** Improved keystroking. Improve speed by 2 *gwam* on 2′ writings; reduce errors to no more than 6 on each 3′ writing.

90c ▶ 30

Measure production skill: letters

Time Schedule

Planning and preparing .... 4′
Production timing .... 20′
Proofreading; computing *n–pram* .... 6′

Type on a separate letterhead [LM pp. 17–20] or plain full sheet each letter shown below. Determine placement: See table, p. 143. Make notes of needed directions. Correct all errors.

If you complete the letters before time is called, start over on plain sheets. Proofread your work. Deduct 15 words from total words for each uncorrected error; divide remainder by 20 to determine *n-pram* (net production rate a minute).

Compare your *n-pram* with your *g-pram* of 89b. If your *n-pram* is much lower, you may need to try to improve your accuracy or give attention to your error correction skill.

modified block style; indented ¶s; mixed punctuation; correct errors

Problem 1

words	parts	total
March 17, 19-- | Mr. Robert King | Administrative Assistant | Salt Lake Supply	15	15
Company | 54 West South Temple | Salt Lake City, UT 84101-6531 | Dear	28	28
Mr. King:	30	30
(¶ 1) I should like to add to the suggestions I sent to you about proofreading.	15	45
Prevention or reduction of typing errors will reduce the time needed for the	30	60
detection and correction of typing errors. (¶ 2) How does a person prevent or	45	75
reduce typing errors as letters are typed, and as a consequence, increase let-	61	90
ter production rates? The first step is to try to keep your eyes on the copy	76	106
from which you are typing. In this way, you can avoid breaks in your typing	92	121
rhythm. Type with your fingers well curved and close to the keys; space	106	136
quickly after each word. When the bell rings, either finish the word you are	122	151
typing, if this can be done in a few keystrokes, or divide it with a hyphen at a	138	168
proper division point. Then make the return and start the new line im-	152	182
mediately. (¶ 3) These suggestions will increase your letter production rates.	167	197
They will help you reduce your typing errors and thus simplify the	181	210
proofreading process. Try them and see.	189	219
Sincerely yours, | Ms. Mercedes Hernandez | Communications Consultant | xx	13	232
(203)		255

Problem 2

words	parts	total
April 10, 19-- | Mr. Scott Sellwood, President | Portland Lumber Products, Inc.	15	15
| 432 Morrison, SW | Portland, OR 97204-3974 | Dear Mr. Sellwood:	27	27
(¶ 1) Planning for the future is the key element for the continuing success of	15	42
any business firm. To paraphrase Abraham Lincoln, you can't be sure of	29	56
getting there unless you determine in advance where it is you are going. (¶ 2)	44	71
When planning for the future of your company, the definition of goals and	59	86
objectives is crucial. Without that, it would not be clear when an opportunity	75	102
was being realized, nor would we know what to do in the face of endless op-	90	117
tions. (¶ 3) All this concern with the importance of planning is by way of in-	104	132
troducing you to our new publication, EFFECTIVE PLANNING. This book has	119	146
received rave reviews from all who have read it. The content of the book is	134	162
described in the enclosed brochure. I know you will want to order a copy for	150	177
yourself and other key executives in your company. It will be an investment	165	193
that will pay immediate dividends.	174	200
Sincerely yours, | Brad Bohnert | Publications Department | xx | Enclosure	13	213
(171)		224

195c ▶ 25 Prepare for measurement: correspondence on special-size stationery

1. Turn to the problems listed below:
page 285, 176b, Problem 2
page 286, 177b, Problem 2
page 287, 178c, Problem 2

2. Select for typing the problem on which you need most additional practice. Follow directions for the problem chosen; circle errors.

3. As time permits, repeat the procedures for other problems for which additional practice is needed.

Note: See LM pp. 105–108 for special-size stationery. For 177b, Problem 2, use half-sheet, short side up.

196

196a ▶ 5 Conditioning practice

Use standard procedure given in 194a, page 309.

alphabet 1 Sylvia Franz wore an exquisite blue jacket to the school dorm pageant.
figures 2 The four dealers reported sales of 84, 95, 207, and 163 new car units.
one-hand 3 rare fear upon junk care wear pump milk dread onion erase poplin craze
fluency 4 The key element of the statement is the big profit of the pencil firm.

| 1 | 2 | 3 | 4 | 5 | 6 | 7 | 8 | 9 | 10 | 11 | 12 | 13 | 14 |

196b ▶ 20 Improve speed/control

1. Two 1′ *speed* writings on each ¶; determine *gwam* on each writing.

2. Two 5′ *control* writings on both ¶s combined; determine *gwam*; circle errors.

all letters used | A | 1.5 si | 5.7 awl | 80% hfw

Text	gwam 1′	5′	
Some of our leading economic experts claim that the type and qual-	13	3	47
ity of life we shall share in the years ahead could very well depend	27	5	50
upon our skill as a nation in finding new sources of energy. There is	41	8	53
strong belief among our known experts that present sources of power are	56	11	55
really neither ample nor adequate to meet the vigorous demands now	69	14	58
required by this complex society. Current expert thought emphasizes	83	17	61
that truism that we have become a strong power-based society, using much	97	19	64
more energy in our daily affairs than we are able to replenish.	110	22	66
The fact that our present energy supplies continue to shrink and	13	25	69
are approaching seriously low levels tends to cause grave concern among	27	28	72
those who are interested in the quality of life that may be realized by	42	30	75
future generations. With energy costs increasing and with supplies of	56	33	77
fuel diminishing, all of us are faced with the problem of making big	70	36	80
adjustments in our way of living. There is a strong possibility that	84	39	83
this generation will be judged by the future ones in terms of how capa-	98	42	86
bly it coped with the big problem of energy and its distribution.	111	44	88

gwam 1′ | 1 | 2 | 3 | 4 | 5 | 6 | 7 | 8 | 9 | 10 | 11 | 12 | 13 | 14 |
5′ | 1 | 2 | 3 |

196c ▶ 25 Prepare for measurement: letters with special features

1. Turn to the problems listed below:
page 292, 181c, Problem 2
page 294, 182d, Problem 2
page 294, 183b
page 296, 184c

2. Select for typing the problem on which you need additional practice. Follow directions for the problem chosen; circle errors.

3. As time permits, repeat the procedures for other problems for which additional practice is needed.

Note: See LM p. 109 for government letterhead for 184c. Use plain full sheets for other problems.

89c ▶ 15
Improve punctuation skill: related learning

full sheet; 1" top margin; 70-space line

Type as directed in 81c, p. 135.

PUNCTUATION GUIDES, continued

10. Dash: Use a dash (a) for emphasis, (b) to indicate an abrupt change of thought, (c) to introduce the name of an author or a reference when it follows a direct quotation, and (d) for other special purposes. *Note:* For the dash, type two hyphens without space before or after.

11. Colon: Use a colon *to introduce* an enumeration or a listing.

12. Colon: Use a colon *to introduce* a question or a long direct quotation.

13. Colon: Use a colon *between* hours and minutes expressed in figures.

14. Hyphen: Use the hyphen *to join* compound numbers from twenty-one to ninety-nine.

learn 10. The icy road--slippery as a fish--made driving hazardous.
learn He was motivated by power--not freedom--in getting his way.
learn "Hitting the wrong key is like hitting me."--Armour.
learn "Well--er--ah," he stammered.

apply She said, "I can explain, at least I hope I can."
apply This vase, don't drop it, dates back to the Ming Dynasty.
apply "The tax cut may turn out to be only a scratch." Glasow.

learn 11. We need the following: a typewriter, a book, and paper.
apply She checked off the items to buy bread, butter, milk, and tea.

learn 12. The question is this: Are you typing with good techniques?
apply This is the question, Did you study for the test?

learn 13. I plan to arrive at 1:30 p.m.
apply United Flight 4 will leave at 8 15 a.m.

learn 14. The ages of the group ranged from twenty-three to seventy-six.
apply Type and spell these numbers: 42, 66, and 91.

90

90a ▶ 5
Conditioning practice

Follow standard directions, p. 143.

alphabet 1 Quincy had to jump over frozen ponds to get to those white lock boxes.
figures 2 Please total 1 and 2 and 38 and 94 and 75 and 62 and 50 and 48 and 10.
space bar 3 If they do the work for us, I may go to the lake and then to the city.
fluency 4 Fix the bicycle for the club, and she may pay both of us for the work.

| 1 | 2 | 3 | 4 | 5 | 6 | 7 | 8 | 9 | 10 | 11 | 12 | 13 | 14 |

90b ▶ 15
Build skill: letter parts

plain full sheets; 1½" margins

1. Four 1' writings on the opening parts (dateline through salutation) of Prob. 1, p. 151.

When you have typed through the salutation, DS, tab for the date, and retype the drill.

2. Four 1' writings on the closing parts (complimentary close through enclosure notation) of Prob. 2, p. 151.

When you have typed through the enclosure notation, DS, tab for complimentary close, and retype the drill.

3. On another sheet of paper, type a 3' writing on the body of the letter of Prob. 1, p. 151. Determine *gwam* by dividing total words typed by 3.

197

197a ▶ 5 Conditioning practice

Use standard procedure given in 194a, page 309.

alphabet	1	Maxine Quigley borrowed five parka jackets for zealous hockey players.
figures	2	There were 460 pliers, 382 wrenches, 75 rulers, and 19 locks in stock.
balanced-hand	3	She may visit the six towns to aid them to pay for half of their work.
fluency	4	They may work with other men and women to make fine elements for them.

| 1 | 2 | 3 | 4 | 5 | 6 | 7 | 8 | 9 | 10 | 11 | 12 | 13 | 14 |

197b ▶ 15 Measure straight-copy skill

two 5′ writings; determine *gwam*; circle errors

all letters used | A | 1.5 si | 5.7 awl | 80% hfw |

	gwam 5′	
Many young people who proclaim an interest in office work give the	3	52
impression that their prime target is to land that initial job--to find	5	55
a place where they can make good money. But what happens after the job	8	58
is secured usually is minimized. Yet, it is important to remember that	11	61
it is not just those qualities enabling one to obtain a job that must be	14	64
cultivated, but abilities crucial for advancement are equally important.	17	66
Those desirous of promotion in an office must learn early to pay	19	69
attention to details. While most of us are quite eager to absorb a	22	72
part of the big tasks that must be done, too many of us disdain those	25	74
smaller, less visible routines. Most office work, however, involves	28	77
taking care of many minor, generally bothersome, duties. Those workers	30	80
who handle the minutia well are those who will move ahead very quickly.	33	83
To merit maximum benefits while working in a business office, an	36	85
employee must be able to demonstrate the ability to follow through on	39	88
tasks assigned. It is most essential that workers show that they can	41	91
be depended upon to finish jobs given them even though some extra time	44	94
may be needed to finish all that is expected. A company will be quick	47	97
to recognize those who are strong in follow-through performance.	50	99

gwam 5′ | 1 | 2 | 3 |

197c ▶ 30 Prepare for measurement: communications of special types

1. Turn to the problems listed below:
- page 302, 188c, Problem 1
- page 303, 189c, Problem 1
- page 308, 193b, Problem 2
- page 306, 191c, Problem 1

2. Select for typing the problem on which you need additional practice. Follow directions for the problem chosen; circle errors.

3. As time permits, repeat the procedures for other problems for which additional practice is needed.

Note: See LM pp. 111–114 for memo form for 188c, Problem 1 and for news release form for 193b, Problem 2. Use half sheet, long side up, for 189c, Problem 1 and plain full sheet for 191c, Problem 1.

88c ▶ 10
Improve punctuation skill: related learning

full sheet; 1" top margin; 70-space line

Type as directed in 81c, p. 135.

PUNCTUATION GUIDES, continued

6. Comma: Use a comma *to separate* two or more parallel adjectives (adjectives that could be separated by the word "and" instead of the comma); however, do not use commas to separate adjectives so closely related that they appear to form a single element with the noun they modify. *Note:* If "and" cannot replace the comma without creating a meaningless effect, the comma should not be used.

7. Comma: Use a comma *to separate* (a) unrelated groups of figures which come together and (b) whole numbers into groups of three digits each; however, *policy, year, page, room, telephone,* and most *serial numbers* are typed without commas.

8. Exclamation mark: Use an exclamation mark *after* emphatic exclamations and *after* phrases or sentences that are clearly exclamatory.

9. Question mark: Use a question mark at the end of a sentence that is a direct question; however, *use a period after* a request in the form of a question.

learn 6. A happy, excited crowd cheered our team to victory.
learn A dozen large red roses were delivered.

apply The hot sticky humid air made our stay uncomfortable.
apply The key is in the small square box in the bottom drawer of my desk.

learn 7. During 1980, 2,375 cars were insured under Policy 123-90645.
apply In 1981 2384 students were enrolled.
apply Please call 825-2,626 if you need more information on Policy #7,204.

learn 8. Gosh, that was a good game!
apply Oh, what a beautiful morning.

learn 9. How much typewriting have you had?
learn Will you please type this letter before you leave.

apply Will you please complete the report in time for the meeting?
apply Did you type the reports.

89

89a ▶ 5
Conditioning practice

Follow standard directions, p. 143.

alphabet 1 Twelve brave, puzzled ibex fought gamely with the noisy, quick jackal.
figures 2 Janet will buy 149 books, 30 pencils, 265 pens, 78 boxes, and 15 pads.
shift key 3 Ms. Edie St. James, President of Zorbett, Inc., visited San Francisco.
fluency 4 He may hand me the clay and then go to the shelf for the die and form.

| 1 | 2 | 3 | 4 | 5 | 6 | 7 | 8 | 9 | 10 | 11 | 12 | 13 | 14 |

89b ▶ 30
Build sustained production skill: letters

plain full sheets

Time Schedule

Planning and preparing .... 4′
Production timing .... 20′
Proofreading; computing *g–pram* .... 6′

Type a 20′ sustained production writing on the problems listed here (make pencil notations of the pages and problems):
page 146, Problems 1 and 2
page 148, Problems 1 and 3

If you complete the letter problems before time is called, start over. Type on the control level; do not correct errors. When time is called, proofread each letter. Compute *g–pram* (gross production rate a minute); *g–pram* = total words ÷ minutes typed.

unit **38** lessons 198-200

Measure office communication skills

Measurement goals

1. To type acceptably* letters on special-size stationery.

2. To type acceptably* letters with special features.

3. To type acceptably* communications of special types.

**Both quality and quantity during a 30' time period.*

Machine adjustments

1. Paper guide at *0*.

2. Ribbon control to type on top half of ribbon.

3. Margins: 70-space line for sentence drills; as required for problems.

4. Tabs: as required for problems.

198

198a ▶ 5 Conditioning practice

each line twice SS (slowly, then faster); DS between 2-line groups; if time permits, retype selected lines

alphabet 1 Jinx Azen made five bright plaid quilts for Kathy Crews last February.

figures 2 The top team saved 863 coupons, 519 labels, 72 stamps, and 40 posters.

fig/sym 3 The bursar wrote checks for $157.82 and $946.30 during the last month.

fluency 4 The goal of the busy auditors is to make a profit by the work they do.

| 1 | 2 | 3 | 4 | 5 | 6 | 7 | 8 | 9 | 10 | 11 | 12 | 13 | 14 |

198b ▶ 45 Measure production skill: letters on special-size stationery

Time schedule

Preparation .... 5'
Timed production ...... 30'
Final check; compute *n-pram* .... 10'

1. Arrange letterheads (with envelopes) and forms [LM pp. 115-120], plain sheets, and carbon paper.

2. Type for 30' when directed to begin; correct all errors neatly.

3. Compute *n-pram*; then turn in completed work, arranged as listed.

words

December 3, 19-- Mr. David J. Green Human Dynamics, Inc. 30 E. Broad 13
Street Columbus, OH 43215-2002 Dear Mr. Green 22

(¶ 1) I am delighted to learn that you will participate in the seminars for 36
junior executives which we have scheduled for next June 5-8. Since we have 51
asked each of our regional offices to send five delegates, our attendance 66
should total about 150 persons. 72

(¶ 2) Enclosed are copies of the seminar programs, listing all the activities 86
planned for the four-day period. I shall soon send you one of the conference 102
kits being prepared for all seminar personnel. 111

Sincerely yours Miss Dorothy Hoehn Seminar Coordinator xx Enclosures 125
142

Problem 1
Half-size letter

block style, open punctuation; 1 cc on plain half sheet; address envelope

Problem 2
Executive-size letter

modified block style, open punctuation; address envelope

December 3, 19-- Miss Viola R. Airgood Executive Talent, Inc. 5101 Madi- 14
son Road Cincinnati, OH 45226-5534 Dear Miss Airgood 25

(¶ 1) We are looking for a person with a data processing and operations 38
management background to administer a multioffice information processing 53
facility in Toledo, Ohio. The person we seek must have a college degree in a 69
related field and experience in data systems. This position provides impres- 84
sive professional status, excellent working conditions, lucrative compensa- 100
tion, and a fine benefits program. It will be titled Assistant Vice President. 115

(¶ 2) I should like to have you help us locate a personable, qualified candidate. 130
For your files, I am enclosing detailed job data and a brochure describing our 146
company profit-sharing plans. 152

Sincerely yours Mrs. Anne G. Butler Vice President xx Enclosures 165/**184**

Problem 3 appears on page 314.

88b ▶ 35

Build production skill: letters

[LM pp. 11-16] or plain full sheets; modified block style; indented paragraphs; mixed punctuation; correct errors

Problem 1

words

March 5, 19-- | Ms. Mercedes Hernandez | Communications Consultant | Office 14
Efficiency, Inc. | 1300 Van Ness Avenue, Suite 1101 | San Francisco, CA 94109- 29
4305 | Dear Ms. Hernandez: 34
(¶ 1) My employer, Mr. Brian Osser, heard you speak at a recent conference. 48
He was impressed with the things you said about improving communication 63
skills. He indicated that if I would write to you, you could give me some 78
suggestions for improving my proofreading skills. (¶ 2) I really do need your 92
help. May I hear from you soon. Sincerely yours, | Robert King | Administra- 107
tive Assistant | xx (65) 110/**137**

Problem 2

Indent numbered items 5 spaces from left and right margins. *Do this:* Type Figure 1 at the ¶ indention point, type the period, space twice, set a tab stop and reset the left margin at this point. After typing Step 1, DS, press the margin release, and move the carriage or element to the left of ¶ indention point; then, tab to point for typing Figure 2. Repeat process for Steps 3 and 4. Remember to reset left and right margins for ¶ 2.

March 10, 19-- | Mr. Robert King | Administrative Assistant | Salt Lake Supply 15
Company | 54 West South Temple | Salt Lake City, UT 84101-6531 | Dear Mr. 28
King: 30
(¶ 1) I'm pleased to respond to your concern about improving your proofread- 44
ing skills. All typed work should be proofread before you remove it from your 59
typewriter. Here are some suggested steps to follow when proofreading the 74
letters you type: 78

1. The first step is to check the placement of the letter on the let- 92
   terhead page. Most employers expect typists to place all letters 105
   properly on the page; therefore, if your typed letter fails this test, 119
   you may have to do it over. 125
2. Second, check the accuracy of all figures used in the letter. This 140
   check should include the date, the street address, and any figures 153
   used in the letter body. 158
3. Third, check to be sure all words are divided correctly at the ends 173
   of lines. When in doubt about the division of a word, the best prac- 186
   tice is to consult a dictionary. 193
4. As a final step, read carefully the entire letter. As you read it for 208
   meaning, check for punctuation, capitalization, grammar, and typ- 221
   ing errors. All such errors must be corrected before the letter is 235
   submitted to your employer for signature. 243

(¶ 2) If you make it a habit to follow these letter proofreading steps, your 258
proofreading skills will improve. Good Luck. Sincerely yours, | Ms. Mercedes 273
Hernandez | Communications Consultant | xx (237) 281/**304**

Problem 3

March 12, 19-- | Mrs. Doris Gerber, Manager | Whittaker Laboratories, Inc. | 14
1510 Westlake Avenue | Seattle, WA 98101-2932 | Dear Mrs. Gerber: 27
(¶ 1) Many business executives complain that they never have time to get done 41
all the things that must be done. Consequently, at the end of a day, they usually 58
take home a briefcase full of work. (¶ 2) If you are one such person, do you 72
realize that with a little planning of your work, you will be able to get more done 89
and avoid having to take work home. Planning means scheduling your work 104
tasks in order of importance and working on them in that order. Planning, then, 120
is the key to more effective use of your time, and that is where it all begins in 134
terms of good management. (¶ 3) We are sending a complimentary copy of our 148
new publication, EFFECTIVE PLANNING, for your review. Instead of taking 163
work home, let reading EFFECTIVE PLANNING be your homework. EFFECTIVE 177
PLANNING is another in our series of publications designed to improve man- 192
agement efficiency. We know you will be pleased with it and that it will change 208
your management style. Sincerely yours, | Brad Bohnert | Publications De- 222
partment | xx | Enclosure (188) 226/**246**

198b, continued

Problem 3
Message/reply memorandum
1 cc; address **COMPANY MAIL** envelope

words

To: Ms. Umeko Soga Director of Media 136 Forsyth Building 11
Date: December 3, 19-- Subject: Systems Analysis Session 19

(¶ 1) For several years, our communications services have been provided 32
through decentralized, independent word processing and data processing cen- 47
ters. We must now critically evaluate our current practices to learn whether 63
we are operating most efficiently and economically. At our top management 78
level, there is some interest in adopting an integrated system to handle the 94
larger function of information processing. 102

(¶ 2) I should like to have you join us in executive session on January 12 to 116
discuss some ideas for systems revision. At that meeting, I want you to give 132
us your reactions to the merits of our present procedures. Signed: George 145
Joyce, Vice President 149

(Reply) Date: December 5, 19-- I shall be at the meeting January 12 ready to 162
discuss some of the issues involved in changing from decentralized to inte- 177
grated information systems. In my opinion, it is appropriate to discuss such 193
matters at this time. We are probably at a point where some change is desir- 208
able. Signed: Umeko Soga, Director of Media 215/**224**

199

199a ▶ 5 Conditioning practice

Use standard procedure given in 198a, page 313.

alphabet 1 Roxey Hazlett broke five records quickly in acquiring wins in jumping.
figures 2 The five students recorded 91, 83, 72, 60, and 54 on the history test.
fig/sym 3 Bill's check for $163.50 is for unpaid interest on a 15%, $3,000 note.
fluency 4 It may be possible for the girls to go to town for the formal socials.

| 1 | 2 | 3 | 4 | 5 | 6 | 7 | 8 | 9 | 10 | 11 | 12 | 13 | 14 |

199b ▶ 45 Measure production skill: letters with special features

Time schedule

Preparation .... 5′
Timed production ...... 30′
Final check; compute *n-pram* .... 10′

1. Arrange letterheads/envelopes [LM pp. 121–126], plain sheets, and carbon paper.

2. Type for 30′ when directed to begin; correct all errors neatly.

3. Compute *n-pram*; then turn in completed work, arranged as listed.

Problem 1
modified block style, open punctuation; 1½″ side margins; 1 cc on plain sheet; address envelope

Problems 2 and 3 appear on page 315.

words

December 4, 19-- CERTIFIED MAIL East Tennessee Manufacturing Company 14
Attention Ms. Nancy L. Watson, President 2103 Cumberland Avenue, SW 28
Knoxville, TN 37916-2133 Ladies and Gentlemen 37

(¶ 1) Have you stopped to consider the impact of a potential energy shortage 51
on your business operations? A dramatic increase in the cost of energy is 66
forecast for the years ahead. Predictions are that electricity costs will triple 82
in the next 20 years, rising from an average of 4.03 to 11.3 cents per kilowatt 98
hour. More costly energy, then, will doubtless result in reduced power for 113
meeting your operational needs, a condition for which you should start to 128
plan now. 130

(¶ 2) We should like to talk with you about planning for an energy-sensitive 144
future. The two confidential reports which are enclosed contain data which 159
should interest you and your directors. 167

Sincerely yours INDUSTRIAL CONSULTING, INC. Miss Mary Beck, Vice Presi- 181
dent xx Enclosures Energy Sources 1985-2000 Projected Energy Consump- 195
tion cc Mr. David Byrne, Controller 202
(PS) We have compiled some interesting data relating to the use of solar 216
energy in firms such as yours. Let's talk about the findings. 228/**257**

87c ▶ 15
Improve punctuation skill: related learning

full sheet; 1" top margin; 70-space line

Certain basic rules or guides must be followed if your writing is to meet acceptable writing standards. Given here and in some of the lessons that follow are basic related learning guides that will help you improve your writing. In typing this drill, follow carefully the *Study/Learn/Apply/Correct* procedures given in 81c, page 135.

PUNCTUATION GUIDES

1. **Comma:** Use a comma *after* (a) introductory words, phrases, or clauses and (b) words in a series; however, do not use commas to separate two items treated as a single unit within a series.
2. **Comma:** Use a comma before short direct quotations.
3. **Comma:** Use a comma *to set off* (a) words which come together and refer to the same person, thing, or idea and (b) words of direct address.
4. **Comma:** Use a comma *to set off* nonrestrictive clauses (not necessary to the meaning of the sentence); however, do not use commas with restrictive clauses (necessary to the meaning).
5. **Comma:** Use a comma *to separate* the day from the year and the city from the state.

learn 1. On our trip, we shall visit London, Paris, Rome, and Stockholm.
learn She ordered ham and eggs, toast, and coffee.

apply Before you leave please wash all dishes pots and pans.
apply She ordered bagels and lox strawberries and tea.

learn 2. She said, "If you try, you can reach your goal."
apply The students said "We'll try."

learn 3. John, the outgoing president, said, "Keep up the good work."
learn I'll look forward, Gina, to seeing you at the meeting.

apply Jean our new president will give the report to the committee.
apply Please try Clifford to be on time.

learn 4. The report, which you typed, was just great. (nonrestrictive)
learn The woman seated in the back row is my mother. (restrictive)

apply Unit 13 which relates to our work is well written.
apply Typists who practice with a purpose will be successful.

learn 5. Jane Fonda gave the keynote address in Cincinnati, Ohio.
learn October 12, 1492, is a special day in history.

apply (Type a complete sentence giving the date, city, and state of your birth.)

88

88a ▶ 5
Conditioning practice

Follow standard directions, p. 143.

alphabet 1 This bright jacket has an amazing weave and is of exceptional quality.
figures 2 The telephone number for your 310 N. Rodeo Drive location is 278-4569.
space bar 3 Is it right to make me sign the forms and then go to the city to work?
fluency 4 They may lend the authentic ancient ivory ornament to the city mentor.

| 1 | 2 | 3 | 4 | 5 | 6 | 7 | 8 | 9 | 10 | 11 | 12 | 13 | 14 |

199b, continued

Problem 2
AMS letter
1½" side margins; 1 cc on plain sheet; address envelope

words

December 4, 19-- Mr. John Velez Director, Administrative Services Univer- 14
sal Engineering Corporation 245 E. Capitol Avenue Jackson, MS 39201-2005 29
EQUIPMENT SELECTION 33

Whether you decide to purchase new equipment might very well depend upon 48
some of the following considerations: 55

1. Time required to recoup the financial outlay--period needed to become 70
cost-effective. 2. Availability of employees skilled in the new technology-- 86
personnel implications. 3. Cost of updating operator performance--need for 102
new training programs. 4. Vulnerability of the new equipment to future 118
technological change--anticipated obsolescence. 127

The enclosed materials contain further ideas and suggestions for equipment 142
selection which you may find helpful. If I may assist you further, please give 158
me an opportunity to do so. 163

MS. GINA R. GRIFFITH xx Enclosures 170/**197**

Problem 3
Informal government letter
1 cc on plain sheet; window envelope

Date: December 4, 19-- Reply to Attn. of: DSMA Subject: INFORMATION PRO- 7
CESSING SYSTEMS To: Miss Robyn L. Frazier Director, Data Management 20
Federal Records Center Washington, DC 20409-2553 30

(¶ 1) Compliance by the business sector to federal government regulations 44
has produced a flood of paperwork. We are now attempting to develop more 59
efficient systems for processing the following kinds of information: 73

a. Financial information--data requested by the Federal Trade Commission 88
for specific lines of business. b. Personnel and benefits information--data 104
required by the Department of Labor on hourly and salaried pension plans. 119
c. Environmental information--data requested by the Environmental Protec- 134
tion Agency on air and water pollution, waste disposal, and drinking water 149
usage. d. Productivity information--data requested by the Bureau of Eco- 164
nomic Analysis on industrial plant operations. 173

(¶ 2) I should like to have you join me on January 17 at a meeting called to 187
discuss methods of reducing the paperwork burden. The enclosed documents 202
will be the basis of our discussions. 209

Richard C. Olson, Director Data Control Systems 2 Enclosures Data Facili- 223
ties Report Needs Assessment Study DSMA: RCOlson:xx 12-4-- 235

200

200a ▶ 5 Conditioning practice

Use standard procedure given in 198a, page 313.

alphabet 1 John Becker first coached an amazingly well-equipped varsity in Texas.
figures 2 The inventory showed 283 cards, 694 books, 50 pens, and 17 jade rings.
fig/sym 3 He ordered 25 of #82057, each priced at $4.98, for a total of $124.50.
fluency 4 The usual civic duty of the attorney is to handle key social problems.

| 1 | 2 | 3 | 4 | 5 | 6 | 7 | 8 | 9 | 10 | 11 | 12 | 13 | 14 |

87b ▶ 30
Build production skill: letters

plain full sheets; modified block style; 5-space ¶ indention; mixed punctuation; your own initials instead of xx as the reference initials

Placement

Use the Letter Placement Table, p. 143, to determine margins and dateline placement. The number of words in the letter body is indicated by the number in parentheses at the end of each letter.

words

Problem 1

February 10, 19-- | Ms. Mercedes Hernandez |Communications Consultant | 13
Office Efficiency, Inc. | 1300 Van Ness Avenue, Suite 1101 | San Francisco, 28
CA 94109-4305 | Dear Ms. Hernandez: 35
(¶ 1) This week all our letters will be typed in the modified block style with 49
indented paragraphs. We plan to compare the production rates achieved with 65
other letter styles before we standardize the letter style to be used by our 80
corporation. (¶ 2) Thanks for sending us a copy of your revised LETTER STYLE 94
MANUAL. It has been reviewed by our administrative staff. The response to 110
it is highly favorable; therefore, we'd like to have 50 copies for distribution to 126
our various communication processing centers. Sincerely yours, | Al Brown, 141
President | xx (101) 143

Problem 2

February 12, 19-- | Mr. Al Brown, President | Solar Corporation | 1080 Westwood 15
Boulevard | Los Angeles, CA 90024-4817 | Dear Mr. Brown: 26
(¶ 1) Fifty copies of our revised Letter Style Manual are being sent to you by 40
United Parcel. (¶ 2) We're pleased by the favorable review it has received from 55
your staff. As a ready reference, it will answer questions your typists may have 72
about letter arrangement. The word-division guides and the letter-placement 87
points given on pages 4 and 5 should be especially helpful to them. (¶ 3) Thanks 102
for giving us this opportunity to be of service to you. Sincerely yours, | Ms. 118
Mercedes Hernandez | Communications Consultant | xx (88) 127

Problem 3

February 20, 19-- | Ms. Betty Ashland, President | Reynolds International | 2500 15
South Harbor Boulevard | Anaheim, CA 92802-4526 | Dear Ms. Ashland: (¶ 1) 28
Information management is one of the prime concerns of every busy execu- 42
tive. No office seems immune to the paperwork explosion that characterizes 58
this decade. And all this is happening despite the advent of modern technol- 73
ogy and the development of sophisticated electronic equipment designed to 88
produce letters, reports, and other communications at fantastic speed. (¶ 2) 102
But that may be our problem. We haven't yet learned how to use most effi- 117
ciently the technology and electronic equipment that is at our disposal. Nor 133
have we learned how to manage our time so as to get maximum time utiliza- 147
tion along with increased productivity. On Wednesday, March 25, our highly 163
skilled staff will be conducting an all-day seminar on the topic "Information 178
and Time Management." The seminar will be held in the Redwood Room of 192
the Century Plaza Hotel in Century City. The topics to be covered are de- 207
scribed in the enclosed brochure. (¶ 3) To insure your reservation, just re- 221
turn to us the enrollment form included in the brochure, along with the 236
names of the persons from your organization who plan to attend. Please note 251
the special rates that apply if five or more persons from your company at- 266
tend. (¶ 4) And here's our special offer. If you or any of your executives do 281
not find the seminar of great value to you, we'll refund the fees you pay. 296
That's how confident we are that you'll like what our staff has to offer. Sin- 312
cerely yours, | C. A. Adams, President | xx | Enclosure (282) 321

200b ▶ 45 Measure production skill: communications of special types

Time schedule

Preparation .... 5′
Timed production ...... 30′
Final check; compute *n-pram* .... 10′

1. Arrange forms [LM pp. 127–130], plain sheets, and carbon paper.

2. Type for 30′ when directed to begin; correct all errors neatly.

3. Compute *n-pram*; then turn in completed work, arranged as listed.

Problem 1
Standard memo on half sheet

1 cc on plain half sheet; address **COMPANY MAIL** envelope

words

TO: Robert Motley, Sales Manager FROM: David Shen, Vice President 11
DATE: December 5, 19-- SUBJECT: New Building Occupancy 19

(¶ 1) Word has just come from the general construction contractor that our 33 new building, now nearing completion, will be ready for occupancy on May 1. 48 We must now make plans to move to the new facility as soon after May 1 as 63 possible. In working out details, I need your help. 73

(¶ 2) To enable our building crews to relocate the equipment in all offices 87 with minimum disruption to our daily routines, all employees must be pre- 101 pared to follow altered schedules during the moving period. I want you to 116 meet with me and all division directors on January 12 to work out procedures 131 to be followed by our employees. Thank you. xx 140/**148**

Problem 2
Simplified memo

plain half sheet; 1 cc on plain half sheet; address **COMPANY MAIL** envelope

December 5, 19-- William Weston, Controller Bids for Typewriters 13

(¶ 1) We plan to replace 120 typewriters currently in use with new ones when 27 we move into our new building next May 1. 36

(¶ 2) By December 15, please submit your cost estimates (specify brand) for 50 replacing 120 type-bar electric typewriters with an equal number of single- 65 element (interchangeable), dual-pitch, correcting machines having single, 80 double, and line-and-a-half spacing. Please indicate the ordering lead time 95 required to assure May 1 delivery. Thank you. 104

David Shen, Vice President xx 110/**117**

Problem 3
News release

1 cc on plain sheet

RELEASE ON RECEIPT 3

(¶ 1) Chicago, December 5, 19--. IBP Corporation announced the purchase on 17 December 1 of Waltex, Inc., an Ohio-based appliance manufacturing firm. 32 The purchase is to expand IBP's corporate operations into an entirely new 47 product line. For the past 35 years, Waltex has compiled an enviable record 62 in the household appliance industry, manufacturing and marketing such 76 products as automatic washers and dryers, refrigerators, freezers, vacuum 91 cleaners, and room air conditioners. 98

(¶ 2) "Acquiring Waltex enables us now to diversify and extend our corporate 112 activities in areas and in ways heretofore not available to us," stated IBP 127 President Joseph Miller, in announcing the new acquisition. "Changes in 142 administrative personnel will be announced later," Miller concluded. 156
Marva Katona xx 159

Problem 4
Phoned telegram

plain full sheet; 1 cc on plain sheet

Use the ¶s in Problem 2 above for a telephoned message. Send as a **PHONED TELEGRAM** signed by **David Shen, Vice President.** Use the current date and **10:45 a.m.** as the time of filing. Send to addressee given at right.

Mr. Robert J. Lewis
Vice President, Sales
Office Equipment, Inc.
801 Park Avenue
New York, NY 10021-3221

Problem 4 word count:
heading 31
¶1 23
¶2 68
closing lines 6

oei

OFFICE EFFICIENCY, INC.
EXPERTS IN OFFICE RESEARCH

1300 VAN NESS AVENUE, SUITE 1101 • SAN FRANCISCO, CA 94109-4305
TEL: (415) 823-4500

		words: parts	total
	Start at horizontal center of paper		
Dateline	Line 16 February 4, 19--	3	3
	4 line spaces (3 blank lines)		
Letter address	Mr. Al Brown, President	8	8
	Solar Corporation	12	12
	1080 Westwood Boulevard	16	16
	Los Angeles, CA 90024-4817	22	22
Salutation	Dear Mr. Brown:	25	25
Body of letter	This letter style is one of three frequently used	10	35
	business letter styles. The style is the same as the modi-	22	47
	fied block letter style, except that each paragraph is	33	58
	indented five spaces. As is true for the modified block	44	69
	letter style, the opening and closing lines are started	55	81
	at the horizontal center point of the letterhead page.	67	92
	Mixed punctuation is used in this letter (a colon	77	102
	after the salutation and a comma after the complimentary	88	113
	close). Since the dictator's name is typed in the closing	100	125
	lines, only the typist's initials need be shown in the	111	136
	reference notation.	115	140
	Enclosed is our revised <u>Letter Style Manual</u>. If y	26	151
	would like additional copies for your office staff, jus	37	162
	let me know.	139	165
Complimentary close	Sincerely yours,	4	168
Signature	*Mercedes Hernandez*		
Typed name	Ms. Mercedes Hernandez	8	173
Official title	Communications Consultant	13	178
Reference initials	le	14	179
Enclosure notation	Enclosure	16	181

Make over Read

Shown in pica type
1 ½″ side margins

Style letter 3: modified block with indented paragraphs and mixed punctuation

phase 9 lessons 201-225

Extend Information Processing Skills

To function successfully in the world of business, a typist must be able to perform tasks involving both word processing and data processing skills. Word/data typing is common to all modern offices; and one preparing to work in an office must be equipped to perform word/data typing tasks efficiently. Phase 9 is designed to provide typists with the skills essential to successful performance in the offices of tomorrow. Specifically, this uniquely structured phase will:

1. Provide drills designed to improve keystroking skill on sentences and paragraphs of straight copy.

2. Develop the ability to type tables of various types having a variety of special features.

3. Develop skill in typing a variety of common business forms and file cards.

4. Provide word processing work assignments drawn from business offices.

5. Provide drills designed to improve composition skills.

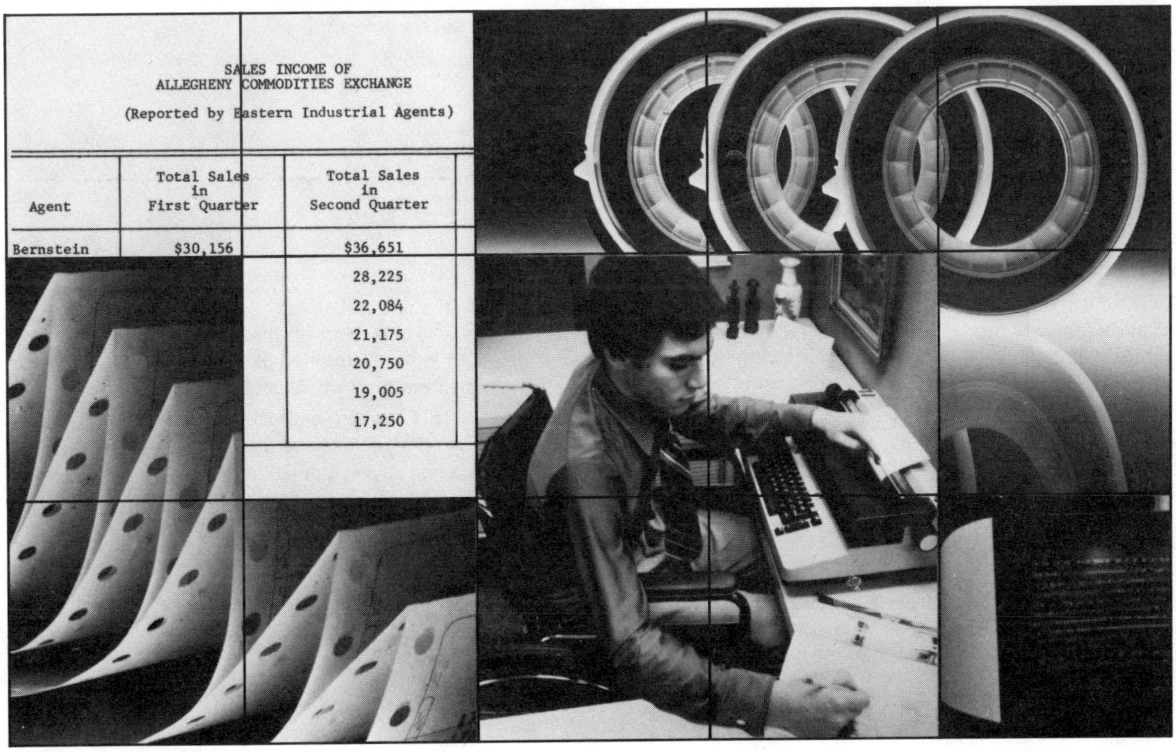
SALES INCOME OF
ALLEGHENY COMMODITIES EXCHANGE
(Reported by Eastern Industrial Agents)
Agent
Total Sales in First Quarter
Total Sales in Second Quarter
Bernstein
$30,156
$36,651
28,225
22,084
21,175
20,750
19,005
17,250

unit 39 lessons 201-206

Improve table typing skills

Learning goals:

1. To improve keystroking on sentence copy.

2. To improve skill in typing business tables.

Machine adjustments

1. Paper guide at *0*.

2. Margins: 70-space line for sentence drills; as directed for problems.

3. Spacing: SS sentence drills; as directed for problems.

4. Tab sets: as needed for problems.

86b ▶ 30
Learn skill applications

plain sheets, 8½″ × 11″

Step 1
Learn letter style

Type Style letter 3, p. 145, in modified block style with 5-space ¶ indention as shown (words in body: 139). Use the Letter Placement Table, p. 143.

In typing the letter in proper form, be guided by the placement and spacing notations given in color.

Type the letter at rough-draft speed (top speed); x-out or strike over any typing errors.

Step 2
Proofread and make rough-draft corrections

Proofread the letter you typed in Step 1. Show by handwritten corrections any changes that you need to make in the copy.

Where you x'd out or struck over any words or letters, write such words correctly.
To make the needed handwritten corrections, use the standard proofreader's marks you learned (Reference Guide, p. ix).

Step 3
Build skill

Using your corrected rough-draft copy, retype the letter. As you type, make the corrections you have indicated in your copy.

Type on the control level; correct neatly any errors you make as you retype the letter. Compare your typed letter with Style letter 3. If your letter is typed in elite type, your lines will end at different points than those in the model, but spacing between letter parts will be the same.

86c ▶ 15
Build skill: letter parts

plain sheets; 1½″ margins

1. Four 1′ writings on the opening parts (dateline through salutation) of Style letter 3, p. 145.

When you have typed through the salutation, DS, tab for the date, and retype the drill. Type these letter parts as many times as you can during the 1′ timings. Leave proper spacing between parts. Type for speed. Determine *gwam*.

2. Using Style letter 3, type four 1′ writings on the closing parts (complimentary close through enclosure notation).

When you have typed through the enclosure notation, DS, tab for the complimentary close, and retype the drill. Type for speed. Determine *gwam*.

3. On another sheet of paper, type a 3′ writing on the body of the letter. Determine *gwam* by dividing total words typed by 3.

Note: On which of the timed writings did you achieve the highest speed: opening lines? closing lines? body of the letter? Why?

87

87a ▶ 5
Conditioning practice

Follow standard directions, p. 143.

alphabet 1 Gentle sailors quickly fixed holes in jibs pummeled by sizeable waves.

figures 2 Pine frames sized 5 × 7, 8 × 10, 9 × 12, and 14 × 16 are 30% off list.

shift keys 3 H. A. McLain and P. T. Hall are employed by the Adams & Brown Company.

fluency 4 They may make them do the work for the city auditor by the end of May.

| 1 | 2 | 3 | 4 | 5 | 6 | 7 | 8 | 9 | 10 | 11 | 12 | 13 | 14 |

201

201a ▶ 5 Conditioning practice

each line twice SS (slowly, then faster); if time permits, retype selected lines

alphabet 1 Marty Alzado acquired six fine print jackets in the big western event.
figures 2 The four team bowlers scored 203, 165, 94, and 87 points respectively.
third row 3 wipe were pity trip treat pupil quiet power youth mirror terror reward
fluency 4 The man may audit six downtown firms for the city if the bid is right.
| 1 | 2 | 3 | 4 | 5 | 6 | 7 | 8 | 9 | 10 | 11 | 12 | 13 | 14 |

201b ▶ 5 Learn to type tables with leaders

Type the table to the right on a full sheet, exact vertical center; SS body; determine spaces between columns. Insert leaders as shown.

To align leaders
Type the first line of the first column; space once: note the position of the printing point indicator (13) (on an odd or even number); type a period, then a space alternately across the line; stop 2 or 3 spaces before the second column. On lines that follow, align the periods with those in Line 1, typing on odd or even numbers.

FORDSON COMPANY QUARTERLY DIVIDENDS
TS

March 31	$ 3.25
June 30	3.40
September 30	3.65
December 31	3.80
Total	$14.10

201c ▶ 10 Arranging column headings

Review centering and tabulating in Reference Guide, pages ix and x. Then type the drills shown at the right as directed below (4 spaces between columns).

Drill 1: Center by column entries.

Drill 2: Center by column headings.

Drill 3: Center by longest item in each column, whether a heading or an entry.

Note: This procedure should be used in future problems unless otherwise specified.

Drill 1

Company	Stocks	Bonds
Continental Insurance	$902,587,049	$95,035,150

Drill 2

Product Classification	Volume of Sales	Annual Increase
Chemicals	$1,075,000	7.5%

Drill 3

Industry	Bonded Indebtedness	Annual Sales
Esposito Fabricators	$2,500,000	$875,000

201d ▶ 30 Type tables with leaders and column headings

Problem 1

full sheet; reading position; DS body; determine spaces between columns, insert leaders

LEADING AREA INDEPENDENT STORES
TS

Company	Sales	words
		6
Company	Sales	12
Anderson and Company	$ 985,000	22
Brown and Wilson	2,015,000	33
Martin, Hershey, and Hulbert	5,875,000	43
McKinzie-Walters Company	853,000	54
Swanson, Inc.	785,000	67
Total	$10,513,000	70

Problem 2 is on page 319.

unit **17** lessons 86-95

Increase letter typing skill

Learning goals

1. To develop and increase skill in arranging and typing letters in modified block (indented paragraphs) and block styles.

2. To maintain good typing technique patterns when typing problem copy.

3. To learn and apply basic punctuation guides.

4. To do all work with a minimum of waste time and motion.

Machine adjustments

1. Paper guide at *0*.

2. 70-space line and single spacing (SS) unless otherwise directed.

3. Line space selector on *1*, or as directed for various activities.

4. Ribbon control on black (*R* on Selectric).

Special letter placement points

Placement table

A placement table is given here to help you place letters properly. With time, you must learn to estimate letter length and place letters properly without using a placement aid.

Stationery

Most business letters are typed on standard-size letterheads (8½" × 11") with the company name, address, and other information printed at the top.

For letters longer than 1 page, plain paper of the same size, color, and quality is used after the first page.

For short letters, smaller letterheads, executive-size (7¼" × 10½") or half-size (5½" × 8½"), may be used.

LETTER PLACEMENT TABLE

Letter Classification	5-Stroke Words in Letter Body	Side Margins	Margin Settings		Dateline Position (from Top Edge of Paper)
			Elite	Pica	
Short	Up to 125	2"	24-78*	20-65*	19
Average	126-225	1 1/2"	18-84*	15-70*	16
Long	226-325	1"	12-90*	10-75*	13
Two-page	More than 325	1"	12-90*	10-75*	13
Standard 6" line for all letters**	As above for all letters	1 1/4"	15-87*	12-72*	As above for all letters

*Plus 3 to 7 spaces for the bell cue—*usually add 5* (see p. 68).

**Use only when so directed. Some business firms use a standard 6" line for all letters.

Placement table pointers

1. Vertical placement of the dateline varies with the letter length. If a deep letterhead prevents typing the date on the designated line, type it on the second line below the last letterhead line.

2. The *letter address* is *always typed on the fourth line* (3 blank line spaces) below the dateline. The *typed name* and/or title in the closing lines is *typed on the fourth line* below the complimentary close. Double spacing is used between all other letter parts.

3. *Special lines* (attention, subject, COMPANY NAME in closing lines, etc.) or features such as tables, lists, extra opening or closing lines may require a higher dateline placement than is shown in the placement table.

86

86a ▶ 5 Conditioning practice

each line twice (slowly, faster); as time permits, retype selected lines for extra credit

alphabet 1 The blitz vexed the famous quarterback whose game plan just went awry.

figures 2 Your Order No. 648 calls for 130 chairs, 29 typewriters, and 75 desks.

3d row 3 You were to quote your best prices on those typewriters, were you not?

fluency 4 If they do the work for us, she may spend the day with me in the city.

| 1 | 2 | 3 | 4 | 5 | 6 | 7 | 8 | 9 | 10 | 11 | 12 | 13 | 14 |

201d, continued

Problem 2

full sheet; DS body; exact vertical center

Leave 16 spaces between Columns 1 & 2; 4 spaces between Columns 2 & 3. Insert leaders.

Problem 3

half sheet, long side up; DS body

Retype Problem 2, omitting the secondary heading and the *Total* line. Insert leaders.

Total words: 100

SALES MANAGEMENT SURVEY OF BUYING POWER

County Retail Sales by Category

	This Year	Last Year	words
SALES MANAGEMENT SURVEY OF BUYING POWER			8
County Retail Sales by Category			14
	This Year	Last Year	21
General merchandise	$ 38,323,000	$ 53,136,000	29
Apparel	6,175,000	9,280,000	34
Automobile	34,817,000	65,503,000	40
Eating, drinking	27,520,000	41,255,000	47
Food	56,230,000	79,604,000	52
Furniture	6,437,000	9,565,000	57
Pharmaceuticals	11,286,000	15,970,000	69
Total	$180,788,000	$274,313,000	75

202

202a ▶ 5 Conditioning practice

Use standard directions given in 201a, p. 318.

alphabet 1 Herbert Gonzales played five excellent games of golf with Jack Quezon.

figures 2 She requested canceled Checks 234, 189, 70, and 65 for the last audit.

1st & 3d rows 3 wiper quiz money bumper mixture bovine metric cement ointment movement

fluency 4 They may go to eight big towns to make an official audit for the firm.

| 1 | 2 | 3 | 4 | 5 | 6 | 7 | 8 | 9 | 10 | 11 | 12 | 13 | 14 |

202b ▶ 5 Improve language arts: error detection and correction

full sheet; 60-space line; DS

1. Read each sentence carefully; then type the number; space twice; and type the sentences, making the necessary corrections.

2. Verify your copy with the teacher.

1. The ferm needed new capitol for its forign operatoins.
2. The superviser ocassionally rote new job discriptions.
3. Won errer ocurred when the cash receits were recorded.
4. The principle point in the recomendation was axcepted.

202c ▶ 10 Learn to type horizontal rules

Study the illustration at the right, observing the spacing between typewritten lines and the single and double rulings. Then type the table on a full sheet, SS body; exact vertical center; determine spacing between columns. Insert rulings at the points indicated.

Horizontal rulings

1. Single rulings: depress the shift lock and use the underline key.

2. Double rulings: type the first line; then use the variable line spacer (3) to move the paper forward slightly. Type the second horizontal line.

EMPLOYMENT IN KEY INDUSTRIES DS

(Figures in thousands) DS

DS

Type	This Year	Last Year
Manufacturing	741.5	740.9
Primary metals	112.1	110.7
Electric machinery	80.4	78.8

SS DS (after heading row); SS DS (after body)

Source: Employment Security Division.

85d ▶ 10
Improve grammar skills: related learning

full sheet; 1″ top margin; 60-space line

Type as directed in 81c, p. 135.

GRAMMAR GUIDES, concluded

C. Other grammatical confusions:

1. Don't confuse *fewer* (meaning number) with *less* (meaning quantity).

2. Don't confuse *bad* (describing health and quality) with *badly* (describing behavior or other action).

3. It is not incorrect to end a sentence with a preposition, but it is incorrect to add a preposition unnecessarily.

4. Avoid faulty pronoun reference.

learn 1. We have had fewer typewriter service calls this year.
learn We have had less typewriter maintenance cost this year.

apply In terms of number, the (fewer, less) the better.
apply In terms of quantity, the (fewer, less) the better.

learn 2. He said that he felt bad. (state of health)
learn He handled the situation badly. (behavior)

apply You did (bad, badly) on the test.
apply I feel (bad, badly) today.

learn 3. WRONG: Where is the office at?
learn RIGHT: Where is the office?
learn WRONG: They went there to rest up.
learn RIGHT: They went there to rest.
learn RIGHT: Where is the new employee from?

In apply sentences, change as necessary.

apply Where are you going to?
apply Is this the house you live in?

learn 4. WRONG: Maria collected scraps of fabric and saved it.
learn RIGHT: Maria collected scraps of fabric and saved them.

In apply sentences, change as necessary.

apply John polished pieces of quartz and sold it for a dime.
apply The girls cut slices of pie and ate them.

85e ▶ 10
Review centering and aligning on lines

half sheet, short side up; 1″ top margin

1. Read the directions at the right.

2. Type a 26-space underline starting 1″ from the left edge of your paper.

3. Center and type your full name on the underline typed in Step 2. Determine center of underline according to formula given at the right.

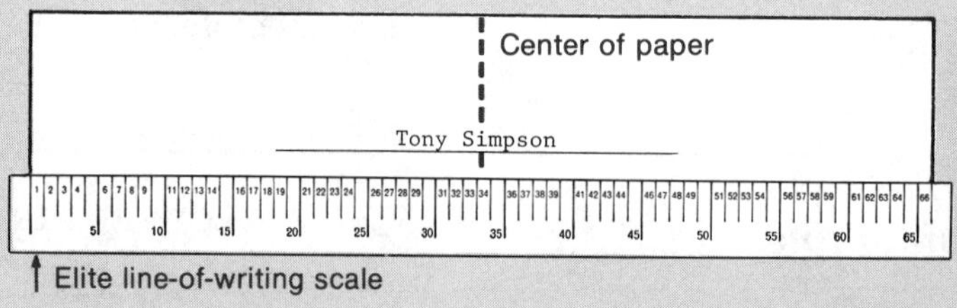

Find center of line or column:	
Read scale at first letter or item	18
Read scale at last letter or item	+48
Total	66
Total ÷ 2 = Center point (66 ÷ 2 = 33)	

Find center of paper:	
Read scale at left edge of paper	0
Read scale at right edge of paper	+66
Total	66
Total ÷ 2 = Center point (66 ÷ 2 = 33)	

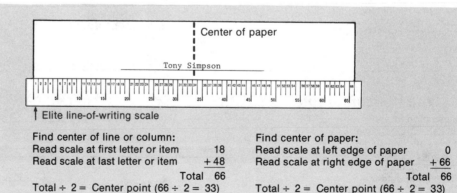

Raquel Rodriguez

4. Study the relationship of typed letters to underline. Note that only a slight space separates the letters of your name from the underline. As shown in the illustration, downstem letters (p, y, q, g) may touch the line. Now note on your typewriter the relationship of the typed letters and underline to the **aligning scale (21).**

5. Space down about 2″ and type a 30-space underline starting 1½″ from the left edge of your paper.

6. Center and type your name on the underline. Remove the paper.

7. Reinsert the paper. Align the paper and type over your name typed in Step 5.

Note: One way to check alignment is to set the ribbon control in stencil position and strike a letter key; then make any needed adjustments in the position of the paper.

202d ▶ 30
Type tables with horizontal rulings

Problem 1
full sheet; exact vertical center; DS body; determine spacing between columns

Problem 2
Retype Problem 1 on a half sheet, long side up, SS body. Arrange the body of the table vertically in 2 groups of 4 items each, separated by a DS.

words

COUNTY PROPERTY TAX RATES 5

(To Nearest 1/10th Cent) 10

20
30

Local Unit	This Year	Last Year	36
			46
Bakersville	$8.144	$8.134	51
Bethel Township	8.076	8.021	56
Forest Park	8.139	8.063	60
Greensburg	7.473	7.402	64
Monroeville	7.023	6.201	68
Oakland City	5.553	5.483	72
Stowe Township	4.513	4.434	77
Wilkinsburg	8.236	8.013	81
			91

Source: County Auditor's Annual Report. 99

Problem 3
full sheet; reading position; SS body; determine spacing between columns

AVERAGE ANNUAL EMPLOYMENT IN COUNTY 7

(Reported by Townships) 12

25
38

Township	Labor Force	Employed	Unemployed	45
				58
Arcadia	40,842	38,033	2,809	63
Benton	40,350	37,550	2,800	68
Davidson	39,454	36,733	2,721	73
Fairborne	39,450	38,050	1,400	78
Harrison	41,050	39,300	1,750	83
Jefferson	38,950	36,300	2,650	88
Wellington	40,650	39,000	1,650	93
				106

Source: Employment Security Division. 114

203

203a ▶ 5
Conditioning practice

Use standard directions given in 201a, p. 318.

alphabet 1 Max Denzil wrote five exquisite essays that were picked by our judges.

figures 2 They stocked 295 tapes, 604 records, 83 cassettes, and 17 new stereos.

double letters 3 fussy noodle rubber hammer butter cannery trigger happiness accessible

fluency 4 He may make a dial for the panel to show elements and handle problems.

| 1 | 2 | 3 | 4 | 5 | 6 | 7 | 8 | 9 | 10 | 11 | 12 | 13 | 14 |

85

85a ▶ 5 Conditioning practice

Follow standard directions, p. 134.

alphabet	1	Brave jockeys and large quarter horses whiz past farmers in box seats.
figures	2	Today we typed 40 letters, 15 reports, 369 orders, and 278 statements.
space bar	3	I'll pay the crew for all this work and then send you the bill for it.
fluency	4	He may sign the usual form by proxy if they make an audit of the firm.

| 1 | 2 | 3 | 4 | 5 | 6 | 7 | 8 | 9 | 10 | 11 | 12 | 13 | 14 |

85b ▶ 15 Measure basic skill: straight copy

two 5′ writings; determine *gwam*; proofread and circle errors; record better rate

Emphasize: Fingers curved and upright; quick, finger-action keystroking.

all letters used | A | 1.5 si | 5.7 awl | 80% hfw |

	gwam 3′	5′
Just what does it mean to be young and when is a person young? To	4	3
be young is perhaps a feeling or disposition, a particular manner of	9	5
looking at things and responding to them. To be young is never a chrono-	14	8
logical period or time of life, although it might be a young person	18	11
examining some material with fascination and pleasure or the composer	23	14
Verdi in his eighties writing his best opera. To be young might be a	28	17
person "hanging ten" on a surfboard or swinging to a musical composi-	32	19
tion. To be young might be Einstein in his seventies still working with	37	22
his field theory, sailing his boat, or playing his cherished fiddle.	42	25
To be young is never the monopoly of youth. It flourishes every-	46	28
where visionaries have stimulated our thinking or amazed us. To be young	51	31
in nature is quite desirable whether you are a young person, a middle-	56	33
aged person, or a chronologically old person. To be young should be	60	36
respected whether the beard is soft and curly or firm and gray. To be	65	39
young has no color; it seems always translucent with its own imaginative	70	42
light. There is no generation space between the young of any age because	75	45
they see things as they ought to be.	77	46

gwam 3′ | 1 | 2 | 3 | 4 | 5 |
5′ | 1 | 2 | 3 |

85c ▶ 10 Improve accuracy

1. Type three 1′ writings of 85b above; start second and third writings at ending point of previous writing. Set goal of no more than 2 errors in each writing.

2. Type a 3′ writing on the ¶s of 85b with a goal of not more than 6 errors. To do this, just start slowly and gradually increase your speed as you feel relaxed. Type with continuity—keep the carriage or element moving.

203b ▶ 15
Learn to type boxed tables

On a full sheet, type the illustration at the right in exact vertical center; SS body; leave 10 spaces between columns.

Boxed tables

1. Type table in usual manner, inserting horizontal rulings as you type.

2. Remove the page and, using a pen (preferably black ink), draw vertical lines at the midpoint between columns.

EARNINGS OF SELECTED RAILROADS DS

(Report of Annual Performance) DS

DS

Company	In Millions	Per Share	
			SS DS
Union Pacific	$404.5	$4.22	
Norfolk & Western	232.4	7.36	
Burlington Northwestern	222.9	7.55	SS DS

Source: The Wall Street Journal.

203c ▶ 30
Type boxed tables

Problem 1

full sheet; reading position; DS body; determine spacing between columns; box table by inserting vertical lines between columns

words

REGISTRATIONS OF DOGS IN THE UNITED STATES 8

19
31

Breed Type	This Year	Last Year	words
			37
			48
Working dogs	286,850	295,949	53
Sporting class	232,250	230,500	59
Non-sporting types	161,500	163,200	65
Toy breeds	105,300	102,600	70
Hound dogs	102,150	106,725	75
			86

Source: Library Animal Collection. 93

Problem 2

full sheet; reading position; DS body; determine spacing between columns; box table by inserting vertical lines between columns

Problem 3

Retype Problem 2 on a full sheet; SS body; exact vertical center. Arrange the body of the table vertically in 4 groups of 2 items each separated by a DS. Box the table by inserting vertical lines between columns.

UNIT CONVERSION TABLE 5

(With Particular Reference to Metrics) 13

25
37

To Convert	Into	Multiply By	words
			39
			42
			54
Inches	Centimeters	2.540	58
Centimeters	Inches	0.3937	63
Feet	Meters	0.3048	66
Meters	Feet	3.281	69
Miles (statute)	Kilometers	1.609	75
Kilometers	Miles (statute)	0.6214	81
Gallons	Liters	3.785	85
Liters	Gallons	0.2642	89
			101

Source: Handbook on Metrics. 107

204

204a ▶ 5
Conditioning practice

Use standard directions given in 201a, p. 318

alphabet 1 Graham Azen quickly broke five records with exceptional juggling acts.

figures 2 She shipped 43 canoes, 80 paddles, 579 life jackets, and 162 whistles.

outside reaches 3 saws poles waxes ploy loop waste swagger monopoly sassafras opposition

fluency 4 The eight big city firms may risk their profits to fight an amendment.

| 1 | 2 | 3 | 4 | 5 | 6 | 7 | 8 | 9 | 10 | 11 | 12 | 13 | 14 |

84c ▶ 35
Type a report with footnotes

full sheet

Side margins: 1"

	Left	Right
elite	12	90*
pica	10	75*

* Plus allowance for bell (see p. 68).

Top margin:
elite, 2"
pica, 1½"

DS report

PRODUCTIVITY

TS

Productivity has been defined as the amount of goods and services produced in an hour of work.[1] The productivity index

DS

> . . . measures the value of goods and services the economy can produce using the labor, machinery, energy, land, and other resources at its disposal. Or to put it another way, the index tells us how efficiently our economy is operating.[2]

Productivity is closely linked with living standards. Gains in real living standards must come primarily from increased productivity. Increased productivity also acts as a potent weapon against inflation, which reduces purchasing power and causes hardship.

The problem, then, is how to increase the output per hour by the average worker. In the past, living standards have been raised by giving workers better education and more efficient tools, along with effective training in ways of using these tools so that more goods can be produced without extra time or effort. The importance of invention and innovation in such an approach to increasing productivity is emphasized by Lipsey and Steiner, who say that "Better organization of production alone can account for increases in productivity."[3] Increased resources will need to be directed to research, modernization, and expansion by business so as to increase the output of goods and services per hour of work.

SS
DS

[1] "Productivity Lower," Los Angeles Times (August 28, 1979), p. 3.

DS

[2] "Productivity and Why It's a Worry," Changing Times (April 1979), p. 31.

SS

[3] Richard G. Lipsey and Peter O. Steiner, Economics, 4th ed. (New York: Harper & Row, 1975), p. 250.

204b ▶ 45
Build table typing skills

Time schedule

Preparation .... 5′
Timed production .... 30′
Final check
compute *n–pram* .... 10′

1. When directed to begin, type the following problems for 30′. Proofread; correct all errors neatly.
2. If you finish all problems in less than 30′, start over and type until time is called.
3. When time is called, compute *n–pram* for the 30′ period.
4. Turn in problems in numbered order.

Problem 1
Ruled table

full sheet; exact vertical center; DS body; determine spacing between columns

Problem 2
Boxed table

Retype Problem 1 on a full sheet in reading position; SS body. Arrange the body of the table in 2 groups of 3 items each separated by a DS. Box the table by inserting vertical lines between columns.

words

CONTRIBUTIONS TO CIVIC OPERA DEVELOPMENT FUND 9

(Donations by Area Patrons) 14

Donor	Location	Amount	words
			27
			40
			44
			57
Asheford Company	Chicago, IL	$ 6,500.75	64
Davidson Corporation	Milwaukee, WI	15,750.00	72
DeCosta, Albert J.	Madison, WI	7,125.50	79
McCullough, Joan	South Bend, IN	11,075.50	87
Sanchez Company	Milwaukee, WI	12,625.50	94
Ziegler Corporation	Chicago, IL	9,865.00	102
			115

Source: Civic Opera Annual Report. 122

Problem 3
Table with leaders

half sheet, long side up; SS body; leave 10 spaces between Columns 1 & 2; 4 spaces between Columns 2 & 3

SUPPLEMENTARY EXPENSE STATEMENT 6
OF EXPENSES CHARGED DIRECTLY TO OPERATIONS 14

(In Thousands of Dollars) 19

Item	Total This Year	Total Last Year	words
			21
			30
Maintenance and repairs	$ 50,924	$ 45,883	43
Taxes, other than income taxes:			49
Payroll taxes	24,265	20,241	61
Property and misc. corporate taxes	7,858	8,406	73
Research and development costs	29,220	26,350	89
Total	$112,267	$100,880	93

Problem 4
Ruled table with leaders

half sheet, long side up; SS body; leave 16 spaces between Columns 1 & 2; 4 spaces between Columns 2 & 3

JOYCE AND McFALLS DEVELOPMENT CORPORATION 8
DS
Statement of Expenses 12

Expense	*This Year (thousands of dollars)*	*Last Year*	words
			25
			38
			42
			48
			61
Operating and other expenses	*$11,214*	*$10,107* DS	73
Interest expense	*7,296*	*6,436*	81
Federal income taxes	*3,742*	*3,461*	89
State income taxes	*209*	*190*	98
Total	*$22,461*	*$20,194*	102

83c ▶ 10
Improve grammar skill: related learning

full sheet; 1" top margin; 60-space line

Type as directed in 81c, p. 135.

GRAMMAR GUIDES, continued

B. Pronouns (he, she, it, they, their, etc.) **and their antecedents.**

1. A pronoun must agree with its antecedent in person (person identifies who is indicated by the pronoun).

2. A pronoun must agree with its antecedent in gender (masculine, feminine, and neuter—his, her, its).

3. A pronoun must agree with its antecedent in number (singular or plural).

learn 1. Luisa, who goes to college, finds she must study.

apply Students who go to college find that (they, you) must study.

learn 2. Everyone in this class has finished his or her work. (mixed group)
learn The class has finished its work. (class as a unit)
learn Each sorority member named her favorite sport.
learn Each fraternity member named his favorite sport.

apply Each member of the Girl Scouts has finished (her, its) project.
apply Each boy will vote for (his, her, its) favorite player.

learn 3. All of us have completed our work.
learn The committee has completed its report. (committee as a group)
learn The committee did not complete their reports. (committee as individuals)

apply Neither Yoko nor Mary has (her, their) book.
apply Janet and Ken have lost (her, his, their) workbooks.

84

84a ▶ 5
Conditioning practice

Follow standard directions, p. 134.

alphabet 1 Monkeys in the quaint park watched a fat lizard devour six juicy bugs.
figures 2 The inventory includes 96 pamphlets, 1,827 books, and 3,450 magazines.
home row 3 J. Kagal asked a lad if he had added a dash of salt to a dish of hash.
fluency 4 They may make the six men pay for the ancient ornament or do the work.

| 1 | 2 | 3 | 4 | 5 | 6 | 7 | 8 | 9 | 10 | 11 | 12 | 13 | 14 |

84b ▶ 10
Type an outline

half sheet, long side up; 1½" side margins:

	Left	Right
elite	18	84*
pica	15	70*

*Plus allowance for bell (see p. 68).

Begin on Line 9; space parts of outline properly (see p. 93).

Learning cue: Remember to release the shift lock to type the hyphen in Item II.

PLANNING AND DECISION MAKING

I. NATURE OF PLANNING
   A. Planning is Choosing the Best Way to Reach a Goal
      1. Wants exceed resources
      2. Some wants must be deferred
   B. Planning Involves Decision Making

II. DECISION-MAKING PROCESS
   A. Identify the Problem
   B. List Alternative Approaches
   C. Evaluate Each Approach
   D. Select the Best Approach

205

205a ▶ 5 Conditioning practice

Use standard directions given in 201a, p. 318.

alphabet	1	Mikey Bazur exchanged exquisite jewels for a very lovely pocket watch.
figures	2	The top teams sold 18, 29, 37, 46, and 50 dozen of Girl Scout cookies.
1st & 3d rows	3	music brick quiver pocket worker bonnet bottom tropics cutlery example
fluency	4	They may work for a big profit to make up for some other slow periods.

| 1 | 2 | 3 | 4 | 5 | 6 | 7 | 8 | 9 | 10 | 11 | 12 | 13 | 14 |

205b ▶ 45 Build sustained production; tables with leaders, rulings, and boxed

Time Schedule

Preparation .... 5′
Timed production .... 30′
Final check;
compute *n-pram* .... 10′

1. Make a list of problems to be typed:

page 318, 201d, Problem 1
page 320, 202d, Problem 3
page 321, 203c, Problem 1
page 322, 204b, Problem 3

2. Arrange supplies: full sheets; half sheets; second sheets; carbon paper; eraser.

3. Make 1 cc for each problem.

4. When directed to begin, type for 30′ from the list of problems, correcting all errors neatly. Proofread before removing the problems from the machine.

5. Determine *n-pram* for the 30′ period.

6. Turn in problems in the order listed.

206

206a ▶ 5 Conditioning practice

Use standard directions given in 201a, p. 318.

alphabet	1	Judge Cazwey got five exceptional lamps for the bankers' headquarters.
figures	2	They delivered 243 desks, 185 tables, 79 lamps, and 60 posture chairs.
double letters	3	loose terror haggle oppose vacuum banner attack saddle plummet success
fluency	4	Those men may go downtown to fight the audit amendment for their town.

| 1 | 2 | 3 | 4 | 5 | 6 | 7 | 8 | 9 | 10 | 11 | 12 | 13 | 14 |

206b ▶ 45 Measure production: tables with leaders, rulings, and boxed

Time Schedule

Preparation .... 5′
Timed production .... 30′
Final check;
compute *n-pram* .... 10′

Supplies: full sheets; second sheets; carbon paper; eraser.

Procedures: Type the problems for 30′ with 1 cc for each problem; correct errors; compute *n-pram*.

Problem 1
Table with leaders

full sheet; reading position; DS body; leave 16 spaces between Columns 1 & 2, and 4 spaces between Columns 2 & 3.

CONSTRUCTION PROJECTS OF LOCAL CONTRACTORS (8)

(In Thousands of Dollars) (13)

	This Year	Last Year	words
			20
Cornetto General Contractors	50,787	47,648	32
Hayes Plumbing, Inc.	27,460	22,513	44
Medrano Electrical Corporation	29,855	28,160	56
Olshavsky Mechanical Engineers	31,609	30,578	68
Pedron Paint and Drywall, Inc.	20,257	19,102	80
Rankin Structural Steel	65,245	47,803	92
Satellite Roofing, Inc.	36,490	30,268	104
Universal Paving Company	78,062	69,435	118
Total	339,765	295,507	122

83

83a ▶ 5 Conditioning practice

Follow standard directions, p. 134.

alphabet 1 Lazy, exotic jellyfish float quietly with mackerel in a very big pond.

figures 2 I ordered 720 pencils, 36 pens, 49 erasers, and 185 cardboard folders.

third row 3 Type upper-row keys properly by making quick reaches with the fingers.

fluency 4 She may pay the firm for the work when they sign the right audit form.

| 1 | 2 | 3 | 4 | 5 | 6 | 7 | 8 | 9 | 10 | 11 | 12 | 13 | 14 |

83b ▶ 35 Type personal/business and business letters

4 full sheets

1. Using your home address in the opening lines and your typed name in the closing lines, type Problems 1, 3, and 4 in personal/business style (see p. 71) to:

Mr. Robert Issacs, Director
Eagle Lake Camp, Box 690
Prescott, AZ 86301-7238

Use a 50-space line and start your street address on Line 17; supply all necessary parts for the letters (salutation, complimentary close, your typed name).

2. On a letterhead [LM p. 5] or plain full sheet, type Problem 2 in modified block style, blocked paragraphs (see p. 83). Use a 60-space line and start the date on Line 16. Supply an appropriate salutation, using your name.

Problem 1

March 10, 19-- (¶ 1) I wish to apply for a job as a counselor at your summer camp. (¶ 2) During the past year, I worked after school as a volunteer in the Vista Park Day Care Program. I taught arts and crafts to the children. (¶ 3) My supervisor, Mrs. Ellen Willette, said she would be happy to recommend me. Her phone number is (use your area code) 277-8829.

Problem 2

May 8, 19-- (Your name and your home address) (¶ 1) Mrs. Willette speaks highly of your work. She said you were conscientious and dependable and that the children enjoyed working with you. (¶ 2) Because of Mrs. Willette's recommendation of you, I am prepared to offer you a summer job as counselor at Eagle Lake Camp. You will be working with children in the 9-12 age group. (¶ 3) If you accept this job offer, I'd like to have you report for work on the afternoon of June 24. I am enclosing a map showing the location of Eagle Lake Camp in relation to the city of Prescott. Sincerely yours | Robert Issacs, Director | jw | Enclosure

Problem 3

May 13, 19-- (¶ 1) Your letter offering me a position as counselor at Eagle Lake Camp arrived today. I am happy to accept your offer. (¶ 2) As you requested, I shall report for work on the afternoon of June 24.

Problem 4

August 28, 19-- (¶ 1) Thank you for the opportunity to work at Eagle Lake Camp. It was a wonderful experience in every way. (¶ 2) I enjoyed working with the children and getting to know you and the rest of the staff.

206b, continued

Problem 2
Ruled table

full sheet; exact vertical center; DS body; decide spacing between columns

Problem 3
Boxed table

Retype Problem 2 on a full sheet; exact vertical center; SS body. Arrange the body vertically in 2 groups of 4 items each separated by a DS. Decide spacing between columns; box the table by inserting vertical lines between columns.

words

EMPLOYMENT TEST PERFORMANCE OF JOB APPLICANTS 9

(Comparative Scores on Typewriting Tests) 17

Applicant	Net Rate Error Deduction	Errors Corrected	words
			30
			43
			45
			53
			66
Connie J. Ashley	87 nwam	79 nwam	72
Beatrice L. Bixler	79 "	68 "	78
Violet L. Chin	74 "	69 "	83
Dominic M. Costello	88 "	76 "	89
Maria D. Gonzalez	89 "	78 "	95
Bryan J. Masumoto	73 "	68 "	101
Yvonne Pawlowski	75 "	67 "	107
Judith Schellenberg	76 "	67 "	113
			126

Source: Personnel Office Reports. 133

Problem 4
Table with leaders

full sheet; reading position; DS body; leave 16 spaces between Columns 1 & 2, and 4 spaces between Columns 2 & 3

U.S. POPULATION BY SELECTED AGE GROUPS 8

(Figures in Thousands) 13

Age Group	Census Bureau Projections 1990	2000	words
			18
			25
10 to 14 years	16,718	20,153	37
15 to 19 years	16,777	19,727	49
20 to 24 years	17,153	16,898	61
25 to 29 years	20,169	16,469	73
30 to 34 years	20,917	17,981	85
40 to 44 years	17,331	20,909	97
50 to 54 years	11,422	16,885	109
60 to 64 years	10,360	10,151	121
All ages	243,513	260,378	132

82c ▶ 30
Recall and improve table typing skills

Problem 1

half sheet, long side up

1. Center problem vertically and horizontally. Leave 8 spaces between columns.

2. DS data of table.

ENERGY SOURCES

TS

natural gas	geothermal
	DS
oil	water
coal	solar
wind	biomass

Problem 2

full sheet

1. Center vertically in reading position (2 spaces above exact center) and horizontally; 10 spaces between columns.

2. DS data of table.

3. SS above and DS below divider line (1 ½" long).

WORD DIVISION REVIEW *

DS

(Preferable Division Points at Ends of Lines)

TS

knowl-edge	mathe-matics
	DS
study-ing	area
oper-ate	highly
planned	enough
sum-mer	run-ning
starter	begin-ning

SS
DS

* If a word is typed without hyphens, it should not be divided.

Problem 3

half sheet, short side up

1. Center vertically and horizontally; 8 spaces between columns.

2. DS data of table.

As time permits, retype Problems 1 and 2 on half sheets, short side up.

CENTURY HIGH SCHOOL, 1983

(Enrollments by Grade Level)

Freshman	508
Sophomore	610
Junior	785
Senior	902

unit **40** lessons 207-212

Master forms typing skills

Learning goals

1. To develop skill in typing purchase orders.
2. To develop skill in typing bills of lading.
3. To develop skill in typing invoices.
4. To develop skill in typing index cards.
5. To reinforce selected language arts skills.

Machine adjustments

1. Paper guide at *0*.
2. Margins: 70-space line for sentence and ¶s; as directed for problems.
3. Spacing: SS sentence drills; DS paragraph activities; as directed for problems.
4. Tab sets: for 5-space ¶ indention; as needed for problems.

207

207a ▶ 5 Conditioning practice

each line twice SS (slowly, then faster); if time permits, retype selected lines

alphabet 1 Marv Brow spoke quietly to experts deciding the fee for the jazz trio.
figures 2 The bowlers on our company team scored 203, 145, 97, and 86 last week.
outside reaches 3 was pop saw old sad ploy warp loop ease open waste plows dwarf opposes
fluency 4 The big problems of the city may end when the key amendment is signed.

| 1 | 2 | 3 | 4 | 5 | 6 | 7 | 8 | 9 | 10 | 11 | 12 | 13 | 14 |

207b ▶ 15 Type a one-page report

full sheet, second sheet, carbon sheet

1. Type the report shown at the right as a leftbound report; make 1 cc. Type the heading **THE WORLD OF TOMORROW** 2" from the top margin. Make changes indicated.

2. Read through the report; then give the original to the teacher and keep the carbon copy for use in 210b, p. 330.

3. Take the carbon copy home with you. Read the report; make pencil notes on the carbon, indicating what you plan to do to prepare for changes in the years ahead. Bring those notes to class for use in 210b.

words

heading 4

Between now and the year 2000, ~~In the years ahead~~, most of us will encounter *drastic* ~~sub-~~ 15
~~tle~~ changes in our *way of life* ~~new life style~~. Business will be 27
conducted in a "cashless" society in which *fund* ~~all~~ transfers 39
will replace *circulating* ~~regular~~ currency. New fabrics will bring 51
exciting changes in *fashions* ~~clothes~~, and new technology will 63
alt*e*~~a~~r substantially *the types of houses in which we shall live. Air* 75
travel will be at fantastically high *speeds,* ~~rates~~, *increasing* ~~moving~~ from 87
supersonic (700 to 3,500 mph) to hypersonic (more than 96
3,500 mph). Present-day automobiles will be replaced by 108
cars having extre*me* ~~am~~ changes in design and performance. 120
Metric measurements will *probably* ~~surely~~ govern our system of 134
weights and measures, pies being baked in pans not 6 x 1 145
inches, but 15 x 3 centimeters; walls being built with 156
38 x 89 millimeter *uprights* ~~beams~~ rather than the old 2 x 4; and 168
s ~~mos~~t typists preparing *reports* ~~letters~~ on station*e*~~a~~ry measuring 182
not 8 1/2 x 11 inches, but 216 x 279 millimeters. 186

82

82a ▶ 5 Conditioning practice

Follow standard directions, p. 134.

alphabet 1 Pam Cejaks dozed at the awards banquet after a very exhausting flight.
figures 2 The shipment included 156 sofas, 132 lamps, 148 desks, and 790 chairs.
shift keys 3 Kimberly A. Patterson spoke on "A Formula for Success in Typewriting."
fluency 4 She may make the goal if she works with vigor and with the right form.

| 1 | 2 | 3 | 4 | 5 | 6 | 7 | 8 | 9 | 10 | 11 | 12 | 13 | 14 |

82b ▶ 15 Improve grammar skill: related learning

full sheet; 1" top margin; 60-space line

Type as directed in 81c, p. 135.

GRAMMAR GUIDES, continued

6. Subjects such as *all* and *some*, as well as fractions and percentages, are plural if their modifiers are plural and singular if their modifiers are singular.

7. If there is confusion whether a subject is singular or plural, consult a dictionary.

8. Pronouns *I, we, you,* and *they*, and *plural nouns* as subjects, require the plural verb *do not* or the contraction *don't*; pronouns *he, she,* and *it*, and *singular nouns* as subjects, require the singular verb *does not* or the contraction *doesn't.*

9. *A number* as the subject is usually plural and requires a plural verb; *the number* is usually singular and requires a singular verb.

learn 6. All the students have been working hard.
learn All the food is frozen.
learn Two thirds of the work is completed.
learn Two thirds of the workers are here.

apply Some of the work (is, are) done.
apply Some of the workers (is, are) going on vacation in two weeks.
apply All of us (is, are) present.

learn 7. The data in your report are erroneous.
learn The national news is good today.
learn The alumni are meeting today.

apply These data (is, are) important.
apply Parentheses (is, are) used in this sentence.

learn 8. The scales don't work properly.
learn They don't want the order.
learn She doesn't want to go with you.
learn The scale doesn't work properly.

apply It (don't, doesn't) matter; use either style.
apply The machine (don't, doesn't) work.

learn 9. A number of students are here for the tour.
learn The number of students is smaller this year.

apply A number of persons (has, have) applied for the position today.
apply The number who qualified (is, are) small.

207c ▶ 30 Learn to type business cards

5″ × 3″ cards or paper cut to size [LM pp. 149-152]

1. Type a card for each customer listed at the right. On one side, type the name and address as shown in the first illustration below; on the reverse side, type the data as shown in the second illustration.

Align the information with the headings as shown. Circle errors.

2. Alphabetize by customer name.

Mrs. Nancy Sakamoto
3107 Diamond Head Road
Honolulu, HI 96815-7321
(Insert name)
271-8811
November 10, 19--
Benson pool sweep
TC-195260
Replace power head

Miss Jean Yuen
1305 Kamehameha Avenue
Aiea, HI 96701-3463
(Insert name)
261-0975
November 10, 19--
Water pump
BX-08621-J
Replace brushes

Mr. Ramon Carvalho
3984 Sunnyvale Street
Kaneohe, HI 96744-4826
(Insert name)
931-4687
November 7, 19--
Water heater
YN-25042-L
Replace thermostat

Mr. Joseph Perry
2659 Fountain Street
Ewa, HI 96706-3826
(Insert name)
683-1704
November 12, 19--
Water filter
QM-56304
Repair backwash valve

Mr. George Mitamura
1036 Hibiscus Drive
Waialua, HI 96791-5726
(Insert name)
822-0317
November 12, 19--
Benson pool sweep
OR-37483-X
Replace rear jets

Miss Susan Okwandu
3791 Floral Avenue
Kahuku, HI 96731-2732
(Insert name)
231-0465
November 8, 19--
Water pump
BZ-91385-K
Replace pressure gauge

Mrs. Grace Moriwaki
2574 Pearl Street
Kailua, HI 96734-5235
(Insert name)
921-3685
November 6, 19--
Electric motor for pump
VI-40715-U
Replace switch

Mrs. Violet Chin
4016 Coast Road
Pearl City, HI 96782-6902
(Insert name)
722-3064
November 9, 19--
Water filter
QN-59184-A
Replace intake valve

Mr. Charles Clark
3829 Paradise Street
Wahiawa, HI 96786-5834
(Insert name)
731-6420
November 8, 19--
Electric motor
VC-58914-Y
Replace armature

```
TS
Sakamoto, Nancy (Mrs.)
                          TS
Mrs. Nancy Sakamoto
3107 Diamond Head Road
Honolulu, HI  96815-7321
3 spaces
```

```
                 POOL SERVICES, INC.

Customer's Name:     Mrs. Nancy Sakamoto

Telephone Number:    271-8811

Date Received:       November 10, 19--

Equipment:           Benson pool sweep

Serial Number:       TC-195260

Repairs:             Replace power head
```

208

208a ▶ 5 Conditioning practice

Use standard directions given in 207a, p. 325.

alphabet 1 Jinx Bouquet carefully mixed vigorous drinks for us on the west plaza.

figures 2 He assigned pages 31, 58, 64, 72, and 90 for extra study by the group.

bottom row 3 van cozy cram bank name mend manner chance moving banner excess boxing

fluency 4 The girl may fix her name to the title form to be signed in city hall.

| 1 | 2 | 3 | 4 | 5 | 6 | 7 | 8 | 9 | 10 | 11 | 12 | 13 | 14 |

81b, continued

Problem 3
Center and type a poem.

half sheet, long side up

Center problem vertically and horizontally. Determine placement by centering longest line of poem (see color arrow); set left margin at this point.

Learning cue: To make author's name end at end of longest line of poem, move carriage or element to the last stroke of the longest line; backspace once for each letter and space in name plus dash (two hyphens); space forward 1 space; type as shown.

```
TYPE CASTING
                TS

Some are the type who do not type,
They write their letters longhand.
And some of these, it would appear,
Write longhand with the wrong hand.
                                  DS
It seems to me that in the time
Their readers spend, perforce,
▶ They could, and would be thanked for this,
Complete a typing course.
                        DS
                        --Richard Armour
```

81c ▶ 15
Improve grammar skill: related learning

full sheet; 1" top margin; 60-space line

Study/Learn/Apply/Correct procedures

1. *Study* explanatory guide.

2. *Type* guide number (with period), space twice, and type *learn* sentence(s) SS, noting guide application at the underline. DS.

3. *Type apply* sentence(s) DS, selecting word (in parentheses) needed to make sentence correct.

4. As your teacher reads the correct sentences, *show* in pencil or pen any corrections that need to be made.

5. Retype any *apply* sentence containing an error, correcting the error as you type. Type the corrected sentence in the space below the *apply* sentence containing the error.

GRAMMAR GUIDES

A. Verbs and subjects: The form of the verb must agree with the subject of the sentence.

1. A singular subject requires a singular verb.

2. Compound subjects (usually joined by *and*) require plural verbs.

3. Indefinite pronouns (each, every, any, everyone, either, and neither) when used as subjects are singular and require singular verbs.

4. Singular subjects linked by *or* or *nor* require a singular verb; however, if one subject is singular, and the other plural, the verb agrees with the one that is closer.

5. Collective nouns (committee, team, class, jury, etc.) when used as subjects are usually singular and require a singular verb.

learn 1. A line of students is waiting to see the counselor.
apply One of the applicants (is, are) here for an interview.

learn 2. My mother and my father are away this week.
apply The president and the manager (is, are) here.

learn 3. Everyone in the class is typing well.
apply Each of the students (is, are) ready to go on the field trip.

learn 4. Either my sister or my brother is going.
learn Neither the teacher nor the students are here.

apply Neither the book nor the pamphlet (is, are) being used.
apply Either the girl or her parents (is, are) going shopping today.

learn 5. The team has gone to the locker room.

apply The jury (has, have) returned its verdict.
apply The board (is, are) in session.

208b ▶ 10
Learn to type common business forms

Study the tips given at the right and the model shown below for pointers on typing business forms.

Purchase order:

a form used to order merchandise.

Bill of lading:

a form used by a common carrier to acknowledge receipt of goods to be shipped.

Invoice:

a form for billing a customer for merchandise purchased.

Tips for typing purchase orders, bills of lading, and invoices

1. Type the address 2 spaces from the left and a DS from the top line in address area; set tab stops for other "columnar" items using the same stop more than once if possible.

2. SS the items in the description column unless there are 3 or fewer lines. Double space (DS) for 2 or 3 single-line items.

3. With an item of more than 1 line, indent the second and succeeding lines 3 spaces.

4. In the *total* column, underline the amount for the last item; then DS and type total.

5. Begin the items in the description column about 2 spaces to the right of the vertical line.

6. Business papers like these are often mailed in window envelopes. (See RG p. vi.)

Note: The total amounts in the forms in this unit are shown without commas separating thousands and hundreds. The use of commas is equally correct.

208c ▶ 35
Learn to type purchase orders

Problem 1
Purchase order

Time schedule

Preparation .... 5′
Problem typing .... 25′
Final check .... 5′

Follow these procedures:

1. Arrange supplies [LM pp. 153–156].

2. Type problems to conform to style shown in model below.

3. Proofread; circle errors.

DPI **Distinctive Pools, Inc.** 716 Poplar Street Macon, GA 31201-7534 (912) 721-3862

Tab

PURCHASE ORDER — words

Purchase order No. B-850374 — 2

Sunbelt Pool Supply Company
265 Parson Drive
Atlanta, GA 30341-6597

Date November 12, 19-- — 11

Terms 2/10, n/30 — 14, 21

Ship Via Lee Transport, Inc. — 25

Quantity	Tab Cat. No.	Tab 2 spaces from rule — Description	Tab Price	Tab Total	words
DS					
10	WX-3856	Deluxe curved pool brush, 18"	15.05	150.50	34
16	TO-1730	Residential pool life line, 20'	14.20	227.20	44
12	HT-2859	Aluminum-frame leaf skimmer,			51
		fiber with fiberglass net	17.25	207.00	56
5	NG-1032	Vacuum hose, 1 1/2" x 30'	43.15	<u>215.75</u>	66
				DS	
				800.45	67
Approximate center	Approximate center	Indent 3 spaces	Approximate center		

By M. McKeown Purchasing Agent — 69

unit **16** lessons 81-85

Recall/improve basic application skills

Learning goals

1. To improve skill in grammar and word division.

2. To review and improve basic application skills: centering, typing tables, personal/business letters, outlines, reports, and aligning and centering on lines.

3. To maintain and improve techniques and basic skill.

Machine adjustments

1. Paper guide at *0*.

2. 70–space line and single spacing (SS) unless otherwise directed.

3. Line–space selector on *1*, or as directed for various activities.

4. Ribbon control on black (*R* on Selectric).

81

81a ▶ 5 Conditioning practice

each line twice (slowly, faster); as time permits, retype selected lines for extra credit

alphabet	1	Turkish women put bezants of quality into an old jug in an excavation.
learning *	2	one, 1; seventy, 70; one twenty-seven, 127; twelve seventy-three, 1273
first row	3	A brave citizen came to help Bonny Kazan move the lynx to the zoo van.
fluency	4	The six busy men may go down to the rifle field to fix the burlap cot.

| 1 | 2 | 3 | 4 | 5 | 6 | 7 | 8 | 9 | 10 | 11 | 12 | 13 | 14 |

* Read, think, and type figures in 2–digit sequences whenever possible.

81b ▶ 30 Recall and improve centering skills

Problem 1

half sheet, long side up

1. Study horizontal centering steps given in problem at right.

2. Determine vertical placement (see solution).

3. Center problem vertically and horizontally (Reference: page 53).

4. TS below the heading; DS between the other lines.

Problem 2

Retype Problem 1; half sheet, short side up.

Line spaces available: 51
Elite center: 33
Pica center: 27

Lines used	
1	CENTERING STEPS
2	TS
3	
4	Find horizontal center of paper:
5	DS
6	add scale reading at left edge of paper
7	
8	to scale reading at right edge of paper;
9	
10	divide sum by 2 to find center point.
11	
12	From center point, backspace 1 for 2
13	
14	and start the line.

Vertical placement solution:

1. Determine lines available on half sheet (long side up): (Recall: 6 lines to vertical inch) 5 1/2″ × 6 = 33 lines available.

2. Count lines used (include all blank line spaces): 14

3. Determine top margin:

$$\frac{\text{Lines available} - \text{lines used}}{\text{Divided by 2}}$$

$$\frac{33 - 14}{2} = 9\ 1/2 \text{ (drop 1/2)}$$

Start on Line 10 from top.

Problem 3 is on page 135.

Proof: 9 (top margin) + 14 (lines used) + 10 (bottom margin) = 33.

208c, continued

Problem 2
Purchase order

					words
		ORDER NO.	B-850377		2
TO:	Aloha Pool Equipment Company	DATE	November 12, 19--		11
	902 Oak Street				14
	Chattanooga, TN 37403-9736	TERMS	2/10, n/30		21
		SHIP VIA	Davis Transit, Inc.		25

QUANTITY	CAT. NO.	DESCRIPTION	PRICE	TOTAL	
3	RO-15639	Pool slide, curved right, 8′	515.00	1545.00	36
5	XU-07428	Benson pool sweep, 3/4 hp	710.00	3550.00	45
24	SI-36921	Low-voltage underwater light	161.25	3870.00	56
6	MD-84057	Standard fiberglass diving			63
		board, 18″ × 2″ × 10′	445.00	2670.00	71
				11635.00	73
		M. McKeown, Purchasing Agent			79

Problem 3
Purchase order

		ORDER NO.	B-850412		2
TO:	Tropic-Air Pool Distributors	DATE	November 12, 19--		11
	814 Walker Street				14
	Augusta, GA 30902-7935	TERMS	2/10, n/30		21
		SHIP VIA	Davis Transit, Inc.		25

QUANTITY	CAT NO.	DESCRIPTION	PRICE	TOTAL	
12	OP-30572	Heavy-duty deck hose, rein-			32
		forced rubber, 5/8″ × 50′	37.50	450.00	39
6	NZ-46198	Water pump, submersible only,			47
		Model No. 4E-34N, 3/4 hp	130.00	780.00	54
2	PR-74821	Water filter, Model XT-729	268.00	536.00	65
				1766.00	66
		M. McKeown, Purchasing Agent			72

209

209a ▶ 5 Conditioning practice

Use standard directions given in 207a, p. 325.

alphabet 1 Quincy and James flew to Santa Cruz for a big public movie exhibition.
figures 2 This exam will cover pages 32, 45, 67, 81, and 90 of the new textbook.
fig/sym 3 He paid a tax of $3,245 ($2,750 plus 18% interest) for the last order.
fluency 4 When the firm pays for the eight elements, they may make a big profit.

| 1 | 2 | 3 | 4 | 5 | 6 | 7 | 8 | 9 | 10 | 11 | 12 | 13 | 14 |

209b ▶ 10 Alignment drill

1. With a pencil and ruler draw 3 horizontal lines about 4″ long and about ½″ apart on a plain sheet of paper.
2. Insert the paper and gauge the line of writing by using the variable line spacer.
3. Check the line alignment, then type the names and bonus figures for each person given at the right, each on a separate ruled line.

15 spaces

Dan Campbell	$12,365
Marcia Colantes	10,470
Mary Wright	9,875

80d ▶ 10
Improve techniques: shift keys/return

1. Lines 1-3: Each line 3 times (slowly, faster, top speed).

2. Lines 4-10: As directed in copy; type for speed.

Technique cue

Manual: Use a quick, flick-of-hand motion to return carriage.

Electric: Make a quick, little-finger reach to the return key.

Emphasize little finger reach; other fingers in typing position

shift keys

1 Ja Ja Ja Jan Jan Jan; F; F; F; Flo Flo Flo; Flo Jantze; Paula McDowde;

2 Janet A. McDuff, President of McDuff & Willis, lives in New York City.

3 Flo James, Jack Dowd, and Mario Diaz visited Los Angeles and Portland.

Emphasize quick return and start of new line

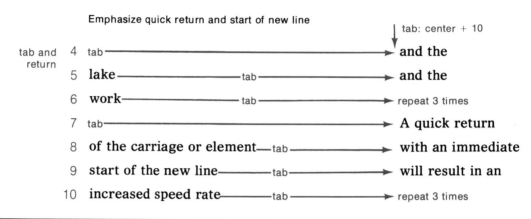

tab: center + 10

tab and return

4 tab → and the

5 lake → tab → and the

6 work → tab → repeat 3 times

7 tab → A quick return

8 of the carriage or element — tab → with an immediate

9 start of the new line — tab → will result in an

10 increased speed rate — tab → repeat 3 times

80e ▶ 15
Measure basic skill: straight copy

two 5′ writings; determine *gwam*; circle errors; record better rate

all letters used | A | 1.5 si | 5.7 awl | 80% hfw

	gwam 3′	5′
It often is so easy to take many things for granted. Consider	4	3
for a moment what amazing equipment our hands really are. Just think	9	5
of the many difficult things, often without conscious thought, our hands	14	8
do for us every day. We utilize our hands for clapping approval, for	18	11
waving goodbye, for tugging at zippers, buttoning buttons, fumbling	23	14
for door keys, or for the quick and skillful operation of the keys of	28	17
a typewriter. Our hands and fingers do all these things for us, and	32	19
we hardly ever give a thought to their wonder and adaptability. It is	37	22
so easy to do this.	38	23
Yet there is more to hands than mere utility. Our hands and fin-	43	26
gers touch the strings of a guitar or the keys of a piano to express	47	28
our mood and feeling. Our hands are used in communicating with another	52	31
individual, whether orally or in writing. We use our hands to draw and	57	34
to paint, and we have created beautiful and individual works of art.	62	37
Combined with our mind, our hands are one of the principal methods we	66	40
use in learning. A youngster touches and feels everything within reach	71	43
to gain knowledge, and this process is continued for a lifetime.	75	45

gwam 3′ | 1 | 2 | 3 | 4 | 5

5′ | 1 | 2 | 3

209c ▶ 35

Learn to type bills of lading

forms[LM pp. 155-158]

Follow time schedule and procedures outlined in 208c, p. 327.

Problem 1
Bill of lading

words

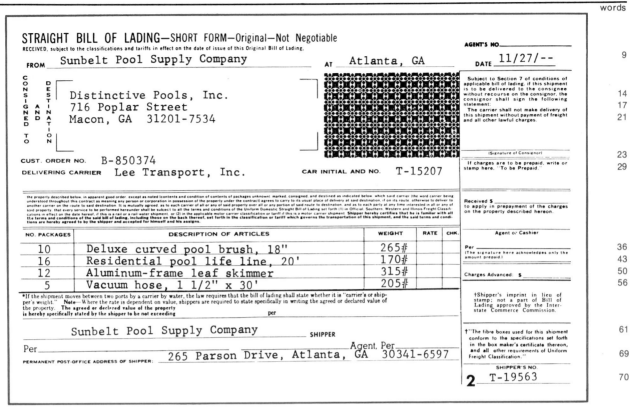

STRAIGHT BILL OF LADING—SHORT FORM—Original—Not Negotiable

RECEIVED, subject to the classifications and tariffs in effect on the date of issue of this Original Bill of Lading,

AGENT'S NO. ______

FROM Sunbelt Pool Supply Company AT Atlanta, GA DATE 11/27/-- 9

CONSIGNED TO AND DESTINATION
Distinctive Pools, Inc. 14
716 Poplar Street 17
Macon, GA 31201-7534 21

Subject to Section 7 of conditions of applicable bill of lading, if this shipment is to be delivered to the consignee without recourse on the consignor, the consignor shall sign the following statement:
The carrier shall not make delivery of this shipment without payment of freight and all other lawful charges.

(Signature of Consignor)

CUST. ORDER NO. B-850374 23
DELIVERING CARRIER Lee Transport, Inc. CAR INITIAL AND NO. T-15207 29

If charges are to be prepaid, write or stamp here, "To be Prepaid."

the property described below, in apparent good order, except as noted (contents and condition of contents of packages unknown), marked, consigned, and destined as indicated below, which said carrier (the word carrier being understood throughout this contract as meaning any person or corporation in possession of the property under the contract) agrees to carry to its usual place of delivery at said destination, if on its route, otherwise to deliver to another carrier on the route to said destination. It is mutually agreed, as to each carrier of all or any of said property over all or any portion of said route to destination, and as to each party at any time interested in all or any of said property, that every service to be performed hereunder shall be subject to all the terms and conditions of the Uniform Domestic Straight Bill of Lading set forth (1) in Official, Southern, Western and Illinois Freight Classifications in effect on the date hereof, if this is a rail or a rail-water shipment, or (2) in the applicable motor carrier classification or tariff if this is a motor carrier shipment. **Shipper hereby certifies that he is familiar with all the terms and conditions of the said bill of lading, including those on the back thereof, set forth in the classification or tariff which governs the transportation of this shipment, and the said terms and conditions are hereby agreed to by the shipper and accepted for himself and his assigns.**

Received $ ______ to apply in prepayment of the charges on the property described hereon.

Agent or Cashier

NO. PACKAGES	DESCRIPTION OF ARTICLES	WEIGHT	RATE	CHK.	
10	Deluxe curved pool brush, 18"	265#			36
16	Residential pool life line, 20'	170#			43
12	Aluminum-frame leaf skimmer	315#			50
5	Vacuum hose, 1 1/2" x 30'	205#			56

Per ______ (The signature here acknowledges only the amount prepaid.)

Charges Advanced: $ ______

*If the shipment moves between two ports by a carrier by water, the law requires that the bill of lading shall state whether it is "carrier's or shipper's weight." Note—Where the rate is dependent on value, shippers are required to state specifically in writing the agreed or declared value of the property. **The agreed or declared value of the property is hereby specifically stated by the shipper to be not exceeding** ______ per ______

†Shipper's imprint in lieu of stamp; not a part of Bill of Lading approved by the Interstate Commerce Commission.

Sunbelt Pool Supply Company SHIPPER 61

Per ______ Agent, Per ______

†"The fibre boxes used for this shipment conform to the specifications set forth in the box maker's certificate thereon, and all other requirements of Uniform Freight Classification."

PERMANENT POST-OFFICE ADDRESS OF SHIPPER: 265 Parson Drive, Atlanta, GA 30341-6597 69

SHIPPER'S NO.
2 T-19563 70

Problem 2
Bill of lading

FROM **Aloha Pool Equipment Company** AT **Chattanooga, TN** DATE **11/27/19--** 10
CONSIGNED TO AND DESTINATION **Distinctive Pools, Inc. 716 Poplar Street** 19
Macon, GA 31201-7534 CUST. ORDER NO. **B-850377** DELIVERING CARRIER 25
Davis Transit, Inc. CAR INITIAL AND NO. **RP-397** 30

NO. PACKAGES	DESCRIPTION	WEIGHT	
			37
3	**Pool slide, curved right, 8′**	**405#**	42
5	**Benson pool sweep, 3/4 hp**	**325#**	49
24	**Low-voltage underwater light**	**430#**	54
6	**Standard fiberglass diving board**	**1110#**	60

SHIPPER **Aloha Pool Equipment Company** PERMANENT POST OFFICE ADDRESS 69
OF SHIPPER **902 Oak Street, Chattanooga, TN 37403-9736** SHIPPER'S NO. 70
T-20174

Problem 3
Bill of lading

FROM **Tropic-Air Pool Distributors** AT **Augusta, GA** DATE **11/27/19--** CON- 9
SIGNED TO AND DESTINATION **Distinctive Pools, Inc. 716 Poplar Street** 17
Macon, GA 31201-7534 CUST. ORDER NO. **B-850412** DELIVERING CARRIER 22
Davis Transit, Inc. CAR INITIAL AND NO. **Y-7205** 27

12 Heavy-duty deck hose, 5/8″ × 50′ 225# | 6 Water pump, Model No. 4E-34N, 42
3/4 hp 475# | 2 Water filter, Model XT-729 270# SHIPPER **Tropic-Air Pool** 48
Distributors PERMANENT POST OFFICE ADDRESS OF SHIPPER **814 Walker** 53
Street, Augusta, GA 30902-7935 SHIPPER'S NO. **T-31895** 61

80

80a ▶ 5
Conditioning practice

each line twice (slowly, faster); as time permits, retype selected lines for extra credit

alphabet 1 Kruczek piqued the Trojan defense with mixed signals and wily bravura.
figures 2 Jane and Lee labeled 10,962 illustrations, 475 tables, and 83 figures.
space bar 3 If what you say is so, then they should find the work very easy to do.
fluency 4 It is the duty of the chair to handle the amendment to the proxy form.

| 1 | 2 | 3 | 4 | 5 | 6 | 7 | 8 | 9 | 10 | 11 | 12 | 13 | 14 |

80b ▶ 10
Type a short report: statistical copy

full sheet, DS copy

1. On Line 13, center the heading:
MOTOR VEHICLE ACCIDENTS
TS below heading.
2. Indent 5 for ¶s.
3. Use 1 1/2" side margins.

	Left	Right
elite	18	84*
pica	15	70*

* Plus allowance for bell (see p. 68).

4. Proofread finished copy and circle errors.

Technique goals

Fingers well curved

Finger-reach action

all figures used

	gwam 1′	3′
During 1973, 55,800 persons were killed in car accidents. There	13	4
were 128.7 million motor vehicles on our highways in 1973. During 1974,	28	9
the number of motor vehicles grew by 7 million to 135.7 million, yet	41	14
the number of highway deaths as a result of car accidents was reduced	55	18
to 46,200. This 17.2% decrease was a direct result of a reduction in	69	23
highway speed. Effective January 1, 1974, the national highway speed	83	28
limit was set at 55 miles per hour as one step in the conservation of	97	32
energy.	99	33
By 1977, the number of motor vehicles on our highways had increased	14	38
to 148.9 million, an increase of 13.2 million vehicles from 1974 to	27	42
1977. Yet the number of highway deaths in 1977 had increased by only	41	47
3,300 to 49,500 in comparison with 1974 when 46,200 persons were killed	56	52
in car accidents. Despite improved safety records, motor vehicle acci-	70	56
dents are still the most frequent cause of death among adolescents and	84	61
young adults. So when you drive, please drive with care. The life you	98	66
save may be your own.	103	67

gwam 1′ | 1 | 2 | 3 | 4 | 5 | 6 | 7 | 8 | 9 | 10 | 11 | 12 | 13 | 14 |
3′ | 1 | 2 | 3 | 4 | 5 |

80c ▶ 10
Improve basic skill: statistical copy

1. Two 1′ writings on ¶1 of 80b above.
2. Repeat Step 1 using ¶2.
3. A 3′ writing using both ¶s.
4. Determine and record *gwam*.

210

210a ▶ 5 Conditioning practice

Use standard directions given in 207a, p. 325.

alphabet	1	Jack Zebendon spoke quietly to the five excited workers making chairs.
figures	2	They returned 214 radios, 583 computers, 70 typewriters, and 69 lamps.
long reaches	3	gym myths behave sympathy minimum numbers mystery celebrate initiative
fluency	4	By the end of the day, the proficient town auditor may sign the forms.

| 1 | 2 | 3 | 4 | 5 | 6 | 7 | 8 | 9 | 10 | 11 | 12 | 13 | 14 |

210b ▶ 10 Composition

full sheet

1. Refer to the carbon copy of the report completed in Lesson 207b, p. 325.

2. Compose (without correcting errors) a paragraph indicating what you plan to do to prepare for "The World of Tomorrow." Begin your paragraph: Yes, the world of tomorrow promises to be a different but challenging one. How exciting to anticipate what I may be doing in the year 2000!

3. Give the completed composition to your teacher.

210c ▶ 35 Learn to type invoices

forms [LM pp. 159-162]

Follow time schedule and procedures outlined in 208c, p. 327.

Problem 1 Invoice

Sunbelt Pool Supply Company
265 Parson Drive
Atlanta, GA 30341-6597 (404) 638-4509

Invoice

	words
Date December 10, 19--	3
Distinctive Pools, Inc.	8
716 Poplar Street / Our Order No. MA-309527	13
Macon, GA 31201-7534	17
Cust. Order No. B-850374	19
Terms 2/10, n/30 — Shipped Via Lee Transport, Inc.	25

Quantity	Description	Unit Price	Total	words
10	Deluxe curved pool brush, 18"	15.05	150.50	33
16	Residential pool life line, 20'	14.20	227.20	42
12	Aluminum-frame leaf skimmer, fiber with			50
	fiberglass net	17.25	207.00	55
5	Vacuum hose, 1 1/2" x 30'	43.15	215.75	64
			800.45	65
	Sales tax		40.02	69
			840.47	70

79c ▶15 Improve techniques: Response patterns/ space bar

Color bars (____) under words indicate *word* response. Read and type these words or word groups for speed.

Color dots (. . .) under words indicate *letter* response. Read and type these words letter by letter.

Technique goal

Quick spacing with down-and-in motion of right thumb

1. Lines 1-3: Each phrase 3 times; type for speed; when bell rings, complete word or divide it at syllable point, return, and continue typing.

Emphasize combination or variable response patterns

phrases

1 and the date | for the address | refer to their address | gave the statement
2 for him | they were | their date | hand weave | she saw | right union | to the tax
3 after the data are you right world opinion address the ancient problem

2. Lines 4-6: Each sentence 3 times; type for speed.

Emphasize combination or variable response patterns

sentences

4 Send a statement of the case to the union for an opinion on the taxes.
5 They gave the statement to the union at the address shown on the card.
6 World opinion is a factor in addressing the ancient problem of growth.

3. Lines 7-9: Each line 3 times; space quickly after each word and type next word without pausing.

Emphasize quick, down-and-in spacing motion with right thumb

phrases/ sentences

7 and the | and the | and the | and the | and the | and the | and the | and the | and to
8 pay them when they | pay them when they work | pay them when they work for
9 They may pay them when they try to help Jim clean the old storm drain.

79d ▶ 15 Apply improved techniques: guided writing

1. Three 1′ writings; determine *gwam*.
2. Add 4 words to best rate; determine 1/4′ goal rates.
3. Three 15″ writings; try to equal or exceed 1/4′ goal rate.
4. Three 30″ writings; try to equal or exceed 1/2′ goal rate.
5. Three 1′ guided writings at goal rate.
6. As time permits, type additional 1′ writings to increase speed.

Technique goals

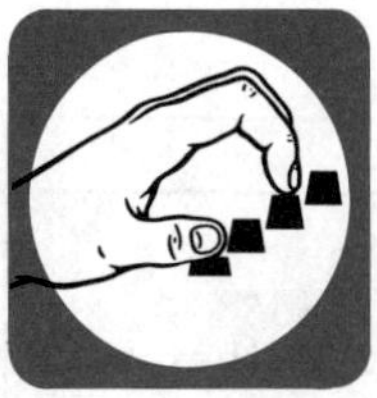

Fingers curved and upright

Finger keystroking action; hands quiet

They will send the statement to the address shown on the card. The union requested that they do this and that the case be referred to the judge for further action. The judge has promised to consider all the facts and the other data of the case. He will probably be able to give us his decision by the end of the week.

210c, continued

Problem 2
Invoice

				words
		DATE	December 11, 19--	3
SOLD TO	Distinctive Pools, Inc.			8
	716 Poplar Street	OUR ORDER NO.	TX-5603	13
	Macon, GA 31201-7534			17
		CUST. ORDER NO.	B-850377	19
TERMS	2/10, n/30	SHIPPED VIA	Davis Transit, Inc.	25

QUANTITY	DESCRIPTION	UNIT PRICE	TOTAL	words
3	Pool slide, curved right, 8′	515.00	1545.00	33
5	Benson pool sweep, 3/4 hp	710.00	3550.00	41
24	Low-voltage underwater light	161.25	3870.00	50
6	Standard fiberglass diving board,			57
	18″ × 2″ × 10′	445.00	2670.00	64
			11635.00	66
	Sales tax		581.75	71
			12216.75	73

Problem 3
Invoice

				words
		DATE	December 11, 19--	3
SOLD TO	Distinctive Pools, Inc.			8
	716 Poplar Street	OUR ORDER NO.	HV-90256	13
	Macon, GA 31201-7534			17
		CUST. ORDER NO.	B-850412	19
TERMS	2/10, n/30	SHIPPED VIA	Davis Transit, Inc.	25

QUANTITY	DESCRIPTION	UNIT PRICE	TOTAL	words
12	Heavy-duty deck hose, reinforced			32
	rubber, 5/8″ × 50′	37.50	450.00	38
6	Water pump, submersible only,			44
	Model No. 4E-34N, 3/4 hp	130.00	780.00	51
2	Water filter, Model XT-729	268.00	536.00	60
			1766.00	61
	Sales tax		88.30	65
			1854.30	66

211

211a ▶ 5 Conditioning practice

Use standard directions given in 207a, p. 325.

alphabet 1 Hank Szabo flew five excellent racquetball players from grand Jamaica.
figures 2 We just sold 178 kites, 925 toys, 60 puzzles, and 43 electronic games.
double letters 3 access puzzle excess oppose rummage balloon battery announce parallels
fluency 4 If they use the fuels to aid the work, they may pay the usual penalty.

| 1 | 2 | 3 | 4 | 5 | 6 | 7 | 8 | 9 | 10 | 11 | 12 | 13 | 14 |

211b ▶ 45 Build sustained production: purchase orders, bills of lading, invoices, cards

Time schedule
Preparation .... 5′
Timed production .... 30′
Final check;
compute *n–pram* .... 10′

1. Make a list of problems to be typed:
page 328, 208c, Problem 2
page 329, 209c, Problem 2
page 331, 210c, Problem 2
page 326, 207c

2. Arrange supplies [LM pp. 161–168], second sheets, carbon paper, eraser.

3. Make 1 cc for each problem.

4. When directed to begin, type for 30′ from the list of problems, correcting all errors neatly. Proofread before removing the problems from the machine.

5. Determine *n–pram* for the 30′ period (count 56 words for each 5″ × 3″ card completed).

6. Turn in problems in the order listed.

78d ▶ 15
Type a short report from rough-draft copy

full sheet, DS copy

1. On Line 13, center the heading:
THE TYPEWRITER AND WRITTEN WORK
TS below heading.

2. Indent 5 for ¶s.

3. Use 1 ½" side margins.

	Left	Right
elite	18	84*
pica	15	70*

* Plus allowance for bell (see p. 68).

4. Proofread finished copy and circle errors.

all letters used

	gwam 1'	3'
lc Many students In preparing the written work for their classes,	13	4
often prepare a first draft which is ten (h) revised. This revision of work	27	9
leads to improvement in the quality of the report or other written work. Some students may type the	48	16
~~first~~ initial draft and then make what ever corrections are ~~that may be~~ needed	60	20
directly on the copy so that it looks very similar to this roug(c)h-	73	24
draft cop y from which you are now typing. Type written copy whcih	86	29
is double spaced is easier to read and to revise.	96	32
lc Amazing as it may seem, Studies indicate that students who type the papers needed for	17	38
their various classes get higher grades ~~than~~ on such work ~~which is handwritten~~	39	45
All of us are impressed with the neatness the and easier-to-read	52	49
characteristics of typewritten copy. Your teachers are no exception. You can earn better grades,	72	56
then, if you will just take extra time to revise carefully ~~with care~~ your written	87	61
work and then to type it in good from before sub mitting it to your	100	65
teachers. as compared with the same work submitted in handwriting.	102	66

79

79a ▶ 5
Conditioning practice

each line twice (slowly, faster); as time permits, retype selected lines for extra credit

alphabet 1 Seventy large fire jumpers quenched forest blazes with picks and axes.
figures 2 In 1982, we had 73 office chairs, 40 office desks, and 56 work tables.
quiet hands 3 Purposeful repetition leads to rapid improvement of stroking patterns.
fluency 4 She may work with them and the others in the ancient city by the lake.

| 1 | 2 | 3 | 4 | 5 | 6 | 7 | 8 | 9 | 10 | 11 | 12 | 13 | 14 |

79b ▶ 15
Improve basic skill: rough draft

70-space line

1. Two 1' writings on ¶1 of 78d above; determine *gwam.*

2. Repeat Step 1 using ¶2.

3. Two 3' writings using both ¶s; determine *gwam.*

4. Record better rate.

212

212a ▶ 5 Conditioning practice

Use standard directions given in 207a, p. 325.

alphabet	1	Max Quigly drove to Santa Cruz just to work with a bass fishing group.
figures	2	He ordered 416 hammers, 392 saws, 80 pliers, and 75 brushes on credit.
one hand	3	ease jump erase onion severe opinion creased union retreat lumpy dread
fluency	4	The problems of the land kept the downtown firm busy with audit forms.
		| 1 | 2 | 3 | 4 | 5 | 6 | 7 | 8 | 9 | 10 | 11 | 12 | 13 | 14 |

212b ▶ 45 Measure production: purchase orders, bills of lading, invoices, cards

Time schedule

Preparation .... 5′
Timed production .... 30′
Final check;
compute *n–pram* .... 10′

1. Arrange supplies [LM pp. 169–174], second sheets, carbon paper, eraser.

2. Make 1 cc of each problem.

3. When directed to begin, type for 30′ from the following problems, correcting all errors neatly. Proofread before removing the problems from the typewriter.

4. If you finish all problems in less than 30′, type the report in 207b, p. 325.

5. Compute *n–pram* for the 30′ period.

6. Turn in all problems in the order shown.

Problem 1
Purchase order

Modern Garden Center
2702 N. Glenstone Avenue • Springfield, MO 65803-5832 • (417) 293-8605

PURCHASE ORDER — words

Purchase order No. J-930762 — 2

Farm and Garden Suppliers, Inc.
913 Elm Place
Kansas City, MO 64133-7851

Date December 14, 19-- — 12
Terms 2/10, n/30 — 17
Ship Via Thrift Trucking, Inc. — 27

Quantity	Cat. No.	Description	Price	Total	words
6	TC-915620	Cord-type hedge trimmer, 22" blade, 110-120 v.	76.75	460.50	35 41
4	NY-862173	Motorized reel mower, 18" width, 3 hp	265.00	1060.00	48 53
10	XP-480362	Wheelbarrow, 6 cu. ft., steel tray, rubber tire	92.75	927.50	61 67
15	NO-526803	Steel-blade spade, 27" handle	15.50	232.50	79
				2680.50	80

By Diane Sears Purchasing Agent — 82

78

78a ▶ 5 Conditioning practice

each line twice (slowly, faster); as time permits, retype selected lines for extra credit

alphabet 1 Gymnasts amaze excited fans and judges with very quick leaps on beams.
figures 2 He bought 51 jackets, 298 blankets, 47 kits, 630 lamps, and 209 tires.
continuity 3 Always examine your aspirations and measure them against your talents.
fluency 4 The key to proficiency is to name the right goals, then work for them.

| 1 | 2 | 3 | 4 | 5 | 6 | 7 | 8 | 9 | 10 | 11 | 12 | 13 | 14 |

78b ▶ 15 Improve technique: response patterns

each line 3 times (slowly, faster, top speed); as time permits, retype selected lines

Goal: To reduce time interval between keystrokes (read ahead to anticipate stroking pattern).

Emphasize curved, upright fingers

one-hand words
1 as in at my be no we on up are you get him was oil dear only were upon
2 date look data pull best link area jump card lump rate hook case water
3 after union state imply great pupil staff nylon extra plump react jump

Emphasize finger action; quiet hands

one-hand phrases
4 you are | my case | in my opinion | were you | great pupil | extra jump | are upon
5 after taxes | were you only | my address | minimum decrease | exaggerate trade
6 only after you were | exaggerated opinion | estate tax | you are in | you read

Emphasize continuity; fingers close to keys with quiet hands

one-hand sentences
7 In our opinion, minimum estate taxes on oil reserves were exaggerated.
8 Only after Julio gave an exaggerated opinion were oil taxes decreased.
9 In Dee's opinion, average water reserve rates are stated at a minimum.

| 1 | 2 | 3 | 4 | 5 | 6 | 7 | 8 | 9 | 10 | 11 | 12 | 13 | 14 |

78c ▶ 15 Apply improved response patterns: guided writing

1. Three 1′ writings (at a controlled rate with a minimum of waste motion); determine *gwam*.
2. Add 4 words to best rate; determine 1/4′ goal rates.
3. Three 15″ writings; try to equal or exceed 1/4′ goal rate.
4. Three 30″ writings; try to equal or exceed 1/2′ goal rate.
5. Three 1′ guided writings at goal rate.
6. As time permits, type additional 1′ writings to increase speed.

It is no exaggeration (4) to say that (8) the decrease in rainfall (12) has resulted in (16) water reserves which (20) are far below the (24) average required for (28) safety. We were told (32) to refer this water (36) problem to the (40) committee for attention. (44) New plans probably (48) will be drafted after (52) this committee has (56) made a minimum (60) study of the water (64) problem.

212b, continued

words

Problem 2
Bill of lading

FROM **Farm and Garden Suppliers, Inc.** AT **Kansas City, MO** DATE 9
12/21/19-- CONSIGNED TO AND DESTINATION **Modern Garden Center** 15
2702 N. Glenstone Avenue Springfield, MO 65803-4129 CUST. ORDER 26
NO. **J-930762** DELIVERING CARRIER **Thrift Trucking, Inc.** CAR INITIAL 32
AND NO. **P-3057-M** 34

NO. PACKAGES	DESCRIPTION	WEIGHT	words
6	Cord-type hedge trimmer, 22″ blade	105#	42
4	Motorized reel mower, 18″ width	420#	49
10	Wheelbarrow, 6 cu. ft.	670#	55
15	Steel-blade spade, 27″ handle	150#	62

SHIPPER **Farm and Garden Suppliers, Inc.** PERMANENT POST OFFICE 68
ADDRESS OF SHIPPER **913 Elm Place, Kansas City, MO 64133-7851** 77
SHIPPER'S NO. **YO-307621** 79

Problem 3
Invoice

SOLD TO **Modern Garden Center** DATE **December 30, 19--** 10
2702 N. Glenstone Avenue OUR ORDER NO. **XT-190567** 14
Springfield, MO 65803-4129 CUST. ORDER NO. **J-930762** 21
TERMS **2/10, n/30** SHIPPED VIA **Thrift Trucking, Inc.** 27

QUANTITY	DESCRIPTION	UNIT PRICE	TOTAL	words
6	Cord-type hedge trimmer, 22″ blade,			34
	110-120 v.	76.75	460.50	38
4	Motorized reel mower, 18″ width, 3 hp	265.00	1060.00	48
10	Wheelbarrow, 6 cu. ft., steel tray,			55
	rubber tire	92.75	927.50	60
15	Steel-blade spade, 27″ handle	15.50	232.50	70
			2680.50	71
	Sales tax		134.03	75
			2814.53	77

Problem 4
Business cards

On one side, type the name and address; on the reverse side, fill in the data provided for each customer. Follow the style used in 207c, p. 326. Use the company name **Artistic Jewelers, Inc.** as heading on back of cards.
Be sure to alphabetize the typed cards by customer name. Allow 57 words for each 5″ × 3″ card completed.

Mr. David Goldberg
789 Beechwood Drive
Fairfax, VA 22031-4789
(Insert name)
366-5409
December 30, 19--
West digital clock alarm
ZT-1804526
Repair alarm-set stem

Mr. George Okoh
807 Laurel Drive
Abingdon, VA 24210-3827
(Insert name)
291-6428
December 31, 19--
Butona wristwatch
TN-8426905
Clean and oil interior

Miss Carmen Portales
1850 Columbia Pike
Arlington, VA 22204-6351
(Insert name)
362-0784
December 29, 19--
Wexford wristwatch
TI-569842
Replace sweep hand

Mrs. Maria Gonzales
397 Chestnut Street
Falls Church, VA 22046-9839
(Insert name)
286-4209
December 30, 19--
Regency stopwatch
SV-6134092
Replace stop-start stem

Miss Kathryn Page
5340 Duke Street
Alexandria, VA 22304-5713
(Insert name)
284-9107
December 29, 19--
Seito wristwatch
X-2915637
Replace battery

Mr. Michael Rosella
1635 Dogwood Lane
Annandale, VA 22003-5734
(Insert name)
367-4802
December 31, 19--
Simco wristwatch
CT-6025874
Replace hour hand

77c ▶ 15
Improve technique: response patterns

1. Lines 1-3: Each word 3 times (slowly, faster, top speed); when bell rings, complete word, return, and continue typing.

2. Lines 4-6: Each phrase 3 times (slowly, faster, top speed); when bell rings, complete word, return, and continue typing.

3. Lines 7-9: Each sentence 3 times (slowly, faster, top speed).

4. As time permits, type lines 4–6 from dictation.

Goal: High-speed typing response (think and type each word or word group as a whole).

Technique goals

Finger reaches, quiet hands

Snappy keystroking

Quick spacing

Emphasize fast finger reaches with hands quiet and relaxed

balanced-hand words

1 to and the for may but pay due did box big end six she cut got fit aid
2 with they them make then when also work such form then wish paid their
3 right field world forms down visit title eight firms chair spend usual

Emphasize high-speed phrase response

balanced-hand phrases

4 and the | and if they | go to the | pay for the work | sign the right form for
5 make right | when they | when they make them | their field | the world of work
6 sign the form | sign the form for them | the right title for the city firm

Emphasize high-speed word-level response; quick spacing

balanced-hand sentences

7 Jake may go to the big city to work with the mentor of the key theory.
8 Pay for the work and then go to the city to sign the field title form.
9 The map of the ancient land forms may aid them when they work with us.

| 1 | 2 | 3 | 4 | 5 | 6 | 7 | 8 | 9 | 10 | 11 | 12 | 13 | 14 |

77d ▶ 15
Apply improved response patterns: guided writing

1. Three 1′ writings; determine *gwam*.
2. Add 4 words to best rate; determine 1/4′ goal rates. (Example: 56 = 14, 28, 42, 56)
3. Three 15″ writings; try to equal or exceed 1/4′ goal rate.
4. Three 30″ writings; try to equal or exceed 1/2′ goal rate.
5. Three 1′ guided writings at goal rate.
6. As time permits, type additional 1′ writings. Try to increase speed.

Technique goals

Fingers curved and upright

Manual

Electric

Quick return and start of new line

Aim for a high goal and then work in the right way to reach such a goal. The right work habits and the right mind set are the format for achieving high goals. It is by working, not wishing, that you can and do reach goals. Start right now to work in the right way so that the right way of working will become a habit.

unit **41** lessons 213-217

Word processing: simulation

Learning goals

1. To learn typical procedures followed in a word processing center.

2. To simulate the use of a self-correcting typewriter.

3. To develop skill in typing letters, memos, and other material in standard formats from handwritten and rough-draft copy.

Machine adjustments

1. Paper guide set at *0*.

2. Margin sets: 70-space line for drills; as required for problems.

3. Spacing: SS sentence drills with a DS between sentence groups; as directed for problems.

213-217

213a-217a ▶ 5 Conditioning practice

each line twice SS (slowly, then faster); if time permits, retype selected lines

alphabet 1 Beverley Jackson was quizzed on many exciting aspects of night flying.

figures 2 Team scores on the dexterity tests were 82, 91, 64, 70, and 53 points.

fig/sym 3 Bill's check for $715.70 ($842 less 15%) was received on September 24.

fluency 4 The usual rush to ride the bus to work is down for eight firms today.

| 1 | 2 | 3 | 4 | 5 | 6 | 7 | 8 | 9 | 10 | 11 | 12 | 13 | 14 |

213b-217b ▶ 45 Word processing jobs

You are a Word Processing Trainee in the Word Processing Center of Twin Cities Industries, Inc., 525 Marquette Avenue, Minneapolis, MN 55402-1234. Your supervisor is Mrs. Elizabeth Muir, Word Processing Supervisor, who will give you specific instructions for each job.

The jobs you will type are prepared in handwritten or rough-draft form by executives or word originators. Documents dictated by executives on tape recorders are transcribed by Word Processing Specialists in the Center.

All letters and memos (except those you are directed to type as rough drafts) are to be typed on printed stationery.

Job 1 Weekly Log Sheet

Mrs. Muir says: Your first job is to prepare for photoduplication a Weekly Log Sheet on which you will record all jobs you complete. Type the log illustrated at the right on 8½" × 11" paper with top, bottom, and side margins of about 1". Use a pen or pencil to draw the vertical lines. The identification number for this log is **132**; be sure to enter it on the Log Sheet.

WEEKLY WORD PROCESSING LOG SHEET

Name________________________ For Week of______________________

Ident. No.	Begin Time	Originator	Department	Total Lines*	End Time	Total Minutes

*Count each line regardless of length (including any titles or subtitles). Count 3 lines for the opening lines of a letter and 3 lines for the closing lines. Count 4 lines for letter envelopes; 1 line for COMPANY MAIL envelopes.

132

76d ▶ 15
Measure basic skill: straight copy

1. Two 5′ writings; determine *gwam*.
2. Proofread; circle errors.
3. Record better *gwam* rate.

all letters used | A | 1.5 si | 5.7 awl | 80% hfw |

	gwam 3′	5′	
In the lessons of this unit, one of your daily purposes should be to	5	3	42
try to improve or to refine your typing form patterns according to the	9	6	45
special techniques that are emphasized in every lesson. These techniques	14	9	48
cover such important areas of typing skill as proper hand-and-finger	19	11	51
position, quick, snappy keystroking with the striking action in the	23	14	54
fingers, proper operation of the space bar after each word, and a fast	28	17	57
return at the end of a line with an immediate start of the new line.	33	20	59
The correct operation of both shift keys is very important, also.	37	22	62
How you type and what you type are fundamental to the rapidity of skill	42	25	65
development. Avoid such unnecessary motions as bouncing hands and arms,	47	28	68
hands moving up and down the keyboard, and that problem of many typing	52	31	71
students--looking. The secret of high-speed typewriting is to keep your	57	34	74
hands and arms very relaxed and to let your fingers do the typing. Every	61	37	77
time you type, just make the effort to progress and you will progress.	66	40	79

gwam 3′ | 1 | 2 | 3 | 4 | 5 |
5′ | 1 | 2 | 3 |

77

77a ▶ 5
Conditioning practice

each line twice (slowly, faster); as time permits, retype selected lines for extra credit

alphabet 1 Five excellent joggers pounded quickly along the beach in a warm haze.
figures 2 She sold 14 watches, 293 rings, 56 clips, 50 tie pins, and 178 clocks.
continuity 3 The prime thing is not whether one can read but whether one does read.
fluency 4 She may go with the widow to the town by the lake to do work for them.

| 1 | 2 | 3 | 4 | 5 | 6 | 7 | 8 | 9 | 10 | 11 | 12 | 13 | 14 |

77b ▶ 15
Improve basic skill: straight copy

1. Add 4 to 8 words to your 76d *gwam* rate. **Goal:** To reach a high speed.

2. Two 1′ guided writings on ¶1 of 76d at your new goal rate as the 1/4′ guides are called.

3. A 2′ guided writing on ¶1. Try to maintain your 1′ goal rate.

4. Repeat Step 2, using ¶2.

5. Repeat Step 3, using ¶2.

6. A 3′ writing using both ¶s. **Goal:** To maintain your new speed rate for 3′.

213b-217b, continued

Job 2
Rough draft of a letter

Mrs. Muir: All of our letters are typed in block style, open punctuation. Use a standard 6" line with the date on Line 13, regardless of the length of the letter. Always use the current date.

Type on plain paper at your best speed and in proper format the letter submitted by Mr. Blackwell of the Sales Department. Add a proper salutation and complimentary close. Do not correct errors. If you make an error, backspace and strike the correct key.*

The identification number for this letter is **149S**, which you will type immediately after your initials (xx:149S). Be sure to record this Job and all future Jobs on your Weekly Log Sheet.

***Note:** On electronic self-correcting typewriters, errors are corrected by backspacing (which eliminates the incorrect character) and striking the correct key. By backspacing and striking over, you are simulating the use of a self-correcting typewriter.

Job 3
Letter in final form
[LM p. 175]

Mrs. Muir: Check the letter typed in Job 2 and make any necessary corrections in pencil. Then, type the letter in final form on a letterhead. Correct errors; address envelope. Enter this Job on your Weekly Log Sheet.

Please type the following letter to Ms. Samantha T. Abrams, who is the Purchasing Agent for ~~the~~ Royal Secretarial Services, 1502 Hewitt Avenue, Saint Paul, ~~Minnesota~~ MN. The ZIP Code is 55104-3823.

(¶) Your kind ~~comments~~ remarks during our telephone conversation today about my presentation at the Office Products Symposium in Minneapolis last week are ~~very~~ much appreciated. As you requested, I am ~~sending you~~ enclosing a brochure that shows all models of the Sovereign Series of electronic typewriters. The prices ~~shown~~ listed in the brochure are, of course, retail prices. Since you ~~customarily~~ usually purchase items in quantity, you will qualify for a 15-percent discount.

(¶) The Sovereign electronic typewriter is a masterpiece of efficiency. The Model HT-100 is a single-element, self-correcting ~~machine~~ typewriter with dual pitch. Its many features include automatic error correction, six repeat character keys, both vertical and horizontal half-spacing, and automatic tabulation. ~~Stenos~~ Secretaries who have ~~utilize~~ used the Model HT-100 ~~have found~~ report that they can do more work with less effort ~~than they ever have before~~.

(¶) May we demonstrate the Sovereign typewriter for your secretarial ~~group~~ personnel? ~~Contact~~ Call me at 487-5200, Extension 512, and I will be ~~glad~~ happy to set up an appointment for one of our representatives to visit your office.

Roy T. Blackwell
Assistant Sales Manager

76

76a ▶ 5
Conditioning practice

each line twice (slowly, faster); as time permits, retype selected lines for extra credit

alphabet 1 Just work for improved basic techniques to maximize your typing skill.

figures 2 Type 1 and 2 and 3 and 4 and 5 and 6 and 7 and 8 and 9 and 10 and 312.

adjacent key 3 Used properly, a typewriter is your friend; used improperly, your foe.

fluency 4 The field work may aid them to make a profit for the eight city firms.

| 1 | 2 | 3 | 4 | 5 | 6 | 7 | 8 | 9 | 10 | 11 | 12 | 13 | 14 |

76b ▶ 15
Improve technique: keystroking

each line 3 times (slowly, faster, top speed); as time permits, retype selected lines

Home row Emphasize curved, upright fingers; wrists low; hands quiet

1 fjfj fjfj dkdk dkdk slsl slsl a;a; a;a; a;sldkfj a;sldkfj a;sldkfj ask

2 a fall; a jag; has a sash; add half a glass; a glad lass shall add gas

3 All lads had half a glass. Ask Jad to add gas. Lalla Jak has a sash.

Third row Emphasize quick, snap strokes; finger reaches

4 y yj u uj i ik o ol p p; t tf r rf e ed w ws q qa aqa; wosl eidk rufj;

5 your quote; we wrote it; your typewriter; you were to try to quote it;

6 You were to try to type our quotation for Pete on your new typewriter.

Bottom row Emphasize curved, upright fingers; finger reaches

7 n nj m mj , ,k . .l / /; b bf v vf c cd x xs z za six can mix; zircons

8 many zebu and bison; six zinc boxes; men and women mix zinc in a cave;

9 Zan Babben can move six boxes of zinc to the cave for Azan and Bonnie.

76c ▶ 15
Apply improved technique: guided writing

1. A 1′ writing (at a controlled rate with good keystroking technique).

2. Determine *gwam*. Add 8 to your *gwam* rate. Determine 1/4′ goals for 1′ writings at new rate. (Example: *48* = 12, 24, 36, 48)

3. Four 1′ writings at your goal rate as 1/4′ guides are called.

4. Two 2′ writings for speed. Try to reach your goal rate.

all letters used (home–, third–, and bottom–row reaches)

. 4 . 8 . 12
To become an expert typist, just be sure to give a purpose to your
. 16 . 20 . 24 .
practice and then type all drill lines at alternating levels of typing
28 . 32 . 36 . 40
speed: sometimes slowly as you concentrate on techniques, such as
. 44 . 48 . 52 .
improved keystroking; then faster or at top speed as you try to reach
56 . 60 . 64 . 68
new speed levels. Work to eliminate all waste motions. You will be
. 72 .
amazed at your skill gain.

213b-217b, continued

Job 4
Interoffice memo [LM p. 177]
Mrs. Muir: Please type this memo from me to **Jose T. Ortez, Chief** of the **Wage and Salary Branch.** Use as a subject **Revised Job Description** and today's date. Correct errors; address **COMPANY MAIL** envelope. The identification number is **483M.**

All memos are typed with a 6-inch line on printed forms. Use current date; type the heading information at the same point as the left margin of the memo.

(¶) In accordance with the provisions of Personnel Bulletin No. 19, we have revised the position of Word Processing Operator to provide for the entry position of Word Processing Trainee as shown on the enclosed job description. This will make it easier for us to recruit and hire personnel for the Word Processing Center.
(¶) Our edition of the Dictionary of Occupational Titles does not include a description for this specific job. However, it is very similar in nature to the position of clerk-typist which is described under D.O.T. No. 203.362-010.

Job 5
Job description full sheet
Mrs. Muir: Type the job description to enclose with the memo to Mr. Ortez. Use a 6-inch line for the body and a top margin of 1½". Correct errors; type the identification number—**192M**—at left margin a DS below the final line.

WORD PROCESSING ~~OPERATOR~~ TRAINEE

Works under the ~~general~~ direct supervision of a Word Processing Supervisor performing recurring duties under established procedures. Supervisor assigns work, provides advice and instruction on policies and procedures, and gives instructions on new or revised work procedures.

Performs the following major duties:

1. Types correspondence, reports, forms, tables, and other matter from handwritten or rough-draft documents in final form except when rough draft is requested by the word originator for his/her further consideration.

~~2. Transcribes dictated material from recordings of all kinds in final form except when intermediate rough draft is requested by the originator for further consideration.~~

~~3~~ 2. Posts information to records, performs timekeeping duties, and executes other simple arithmetic procedures, using adding or calculating machine.

~~4~~ 3. Substitutes, when necessary, for the mail clerk by sorting and distributing mail, answering telephone, and performing similar duties.

Performs other related duties as directed by the Word Processing Supervisor.

phase **4** lessons 76-100

Build communication skills

These lessons represent a *planned program* to help you improve your typing skills. Here are the key steps to improving typing skill:

1. Position: Maintain good typing posture and proper hand-and-finger position.

2. Purpose: Give a purpose to all typing practice as directed in the various lessons.

3. Practice: Use alternating levels of practice speed in typing drill lines—slowly, then faster, etc.

4. Goals: Set daily and weekly goals with the emphasis on improvement.

The 25 lessons of Phase 4 reflect this *planned program* to help you:

1. Improve technique and practice patterns.

2. Increase basic skill on straight, statistical, and rough-draft copy.

3. Improve basic English skills and composing skills.

4. Reinforce basic application skills.

5. Increase application skill on personal/business letters.

unit **15** lessons 76-80

Refine techniques and improve basic skills

Learning goals

1. To improve technique and practice patterns.

2. To transfer or apply improved technique patterns to straight-copy typing.

3. To improve basic skill on straight, statistical, and rough-draft copy.

Machine adjustments

1. Set paper guide at *0* on most typewriters.

2. Set paper-bail rolls at even intervals across paper.

3. Set ribbon control to type on upper portion of ribbon (on black; *R* on Selectric).

Use:

- 70-space line and single spacing (SS) for drills
- 5-space ¶ indention
- double spacing (DS) for all timed writings of more than 1 minute (1′)
- double spacing (DS) below each single-spaced (SS) group of drill lines
- triple spacing (TS) below drills and lesson parts

213b-217b, continued

Job 6
Letter [LM p. 179]

Mrs. Muir: **Harry W. Neal**, one of our **Sales Representatives**, has submitted this letter to be typed in final form. Type the letter and envelope, following the directions I gave you earlier. Be sure to proofread and correct your copy carefully before you remove it from the typewriter.

Letter to Miss Mary Dolores Weir, Director of Administration, Consolidated Manufacturing, Inc., 300 West
Superior Street, Duluth, MN 55802-2731

Roy T. Blackwell, our assistant sales manager, has
asked me to *answer* ~~reply to~~ the questions you raised during his
presentation at the Office Products Symposium in Minneapolis last week about dictating machines.

There are a number of different *types* ~~kinds~~ of dictating
equipment on the market. The portable *machine* ~~one~~, however, is
by far the most convenient and versatile. Take, for *example* ~~in-
stance~~, our portable dictation/transcription machine--
the "Traveler." It can and will travel wherever the
word originator must go. It *permits* ~~lets~~ busy executives *to* dictate at their own convenience, during or after hours.
It requires the *attention* ~~time~~ of just one person at a time--the
executive's when dictating, the transcriber's when tran-
scribing. *It also permits any transcriber to type the dictation.*

Executives ~~Companies~~ who have *used* ~~bought~~ the "Traveler" during the
past several years have been enthusiastic in their *assessment of its value* ~~praise~~.
They report that errors in transcription have decreased
since the secretary no longer must decipher illegible
handwritten or stenographic notes. *More important,* all companies report that the use of ~~the~~ dictating machines has saved both
time and money.

May we demonstrate the value of the "Traveler" at
your ~~our mutual~~ convenience? Please call me at 487-5200, Ext.
358, to make the necessary arrangements.

xx:186S

75c, continued

Problem 2

half sheet, short side up

Center and type the table DS in reading position. Decide spacing between columns. Correct errors.

		words
MAIL DISTRIBUTION SCHEDULE		5
For Week Beginning January 17		11
Monday, January 17	Delia Ortiz	18
Tuesday, January 18	Joshua Weber	24
Wednesday, January 19	Oramae Williams	32
Thursday, January 20	Akeo Chiba	38
Friday, January 21	Wanda Marcus	44

Problem 3

full sheet

Center and type the table DS in reading position. Decide spacing between columns. Correct errors.

Problem 4

half sheet, long side up

If time permits, retype Problem 2 in exact vertical center. Correct errors.

			words
MS. TOBIN'S TUESDAY INTER VIEW SCHEDULE			8
(Aplicant, Time, and Position)			14
Marie Tallchief	8:30	Junior stenographer	23
Terry Tellfer	9:15	File Clerk	29
Cynthia Staun	10:00	Administrative Assistant	38
Louis Jimenez	10:45	Key punch Operator	45
Karen Knott	1:03	Word processor	52
John Devlin	2:15	Executive Secretary	55
Po-ling Chow	3:00	Accounting Clerk	66
Samuel Gordon	3:45	Mt/St Operator	73

Supplemental practice/evaluation

Basic skill improvement

To prepare for formal measurement, you may want to do additional practice on the following materials.

Techniques: 63d, p. 104; 64b, p. 104.

Timed writings: 51c, p. 81; 56c, p. 89; 57b, p. 92; 63c, p. 103; 70b, p. 113; 73b, p. 118.

Problem skill improvement

If you had difficulty with any of the problems in Lessons 73–75, you may want to practice on problems selected from those below and at the right.

Centering: 63d, p. 104; 64b, p. 104; 32c, p. 53.

Personal/business letter: 44c, pp. 70–71.

Business letter: 52c, pp. 82–83.

Envelope addressing: 53c, p. 85.

Reports/footnotes: 58c, p. 94; 59d, p. 97; 60d, p. 99.

Tables: 64c, p. 105; 67b, p. 108; 67c, p. 109.

Final performance evaluation

Progress Checkup 3, covering the basic skill and problem learnings presented in Cycle 1, appears on LM pp. 93–96 and may be given at this time.

Performance Test 3, available separately from the publisher, may be used for formal measurement and evaluation instead of or in addition to the progress checkup mentioned above.

213b-217b, continued

Job 7

Magazine article 3 full sheets

Mrs. Muir: Ms. Andrea T. Shea, the company's Word Processing Manager, has completed the first draft of an article she is writing for Tomorrow's Office magazine. She would like to have the article typed in final form as a leftbound manuscript. Correct all errors as you type.

Type the footnotes at the bottom of the appropriate page so that there is a bottom margin of about 1". Type the identification number—**15M**—at left margin a DS below the final line of the article. This Job will probably require more than one class period to complete. When recording Job 7 on your Weekly Log Sheet, indicate the date as well as the time under *Begin Time*, *End Time*.

WORD PROCESSING AND THE ELECTRONIC OFFICE

by Andrea T. Shea
Word Processing Manager
Twin Cities Industries, Inc.
Minneapolis, Minnesota

Word processing is merely the transfer of ideas into typewritten or printed type. The function of word processing is not new to business because typists and stenographic workers have been processing words in offices since the turn of the Century. What is new about word processing are currant efforts to make the function run more systematically and efficiently by using electronic machines, specialized people, and centralized word-processing stations.

A big incentive for the electronic word processing movement is the cost of correspondence. Getting words onto paper is becoming more and more expensive.[1]

> In 1952, the average one-page business letter was produced for about $1.15. By 1970, that page was costing the businessman a little over $3.00 and in 1974, a study in one midwestern company showed a cost of well over $6.00 per page. A consultant from that same part of the country reports that page costs up to $18.00 exists.

[1]Gilbert J. Konkel and Phyllis J. Peck, The Word Processing Explosion (Stamford, Conn.: Office Publications, Inc., 1976), p. 5.

Electronic equipment provides the heart of any word processing system, including dictation devices and and

(continued, page 339)

75a ▶ 7 Conditioning practice

Use standard procedure given in 73a, page 118.

alphabet	1	Fumiaki quickly amazed us by his jovial spirit and his relaxing views.
figures	2	Add 14 meters 25 centimeters, 89 meters 36 centimeters, and 70 meters.
fig/sym	3	Will we receive a discount of 2% when we pay Invoice #847603 for $915?
fluency	4	A proficient auditor may use a visual aid to make the six risks vivid.

| 1 | 2 | 3 | 4 | 5 | 6 | 7 | 8 | 9 | 10 | 11 | 12 | 13 | 14 |

75b ▶ 8 Check statistical-copy typing skill

1. A 1′ writing on each ¶; determine *gwam* and errors on each writing.

2. A 3′ writing on ¶s 1–2 combined; determine *gwam* and errors.

To determine % of transfer:

3′ *gwam* ÷ 3′ *gwam* of 73b

Goal: *at least* 75% transfer

all figures used | A | 1.5 si | 5.7 awl | 80% hfw |

	gwam 3′	5′
When President Ford signed Public Law 94-168 on December 23, 1975,	4	3
it indicated the start of the official changeover to the metric system	9	6
of weights and measures in this country. Although the system is quite	14	8
simple, it may seem difficult to you the first few times you must	18	11
remember to refer to such things as using 10 liters of gas, living 188	23	14
meters above sea level, or driving in the Indianapolis 805.	27	16
During the time of changeover, you may be required at times to find	32	19
an equivalent value. For instance, how many kilometers are there in the	36	22
1,141 miles between Boston and St. Louis--2,597, or 1,836, or maybe 890?	41	25
To find the nearest whole number of kilometers in 1,141 miles, you sim-	46	28
ply divide the miles by .6214, the number of miles in a kilometer. The	51	31
answer is 1,141 miles divided by .6214, or 1,836 kilometers.	55	33

gwam 3′ | 1 | 2 | 3 | 4 | 5 |
5′ | 1 | 2 | 3 |

75c ▶ 35 Check centering and table typing skills

3 half sheets
1 full sheet
correction supplies

Problem 1

half sheet, long side up

Type the announcement DS in exact vertical center; center each line horizontally. Correct errors.

	words
QUEEN CITY SCHOOL OF DESIGN	6
cordially invites you to attend its	13
Open House	15
on Friday, the twenty-ninth of March	22
at 2324 Victory Parkway	27
Cincinnati, Ohio	31

Job 7
Magazine article,
continued

typewriters, specifically text-editing typewriters. A term "text editing" ~~refers to~~ "the capability the machine provides for making type corrections and editoriel changes during and after copy is key boarded."[2]

[2]J Marshall Hanna, Estelle L. Popham, Rita Sloan Tilton, Secretarial Procedures and Administration, 7th edition (Cincinnati: South-Western Publishing Co., 1978), p. 70.

Mrs. Muir: Ms. Shea informs me that the Table 1 she mentions in her article is a one-page table which she will submit for completion in a very few days. The table will appear on a separate sheet at the end of the article.

As the copy is typed, it is recorded on magnetic ~~devices~~ which can easily be corrected or changed. After the copy has been recorded, it can be "played back" (retyped) on the typewriter or a special printer ~~very quickly~~.

Although electronic word processing centres are ~~very~~ expensive to install and equip, "power" typing equipment such as that mentioned ~~previously~~ increases productivity in ~~a number of very~~ important ways:

1. It greatly speeds up the correction of typeing errors.
2. It eliminates the manuel re typing of an entire message or page when editorial corrections are necessary.
3. It minimizes the reduction in typing speed caused by the "feer of making an error."
4. It permits the high-speed ~~reproduction~~ of messages, each with ~~individualized~~ inserts such as names, addresses, and amounts.
5. It reduces the time required to type tables, letters, and other documents by the use of special format programs that automatically format the typed material.

(continued, page 340)

74c, continued

Problem 2

Page 2 of an unbound report

Type the rough-draft copy shown at the right as page 2 of an unbound report. Position footnotes to leave a bottom margin of approximately 1". Correct any errors you make as you type.

words

2

v n the economic
Increasing gobernment involvement in ~~this~~ process by way 338
tax
of regultatory measures, laws, and deficit provision of social 351
and programs
services during the last quarter century has added not only to 366
production on
the cost of ~~manufacturing~~ and distributing but also to the 377
consumer
price of goods. Since, as the friedman's have said, "There 391
u
is no such thing as a free linch," the study of economics is 403
intended to help n
also ~~aimed at helping~~ producers, distributors, and comsumers 415
monitor elected
~~check~~ the socioeconomic choices made by officials. these 429
a citizens
choices effect the lives of all ~~people~~. 438
m surveys of
Wakin,[3] in sumarizing the findings of ~~charts on~~ economic 449
7
literacy, reports that only 1 in 6 Americans can explain how 462
labor intertwined
business, ~~workers~~, and investors are ~~combined~~. He further 474
only 1 d labor
reports that 1 in 200 can hescribe how business, ~~workers~~, 486
operate in the economy
consumer, investor, and advertising ~~work~~. 498

In terms of opportuinties to become economically liter- 509
points out sp
ate, Wakin ~~states~~ that only 8% of high-school seniors take 523
an
economics courses and that only one-fourth of college-bound 535
u contends
stidents do so. He ~~further states~~ that teachers are not very 546
social studies
far ahead: only half of all ~~sociology~~ teachers have ever 559
taken a course in economics and very few of these have taken 571
more than one
~~others~~. 574

d
The beleif of the writers and economists cite here, as 586
growing numbers of raising
well as others, is that ~~increasing~~ the economic quotient (eq)-- 601
in Grades K
increasing economic literacy--by formal programs ~~from kinder-~~ 613
essential
~~garden~~ through 14 is ~~necessary~~ to preserving the individuals 624
choices
freedom to make wise socio-economic ~~selections~~. 633

_______________ 637

[3]Edward Wakin, "Raising the National eq," American Way 648
(July 1908), pp. 1-2. 652

213b-217b, continued

Job 7
Magazine article,
continued

The growth ~~increase~~ in word processing has opened new doors in business for individuals ~~anyone~~ who possesses~~es~~ key boarding skills. "Companies that offer~~s~~ career paths provide an opportunity for employees to work their way up to management positions."[3] Table 2 displays a typical career ladder that permits a word processing trainee who prepares carefully to progress up the ~~career~~ ladder to ~~the position of~~ Word Processing Manager and to even higher levels in the executive chain of command.

[3]Mona Casady, Word Processing Concepts (Cincinnati: South-Western Publishing Co., 1980), p. 169.

Table 2

A TYPICAL WORD PROCESSING CAREER LADDER

Director of Administration
Word Processing Manager
Word Processing Center Manager
Correspondence Supervisor
Assistant Correspondence Supervisor
Senior Word Processing Operator
Word Processing Operator
Word Processing Trainee

These opportunities for growth present a challenge to the keyboard operator who seeks greater fulfillment in the business office. Each step in the career ladder provides greater responsibilities and more difficult intellectual ~~mental~~ tasks. At the same time, each step provides greater rewards in terms of higher salaries, more ~~and greater~~ fringe benefits, and increased job satisfaction.

15M

74c ▶ 35
Check report typing skill

Problem 1

Type the copy shown at the right as page 1 of an unbound report; listen for bell as signal to return. Use a page line gauge [LM p. 79] to position the footnotes to leave a bottom margin of approximately 1". Correct any errors you make as you type.

words

THE NEED FOR ECONOMIC LITERACY 6

"Economics is a study of the process by which people 17
make and spend their incomes."[1] Most people work to earn 28
money so that they can buy the goods and services they want 40
and need. Although a high percentage of people are able to 52
buy most of the goods they <u>need</u>, few are able to buy all 64
the goods and services they <u>want</u>. As a result, economics 75
involves a study of how individuals and nations make choices, 88
within the limits of their incomes, from the vast array of 100
goods and services that are available. 108

The economic process by which people satisfy their 118
wants and needs includes the production, distribution, and 130
consumption of goods and services. The costs of production 142
and distribution (including profits and taxes) largely de- 153
termine the prices people pay for the economic goods they 165
consume. 167

Because people want many services they cannot individu- 178
ally afford or have chosen not to provide for themselves, 189
the government provides them out of money collected as taxes. 202
Increasingly in recent years, these services have cost more 214
than the government has taken in as tax revenue and have 225
led to deficit government spending and larger and larger un- 237
balanced annual budgets. These shared services include so- 249
cial security, health, education, welfare, public roads, 260
and public housing, to name only a few major ones.[2] 271

_______________ 274

[1]Eugene Wyllie and Roman Warmke, <u>Free Enterprise in</u> 285
<u>the United States</u> (Cincinnati: South-Western Publishing Co., 297
1980), p. 2. 300

[2]Milton and Rose Friedman, <u>Free to Choose, A Personal</u> 311
<u>Statement</u> (New York: Harcourt Brace Jovanovich, 1980), 322
pp. 100-127. 324

Problem 2 is on p. 122.

213b-217b, continued

Job 8
Table full sheet

Mrs. Muir: Ms. Shea has submitted this material to be included in the magazine article previously typed. She has requested that the material be typed in the form of a table with two columns. In Column 1, list the type of equipment under the heading **Type**. Do not underline each type of machine. In Column 2, list the capabilities of each machine under the heading **Capabilities**.

Since this is a part of the manuscript, it should be typed in the same manner as the second page of a leftbound manuscript. Type the identification number—**15MA**—at left margin a DS below the final line of the table.

Table 1

ELECTRONIC KEYBOARDING MACHINES

Self-Correcting Typewriters

Quick error correction and automatic features permit rapid keyboarding of most business documents, particularly correspondence and reports.

Electronic Typewriters with Memory

Limited storage of data permits automated repetition of short documents such as letters and the assembly of form paragraphs into form letters.

Blind Text-Editing Machines

Information stored on removable media (magnetic tape or discs) permits limited-to-moderate revisions on short and average-length documents.

Keyboard with Linear Display

Line display window into memory permits verification of instruction codes as well as limited-to-moderate revisions on short and average-length documents.

Keyboard with Video Display

Includes CRT (Cathode Ray Tube) display, keyboard, disc drive, and printer which permit unlimited revision and numerous applications restricted only by software programs available.

74

70-space line

74a ▶ 7 Conditioning practice

Use standard procedure given in 73a, page 118.

alphabet	1	Mac learned that various jobs emphasized quality work for extra wages.
figures	2	The ten jobs will be done by May 30, 1987, at a cost of 256.4 million.
fig/sym	3	Jacqueline has had Social Security Card #293-48-0752 since she was 16.
fluency	4	Lana is to inform them by six if she is too sick to chair their panel.

| 1 | 2 | 3 | 4 | 5 | 6 | 7 | 8 | 9 | 10 | 11 | 12 | 13 | 14 |

74b ▶ 8 Check rough-draft typing skill

line: 70; listen for bell

1. A 1′ writing on each ¶; determine *gwam* and errors on each writing.

2. A 3′ writing on ¶s 1–2 combined; determine *gwam* and errors.

To determine % of transfer:

3′ *gwam* ÷ 3′ *gwam* of 73b

Goal: *at least* 80% transfer

all letters used | A | 1.5 si | 5.7 awl | 80% hfw |

	gwam 1′	3′	5′
You are now ~~well~~ on your way to *becoming* ~~being~~ a real typist.	10	3	2
You have *built* ~~developed~~ your *basic* skill to a minimum level with	21	7	4
acceptable ~~good~~ technique. You have sohwn that you can *type* ~~work~~ from	34	11	7
~~both~~ handwritten and *corrected* ~~rough-draft~~ copy with a reasonable	43	14	9
degree ~~level~~ of skill. # You ~~have demonstrated that you~~ can type	50	17	10
copy *that contains* ~~with~~ figures and common symbols with out *often* looking at	64	21	13
the keys. *Finally,* You have learned, ~~in addition,~~ to *arrange and* type copy in	77	26	15
the com*m*on forms. ~~What are your plans now? Do you plan~~	80	27	16
~~to drop typing or to continue for another term?~~			
If ~~When~~ your *basic* skill level is just barely thirty *words a minute* ~~w.a.m.~~,	13	31	19
you should by all means take *another* ~~one more~~ term of typewrit-	24	35	21
ing ~~in order~~ to add another *ten* ~~10~~ words to your rate. If	33	38	23
you *now exceed* ~~are pushing a rate of~~ forty words a minute, one more	42	41	24
term ~~semester~~ should help you *reach* ~~acquire a skill of~~ fifty--the	50	43	26
minimum *level* for *really* effective us~~e~~ability. ~~And~~ if you desire to	63	48	29
be*come* a *vocational typist,* ~~well paid office worker,~~ realize that you need *all* the	74	51	31
advantages *of* ~~that come from~~ a vocational co*u*~~a~~rse offer~~r~~ed	83	54	32
in a second year. ~~of typewriting.~~	86	55	33

213b-217b, continued

Job 9

Letter with table [LM p. 181]

Mrs. Muir: **Carlos R. Medina**, our **Promotion Director**, has submitted this letter to be typed in final form. Type the letter, following the directions I gave you earlier. Be sure all errors have been corrected before you remove the letter from the typewriter; address envelope.

Letter to Mrs. Pauline T. Woodburn, President of the Plymouth Manufacturing Co., 2400 Minnehaha Avenue, Minneapolis, MN 55404-~~1234~~ 8016

The questions you ~~asked~~ raised in your recent ~~correspondence~~ letter about the Sovereign family of Electronic Typewriters (l.c.) and word processers (o) can best be ~~satisfied~~ answered through a display and demonstration of our cost-efficient, versatile, equipment. We have a special ~~demonstration~~ program we can present to your ~~WP~~ key personnel in our downtown office or, if you prefer, at your headquarters. The program can be scheduled as follows:

SS

9:00	- 9:15	Introductory Remarks
~~9:30~~ 9:15	- 10:~~3~~0	Demonstration of Model HT-100
10:00	- 10:30	Coffee Break
10:30	- 11:00	Demonstration of Model HT-200
11:00	- 11:30	Film, "The Versatile Sovereign WP Work Station"

If the ~~demonstration~~ program is held in our office, we can demonstrate the Sovereign WP Work Station in operation instead of the film.

During the afternoon hours, we can ~~give~~ provide a hands-on orientation for your supervisors and word processing personnel on the HT-100 and HT-200. If you have any ~~specific~~ special operations or problems you would like to have processed on either of these machines, please let ~~us~~ me know in advance.

If you call me within the next few days ~~(487-5200,~~ on Extension 452~~)~~, we can schedule your demonstration for sometime next month.

xx:213S

73c ▶ 34 Check letter typing skill

3 plain full sheets
2 letterheads [LM pp. 87-90]
1 carbon sheet
correction supplies

Problem 1
Personal/business letter

plain sheet; 50-space line; return address on Line 17; open punctuation; correct errors; *do not prepare a carbon copy*

words
5492 Sandpiper Lane Las Vegas, NV 89102-2630 October 3, 19-- Mr. Louis 14
Japonica One Don Salvador Avenue Salt Lake City, UT 84118-2140 Dear Louis 29

The first week of November I will be in Salt Lake City to attend our regional 45
sales conference at the Hotel Utah. 52

Is there a chance that you could get me two tickets for one of the games to be 68
played that week by the Utah Jazz? Any location and any price will be fine. I'll 85
send a check when I know the cost. 92

I know that Salt Lake City is an avid basketball city, so I won't be too dis- 107
appointed if you must say "no." But I'd be mighty happy if I could attend one of 124
the Utah Jazz games. 128

Sincerely Clarissa Beauclaire 134

Problem 2
Business letter

letterhead, 1 cc; 60-space line; date on Line 16; mixed punctuation; address envelope; correct errors

Problem 3
Business letter

Use Problem 2 directions, but address the letter to:

Mrs. Ivalee Jones, Manager
Family Stores, Inc.
1027 South Atlantic Avenue
Daytona Beach, FL 32018-4765

Use an appropriate salutation.

January 20, 19-- 3

Mr. Gerard L. Wilkins 8
Kensington Manufacturing Co. 14
3849 North Wickham Road 18
Melbourne, FL 32935-3746 24

Dear Mr. Wilkins: 27

All who hire workers must be alert to recent state and federal rules and 42
regulations that govern employment practices. 51

As a result of government action, some of the personal information formerly 66
asked for can no longer be requested. For example, a firm cannot ask those who 82
apply for work to specify their race, national origin, sex, religion, or creed. 99

To encourage everyone to comply with the intent of equal opportunity goals, 114
firms have had to develop affirmative action plans. Such plans require a firm 130
to analyze, and correct if necessary, its distribution of jobs by national origin, 146
sex, and race in relation to essential job requirements and employee qualifica- 162
tions. 163

The enclosed booklet should help you to assess the degree to which your firm 179
is complying with the government guidelines. 188

Sincerely yours, 191

Ms. Victoria Rivera 195
Assistant Manager 199

xx 200

Enclosure 201
221

213b-217b, continued

Job 10
Memo with table [LM p. 183]

Mrs. Muir: Mr. Medina has submitted this memorandum to be typed in final form. Please follow the directions I gave you previously for typing memos; address **COMPANY MAIL** envelope. The identification number is **507M.**

TO: Sandra T. Phillips, Chief Demonstrator

FROM: Carlos R. Medina, Promotion Director

DATE:

SUBJECT: Plymouth Manufacturing Co. Demonstration

(¶) Mrs. Pauline T. Woodburn, President of Plymouth Manufacturing Co., has ~~asked~~ requested that we schedule our program on Sovereign electronic typewriters and word processors at our downtown office sometime during the ~~third~~ second week of next month. There will be ~~about~~ approximately 30 Plymouth ~~people~~ employees at the presentation.

(¶) Mrs. Woodburn ~~says that~~ indicates they are not interested in the Model HT-100 but would like to have ~~time for questions~~ a question and answer period at the ~~close~~ end of the ~~program~~ presentation. The schedule for the program, therefore, will be:

SS

9:00 - 9:15	Introductory Remarks
9:15 - 10:00	Demonstration of Model HT-200
10:00 - 10:30	Coffee Break
10:30 - 11:15	Demonstration of Sovereign WP Station
11:15 - 11:45	Questions and Answers

In addition, the Plymouth people are particularly interested in ~~seeing~~ observing the HT-200 prepare individualized form letters from stock paragraphs in memory and the ~~ability~~ capability of the WP Work Station to store, retrieve, ~~change~~ modify, and retype documents.

(¶) Will you please ~~contact~~ call Mrs. Woodburn and make the final arrangements for this ~~program~~ presentation. As soon as you have done so, please let me know.

unit **14** lessons 73-75

Measure your skills: basic/applied

Measurement goals

1. To demonstrate that you can type for 3′ on straight copy, rough draft, and statistical copy at acceptable speeds within an error tolerance specified by your teacher.

2. To demonstrate that you can arrange and type in proper form (with errors corrected) letters, reports, and tables.

Machine adjustments

1. Paper guide at *0*.

2. Ribbon control to type on top half of ribbon.

3. Margin sets: 70–space line (center – 35; center + 35 + 5) unless otherwise directed.

4. Line–space selector on *1* (SS) for drills, on *2* (DS) for ¶s; as directed for problems.

73

70-space line

73a ▶ 7 Conditioning practice

each line twice SS (slowly, then faster); DS between 2-line groups; if time permits, retype selected lines

alphabet	1	As jet black clouds filled the hazy sky, quite vexed men kept working.
figures	2	I shall print 173 calendars, 850 cards, 96 leaflets, and 24 circulars.
fig/sym	3	Strikes in 1982 delayed delivery of 624,350# (or 7% of all shipments).
fluency	4	Audit the work forms and then pay the six girls for the work they did.

| 1 | 2 | 3 | 4 | 5 | 6 | 7 | 8 | 9 | 10 | 11 | 12 | 13 | 14 |

73b ▶ 9 Check straight-copy typing skill

1. A 1′ writing on each ¶; determine *gwam* and errors on each writing.

2. A 3′ writing on ¶s 1–3 combined; determine *gwam* and errors. Record your rate for use in Lessons 74 and 75.

all letters used | A | 1.5 si | 5.7 awl | 80% hfw

	gwam 3′	5′
Someone once said that the hardest thing about holding a job is the	5	3
work it requires. That may be clever; however, as an expression of the	9	6
attitudes some people have regarding their work, it points up the tragic	14	9
situation of people who fail to match interest and ability with available	19	11
jobs when they place themselves on the job market.	22	13
Almost everyone has to work at one time or another in life. Over	27	16
fifty percent of us must work during all of our eligible working years.	32	19
Many people work with joy in what they do, whereas others consider their	37	22
jobs boring regardless of the work they are assigned. Bored workers let	41	25
their work master them instead of mastering their work.	45	27
Whether the work is a chore or a satisfaction depends more upon you	50	30
than upon the work itself. Every day has both a routine and an exciting	55	33
period. Fortunate are the workers who get enough pleasure from the ex-	59	36
citing period to be able to accept the routine one. The bored workers	64	38
should consider changing jobs in order to realize job satisfaction.	68	41

gwam 3′ | 1 | 2 | 3 | 4 | 5 |
5′ | 1 | 2 | 3 |

unit **42** lessons 218-220

Improve basic skills

Learning goals

1. To improve keystroking on goal-selection sentences.
2. To improve straight-copy typing on ¶s of varied difficulty.
3. To improve keystroking skill on straight-copy ¶s (220b, page 347).
4. To prepare for measurement on tables, business forms, letters, and reports.

Machine adjustments

1. Paper guide at *0*.
2. Margin sets: 70-space line for sentence and ¶ activities; as required for problems.
3. Spacing: SS sentence drills with a DS between sentence groups; DS paragraph activities; as directed for problems.
4. Tab sets: for 5-space ¶ indention; as needed for problems.

218

218a ▶ 5 Conditioning practice

each line twice SS (slowly, then faster); if time permits, retype selected lines

alphabet	1	Jack Elzay had experts review the first quarter gold and bond markets.
figures	2	The leading players scored 29, 38, 46, 51, and 70 points respectively.
long reaches	3	gym myth break money onions cruise numbers minimum exercise celebrates
fluency	4	The name of the man who paid for half of the land is held by an agent.

| 1 | 2 | 3 | 4 | 5 | 6 | 7 | 8 | 9 | 10 | 11 | 12 | 13 | 14 |

218b ▶ 10 Improve speed

The first column at the right of the sentences shows the rate at which you are typing if you complete each sentence the number of times (4) indicated at the top of the column. Column 3 shows the rate if you type the sentence 8 times.

1. Select a speed goal rate from the columns at the right.
2. Using the sentence at the left of that speed rate, type a 1′ writing, trying to complete the sentence the number of times indicated at the top of the column.
3. If you are unable to type the sentence the specified number of times, type two additional writings on the sentence.
4. If in the first writing you reach your speed goal, select the next higher speed rate from the columns and type two more 1′ writings to reach your new goal.
5. Finally, type a 1′ writing on Line 17; compare your rate with the rate attained on Line 17 in 219c, page 346.

		times per minute to type sentence: 4	6	8
1	He may wish to aid their town.	gwam 24	36	48
2	The risk to the firm is also cut.	26	40	53
3	She has the right to own city land.	28	42	56
4	The name of the man who paid is known.	30	46	61
5	They may audit our plans for the bridge.	32	48	64
6	Their handy work paid off in good contacts.	34	52	69
7	They may wish to form a town theater project.	36	54	72
8	The problem did cause anxiety for the other men.	38	58	77
9	The maid can burn the corks to form a new element.	40	60	80
10	The name and title of the paper will go to the coach.	42	64	85
11	Our world venture may cut down on many of our problems.	44	66	88
12	I will also spend half of the funds to fix our worn roads.	46	70	93
13	It is right to handle and to pay for the work of their town.	48	72	96
14	They will spend other funds to do some work for the town board.	50	76	101
15	There may be an element of anxiety in their talk of world travel.	52	78	104
16	They may wish to sign the title for the firm when some work is done.	54	82	109
17	The auditor was worn down by the problems and anxiety of some workers.	56	84	112

| 1 | 2 | 3 | 4 | 5 | 6 | 7 | 8 | 9 | 10 | 11 | 12 | 13 | 14 |

72c ▶ 25
Recall/extend centering and table typing skills

References
horizontal centering, p. 52
vertical centering, p. 53
centering columns, p. 105

Problem 1
half sheet, long side up

Type the announcement DS in exact vertical center; center each line horizontally. Correct errors.

	words
BALI HAI SHOWCASE PRESENTS	5
Native Dances of the Indonesian Islands	13
November 9 Through December 13	20
All Seats $6.50	23
Reservations Assure Preferred Seating	30
(808) 721-4937	33

Problem 2
half sheet, short side up

Center and type the table in reading position; SS the groups of columnar entries, DS between them. Decide spacing between columns. Align figures in Column 2 at the decimal (.). Correct errors.

COMMON U.S.-METRIC EQUIVALENTS (words: 6)

Approximate Values (words: 10)

		words
1 inch	25.4 millimeters (mm)	16
1 inch	2.54 centimeters (cm)	22
1 foot	0.305 meters (m)	27
1 yard	0.91 meters (m)	31
1 mile	1.61 kilometers (km)	37
1 pint	0.47 liters (l)	41
1 quart	0.95 liters (l)	46
1 gallon	3.785 liters (l)	51
1 ounce	28.35 grams (g)	56
1 pound	0.45 kilograms (kg)	62

Problem 3
full sheet

Center and type the table in reading position. DS items in columns. Decide spacing between columns. Correct errors.

To type totals

1. Type an underline the length of the longest item in the column.

2. DS and type the total figure.

DECEMBER SALES REPORT (words: 4)

(Showing Estimated and Actual Sales) (words: 12)

			words
Abramson, Stanley	$ 6,500	$ 6,750	19
Chiang, Kuang-fu	5,000	4,950	25
Delgado, Dolores	5,700	5,740	31
Guzman, Eduardo	4,750	5,000	37
Jackson, Rosie Lee	5,500	5,600	43
McClain, Malcom	7,200	7,150	48
O'Malley, Christopher	8,750	9,000	55
St. John, Donald	5,250	5,350	61
Thornton, Lavonne	6,500	6,590	67
Watanabe, Michi	8,500	8,650	75
	$63,650	$64,780	78

218c ▶ 10
Improve control

Three 2′ timings on the ¶ at the right; try to improve your control with each timed writing.

Goal: 3 or fewer errors on each writing.

all letters used | HA | 1.7 si | 6.0 awl | 75% hfw

	gwam 2′	
To realize your ambition to work as a typist in a modern office,	7	56
you must direct serious attention to many important factors influencing	14	63
your typing power. High stroking skill is the result of many hours of	21	70
active practice on basic elements called techniques, and ability in	28	77
typing office problems is the product of learning how to apply your	35	84
stroking skill to typical job situations. The abilities sought by an	42	91
employer are the same as those emphasized by an expert teacher.	49	98

gwam 2′ | 1 | 2 | 3 | 4 | 5 | 6 | 7 |

218d ▶ 25
Prepare for measurement: tables

1. Make a list of the problems to be typed:
page 318, 201d, Problem 1
page 320, 202d, Problem 1
page 321, 203c, Problem 2

2. Arrange full sheets for easy handling.

3. Follow the directions given for each problem; correct errors neatly.

4. As time permits, repeat the procedures for other problems for which additional practice is needed.

219

219a ▶ 5
Conditioning practice

Use standard directions given in 218a, p. 344.

alphabet 1 Tony Perez required worthy behavior from lucky students judged expert.
figures 2 A junk dealer found 327 hubcaps, 604 tires, 115 bumpers, and 89 locks.
double letters 3 pass seed poor happy worry robber assess access runner success suggest
fluency 4 They may make us visit the firm to pay for the title to the town land.

| 1 | 2 | 3 | 4 | 5 | 6 | 7 | 8 | 9 | 10 | 11 | 12 | 13 | 14 |

219b ▶ 10
Guided writing: paragraph

1. Take a 1′ timing to establish your base rate.

2. Add 4 words to base rate to set your new speed goal.

3. Determine your speed goal for quarter minutes; mentally note your 1/4′ goals in the copy at right.

4. Take four 1′ speed timings, trying to reach your goal. Each time you reach your goal, reset your speed goal 2 words higher.

all letters used | A | 1.5 si | 5.7 awl | 80% hfw

	gwam 2′	
To get ready for the kind of office job requiring much typing, you	7	56
must prepare to do well a variety of typewriting activities. You need	14	63
the best stroking skill possible; and you must develop power to utilize	21	70
that skill in a number of complex typing tasks. There is no place in	28	77
business for modest skill or limited ability to complete work in minimum	36	85
time periods. Now is the time to prepare yourself for the kind of office	44	93
position you really desire upon finishing school.	49	98

gwam 2′ | 1 | 2 | 3 | 4 | 5 | 6 | 7 |

71c, continued

Problem 2
Page 2 of report

Beginning with the final ¶ of the report typed as Problem 1, type the copy as page 2 of an unbound report. Place the footnote immediately below the table *or* at the foot of the page as your teacher directs.

	words
off as it was in 1970 (Column 1), ~~if~~ provided the curr~~a~~ent upward trend	214
of inflation and taxes ~~continues~~ prevails for the next ~~few~~ several years.[2]	226

DS

$10,000	$22,552	$ 55,941	232
20,000	46,744	118,689	236
30,000	73,171	177,405	240

———————— 244

[1]"Economic Road Maps," Nos. 1876-1877, the Conference Board (April 1980), p. 1. 255 / 260

[2]"The Double Whammy of ~~Texas~~ Taxes and Inflation," U.S. News & World Report (July 14, 1980), p. 47. 274 / 284

72

70-space line

72a ▶ 7 Conditioning practice

Use standard procedure given in 70a, page 113.

alphabet	1	**High expenses led them to centralize equipment for every woodwork job.**
figures	2	**Of 1,089 pages, 764 were textual pages and 325 were appendix material.**
fig/sym	3	**Both start today (2/14): Jay Moya at $98.75/wk.; Emi Doi at $3.60/hr.**
fluency	4	**It is their duty to sign the amendment if he is to handle the problem.**

| 1 | 2 | 3 | 4 | 5 | 6 | 7 | 8 | 9 | 10 | 11 | 12 | 13 | 14 |

72b ▶ 18 Check/improve statistical typing skill

1. A 1′ writing on ¶ 1, then on ¶ 2; determine *gwam* on each.

2. A 3′ writing on ¶s 1–2 combined; determine *gwam*.

3. Set a speed goal 4–5 *gwam* above your ¶ 1 rate; type two 1′ goal writings on ¶ 1.

4. Set a speed goal 4–5 *gwam* above your ¶ 2 rate; type two 1′ goal writings on ¶ 2.

5. A 3′ writing on ¶s 1–2 combined; determine *gwam*.

Determine % of transfer: Step 5 *gwam* ÷ 3′ *gwam* of 70c.

Goal: *at least* 75% transfer

all letters/figures used | A | 1.5 si | 5.7 awl | 80% hfw |

	gwam 1′	3′
Figures are utilized daily in typing business forms. They are used	14	5
to specify dates, as August 26, 1982; to identify orders, as JX-384069;	28	9
to specify terms of an invoice, as 2/10, n/30; to indicate dimensions,	42	14
as 5 × 3 cards or 8 1/2 × 11 paper; and so on. To be a business typist,	57	19
it is essential that you be able to type figures quickly and precisely.	71	24
Certain symbols are often used with figures in office typing, too.	14	28
They are used to specify amounts ($7.50 and $265); to designate percent	28	33
(12.6%); to make dimensions specific (4′ × 7′5″); and so forth. Even	42	38
though symbols may not be used as often as figures, they can lower the	56	42
typing rate if you cannot locate them easily and quickly.	68	46

gwam 1′ | 1 | 2 | 3 | 4 | 5 | 6 | 7 | 8 | 9 | 10 | 11 | 12 | 13 | 14 |
3′ | 1 | 2 | 3 | 4 | 5 |

219c ▶ 10 Improve speed

The first column at the right of the sentences shows the rate at which you are typing if you complete each sentence the number of times (4) indicated at the top of the column. Column 3 shows the rate if you type the sentence 8 times.

1. Select a speed goal rate from the columns at the right.

2. Using the sentence at the left of that speed rate, type a 1′ writing, trying to complete the sentence the number of times indicated at the top of the column.

3. If you are unable to type the sentence the specified number of times, type two additional writings on the sentence.

4. If in the first writing you reach your speed goal, select the next higher speed rate from the columns and type two more 1′ writings to reach your new goal.

5. Finally, type a 1′ writing on Line 17; compare your rate with the rate attained on Line 17 in 218b, page 344.

	Sentence	times per minute to type sentence 4	6	8
1	The men will work with us now. gwam	24	36	48
2	They make other styles for teams.	26	40	53
3	He paid for eight knives and forks.	28	42	56
4	Doc may sign six copies of her manual.	30	46	61
5	Rob held a jam session for the students.	32	48	64
6	She will spend their money for new clothes.	34	52	69
7	Helene may be idle for a long period of time.	36	54	72
8	If he is to run with them, he must sign up soon.	38	58	77
9	They will make a rock fountain for their building.	40	60	80
10	It is a worthy goal to work for high speed in typing.	42	64	85
11	They may work when they find keys for the field office.	44	66	88
12	They paid half the cost for the right to make a rock path.	46	70	93
13	The big city firm may wish to visit with some title holders.	48	72	96
14	They may wish to cut their safety risks by staying in the city.	50	76	101
15	She will pay half the fee due on the land she owns with the firm.	52	78	104
16	The title held by the firm cut the risks of owning land in the city.	54	82	109
17	The man may go to sign the title for the land he owns when he is paid.	56	84	112

| 1 | 2 | 3 | 4 | 5 | 6 | 7 | 8 | 9 | 10 | 11 | 12 | 13 | 14 |

219d ▶ 25 Prepare for measurement: business forms

1. Make a list of the problems to be typed:
page 328, 208c, Problem 3
page 329, 209c, Problem 3
page 331, 210c, Problem 3

2. Arrange forms [LM pp. 185–188] for efficient handling.

3. Follow the directions given for each problem; correct errors neatly.

220

220a ▶ 5 Conditioning practice

Use standard directions given in 218a, page 344.

alphabet	1	Jayne Zinman spoke about the exquisite golf carts Vera Kowles ordered.
figures	2	The teacher asked the math class to read pages 26, 39, 47, 50, and 81.
adjacent keys	3	sad was ask buy few build quite fever policy bruise oppose onion tread
fluency	4	They will make a big profit if they double the quantity of their work.

| 1 | 2 | 3 | 4 | 5 | 6 | 7 | 8 | 9 | 10 | 11 | 12 | 13 | 14 |

71b ▶ 18
Check/improve rough-draft typing skill

line: 70; listen for bell

1. A 1′ writing on ¶ 1, then on ¶ 2; determine *gwam* on each.

2. A 3′ writing on ¶s 1–2 combined; determine *gwam*.

3. Set a speed goal 4–5 *gwam* above your ¶ 1 rate; type two 1′ goal writings on ¶ 1.

4. Set a speed goal 4–5 *gwam* above your ¶ 2 rate; type two 1′ goal writings on ¶ 2.

5. A 3′ writing on ¶ 1–2 combined; determine *gwam*.

Determine % of transfer:

Step 5 *gwam* ÷ 3′ gwam of 70c.

Goal: *at least* 80% transfer

all letters used | A | 1.5 si | 5.7 awl | 80% hfw |

gwam 1′ | 3′

The ~~major~~ *primary* reason for f*i*ling some thing is to be able to 11 | 4
~~find~~ *locate* the information *readily* the next time the need arises. *#* Therefore*,* 26 | 9
one test of ~~an effective~~ *a useful* filing syst~~o~~*e*m simply is how fast you 38 | 13
can ~~locate~~ *find* material when ~~they are~~ *it is* needed. The more time you 49 | 16
~~lose~~ *squander* searching for ~~important~~ *needed* records*,* the more your filing 61 | 20
habits and *filing* system need~~s~~ a good ~~overhaul~~ *review*. 70 | 23

If you ~~don't~~ *do not* store ~~papers~~ *documents* correctly, you are hiding them*, not filing them.* 16 | 29
Furthermore, permit*t*ing papers that ~~should~~ *ought to* be filed to ~~stack up~~ *accumulate* 30 | 33
in a jumbled pile ~~on~~ *in* the ~~desk~~ *office* forces you to make a ~~puzzling~~ *haphazard* 42 | 37
search for ~~the~~ material that is ~~needed~~ *requested*. File promp*t*ly; think 54 | 41
~~while~~ *as* you do so; and follow a standard set of ~~guides~~ *rules* so you 66 | 45
can find ~~any of your~~ papers quickly. 70 | 47

71c ▶ 25
Recall/extend report typing skill

References

report form, p. 94
footnote placement, p. 97

Problem 1

1-page report/footnotes

Type the rough-draft copy shown at the right and on p. 116 as a 1-page report. DS above the table. Center the columnar material horizontally; leave 8 spaces between columns. Correct any errors you make as you type.

words

THE TWO*-*WAY SQUEEZE 4

A ~~before tax~~ *pretax* income of $10,000 ~~was~~ *represented* just about the average 16
for American families in 1970. Ac*c*ording to a report of the 29
conference board, in order to have *in 1980* the same real purchasing 42
power after ~~taxes~~ *tax deductions* that a $10,000 income yei~~l~~lded only ~~10~~ *ten* years 57
before*,* a family needed a pretax *total* income *somewhat* over $20,000.[1] 71

~~As~~ *While* inflation eats up the ~~buying~~ *purchasing* power of the family ~~in-come~~ *paycheck*, millions of Americans are being ~~eaten up~~ *taken to the cleaners* by *f*ederal, 83
98
state, and local ~~taxes~~ *tax collectors*. Because higher wages ~~are pushing~~ *push* 110
~~employees~~ *workers* into higher *income* tax brackets and into ~~bigger~~ *larger* social 122
security tax payments, *many* families are finding that they can not 136
keep up with living cost*s* simply by get*t*ing wage ~~increases~~ *gains* that 148
match *steadily* increasing consumer prices. As a ~~consequence~~ *result* of growing 161
inflation *and taxes*, the American worker has lost *real* purchasing power. 176
¶ The table following ~~presents~~ *shows* the ~~earnings~~ *income* a family of four 187
needed in 1980 and *predicts what it* will need in 1990 ~~in order~~ to be as well 200

(continued, p. 116)

220b ▶ 15
Measure straight-copy skill

1. Type two 5′ writings; proofread and circle errors.

2. Determine *gwam* for each writing; record the better of the two writings.

all letters used | A | 1.5 si | 5.7 awl | 80% hfw

gwam 1′ | 5′

The day in which we live is often referred to as the age of the 13 3
computer. Most of us have been or soon will be influenced in some way 27 5
by this marvel of modern technology. There are some workers who state 41 8
that the computer represents the greatest application of inventive genius 56 11
known to our civilized world, a claim hard to deny. While some persons 71 14
think the computer performs in some magic way, those who understand the 85 17
way in which it operates know it functions in a very logical, orderly 99 20
manner, responding very reliably to established controls. All of us 113 23
must be prepared to live and work in a world influenced by computers. 126 25

Actually, a computer is just a machine--one made to utilize raw data 14 28
with amazing speed. Most computers are so quick in doing their assigned 28 31
work that they can go through millions of arithmetic problems in a matter 43 34
of seconds; and because of this exceptional ability, computers have been 58 37
called electronic brains. But a computer cannot think; it can do only 72 40
those things it is told to do. A human operator must put all facts and 86 43
figures into the machine and then tell it, in a precise way, what to do 101 45
with the information. It is true that computers work only as programmed. 116 48
The way in which they are programmed determines the quality of responses 130 51
they are able to give. 135 52

gwam 1′ | 1 | 2 | 3 | 4 | 5 | 6 | 7 | 8 | 9 | 10 | 11 | 12 | 13 | 14 |
5′ | 1 | 2 | 3 |

220c ▶ 5
Improve control

three 1′ writings; try to improve control with each writing

Goal: 2 or fewer errors on each writing.

all letters used | HA | 1.7 si | 6.0 awl | 75% hfw

gwam 1′

Able managers seldom ask their staff of office workers to operate 14 84
singly; more typically, an expert manager organizes an office force 28 98
into units or work groups. Employers tend to expect that workers cho- 42 112
sen will have initially, or acquire soon after joining the staff, a 56 126
sense of group, as well as personal, duty and loyalty to the company. 70 140

| 1 | 2 | 3 | 4 | 5 | 6 | 7 | 8 | 9 | 10 | 11 | 12 | 13 | 14 |

220d ▶ 25
Prepare for measurement: letters, memos, message/reply memos

1. Make a list of the problems to be typed:
page 287, 178c, Problem 1
page 292, 181c, Problem 1
page 302, 188c, Problem 1

2. Arrange materials [LM pp. 188–192] for efficient handling.

3. Follow directions given for each problem; correct errors neatly.

4. As time permits, repeat the procedures for other problems for which additional practice is needed.

70d ▶ 25 Recall/extend letter typing skill

1 plain full sheet
2 letterheads [LM pp. 83-86]
1 carbon sheet
correction supplies

References
personal/business letter, p. 71
business letter, p. 83
addressing envelope, p. 85

Problem 1
Personal/business letter
50-space line; begin on Line 17; modified block style; address envelope; correct errors

	words
P.O. Box 1304 Macon, GA 31207-9210 July 15, 19-- Ms. Frances Jablonski	14
Athens Vocational/Technical School 100 East Campus Road Athens, GA	28
30602-3812 Dear Ms. Jablonski	34
Thank you for sending me the literature about programs and course offerings	49
in office education at Athens Vocational/Technical School. The booklets are	65
quite informative.	69
Next month I shall visit friends in Athens. While there, I want to explore	84
housing accommodations near the school. Does your office maintain a list-	98
ing of families who wish to rent rooms to students?	109
Any assistance you can provide will be appreciated, for I do not want to wait	125
until the last minute to locate housing for the fall term.	137
Sincerely yours Your name	144
	174

Problem 2
Business letter
1 cc; 60-space line; date on Line 16; modified block style; address envelope; correct errors

March 17, 19-- Mr. Jason L. Riggens Hopewell Retraining Center 346 River-	14
side Mall Baton Rouge, LA 70801-5214 Dear Mr. Riggens:	26
Enclosed is a summary of the "measured" reading difficulty levels of the	40
"Essential Life Skills" learning activity packages you are considering for	55
use in your retraining program.	62
On the basis of recent reading vocabulary test results, Dale and O'Rourke	77
report that learning materials designed for use by students of a given reading	92
level can safely include some words--without definitions--from the next higher	108
grade level category. Grade 8 words, for example, can be used with students	124
who have a Grade 6 reading level.	131
Students are not likely to progress from one reading level to the next if the	146
words they read are restricted to those they already know. Further, students	162
cannot be said to have learned a skill until they have mastered its "language."	178
I hope these comments will be helpful in your evaluations.	190
Sincerely yours, Mrs. Jolene Wilson Marketing Manager xx Enclosure	203
	221

71

70-space line

71a ▶ 7 Conditioning practice

Use standard procedure given in 70a, page 113.

alphabet	1	Alex was amazed by the seven major forgery problems he quickly solved.
figures	2	The index slipped 1.79 points to 86.34 as sales hit 13,725,000 shares.
fig/sym	3	There was a credit on May 29 for $487 and a debit on June 15 for $360.
fluency	4	Both of us may wish to bid for the antique bicycle or the ivory whale.

| 1 | 2 | 3 | 4 | 5 | 6 | 7 | 8 | 9 | 10 | 11 | 12 | 13 | 14 |

unit **43** lessons 221-225

Measure basic / production skills

Learning goals

1. To improve your straight-copy speed and accuracy.

2. To type acceptably* a variety of business letters.

3. To type acceptably* typical business tables.

4. To type acceptably* basic business forms.

5. To type acceptably* reports and memos.

Machine adjustments

1. Paper guide at *0*.

2. Ribbon control on black.

3. Margins: 70-space line for sentence drills and ¶ timed writings; as required for problems.

4. Tab sets: as required for individual problems.

**Both quality and quantity during a 30′* time period.

221

221a ▶ 5 Conditioning practice

each line twice SS (slowly, then faster); if time permits, retype selected lines

alphabet 1 Louise Zabel worked five months on projects requiring expert analysis.

figures 2 Marilyn visited four art classes having 230, 185, 79, and 64 students.

fig/sym 3 The bank loan of $7,280 was due August 15 ($6,500 plus $780 interest).

fluency 4 She may visit the foreign city to buy a cow and eight bushels of corn.

| 1 | 2 | 3 | 4 | 5 | 6 | 7 | 8 | 9 | 10 | 11 | 12 | 13 | 14 |

221b ▶ 23 Check language arts

2 plain full sheets; block style, open; 1½″ side margins; begin on Line 16

1. Type the letter, correcting any errors you detect in the copy as you type.

2. Remove the paper; proofread; mark any additional errors for correction.

3. Type a final copy from your corrected copy with all errors corrected.

November 27 19--

Ms. Virginia Ward President
PennsylvaniaIndustrials, Inc.
2153 Library rd
Pittsburg PA 15234-3200

dear ms. Ward:
Managers today deel with countless numbers and statistics; and teh time required to sort, clasify, and interpret data involved in decision-making can be both costly and time consuming.most executives need relief from cumbersome data handeling.
Integrating computer graphics inot the management process can facilitate planning and forecasting, evaluating performance, measuring productivity, determining financial status, and many other managemetn functions. Tons of unwieldy statistics essential tomanagement operations can become more manageable through the utilization of meaningful graphics.

May I meet with you soon to discuss the possibility of incorporating computer graphics into your datasystems?

sincerely yours,

Jeff Thomas, director
Data Applications

xx

unit **13** lessons 70-72

Recall/improve basic and problem skills

Recall/improvement goals

1. To improve skill (increase speed or reduce errors) when typing straight copy, rough draft, and statistical copy.
2. To recall and extend copy arrangement skills: letter typing, report typing, and centering announcements and tables.

Machine adjustments

1. Paper guide at *0*.
2. Ribbon control to type on top half of ribbon.
3. Margin sets: 70-space line (center − 35; center + 35 + 5) unless otherwise directed.
4. Line-space selector on *1* (SS) for drills, on *2* (DS) for ¶s; as directed for problems.

70 — 70-space line

70a ▶ 7 Conditioning practice

each line twice SS (slowly, then faster); DS between 2-line groups; if time permits, retype selected lines

alphabet 1 The vote forced the town board to combine six zoning projects quickly.
figures 2 They replaced at cost 50 plates, 194 forks, 362 spoons, and 78 knives.
fig/sym 3 The price quoted on May 26 was $153.80 per 100 or $1,149.75 per 1,000.
fluency 4 Pamela may do the work for the city if the clerk signs the work forms.

| 1 | 2 | 3 | 4 | 5 | 6 | 7 | 8 | 9 | 10 | 11 | 12 | 13 | 14 |

70b ▶ 8 Check straight-copy typing skill

1. A 1′ writing on ¶ 1; determine *gwam* and errors.
2. A 1′ writing on ¶ 2; determine *gwam* and errors.
3. A 3′ writing on ¶s 1–2 combined; determine *gwam* and errors.

all letters used | A | 1.5 si | 5.7 awl | 80% hfw

	gwam 1′	3′
A career is vastly more divergent than a job. If you talk about	13	4
landing a job when you finish school, you are saying that all you are	27	9
interested in is some kind of work with regular wages. A career, how-	41	14
ever, has larger implications. It implies a life's work in which you	55	18
have interest and in which you have received some training and educa-	69	23
tion. But within any one career field, there may be numerous and dis-	83	28
tinct choices.	86	29
In almost any of the careers you may choose, two basic items are	13	33
required for the career to grow--flexibility and an openness for learn-	27	38
ing. Nowhere is this more true than in the world of business. There	41	42
are millions of workers in business today, and their jobs range from	55	47
accountants to zoologists. Regardless of your desires, a career in	69	51
business is open to just about all men and women of nearly every field	83	56
of interest.	85	57

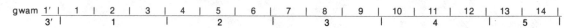

gwam 1′ | 1 | 2 | 3 | 4 | 5 | 6 | 7 | 8 | 9 | 10 | 11 | 12 | 13 | 14 |
3′ | 1 | 2 | 3 | 4 | 5 |

70c ▶ 10 Improve straight-copy typing skill

1. Choose a goal of speed or of control based on performance on 70b above. Work for *control* if you made more than 2 errors on either of the 1′ writings; otherwise, work for *speed*.
2. Two 1′ writings on each ¶ of 70b above, according to your selected goal.
3. A 3′ writing on ¶s 1–2 combined; determine *gwam* and number of errors.
4. Compare your two 3′ scores. Did you improve either speed or accuracy?
5. Record the better 3′ *gwam* for use in Lessons 71 and 72.

221c ▶ 22 Measure straight-copy skill

three 5′ writings; determine *gwam*; circle errors

all letters used | A | 1.5 si | 5.7 awl | 80% hfw

	gwam 1′	5′
Management as a profession is a relative newcomer to the world of	13	3
business. There are many who assume that management is a science, but	27	5
it is much more than that. Management is a skill, an art, a process, a	42	8
practice, and an occupation. Management is an essential element of any	56	11
concerted endeavor, be it politics, religion, or business. Management is	71	14
the activity that sets the objectives, plans what work is to be done,	85	17
how and when it is to be done, and who will do it. It also establishes	99	20
the essential controls to insure that the work is done correctly.	113	23
Most colleges offer courses in management, and some of them offer	13	25
it as a major field. A special area of interest in the field of man-	27	28
agement is office management which deals with the flow of data, usually	41	31
in the form of paperwork, in an office. So that executives can acquire	55	34
timely and accurate data when it is needed, there must be those who	69	36
collect, process, record, and transmit data in a proper manner. It is	83	39
the duty of an office manager to oversee these workers and tasks so	97	42
that busy executives can focus their minds on more specialized matters.	112	45
As the systems and the technology used in the office grow more	13	47
complex, business is insisting that only those with formal training can	27	50
qualify as an office manager. Despite this trend, there are many office	42	53
managers who began a career as a clerk or as a typist and who worked	55	56
their way up through the ranks. By extensive experience and, in many	69	59
cases, by taking a special management program on the college level, they	84	62
qualified for the job. As time goes by, though, this road to the top	98	64
may be closed and only those with the college degree may be acceptable.	112	67

gwam 1′ | 1 | 2 | 3 | 4 | 5 | 6 | 7 | 8 | 9 | 10 | 11 | 12 | 13 | 14 |
5′ | 1 | 2 | 3 |

222

222a ▶ 5 Conditioning practice

Use standard directions given in 221a, p. 348.

alphabet	1	Joe Bevin walked six furlongs each day to qualify for the major prize.
figures	2	The girls made 57, 48, 30, 26, and 19 points when shooting basketball.
fig/sym	3	Karen's bill totaled $1,146.25 ($937.50 plus $208.75 finance charges).
fluency	4	If she makes room for them to do the work, they may mend the worn rug.

| 1 | 2 | 3 | 4 | 5 | 6 | 7 | 8 | 9 | 10 | 11 | 12 | 13 | 14 |

69c, continued

Problem 3

full sheet

reading position; DS columnar entries; decide spacing between columns

Note: Space in once before setting left margin stop to position single-digit numbers in Column 1; use margin release and backspace to position *10*.

			words
MOST COMMON AMERICAN SURNAMES			6
(Showing Rank, Surname, and No. of People)			15
1	Smith	2,382,509	18
2	Johnson	1,807,263	22
3	Williams (on)	1,568,939	27
4	Brown	1,362,910	31
5	Jones	1,331,205	34
6	Miller	1,131,861	38
7	Davis	1,047,848	42
8	Martin (ez), (son)	1,046,297	48
9	Anders(on)	825,648	52
10	Wilson	787,825	56

Enrichment activities: tables

Problem 1

half sheet, long side up

exact center; DS columnar entries; decide spacing between columns; correct any errors you make

			words
RECENT HEISMAN TROPHY WINNERS			6
1976	Tony Dorsett	Pittsburgh	12
1977	Earl Campbell	Texas	17
1978	Billy Simms	Oklahoma	22
1979	Charles White	Southern California	30
1980	George Rogers	South Carolina	36

Problem 2

full sheet

reading position; DS columnar entries; decide spacing between columns; align Roman numerals at the right; correct any errors you make

			words
SUMMER OLYMPIC GAMES			4
(Olympiad, Site, and Year)			10
XXIII	Los Angeles	1984	14
XXII	Moscow	1980	18
XXI	Montreal	1976	21
XX	Munich	1972	24
XIX	Mexico City	1968	28
XVIII	Tokyo	1964	32
XVII	Rome	1960	35
XVI	Melbourne	1956	39
XV	Helsinki	1952	42

Problem 3

half sheet, short side up

Retype Problem 1 in reading position; DS columnar entries; decide spacing between columns.

Additional enrichment material appears on LM p. 82.

222b ▶ 45
Measure production skill: letters

Time schedule

Preparation .... 5′
Timed production .... 30′
Final check:
compute *n-pram* ... 10′

1. Arrange letterheads (LM pp. 193–200), carbon paper, second sheets, and correction materials for ease of handling.

2. Type Problems 1–4 for 30′. Type 1 cc for each letter; correct errors. If you complete the letters before time is called, start over again with Problem 1 on plain paper.

3. Proofread, circle any uncorrected errors, compute *n-pram*.

Problem 1
Block style letter
[LM p. 193]
open punctuation, address envelope

words

December 4, 19-- Mrs. Delia F. Preston, 3204 Robin Road, 11
Louisville, KY 40213-5230 Dear Mrs. Preston Subject: 22
Policy 30 464 589 25

(¶) In your letter of November 24, you raised a question 36
regarding the settlement of this policy under Option 5. 47
Under this option, you may leave the matured value of 58
the policy with the company and receive payments at the 69
rate of $500 per month. Also, while these proceeds 79
remain with the company you may, upon written 88
request, make additional withdrawals from any un- 98
paid sum in amounts of not less than $500. 106

(¶) If you are interested in this option, please notify Mr. 117
Paul Rothman of our Annuities Division. At the same time, 129
please furnish the names and relationships of any persons you 141
may wish to name as beneficiaries. 148

Sincerely yours LINCOLN MUTUAL LIFE INSURANCE COMPANY 159
Martin B. Bergraf, Correspondent Customer Service Division xx 172
185

Problem 2
Executive-size letter
[LM p. 195]
modified block, mixed punctuation; listed enclosures; address envelope

December 8, 19-- Mr. Alexander C. Willing 8530 North High Street Colum- 14
bus, OH 43085-6127 Dear Mr. Willing Subject: Claim 347 020 26

I am pleased to tell you that your claim for disability benefits has been 41
approved and that the annual premium due on your Policy 30 764 649 has 55
been waived as of November 28. Your Certificate of Disability is enclosed. A 71
refund of any premium waived and already paid will be made within the next 86
two weeks. 88

Your claim for benefits will be processed within 30 days, and benefits will be 104
paid in accordance with the enclosed schedule. In the meantime, if you have 120
any questions about your policy or your claim, please write us, using Claim 135
Number 347 020 in your correspondence. 143

Sincerely yours Marc M. Whiteside Executive Vice President xx Enclo- 156
sures Certificate of Disability Schedule of Payments 167/**181**

Problems 3 and 4 are on page 351.

69a ▶ 7 Conditioning practice

Use standard procedure given in 63a, page 103.

alphabet	1	Joel found that good executives were able to analyze problems quickly.
figures	2	Ozark has a flight at 8:26; Delta, at 9:37; and Continental, at 10:54.
fig/sym	3	The cost of $6,948 he quoted on Order 30721 included the 5% sales tax.
fluency	4	Is she to pay the six firms for all the bodywork they do on the autos?

| 1 | 2 | 3 | 4 | 5 | 6 | 7 | 8 | 9 | 10 | 11 | 12 | 13 | 14 |

69b ▶ 13 Improve keystroking control

1. A 1′ *speed* writing on the ¶; note *gwam*.

2. From *gwam*, subtract 4–6 words to set a *control* rate.

3. Three 1′ writings at your *control* rate, trying not to exceed 1 error a minute.

4. Repeat Steps 1–3, but type for 2′ on each writing.

gwam 2′

As you learn to type, there is a time to work for speed and a time 7
to work for accuracy. During the early weeks, technique--not speed, not 14
accuracy--is the major goal. Then speed through improved technique be- 21
comes the primary thrust for a time. Toward the end of the term, ac- 28
curacy of copy (with error correction if necessary) is emphasized. The 35
final goal of speed with accuracy can never be served before its time. 42
Until proper technique is developed, the final goal cannot be realized. 50

gwam 2′ | 1 | 2 | 3 | 4 | 5 | 6 | 7 |

69c ▶ 30 Check table typing skill

Problem 1

half sheet, long side up

exact vertical center; DS columnar entries; decide spacing between columns (4, 6, 8, etc.); correct errors

SOME POSTAL TERMS/ABBREVIATIONS

		words
SOME POSTAL TERMS/ABBREVIATIONS		6
Bar Code Reader	BCR	10
Letter Sorting Machine	LSM	16
Optical Character Reader	OCR	22
United States Postal Service	USPS	28

Problem 2

half sheet, short side up

reading position; DS columnar entries; decide spacing between columns; correct errors

		words
CIRCULATION OF LEADING U.S. MAGAZINES		8
(In Millions)		10
TV Guide	18,871	14
Reader's Digest	18,193	18
National Geographic	10,561	24
Better Homes & Gardens	8,057	30
Woman's Day	7,574	33
Family Circle	7,366	38

Problem 3 is on page 112.

222b, continued

Problem 3
Modified block style letter [LM p. 197]
mixed punctuation, address envelope

Problem 4
AMS letter [LM p. 199]
Type the Problem 3 letter in AMS style; address envelope.

Total words: 196/**210**

words

December 12, 19-- 3

CERTIFIED
~~REGISTERED~~ MAIL 6

Mr. David L. DeProphitis 11
1603 North University Drive 16
Fargo, ND 58102-0364 20

Mr. DeProphitis: 24
Dear ~~Sir:~~ 30
Subject: Your Claim No. 180-2143

completing
Thank you ~~very much~~ for ~~filling out~~ the Application for 40

Payment of benefits for the injury you sustained on October 7, 53

hospital
which resulted in treatment and surgery. Before we are able to 68

process *additional information*
~~consider~~ this claim, however, we need some ~~clarifying data~~. 79

indicate
In your statement, you ~~state~~ that you were injured while 91

ing
~~at~~ work, at the Wahpeton Manufacturing Co. In answer to the 115

question about workmen's compensation, however, you indicate 128

a
that no claim was processed and that no benefits are payible. 137

It appears to us that your accident, which occurred while 149

on the job, *through Workmen's Compensation*
you were ~~at work~~ would be compensible. If it is not, we must 169

lc
have a statement from your Employer explaining why this is not 181

so. 192

matter *review*
After you have clarified this ~~situation~~, we will ~~consider~~ 195

your claim ~~once~~ again. 198

Sincerely yours, 204
3 blank lines
Ms. Ann Castle, Claims Examiner 205/**219**

xx

223

223a ▶ 5
Conditioning practice
Use standard directions given in 221a, p. 348.

alphabet 1 Max Bozzuto played five games of racquetball with Jack Ferguson today.
figures 2 The class was asked to read pages 59, 78, 136, and 240 by next Monday.
fig/sym 3 Smith & Miller sold a computer for $3,028 ($3,495 less $467 discount).
fluency 4 The angle of the oak panel in the cubicle is right for the handy maps.

| 1 | 2 | 3 | 4 | 5 | 6 | 7 | 8 | 9 | 10 | 11 | 12 | 13 | 14 |

68c ▶ 30
Type 3-column tables

Problem 1

half sheet, long side up

exact vertical center; DS columnar entries; 6 spaces between columns

			words
SELECTED U.S. INVENTIONS			5
(Dates and Inventors)			9
Adding machine	1885	W. S. Burroughs	17
Automatic sequence computer	1943	H. H. Aiken	26
Liquid paper	1954	Bette Graham	32
Telephone	1876	Alexander Bell	38
Typewriter	1867	Christopher Sholes	45

Problem 2

half sheet, short side up

reading position; DS columnar entries; 4 spaces between columns; align figures of Column 2 at the right; erase and correct errors

AMERICANS OF SPANISH ANCESTRY			6
(Estimated Population and % of U.S. Total)			15
Mexican	7,151,000	2.4	19
Puerto Rican	1,823,000	0.6	24
Central/South American	863,000	0.3	32
Cuban	689,000	0.2	36
Other Spanish	1,519,000	0.5	41

Problem 3

full sheet **(extra credit)**

reading position; DS columnar entries; 10 spaces between columns

If time is called before you complete Problem 3, finish the line on which you are typing. Your teacher will tell you if you are to complete the table in the next class period.

THE ORIGINAL THIRTEEN STATES OF THE U.S.			8
(With Date of Constitution Ratification and Original Capital)			21
Delaware	December 7, 1787	Dover	27
Pennsylvania	December 12, 1787	Harrisburg	35
New Jersey	December 18, 1787	Trenton	43
Georgia	January 2, 1788	Atlanta	49
Connecticut	January 9, 1788	Hartford	57
Massachusetts	February 6, 1788	Boston	64
Maryland	April 28, 1788	Annapolis	71
South Carolina	May 23, 1788	Columbia	78
New Hampshire	June 21, 1788	Concord	86
Virginia	June 25, 1788	Richmond	92
New York	July 26, 1788	Albany	98
North Carolina	November 21, 1789	Raleigh	106
Rhode Island	May 29, 1790	Providence	113

223b ▶ 45
Measure production skill: interoffice memorandums and reports

Follow the timing procedures and time schedule given for 222b, p. 350.

Problem 1
Unbound report with side headings
full sheet

words

TYPES OF LIFE INSURANCE AVAILABLE 7

TS

DS Life insurance is one way a person can be sure 16
that his or her depend~~s~~*ents* will have enough money to 27
support them after he or she has died. There are 37
several different types of policies available. 46

TS

<u>Whole Life Policy</u> 53

A whole life policy pays its *face* value to the bene- 63
ficiary when the *insured* ~~individual~~ dies. If premiums are 73
payable for *the* life of the insured, the policy is *known as* ~~called~~ 85
a <u>straight</u> <u>life</u> policy; if the premiums are payable 98
for a *given* ~~set~~ number of years, the policy is called a 109
<u>limited</u> <u>payment</u> policy. Since a whole life policy 122
combines protection with savings, it is the most 132
widely used *form* ~~kind~~ of life insurance. 139

TS

<u>Endowment Policy</u> 145

An endowment policy insures a person's life for 155
a *stated* ~~given~~ number of years. At the end of that *time* ~~period~~, 165
the full amount of the policy is *paid* ~~payed~~ to the in- 174
sured. If the insured dies before the *end* ~~close~~ of the 184
period, the full amount is paid to *his or her* ~~the~~ beneficiary. 196

TS

<u>Term Policy</u> 200

This type of policy also protects an individ- 209
ual for a *stated* ~~given~~ number of years. Term *insurance* offers the 221
same protection as other types of policies, but 231
when the term *ends* ~~runs out~~, so does the coverage. Al- 240
though the *initial* cost of this policy is very low, ~~at~~ 250
~~first,~~ the cost *increases* ~~grows~~ as the insured grows older. 259

Problems 2, 3, and 4 are on page 353.

67c ▶ 30 Type 3-column tables

3 half sheets

Problem 1

half sheet, long side up

Center and type the table in exact vertical center. DS items in columns; leave 14 spaces between columns. Align figures at right.

			words
SAMPLE CONVERSION OF WOMEN'S CLOTHING SIZES			9
U.S. to Metric			12
Shoes	6	36	14
Hosiery	9	2	17
Blouses	36	42	20
Dresses	12	40	22

Problem 2

half sheet, long side up

Center and type the table in exact vertical center. SS items in columns; leave 8 spaces between columns.

Problem 3

half sheet, short side up

Center and type the table of Problem 1 in *reading position* (2 spaces above exact center). DS items in columns; leave 12 spaces between columns.

			words
THE FIVE NEWEST STATES OF THE U.S.			7
(With Date of Entry and Capital)			14
Hawaii	August 21, 1959	Honolulu	20
Alaska	January 3, 1959	Juneau	26
Arizona	February 14, 1912	Phoenix	33
New Mexico	January 6, 1912	Santa Fe	40
Oklahoma	November 16, 1907	Oklahoma City	48

68

70-space line

68a ▶ 7 Conditioning practice

Use standard procedure given in 63a, page 103.

alphabet 1 Wise judges of the market expect a big zoom in our quarterly dividend.

figures 2 I ordered 36 desks, 49 chairs, 15 tables, 80 lamps, and 72 file trays.

fig/sym 3 Order 21846 (File 957-20) must be shipped to Tsai & O'Day by March 31.

fluency 4 The firm may wish to bid by proxy for title to the lake and the docks.

| 1 | 2 | 3 | 4 | 5 | 6 | 7 | 8 | 9 | 10 | 11 | 12 | 13 | 14 |

68b ▶ 13 Determine cost of an error

1. A 1′ writing on the ¶; determine *gwam*.

2. Another 1′ writing on the ¶, but this time erase and correct any errors you make as you type; determine corrected words a minute (*cwam*).

3. Subtract your *cwam* from your *gwam*. The difference is the cost of your errors.

4. Two 2′ writings on the ¶ in the same way; determine the cost of errors.

5. Two more 2′ writings at reduced speed to improve control (reduce errors).

gwam 2′

· 4 · 8 · 12

The number of words you can type in the time it takes you to stop 7

· 16 · 20 · 24 ·

and correct an error is one index of error cost. To see how much your 14

28 · 32 · 36 · 40

errors cost you, type a timed writing on a paragraph and determine your 21

· 44 · 48 · 52 · 56

rate. Then, type the paragraph again; but when you are aware you have 28

· 60 · 64 · 68 ·

made an error, stop and correct it before you resume typing. Determine 35

72 · 76 · 80 · 84

your new rate. The difference in rates on the two writings is the cost 42

· 88 · 92 · 96 ·

of the errors you made. The more errors you make, the higher the cost. 50

gwam 2′ | 1 | 2 | 3 | 4 | 5 | 6 | 7 |

223b, continued

Problem 2
Interoffice memorandum
[LM p. 201]
Address **COMPANY MAIL** envelope.

Problem 3
Interoffice memorandum
[LM p. 203]
Retype the memo in Problem 2. Address the memo to **Eric Gomez, Senior Correspondent.**
Total words: 136/**143**

Problem 4
Leftbound report with ¶ headings
full sheet
Retype the report in Problem 1 as a leftbound report. Change the side headings to ¶ headings.

words

TO: Irene T. Michaels, Contract Division 7
FROM: Harriet M. Lowe, Employee Services 14
DATE: December 14, 19-- 17
SUBJECT: Establishing Dependency 22

In order for an insured employee to claim an indi- 32
vidual other than his or her spouse or minor children 43
as dependents, we must have answers to these 53
three questions: 55
1. Is the individual living with the employee? 64
2. Is the individual dependent on the employee for at 73
least 50% of his or her support? 81
3. Is the individual claimed as an exemption on 91
the employee's federal income tax? 98
If you will have the employee answer these questions 108
in writing, complete the enclosed Form 62A in 120
triplicate, and send both documents to this office, 130
we will establish the dependency. 134
xx 135
Enclosure 137/**144**

224

224a ▶ 5 Conditioning practice

Use standard directions given in 221a, p. 348.

alphabet 1 Zoe Wickley exhibited two quaint lamps in five galleries for the jury.
figures 2 She sold 305 records, 194 tapes, 72 stereos, and 86 new movie cameras.
fig/sym 3 Hall & Ray's new computer (Model BK-98064) cost $23,175 with discount.
fluency 4 It is their goal to double the quantity of work in the town by spring.

| 1 | 2 | 3 | 4 | 5 | 6 | 7 | 8 | 9 | 10 | 11 | 12 | 13 | 14 |

66c ▶ 30
Type 2-column tables with secondary headings

Problem 1

half sheet, long side up

Center and type the table in exact vertical and horizontal center. DS between main and secondary headings; TS between secondary heading and body of table; SS items in columns. Leave 10 spaces between the two columns.

TELEPHONE EXTENSIONS (DS)

By Department (TS)

		words
TELEPHONE EXTENSIONS		4
By Department		7
Accounting	260	10
Advertising	270	13
Information Processing	280	19
Marketing	290	21
Personnel	310	24
Purchasing	340	27
Shipping	350	30

Problem 2

half sheet, long side up

Type the table using Problem 1 directions, but leave 14 spaces between the two columns. Erase and correct any errors you make.

Problem 3

half sheet, long side up

Retype Problem 1, but DS the columnar entries and leave 12 spaces between columns.

		words
SELECTED SYMBOLS		3
Names and Examples		7
Ampersand (and)	B&O	11
Diagonal	5/8	14
Dollar/dollars	$92	18
Number	#73	20
Percent	10%	22
Pound/pounds	46#	25

67

70-space line

67a ▶ 7
Conditioning practice

Use standard procedure given in 63a, page 103.

alphabet 1 Margie expertly sewed five square white buttons on a jet black blazer.

figures 2 Joe must sell 27 to 28 tickets for the 19th and 35 to 40 for the 26th.

fig/sym 3 "No-fault"* Policy 796-380 had a $150 deductible (42% of the premium).

fluency 4 The goal of this firm is to cut the delay for corn, cocoa, and burlap.

| 1 | 2 | 3 | 4 | 5 | 6 | 7 | 8 | 9 | 10 | 11 | 12 | 13 | 14 |

67b ▶ 13
Learn to center on off-size paper

2 half sheets, short side up

1. Insert a half sheet, short side up.

2. Study "How to find horizontal center" and "How to determine vertical placement" at the right.

3. Center and type your name in exact vertical and horizontal center of half sheet.

4. Insert another half sheet, short side up.

5. Center and type the table of Problem 1, above. Use Problem 1 directions, but DS items in columns.

How to find horizontal center

1. On line-of-writing scale, read figures at left and right edges of the paper.

2. Add the 2 figures; divide total by 2.

3. The resulting figure is the horizontal center of the sheet.

4. Use this figure as the point at which to begin backspacing to center lines horizontally.

How to determine vertical placement

1. Measure the sheet from top to bottom (in inches).

2. Multiply 6 times the number of inches.

3. The resulting figure is the number of lines available for typing.

4. Subtract from this figure the number of lines needed and divide the resulting number by 2.

224b ▶ 45
Measure production skills: tables

Follow the time schedule for 222b, p. 350. Center the longest item in each column, whether it is a column heading or a columnar item.

Problem 1
Three-column table with footnote

full sheet; DS; center vertically in reading position; 10 spaces between columns

words

WHO WATCHES TELEVISION THE MOST?* 7

Average Weekly Viewing Time in Hours and Minutes 17

Person	Age	Time	words
			23
Women	55+	37:55	26
Women	25-54	33:54	29
Men	55+	33:28	31
Women	18-24	32:53	34
Children	2- 5	31:23	37
Children	6-11	27:16	40
Male	Teens	27:12	43
Men	25-54	26:42	46
Men	18-24	23:32	49
Female	Teens	23:25	52

55

*Based on an A. C. Nielsen survey. 62

Problem 2
Three-column table with totals

full sheet; DS; exact vertical center; 10 spaces between Cols. 1 & 2; 4 spaces between Cols. 2 & 3

COMPARISON OF AREA FINANCIAL INSTITUTIONS 8

(In Thousands of Dollars) 13

	Assets	Deposits	words
			19
American Federal	77,112,434	55,651,250	27
Bankers Trust	53,180,295	43,508,258	34
Citizens Savings	35,787,568	29,782,691	42
Manufacturers Trust	31,663,815	23,831,026	50
First National	25,800,280	18,753,785	57
Farmers Mutual	22,613,959	17,054,104	64
Home Savings and Loan	18,735,845	14,833,657	77
Total	264,894,196	203,414,771	83

Problem 3
Four-column ruled table with source note

full sheet; DS; exact vertical center; 6 spaces between columns

Problem 4
Four-column boxed table with source note

If time permits, retype Problem 3 SS as a boxed table. Arrange the body in 2 groups of 5 items each; DS between groups.

INVENTIONS OF MAJOR SOCIETAL SIGNIFICANCE 8

(Selected by Panel of Students) 14

28
42

Invention	Inventor	Date	Country	words
				48
				62
Bicycle	K. D. von Sauerbronn	1816	Germany	70
Bifocal lens	Benjamin Franklin	1780	United States	78
Cathode-ray tube	William Crookes	1878	England	86
Electric motor	Michael Faraday	1822	England	94
Gyrocompass	Elmer A. Sperry	1911	United States	103
Laser	T. H. Naiman	1960	United States	110
Parachute	L. S. Lenormand	1783	France	117
Radar	R. A. Watson-Watt	1935	England	124
Safety pin	Walter Hunt	1849	United States	132
Typewriter	Henry Mill	1714	England	138

152

Source: Science Facts. 157

65d ▶ 20 Type 2-column tables

2 half sheets

Problem 1

half sheet, long side up

Center and type the table in exact vertical and horizontal center. DS items in columns. Leave 12 spaces between the two columns.

		words
REGIONAL OFFICE MANAGERS		5
Atlanta	Marla Simpson	9
Boston	John O'Donnell	14
Chicago	Kevin Jablonski	19
Denver	Sybil Duarte	23
San Francisco	Han Song Ki	28
Toronto	Paula Killy	32

Problem 2

half sheet, long side up

Center and type the table in exact vertical and horizontal center. SS items in columns. Leave 10 spaces between columns.

		words
SUPERLATIVE U.S. STATISTICS		6
Largest state	Alaska	10
Largest national park	Yellowstone	17
Highest city	Leadville, Colorado	23
Highest waterfall	Yosemite Falls	30
Highest mountain	Mount McKinley	36
Highest bridge	Royal Gorge	42
Deepest gorge	Hell's Canyon	47

66

70-space line

66a ▶ 7 Conditioning practice

Use standard procedure given in 63a, page 103.

alphabet 1 My sizable rebate check was given to adjust for a parish tax inequity.

figures 2 Those 76 buildings house 1,420 offices, 389 apartments, and 51 stores.

fig/sym 3 The new dealership (J & B Agency) sold 157 new cars and 246 used ones.

fluency 4 The eighty girls did rush onto the field with usual and visible vigor.

| 1 | 2 | 3 | 4 | 5 | 6 | 7 | 8 | 9 | 10 | 11 | 12 | 13 | 14 |

66b ▶ 13 Learn to align figures

Type the table twice DS; center according to the KEY on 50-space line.

To align figures at right: Set a tab stop for the digit in each column (after Column 1) that requires the least forward and backward spacing. Do not consider fractions as part of the column. To align the figures, space forward ▶ or backward ◀ as necessary.

ALIGNING FIGURES

margin ↓	tab ↓	tab ↓	tab ↓
406	1384	305	1209
294	▶730	413	▶627
▶56	▶23 4/5	▶50 3/8	▶83
105	4039	◀2703	1560

key| 3 | 12 | 4 | 12 | 4 | 12 | 4 |

225

225a ▶ 5 Conditioning practice

each line of 224a, page 353, twice SS; repeat selected lines as time permits

225b ▶ 45 Measure production skills: forms

Follow the time schedule given for 222b, page 350. [LM pp. 207–211]

Problem 1 Message/reply memo [LM p. 207]

words

TO: Ramona T. Ramirez, Sales Director 23 Administration Building 12
DATE: August 19, 19-- SUBJECT: Expected Production Delay 20
(¶) Due to an unexpected delay in receiving press-brake dies for the 33
press used in manufacturing parts for our 4-drawer file cabinet (Cat. 47
No. 4A6927), we have temporarily stopped production of these cabinets. 61
We expect the press to be shut down for a period of 3 to 4 weeks. We 75
have enough cabinets presently in stock to cover existing orders. 88
However, your sales force should inform customers when taking new 101
orders for these cabinets that a 3- to 4-week delay in delivery should 115
be expected. SIGNED: Xavier Montano, Production Manager 124

(Reply) DATE: August 20, 19-- (¶) The sales force has been informed 134
of the problem halting production of our 4-drawer file cabinets, and 148
they will tell prospective customers to expect a 3- to 4-week delay 162
in delivery. If there is any change in when you expect to resume 175
production of these cabinets, please let me know immediately. 187
SIGNED: Ramona T. Ramirez, Sales Director 194

Problem 2 Purchase order [LM p. 209]

Reliable Hardware, Inc. 565 N. Addison Street, Indianapolis, IN 46222-5387, (317) 751-6200

PURCHASE ORDER

Purchase order No. T66-9420 2

Oakland Tool & Die Company
4000 Lincoln Road
Indianapolis, IN 46208-1134

Date August 21, 19-- 10
Terms 2/10, n/30 16
Ship Via Sunset Freight 24

Quantity	Cat. No.	Description	Price	Total	words
20 ea.	8A55549	Sockets, 6-point, 14 mm	3.10	62.00	34
6 sets	8A55258	Socket sets, 9-15 mm	21.30	127.80	43
20 ea.	8A44287	Wrenches, 10 x 11 mm	.79	15.80	52
6 sets	8A44292	Wrench sets, 6-15, 17 mm	41.99	251.94	63
				457.54	64

By Samuel T. Gottlieb Purchasing Agent 68

Problems 3 and 4 are on next page.

65a ▶ 7 Conditioning practice

Use standard procedure given in 63a, page 103.

alphabet	1	We requested twelve cans of zone marking paint expressly for that job.
figures	2	Their team took some close games: 97 to 96, 84 to 83, and 105 to 102.
fig/sym	3	Poe & Co. is 364th of 1,780 top firms rated in <u>Fortune</u>, June 15, 1982.
fluency	4	Key firms of both towns may risk a penalty if the fuel profit is down.

| 1 | 2 | 3 | 4 | 5 | 6 | 7 | 8 | 9 | 10 | 11 | 12 | 13 | 14 |

65b ▶ 8 Improve technique: response patterns

1. Type Line 1 once from dictation; then type a 1′ writing on Line 2.

2. Type the other sets of lines in the same way.

3. If time permits, type Lines 1, 3, and 5 again to increase speed.

word response	1	the dial | is worn | paid half | may throw | their bid | eight pens | right height
	2	Did the chair signal the man to name the auditor of the downtown firm?
letter response	3	my ad | at you | see him | pop art | milk case | poppy seed | water pump | extra ink
	4	You saw him test a rated water pump on my extra car at a union garage.
combination response	5	see us | if you | as she | my bid | and oil | for gas | upon the | did join | the pump
	6	It is up to you and him to start the leprosy treatment in my big ward.

| 1 | 2 | 3 | 4 | 5 | 6 | 7 | 8 | 9 | 10 | 11 | 12 | 13 | 14 |

65c ▶ 15 Improve skill transfer

line: 70; listen for bell

1. A 1′ writing on ¶ 1, then ¶ 2, then ¶ 3. Determine *gwam* on each.

2. A 1′ writing on each of the 2 slowest ¶s to increase speed.

3. A 2′ writing on each of the 3 ¶s. If you finish a ¶ before time is called, start over.

Determine % of transfer, using the 2′ rates:

¶ 2 *gwam* ÷ ¶ 1 *gwam*
¶ 3 *gwam* ÷ ¶ 1 *gwam*

Goals

¶ 2, *at least* 75% of ¶ 1
¶ 3, *at least* 80% of ¶ 1

all letters/figures used | A | 1.5 si | 5.7 awl | 80% hfw

	gwam 1′	2′
Some people can find something good in virtually every situ-	12	6
ation. Even when things go amiss, they believe every dark cloud	25	12
hides a silver lining. No matter what the origin of this point	38	19
of view, it results in the power of positive thinking. A great	50	25
deal of praise should be given the person who can be identified	63	32
as a positive thinker.	68	34
The right attitude helps when you check your work. It is	12	6
easy to miscue when typing figures and symbols (for example, 7201	25	12
for 7021, $485 for $458, and 1673 for 1573) and just as easy to	38	19
overlook such mistakes when proofreading. If you look upon the	50	25
discovery of errors as an opportunity to correct them, you can	63	32
find 99-100% of your mistakes.	69	35
Realize that (many) errors are but ~~indexes~~ (symptoms) of something more basic:	14	7
Lack (lc) of attention, ~~weak~~ (poor) reading habits, or ~~poor~~ (inadequate) technique. ~~The~~ (A)	27	14
positive person will work to corect (r) these ~~causes~~ (reasons) for error ~~when~~ (in)	40	20
typing and ~~checking~~ (proofreading). In addition, a positive ~~thinker~~ (person) will laern	54	27
to correct errors be fore taking work outof the ~~typewriter~~ (machine) so	65	33
that a job ~~won't~~ (will not) have tobe done ~~again~~ (over.)	74	37

225b, continued

words

Problem 3
Bill of lading
[LM p. 209]

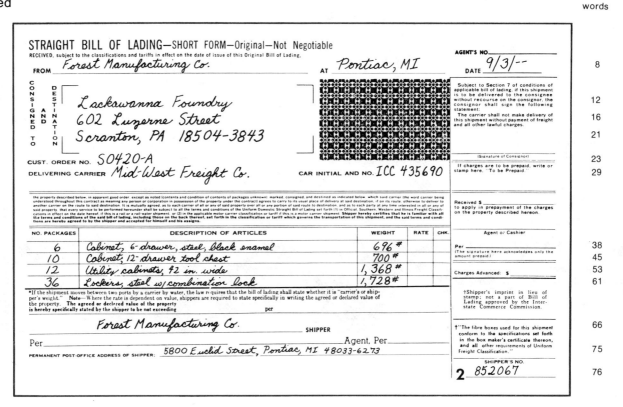

STRAIGHT BILL OF LADING—SHORT FORM—Original—Not Negotiable

RECEIVED, subject to the classifications and tariffs in effect on the date of issue of this Original Bill of Lading,

AGENT'S NO. ______

FROM *Forest Manufacturing Co.* AT *Pontiac, MI* DATE *9/3/--* 8

CONSIGNED TO AND DESTINATION:
Lackawanna Foundry 12
602 Luzerne Street 16
Scranton, PA 18504-3843 21

Subject to Section 7 of conditions of applicable bill of lading, if this shipment is to be delivered to the consignee without recourse on the consignor, the consignor shall sign the following statement:
The carrier shall not make delivery of this shipment without payment of freight and all other lawful charges.

______ (Signature of Consignor)

CUST. ORDER NO. *S0420-A* 23
DELIVERING CARRIER *Mid-West Freight Co.* CAR INITIAL AND NO. *ICC 435690* 29

If charges are to be prepaid, write or stamp here, "To be Prepaid."

the property described below, in apparent good order, except as noted (contents and condition of contents of packages unknown) marked, consigned, and destined as indicated below, which said carrier (the word carrier being understood throughout this contract as meaning any person or corporation in possession of the property under the contract) agrees to carry to its usual place of delivery at said destination, if on its route, otherwise to deliver to another carrier on the route to said destination. It is mutually agreed, as to each carrier of all or any of said property over all or any portion of said route to destination, and as to each party at any time interested in all or any of said property, that every service to be performed hereunder shall be subject to all the terms and conditions of the Uniform Domestic Straight Bill of Lading set forth (1) in Official, Southern, Western and Illinois Freight Classifications in effect on the date hereof, if this is a rail or a rail-water shipment, or (2) in the applicable motor carrier classification or tariff if this is a motor carrier shipment. **Shipper hereby certifies that he is familiar with all the terms and conditions of the said bill of lading, including those on the back thereof, set forth in the classification or tariff which governs the transportation of this shipment, and the said terms and conditions are hereby agreed to by the shipper and accepted for himself and his assigns.**

Received $ ______ to apply in prepayment of the charges on the property described hereon.

______ Agent or Cashier

NO. PACKAGES	DESCRIPTION OF ARTICLES	WEIGHT	RATE	CHK.	
6	*Cabinet, 6-drawer, steel, black enamel*	*696#*			38
10	*Cabinet, 12-drawer tool chest*	*700#*			45
12	*Utility cabinets, 42 in. wide*	*1,368#*			53
36	*Lockers, steel w/combination lock*	*1,728#*			61

Per ______
(The signature here acknowledges only the amount prepaid.)

Charges Advanced: $ ______

*If the shipment moves between two ports by a carrier by water, the law requires that the bill of lading shall state whether it is "carrier's or shipper's weight." **Note**—Where the rate is dependent on value, shippers are required to state specifically in writing the agreed or declared value of the property. **The agreed or declared value of the property is hereby specifically stated by the shipper to be not exceeding** ______ per ______

†Shipper's imprint in lieu of stamp; not a part of Bill of Lading approved by the Interstate Commerce Commission.

Forest Manufacturing Co. SHIPPER 66

Per ______ ______ Agent, Per ______

†"The fibre boxes used for this shipment conform to the specifications set forth in the box maker's certificate thereon, and all other requirements of Uniform Freight Classification."

PERMANENT POST-OFFICE ADDRESS OF SHIPPER: *5800 Euclid Street, Pontiac, MI 48033-6273* 75

SHIPPER'S NO.
2 *852067* 76

Problem 4
Invoice
[LM p. 211]

FM Forest Manufacturing Co.
5800 Euclid Street
Pontiac, MI 48033-6273

Invoice

McKinley Products, Inc.
4500 Daniels Street
Vancouver, WA 98663-7563

Date *August 30, 19--* 8
Our Order No. *70583-K* 13
Cust. Order No. *MP-9420* 19
Terms *2/10, n/30* Shipped Via *Coastal Trucking* 24

Quantity	Description	Unit Price	Total	
20 ea.	*Cabinets, 13 x 6 1/4 x 9 1/4*	*9.05*	*181.00*	33
20 ea.	*Mechanic's tool box, 27 1/8 x 8 3/8 x 10*	*28.95*	*579.00*	44
15 ea.	*Storage units, 20 1/2 x 25 x 31 1/4*	*54.90*	*823.50*	54
25 ea.	*Steel storage units, 42 x 30 x 12 in. deep,*			64
	gray	*14.39*	*359.75*	69
			1,943.25	71

64c ▶ 25

Learn to center a table horizontally and vertically

Steps in horizontal centering of columns

1. Preparatory steps
a. Move margin stops to ends of scale.
b. Clear all tabulator stops.
c. Move carriage (element) to center of paper.
d. Decide spacing between columns (if spacing is not specified)—preferably an even number of spaces (4, 6, 8, 10, 12, etc.).

2. Set left margin stop
From center of paper, backspace once for each 2 characters and spaces in longest line of each column, then for each 2 spaces to be left between columns. Set the left margin stop at this point.

If the longest line in one column has an extra letter or number, combine that letter or number with the first letter or number in the next column when backspacing by 2's, as in paper (4) pen.

◀ 1 1 1 1 1 1
pa| pe| rp| en| ##| ##

If you have 1 stroke left over after backspacing for all columnar items, disregard it.

3. Set tabulator stops
From the left margin, space forward once for each letter, figure, symbol, and space in longest line in the first column and for each space to be left between first and second columns. *Set tab stop at this point for second column.* Follow similar procedure for additional columns to be typed.

Type the table below on a half sheet, centering it vertically and horizontally.
If time permits, retype the problem. (See page 53 for a review of vertical centering.)

Center

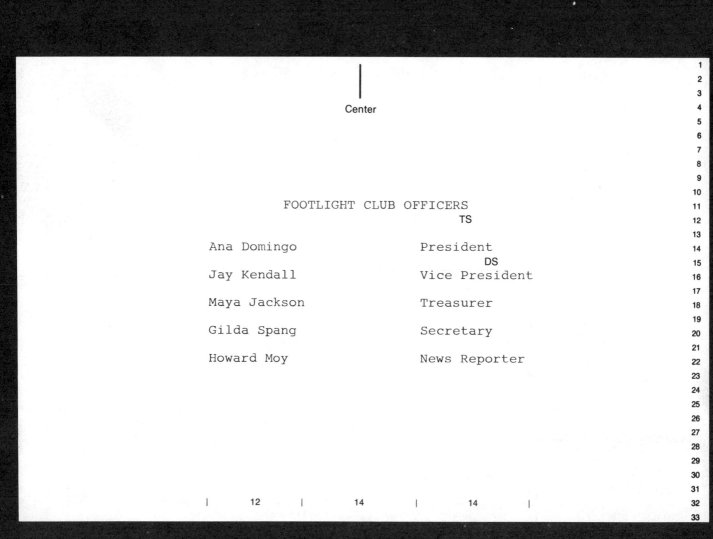

FOOTLIGHT CLUB OFFICERS

TS

Ana Domingo	President
Jay Kendall	Vice President
Maya Jackson	Treasurer
Gilda Spang	Secretary
Howard Moy	News Reporter

DS

| 12 | 14 | 14 |

Table centered vertically and horizontally

phase **10** lessons 226-250

Improve basic/production skills

Phase 10 begins with a series of pretests to measure your basic and production skills. The scores on these tests will provide the basis for you and your teacher to plan the learning experiences you need to improve your typing ability. After you have finished a series of drills and problems, a set of posttests will measure the degree of progress you have made.

In general terms, the 25 lessons of Phase 10 are designed to give you an opportunity to:

1. Increase speed and accuracy on straight copy, rough-draft copy, and statistical copy;

2. Improve the transfer of straight-copy skill to the typing of rough-draft and statistical copy;

3. Improve skill in typing a wide variety of business correspondence;

4. Increase ability to type several kinds of business reports, including tabulated reports;

5. Improve speed and accuracy in typing tables and a number of typical business forms.

unit **44** lessons 226-229

Assess basic/production skills

Assessment goals

1. To determine your speed and accuracy on straight copy, rough draft, and statistical copy.

2. To determine your production rate when typing business correspondence, reports, tables, and business forms.

Machine adjustments

1. Line: 70 for drills and timed writings; as required for production problems.

2. Spacing: SS sentence drills with a DS between sentence groups; DS ¶s; space problems as required.

63d ▶ 16 Review/improve techniques

each line 3 times SS (slowly, faster, top speed); DS between 3-line groups; if time permits, type selected lines again

Lines 1-3: Curved, upright fingers; quiet hands.

Lines 4-6: Space *immediately* after words; use down-and-in motion of thumb.

Lines 7-9: Easy words at high speed; difficult words at a slower, continuous pace.

Keystroking

adjacent 1 We built a radio forum on the premise that expert opinion was popular.
long direct 2 The recent survey is summarized in a brochure she found in my library.
fingers 3/4 3 Allison has quit work at the plaza shop to expand the place next door.

Spacing

4 by it my am is on go an do me in so no but may get pay sum sun buy any
5 if my | do my work | if any go | so they are | to buy it | go by the | so many men
6 If you want to buy the pony for the boy, you may come for it any time.

Response patterns

word 7 Eighty firms may bid for the right to make the big signs for the city.
letter 8 As you are aware, only a fast rate on a test gets a pin in my opinion.
combination 9 The panel agreed to award to the union the deed to the vast lake land.

| 1 | 2 | 3 | 4 | 5 | 6 | 7 | 8 | 9 | 10 | 11 | 12 | 13 | 14 |

64

70-space line

64a ▶ 7 Conditioning practice

Use standard procedure given in 63a, page 103.

alphabet 1 Jo climaxed her talk by awarding the prized silver plaque for service.
figures 2 The 405 members voted 267 to 138 to delay the tax increase until 1987.
fig/sym 3 Their statement read, "Payment #6 will be $50.73 plus 12.4% interest."
fluency 4 The duty of the auditor is to sign the usual audit forms for the city.

| 1 | 2 | 3 | 4 | 5 | 6 | 7 | 8 | 9 | 10 | 11 | 12 | 13 | 14 |

64b ▶ 18 Review/improve techniques

each set of lines twice SS (slowly, then faster); DS between 6-line groups; if time permits, type selected sets again

Lines 1-3: Shift, type, and release without moving the hands down.

Lines 4-6: Turn platen *down* for superscripts, *up* for subscripts.

Lines 7-9: Start at center point of paper and backspace to center each line horizontally.

Lines 10-12: Beginning at left margin, use the KEY to set tab stops. Tab quickly from column to column; return without pausing.

Shifting

1 Monday or Tuesday | March and April | Dover or Nassau | Florida and Oklahoma
2 A cruise to the Caribbean leaves Port Everglades on Monday, October 9.
3 Marsha and Alton left with Janet and Appley on a South Pacific cruise.

Automatic line finder

4 See Saunders and Biggs,[1] Cunningham,[8] and Martinez [13] for descriptions.
5 Use the chemical formulas for benzene (C_6H_6) and for ethanol (C_2H_5OH).
6 One square inch equals 6.4516 cm^2. One square mile equals 2.5900 km^2.

Backspacer

7 Find center point of paper;
8 backspace once for each two strokes;
9 begin typing where backspacing ends.

Tabulator and return

10 if it is	*Tab*	go with them	*Tab*	sign the form	*Tab*	with the work
11 is to go		of the firms		they lent the		they may lend
12 to do it		she may work		all the forms		kept the land
Key 8	8	12	8	13	8	13

226

226a ▶ 5 Conditioning practice

each line twice SS (slowly, then faster); DS between 2-line groups; if time permits, retype selected lines

alphabet 1 An objective of the odd exercise was to analyze quickly a small graph.
figures 2 Our new Model 28548 has 15 digits, 30 memories, and 976 program steps.
fig/sym 3 Multiply $9,640 (the base) times 7 1/2% (the rate) times 5 (the time).
fluency 4 If they wish me to do so, I shall rush the keys for the trucks by air.

| 1 | 2 | 3 | 4 | 5 | 6 | 7 | 8 | 9 | 10 | 11 | 12 | 13 | 14 |

226b ▶ 15 Assess basic skill: straight copy

1. Type two 5′ writings on the 3 ¶s combined.
2. Record *gwam* and errors on better writing. Keep a record for comparison with scores achieved on 242c, page 380, 246b, page 384, and on 295c, page 452.
3. If time permits, type a 1′ writing on each ¶ to improve speed.

all letters used | A | 1.5 si | 5.7 awl | 80% hfw

gwam 3′ | 5′

Books, magazines, newspapers, and other printed material are so 4 3
common today that we rarely give them a second thought. Imagine for 9 5
a minute, however, what your life might be like if printing had never 14 8
been invented. There would be no newspapers to inform us about what 18 11
is happening anywhere. Since there would be few books, schools for 23 14
the general public would not exist. In all probability, you would not 27 16
be typing this paragraph because you would not know how to read at all. 32 19

Thousands of years before printing was developed, people began to 37 22
communicate through writing. At first, perhaps, they just made signs 41 25
on trees or rocks to direct others to the nearest water or town or to 46 27
warn of dangerous animals in the area. Later came pictures on the wall 51 30
or tablets to record history or an interesting story. It is said that 55 33
the Greeks were the first civilized group to develop an alphabet by 60 36
using separate letters for the consonants and the vowels. 64 38

Books were first printed on paper in China and Korea more than two 68 41
thousand years ago. Large libraries could be found in the Far East long 73 44
before printing was commonplace in Europe. Paper was not used in the 78 47
West until the twelfth century and was not available in quantity until 82 49
two hundred years later. After the invention of the printing press 87 52
with movable type in the middle of the fifteenth century, however, the 92 55
production of books in the western world spread like wildfire. 96 57

gwam 3′ | 1 | 2 | 3 | 4 | 5 |
5′ | 1 | 2 | 3 |

unit **12** lessons 63-69

Learn to type simple tables

Learning goals

1. To learn to center, arrange, and type 2- and 3-column tables.
2. To learn to align figures at the right.
3. To improve skill in typing copy containing figures and symbols.
4. To improve typing speed and control.

Machine adjustments

1. Paper guide at *0*.
2. Ribbon control to type on top half of ribbon.
3. Margin sets: 70-space line (center − 35; center + 35 + 5) unless otherwise directed.
4. Line-space selector on *1* (SS) for drills, on *2* (DS) for ¶s; as directed for problems.

63 — 70-space line

63a ▶ 7 Conditioning practice

each line twice SS (slowly, then faster); DS between 2-line groups; if time permits, retype selected lines

alphabet 1 Keifka was just amazed that everyone expected a large quarterly bonus.
figures 2 The shop is 278.4 meters long, 90.6 meters wide, 13.5 meters high.
fig/sym 3 Terms on Devlin & Arnold's order dated 4/6 for $587.90 are 2/10, n/30.
fluency 4 Make them pay us the penalty they owe or cut the profit for the cycle.

| 1 | 2 | 3 | 4 | 5 | 6 | 7 | 8 | 9 | 10 | 11 | 12 | 13 | 14 |

63b ▶ 5 Align and type over words

(Reference: 60c, page 98)

1. Remove your paper from the typewriter.
2. Reinsert the paper; gauge the line and letters and type over Line 1 of 63a.
3. Repeat Steps 1–2, but type over Line 3 of 63a.

63c ▶ 22 Improve keystroking skill: guided writing

1. A 1′ writing on ¶ 1; determine *gwam*. Add 2–4 words to set a new goal.
2. Two 1′ writings on ¶ 1 at your new goal rate, guided by ¼′ guide call.
3. Type ¶ 2 in the same way.
4. A 2′ writing on ¶ 1, then on ¶ 2. If you finish a ¶ before time is called, begin retyping it.
5. A 3′ writing on ¶s 1–2 combined; determine *gwam*.

gwam	¼′	½′	¾′	1′
20	5	10	15	20
24	6	12	18	24
28	7	14	21	28
32	8	16	24	32
36	9	18	27	36
40	10	20	30	40
44	11	22	33	44
48	12	24	36	48
52	13	26	39	52
56	14	28	42	56

all letters used | A | 1.5 si | 5.7 awl | 80% hfw |

Text	gwam 2′	3′
We live in a society of numbers. From the number of a birth cer-	7	4
tificate to the number of a death certificate, numbers play a very vital	14	9
role in the daily life of each of us. Virtually all typed business and	21	14
personal papers contain figures. Quite often these documents contain	28	19
some commonly used symbols, also. Therefore, skill in typing on the top	35	24
row is critical to your future use of the machine.	40	27
Data arranged in table form shows a common use of figures and sym-	7	31
bols. Although some tables include no figures, a very high percentage	14	36
of them do. Just as top skill on a letter keyboard may pay well, expert	21	41
skill on figure copy may land you a prized job as a statistical typist	28	46
that will pay even better. Workers in accounting and data processing	35	50
offices must know how to operate the top row with efficiency.	41	54

gwam 2′ | 1 | 2 | 3 | 4 | 5 | 6 | 7 |
3′ | 1 | 2 | 3 | 4 | 5 |

226c ▶ 15
Assess basic skill: rough draft

1. Two 5′ writings on the 3 ¶s combined.
2. Record *gwam* and errors on better writing. Keep a record for comparison with scores achieved on 243c, page 381.
3. If time permits, type a 1′ writing on each ¶ to improve speed.

all letters used | A | 1.5 si | 5.7 awl | 80% hfw

	gwam 1′	5′
Until the use of the printing press with moveable type	12	2
in the 15th century, there were few books printed. The first	26	5
manuscripts were written by hand and were very costly. As	39	8
a result, the only persons who possessed them were rich ones,	53	11
members of the ruling family, and religious orders. The major	67	13
tasks pupils faced in school was to make their own copies of	80	16
the books needed. These pupils were usually the sons of rich	93	19
people who spent thier time in school, or "schole," an Old Greek	107	21
word that means "leisure." The major factor in the making of	112/7	24
books was that of moveable type for the presses. Under this	21	27
way, stamps were made for letters on a seperate base so that	34	29
letters could be arranged to make a page and, after the needed	48	32
number of pages was made, the stamps could be taken apart and	61	35
reformed again to make a second page.	68	36
The use of printing with movable type has been named	12	47
one of the notable developments of the middle ages. It is	26	50
very difficult to emphasize too much the value of printing	39	52
in the progress of the world. Formerly, all knowledge had	52	55
been the right of only a small and selective group. The	65	58
possession of books led not just to schooling for the general	77	60
public, but to the rise of great nations.	94	63
This method had been used many years before in China but was	80	38
discontinued because there were so many different characters in	93	41
the Chinese dialects. The first book printed using movable	105	43
type was an edition of the Bible.	112	45

62c ▶ 35
Type a 2-page report with footnotes

1. Adjust your machine for typing an unbound report.

2. Use a *page line gauge* to plan vertical spacing, page number location, and footnotes [LM p. 79]. Type the footnotes on the same page as their reference figures.

3. Erase and correct any errors you make as you type. Before you remove a page from the machine, proofread it once more and correct any additional errors you find.

Enrichment material appears on LM p. 81.

words

PRACTICE LEVELS IN TYPEWRITING 6

In learning to type, how you practice is just as important as what you 22
produce (words on paper). How you practice is largely determined by the 36
level (speed) of your practice effort. There are three levels of practice in 52
typewriting: (1) the exploration level, (2) the control level, and (3) the op- 68
timum level.[1] 71

When the goal of practice is to go beyond the speed at which you can 84
type accurately and to discover new and faster patterns of keystroking, type 100
on the exploration (high-speed) level. On this level you should try to force 119
letter-sequence motions closer together in time even though you may make 133
many errors. 136

When the purpose of practice is to type with acceptable accuracy, drop 150
back in speed from two to four words a minute and type with ease and con- 165
fidence on the control level. "Control" means more than absence of error in 183
copy produced, however; it means control over reading habits as well as the 198
precise finger movements that lead to accurate typescript. 210

The optimum (in-between) level of practice is somewhere between the 226
exploration level and the control level. It is a level of performance speed 241
that is fairly easy to maintain without undue tension or stress. When you at- 257
tempt to work at this in-between rate, you should make every effort to keep 272
the carriage (element) moving steadily and to eliminate "jerks" and pauses. 287

When you practice first on the exploration level and then on the control 302
level, you are desirably separating the two goals of speed and accuracy. 317
When you type on the optimum level, however, you attempt to type at your 331
best (but not highest) speed within an error tolerance that is acceptable. Ac- 347
cording to the findings of an experimental study by Weise,[2] it is the correct 362
and timely use of levels of practice (rather than the use or nonuse of repeti- 378
tion) that leads most quickly to the final goal of speed with accuracy. 393

The exploration and control levels are used primarily in building the 407
skill; the optimum level is used periodically to measure the skill you have 422
built. 424

________________ 428

[1] Jerry W. Robinson et al., Typewriting: Learning and Instruction 448
(Cincinnati: South-Western Publishing Co., 1979), pp. 62, 93. 461

[2] Barbara S. Weise, "The Effects of Repetition and Alternating Levels 475
of Practice on Learning to Typewrite" (Doctoral dissertation, University of 490
California, Los Angeles, 1975), pp. 62-63. 499

226d ▶ 15
Assess basic skill: statistical copy

1. Two 5′ writings on the 3 ¶s combined.

2. Record *gwam* and errors on better writing. Keep a record for comparison with scores achieved on 244b, page 382.

3. If time permits, type a 1′ writing on each ¶ to improve speed.

all letters/figures used | A | 1.5 si | 5.7 awl | 80% hfw |

	gwam 3′	gwam 5′
After the invention of the printing press between 1450 and 1456,	4	3
the printing of books, magazines, and other matter increased at an	9	5
amazing pace which continues today. Take, for example, the period be-	13	8
tween 1960 and 1980. In 1960, 15,012 new books or titles were put out.	18	11
In 1980, 63,124 new titles were printed--an increase of more than 320%.	23	14
In 1960, an average of 96.9 million newspapers were issued each day;	28	17
in 1980, this number had jumped to 128 million--a rise of 117%.	32	19
In spite of the increase in printed matter, literacy--the ability	37	22
to read and write--was not accomplished by the majority of our citizens	41	25
until the 20th century. During World War I, the U.S. Government found	46	28
that 700,000 men were unable to sign their draft registrations. As	51	30
late as 1960, there were 2.6 million illiterates in this country. By	55	33
1970, this number had decreased to 1.0 million. Today more than 99%	60	36
of our people can read and write--one of the highest rates in the world.	65	39
The credit for the rise in literacy belongs almost entirely to our	69	42
educational system. In 1940, 13.7% of all individuals over 25 years of	74	45
age had less than 5 years of schooling, 24.5% had a high school diploma,	79	47
and only 4.6% had finished college. In 1960, 8.3% had less than 5 years	84	50
of schooling, 41.1% had a high school diploma, and 7.7% had completed	89	53
college. By 1980, a mere 2% had less than 5 years of schooling, 90%	93	56
had a high school diploma, and 25% had acquired a college degree.	98	59

gwam 3′ | 1 | 2 | 3 | 4 | 5 |
5′ | 1 | 2 | 3 |

227

227a ▶ 5
Conditioning practice

Use standard directions given in 226a, page 358.

alphabet 1 Vicky will quiz the group about the rate of the latest tax adjustment.

figures 2 Please check the latest prices on Items 804, 781, 252, 9530, and 2586.

fig/sym 3 The total (as of July 31, 1981) was $14,250,700--an increase of 36.4%.

fluency 4 They must sign and mail the form today if they want to sell the stock.

| 1 | 2 | 3 | 4 | 5 | 6 | 7 | 8 | 9 | 10 | 11 | 12 | 13 | 14 |

61c, continued

On page 2, type footnotes immediately following last line of text.

If you have not completed the report when the class period ends, complete the line you are typing. Your teacher will tell you if you are to complete the report in the next class period.

words

efficient either is, however, remains a moot question. Many claims are made, 362
but there is little proof that is based on valid, reliable research. 376

In 1956, Strong reported on the basis of his data that to retrain a typist 391
skilled on the traditional keyboard to use a "Simplified" keyboard with equal 406
facility required about one hundred hours! Further, he reported that "tra- 421
ditional" typists outgained "simplified" typists during a period of further 436
training to improve skill. He concluded that "A recommendation for the 451
adoption of the Simplified Keyboard for use by the Federal Government can- 465
not be justified based on the findings of this experiment."[3] 478

It is unfortunate that Dvorak and later proponents of his keyboard did 492
not provide dependable comparative data from which viable conclusions can 507
be drawn. Until such data are available--and no carefully controlled experi- 522
ments appear to be under way to provide them--the currently rekindled 536
interest in keyboard "reform" is likely to remain in the heads of a limited 551
group of Dvorak devotees.[4] 557

________________ 560

[3] Earl P. Strong, A Comparative Experiment in Simplified Keyboard Re- 584
training (Washington: General Services Administration, 1956), p. 41. 600

[4] Shirley Boes Neill, "Dvorak vs. Querty: Will Tradition Win Again?" 614
Phi Delta Kappan (June 1980), pp. 671-73. 625

62

70-space line

62a ▶ 7 Conditioning practice

Use standard procedure given in 57a, page 92.

alphabet 1 Al criticized my six workers for having such quick tempers on the job.
fig/sym 2 Does Ms. Beecham's Policy #304156 for $18,500 expire on June 27, 1987?
br/ui 3 Brig may bring suit against the bricklayer for ruining the brick wall.
fluency 4 Both of them may also wish to make a formal bid for the big auto firm.

| 1 | 2 | 3 | 4 | 5 | 6 | 7 | 8 | 9 | 10 | 11 | 12 | 13 | 14 |

62b ▶ 8 Improve technique: response patterns

1. Line 1 twice at increasing speed.
2. Line 3 then Line 5 in the same way.
3. A 1' writing on Line 2, then on Line 4, then on Line 6; determine *gwam* on each.
4. If time permits, type another 1' writing on each of the 2 slowest lines.

word response 1 of the | the world | of the world | to the | the problem | to handle the problem
2 The goal of the panel is to handle the big fuel problem for the towns.

letter response 3 as you | you set | as you set | set up | you set up | as you set up | set up rates
4 Get him a few oil tax cards only after you set up a minimum base rate.

combination response 5 is up | up to | is up to | he was | was to | he was to | if you | you did | if you did
6 He is quite great when he bases firm opinion on the facts of the case.

| 1 | 2 | 3 | 4 | 5 | 6 | 7 | 8 | 9 | 10 | 11 | 12 | 13 | 14 |

227b ▶ 45
Assess production skill: correspondence

1. Type the problems at the right and on p. 362 for 30′; correct errors as you type. If you finish all problems before time is called, start over.

2. After time is called, go over each page carefully and circle any errors you did not correct. Compute *o-pram* (Office Production Rate a Minute) as directed on p. 362.

Problem 1
Short letter

plain full sheet; modified block style, mixed punctuation

Type the letter to the **Madison Manufacturing Co., Inc., 3602 W. Broad Street, Richmond, VA 23230-4437** directed to the attention of **Ms. Joanne W. Hines, Purchasing Agent.** Date the letter **April 27**; use an appropriate salutation and complimentary close. The letter will be signed by **Russell C. Reese**, who is the **Sales Manager** of **Melrowe Distributors, Inc.** Use the company name in the closing lines.

words

opening lines 32

As soon as we received your letter of April 23, our expediter 45
began to trace your Order 69310 which was shipped by us on 56
March 31. At first, the carrier insisted that the order had been 70
delivered as scheduled. A closer check revealed, however, 81
that the order had been shipped to Richmond, CA, instead of 93
Richmond, VA. The carrier reshipped your order on April 25. 106
Thank you for bringing this matter to our attention. 116
We hope that you have not been seriously inconvenienced 127
by the delay. 130

closing lines 144

Problem 2
Interoffice memorandum
[LM p. 7]

TO: Mario X. Cordera, Traffic Manager FROM: Russell C. Reese, Sales Manager 13
DATE: April 27, 19-- SUBJECT: Blake Motor Freight Company (¶ 1) On March 31 24
we shipped a large order to the Madison Manufacturing Co., Inc., in Richmond, 40
VA, via the Blake Motor Freight Company. After the Madison Company notified 55
us on April 23 that the shipment had not been received, we discovered that the 71
freight company had misshipped the goods to Richmond, CA. (¶ 2) This is the 85
fourth time in the past two months that the Blake Motor Freight Company has 100
either lost or misshipped one of our orders. Unless the Blake Company can 115
assure us that this situation will be remedied, may I suggest that they be 130
dropped from our list of acceptable carriers. 140

Problem 3
Average-length letter

plain full sheet; block style, open punctuation

Type the letter to **Ms. Mary Kay Benton, Manager** of the **Dixie Bell Boutique, 329 N. Elm Street, Greensboro, NC 27401-3218.** Date the letter **May 2**; use an appropriate salutation and complimentary close. **Subject: Your Purchase Order 4275.** The letter will be signed by **Mark W. Shapiro**, who is the **Director of Customer Relations.**

opening lines 31

We owe you an apology for returning your purchase order of April 27 without an 47
explanation. Unfortunately, the letter which was to accompany your order was 62
placed in your file rather than in the envelope addressed to you. The reasons we 79
returned your order are quite simple. First, we no longer carry the woolen 94
sweaters you requested (Item 1497A); nor do we have a comparable sweater to 109
offer you. Second, the synthetic blouses you ordered (Item 93210) have not been 125
included in our line of merchandise for several years. Third, the women's slacks 142
you requested (Item 1562B) are out of stock but may be reordered in July of this 158
year. 159

A copy of our current catalog is enclosed. Please note the special sale we are 175
having on colorful slacks and jeans for teenagers. You may also be interested in 191
the wide selection of costume jewelry--a new addition to our catalog. This 206
catalog will be in effect until August 31. 215

Please let us have your order soon. We shall see to it that it receives prompt 231
and special attention. 236

closing lines 251

Problem 4 is on the next page.

61

70-space line

61a ▶ 7
Conditioning practice

Use standard procedure given in 57a, page 92.

alphabet 1 James quickly paid a ticket received for a wrong turn by the zoo exit.
figures 2 FOR URGENT CALLS: Fire, 561-3723; Police, 461-7022; Doctor, 841-5839.
my/ny 3 Myrna says that any one of my army poems may win a zany company prize.
fluency 4 The amendment did signal an end to the rigid social theory of the day.

| 1 | 2 | 3 | 4 | 5 | 6 | 7 | 8 | 9 | 10 | 11 | 12 | 13 | 14 |

61b ▶ 5
Align and type over words

1. Remove your paper from the typewriter.

2. Reinsert the paper; gauge the line and letters (see 60c, page 98, if necessary) and type over Line 1 of 61a.

3. Repeat Steps 1–2, but type over Line 3 of 61a.

61c ▶ 38
Type a 2-page report with footnotes

1. Adjust your machine for typing an unbound report.

2. Use a *page line gauge* to plan vertical spacing, page number location, and footnotes [LM p. 79]. Type the footnotes on the same page as their reference figures.

3. Proofread each page; correct errors.

words

THE TRADITIONAL VS. THE "SIMPLIFIED" KEYBOARD 9

The first practical American typewriter was patented in 1868 by Sholes, 24
Glidden, and Soule. It was produced and sold, after many improvements, by 39
Remington & Sons in 1874. The location of the keys on the Remington type- 53
writer soon became the standard arrangement for keyboards of nearly all 68
other makes. This keyboard, with minor changes and additions, is almost the 83
same as that of the millions of typewriters used in offices, schools, and 98
homes even today.[1] 102

Keyboard "reform"--efforts to make the keyboard more efficient and 115
easier to operate--has a long history. Hammond, for example, in 1881 mar- 130
keted a typewriter with an "improved" keyboard. Hoke in 1924 was issued a 145
patent for a keyboard arranged according to frequency of letter use and 159
facility of the various fingers. In 1932, Dvorak and Dealey received a patent 175
for still another keyboard arrangement called the "Simplified" keyboard 189
(quotation marks theirs).[2] Not one of these attempts to improve the ar- 209
rangement of the letter keys received more than passing interest. 217

From time to time, a new spark of interest in simplifying the traditional 232
keyboard is ignited, flames for a while, then dies. This may be true today 247
regarding the Dvorak-Dealey keyboard. It is generally agreed that the Hoke 262
and the Dvorak keyboards are more scientific in design than is the "Univer- 277
sal" keyboard and <u>should</u> be more efficient to operate. Just how much more 293

________________ 297

[1] Bruce Bliven, Jr., <u>The Wonderful Writing Machine</u> (New York: Ran- 316
dom House, 1954), p. 114. 321

[2] Jerry W. Robinson, "An Idea Whose Time Has Come . . . Again?" <u>Cen-</u> 335
<u>tury 21 Reporter</u> (Spring 1975), p. 2. 346

Note: To type the ellipsis in Footnote 2, alternate 3 periods and spaces. Leave a space before and a space after the ellipsis.

(continued, page 101)

227b, continued

Problem 4
Long letter

plain full sheet; modified block style with indented ¶s, mixed punctuation

Type the letter dated **June 24** to **Ms. Deborah M. Scottfield, 2400 Royal Palms Boulevard, Charleston, SC 29407-2172.** Use an appropriate salutation and complimentary close. The letter will be signed by **John F. Schofield, Director of Human Resources.**

How to Compute Office Production Rate a Minute (o-pram):

1. List number of words typed on each page on which all errors have been corrected (correct words). Total these figures to determine *Total Correct Words*.

2. Then list number of words typed on each page on which there are errors that can be corrected. From this number, deduct 40 words for the first uncorrected error on the page and 10 words for each additional error on the same page. The remainder is *correctable words* per page. Add *corrected words* per page to find *Total Correctable Words*.
No credit is given for any page which contains an error that cannot be corrected.

3. Use this formula to find *o-pram*: Total Correct Words *plus* Total Correctable Words divided by time (30 minutes).

opening lines 23

SS ¶ 1

Dr. Karl S. Cook, dean of the School of Business at 33
Bradford University, has suggested I ~~contact~~ write you about a 44
rewarding and challenging position with our company. As a result of our 59
tremendous growth and ~~development~~ expansion, we have ~~an immediate~~ 67
a career opportunity for a Senior Systems Analyst with the 79
following technical qualifications: 86

1. A bachelor's degree in Computer Science with a minor 98
in business as a minimum; a master's degree in computer 109
science with a bachelor's degree in business ~~quite~~ highly de- 120
sirable. 122

2. A minimum of three years' experience as a systems 133
analyst in a software development ~~situation~~ environment 142

3. A thorough knowledge of multiple languages such as 153
COBOL, RPG II, ASSEMBLER, and PL 1. 160

4. Experience and/or knowledge of the IBM 360/370, HP 171
3000, DEC 1170, and SIGMA VI hardware and software. 182

From a personal ~~standpoint~~ viewpoint, the individual must be 192
a self-starter with excellent communications skills and an 204
analytical mind plus a demonstr ated background of crea- 215
tivity and accomplishments. 231

This ~~position~~ job includes a full range of company-paid 241
benefits and numerous opportunities for career advance- 252
ment. The salary will be commensurate with experience 263
and ability. 266

If you are interested in this position, will you please forward your 280
resume to me in confidence within the next week. 290

The ability to get along well with others is a must.

closing lines 302

228

228a ▶ 5 Conditioning practice

Use standard directions given in 226a, p. 358.

alphabet 1 Jimmy quickly alphabetized sixteen letters we received Friday morning.

figures 2 Check the gas mains at 2854, 3890, 4217, 5673, and 6091 Market Street.

fig/sym 3 On 8/21/79, my account totaled $19,141.36 (931 shares at $20.56 each).

fluency 4 During their visit to the city, they may go to the auto show downtown.

| 1 | 2 | 3 | 4 | 5 | 6 | 7 | 8 | 9 | 10 | 11 | 12 | 13 | 14 |

60d ▶ 22 Type an unbound report with footnotes

Margins

top: 2" elite
1½" pica
side: 1"
bottom: approx. 1"

Problem 1

Type the 1-page report given at the right. Make the indicated corrections and correct any errors you make as you type.

Problem 2

If time permits, type the final ¶ as page 2 of an unbound report. Recall: Page 2 should have a 1" top margin.

Note: Footnotes on a partially filled page may immediately follow the last line of the body of the report, or they may be placed to end 1" from the bottom of the page.

words

ARE YOU LISTENING? 4

To hear means to perceive by the ear. To listen means 17
hear with thoughtful attention. Hearing is easy. Listening 38
on the contrary is a dificult skill which can be perfected by 55
practice. 57

More time is spent in speaking and listening than reading 74
and writing. Oral communication is a 2-way process: it re- 86
quires a sender and a receiver. If the listener does~~n't~~ hear 104
~~or~~ understand what is said, ~~their~~ is no communication. Poor 116
listening skills are indicated by such comments as "My sugges- 130
tions fell on deaf ears" and "My directions went in one ear 142
and out the other. 146

To listen ~~carefully~~, one must <u>intend</u> to hear and must con- 161
centrate on what is bieng said. Do~~n't~~ permit you mind to wan- 174
der. Use your spare time to note the ideas being presented. 193
Resist the temptation tobe distracted by the aearance and man- 206
nerisms of the speaker or by noise in the immediate environment; 221
concentrate on the message. Avoid the tendency to react to 236
what is being said; "hear the speaker out" and then react. 249
The foregoing suggestions from Bonner and Voyles[1] and from 261
Lesikar[2] if practiced daily will lead to better skills. 275

---------- 278

[1]William Bonner and Jean Voyles, <u>Communication in Business: Key to Success</u> (Houston: Dame Publications, Inc., 1980), p. 314. 296 312

[2]Raymond V. Lesikar, <u>Business Communication: Theory and Application</u>, 4th ed. (Homewood: Richard D. Irwin Inc., 1980), p. 505. 333 347

228b ▶ 45
Assess production skill: report manuscripts

1. Type the problems at the right and on page 364 for 30′; correct errors as you type. If you finish all problems before time is called, start over.

2. After time is called, go over each page carefully and circle any errors you did not correct. Compute *o-pram*.

Problem 1
Unbound report with footnote

Use as a main heading, **Automated Cash Registers.** The footnote will be: **U.S. Department of Commerce, Automation in the Marketplace (Washington, D.C.: U.S. Government Printing Office, 1978).** Type the footnote so that there will be a margin of approximately 1 inch at the bottom of the page.

Problem 2
Topbound report

Type ¶s 2 and 3 *only* of Problem 1 as a topbound report. Use as a main heading, **Automated Cash Registers,** and as a secondary heading, **Point-of-Sale Terminals.** DO NOT include the footnote and DO NOT type the superior figure shown in ¶2.

Total words: 156

words

main heading 5

The Executive Planning committee strongly recommends 12
that ~~very~~ serious consideration be given to replacing our 22
conventional cash registers with point-of-sale terminals-- 34
electronic cash registers--which can be linked to our 45
existing computer ~~set ups~~ system. 50

According to a publication of the U. S. Government, 60
the National Retail Merchants Association has devised a 72
standard system for marking merchandise.[1] This system 83
uses a ~~newly~~ specially designed set of numbers and letters, very 94
similar to the letters of the alphabet and the ~~numbers~~ numerals 106
we use every day, that can be read by ~~an~~ automatic 115
scanning devices as well as by the customer. 124

At the point of sale, the clerk uses a hand-held 134
scanner (or "wand") which is connected to the computer 145
terminal to scan the markings on each label. When all 156
items have been scanned, the terminal adds the customer's 168
bill and computes ~~the~~ any tax. The computer can keep a run- 179
ning total of sales by department and, at the same 189
time, update the inventory records. 197

The advantages of this system are ~~apparent~~ obvious. The auto- 207
mated reading of merchandise labels will be ~~quicker~~ faster and 218
more accurate than manual operations. Better inventory 230
control will also permit us to improve and streamline 240
our purchasing and storage ~~transactions~~ operations. In short, 250
the use of electronic registers will greatly increase the 262
~~effectiveness~~ efficiency of our ~~entire~~ overall operations. 270

footnote 303

Problem 3 is on the next page.

60 — 70-space line

60a ▶ 7 Conditioning practice

Use standard procedure given in 57a, page 92.

alphabet 1 Quite a few very big men like to jump and do exercises on the trapeze.
fig/sym 2 O'Day & Sills has discounted these items: *C2847, *M1395, and *X6402.
um/mu 3 Sumi must add a column of numbers to get the sum owed the new plumber.
fluency 4 The panel may then work with the problems of the eight downtown firms.

| 1 | 2 | 3 | 4 | 5 | 6 | 7 | 8 | 9 | 10 | 11 | 12 | 13 | 14 |

60b ▶ 8 Improve technique: machine parts

exact 60-space line; from left margin, set 2 tab stops 23 spaces apart.

Type drill once; retype if time permits.

Lines 7–8: Release margin and backspace 4 times to start line.

tabulator and return
1 paid the firm——tab——▶ owns the land——tab——▶ sign the forms
2 she kept it fix the dial a big risk

shift keys
3 Apt. 3 | May or June | Box 214 | Apel & Marx | Epson and Yates | #1526
4 Ruby Yates sent the order to Marx & Epley at 3629 Hays Road.

automatic line finder
5 Pope,[1] centuries after Plutarch,[2] wrote: "To err is human."
6 Were heavy doses of B_1 and B_6 prescribed by Dr. Mark Gorham?

margin release and backspacer
7 A. I can use the margin release and backspace four times to type A.
8 I will now apply my typing skill when composing letters and reports.

60c ▶ 13 Learn to align and type over words

1. Type the sentence as shown below.

I can align this copy.

2. Study and follow the numbered steps given at the right.

Your typed line should look like this:

I can align this copy.

Not like this:

I can align this copy.

I can align this copy.

3. If time permits, repeat the drill to develop skill in aligning and typing over to make corrections in copy.

Aligning and typing over words

It is sometimes necessary to reinsert the paper to correct an error. The following steps will help you learn to do so correctly.

1. Type a line of copy in which one or more *i's* appear (such as *I can align this copy*, which you have just typed). Leave the paper in your typewriter.

2. Locate **aligning scale (21)** and **variable line spacer (3)** on your typewriter.

3. Move carriage (element) so that a word containing an *i* (such as *align*) is above the aligning scale. Be sure that a vertical line points to the center of *i*.

4. Study the relation between top of aligning scale and bottoms of letters with downstems (*g, p, y*). Get an exact eye picture of the relation of typed line to top of scale so you will be able to adjust the paper correctly to type over a word with exactness.

5. Remove the paper; reinsert it. Gauge the line so bottoms of letters are in correct relation to top of aligning scale. Operate the *variable line spacer*, if necessary, to move the paper up or down. Operate the *paper release lever* to move paper left or right, if necessary, when centering the letter *i* over one of the lines on the aligning scale.

6. Check accuracy of alignment by setting the *ribbon control* in stencil position and typing over one of the letters. If necessary, make further alignment adjustments.

7. Return ribbon control to normal position (to type on black).

8. Type over the words in the sentence.

228b, continued

Problem 3
Leftbound report with side headings

Use as a main heading, **Dictation Equipment for a Proposed Word Processing Center**. Side headings to be used are underlined.

words

main heading 12

(¶ 1) Under the provisions of Paragraph 10.3 of the "Proposal to Establish a 26
Word Processing Center," the Purchasing Committee has investigated the types 41
and specifications of dictation equipment available. The three basic types now 57
on the market are (1) portable models, (2) desk-top models, and (3) centralized 73
systems. 75

(¶ 2) Portable units are designed for dictation performed in and away from the 90
office. Desk-top models are best suited for heavy use within individual offices 107
of an organization. Centralized systems are designed for a central transcription 124
site (a typing pool or word processing center) where a group of transcribers do 140
the typing. The latter type is considered to be best suited for our proposed 155
center. 157

(¶ 3) The Purchasing Committee studied 15 different centralized transcription 172
systems; and they believe that, all factors considered, the following three sys- 188
tems are the best on the market: 194

<u>Phonomatic Model 411</u> (¶ 4) This system uses only a standard cassette with 30 213
minutes of recording time per side, but it can be operated through both a PBX 227
and a private wire. Features include an indicator of availability, an automatic 244
signal to indicate the end of a cassette side, a fast reverse, a fast forward, and an 261
automatic changer to switch from one side of the cassette to the other. 275

<u>Memotype Model MT-90</u> (¶ 5) Minicassettes with 24 minutes of recording time 294
per side are the standard media for this system which uses only a private wire. 310
Features include an indicator of availability, a warning unit to show the end of 326
the cassette, a fast reverse, a fast forward, and an automatic changer. 341

<u>Stenotape SX 300</u> (¶ 6) Only a standard cassette can be used with this private 359
wire system with 45 minutes per side recording time. Standard features include 375
an availability indicator and a fast reverse but not a fast forward or an automa- 391
tic changer. Although this system includes the fewest automatic features, the 407
cassettes used provide the longest recording time of any unit. 419

(¶ 7) The technical specifications of these systems are included in Appendix A. 434
In addition, a detailed cost analysis of the three systems, including initial instal- 451
lation and operating costs, is included in Appendix B. 462

229

229a ▶ 5 Conditioning practice

Use standard directions given in 226a, page 358.

alphabet 1 Weber analyzed the cost of manufacturing the expensive quilted jacket.
figures 2 Please phone Mr. Robinson at 215-876-9425 on December 13 at 12:30 p.m.
fig/sym 3 In shorthand, May has quiz grades of 92%, 85%, 71%, 94%, and 86%.
fluency 4 Did she ask one of the girls who work for her to mail the check to us?

| 1 | 2 | 3 | 4 | 5 | 6 | 7 | 8 | 9 | 10 | 11 | 12 | 13 | 14 |

59c ▶ 23 Learn to type footnotes

1. Adjust your machine for typing an unbound report.

2. Study the guides and illustrations for typing report footnotes.

3. From the appropriate model (pica or elite), type the last 2 lines of the report and the footnotes beneath them. Begin on Line 51 from top edge (16 lines from bottom edge) of the page.

4. Check the spacing of your completed work.

5. Retype the drill.

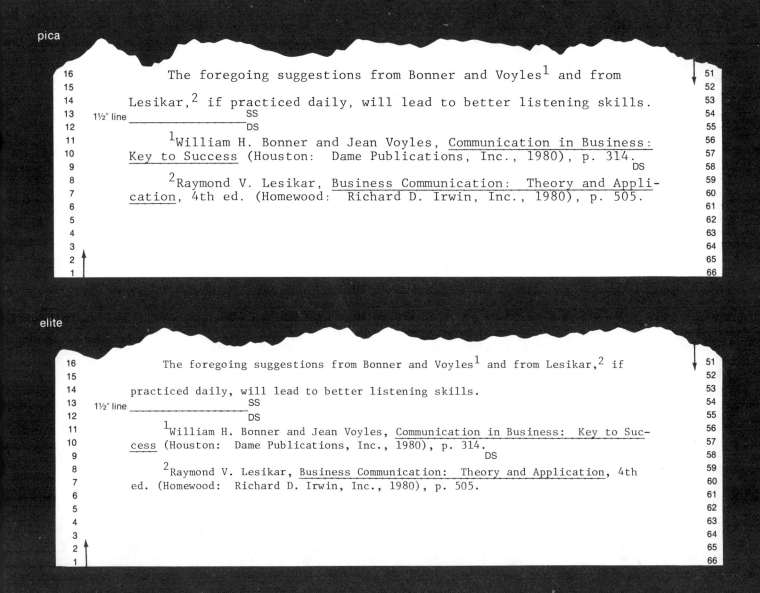

Guides for typing footnotes

1. Type a superior figure (superscript) in the text to indicate each footnote reference.

2. In planning a manuscript page, save 2 lines for a divider line and the spaces before and after it. Save 3 or 4 lines for each footnote to be typed on the page and 6 lines for the bottom margin.

3. Type a footnote on the same page with its corresponding superior figure.

4. After typing last line of text on a page, SS and type a 1½" divider line (15 pica or 18 elite spaces); then DS and type the footnote SS with a 5-space indention.

5. If two or more footnotes are to be typed on same page, DS between them.

6. A *page line gauge* will help in planning footnotes. (See LM p. 79.) Place it back of a full sheet with the line numbers extending to the right; insert the two sheets; note the number of lines to be left for the divider line and footnotes; make a light pencil mark at that point on your copy sheet.

pica

The foregoing suggestions from Bonner and Voyles[1] and from

Lesikar,[2] if practiced daily, will lead to better listening skills.

1½" line _______________ SS

DS

[1]William H. Bonner and Jean Voyles, Communication in Business: Key to Success (Houston: Dame Publications, Inc., 1980), p. 314.

DS

[2]Raymond V. Lesikar, Business Communication: Theory and Application, 4th ed. (Homewood: Richard D. Irwin, Inc., 1980), p. 505.

elite

The foregoing suggestions from Bonner and Voyles[1] and from Lesikar,[2] if

practiced daily, will lead to better listening skills.

1½" line _______________ SS

DS

[1]William H. Bonner and Jean Voyles, Communication in Business: Key to Success (Houston: Dame Publications, Inc., 1980), p. 314.

DS

[2]Raymond V. Lesikar, Business Communication: Theory and Application, 4th ed. (Homewood: Richard D. Irwin, Inc., 1980), p. 505.

229b ▶ 45
Assess production skill: forms and tables

1. Type the problems for 30′; correct errors as you type.

2. After time is called, go over each page carefully and circle any errors you did not correct. Compute *o-pram*.

Problem 1
Purchase order [LM p. 7]

words

PURCHASE ORDER NO. S-7932 1

TO: National Business Forms, Inc. — DATE July 31, 19-- 10
8720 Colesville Road 15
Silver Spring, MD 20910-7232 — TERMS Net 21

SHIP VIA UPS 22

QUANTITY	CAT. NO.	DESCRIPTION	PRICE	TOTAL	words
10,000 ea.	SF196	Sales forms, all-purpose, 3-part	.0245	245.00	32
250 ea.	RE032	Sales registers, portable	4.90	1,225.00	43
80 ea.	FB836	File storage boxes, legal size	1.19	95.20	54
125 bks.	SR297	Sales receipts, carbonless, 2-part	3.75	468.75	66
5,000 ea.	MR975	Message/reply forms, 3-part	.0195	97.50	78
300 ea.	PP632	Page protectors, 8 1/2″ x 11″			86
		for 3-ring binder	.125	37.50	91
				2,168.95	92

Problem 2
Invoice [LM p. 9]

DATE August 16, 19-- 3

TO: Keystone Hardware Company 8
402 Duquesne Boulevard — OUR ORDER NO. 522631 15
Pittsburgh, PA 15222-1151 19

CUST. ORDER NO. K9041 21

TERMS: 2/10, n/30 — SHIPPED VIA D & L Freight Line 27

QUANTITY	DESCRIPTION	UNIT PRICE	TOTAL	words
50	Wood extension ladders, heavy-duty, indus-			36
	trial, 24 feet	98.90	4,945.00	42
100	Step stools, aluminum, Type III	9.55	955.00	51
60	Paint spray guns, 7 1/2 fl. oz./min.	63.71	3,822.60	62
10	Electric sprayer/compressors, 1/2 HP motor	115.40	1,154.00	75
5	Sand blasters, heavy-duty, 100# capacity	62.99	314.95	86
			11,191.55	88

Problem 3
Table
full sheet; reading position; DS items; decide intercolumn spacing

Problem 4
Table
half sheet, long side up; type table in Problem 3 in exact center; SS items

MELROWE DISTRIBUTORS, INC. 6

Monthly Sales by Division for Year to Date 14

(In Thousands of Dollars) 19

Month	Division I	Division II	Division III	words
				28
January	76.4	27.8	41.9	32
February	37.7	27.7	21.9	37
March	46.8	36.0	20.6	41
April	49.0	38.1	25.3	46
May	54.9	39.2	30.1	49
June	57.3	39.1	27.1	53
July	37.6	54.3	21.5	57
August	49.7	34.6	25.2	62
September	48.9	36.4	29.9	67
Total	458.3	333.2	243.5	72

59

70-space line

59a ▶ 7 Conditioning practice

Use standard procedure given in 57a, page 92.

alphabet 1 Jan very quickly seized the wheel as big cars pulled out from an exit.

figures 2 We have stores at 472 Avon Court, 591 Opera Place, and 3068 Rich Road.

line finder 3 Juanita cited (Martinez, 1980) [1] and (Gorbea, 1981) [2] as her references.

fluency 4 It is their wish to name a panel to shape the theme for a town social.

| 1 | 2 | 3 | 4 | 5 | 6 | 7 | 8 | 9 | 10 | 11 | 12 | 13 | 14 |

59b ▶ 20 Type page 2 of an unbound report

1. Type page number—2—on Line 4 from top edge.
2. TS and continue body of report begun in Lesson 58. Correct errors.
3. If you finish report before time is called, proofread your copy and correct any additional errors you find.

elite

pica

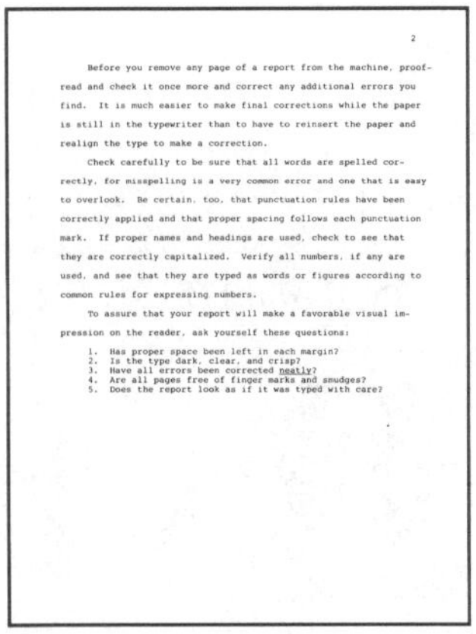

words

2

Before you remove any page of a report from the machine, 11
proofread and check it once more and correct any additional 23
errors you find. It is much easier to make final corrections 36
while the paper is still in the typewriter than to have to 48
reinsert the paper and realign the type to make a correction. 60

Check [carefully] to be sure that all ~~your~~ words are spelled cor- 72
rectly, for mi[s]spelling is a [very] common error and one that is easy 85
to overlook. [#] Be certain[,] too, that punct[ua]tion rules have been 98
[correctly] applied and that proper spacing follows each punctuation mark. 113
If proper names [and headings] are used[,] check to see [that] ~~if~~ they are correctly 128
capitali[z]ed. [Verify] ~~Check~~ all numbers, [if any are used,] and see that they are typed 144
as words or figures according to com mon [close up] rules for expressing 156
numbers[.] 158

To assure that [your] ~~the~~ report will make a favorable [visual] impres- 170
sion on the reader[,] ask your self [close up] these questions: 181

Indent 5 spaces from left margin and SS.

1. Has proper space been left in each margin? 190
2. Is the type dark, clear, and crisp? 198
3. Have all errors been corrected <u>neatly</u>? 208
4. Are all pages free of finger marks and smudges? 219
5. Does the report look as if it was typed with care? 230

unit **45** lessons 230-233

Refine problem skills: correspondence

Learning goals

1. To increase your ability to plan, organize, and type business correspondence.

2. To increase your rate in typing business letters and interoffice memorandums.

Machine adjustments

1. Line: 70 for drills; as necessary for production problems.

2. Spacing: SS sentence drills with a DS between sentence groups; space problems as required.

230

230a ▶ 5 Conditioning practice

each line twice SS (slowly, then faster); DS between 2-line groups; if time permits, retype selected lines

alphabet 1 Peg Vega quickly explained the hazardous job of atomic waste disposal.

figures 2 Item No. 95753 will be offered in Sizes 8, 10, 12, 14, 16, 18, and 20.

fig/sym 3 John won bonuses of $2,413, $4,675, and $5,980 on sales of $2,960,317.

fluency 4 Michael can plan on a major truck and auto sale during the final days.

| 1 | 2 | 3 | 4 | 5 | 6 | 7 | 8 | 9 | 10 | 11 | 12 | 13 | 14 |

230b ▶ 45 Refine problem skills: letters

1. Before typing each of the following problems, review the appropriate letter style on page v of the Reference Guide.

2. After you type each letter, check it for proper style and format.

Problem 1

Short letter
plain full sheet

Type Letter 1 in block style with open punctuation. Do not correct errors.

Problem 2

Average-length letter
plain full sheet

Type Letter 2 in modified block style with mixed punctuation. Do not correct errors.

Problem 3

Type Letter 1 in modified block style with indented ¶s, mixed punctuation. Do not correct errors. Modify the letter as follows:

1. Add the company name in the closing lines;
EAGLE PUBLISHING CO.

2. Omit the third ¶ from the *body* of the letter and add it as a postscript. Add 4 words for the company name in the closing lines.

Letter 1 words

May 8, 19-- Keystone Variety Stores, Inc. Attention Miss Betty C. Reese, 15
Sales Manager 2 Penn Plaza Philadelphia, PA 19102-2636 Ladies and Gentle- 29
men (¶ 1) It has been two years since we last raised our advertising rates. 44
Since then our expenses have risen steadily. Reluctantly, therefore, we must 59
raise our rates on the first of June. (¶ 2) As the enclosed rate schedule shows, 74
rates will increase little more than 7%. So that you may plan your advertis- 90
ing budget, these rates will remain in effect for at least a year. (¶ 3) If you 105
need any assistance in planning your next advertising campaign, one of our 120
experts will be happy to help you. Sincerely yours Jon C. Parke Advertising 135
Director xx Enclosure 139

Letter 2

May 1, 19-- Mr. Alex T. Rich, President Allied Industries, Inc. 300 N. State 15
Street Chicago, IL 60610-7767 Dear Mr. Rich: Subject: Honorarium, National 31
Business Conference (¶ 1) The National Business Conference held April 4-8 44
in Los Angeles was the largest and most diverse business conference and ex- 59
position ever held in the United States. It included the largest exhibit of 75
business products ever shown under one roof. The total attendance exceeded 90
50,000 persons representing business firms from all parts of the United 104
States, Canada, and Mexico. (¶ 2) As the keynote speaker, you played a large 119
part in the success of the conference. The interesting and timely comments 134
you made in your address were well received by the audience. As an ex- 148
pression of our appreciation for your presentation, enclosed is an honorarium 164
for $2,500. (¶ 3) It was a personal pleasure for me to welcome you. Please 178
accept my thanks for your contribution to a highly successful endeavor. 192
Cordially yours, Karl M. Gray Executive Director xx Enclosure 204

58d ▶ 20 Type page 1 of an unbound report

Margins

top: 2″ elite (Line 13)
1½″ pica (Line 10)
side: 1″
bottom: approx. 1″

1. Type the copy as an unbound report DS, correcting any errors you make.

2. Proofread your copy before removing it from the typewriter and correct any additional errors you find.

elite

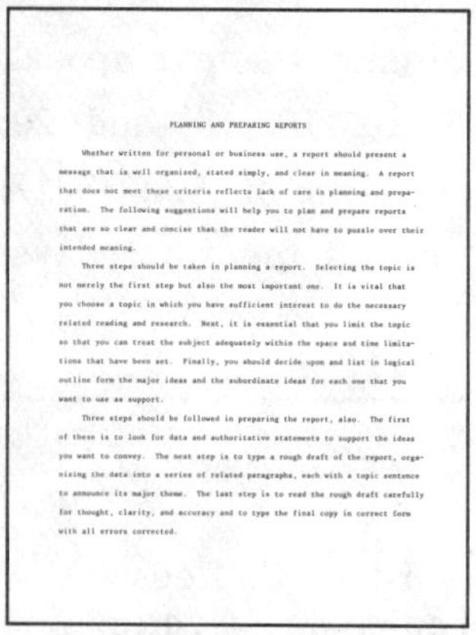

pica

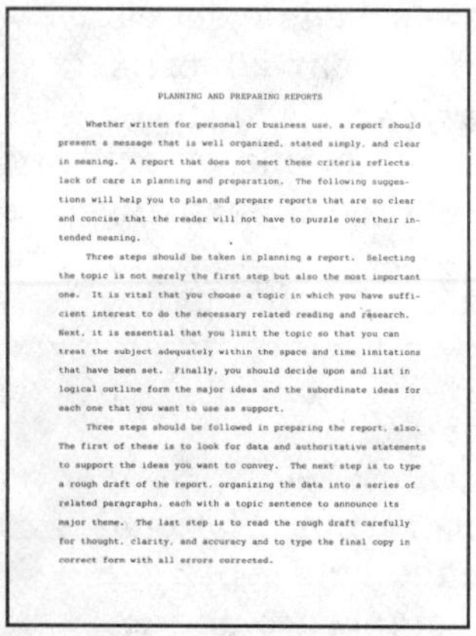

words

PLANNING AND PREPARING REPORTS 6

TS

Whether written for personal or business use, a report 17
should present a message that is well organized, stated simply, 30
and clear in meaning. A report that does not meet these cri- 42
teria reflects lack of care in planning and preparation. The 54
following suggestions will help you to plan and prepare re- 66
ports that are so clear and concise that the reader will not 78
have to puzzle over their intended meaning. 87

Three steps should be taken in planning a report. Se- 98
lecting the topic is not merely the first step but also the 110
most important one. It is vital that you choose a topic in 122
which you have sufficient interest to do the necessary related 134
reading and research. Next, it is essential that you limit 146
the topic so that you can treat the subject adequately within 159
the space and time limitations that have been set. Finally, 171
you should decide upon and list in logical outline form the 183
major ideas and the subordinate ideas for each one that you 195
want to use as support. 200

Three steps should be followed in preparing the report, 211
also. The first of these is to look for data and authorita- 223
tive statements to support the ideas you want to convey. The 235
next step is to type a rough draft of the report, organizing 248
the data into a series of related paragraphs, each with a 259
topic sentence to announce its major theme. The last step is 272
to read the rough draft carefully for thought, clarity, and 284
accuracy and to type the final copy in correct form with all 296
errors corrected. 299

231a ▶ 5 Conditioning practice

Use standard directions given in 230a, page 366.

alphabet 1 The blaze badly damaged a large quantity of women's expensive jackets.
figures 2 He will give performances on October 2, 5, 6, 7, 8, 9, 13, 14, and 20.
fig/sym 3 They will need two pieces of carpet: 12′6″ × 15′8″ and 17′4″ × 30′9″.
fluency 4 They did not make a big profit during the special sale held this week.
| 1 | 2 | 3 | 4 | 5 | 6 | 7 | 8 | 9 | 10 | 11 | 12 | 13 | 14 |

231b ▶ 15 Refine problem skills: interoffice memorandum

[LM p. 9]

1. If necessary, refer to page 302 for format of an inter-office memorandum.

2. Type a 10′ writing on the memorandum at the right; correct errors as you type.

3. When you have finished typing, check the memorandum carefully for errors in format.

Goal: a completed memo with all errors corrected in 10′ or less.

words

TO: Harry F. Ames, Director of Administration FROM: Marie T. Ortego, Pur- 13
chasing Agent DATE: June 26, 19-- SUBJECT: Tex-Ed Electronic Typewriters 24

(¶ 1) The contract for the supply of 24 Tex-Ed Electronic Typewriters is being 39
prepared in final form. The Tex-Ed people have indicated that they can begin 54
delivery of these typewriters any time after August 1. They have further in- 70
dicated that they can provide, if desired, a maximum of three on-site training 86
sessions of six hours each on the use of these machines at a time convenient to 102
you. 103

(¶ 2) Will you please let us know as soon as possible the date or dates on which 132
you want to have these machines delivered. Further, if you decide to take 147
advantage of the training sessions, please give us the dates on which you wish 163
to have them conducted. xx 168

231c ▶ 15 Timed drills on business letters

short letter

1. Type a 5′ writing on the letter in *straight-copy* form, beginning with the date. Compute *gwam*.

2. Type a 5′ writing in letter form: modified block, mixed punctuation. Do not correct errors. Compute *gwam*.

3. Compare *gwam* on the two writings. Check the second writing for correct letter format.

gwam 5′

July 13, 19-- Ogden-North Appliance Manufacturing Co., Attention 3 | 34
Mr. Charles T. Barnes, Sales Manager 852 Euclid Avenue Cleveland, OH 5 | 37
44114-3732 Ladies and Gentlemen: Subject: Your Model 4605 Toaster Oven 8 | 40

During the past several weeks, six of our customers have returned your 11 | 43
Model 4605 Toaster Oven. They have complained that the thermostat is set too 14 | 46
high, causing burnt toast and baked items. We checked these toaster ovens 17 | 49
carefully and found that the customers are correct. A complete report of our 20 | 52
tests is enclosed. 21 | 53

We have removed these toaster ovens from our stores, although we have 24 | 55
136 of them in stock. Please let us know soon what action you would like us to 27 | 59
take in this matter. 28 | 60

Sincerely yours, DIAMOND DEPARTMENT STORES Ms. Rose M. Williams 31 | 62
Chief Buyer xx Enclosure 32 | 63

58

70-space line

58a ▶ 7 Conditioning practice

Use standard procedure given in 57a, page 92.

alphabet 1 Luci Kwan said the boutique might have jade, onyx, and topaz for sale.
fig/sym 2 Su & Wong's order (#29413) for 750 sets of 6-ply NCR paper came May 8.
un/nu 3 Unsel said the annual account of the gun shop was bound to be unusual.
fluency 4 The six girls spent their profit for an ancient memento of the island.

| 1 | 2 | 3 | 4 | 5 | 6 | 7 | 8 | 9 | 10 | 11 | 12 | 13 | 14 |

58b ▶ 8 Learn to type superscripts/subscripts

1. Study the steps given at the right.

2. Type twice the sentences at right, below.

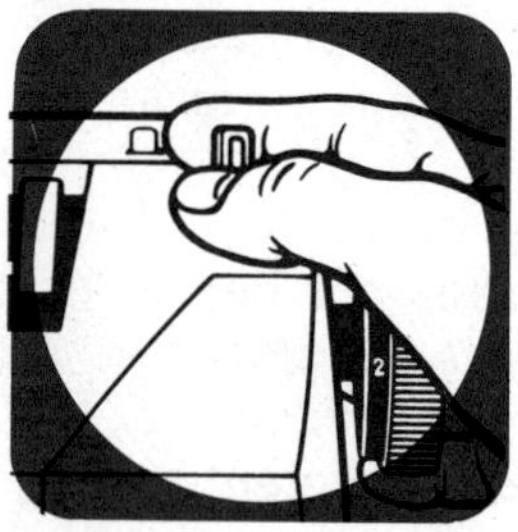

Superscript

To type a figure or symbol above the line:

1. Operate *ratchet release* or *automatic line finder* (6);

2. Turn platen *backward* (toward you);

3. Type the figure or symbol, then return automatic line finder and platen to normal position.

Subscript

To type a figure or symbol below the line, follow the same procedure *except* turn the platen *forward* (away from you).

1 The exponent of x is 4 in the monomial $10x^4$ (10x to the fourth power).
2 A discussion of vitamin B_6 is given on page 8 of Vol. 23, <u>Britannica.</u>[1]

58c ▶ 15 Type an outline

full sheet;
65-space line:
(center − 32; center + 33);
begin on Line 10;
correct errors

1. Space forward once from margin to type Roman numeral **I.** Reset margin 2 spaces to right of period in **I.** for subheadings **A.** and **B.**

2. Beginning at left margin, set 3 tab stops 4 spaces apart for typing subheadings; use margin release and backspace to type **II.**

Note: Space once after closing parenthesis

	words
UNBOUND MANUSCRIPTS	4
I. MARGINS AND SPACING	9
A. Margins	11
1. Side and bottom margins: approximately 1″	21
2. Top margin, first page: elite, 2″; pica, 1 1/2″	32
3. Top margin, additional pages: 1″	40
B. Spacing	42
1. Body of manuscript: double	49
2. Paragraph indentions: 5 or 10 spaces uniformly	59
3. Quoted paragraph	64
a. Four or more lines	69
(1) Single-spaced	73
(2) Indented 5 spaces from each margin	81
(3) Quotation marks not required--may be used	91
b. Fewer than 4 lines	96
(1) Quotation marks used	102
(2) Not separated from text	108
(3) Not indented from text margins	116
II. PAGE NUMBERING	121
A. Page 1: Usually Not Numbered, but Number <u>May</u> Be Centered	134
1/2″ from Bottom Edge	138
B. Other Pages: Number Typed at Right Margin, 1/2″ from Top	151
Edge of Paper	153

231d ▶ 15
Refine problem skills: letters

short letter
plain full sheet

1. Type the letter in block style, open punctuation.

2. Use the current date; address the letter to **Samson Clothiers, Inc., 1001 Grand Avenue, Kansas City, MO 64106-4300**; provide an appropriate salutation and include a subject line: **Your Order 9320.**

3. Provide a proper complimentary close. The letter will be signed by **Ms. Alyce T. King, Sales Manager.**

From this point, the two x's will not be used to indicate reference initials, but you will continue to use your initials as the typist on all correspondence. In addition, you will not be told when an enclosure notation is needed; if the letter body indicates material is to be enclosed, be sure to include an enclosure notation.

	words
opening lines	20
(¶ 1) Based on the detailed information you provided in your recent letter, we	35
were able to trace your Order 9320. (¶ 2) We discovered that the order was	49
ready for shipment except for the men's leisure jackets which are no longer	64
available in blue corduroy. To avoid further delay, we have substituted jackets	80
in brushed denim--an item that has proven extremely popular. If these jackets	96
do not move quickly, please return them at our expense. (¶ 3) Your order was	111
shipped yesterday by American Parcel Service, and you should receive it within	126
the next week.	129
closing lines	139

232

232a ▶ 5
Conditioning practice

Use standard directions given in 230a, page 366.

alphabet 1 Max Golden's objective was to increase quickly the size of his biceps.

figures 2 We produced 987 units on May 5; 1,342 on June 6; and 3,890 on July 16.

fig/sym 3 M & R Co. (formerly T & M Co.) has changed its name to Mel & Ray, Inc.

fluency 4 She told us to thank both girls for the ticket they got for her today.

| 1 | 2 | 3 | 4 | 5 | 6 | 7 | 8 | 9 | 10 | 11 | 12 | 13 | 14 |

232b ▶ 15
Refine problem skills: letters

average-length letter
plain full sheet

1. Type the letter in modified block style, mixed punctuation.

2. Use the current date; address the letter to **Mr. Mark L. Balsam, Manager** of the **Allied Tire & Auto Service, 5010 Washington Avenue, Evansville, IN 47715-2601**; provide an appropriate salutation.

3. Use an appropriate complimentary close and the company name **DETROIT AUTO SERVICE** in the closing lines. The letter will be signed by **Frank T. Ryan,** who is the **Chief of Customer Relations.**

	words
opening lines	27
(¶ 1) Thank you for your recent inquiry about changes in auto tire designa-	41
tions. We can understand your confusion about the new designations for au-	56
tomobile tires and believe that we can clarify them for you. (¶ 2) The tire	70
which was previously designated as 6.50-13 is now 78-13. It is preceded by the	86
letter A, B, or C, which refers to the tire's size/load range (a tire with a letter A	104
has a smaller limit than a tire with the letter C). If the tire is a radial tire, the	121
letter R is included in the designation. Thus, a tire marked "AR 78-13" indi-	137
cates a radial tire with a tire limit of 1,060 pounds and a 13-inch rim diameter.	153
(¶ 3) Some tires made in Europe will have a size rating that reads "155-13" or	168
"175-14." These are sizes expressed in metric units: The first number refers	184
to the cross section of the tire measure in millimeters; the second refers to the	200
rim diameter in inches. (¶ 4) If you still find this somewhat confusing, I am	215
sure that the enclosed table comparing the "old" designations with the "new"	230
and "metric" designations will further clarify the situation.	242
closing lines	261

57c ▶ 8
Learn to align Roman numerals

half sheet

1. Set left margin stop for a 40-space line.

2. Clear all tab stops; from left margin, space forward to set new tab stops as indicated by the KEY below and the guides above the table.

3. Center the heading on Line 11.

4. Align the columns of Roman numerals at the right. Tabs should be set to require the least forward and backward spacing.

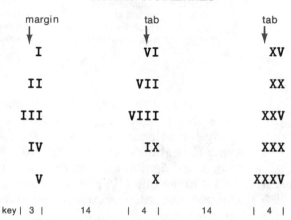

ROMAN NUMERALS

margin	tab	tab
I	VI	XV
II	VII	XX
III	VIII	XXV
IV	IX	XXX
V	X	XXXV

key | 3 | 14 | 4 | 14 | 4 |

57d ▶ 15
Learn to type a topic outline

full sheet; 65-space line: (center − 32; center + 33); begin on Line 20; space as directed; correct errors

First-order subheadings preceded by **A.**, **B.**, etc.

Second-order subheadings preceded by **1.**, **2.**, etc.

words

TOPIC OUTLINES 3

TS

(Space forward once from margin; 2 spaces)

I. CAPITALIZING HEADINGS IN TOPIC OUTLINES 12

DS

(Reset margin; 2 spaces)

A. Title of Outline in ALL CAPS (<u>May Be Underlined</u>) 26
B. Major Headings in ALL CAPS (Not Underlined) 35
C. Important Words of First-Order Subheadings Capitalized 47
D. Only First Word of Second-Order Subheadings Capitalized 59

DS

(Use margin release; backspace 5 times)

II. SPACING TOPIC OUTLINES 66

DS

A. Horizontal Spacing 70

(Set 2 tab stops 4 spaces apart. 1st tab; 2d tab)

1. Title of outline centered over the writing line 91
2. Identifying numerals for major headings typed at the 93
left margin (periods aligned), followed by 2 spaces 103
3. Identifying letters and numerals for each subsequent 115
level of subheading aligned beneath the first word of 126
the preceding heading, followed by 2 spaces 135

B. Vertical Spacing 140

1. Title of outline followed by 2 blank line spaces 151
2. Major headings (except the first) preceded by 1 blank 162
line space; all followed by 1 blank line space 172
3. All subheadings single-spaced 179

232c ▶ 30
Refine problem skills: letters

average-length letter
plain full sheet

1. Type the letter for 10′ in modified block style with indented ¶s, open punctuation. Do not correct errors as you type. Date the letter **March 17, 19--** and make a notation that the letter is to be sent by **Registered Mail.** Address the letter to **Ms. Mary C. Conley, Treasurer, Dixie Manufacturing Co., 230 West Jefferson Street, Louisville, KY 40202-8871.** Provide an appropriate salutation and complimentary close. The letter will be signed by **Jason T. Scott, Auditor.**

2. When you have finished typing the letter, correct in pencil all typographical and style errors.

3. From your corrected copy, retype the letter, correcting errors as you type.

Goal: to type the edited letter with all errors corrected in 10′ or less.

words

opening lines 7

~~We have received~~ Thank you very much for your letter of March 3 ~~showing in detail~~ detailing 18
the payments you have made on your Account 49321J. We find 30
that your ~~data~~ figures are correct except for the ~~one~~ payment you in- 42
dicate you made on February 16. According to your records, a 54
payment of $1,245 was made on that date; however, our ~~books~~ records 67
show that the payment made was $524. Originally, because of 79
a ~~typographical~~ keyboarding error~~s~~, you were credited with only $254. On 91
February 23, however, we found the ~~mistake~~ error and credited 103
your account for the difference of $270. 110

Based on your Check 52416, the First National Bank of 121
North Carolina has credited our account for $524. This sub- 133
stantiates the fact that the payment you made was $524. As a 145
result, your balance is now $721 plus, ~~naturally~~ of course, the 2% pen- 157
alty of $14.42 imposed when your account was not paid in 168
full on February 28, as shown on the enclosed statement. 180

We ~~regret that an~~ are sorry for the error ~~was~~ we made in your account, but 191
hope that this detailed ~~accounting~~ explanation will clarify the matter. 203

closing lines 214

233

233a ▶ 5
Conditioning practice

Use standard directions given in 230a, page 366.

alphabet 1 Max Forrester jogged very quickly between the benches in the zoo park.
figures 2 Clinics will be held at 1:30 p.m. and 7:45 p.m. on May 26, 28, and 29.
fig/sym 3 The trade discount was decreased from 20% and 10% to 15%, 10%, and 3%.
fluency 4 The man told a story about the major labor problems in the big cities.

| 1 | 2 | 3 | 4 | 5 | 6 | 7 | 8 | 9 | 10 | 11 | 12 | 13 | 14 |

233b ▶ 45
Sustained production: correspondence

1. Make a list of the problems below:
page 366, 230b, Problem 3
page 367, 231b [LM p. 13]
page 368, 231d
page 368, 232b

2. Type the problems for 30′, each problem on plain sheet, except for 231b. Proofread each problem before you remove it from the typewriter and correct any errors you may have missed.

If you finish before time is called, start over.

3. Compute *o-pram* as explained on page 362.

unit **11** lessons 57-62

Learn to type outlines and reports

Learning goals

1. To learn to arrange and type topic outlines.
2. To learn to arrange and type reports (with and without footnotes) in unbound format.
3. To learn to align copy vertically and horizontally.
4. To improve your basic keystroking skills.

Machine adjustments

1. Paper guide at *0*.
2. Ribbon control to type on top half of ribbon.
3. Margin sets: 70–space line (center – 35; center + 35 + 5) unless otherwise directed.
4. Line–space selector on *1* (SS) for drills, on *2* (DS) for ¶s; as directed for problems.

57

70-space line

57a ▶ 7 Conditioning practice

each line twice SS (slowly, then faster); DS between 2-line groups; if time permits, retype selected lines

alphabet	1	Jacki Veloz hung exquisite paintings on a wall of the academy library.
figures	2	On April 6 you ordered 5 TABCO filing cabinets: 2 HC-7850; 3 VC-9146.
ce/ec	3	Cecil was once elected to the office of secretary of the police force.
fluency	4	She did signal the chair to hand the proxy to the auditor of the firm.

| 1 | 2 | 3 | 4 | 5 | 6 | 7 | 8 | 9 | 10 | 11 | 12 | 13 | 14 |

57b ▶ 20 Improve keystroking skill: guided writing

1. A 1′ writing on ¶ 1; determine *gwam*. Add 2–4 words to set a new goal rate.
2. Two 1′ writings on ¶ 1 at your new goal rate, guided by ¼′ guide call.
3. Type ¶ 2 in the same way.
4. A 2′ writing on ¶ 1; then on ¶ 2. If you finish a ¶ before time is called, begin retyping it.
5. A 3′ writing on ¶s 1–2 combined; determine *gwam*.

gwam	¼′	½′	¾′	1′
20	5	10	15	20
24	6	12	18	24
28	7	14	21	28
32	8	16	24	32
36	9	18	27	36
40	10	20	30	40
44	11	22	33	44
48	12	24	36	48
52	13	26	39	52
56	14	28	42	56
60	15	30	45	60

all letters learned | A | 1.5 si | 5.7 awl | 80% hfw |

	gwam 2′	3′
It certainly pays to be skillful in correcting errors; however, it	7	4
will pay better when you learn to pace the typing at just the level you	14	9
can control with accuracy and remove the need to correct so many errors.	21	14
About twenty seconds are required to correct an error. If you make five	29	19
errors in five minutes and must stop to correct them, you cut your speed	36	24
over thirty percent. Realize this now and begin pacing yourself.	42	28
Office typists are expected to correct every error. Making correc-	7	33
tions takes time and skill. The greater the skill, the less time needed	14	38
to make a correction and the lower the cost of an error. Accordingly,	21	42
you are sometimes being told now to erase and correct every error made	28	47
during the typing of a letter or a report in the daily work. Learning	35	52
to do so quickly should be one of your important goals.	41	55

gwam 2′ | 1 | 2 | 3 | 4 | 5 | 6 | 7 |
3′ | 1 | 2 | 3 | 4 | 5 |

unit **46** lessons 234-237

Refine problem skills: reports

Learning goals

1. To increase your ability to plan, organize, and type reports.

2. To increase your rate in typing reports of various styles.

Machine adjustments

1. Line: 70 for drills; as necessary for production problems.

2. Spacing: SS sentence drills; space problems as required.

234

234a ▶ 5 Conditioning practice

each line twice SS (slowly, then faster); DS between 2-line groups; if time permits, retype selected lines

alphabet 1 Rex quickly memorized jokes for the performance he will give publicly.

figures 2 Table 430 indicates that a mile is 5,280 ft., 1,760 yds., or 1.609 km.

fig/sym 3 To order, call 621-3590 (Tampa), 467-8217 (Miami), or 459-8306 (Alva).

fluency 4 The panel of editors has the authority to plan the format of the play.

| 1 | 2 | 3 | 4 | 5 | 6 | 7 | 8 | 9 | 10 | 11 | 12 | 13 | 14 |

234b ▶ 20 Refine problem skills: unbound report

1. Type the report as an unbound manuscript; correct errors as you type.

2. SS and indent the enumerated items; DS between them.

How to "make" special symbols

Minus
Space; hyphen; space

5 - 2

Plus
Hyphen; backspace; diagonal

+

Divide
Colon; backspace; hyphen

÷

Times
Space x space

5 x 2

Equals
Hyphen; backspace; roll platen forward slightly; hyphen

=

words

CENTERING MATERIAL IN COLUMNS MATHEMATICALLY 9

Many keyboard operators prefer to use a mathematical method of cen- 22
tering columnar material horizontally instead of the backspace-from-center 37
method. To center material in columns using the mathematical method, follow 53
these steps: 55

1. Count the strokes in the longest item in each column. (Remember, the 70
heading may be the longest item.) Add these numbers. 81

2. Determine by judgment the number of spaces to be left between col- 95
umns. Add the <u>total</u> spaces to be left between columns to the total 110
obtained in Step 1 (Step 1 + Step 2). 117

3. Subtract the total of Steps 1 and 2 from the spaces available (85 pica 132
spaces or 102 elite spaces on standard 8 1/2″ × 11″ paper). Divide the 147
remainder by 2, ignoring any fraction, to find the left margin setting 161
(102 <u>or</u> 85 − total spaces ÷ 2). 168

4. To determine tab stops: 173
a. Add the number of spaces in the left margin to the sum of spaces 187
required for the first column and the number of spaces between the 200
first and second columns. This will be the first tab stop (left margin + 215
Column 1 + spaces between columns). 222
b. To the number found in 4a, add the sum of spaces required for the 236
second column and the spaces between the second and third columns. 250
This figure will be the second tab stop (first tab stop + Column 2 + 263
spaces between columns). 268
c. Continue in this manner for each additional column to be typed. 282

5. Main and secondary headings should be centered by the backspace- 296
from-center method even when the mathematical method is used 308
to center columns of material horizontally. 317

Problem 2

2 plain sheets;
1 letterhead [LM pp. 77, 78];
1 sheet carbon paper;
1 typewriter eraser;
1 soft (pencil) eraser;
1 protective card;
line: 60

1. On plain paper, arrange and type the letter in modified block style, mixed punctuation, beginning on Line 16. Type at high speed without concern for errors.

2. Remove your letter from the typewriter; proofread it and mark all errors for correction.

3. Assemble a letterhead carbon pack; type a final copy from your rough draft, erasing and correcting all errors you make as you type.

4. Before you remove the letter from the typewriter, proofread it and correct any remaining errors.

5. Prepare an envelope.

words

January 12, 19-- Mrs. Katherine Messman Glos, Steade & Lowry, Inc. 2464 14
Soloman Island Road Baltimore, MD 21401-3875 Dear Mrs. Messman: 27

Many people think that word processors type most frequently from "copy" that 43
has been recorded on some kind of electronic medium--tape, belt, or floppy disk. 59
This belief is wrong. 64

Much of the copy typed by WP operators is presented to the typist in long- 78
hand. This practice is not efficient because an executive's time is costly and 94
handwriting is slow. In addition, the time required by a WP operator to read and 111
type poorly written longhand is expensive, and many executives do not write 126
legibly. 128

Whatever their "input" medium, executives should have major concern for 142
cost. They should learn to type and to dictate so that their time as well as that 159
of the WP operator is used efficiently. 167

The enclosed pamphlet offers some helpful pointers on planning for dicta- 182
tion, dictating, and making corrections. If you need multiple copies, we have 197
them at nominal cost. 202

Sincerely yours, Stanley B. Moses Research & Development xx Enclosure 216
235

Suggestions for optional compose-as-you-type activities

When directed by your teacher, choose a "Thought Starter" from those listed below. Develop the idea into a 2- or 3-paragraph theme, giving reasons for what you would do.

1 If I had it to do over, I would . . . .
2 If I could have just one wish, I would . . . .
3 If I were President, I would . . . .
4 If I had my choice of career, I would . . . .
5 If I could attend the college or school of my choice, I would . . . .
6 If I had a lot of money, I would . . . .
7 If I could be the person I want to be, I would . . . .
8 If I could participate in the extracurricular activity of my choice, I would . . . .

When your teacher directs, choose a letter-writing situation from those listed below and prepare a rough draft of a suitable letter.

1. Compose a letter to invite a friend or relative who lives some distance away to be your houseguest for a weekend. State your plans for the weekend positively so that your friend or relative will be highly motivated to visit you.

2. Compose a letter to a business acquaintance who might help you get a job for the summer. Indicate the kind of work you want to do and what your qualifications are for the job.

3. Compose a letter to your teacher, summarizing what you have learned in typewriting thus far and in what ways you think it will help you in the future.

4. Compose a letter to the U.S. Department of Labor, requesting information in pamphlet or booklet form about job prospects, qualifications, and salary for a career in which you are interested.

234c ▶ 25 Refine problem skills: unbound report with table

1. Type the report as an unbound manuscript; correct errors as you type.
2. Use the mathematical method to center the table, following the directions given in 234b, page 370.

words

SPENDING PATTERNS OF THE AMERICAN PEOPLE 8

Any study of the spending patterns of the American people is a very 22
difficult one because of the difference in money income and real income. 37
Money income is the number of dollars individuals receive; real income is the 52
goods and services that the money received will buy at any given time. Over 68
the years, money income has risen at a far greater pace than real income. 83

In 1967, for example, Americans consumed $492,265 millions worth of 96
products; in 1977, the consumption had risen to $1,206,507 millions. The table 112
below shows the amount spent on a few selected products in dollars and as a 127
percent of the total for each year. Note that although dollar expenditures in- 143
creased in all cases, the American people were actually spending less of their 159
total incomes on some products. 166

DS

PERSONAL CONSUMPTION OF SELECTED PRODUCTS 174

(In Millions of Dollars) 179

Product	1967	1977	Percent Change	
Food and tobacco	117,395	261,763	– 1.9%	199
	(23.8%)	(21.9%)		202
Clothing	51,054	95,561	– 2.5%	208
	(10.4%)	(7.9%)		211
Housing	71,808	184,592	+ .7%	217
	(14.6%)	(15.3%)		220
Recreation	30,903	81,200	+ .4%	227
	(6.3%)	(6.7%)		229

(header line: 191)

__________________ 233

Source: U.S. Department of Commerce. 240

235

235a ▶ 5 Conditioning practice

Use standard directions given in 234a, page 370.

alphabet 1 Victoria said her new boutique might market the fuzzy panda next July.
figures 2 Ronald scored 238.1, 246.7, and 250.1 points on the 90-meter ski jump.
fig/sym 3 The invoice showed credits of $20, $13.95, $42.87, $66, $92, and $121.
fluency 4 If the clerk did not pay the bill on time, they may owe a big penalty.

| 1 | 2 | 3 | 4 | 5 | 6 | 7 | 8 | 9 | 10 | 11 | 12 | 13 | 14 |

56d ▶ 21 Check letter typing skill

2 letterheads [LM pp. 71-74]; 1 carbon copy sheet; 1 sheet carbon paper; 1 typewriter eraser; 1 pencil eraser; 1 protective card; line: 60; date on Line 19

Problem 1

1. Type in modified block style, mixed punctuation, the letter at the right; do not prepare a carbon copy or correct errors; prepare an envelope.

2. Check your completed letter for placement and spacing only.

words

January 8, 19-- Miss Hilda Jacobs, Manager Information Processing Center 15
Global Insurance Company 420 Boulevard of Allies Pittsburgh, PA 15219- 29
3647 Dear Miss Jacobs: 33

Thank you for your interest in discussing information processing equipment 48
with a member of our company. 55

Mr. Goro Shinoda, one of our regional consultants, plans to be in Pittsburgh 70
next week. He will be glad to confer with you either Wednesday or Friday 85
morning, whichever is more convenient for you. 94

Will you please let me know on which of these days and at what time you 109
would like to have Mr. Shinoda meet with you. 118

Sincerely yours, Ralph H. Bruckman National Sales Manager xx 130/**156**

Problem 2

1. Type the letter in the same style as Problem 1; prepare a carbon copy; erase and correct any errors you make as you type.

2. Proofread your copy before removing it from the typewriter; correct any additional errors you find; prepare an envelope.

January 10, 19-- Mr. Stanley B. Moses Research & Development Multimedia 14
Corporation 100 South Wacker Drive Chicago, IL 60606-2174 Dear Mr. 28
Moses: 29

Thank you very much for the suggestions you offered in your letter of 43
December 15. Their application has already made some real differences, 58
and I am sure their improved use will bring even greater efficiency. 72

I find that by making pencil notations on incoming letters as I read them 87
and placing the letters in a logical sequence, I can dictate more letters in less 103
time. Further, I need to make fewer corrections. 113

The word processors are giving me more accurate transcripts than ever before. 129
In addition, they say that the tapes are easier to understand and that the letters 146
are easier to type in correct form the first time. 156

Most sincerely yours, Ms. Gwynne Glisson, Manager Customer Service 169
Department xx 172/**194**

Enrichment activities: business letters

Problem 1

1 letterhead [LM pp. 75, 76]; line: 60; modified block style, mixed punctuation; date on Line 19; use the following letter address:

Reservations Manager
Town & Country Hotel
500 Hotel Circle
San Diego, CA 92138-1476

Use your name and the title Secretary to Mr. Bruckman in the closing lines. Prepare an envelope; correct errors.

December 30, 19--

Dear Sir or Madam:

¶ In the name of Ralph H. Bruckman, please reserve a single room with full-size bed for the nights of January 13, 14, and 15.

¶ Because Mr. Bruckman will not arrive until after six o'clock, please mark the reservation LATE ARRIVAL. The reservation is guaranteed by Multimedia Corporation. A written confirmation will be appreciated.

Sincerely yours,

235b ▶ 45
Refine problem skills: reports

1. Study the material in both problems carefully before you begin to type.

2. Type Problem 1 as a leftbound manuscript, DS. Correct errors as you type. The title will be:

TYPING REPORT MANUSCRIPTS

Note: Side headings are shown preceding (before) the paragraph numbers.

3. Type Problem 2 as a topbound manuscript, SS. Correct errors as you type. The title will be:

TYPING HEADINGS AND FOOTNOTES IN MANUSCRIPTS

The footnote will be as follows:

[1] Morris P. Wolf, Dale F. Keyser, and Robert P. Aurner, <u>Effective Communication in Business</u>, 7th ed. (Cincinnati: South-Western Publishing Co., 1979), p. 399.

Type the footnote so that there will be a bottom margin of approximately 1 inch.

Note: Paragraph headings are shown after the paragraph numbers.

4. If time permits, retype Problem 1 as an unbound manuscript, DS. Correct errors as you type.

words

Problem 1: Report with side headings

main heading 5

(¶ 1) Typing report manuscripts is not at all difficult once you learn a few basic 21
spacing and placement rules. Manuscripts to be printed and most school re- 36
ports are double-spaced; many business reports, however, are single-spaced. 51
Paragraphs are usually indented 5 spaces, but they may be indented 7 or 10 66
spaces. Following is the format for each of the major report types: 80

<u>Unbound Manuscript</u> (¶ 2) The top margin of the first page of an unbound manu- 98
script is 1 1/2 inches (pica) or 2 inches (elite). All other margins are 1 inch. All 115
margins on the second and succeeding pages are 1 inch. Beginning with page 2, 131
number the pages on the fourth line from the top, 1 inch from the right edge of 147
the paper. 149

<u>Leftbound Manuscript</u> (¶ 3) Since this report is bound on the left, the left margin is 1 169
1/2 inches. All other margins and page numbers are the same as on an unbound 185
manuscript. 188

<u>Topbound Manuscript</u> (¶ 4) To allow for binding, the top margin of the first page 207
is 2 inches (pica) or 2 1/2 inches (elite). The top margin on the second and 222
succeeding pages is 1 1/2 inches. All other margins are 1 inch. The page num- 238
bers are centered and typed a half inch from the bottom edge of each page. 253

Problem 2: Report with side headings, ¶ headings, and footnote

main heading 9

<u>Main and Secondary Headings</u> (¶ 1) <u>Main heading</u>. The main heading of a report 31
is centered over the line of writing in ALL CAPS. To center headings, backspace 47
from the center point for unbound and topbound reports; for leftbound reports, 63
begin backspacing from 54 on the elite scale or 45 on the pica scale. 77

(¶ 2) <u>Secondary headings</u>. Secondary headings are typed with only the main 95
words capitalized. Double-space between headings, but triple-space after the 110
final heading before typing the body of the report. 121

<u>Side Headings and Paragraph Headings</u> (¶ 3) Side headings are typed even with 143
the left margin and underlined with main words capitalized. Triple-space be- 158
fore and double-space after typing a side heading. Paragraph headings are 176
indented and underlined with only the first word capitalized. 188

<u>Footnotes</u> (¶ 4) On a filled page, footnotes are typed so there is a margin of 204
approximately 1 inch at the bottom of the page. On a partially filled page, 220
footnotes may be typed in the same manner or typed immediately below the last 235
line of the body of the report. Footnotes are single-spaced with a double space 252
between them and are indented in the same manner as the manuscript. The line 267
which divides the body of the manuscript from the footnote is 1 1/2 inches in 283
length and is always a double space above the first footnote. 296

(¶ 5) In formal manuscripts, footnotes are numbered with superscript figures. 310
However, "Asterisks, daggers, or other symbols are used instead of Arabic 325
numerals occasionally, particularly in statistical tables." [1] 337

footnote 380

56

70-space line

56a ▶ 7 Conditioning practice

Use standard procedure given in 51a, page 81.

alphabet 1 Marvin, the tax clerk, was puzzled by the quaint antics of the judges.
fig/sym 2 Jo paid a $94.30 premium on a $5,000 insurance policy (dated 6/12/78).
uy/ui 3 Quin may buy yucca plants from the guy at a shop at the Yucatan ruins.
fluency 4 The city auditor is due by eight and she may lend a hand to the panel.

| 1 | 2 | 3 | 4 | 5 | 6 | 7 | 8 | 9 | 10 | 11 | 12 | 13 | 14 |

56b ▶ 12 Check keystroking speed: skill comparison

1. A 1′ writing on each line; determine *gwam* on each writing.
2. Compare *gwam* on the 5 writings to identify the 3 slowest lines.
3. If time permits, type these 3 lines again.

all letters/figures used

balanced-hand 1 Eighty of the city firms may form a panel to handle the fuel problems.
combination 2 An audit crew is due by noon; we shall look into the tax problem then.
adjacent-key 3 Troy said he was at the arena for a pop concert when the lion escaped.
direct-reach 4 Brenda checked both number columns twice before she plotted the curve.
figure 5 Our ZIP Code was expanded from 45236 to 45236-1058 on August 17, 1981.

| 1 | 2 | 3 | 4 | 5 | 6 | 7 | 8 | 9 | 10 | 11 | 12 | 13 | 14 |

56c ▶ 10 Check straight-copy skill

1. A 1′ writing on ¶ 1, then on ¶ 2; determine *gwam* on each writing.
2. A 2′ writing on ¶s 1–2 combined; determine *gwam*.
3. A 3′ writing on ¶s 1–2 combined; determine *gwam*.

all letters used | A | 1.5 si | 5.7 awl | 80% hfw

gwam 2′ | 3′

A great many people alibi that if they could only stop the clock 7 4
or hold the hands of time, they could accomplish whatever they desire 14 9
to do. Unfortunately, time marches on whether human beings do or not. 21 14
The question therefore becomes not how can we acquire more time for 28 18
ourselves, but how can we utilize more productively the time allotted 35 23
us. Learning to use time wisely is a major step toward success. 41 27

Time is a constant, for everyone has an equal amount of it. How 47 32
we use time, however, is a critical variable in the equation of ex- 54 36
cellence. Thinking requires time, of course; but we can conserve our 61 41
time by taking time to plan before beginning our work. The likelihood 68 45
of having to do work over is decreased by thinking through all related 75 50
problems and planning the project before starting work. 81 54

gwam 2′ | 1 | 2 | 3 | 4 | 5 | 6 | 7 |
3′ | 1 | 2 | 3 | 4 | 5 |

236

236a ▶ 5 Conditioning practice

Use standard directions given in 234a, page 370.

alphabet 1 We have a joint group of experts analyze the bond market each quarter.
figures 2 Published in 1982, this book has 856 pages, 234 pictures, and 70 maps.
fig/sym 3 The tax was 3% in 1956, 5.2% in 1967, 8.3% in 1978, and 10.2% in 1982.
fluency 4 If they ask her to do so, the author may change the title of the play.

| 1 | 2 | 3 | 4 | 5 | 6 | 7 | 8 | 9 | 10 | 11 | 12 | 13 | 14 |

236b ▶ 30 Timed drills on reports

Type four 5' writings on the report at the right as directed below; do not correct your stroking errors. Check carefully for errors in style and format. Compute *g-pram*.

1. As an unbound report.

2. Beginning with ¶ 2, as the second page of a leftbound report.

3. As a topbound report.

4. Beginning with ¶ 2, as the second page of a topbound report.

Note: Type the footnote (or footnotes) so that there will be a bottom margin of approximately one inch.

	words Problems 1 & 3	Problems 2 & 4
REPORTS IN THE EVERY DAY WORLD OF BUSINESS	8	
TS		
Importence [a] of Reports	17	
[modern] ~~Today's~~ managers thrive on a continuous flow of [data] ~~facts~~ in	28	
report form about such [vital functions] ~~essential tasks~~ as sales, finance,	40	
production, research, and [purchasing] ~~marketing~~. Hanna, Popham, and	51	
Tilton assert that, "For every business, large or small, what-	64	
ever the orientation, today can aptly be described as the age	76	
of reporting."[1] No business can [survive] ~~last~~ for every long with out	89	
reports of [many] ~~numerous~~ kinds.	93	
TS		
Use of Reports	99	6
"Reports are used by managers as an aid in making decisions	111	18
DS and as a source of information for placing responsibility, for	124	30
modifying policies, or merely as a matter of history."[2] Reports	137	43
also [establish] ~~set up~~ a double channel of communication through which	149	56
data [essential] ~~necessary~~ to the efficient [conduct] ~~operation~~ of the business can	161	68
flow. [These] ~~This~~ vital data canbe [#] used to assess results, to solve a	175	81
[wide variety] ~~great mixture~~ of problems, and to make changes [necessary] ~~required~~ to	186	93
improve operatoins.	191	97
	194	101
[1] J Marshall Hanna, Estelle L. Popham, and Rita Sloan Tilton,	207	
Secretarial Procedures and Administration, 7th ed. (Cincinnati:	225	
South-Western Publishing Co., 1978), p. 480.	237	
[2] B. Lewis Keeling, Norman F. Kallaus, and John J. W. Neuner,	249	113
Administrative Office Management, 7th ed. (Cincinnati: South-	268	132
Western Publishing Co., 1978), p. 724.	276	140

55c ▶ 14 Learn to assemble, insert, and correct a carbon pack

2 plain sheets; 1 carbon sheet; line: 60; DS

1. Read ¶ 1 at the right; assemble a carbon pack as directed there.

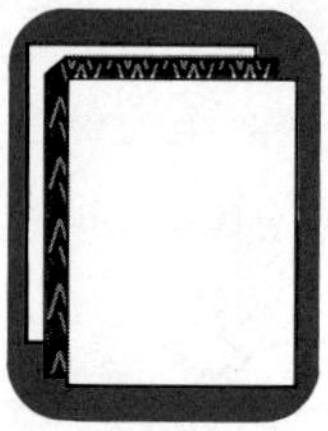

2. Read ¶s 2 and 3; then insert the pack as directed.

3. Type the material as given at the right. Begin on Line 13. Erase and correct your errors.

To correct errors

1. Pull original sheet forward and place a 5" × 3" card or a plastic erasing shield in front of carbon sheet. Erase error on original with a hard (typewriting) eraser.

2. Remove card; then with a soft (pencil) eraser, erase error on carbon (file) copy.

words

ASSEMBLE AND INSERT A CARBON PACK 7
TS

Place on the desk the sheet of paper on which the carbon 18
(file) copy is to be made; then place a sheet of carbon paper, <u>carbon</u> 33
<u>side down</u>, on top of the first sheet. Finally, place the sheet for the 50
original on top of the carbon paper. 57

Pick up the carbon pack so that the original copy sheet is to 70
the back and the carbon copy sheet is to the front. Tap the bottom 83
edge of the pack lightly on the desk to align the edges. With 96
the <u>carbon copy sheet toward you</u>, place the pack between the 114
platen and the paper table; then turn the pack into the typewriter. 127

Position the pack for typing; then check the top left and 139
right corners to see whether they are properly aligned. If they are 153
not, operate the paper-release lever to straighten them; then 165
return the pack to typing position. 172

55d ▶ 16 Type a business letter with a carbon copy

1 letterhead [LM pp. 69, 70]; 1 plain sheet; 1 carbon sheet; line: 60; date on Line 19; prepare envelope

1. Assemble a carbon pack as directed in 55c, above; insert it into typewriter.

2. Type in modified block style, mixed punctuation, the letter at the right. Arrange opening and closing lines as appropriate. Listen for the bell as a signal to divide words and return at line endings in body.

3. Proofread your copy before removing paper from typewriter; correct any errors you find.

words

January 6, 19-- | Mr. Charles D. Henry | 357 Conde Street | West Chicago, IL 14
60185-1147 | Dear Mr. Henry: 20

Thank you for sending your completed application form. We are pleased that 35
you are interested in joining our data/word processing staff. 48

Can you come to this office some afternoon during the week of January 12 to 63
take the aptitude and proficiency tests I discussed with you? So that you will 79
not have to miss any of your classes at school, we can have the tests given 94
between 3:30 and 5:00 p.m. We allow an hour to complete the tests. 108

Please fill in and return the enclosed card indicating the date and time you 123
wish to take the tests. Mr. Garcia, our training director, can then arrange to 139
be here to help you. 144

Sincerely yours, | Mrs. Eloise Johnson | Personnel Director | xx | Enclosure 157
170

236c ▶ 15
Refine problem skills: leftbound report with footnote

Type the report at the right as a leftbound manuscript. The title will be: **PREPARING BUSINESS REPORTS.**

Provide an appropriate footnote. The quote is from **page 114** of **Communication for Management and Business** by **Norman B. Sigband, 2d ed.**, published in **1976** by **Scott, Foresman and Company, Glenview, IL.** Type the footnote so that there will be a bottom margin of approximately 1 inch.

words
title 5

The business report is an essential tool in planning, 16
organizing, directing, and controlling business operations. 28
Although many reports are presented orally or informally in 40
writing, most major reports are prepared in manuscript form. 53
It is essential that these reports make a favorable impres- 64
sion, with no strikeovers or poor erasures. 73

The typist can do a great deal to insure the favorable 84
reception of a report by arranging and typing it so that it 96
is neat and attractive. Special attention should be given to 109
the format of a report, especially the margins and spacing. 121
As Sigband indicates, "The well-balanced page looks invit- 133
ing; the material is easy to read and easy to assimilate."[1] 144

footnote 183

237

237a ▶ 5
Conditioning practice

Use standard directions given in 234a, page 370.

alphabet 1 We have begun a check of quarterly expenses itemized in their journal.
figures 2 Remove pages 736, 852, 1079, 1826, 2564, and 3690 from the manuscript.
fig/sym 3 The men's case (Item 5139-874) is 24″ × 15″ × 7″ and sells for $26.98.
fluency 4 Perhaps he can write me a check so that we can pay for the auto today.

| 1 | 2 | 3 | 4 | 5 | 6 | 7 | 8 | 9 | 10 | 11 | 12 | 13 | 14 |

237b ▶ 45
Sustained production: report manuscripts

1. Make a list of the problems below:
page 372, 235b, Problem 1
page 373, 236b, Direction 1
page 372, 235b, Problem 2
page 370, 234b

2. Type the reports for 30′ *in the order indicated*. Proofread each page before you remove it from the typewriter and correct any errors you may have missed.

3. If you finish before time is called, start over.

4. Compute *o-pram* as explained on page 362.

54d ▶ 25
Type business letters from semiarranged copy

3 letterheads [LM pp. 63-68]; line: 60; date on Line 19; prepare envelopes; correct errors

Problem 1

Type in modified block style, mixed punctuation, the letter at the right. Color bars indicate line endings in opening and closing lines. Listen for bell as signal to divide words and return at line endings in body.

Do not type line-end indicators in opening/closing lines.

	words parts	total
January 3, 19-- | Mr. Kenneth J. Willingham | 2638 Silver Oaks Way |	13	13
Spring Valley, CA 92077-4830 | Dear Mr. Willingham:	23	23
I am glad you will be able to meet me in San Diego to discuss the position	15	38
of sales representative in the Southern California area.	27	49
While in San Diego, I shall stay at the Town & Country Hotel. Why don't	41	64
you meet me there for lunch at 11:30 on January 15. If either the	55	77
suggested time or place is not convenient for you, we can make other	68	91
arrangements for the interview.	75	98
As soon as I arrive in San Diego on January 13, I shall telephone you to	90	112
confirm the interview appointment.	96	120
Sincerely yours, | Ralph H. Bruckman | National Sales Manager | xx	12	132
		147

Problem 2

Use Problem 1 directions for typing the letter given at the right.

Problem 3 (extra credit)

If time permits, type Problem 2 addressed to:

Mr. Benito R. Guzman
Head, English Department
Blue Bonnet High School
643 East Durango Boulevard
San Antonio, TX 78206-1529

	words parts	total
January 4, 19--| Ms. Cynthia Blockhaus| Language Arts Training Center|	14	14
3133 Lawton Road| Orlando, FL 32803-4567| Dear Ms. Blockhaus:	26	26
Series 8 of "The Right to Read" filmstrips was shipped to you this morn-	14	40
ing by Emery Express.	19	45
You and your students will be especially pleased with the improvement	33	59
in reading skill that results from the addition of sound to the visual	47	73
presentation. Our test results show that the use of dual response cues not	62	88
only speeds up the reading rate but also helps students pronounce words	77	102
correctly.	79	105
Your continued use of our materials is appreciated. The enclosed	92	118
brochure describes other items that may interest you.	103	129
Sincerely yours,| Miss Kathy Simms, Manager| Educational Media Di-	13	142
vision| xx| Enclosure	16	145
		164

55

70-space line

55a ▶ 7
Conditioning practice

Use standard procedure given in 51a, page 81.

alphabet 1 Barth was given a big prize for completing six quick high jumps today.
figures 2 Our group read 45 plays, 176 books, and 203 articles during 1981-1982.
tr/rt 3 Trujillo tried to sell part of the art assortment to the trust expert.
fluency 4 When did the widow make the eighty formal gowns for the downtown firm?

| 1 | 2 | 3 | 4 | 5 | 6 | 7 | 8 | 9 | 10 | 11 | 12 | 13 | 14 |

55b ▶ 13
Build skill in typing business letters

plain paper

1. Two 1' speed writings (in letter form) on opening lines of Problem 1, 54d, above. If you finish before time is called, start over.

2. Two 1' speed writings (in letter form) on closing lines of Problem 1, 54d, above. If you finish before time is called, start over.

3. A 5' writing (in letter form) on Problem 1, 54d, above. Tab, return, and space forward quickly.

unit **47** lessons 238-241

Refine problem skills: forms and tables

Learning goals

1. To increase your ability to plan, organize, and type forms and tables.

2. To increase your rate in typing forms and tables.

Machine adjustments

1. Line: 70 for drills; as necessary for production problems.

2. Spacing: SS sentence drills; space problems as required.

238

238a ▶ 5 Conditioning practice

each line twice SS (slowly, then faster); DS between 2-line groups; if time permits, retype selected lines

alphabet 1 Jack Gilford requested us to buy an expensive camera with a zoom lens.

figures 2 Dial 011-39-6 for Rome, 011-87-78 for Kobe, and 011-254-2 for Nairobi.

fig/sym 3 Use the "and" sign (&) in company names: D & R Motors; Barton & Sons.

fluency 4 Did he claim that she can handle the problem of the special amendment?

| 1 | 2 | 3 | 4 | 5 | 6 | 7 | 8 | 9 | 10 | 11 | 12 | 13 | 14 |

238b ▶ 25 Refine problem skills: business forms

Problem 1
Purchase order [LM p. 21]

1. Type the purchase order; do not correct errors as you type.

2. When you finish, correct errors in pencil. Pay close attention to correct format.

3. Retype the purchase order from your corrected copy; correct all errors as you type.

Goal: an acceptable form typed in 5′ or less.

words

PURCHASE ORDER NO. X-7492 1

TO: LaSalle Manufacturing Company, Inc. DATE July 31, 19-- 11
1251 South Wabash Avenue 16
Chicago, IL 60605-3732 TERMS 2/10, n/30 23

SHIP VIA Midland Freight 26

QUANTITY	CAT. NO.	DESCRIPTION	PRICE	TOTAL	words
25	82 S 81492	AM/FM stereo receiver, 9 watts	199.50	4,987.50	39
50	85 S 92506	Speaker, 10-inch, 3-way	107.00	5,350.00	48
25	86 T 92507	Turntable, 2-speed, belt-drive	79.75	1,993.75	61
30	87 T 92564	Record changer, automatic			69
		w/ceramic cartridge	55.95	1,678.50	78
				14,009.75	80

Problem 2
Invoice [LM p. 23]

Type the invoice in the same manner as Problem 1.

DATE August 16, 19-- 3

8

SOLD TO: Memphis Music Academy OUR ORDER NO. MP50502 13
4820 Walnut Grove 17
Memphis, TN 38117-3330 CUST. ORDER NO. 49963-T 19

TERMS Net SHIPPED VIA Local Transfer 21

QUANTITY	DESCRIPTION	UNIT PRICE	TOTAL	words
2	Tape deck, player/recorder	307.90	615.80	29
1	Microphone, omni-directional	37.50	37.50	38
6	Patchcord/connector kits	5.85	35.10	45
2	Speaker cables	3.75	7.50	51
1	Turntable, w/electronic speed control	79.50	79.50	63
			775.40	64

54a ▶ 7 Conditioning practice

Use standard procedure given in 51a, page 81.

alphabet 1 Zig will do extra jobs for the antique clock firm if it pays overtime.
fig/sym 2 I said, "The quiz covering pages 35-149 and 168-270 will be on May 6."
oi/io 3 Lionel has the option of joining an oil firm; Lois has a choice, also.
fluency 4 Both of the girls may go with the busy auditor to visit the auto firm.

| 1 | 2 | 3 | 4 | 5 | 6 | 7 | 8 | 9 | 10 | 11 | 12 | 13 | 14 |

54b ▶ 8 Improve technique: response patterns

1. A 1′ writing on each of Lines 3, 6, and 9; determine *gwam* on each.

2. Beginning with Line 1, type as much of the drill as you can, trying to improve your key-stroking response patterns.

word response
1 of dot pen lay eye tie bus rug bit key oak map bid via aid got fit air
2 the man | due them | six pens | worn fur | such aid | she kept | the hand | big auto
3 Zorn is to go for the auto keys; then they may go to the lake to fish.

letter response
4 as you are him was ill get oil few ink tax pop set kin ads hip raw pin
5 at him | in case | on edge | no fear | my fare | we join | as only | my data | be safe
6 Molly gave him a few wage cards only after you set a safe rate on oil.

combination response
7 we the you and are for was may get but tax pay few due him own set men
8 a pair | is ever | on hand | if only | to join | no fuel | we kept | as busy | so vast
9 Sign the pink form and turn it in by six if you wish to join the cast.

| 1 | 2 | 3 | 4 | 5 | 6 | 7 | 8 | 9 | 10 | 11 | 12 | 13 | 14 |

54c ▶ 10 Improve skill transfer

1. A 1′ writing on ¶ 1; determine *gwam*.

2. Type figure/symbol combinations from ¶ 2 from your teacher's dictation.

3. Two 1′ writings on ¶ 2, trying to maintain your ¶ 1 rate.

4. A 2′ writing on ¶ 1; determine *gwam*.

5. A 2′ writing on ¶ 2, trying to maintain your ¶ 1 2′ rate.

all letters/figures used | A | 1.5 si | 5.7 awl | 80% hfw |

	gwam 1′	2′
Words are the major component of written communication, and the	13	6
typewriter is a very vital tool we use to put those words on paper with	27	14
ease and speed. To exchange information effectively, the words we use	41	21
must be chosen quite carefully and typed in a neatly arranged form. We	56	28
should keep in mind that the selection of the precise word is even more	70	35
important than the size of the word because clarity is crucial.	83	41
One study of a national sample of business messages reveals that	13	7
over 56% of all typed letters are brief (125 words or fewer), over 26%	27	14
are of medium length (126-225 words), and somewhat under 18% are long	41	21
(over 226 words). Other studies--these dealing with message cost--	55	27
show that letters range in cost from $4 to $7, depending on length.	68	34
Message cost is likely to continue a trend upward from 1983 to 1990.	82	41

gwam 1′ | 1 | 2 | 3 | 4 | 5 | 6 | 7 | 8 | 9 | 10 | 11 | 12 | 13 | 14 |
2′ | 1 | 2 | 3 | 4 | 5 | 6 | 7 |

238c ▶ 25
Refine problem skills: tables

1. Center the table horizontally and vertically in reading position on a full sheet of paper. Use the mathematical method to determine horizontal placement. DS the items.

2. Correct errors as you type. If necessary, refer to page 319 for spacing horizontal rules.

				words
U.S. MOTOR FUEL SUPPLY AND DEMAND				7
(In Thousands of 42-Gallon Barrels)				14
				26
				39
Year	Annual Production	Daily Average	Domestic Demand	49
				62
1950	1,024,481	2,806	994,290	68
1955	1,373,950	3,764	1,329,788	74
1960*	1,522,497	4,171	1,511,670	80
1965	1,733,258	4,749	1,750,028	86
1970	2,135,838	5,852	2,162,642	93
1975	2,420,962	6,633	2,477,786	99
1980	2,629,482	7,048	2,528,478	105
				118
* Beginning with 1960, Alaska and Hawaii are included.				129
Source: Energy Information Administration, U.S. Energy Department.				142

239

239a ▶ 5
Conditioning practice

Use standard directions given in 238a, page 375.

alphabet 1 Jacques explained why he memorized the various passages from the book.

figures 2 One ounce is 16.0 drams, 437.5 avoirdupois grams, 28.349 metric grams.

fig/sym 3 The R & W Lathe (Model 23687A) is listed at $945, less a 10% discount.

fluency 4 Some of the items on display may not be sold during this special sale.

| 1 | 2 | 3 | 4 | 5 | 6 | 7 | 8 | 9 | 10 | 11 | 12 | 13 | 14 |

239b ▶ 25
Refine problem skills: tables

1. In pencil on a sheet of scrap paper, complete the information for the table at the right. See Problem 1 on page 372 for the information, if necessary.

2. Use the heading: **MARGINS FOR REPORTS** Center the table horizontally and vertically in reading position on a full sheet of paper. DS the items; correct errors as you type.

3. Keep the table for future reference.

				words
			heading	4
Margins	Unbound	Leftbound	Topbound	17
Left margin, in inches	1″			24
Right margin, in inches	1″			31
Left margin and exact right				37
margin in pica spaces	10-75*			46
Left margin and exact right				52
margin in elite spaces	12-90*			62
Top margin, page 1, in				67
inches (pica)	1 1/2″			73
In pica type, begin typing				78
page 1 on line	10			83
Top margin, page 1, in				88
inches (elite)	2″			93
In elite type, begin typing				98
page 1 on line	13			103
Bottom margin, all pages,				108
in inches	1″			112
Top margin, page 2, in inches	1″			121
Begin typing page 2 on line	7			128
				132
* Plus 3-7 spaces for bell cue				138

53c ▶ 18 Learn to address envelopes and fold letters

1. Study the guides at the right and the illustrations below.

Envelope address	**Style**	**Special notations**
Set a tab stop 10 spaces left of center of small envelope, 5 spaces for a large envelope. Space down 12 lines from top edge of small envelope, 14 spaces for a large envelope. Begin the address at the tab stop position.	Use *block style*, SS. Type in all capitals; omit punctuation. Type city name, 2–letter state name abbreviation, and ZIP Code on last address line. Two spaces precede the ZIP Code.	Type *mailing* notations such as REGISTERED and SPECIAL DELIV–ERY below the stamp position on Line 8 or 9. Type *addressee* notations such as PERSONAL and HOLD FOR AR–RIVAL a TS below return address and 3 spaces from left edge of en–velope.

Addressing business envelopes as recommended by U.S. Postal Service

small, number 6¾ (6½″ × 3⅝″)

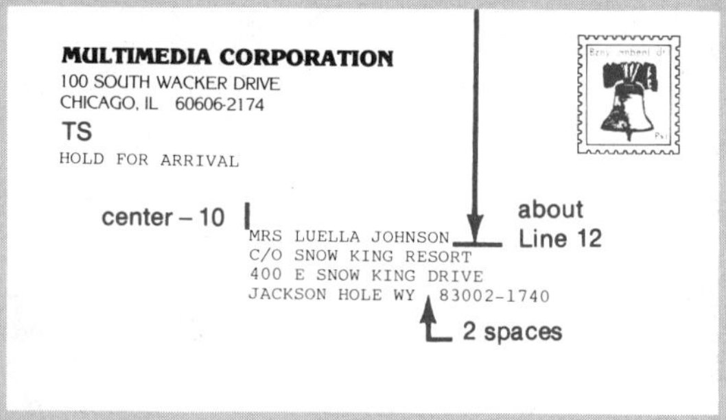

large, number 10 (9½″ × 4⅛″)

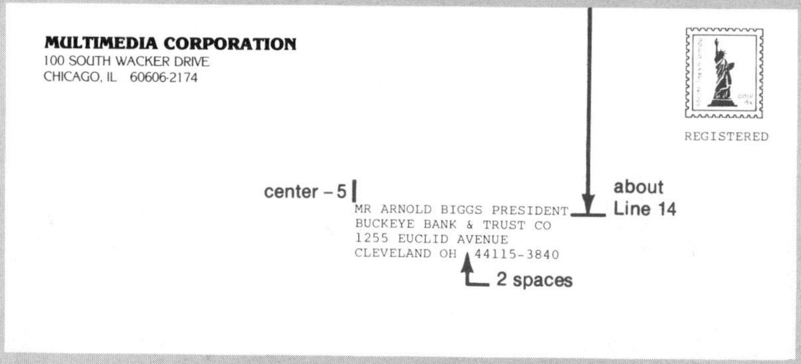

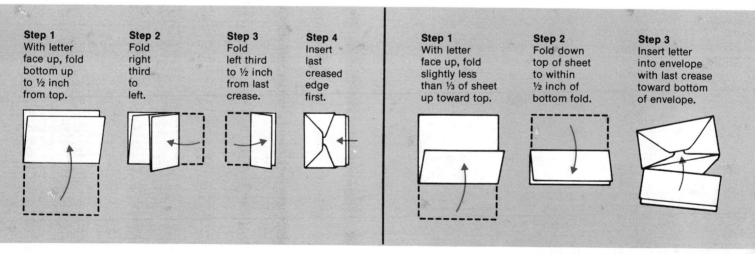

Step 1
With letter face up, fold bottom up to ½ inch from top.

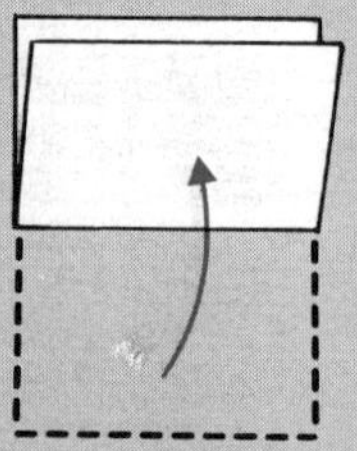

Step 2
Fold right third to left.

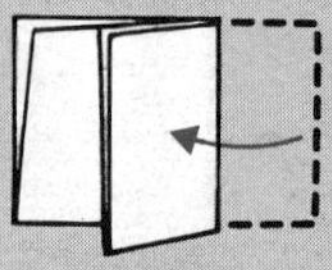

Step 3
Fold left third to ½ inch from last crease.

Step 4
Insert last creased edge first.

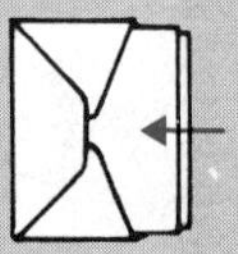

Step 1
With letter face up, fold slightly less than ⅓ of sheet up toward top.

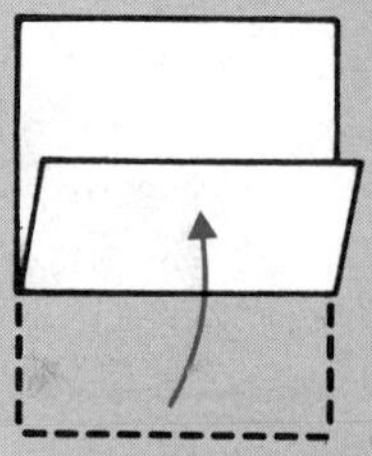

Step 2
Fold down top of sheet to within ½ inch of bottom fold.

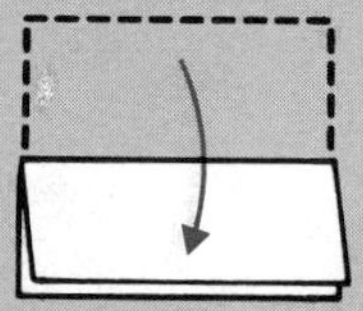

Step 3
Insert letter into envelope with last crease toward bottom of envelope.

2. Type a small (No. 6 3/4) and a large (No. 10) envelope for each of the addresses given at the right [LM pp. 53–62].

3. If time permits, practice folding and inserting standard–size sheets of paper for both large and small envelopes.

MS MARIE OLDHAM
1746 SHAWMUT AVENUE
NEW BEDFORD MA 02746-1020

MR FRANK PEREZ MANAGER
EMPIRE STATE TOWERS
122 JAMES STREET SUITE 8C
SYRACUSE NY 13202-1856

DR EVELYN SCHWARTZ CHAIR
DIVISION OF BUSINESS STUDIES
LONE STAR TECHNICAL SCHOOL
6410 FANNIN STREET
HOUSTON TX 77030-9421

MR J EVAN ARMSTRONG
5849 POWERS BLVD APT 3
COLORADO SPRINGS CO 80917-1427

239c ▶ 20
Refine problem skills: forms

Problem 1
Statement of account
[LM p. 25]

Type the statement of account at the right; correct errors as you type.

words

DATE August 31, 19-- 3

TO Old Hickory Junior College 9
700 Church Street 12
Nashville, TN 37203-4556 17

			DEBITS	CREDITS	BALANCE	words
August	1	Balance due			394.80	23
	5	Invoice 564349	1,921.50		2,316.30	31
	7	Payment on account		394.80	1,921.50	38
	17	Invoice 564392	560.90		2,482.40	45
	22	Invoice 564409	364.85		2,847.25	52
	28	Credit Memorandum 4728		207.90	2,639.35	61
	30	Payment on account		1,921.50	717.85	68

Problem 2
Bill of lading
[LM p. 25]

Type the bill of lading at the right; correct errors as you type.

FROM **LaSalle Manufacturing Company, Inc.** AT **Chicago, IL** DATE **11/1/19--** 12
CONSIGNED TO AND DESTINATION **The Entertainment Center 145 Jefferson** 19
Street, Memphis, TN 38103-2244 CUST. ORDER NO. **8156** DELIVERING 27
CARRIER: **Mid-West Express Line** CAR INITIAL AND NO. **ICC-29378** 33

NO. PACKAGES	DESCRIPTION	WEIGHT	words
3	Television antennas	420#	39
1	Antenna rotators	300#	43
3	Television sets, color	1,260#	50
3	Television amplifiers	60#	55

SHIPPER **LaSalle Manufacturing Company, Inc.** PERMANENT POST OFFICE 63
ADDRESS OF SHIPPER **1251 South Wabash Avenue, Chicago, IL 60605-3732** 73
SHIPPER'S NO. **48395** 74

240

240a ▶ 5
Conditioning practice

Use standard directions given in 238a, page 375.

alphabet 1 Kate adjusted a few valves to equalize pressure in the oxygen chamber.
figures 2 Truck 62081 traveled at a rate of 46.9 MPH for a total of 375.2 miles.
fig/sym 3 The temperature on May 17 rose from 20° C to 35° C (68° F. to 95° F.).
fluency 4 The fight for the world title will be held at the downtown civic hall.

| 1 | 2 | 3 | 4 | 5 | 6 | 7 | 8 | 9 | 10 | 11 | 12 | 13 | 14 |

53a ▶ 7 Conditioning practice

Use standard procedure given in 51a, page 81.

alphabet	1	Pivone will get quite old junk from his uncle for my next lawn bazaar.
figures	2	The data are given in Figures 26 and 27 of Part 14, Unit 39, page 508.
we/ew	3	We knew our new weekly journal would give a powerful view of the news.
fluency	4	It is the wish of all of us to lend a hand to the visitor to the city.

| 1 | 2 | 3 | 4 | 5 | 6 | 7 | 8 | 9 | 10 | 11 | 12 | 13 | 14 |

53b ▶ 25 Type business letters from arranged copy

2 plain sheets;
1 letterhead [LM p. 51];
line: 60; date on Line 16

1. On a plain sheet, type line for line (in letter form) a 1′ writing on the opening lines of letter (date through salutation). If you type the salutation before time is called, start over.

2. Type line for line (in letter form) a 1′ writing on the closing lines (complimentary close through reference initials). If you type the initials before time is called, start over.

3. Insert a letterhead and type the complete letter, correcting any errors you make as you type.

4. Proofread your copy and mark any uncorrected errors using proofreader's marks.

5. If time permits, type additional 1′ writings on the opening lines and on the closing lines to build speed.

	words: parts	total
December 29, 19--	4	4
Miss Emi Yamaguchi	7	7
2148 Forest View Road	12	12
Rockford, IL 61108-1375	17	17
Dear Miss Yamaguchi:	21	21
On the basis of your interest in records management and your	12	33
proficiency in typing, shorthand, and related skills, I am	24	45
pleased to offer you a position as a secretary in our firm.	36	57
You will be working under the direct supervision of Ms. Janet	49	69
Miller, Systems Consultant. Although your duties will in-	60	81
volve general secretarial work, much of your time will be	72	92
spent in handling problems and correspondence in the area of	84	105
records storage and retrieval.	90	111
We should like to have you begin work on Monday, January 12.	103	123
This will give you about two weeks of vacation before you	114	135
begin work with us.	119	139
If that date is agreeable to you, we shall look forward to	130	151
welcoming you into the Records Management Department and into	143	163
the company on January 12.	148	169
Sincerely yours,	3	172
Mrs. Eloise Johnson	8	176
Personnel Director	11	180
xx (use your initials)	12	180

240b ▶ 45
Refine problem skills: forms and tables

Problem 1
Table

Center the table horizontally and vertically in the reading position on a full sheet. DS the items; correct errors.

Problem 2
Purchase order [LM p. 27]

Using the table prepared in Problem 1, type Purchase Order No. **41328**, dated **May 14, 19--**, to the **LaSalle Manufacturing Company, Inc.**, for the items below. Terms: **net**; goods will be shipped by **United Freight.**

No.	Catalog No.
10	29405
10	29409
10	29410
20	29414

Problem 3
Invoice [LM p. 27]

Using the purchase order typed in Problem 2, type an invoice (Our Order No. **EE72714**) to the **Entertainment Center, 145 Jefferson Street, Memphis, TN 38103-2244** dated **May 31, 19--**, for the items ordered. Obtain all necessary information from the purchase order.

words

LaSalle Manufacturing Company, Inc. 7
1251 South Wabash Avenue 12
Chicago, IL 60605-3732 17

NEW PRODUCTS AVAILABLE* 21

CATALOG NUMBER	DESCRIPTION	WEIGHT	UNIT PRICE	words
				23
				34
29405	AM/FM Intercom System w/1			41
	master and 2 remotes	18 lbs.	$319.00 set	49
29406	Intercom System, Desk Top	2 lbs.	21.50 ea.	59
29407	Telephone Answering System			65
	(Model 10, 60′ capacity)	12 lbs.	139.00 ea.	74
29408	Telephone Answering System			80
	(Model 20, 120′ capacity)	12 lbs.	189.00 ea.	89
29409	Automatic Dial Telephone			95
	w/10 number capacity	4 lbs.	164.95 ea.	103
29410	Modular Telephone Plug/Jack	8 oz.	3.75 ea.	113
29411	Telephone Amplifier	1.5 lbs.	7.80 ea.	122
29412	Deluxe Telephone Amplifier	3 lbs.	21.95 ea.	132
29413	Telephone Extension Cord, 25′	12 oz.	7.75 ea.	142
29414	Telephone Extension Cord, 50′	1 lb.	8.90 ea.	152

_______________ 156

*Available May 1. For additional information and quantity discounts, call 171
1-800-555-9400. 174

241

241a ▶ 5
Conditioning practice

Use standard directions given in 238a, page 375.

alphabet 1 Wingate quickly emphasized the values of expert analysis to rank jobs.
figures 2 The tax rates rose in 1963, 1968, 1972, 1974, 1978, and again in 1981.
fig/sym 3 Item 63-4729 will measure exactly 50.80 cm by 68.58 cm (1′8″ by 2′3″).
fluency 4 Did the worker dismantle the light panel and fix the lock on the door?
| 1 | 2 | 3 | 4 | 5 | 6 | 7 | 8 | 9 | 10 | 11 | 12 | 13 | 14 |

241b ▶ 45
Sustained production: forms and tables

1. Make a list of the problems below:

page 375, 238b, Prob. 1 [LM p. 29]
page 375, 238b, Prob. 2 [LM p. 29]
page 376, 238c
page 378, 240b, Prob. 1

2. Type the problems for 30′ in the order given; correct errors as you type. Proofread each problem carefully before you remove it from the typewriter and correct any errors you may have missed. If you finish before time is called, type 239b, page 376, as directed.

3. Compute *o–pram* as explained on page 362.

MULTIMEDIA CORPORATION

100 SOUTH WACKER DRIVE / CHICAGO, IL 60606-2174
TELEPHONE 312/871-5050

Tabulate to center
to type date

		words: parts	total
Dateline	Line 19 November 15, 19--	4	4
	Operate return 4 times to leave 3 blank line spaces		
Letter address	Mr. Roger L. Murray, Director	10	10
	Vocational Education Center	15	15
	2836 West Jefferson Road	20	20
	Joliet, IL 60435-2730	25	25
	DS		
Salutation	Dear Mr. Murray:	28	28
	DS		
Body of letter	A copy of the training film ARE YOU LISTENING? is on its way	12	40
	to you by Intercity Parcel Service. You should have ample	24	52
	time to plan your program around it.	32	60
	DS		
	Listening is one of the most important, yet one of the least	44	72
	developed, skills needed by everyone. In the world of work,	56	84
	many people spend much more time listening than they do writ-	68	96
	ing, speaking, or even reading. Few people, however, listen	80	108
	skillfully.	83	111
	Enclosed is a list of pamphlets and training packets that we	95	123
	offer at nominal cost. You might find these useful, also.	107	135
	DS		
Complimentary close	Tab Sincerely yours,	3	138
	Kathy Simms Operate return 4 times		
Typed name and title	Miss Kathy Simms, Manager	9	143
Department or division	Educational Media Division	14	149
	DS		
Initials of typist	jr	15	149
	DS		
Enclosure notation	Enclosure	16	151

Shown in pica type
(60–space line)

In *mixed* punctuation,
a colon follows the salutation
and a comma follows the complimentary close.

Style letter 2: business letter in modified block style, block paragraphs

unit **48** lessons 242-245

Refine basic skills

Learning goals

1. To increase your speed and accuracy on straight copy, rough-draft copy, and statistical copy.

2. To increase your percent of transfer from straight copy to rough-draft copy and statistical copy.

Machine adjustments

1. Line: 70 for all drills.

2. Spacing: SS sentence drills with a DS between groups; DS timed writings.

242

242a ▶ 5 Conditioning practice

each line twice SS (slowly, then faster); DS between 2-line groups; if time permits, retype selected lines

alphabet 1 Working quickly, Juan Sanchez solved the problem by a complex formula.

figures 2 Joe bowled 198, 235, and 246; but Peg's scores were 197, 209, and 237.

fig/sym 3 Read pages 107, 256, and 398 in Finance by Goss & May (4th ed., 1981).

fluency 4 This manual shows both the cost and the quantity of the items on hand.

| 1 | 2 | 3 | 4 | 5 | 6 | 7 | 8 | 9 | 10 | 11 | 12 | 13 | 14 |

242b ▶ 15 Skill-comparison typing

1. Three 2′ writings on ¶ 1; compute *gwam*. Note highest speed typed.

2. Three 2′ writings on ¶ 2; compute *gwam*. Note highest speed typed.

Goal: To equal or exceed on ¶ 2 the highest speed typed on ¶ 1.

all letters used ¶ 1: E | 1.2 si | 5.1 awl | 90% hfw — ¶ 2: D | 1.8 si | 6.3 awl | 70% hfw

Text	gwam 1′	2′	
Almost all companies are in business to make a profit. This means	13	7	55
that a firm must strive to supply goods and services so well that after	28	14	62
all the costs have been paid there will be money remaining which it can	42	21	69
pay to the owners of the firm as a return on the money they invested.	56	28	76
In our economic system, if a business is not run well and does not earn	71	35	84
a profit, it is almost sure to fail. Under these conditions, only the	85	42	91
best and most efficient firms are left to serve the public.	97	48	97
Since efficiency promotes larger profits, every organization is	13	6	56
concerned about productivity. As a key administrative employee, it will	27	14	62
be your function to strive to work efficiently and effectively at all	41	21	69
times. Not only should you maintain a high level of productivity, you	56	28	76
must also be alert to discover new ways to improve the operations of the	70	35	83
office. Improvements lead to greater efficiency which, in turn, leads	84	42	90
to a more profitable business and, perhaps, higher salaries.	96	48	96

gwam 1′ | 1 | 2 | 3 | 4 | 5 | 6 | 7 | 8 | 9 | 10 | 11 | 12 | 13 | 14 |
2′ | 1 | 2 | 3 | 4 | 5 | 6 | 7 |

51d ▶ 13
Type a report about correcting errors

full sheet; line: 70; begin on Line 13; DS the paragraph; indent numbered items 5 spaces from both margins; SS the items but DS between them

GUIDES FOR ERASING ERRORS

TS

Liquid paper, lift-off tape, and the eraser are some of the devices used to correct typing errors. The oldest and most basic of these correction devices is the typewriter eraser. The following guides will help you learn to erase and correct errors neatly:

1. Use a plastic erasing shield, if you have one, and a typewriter (hard) eraser.
2. Lift the paper bail and turn the paper forward (up) if the error is on the upper two thirds of the page or backward (down) if the error is on the lower third of the page.
3. Move the carriage to the left (element to the right) as far as you can if the error is left of center; move the carriage to the right (element to the left) if the error is right of center.
4. Erase lightly--don't "scrub" the error. Blow eraser particles away as you erase.
5. After erasing, return the paper to typing position and type the correction.

52

70-space line

52a ▶ 7
Conditioning practice

Use standard procedure given in 51a, page 81.

alphabet	1	Suzi can equal a track record by jumping twelve feet at the next meet.
fig/sym	2	Check #84 (dated 6/5) for $93 covers Invoice #275 less a 10% discount.
po/op	3	Polly said she saw a copy of a policy report on the open rolltop desk.
fluency	4	He may visit the firm to work with the title forms they handle for me.

| 1 | 2 | 3 | 4 | 5 | 6 | 7 | 8 | 9 | 10 | 11 | 12 | 13 | 14 |

52b ▶ 8 Erase and correct errors

1. Type the sentences *exactly* as shown at the right.

2. Review the erasing guides in 51d, above.

3. Erase and correct each error in your copy.

1 Recognive that the first step in error corretcion is error detection.

2 Always proofreed and correct your errors befoer removing a typed job.

3 Erase and correct aech error so taht the corrections are not visible.

4 Use a typewriter eraser for the orignial, a soft erasre for a carbon.

52c ▶ 35
Learn to type business letters

3 plain sheets; line: 60; date on Line 19

1. Study Style Letter 2 (page 83) illustrating *modified block style, block ¶s, mixed punctuation.* Note the vertical and horizontal placement of letter parts.

2. On plain paper (8½" × 11") type line for line a copy of the letter on page 83.

3. Proofread your copy, mark it for correction, and retype it in final form, correcting all errors.

4. If time permits, type a 2' writing on opening lines (date through salutation); then a 2' writing on closing lines (complimentary close through enclosure notation). If you complete the copy before time is called, start over.

242c ▶ 30
Refine basic skill: straight copy

1. One 5′ writing on ¶s 1–3 combined. Compute *gwam* and errors.

2. Two 1′ guided writings on each ¶.

3. Two 5′ writings on ¶s 1–3 combined. Compute *gwam* and errors. Compare the better of the two scores with those attained on 226b, page 358.

gwam	¼′	½′	¾′	1′
32	8	16	24	32
36	9	18	27	36
40	10	20	30	40
44	11	22	33	44
48	12	24	36	48
52	13	26	39	52
56	14	28	42	56
60	15	30	45	60
64	16	32	48	64
68	17	34	51	68
72	18	36	54	72
76	19	38	57	76
80	20	40	60	80

all letters used | A | 1.5 si 5.7 awl 80% hfw — gwam 5′

A telephone system provides us with a great deal more than verbal 3 59
contact between two points. Our radio and television networks rely 5 61
heavily on telephone service. By the use of telephone wires, it is 8 64
possible to send radio and television shows from the point of origin 11 67
to far and remote spots. If we did not have this service, many people 14 70
would not be able to enjoy national sports contests such as the Super 16 72
Bowl or important events such as a special address by the President. 19 75

A special portable telephone which is known as the data phone 22 78
serves many useful purposes. This phone can be used by a doctor to 24 80
send data from the bedside of a patient to laboratories or specialists 27 83
for immediate analysis. This telephone can also be used to obtain in- 30 86
formation from centralized data banks of all types. When tied in with 33 89
a computer, the telephone can be used to process data and to solve many 36 92
complex problems. 37 93

You will find a variety of telephonic devices in a business office. 39 95
Correspondence, reports, and documents of all kinds can be sent from 42 98
place to place by use of a telefax machine. Telephone answering 45 100
sets, which record messages on tape, can be used to answer the phone 47 103
when no one is present. Equipment of this type can also be used 50 106
by out-of-town sales agents to report and record sales. Similar 52 108
devices are used by executives to dictate material to a central word 55 111
processing center. 56 112

gwam 5′ | 1 | 2 | 3 |

243

243a ▶ 5
Conditioning practice

Use standard directions given in 242a, p. 379.

alphabet 1 The joint executive board will analyze their request for more parking.

figures 2 Check pages 45, 73, 86, and 92 in the 1980-1981 edition of the manual.

fig/sym 3 She wrote checks for $2,179, $82.87, $61.50, $2.95, $63.41, and $8.94.

fluency 4 She may work with me to plan the theme for the big spring floral show.

| 1 | 2 | 3 | 4 | 5 | 6 | 7 | 8 | 9 | 10 | 11 | 12 | 13 | 14 |

51a ▶ 7 Conditioning practice

each line twice SS (slowly, then faster); DS between 2-line groups; if time permits, retype selected lines

alphabet	1	Jen can get five quiet days off, for she works extra at my plaza club.
figures	2	Of 1,303 persons who took the test in 1982, 847 passed and 456 failed.
er/re	3	All three of them were there for the reading of the terms of her sale.
fluency	4	I wish to do the work so the girls may go with them to make the signs.

| 1 | 2 | 3 | 4 | 5 | 6 | 7 | 8 | 9 | 10 | 11 | 12 | 13 | 14 |

51b ▶ 10 Improve technique: machine parts

each set of lines twice SS; DS between 4-line groups

Lines 1–2: Clear tab stops; from left margin, set a tab stop 30 spaces to the right; set another tab stop 30 spaces beyond the first one.

tab and return	1	for me —tab→ is due —tab→ he may
	2	the forms city firm she works
space bar	3	if so | he or she | but it is | pay for it | a key map | fix the bus | she may cut
	4	If we are to take a cut in pay, the hours of work should be cut, also.
shift keys	5	Luisa and Andres | Michi and Sumio | Lu-yin and San-li | Kermit and Drucilla
	6	Sumio and Luisa beat Drucilla and Michi in the tournament in San Juan.
shift lock	7	The USPS did expand the old ZIP Code to 9 digits (45227-1021) in 1981.
	8	Special notations, such as PERSONAL and REGISTERED, are typed in CAPS.

| 1 | 2 | 3 | 4 | 5 | 6 | 7 | 8 | 9 | 10 | 11 | 12 | 13 | 14 |

51c ▶ 20 Improve keystroking skill: guided writing

1. A 1′ writing on ¶ 1; determine *gwam*. Add 2–4 words to set a new goal.
2. Two 1′ writings on ¶ 1 at your new goal rate, guided by ¼′ guide call.
3. Type ¶ 2 in the same way.
4. A 2′ writing on ¶ 1, then on ¶ 2. If you finish a ¶ before time is called, begin retyping it.
5. A 3′ writing on ¶s 1–2 combined; determine *gwam*.

gwam	¼′	½′	¾′	1′
20	5	10	15	20
24	6	12	18	24
28	7	14	21	28
32	8	16	24	32
36	9	18	27	36
40	10	20	30	40
44	11	22	33	44
48	12	24	36	48
52	13	26	39	52

all letters used | A | 1.5 si | 5.7 awl | 80% hfw |

	gwam 2′	3′
How will you know that you have learned to type a business letter?	7	5
First, you will be able to position all items of the seven basic parts	14	9
in the proper sequence. You will demonstrate that you know the exact	21	14
number of vertical spaces to leave between the various parts, too. You	28	19
will also demonstrate that you know the right horizontal placement of	35	23
each item that is positioned according to a specified layout guide.	42	28
As soon as you have demonstrated the ability to sequence, space,	7	32
and place every letter part properly, you will also learn how to judge	14	37
letter length, to set the margin stops accordingly, and to use appropri-	21	42
ate spacing in the top and bottom margins. Finally, you will demonstrate	28	47
that you can type, proofread, and correct the copy so that it will make	35	51
a good impression on the person who will receive and read the letter.	42	56

gwam 2′ | 1 | 2 | 3 | 4 | 5 | 6 | 7 |
3′ | 1 | 2 | 3 | 4 | 5 |

243b ▶ 15
Refine skill transfer

Type two 1′ writings on each sentence: first for speed; second, for control. Compute *gwam*.

straight copy 1 She says that both of them show a special aptitude for this work.

rough draft 2 The price ~~cost~~ of this item ~~the merchandise~~ will depend upon ~~on~~ the quantity ~~amount~~ she desires ~~orders~~.

statistical 3 The index rose 18.7 points on June 25 and 46.9 points on July 30.

straight copy 4 I told the two workers to throw the bushels of corn on the truck.

rough draft 5 He plans to take ~~make~~ a spedail inventory ~~count~~ today of all items ~~goods~~ in stock ~~the store~~.

statistical 6 On May 16, I ordered Item 4197; on July 23, I received Item 4806.

243c ▶ 30
Refine basic skill: rough-draft copy

1. One 5′ writing on ¶s 1–3 combined. Compute *gwam* and errors.

2. A 1′ writing on each ¶ for speed; then type a 1′ writing on each ¶ for control.

3. Two 5′ writings on ¶s 1–3 combined. Compute *gwam* and errors. Compare better of the two scores with those attained on 226c, page 359.

all letters used | A | 1.5 si | 5.7 awl | 80% hfw

gwam 1′ | 5′

DS

The telephone is the most widely used instrument ~~equipment~~ for 11 2
communication in a business office. As an employee in an 22 4
office, you will be asked to make and answer many kinds of 34 7
phone calls daily. How effective you are in using the 45 9
phone depends to a large extent upon how well your callers 57 11
raect to you and comprehend you. It is vital, therefore, 68 14
that you master the proper techniques for using the tele- 80 16
phone. 81 17

using the telephone is not a very difficult task. Talk ~~You~~ 11 18
~~speak~~ directly into the reciever in your normal tone; it is 22 21
not necessary to shout. Speak naturally, but emphasize ~~stress~~ your 34 23
~~key~~ ideas by the use of inflection, by stressing key ~~main~~ 44 25
words and phrases, and by varying the rate ~~speed~~ at which you 55 27
talk ~~speak~~. Speak simply; donot confuse the other person ~~caller~~ with techni- 68 30
cal jargon. 84 33

Your telephone manner is just as important ~~vital~~ as ~~is~~ your 10 35
voice. If you wish to impress your callers, you should be 22 37
pleasant, courteous ~~friendly~~, and helpful. You must show ~~display~~ a sin- 33 40
cere interest in the inquiries ~~questions~~ and ideas of your callers. 45 42
You must be a good listener as well as an good ~~interesting~~ 54 44
conversationalist. ~~speaker~~. Using the phone is not just a routine task ~~job~~. You 68 47
can help build valuable goodwill for your company ~~organization~~ if 78 49
you use it properly ~~correctly~~. 82 50

Since you cannot be seen, you must make the best use of your voice.

phase 3 lessons 51-75

Learn to arrange and type personal/business papers

People who learn to type for personal use often use the skill for a part-time job in a club, school, or business office. There they must arrange and type papers of various kinds—letters, envelopes, reports being the most common. It is important, then, that you learn these basic applications.

In the 25 lessons of Phase 3, you will:

1. Learn to arrange and type business letters in one of the commonly used styles.

2. Learn to type reports—with as well as without footnotes.

3. Learn to arrange and type tables for personal and business uses.

4. Continue to improve your basic typing skills.

unit 10 lessons 51-56

Learn to type business letters

Learning goals

1. To learn to type business letters and envelopes.

2. To learn to erase and correct errors.

3. To learn to prepare and correct carbon copies.

4. To improve keystroking speed and control.

Machine adjustments

1. Paper guide at *0*.

2. Ribbon control to type on top half of ribbon.

3. Margin sets: 70-space line (center − 35; center + 35 + 5) unless otherwise directed.

4. Line-space selector on *1* (SS) for drills, on *2* (DS) for paragraphs; as directed for problems.

244

244a ▶ 5 Conditioning practice

Use standard directions given in 242a, p. 379.

alphabet	1	Maybe the experts realized we can judge the value of the unique books.
figures	2	In 1981, they produced 432,564 units as compared with 265,737 in 1980.
fig/sym	3	The single discount equivalent of 33 1/3%, 10%, and 2 1/2% is 41 1/2%.
fluency	4	He may go with them when they cycle to the lake if he is not too busy.

| 1 | 2 | 3 | 4 | 5 | 6 | 7 | 8 | 9 | 10 | 11 | 12 | 13 | 14 |

244b ▶ 30 Refine basic skill: statistical copy

1. One 5′ writing on ¶s 1–3 combined. Compute *gwam* and errors.

2. A 1′ writing on each ¶ for speed; then, type a 1′ writing on each ¶ for control.

3. Two 5′ writings on ¶s 1–3 combined. Compute *gwam* and errors. Compare better of the two scores with those attained on 226d, page 360.

gwam	¼′	½′	¾′	1′
32	8	16	24	32
36	9	18	27	36
40	10	20	30	40
44	11	22	33	44
48	12	24	36	48
52	13	26	39	52
56	14	28	42	56
60	15	30	45	60
64	16	32	48	64
68	17	34	51	68
72	18	36	54	72
76	19	38	57	76
80	20	40	60	80

all letters and figures used | A | 1.5 si | 5.7 awl | 80% hfw |

	gwam 5′	
The vision of a means of voice communication over great distances	3	51
was realized with the invention of the telephone in 1876. In 1878, the	6	54
first telephone exchange was opened, and action was taken in 1900 to	8	57
connect the various city exchanges that had been set up. The first	11	60
coast-to-coast telephone call was made in 1915, and by 1970 there were	14	63
105 million phones in the United States with 628 million miles of wire.	17	66
In 1920, the first public radio program started a new era of voice	19	68
communication. By 1922, close to 600 radio stations were on the air;	22	71
and in 1926, the first coast-to-coast service was begun with a network	25	74
of 25 stations. By 1970, just 50 years after the first broadcast, there	28	78
were 4,898 radio stations in the nation serving more than 63 million	31	80
homes and over 96% of all families in America.	33	82
The telephone and radio were combined as early as 1915 to send the	35	84
spoken word over 3,000 miles. It was not until 1927, though, that pub-	38	87
lic service had begun. By 1950, a total of 60 radiotelephone nets were	41	90
in use which linked America with over 90 other nations. Today, a series	44	93
of satellites that hover 22,000 miles over set spots on the equator pro-	47	96
vide verbal contact with most parts of the globe.	49	98

gwam 5′ | 1 | 2 | 3 |

50b ▶ 12 Measure statistical-copy skill

1. A 1′ writing on each ¶; determine *gwam* and number of errors on each. Record the better *gwam*.

2. Two 3′ writings on ¶s 1–2 combined; determine *gwam* and number of errors on each. Record the better *gwam*.

1′ goal: At least 19 *gwam*.
3′ goal: At least 17 *gwam*.

all figures used | A | 1.5 si | 5.7 awl | 80% hfw |

gwam 1′ | 3′

Immigration to the United States is limited to 290,000 11 4
people a year. This ceiling is divided into an annual limit 23 8
of 170,000 for the eastern and 120,000 for the western hemi- 35 12
sphere. Within each of these groups there is a further limit 48 16
of 20,000 people for each country (P.L. 94-571, 1976). 58 19

To apply to become a naturalized citizen of the United 11 23
States, an immigrant must be at least 18 years old. He or 23 27
she must have been a legal resident of this country on a con- 35 31
tinuous basis for 5 years. For spouses of citizens, this 47 35
requirement is merely 3 years in most instances. 56 38

gwam 1′ | 1 | 2 | 3 | 4 | 5 | 6 | 7 | 8 | 9 | 10 | 11 | 12 |
3′ | 1 | 2 | 3 | 4 |

50c ▶ 32 Check letter typing skill

2 letterheads [LM pp. 43-46] or plain full sheets; line: 50; return address on Line 16; address small envelopes

Problem 1

Type the letter given at the right and address an envelope. Be guided by the bell as a signal to complete or divide words and return.

Problem 2

Proofread your typed copy, mark errors for correction, and retype the letter from your rough draft if time permits.

words

1764 Seminole 3
Detroit, MI 48214-1367 8
April 15, 19-- 11

Miss Sophie Palmer 14
4857 Van Dyke 17
Detroit, MI 48214-1539 22

Dear Sophie 24

As president of our Business Education Club, let me congratulate 37
you on winning first place in the Metropolitan Typewriting 49
Contest last week. 53

All the club members know that your excellent performance was 66
made possible only by long, hard hours of practice. That 77
personal investment really paid off. 85

We're proud of you for the honor you have earned for yourself, 97
for our club, and for our school. 104

Cordially 106

Gary M. Badowski 110/132

244c ▶ 15
Refine skill transfer

1. Three 1′ writings on each ¶. Compute *gwam* on best writing.

2. Determine percent of transfer from ¶ 1 to ¶ 2 and ¶ 1 to ¶ 3 (See Direction 2 in 245b, below).

3. Type additional 1′ writings on ¶s 2 and 3 to increase percent of transfer as time permits.

LA	1.4 si	5.4 awl	85% hfw

gwam 1′

There is no question that the automobile is the most popu- 12
lar form of transportation in the United States today. Less 24
than a hundred years ago, though, the bicycle was one of the 36
principal means of transportation. At the turn of the century, 49
more than a million bicycles were built in this country each 61
year. It was the great use of bicycles that led to a cry for 73
better roads. 76

When [people] ~~customers~~ began to buy and use [automobiles] ~~cars~~, the demand for 12
bicycles began to [drop] ~~decrease~~. [For that reason] ~~As a result~~, there were very few 25
bicycles [made] ~~sold~~ in this country for [a number of] ~~many, many~~ years. After the 37
[second] ~~days of~~ World War ~~II~~, though, the [use] ~~sales~~ of [the] bicycles grew until 49
today more than five million are made [each year] ~~annually~~. Dispite that 62
fact, though, cars outnumber bikes by more than [a] 2-to-1 margin. 76

The increase in the use of the automobile through the 11
years has been amazing. In 1900, 4,192 passenger cars were 23
sold. By 1920, a mere 20 years later, this number had risen 35
to 1,905,560. In 1940, the number grew to 3,717,385; in 1960, 48
sales had risen to 6,674,796; and, in 1980, sales were well 60
over 9,500,000 automobiles--an increase of more than 50% in a 72
period of just 20 years. 77

245

245a ▶ 5
Conditioning practice

Use standard directions given in 242a, p. 379.

alphabet 1 Wise executives will analyze the facts before passing quick judgments.
figures 2 Read the material underlined on pages 18, 23, 49, 65, 70, 85, and 129.
fig/sym 3 On May 17, she paid the interest on $3,895 for 40 days at 6% ($25.97).
fluency 4 He named a special panel to study the problem of the acid in the lake.

| 1 | 2 | 3 | 4 | 5 | 6 | 7 | 8 | 9 | 10 | 11 | 12 | 13 | 14 |

245b ▶ 45
Refine skill transfer

1. Type a 5′ writing on each of these exercises:
p. 380, 242c, straight copy
p. 381, 243c, rough draft
p. 382, 244b, statistical

2. Compute percent of transfer: Divide straight copy *gwam* INTO *gwam* on rough-draft copy and statistical copy.

Your percent-of-transfer goals are shown below:
Rough draft 70–90%
Statistical copy 65–85%

3. As time permits, type additional 5′ writings on selected copy to increase your percent of transfer.

49d ▶ 22

Check report typing skill

full sheet; line: 60; heading on Line 10 (1½" top margin); DS (double spacing)

Listen for bell as signal to complete or divide words and return.

Abbreviations such as U.S. and N.Y. are typed solid (without internal spacing).

words

THE UNITED STATES PASSPORT 5

More than six million U.S. citizens travel each year in other 18
countries. To be admitted into many countries, a passport is 30
required. A passport is an official document issued by the U.S. 43
Department of State that identifies you by photograph and a brief 56
description as a U.S. citizen. A passport permits you to leave and 70
to return to the United States. 77

To apply for your first passport, you must appear in person 89
at one of the passport agencies. These agencies are often located 102
in local federal buildings. You must present the following 114
papers:* 116

1. The completed passport application. 124
2. Proof of U.S. citizenship (a birth certificate or a 135
certificate of naturalization, usually). 144
3. Proof of identification bearing your signature and 155
description (often a driver's license). 163
4. Two signed duplicate photographs taken by a 174
photographer within the past six months. 185
5. The required passport fee. 192

A passport is valid for five years from date of issue. When 204
you receive your passport, you should sign it and fill in the 216
information requested on the inside cover. During foreign 228
travel, always carry your passport on your person; NEVER leave 241
it in a hotel room. 244

________________ 248

*The World Almanac & Book of Facts 1981. 264

50

60-space line

50a ▶ 6

Conditioning practice

each line twice SS (slowly, then faster); DS between 2-line groups; if time permits, retype selected lines

alphabet 1 Marquis has just solved the exciting new puzzle from Byke's.

fig/sym 2 She filed the invoice (#9304) and the contract (#17-48-562).

fluency 3 He lent the field auditor a hand with the work for the firm.

| 1 | 2 | 3 | 4 | 5 | 6 | 7 | 8 | 9 | 10 | 11 | 12 |

unit **49** lessons 246-250

Measure basic/ production skills

Measurement goals

1. To demonstrate improvement in speed and accuracy in typing straight-copy material of average difficulty.

2. To demonstrate improvement in production rates in typing letters, reports, tables, and business forms.

Machine adjustments

1. Line: 70 for drills; as necessary for problems.

2. Spacing: SS sentence drills with a DS between sentence groups; DS timed writings; space problems as directed or necessary.

246-247

246a-247a ▶ 5 Conditioning practice

each line twice SS (slowly, then faster); DS between 2-line groups; if time permits, retype selected lines

alphabet	1	Peggy Black was amazed when she qualified to serve as an expert judge.
figures	2	The fraction 15/16 equals .9375; 11/32 is .34375, and 3/64 is .046875.
fig/sym	3	A teaspoon = 5 milliliters (ml); 1 tablespoon = 15 ml; 1 cup = 250 ml.
fluency	4	Can the city auditor block the proxy sale of the land to the attorney?

| 1 | 2 | 3 | 4 | 5 | 6 | 7 | 8 | 9 | 10 | 11 | 12 | 13 | 14 |

246b-247b ▶ 15 Measure basic skill: straight copy

1. Two 5′ writings on ¶s 1–3 combined.

2. Compute *gwam* and errors on better writing. Compare with scores achieved on 226b, page 358.

all letters used | A | 1.5 si | 5.7 awl | 80% hfw |

	gwam 1′	5′	
Many changes are being made in the modern office as a result of	13	3	58
technological advances in equipment and methods. The use of the com-	27	5	61
puter continues to grow by leaps and bounds because of its ability to	41	8	64
process figures with amazing speed and accuracy. In a matter of sec-	54	11	66
onds or minutes the computer can process numerical data which, in the	68	14	69
past, took hours or days. These data, in turn, help people to make	82	16	72
judgments or decisions which a computer is unable to do.	93	19	74
New equipment is also available that will improve the processing of	14	21	77
words. Included are typewriters which permit a person to correct errors	28	24	80
and make changes when or after the copy is typed. Magnetic cards or	42	27	83
tapes record the copy as it is typed; errors can be corrected merely by	56	30	86
backspacing and typing the correct data. When the material has been com-	71	33	88
pleted, the keyboard operator can put paper in the machine, press a but-	85	36	91
ton, and the copy will be typed at a high rate of speed with no errors.	100	39	94
Most types of new equipment for processing figures and words have one	14	41	97
thing in common--they are operated through the use of a typewriter key-	28	44	100
board. Although these keyboards may not be identical, the location of	42	47	103
the letter keys is almost always the same. As a result, a typist can	56	50	105
learn to run one of these new machines with little or no difficulty.	70	53	108
Thus, the machines open new horizons for the speedy and accurate typist.	85	56	111

gwam 1′ | 1 | 2 | 3 | 4 | 5 | 6 | 7 | 8 | 9 | 10 | 11 | 12 | 13 | 14 |
5′ | 1 | 2 | 3 |

unit **9** lessons 49-50

Measure your skills: basic/applied

Performance goals

Goals (to be supplied by your teacher) include: 1′ straight-copy goal; 3′ straight-copy goal; 3′ statistical-copy goal; time-limit goals for completing problems: centered announcement, report, letters.

Machine adjustments

1. Paper guide at *0*.

2. Ribbon control to type on top half of ribbon.

3. Margin sets: 60-space line (center − 30; center + 30 + allowance for bell).

4. Line-space selector on *1* (SS) for drills; on *2* (DS) for ¶s; as directed for problems.

49

60-space line

49a ▶ 6 Conditioning practice

each line twice SS (slowly, then faster); DS between 2-line groups; if time permits, retype selected lines

alphabet 1 Ella may have Jack retype parts two and six of the big quiz.

fig/sym 2 I'm told 17% of them make $849.25 a month; 83% make $826.50.

fluency 3 I did rush the die to shape the auto panels to the big firm.

| 1 | 2 | 3 | 4 | 5 | 6 | 7 | 8 | 9 | 10 | 11 | 12 |

49b ▶ 12 Measure straight-copy skill

1. A 1′ writing on each ¶; determine *gwam* and number of errors on each. Record the better *gwam*.

2. Two 3′ writings on ¶ 1–2 combined; determine *gwam* and number of errors on each. Record the better *gwam*.

1′ goal: At least 24 *gwam*.
3′ goal: At least 21 *gwam*.

all letters used | A | 1.5 si | 5.7 awl | 80% hfw |

	gwam 1′	3′
It is a satisfying feeling to be a winner. Every person	11	4
prefers to serve on a winning team. Although the prize might	24	8
not be worth either the time or effort involved, the desire to	36	12
excel may justify both. Realize that team members must meet	48	16
the requirements for a winning exhibition each time they play.	61	20
An office work force is a team, also; and the same basic	11	24
principles apply there as apply on an athletic field. A major	24	28
difference, however, is that in the office the rewards are in-	36	32
creased pay and promotions instead of trophies and letters.	48	36
Winning is fun on any team, but winning takes effort from all.	61	41

gwam 1′ | 1 | 2 | 3 | 4 | 5 | 6 | 7 | 8 | 9 | 10 | 11 | 12 |
3′ | 1 | 2 | 3 | 4 |

49c ▶ 10 Check centering skill

1. Center and type the announcement vertically on a half sheet; center each line horizontally.

2. Proofread and mark errors for correction.

3. Retype problem from your rough draft if time permits.

	words
BUSINESS EDUCATION CLUB	5
will see	7
Richard Holland, Typewriting Champion	14
demonstrate championship techniques	21
Student Union	24
Friday, December 9, 3 p.m.	29

246c ▶ 30
Premeasurement drills: correspondence and forms

1. Type the problems as quickly as possible. Correct errors as you type.

2. When completed, check each problem carefully for errors in stroking and format.

Goal: To complete the 3 problems correctly in the time alloted.

Problem 1
Average-length letter
plain full sheet; modified block style

Type the letter to the attention of **Mrs. Nancy Houlton, Controller, Lamar Industries, Inc., 802 Walker Street, Houston, TX 77002-7767.** Date the letter **February 8, 19--**; provide an appropriate salutation and complimentary close. Use the company name **JEFFERSON WHOLESALERS, INC.** in the closing lines. The letter will be signed by **Ms. Helen C. Williams,** who is the **Marketing Manager.**

words

opening lines 29

(¶ 1) Are you looking for ways to speed your operations and decrease your 42
administrative costs? If so, please consider the new Model X21 Jefferson 57
Calculator. 60

(¶ 2) The Model X21 is a fully automatic calculator which offers amazing 73
shortcuts in payroll calculations, percentages, invoicing, and discounts. It 89
speeds the computation of taxes, interest, inventory, and engineering prob- 104
lems of all kinds. 108

(¶ 3) Enclosed is our catalog describing this amazing new calculator and other 122
quality business machines and equipment we offer. Please call us collect for 138
any further information you may like to have. 147

closing lines 166

Problem 2
Interoffice memorandum [LM p. 33]

Type the memo to **Paul C. Roberts, Chief of Administration,** from **Martha K. Barnes, Purchasing Clerk.** Date the memo **June 24, 19--,** and use the subject: **Invoice 94821-A.**

opening lines 21

(¶ 1) Enclosed is a copy of our Purchase Order 94821-A 31
which has been prepared in response to your Purchase 42
Requisition 241 of June 2. 47
(¶ 2) In preparing this purchase order, we had to 56
make several substitutions. Will you please check 66
the items ordered to insure that they will meet 76
your needs and return the purchase order to me 85
as quickly as possible. 90

closing lines 92

Problem 3
Purchase order [LM p. 33]

PURCHASE ORDER NO. 94821-A 2

TO: National Business Forms, Inc.
8720 Colesville Road
Silver Spring, MD 20910-7232

DATE June 24, 19-- 10
15
TERMS Net 21

SHIP VIA UPS 22

QUANTITY	CAT NO.	DESCRIPTION	PRICE	TOTAL	
6	721231	Automatic paper shredders	79.70	478.20	32
50	424950	Plastic ring binders,			38
		8 1/2″ × 11″	2.40	120.00	43
10 bxs.	305476	Kraft envelopes, heavy-duty			52
		w/metal clasp, 10″ × 15″	14.64	146.40	59
10	960000	Portable cassette recorders	86.50	865.00	71
				1,609.60	73

48c ▶ 10 Improve typewriting techniques

each line twice SS (slowly, then faster); DS between 2-line groups

Technique goals

- fingers curved, upright
- finger-action stroking; hands and arms quiet
- wrists low and relaxed
- quick down-in spacing
- shift-type-release without wasting time
- swift return and quick start of new line
- eyes on book copy as you return

all letters/figures used

balanced-hand	1	If they make such a visit, it may end a fight for the title.
combination	2	It was then up to us to set the right rate on the big crate.
double-letter	3	I need to use a little more effort to boost my typing skill.
3d row	4	A superior figure should follow the quote if they quote her.
3d/1st rows	5	Zubin directed a plumbing project next to the valve company.
adjacent-key	6	Violet reads the meters on the oil heaters in the warehouse.
outside-reach	7	Zoe won a quick game of croquet from Shep and amazed us all.
direct-reach	8	My group collected a large sum for her musical concert fund.
fig/sym	9	Issue #3 was rejected by 50,375 (64%) of the voters in 1982.
fig/sym	10	"Don't be surprised," he said, "if O'Toole & Sons hits $50."

| 1 | 2 | 3 | 4 | 5 | 6 | 7 | 8 | 9 | 10 | 11 | 12 |

48d ▶ 20 Type personal-business letters

2 letterheads [LM pp. 37-40] or 2 plain full sheets
line: 50; SS;
return address on Line 16;
address small envelopes

Problem 1

Type the letter given at the right, using the bell as a signal to complete or divide words and return. Leave correct spacing between letter parts.

Problem 2

Proofread your copy, using proofreader's marks to indicate needed corrections. If time permits, type another copy of the letter from your marked copy.

	words
One Ridge Court	3
Evanston, IL 60202-3542	8
November 26, 19--	12
Ms. Nina Ziegler, Chairperson	18
Foreign Exchange Committee	23
Rotary, International	28
1600 Ridge Avenue	31
Evanston, IL 60201-3475	36
Dear Ms. Ziegler	40
Here are my completed application forms for a Rotary Founda-	52
tion Scholarship to study one year in a European country.	63
I would especially like to study in Germany. As my application	76
indicates, my minor course of study is German. My career goal	89
is to become a medical doctor, and I am told that fluency in	101
German might prove beneficial during training.	111
Further, I toured Germany with my family last year, and I en-	123
joyed the country and its people very much.	132
Sincerely yours	135
Kathryn Kirkland	138/**174**

Enrichment material appears on LM p. 42.

Preparation for Measurement

Listed at the right are appropriate review/practice materials to prepare you for measurement in Lessons 49–50.

1. *Centering*: Do Step 4 of 32c, p. 53.

2. *Personal note*: Do Step 1 of 41d, p. 66.

3. *Report*: Do 44b, p. 70.

4. *Personal-business letter*: Do Step 2 of 44c, p. 70.

5. *Basic skill*: Select drills and timed writings from previous lessons for practice.

247c ▶ 30
Premeasurement drills: reports and table

3 full sheets

1. Type the problems as quickly as possible. Correct errors as you type.

2. When completed, check each problem carefully for errors in stroking and format.

Goal: To complete the 3 problems correctly in the time allotted.

Problem 1
Topbound report with side headings and footnote

Use as a main heading: **THE CHALLENGE OF PROMOTING HUMAN RESOURCES** and the following side headings:

¶ 1: **A Human Resources Department**
¶ 2: **Organization**
¶ 3: **Purpose**

Problem 2
Page 2 of a leftbound report with footnote

Type the final ¶ and the footnote in Problem 1 as the second page of a leftbound report. Do *not* type the side heading for the ¶.

Total words: 89.

Note: Type the footnote so that there will be a bottom margin of approximately one inch.

words

main heading 9

side heading 20

In ~~the middle~~ June of this year, ~~we set up~~ Comex Industries established an important new 34

managerial ~~office~~ entity designated as the Human Resources Depart- 45

ment to bring together the ~~vital~~ key corporat~~ion~~e functions ~~that are~~ 56

~~responsible for~~ which affect people: our employees, our customers, and 68

those in the communities in which we ~~function~~ operate. 77

side heading 82

The new Human Resources Department includes the follow- 93

ing Sections: Labor Relations, ~~Consumer~~ Customer Relations, Personnel, 106

Safety, Medi~~a~~cal, and Government ~~Relations~~ Liaison. 114

side heading 117

This new department was ~~set up~~ established because we ~~believe~~ feel that 128

these functions, although discrete, have many interrelated 140

~~purposes~~ objectives and tasks. Putting them under "one umbrella," we 152

are convinced, will provide the leadership and ~~forces~~ impetus to deal 165

effectively with the numerous ~~vital~~ significant problems in the ~~arena~~ area of 178

human resources.* 182

rule 185

*For a discussion of our efforts to meet the challenge of 197

promoting environment~~~~al resources, see page 9. 206

Problem 3
Table

Center the table horizontally and vertically in reading position; DS the items. Decide intercolumn spacing.

COMEX INDUSTRIES, INC. 5

Net Foreign Sales for First Half of 19-- 13

(In millions) 16

Month	Canada	South America	Europe	
				28
January	23.5	14.2	51.6	33
February	21.2	12.3	52.7	38
March	22.9	13.5	53.8	42
April	24.1	14.9	55.7	46
May	25.3	15.0	55.9	50
June	25.8	15.4	56.3	54

47d ▶ 20
Type personal letters

2 plain full sheets;
line: 50; SS;
date on Line 20;
in body of letters, listen for bell as signal to complete or divide words and return carriage (element)

Problem 1

Leave 3 blank line spaces (QS) between the date and the salutation. DS between ¶s. Proofread your completed letter and circle your errors.

words

November 18, 19-- 4

Dear Marcella 6

On December 18, our Music/Drama Club is sponsoring a special 19
event, "Holiday Sounds," at Emory Center. Instrumental, vocal, 31
and dramatic selections are to be featured. 40

Even though I have only a minor role, I'd like to know that you are 54
in the audience applauding our performance. I really hope that 67
you can be here for the holidays and that you will come to see our 80
show. 82

I have a super ticket for you. And your good friend, Kevin, will 95
see that you're properly escorted. We hope to see you on the 18th 108
and throughout the holiday season. 115

Cordially 117

Problem 2

Use Problem 1 directions.

November 23, 19-- 4

Dear Cory 6

Thank you for inviting me to your "special event" on December 18
18. Having been a part of your group for two years, I wouldn't 31
miss it! 33

Our holiday break begins December 12. I have a report to com- 45
plete here before I leave, but I should be home no later than the 58
15th. 60

It will be great to see all of you do your theatrics. Perhaps there 74
will be time for some skiing, too. See you soon. 84

Sincerely 86

48

60-space line

48a ▶ 6
Conditioning practice

each line twice SS (slowly, then faster);
DS between 2-line groups;
if time permits, type each line again

alphabet 1 Jinx Maze worked to improve the quality of her basic typing.

fig/sym 2 Please see "Think Metric!" in Vol. 47, No. 12 (pp. 598-603).

fluency 3 When did the field auditor sign the audit form for the city?

| 1 | 2 | 3 | 4 | 5 | 6 | 7 | 8 | 9 | 10 | 11 | 12 |

48b ▶ 14
Compose as you type

full sheet; DS;
line: 60

Read the 2 ¶s of 46c, p. 74; then summarize in a short paragraph what the message means to you as a typist.

1. List the points you wish to make.

2. Compose your message as you type.

As you compose, x-out and immediately retype any words in which you make errors.

248-250

248a-250a ▶ 5 Conditioning practice

Use standard directions given in 246a–247a, p. 384.

alphabet	1	The judge observed as the expert workers quickly froze the boned meat.
figures	2	Items 16, 35, 46, 70, 78, 90, 92, and 208 were sold on June 14 and 15.
fig/sym	3	The TV was sold for $479 less discounts of 33 1/3% and 25% or $239.50.
fluency	4	It is time for the tour bus to take the women to the park in the city.

| 1 | 2 | 3 | 4 | 5 | 6 | 7 | 8 | 9 | 10 | 11 | 12 | 13 | 14 |

248b ▶ 45 Measure production skill: correspondence

1. Type problems at the right and at the top of page 388 for 30′; correct errors as you type. If you finish all problems before time is called, start over.

2. After time is called, go over each page carefully and circle any errors you did not correct. Compute *o-pram* (Office Production Rate a Minute). Compare score with that attained on 227b, page 361.

Problem 1
Short letter

plain full sheet; modified block, mixed

Type the letter to **Cooperman, Reilly, and Barker,** who are **Attorneys-at-Law** located at **1400 Investors Building, 733 Marquette Avenue, Minneapolis, MN 55402-2318** to the attention of **Mr. Patrick Reilly.** Date the letter **May 23, 19--;** use an appropriate salutation and complimentary close. The letter will be signed by **Marcus H. Windham,** who is the **Treasurer** of **Midwestern Industries, Inc.** Use the company name in the closing lines.

words

opening lines 38

Enclosed is a draft copy of the prospectus we have pre- 49
pared for the issue of stock planned for the beginning of 60
our next fiscal year. 65

Will you please check this prospectus very carefully to 76
insure that it is legally correct and proper in every respect. 89

Since our deadline for submitting this prospectus to 99
the printer is June 15, may we have your comments and any 111
corrections at the earliest possible date. 119

closing lines 137

Problem 2
Interoffice memorandum
[LM p. 35]

Type the memorandum to **Marcus H. Windham, Treasurer,** from **Mary C. Babcock, Controller,** dated **May 17, 19--** Subject: **Sale of Securities.**

opening lines 18

The Securiteis and Exchange commission (SEC), which 28
~~carefully watches~~ closely monitors the Securities and Financial markets, has 40
~~decreed~~ ruled that a ~~firm~~ company may ~~dispose of~~ sell up to $100,000 of it s 50
securities ~~in~~ within a year with out registering the sale with that 63
Agency. ¶ The securities to be sold, ~~though~~ however can not be of- 75
fered or sold through general advertiseing or solicitation. 87
Further, the Company can not have more than 100 beneficial 99
~~stock holders~~ owners of shares and the securities sold must be ~~kept~~ held for at 111
least ~~a period of~~ two years. 114

~~Inasmuch as~~ Since we ~~now~~ currently have more than 100 beneficial owners 126
of shares, our proposed stock issue doesnot fall under the~~se~~ 138
provisions of this new ruling. 144

Problem 3 is on the next page.

46c ▶ 20 Improve keystroking skill: guided writing

60-space line

1. A 1′ writing on ¶ 1; determine *gwam*.
2. Add 4 *gwam* to set a new goal rate.
3. Two 1′ writings on ¶ 1, trying to maintain your goal rate each ¼ minute.
4. Type ¶ 2 in the same way.
5. A 2′ unguided writing on ¶ 1; if you complete ¶ before time is called, start over.
6. A 2′ writing on ¶ 2 in the same way.
7. A 3′ writing on ¶s 1–2 combined; determine *gwam*.

all letters used | LA | 1.4 si | 5.4 awl | 85% hfw

	gwam 2′	3′
Those who have pencils but no erasers can never make a	5	4
mistake. They must never, of course, try anything of great	11	8
importance either. Don't be ashamed of making an error now	17	12
and then, but try not to make the same one again and again.	23	16
Follow this excellent rule to become a careful worker.	29	19
As you try to develop your typing power, you will make	5	23
quite a few errors when you try out new or improved methods	11	27
of stroking. Just as in other skills, though, many of your	17	31
errors will fall away as you further your ability. Realize,	23	35
also, that even the best workers often need an eraser.	29	39

gwam 2′ | 1 | 2 | 3 | 4 | 5 | 6 |
3′ | 1 | 2 | 3 | 4 |

47 — 60-space line

47a ▶ 6 Conditioning practice

each line twice SS (slowly, then faster); DS between 2-line groups; if time permits, type each line again

alphabet 1 Dirk Bux can have a jeweler size my antique ring to fit Peg.

fig/sym 2 My policy (#L-48356-G) for $50,000 was paid up May 27, 1982.

fluency 3 They risk a big penalty if they throw a fight for the title.

| 1 | 2 | 3 | 4 | 5 | 6 | 7 | 8 | 9 | 10 | 11 | 12 |

47b ▶ 14 Improve keystroking skill: guided writing

Repeat Steps 1–4 and 7 of 46c, above.

Goal: 2 *gwam* increase.

47c ▶ 10 Learn to compose as you type

plain sheet; line: 60; DS

Type the sentences at the right, filling in the missing information. X-out and immediately retype words in which you make errors.

1 **My full name is** (first, middle, last).

2 **I live in** (names of city and state).

3 **My address is** (house number and street name or route number).

4 **My telephone number is** (area code and telephone number).

5 **I am a** (grade level) **at** (name of school).

6 **I can type for 3 minutes at** (typing speed) **gwam.**

7 **My goal for the end of the semester is** (typing speed) **gwam.**

8 **This goal is** (number of words) **gwam above my current rate.**

248b, continued

Problem 3
Average-length letter

plain full sheet; block style, open

Type the letter to **Mr. Luis C. Ortiz, Office Manager** of the **Ludlam Industries, Inc., 102 Biscayne Boulevard, Miami, FL 33132-4401.** Date the letter **April 5, 19--**; provide an appropriate salutation and complimentary close. **Subject: Your New Document Storage System.** The letter will be signed by **H. Edward Randolph, President.**

words

opening lines 35
(¶ 1) Our experts have completed their study of your document storage and 48
retrieval procedures. You will find a detailed explanation of their findings in 64
the enclosed report. (¶ 2) In essence, our experts found that you have approx- 79
imately one million hard-copy documents filed in 1,800 square feet of space 94
and that you are adding about 600,000 documents each year. The average re- 109
trieval time for a document is 4.5 minutes and the annual document loss is 124
almost 5%. (¶ 3) We recommend that you convert your hard-copy documents 138
to microfilm at a cost of less than $50,000. This will reduce the filing space 154
required from 1,800 square feet to 500 square feet. The average retrieval 169
time will be cut from 4.5 minutes to less than 30 seconds. The new system is 184
so simple that it will take less than one day to train your clerks to use it. (¶ 4) 200
As soon as you have had an opportunity to study our report, please let us 215
have your decision. In the meantime, if you have any questions, please call 230
me or Ms. Jenkins, who prepared the report. 239
closing lines 250

249b ▶ 45
Measure production skill: reports

5 full sheets

1. Type the problems at the right and on page 389 for 30′; correct errors as you type. If you finish all problems before time is called, start over.

2. After time is called, go over each page carefully and circle any errors you did not correct. Compute *o-pram*. Compare score with that attained on 228b, page 363.

Problem 1
Unbound report with side headings

Use as a main heading: **CONSOLIDATED CONTINENTAL INDUSTRIES:** as a secondary heading: **Utilizing Human Resources.** Side headings to be used are underlined.

opening lines 12
(¶ 1) The groups involved in the success of our industries--our customers, 26
stockholders, employees, and the people in the communities in which we 40
operate--must be treated with fairness and served with consideration and 55
integrity. The following highlights reflect our desire to utilize these human 71
resources to the fullest: 76

<u>Our Customers</u> (¶ 2) Our customers deserve products of the highest quality at 93
the lowest possible cost, together with efficient and courteous service. The 108
success of our operations depends upon profits; no profits are possible, how- 124
ever, unless we meet the needs of our customers efficiently and effectively. 139

<u>Our Employees</u> (¶ 3) The foundation of the success of our industries is the 156
talent, dedication, and motivation of our employees. One of our highest 170
priorities is to encourage our employees to develop their talents and skills to 186
the highest possible degree so that they can derive the greatest potential 201
satisfaction from their jobs. Another major goal is to provide an environ- 217
ment in which all employees feel free to offer constructive suggestions to 232
improve our operations. 237

<u>Our Stockholders</u> (¶ 4) We are fully committed to provide our stockholders 253
with the highest feasible return on their investment which can be attained in 269
an honest and socially responsible manner. We will continue to keep our 284
stockholders fully informed on all matters pertinent to the operations of the 299
company and pledge to improve our communications so that all stockholders 314
will be kept informed of any changes in our objectives and operations. 328

<u>The Public</u> (¶ 5) To the citizens of the communities in which we operate, we 344
pledge to do business in a manner which will conserve and promote all 358
human and ecological resources. In partnership with all groups involved 373
in our extensive operations, we emphasize service to the community in all 387
activities which will promote the utmost benefits to the general public. 402

Problems 2 and 3 are on the next page.

45d ▶ 20 Type personal-business letters

2 letterheads [LM pp. 33–36] or 2 plain full sheets; 50–space line; SS; return address on Line 16; address small envelopes

Problem 1

Type line for line the letter given at the right. *Be sure to set a tab stop at horizontal center and tab to begin the opening and closing lines.*

Problem 2

Type a second copy of the letter, but address it to:

Ms. Marcia Vallejo, Manager
Western Office Machines, Inc.
1612 Tremont Place
Denver, CO 80202-1536

Supply an appropriate salutation.

	words parts	total
5137 Rosada Way	3	3
Las Vegas, NV 89108-7243	8	8
December 6, 19--	12	12
QS (Return 4 times)		
Mr. Cyrus P. Mann, Manager	17	17
Ultramatic Typewriter Company	23	23
15 Columbus Circle	27	27
New York, NY 10023-8952 DS	32	32
Dear Mr. Mann DS	35	35
Thank you for sending me the materials on typewriting	11	45
champions that I requested. The bulletin board post-	21	56
ers my committee prepared from these materials have	32	66
created a lot of interest among the typing students. DS	43	77
It is hard to believe that anyone can type 149 words	53	88
a minute for an hour! Such a speed makes our rates	64	98
of 25 to 40 words a minute for 3 minutes seem poor,	74	109
but many of us are now determined to do better. DS	84	118
We really appreciate your sharing this information	94	129
with us. Maybe someday one of us will be a champion	105	139
and get featured on a "Typewriting Champions" poster. DS	115	150
Sincerely yours	3	153
QS (Return 4 times)		
Rilla Raintree	6	156
		187

The final figure in the word count column includes the count for the envelope address.

46

60-space line

46a ▶ 6 Conditioning practice

each line twice SS (slowly, then faster); DS between 2-line groups; if time permits, type each line again

alphabet 1 Jack Wilford may have enough cash for six quite big topazes.

fig/sym 2 The 3-year loan of $5,078 (9 1/4% interest) was made May 26.

fluency 3 The audit by the city signals the end of their profit cycle.

| 1 | 2 | 3 | 4 | 5 | 6 | 7 | 8 | 9 | 10 | 11 | 12 |

46b ▶ 24 Improve skill in typing personal-business letters

3 plain full sheets; line: 50; SS; tab stop at center point

1. On a plain sheet type the opening lines (return address through salutation) of the letter in 45d, above. Try to complete them in 1′.

2. TS; then type a 3′ writing on the 3 ¶s of the letter; determine *gwam*:

gwam = total words typed ÷ 3

3. TS, then type the closing lines (complimentary close and typed name) as many times as you can in 1′.

4. Insert a clean full sheet. Starting on Line 16, type the entire letter. Use your own return address; use your name in the closing lines.

5. Proofread your copy; mark errors for correction, using proofreader's marks.

6. If time permits, type a final copy of the letter from your marked copy.

249b, continued

Problem 2
Leftbound report with footnote

Use as a main heading: **FLEXIBLE WORK SCHEDULING.** The footnote will be:

B. Lewis Keeling, Norman F. Kallaus, and John J. W. Neuner, Administrative Office Management, 7th ed. (Cincinnati: South-Western Publishing Co., 1978), p. 359.

Type the footnote so that there is a 1-inch margin at the bottom of the page.

Problem 3
Topbound report

Type ¶s 1 and 2 of the report in Problem 2. Use as a main heading: **FLEXIBLE WORK SCHEDULING.**

words
heading 5

"Flextime" is a name given to a number of plans which 17
provide for a flexible ~~time~~ work schedule. Under most plans, all em- 29
ployees are required to be at work during ~~set~~ specified hours. This is 42
known as "core time." "Flexible time" includes the hours employ- 55
ees may ~~elect~~ choose for their arrival and departure times. For 67
example, a worker may elect to arrive at any time from 7 to 80
10 a. m. and ~~depart~~ leave at any time from 3 to 7 p. m. Under this plan, 92
"core time" is from 10 a. m. to 3 p. m. Employees may work as 104
few as 5 hours a day and as many as 12 hours ~~so long as~~ provided 116
they work at least 36-40 hours in a ~~given~~ calendar week. 125

A number of advantages are claimed for flextime. Employ- 137
ers ~~indicate~~ report that ~~lateness~~ tardiness is almost eliminated and that 149
absenteeism is ~~quite~~ very rare. Most workers like the plan, moreover, 162
because they can attain a better balance among worktime, time at 173
home, and leisure ~~pursuits~~ activities. Unions fear, however, that flextime 187
may lead to the loss of ~~extra~~ overtime pay. 194

There is some question, however, about the ~~affect~~ impact of flex- 206
time on productivity. "Companies that have converted to flex- 218
time note significant gains in productive hours. . . . The 229
output per hours worked increases because employees gain more 242
satisfaction, which typically means better production."[1] Other 255
experts report, however, that employees who work a 10- or 267
12-hour day do not ~~raise~~ increase their rate per hour. Employees simply 280
pace themselves to put forth as much ~~work~~ effort in 10 hours as they 292
would have in 8. Further, it has been ~~discovered~~ found that a 304
10-~~hour~~ to 12-hour day takes a ~~big~~ heavy toll in both fatigue and
boredom. 317

footnote 360

45a ▶ 6
Conditioning practice

each line twice SS (slowly, then faster); DS between 2-line groups; if time permits, type each line again

alphabet 1 Cheryl was pleased with the quartz box Jake Forman gave her.
fig/sym 2 Ramo & Lo used * to identify "best buys": #17285*; #30496*.
fluency 3 Diana is to handle all title forms for the eight auto firms.

| 1 | 2 | 3 | 4 | 5 | 6 | 7 | 8 | 9 | 10 | 11 | 12 |

45b ▶ 9
Practice using margin release

1. Set margin stops for an *exact* 50-space line.
2. Center and type the heading of the list given at the right; TS.
3. Depress margin release; then backspace 4 times into left margin and type the number "1."
4. Type the line until carriage (element) locks; then depress margin release and complete line.
5. Type Items 2-4 in the same way.

SPACING WITH PUNCTUATION MARKS

TS

1. Space once after , and ; used as marks of punctuation. DS
2. Space twice after . ending a sentence. Space once after . following an initial (J. W. Lee) or an abbreviation, but not after . within an abbreviation (The candidate has a Ph.D. in education.).
3. Space once after ? within a sentence (Was it Al? or Dee?), twice after ? at the end of a sentence (Is the meeting at ten o'clock? If so, please have coffee set up.).
4. Space twice after : used to introduce a list, an example, or a quotation (He said: "Return my call at 3 p.m."); do not space after : used to express time (3:15 p.m.).

45c ▶ 15
Learn to address small envelopes and fold letters

Return address. Use block style SS, as shown. Begin on second line space from top edge of envelope and 3 spaces from left edge. Type writer's name, house number and street name (or box number), city, state (followed by 2 spaces), and ZIP Code in upper left corner (unless envelope with printed return address is being used).

Envelope address. Use block style SS, as shown. Set a tab stop about 10 spaces to left of horizontal center of envelope to begin lines. Type first line of address on 12th line from top edge. Type city name, state name abbreviation, and ZIP Code on last line of address.

Direction names (North, South, East, and West) may be abbreviated (N., S., E., W.) to shorten lines and improve address balance.

Problems [LM pp. 29, 30]

Address a small envelope to each addressee; use your own return address.

Mrs. Shelly Toshiba
16954 Strawberry Drive
Encino, CA 91436-2052

Mr. Dwayne LaCoss
619 E. Audubon Drive
Bloomington, IN 47401-9710

If time permits, practice folding 8½" by 11" paper for insertion into small envelopes.

Miss Cheryl Sanudo
933 Putnam Boulevard
Wallingford, PA 19086-3724

Dr. J. Evan Townsend
3672 Beecham Lane, Apt. B
Cincinnati, OH 45208-1739

Addressing a small (No. 6 3/4) envelope (6 1/2" × 3 5/8")

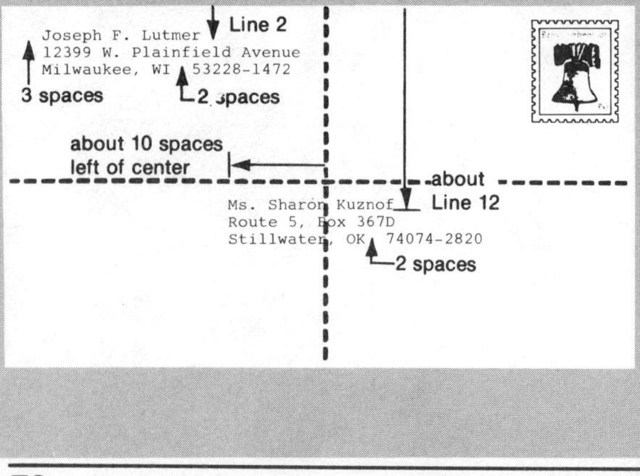

Folding and inserting letters into small envelopes

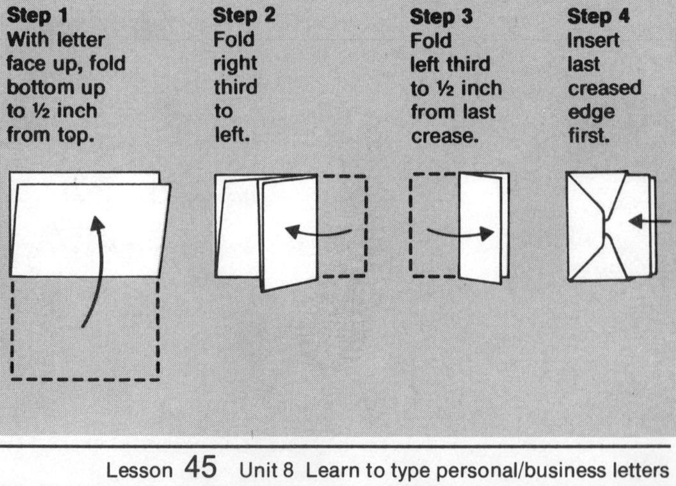
Step 1
With letter face up, fold bottom up to ½ inch from top.
Step 2
Fold right third to left.
Step 3
Fold left third to ½ inch from last crease.
Step 4
Insert last creased edge first.

250b ▶ 45

Measure production skill: forms and tables

1. Type the problems for 30′; correct errors as you type.

2. After time is called, go over each page carefully and circle any errors you did not correct. Compute *o-pram*. Compare score with that attained on 229b, page 365.

Problem 1
Purchase order [LM p. 39]

			words
	PURCHASE ORDER NO.	8043C	1
TO: Industrial Suppliers, Inc.	DATE	August 26, 19--	10
145 W. Van Buren Street	TERMS	3/10, n/60	17
Chicago, IL 60605-3733	SHIP VIA	Erie Motor Freight	25

QUANTITY	CAT. NO.	DESCRIPTION	PRICE	TOTAL	words
6	744-102C	Storage cabinets,			31
		36″ × 18″ × 78″	119.90	719.40	37
2	321-102S	Bin shelving, 21-bin units	85.70	171.40	47
10	730-102S	Cabinets w/steel drawers	96.50	965.00	57
8	111-022C	Service carts, steel,			64
		20″ × 28″	47.25	378.00	68
15	113-320C	Containers, plastic,			75
		48″ × 42″ × 30″	78.00	1,170.00	81
5	320-915T	Trucks, reinforced canvas,			89
		24 bu capacity	164.50	822.50	96
				4,226.30	98

Problem 2
Invoice [LM p. 39]

				words
SOLD TO:	Mo-Kan Suppliers, Inc.	DATE	September 3, 19--	8
	221 Pershing Road	OUR ORDER NO.	633742	13
	Kansas City, MO 64108-8810	CUST. ORDER NO.	8930L	20
TERMS:	Net	SHIPPED VIA	Lincoln Van Lines	25

QUANTITY	DESCRIPTION	UNIT PRICE	TOTAL	words
3	Ladders, fiberglass, reinforced, 12′	225.60	676.80	36
3	Work platforms, steel, 500# load capacity,			45
	50″ × 36″ × 48″ platform	310.75	932.25	52
12	Flashing warning lights, truck	49.40	598.80	62
48	Fire extinguishers, chemical	62.50	3,000.00	71
160	Hearing protectors, thermal plastic	4.95	792.00	83
			5,999.85	85

Problem 3
Table
full sheet
reading position; DS items

Problem 4
Table
half sheet, long side up
Type table in Problem 3 in exact center; SS items.

JEFFERSON WHOLESALERS, INC. 6

Monthly Average Number of Employees 13

Month	District A	District B	District C	words
				28
January	3,980	2,061	1,642	34
February	4,021	2,457	1,321	39
March	4,009	2,439	1,461	44
April	3,990	2,462	1,580	49
May	4,162	2,597	1,609	53
June	4,258	2,603	1,594	58
July	4,249	2,508	1,621	62
August	4,310	2,721	1,654	67
September	4,299	2,786	1,648	73
October	4,312	2,801	1,673	78
November	4,305	2,854	1,702	84
December	4,110	2,910	1,743	89

Shown in pica type
50–space line

Tabulate to center to type
return address and date

Return address — Line 16 — 9248 Socorro Road — words 4
El Paso, TX 79907-1312 — 8
Dateline — November 10, 19-- — 12

Operate return 4 times
(3 blank line spaces)

Letter address
Mrs. Suzanne Rios, Director 18
Graphic Arts Institute 22
22004 La Paz Road 26
Laguna Beach, CA 92766-2140 32

DS

Salutation
Dear Mrs. Rios 35

DS

Body of letter
A graduate of your school, Ms. San-li Chou, has sug- 45
gested that I write to you because of my interest in 56
a career in graphic design. 61

DS

To keep my choices open, I am taking a college-prep 72
program. All my electives, though, are being chosen 83
from courses in art, design, and graphics--including 94
photography. I do unusually well in these courses. 104

DS

Can you send me a catalog that outlines the special 115
graphics programs now being offered by your school. 126
I shall appreciate your doing so. 133

DS

Complimentary close — Tab — Cordially yours 136

Miguel Blanco

Typed name — Miguel Blanco 139

In *open* punctuation,
no punctuation follows
the salutation or the
complimentary close.

Style letter 1: personal-business letter in modified block style

phase **11** lessons 251-275

Specialized office simulations

In Phase 11 are four units of simulated activities which provide realistic practice on typing tasks found in typical specialized offices: the administrative office, the finance office, the sales/purchasing office, and the executive office. Employment activities similar to those you will encounter when you look for a job, including an employment test, are also included. In addition, a separate unit is included to build your speed and accuracy.

These 25 lessons will give you an opportunity to:

1. Apply—in realistic business situations—the basic knowledge, skills, and concepts you have previously developed.

2. Improve your ability to read and follow directions.

3. Plan and organize your work using data from a variety of documents and sources in order to complete assigned tasks.

4. Increase your knowledge of typical tasks found in business.

5. Improve your speed and accuracy in typing production materials.

6. Build your basic skill on straight copy, rough-draft, and statistical copy.

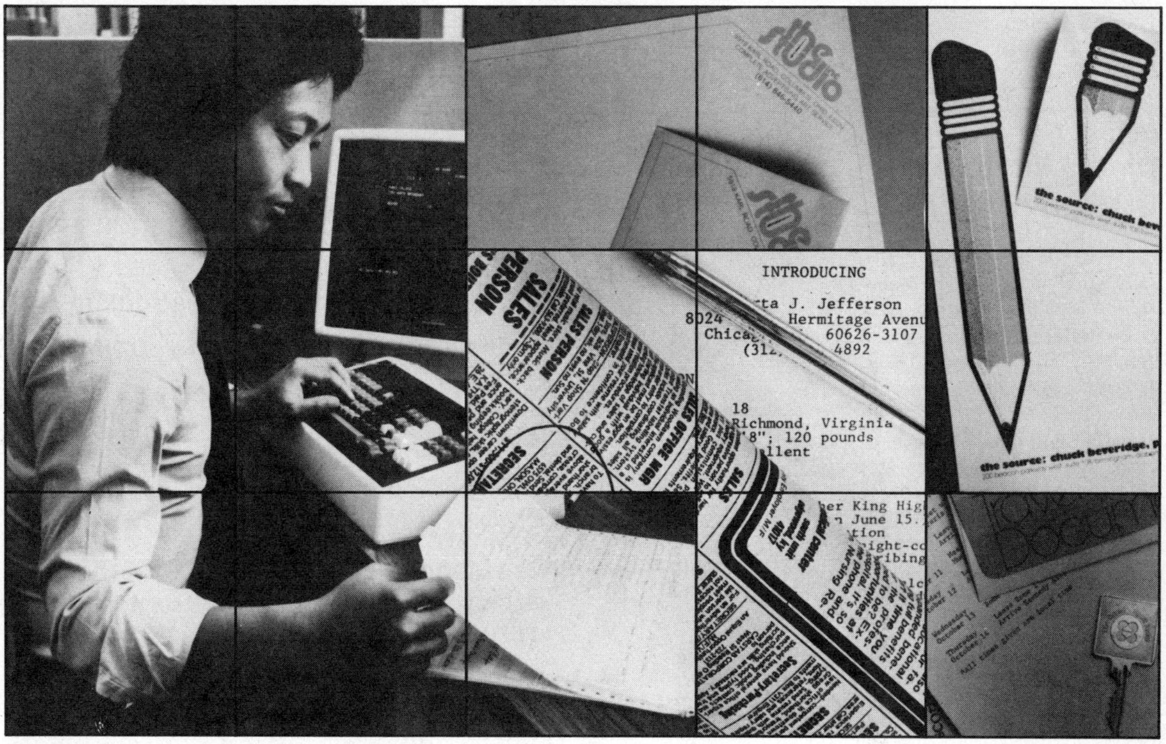

unit **50** lessons 251-254

Administrative office

Learning goals

1. To type in an acceptable form with all errors corrected a series of typical job tasks found in an administrative office.

2. To improve your skill in planning, organizing, and typing a variety of production materials.

Machine adjustments

1. Line: 70 for drills and timed writings; as required for production problems.

2. Spacing: SS sentence drills with a DS between sentence groups; space problems as required.

unit **8** lessons 44-48

Learn to type personal/business letters

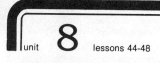

Learning goals

1. To learn to type personal and personal–business letters on full sheets.

2. To learn to address small envelopes.

3. To learn to compose as you type.

4. To improve speed and control.

Machine adjustments

1. Paper guide at *0*.

2. Ribbon control to type on top half of ribbon.

3. Margin sets: 60–space line (center – 30; center + 30 + 5) except as otherwise directed.

4. Line–space selector on *1* (SS) for drills; on *2* (DS) for ¶s; as directed for other tasks.

44

60-space line

44a ▶ 6 Conditioning practice

each line twice SS (slowly, then faster); DS between 2-line groups; if time permits, type each line again

alphabet 1 Jack Hud won first prize by solving a tax quiz in less time.

fig/sym 2 Ida bought a 9′ × 12′ rug for a 13′6″ × 15′8″ room for $470.

fluency 3 Six of the big firms may bid for the right to the lake land.

| 1 | 2 | 3 | 4 | 5 | 6 | 7 | 8 | 9 | 10 | 11 | 12 |

44b ▶ 14 Type a short report

full sheet; line: 60; heading on Line 10

1. Locate **margin release (32)** on your typewriter; practice reaching the little finger to it.

2. Center and type the report heading; TS, then type ¶ 1 DS.

3. Reset line–space selector on **1** (SS).

4. Indent and type **1.**, space twice, then reset left margin stop at this point and move right margin stop 5 spaces toward center of paper.

5. After typing Item 1, DS, operate margin release, and backspace 4 times; then type **2.** and the item.

6. Type Item 3 in same way.

7. Check placement points given in report against model letter shown on page 71.

PERSONAL AND PERSONAL-BUSINESS LETTERS
TS

Personal as well as personal-business letters are often typed. Some people use special-size stationery (7 1/4″ by 10 1/2″); others use standard-size stationery (8 1/2″ by 11″). Most people use a letter style known as Modified Block for such letters. Features of modified block style include: DS

(2 spaces) (Reset left margin stop →)

1. The return address and the date begin at the horizontal center point of the stationery. A strictly personal letter often does not include a return address. DS

(Backspace 4 times to type **2.** →)

2. The letter address, the salutation, and every line of the paragraphs begin at the left margin. A letter address is often not included in a strictly personal letter.

3. The complimentary close and the typed name of the writer (if one is used) begin at the horizontal center point of the stationery.

44c ▶ 30 Learn to type personal-business letters

2 plain full sheets; line: 50; SS

1. Study Style Letter 1 (p. 71), which illustrates *modified block style* and *open punctuation*. Note horizontal and vertical placement of parts.

2. On standard–size paper (8½″ by 11″) type line for line a copy of the model letter. Follow the spacing directions given in color on the letter.

3. Proofread and mark your copy for correction, using proofreader's marks; then retype the letter from your marked copy.

251-254

251a-254a ▶ 5 Conditioning practice

each line twice SS (slowly, then faster); DS between 2-line groups; if time permits, retype selected lines

alphabet 1 Liz Welk adjusted the cable axis to improve the quality of the signal.

figures 2 Models 85642 and 97031 will be replaced by Model 26490 on November 15.

fig/sym 3 Use the hyphen (-) for dividing words, as: in-ter-est and re-ac-tion.

fluency 4 Any individual from six to sixty can play the game and win the prizes.

| 1 | 2 | 3 | 4 | 5 | 6 | 7 | 8 | 9 | 10 | 11 | 12 | 13 | 14 |

251b-254b ▶ 45 Production typing

You have been hired as a junior typist in the Administrative Division of the Webster Manufacturing Co., 9543 Edmund Drive, St. Louis, MO 63114-5270. Your supervisor is J. Clark Mansfield who is an assistant to Mary K. Scott, Director of Administration.

Follow the directions for each job carefully. Make carbon copies when directed to do so; address envelopes when appropriate. Use your initials in letters and memos. Correct errors neatly; strive for copy that would be acceptable in a business office.

Job 1
Partial draft of speech

full sheet

Mr. Mansfield is preparing a speech of welcome to be given to new employees during their initial orientation. Type the partial draft given at the right as an unbound manuscript; use the title:

WELCOME TO WEBSTER MANUFACTURING

The Administrative Office is the nerve center of ~~the~~ any company. The office performs ~~duties~~ functions that are ~~vital~~ essential to the smooth, efficient operation of the business. Among the ~~chief~~ major functions we perform in this office are word processing, data processing, records management, and ~~duplication~~ reprographics.

As employees in an Administrative (l.c.) Office (l.c.), you will be asked to perform a wide variety of ~~duties~~ tasks. A few of the more common tasks that you will perform are typing letters, reports, and forms; filing ~~letters~~ correspondence; using the telephone; processing mail; and using office machines of all kinds. These tasks call for a high ~~level~~ degree of skill, especially at the keyboard.

Members of this office are in frequent contact with the public and with other employees at all ~~levels~~ echelons of the company. For this reason, your grooming, ~~and~~ dress, and manner are of the utmost importance. Although you may want to "do your own thing" in your ~~everyday~~ personal life, you must remember that business, in general, is ~~very~~ quite conservative when it comes to grooming and dress~~ing~~. In your ~~dealings~~ contacts with others, you must also ~~make an effort to~~ be courteous, tactful, ~~and~~ discreet, and cheerful.

43d ▶ 20 Type a short report

full sheet; 60-space line (center − 30; center + 30 + allowance for bell); DS; heading on Line 10 (1½" top margin)

1. Type a copy of the short report given at the right. As you type, be guided by the bell as a cue to divide words and return.

2. Proofread your copy; circle your errors.

EVEN EXECUTIVES USE THE TYPEWRITER

TS

In a copyrighted column,* Joyce Lain Kennedy said that there are at least two rules to follow in order to survive in tomorrow's world: "Never stand up in a canoe, and never sit down at a minicomputer without being able to type." She also said that high technology is invading offices everywhere, including the executive suite.

It isn't only clerical workers who need keyboard agility. Rather, she continued, managers and professionals are fingering machines and minicomputers as a way to expand their business and personal productivity, too.

She describes an office in which the "boss" taps a key to flash staff reports on a video screen, then fires off messages to co-workers on an attached computer keyboard. In addition, minicomputers can be used as a combination card file, telephone log, and filing cabinet with an executive being able to call up anything from business letters to expense reports simply by operating a keyboard.

Kennedy concludes that those who wish to "paddle their own canoes" with style and efficiency ought to learn their way around a keyboard.

SS

DS

* Published by Suburban Features, Inc., 1979.

An additional short report is provided on LM p. 28 for enrichment practice.

Enrichment activities

As time permits, type the sentences in the following ways:

1. A 1′ writing on each sentence; determine and compare *gwam* on each. Then, type the slower sentences several times to improve your keystroking patterns; or

2. Type each line 3 times (slowly, faster, then at top speed) to improve your techniques and speed.

balanced-hand	1	The auto firm owns the big signs by the downtown civic hall.
combination	2	We may amend the rate if the union agrees to the work risks.
double-letter	3	All had used the school soccer ball, but no one had seen it!
3d row	4	We will type figures quite fast if we try this for our goal.
adjacent-key	5	Cass tried various copiers to find one that suits her needs.
one-hand	6	You deferred my tax case after my union traced my wage card.
outside-reach	7	Perhaps the new printing press will require new paper sizes.
direct-reach	8	A great many people must make payment at the central branch.
figure	9	Of the 1,278 hikers, 1,036 had reached the camp by 9:45 p.m.
fig/sym	10	Tina asked, "Can't you touch-type 56, 73, $480, and 9 1/2%?"

| 1 | 2 | 3 | 4 | 5 | 6 | 7 | 8 | 9 | 10 | 11 | 12 |

251b-254b, continued

Job 2
Material for an office procedures manual

full sheet

Mr. Mansfield has been revising the company Office Procedures Manual and has asked you to type the final copy of page **9** from the draft at the right. Type the material as a leftbound manuscript. Keep the page for future reference.

9

<u>Typing index cards</u>

1. Type the name of the individual ~~person~~ or company ~~business organization~~ on the third line from the top edge of the card beginning ~~starting~~ three spaces from the left side. Type the name of an individual ~~a person~~ in inverse ~~reverse~~ order --family name ~~is~~ first, given name ~~is~~ second, and middle name or initial ~~is~~ last. Type a title, such as <u>Ms</u>. or <u>Dr</u>., in parentheses immediately after ~~following~~ the given name or initial.

2. Triple-space after typing the name of the individual ~~person~~ or company ~~organization~~ and type the information ~~data~~ in postal order--name, address, city, state and ZIP code. TS

<u>Typing mailing labels</u>

1. Type the name of the individual ~~person~~ or company ~~organization~~ on the second line from the top edge of the label beginning just three spaces from the left edge.

2. Type the local address on the next ~~second~~ line and the city, state, and ZIP code on the following ~~third~~ line.

<u>Typing file folder labels</u> TS

1. Type the name of the individual ~~person~~ (in inverse ~~reverse~~ order) or company ~~organization~~ on the second line from the top edge of the label beginning just three spaces from the left edge.

2. Type the city, state, and ZIP code on the next ~~second~~ line, followed by the local address, if necessary ~~desired~~, on the following ~~next~~ line.

43

60-space line

43a ▶ 6 Conditioning practice

each line twice SS (slowly, then faster); DS between 2-line groups; if time permits, type each line again

alphabet 1 Pam Fyle was quite excited when Jack bought the bronze vase.

fig/sym 2 B&O car #630-2847 (Track 1) leaves for St. Paul at 9:15 a.m.

fluency 3 A neighbor paid the girl to fix the turn signal of the auto.

| 1 | 2 | 3 | 4 | 5 | 6 | 7 | 8 | 9 | 10 | 11 | 12 |

43b ▶ 14 Learn to use the typewriter bell

1. Set margin stops for exact 60-space line: center − 30; center + 30.

2. Type sentence given at right at a slow pace; stop as soon as typewriter bell rings. Instead of typing remainder of sentence, type figures—1234 etc.—until the carriage locks. Subtract 5 (the desired warning) from final figure; move right stop one space to the right for each remaining figure (usually 3 to 10 spaces). See the illustrative example under the sentence at the right.

3. Type sentence again to check accuracy of your setting of the right margin stop.

4. Using same margin settings, type the ¶ given at the right. Be guided by bell as cue to complete a word or divide it, type another word, or return.

```
Move stop so bell rings 5 spaces before desired line ending.
                                                 ▼ bell
▶ Move stop so bell rings 5 spaces before desired liB123456789
  Move stop so bell rings 5 spaces before desired line en////.
                                                       ▲
                                                      bell
                                                       ▼
```

Typewriters vary widely in terms of the number of characters they will permit to be typed between the point where the warning bell rings and the point at which the carriage or carrier locks. Set the right margin stop at that point which causes the bell to ring exactly 5 spaces before the line ending desired. This guide means that you will move the right margin stop 3-10 spaces, usually, to the right of the exact setting for a specified line length. You can then type from 1 to 7 spaces after the warning bell and before the carriage locks without creating an unduly ragged right margin.

43c ▶ 10 Type a personal note

half sheet, long side up; 60-space line; SS; begin on Line 7 (1" top margin)

1. Set right margin stop so bell rings on 5th space before exact 60-space line ending.

2. As you type the note, listen for the bell as a cue to return. If necessary, divide words to have a fairly even right margin.

▶ Your lines will not end at the same points as those in the copy.

June 28, 19--

Dear Diana

After all the trouble I had in Mr. Dodd's class, I have a typing job for the summer.

I hate to admit it, but Mr. Dodd was right: Figures and symbols <u>are</u> important. Hunt-and-peck doesn't cut it at Royer & Fink (public accountants)--even on the top row!

When we take Typing 2, we'd better listen more and "advise" less. After two weeks on this job, I think Mr. Dodd "has a better idea."

Cordially

251b-254b, continued

A card file and a folder are set up for each person who applies for a job with the Webster Manufacturing Company. For cross-reference purposes, each application, index card, file folder label, and address label is numbered in the upper right-hand corner.

Job 3
Index cards [LM. pp. 41–48]

Type 5″ × 3″ index cards (like the one illustrated) for the job applicants. Type the title of the job for which the person applied on the sixth line below the city and state. After the cards are typed, arrange them in alphabetical order.

Job 4
Address labels [LM pp. 49–52]

Type an address label (similar to the one illustrated) for each job applicant. Type the labels in alphabetical order, using the cards prepared in Job 3.

Job 5
File folder labels [LM pp. 51–54]

Rearrange the cards prepared in Job 3 in numeric order; then type a label (similar to the one illustrated) for the file folder of each job applicant.
Note: The top part of these gummed labels is folded over to the back when they are fastened to the file folder.

Index card

```
Benton, Joyce L. (Ms.)                    1403

Ms. Joyce L. Benton
1548 Rozelle Street
Memphis, TN  38106-7635

Administrative Assistant
```

Address label

```
Ms. Joyce L. Benton                       1403
1548 Rozelle Street
Memphis, TN  38106-7635
```

File folder label

```
Benton, Joyce L. (Ms.)                    1403
Memphis, TN  38106-7635
1548 Rozelle Street
```

1403
Mrs. Margaret C. Hoffman
7203 Anna Avenue
St. Louis, MO 63143-3171
Chemical Operator

1404
Mr. Oren F. Brubaker
309 Mascoutah Avenue
Belleville, IL 62221-8998
Administrative Assistant

1405
Mr. Alex V. Molyneux
640 Madison Road
Granite City, IL 62040-5953
Laboratory Technician

1406
Mr. Andrew C. Van Buren
3612 Bellerive Boulevard
St. Louis, MO 63116-3273
Transportation Specialist

1407
Mr. Ronald R. Leverette
10608 Bruno Avenue
St. Louis, MO 63114-3663
Utility Operator

1408
Dr. Marian W. O'Leary
681 Waterville Road
Edwardsville, IL 62025-5101
Chemical Engineer

1409
Mr. Alfred M. Conti
29 St. Charles Place
Alton, MO 65606-6767
Junior Clerk

1410
Ms. Lucia I. Morales
1819 Martin Luther King Drive
East Saint Louis, IL 62205-2504
Reprographic Supervisor

1411
Ms. Alverna M. Schultz
6130 Eaton Avenue
St. Louis, MO 63134-4733
Stenographer

1412
Mrs. Rosa R. Fernandez
985 Chesterfield Avenue
Ballwin, MO 63011-2001
Utility Operator

1413
Mr. Leonard C. Marcus
4056 Webster Road
Kirkwood, MO 63122-4261
Security Guard

1414
Mr. Yuan K. Cheng
5426 January Avenue
St. Louis, MO 63109-4601
Catalyst Operator

1415
Miss Susan A. Wetzel
237 Chestnut Street
Creve Coeur, MO 63141-2900
Weigher Operator

1416
Mr. Albert T. Monahan
908 Elm Street
East Saint Louis, IL 62003-2745
Administrator

1417
Ms. Louise A. Benedetti
1120 Wilson Avenue
St. Louis, MO 63130-4523
Laboratory Technician

1418
Miss Mary Ann Kowalski
8452 Tennessee Avenue
St. Louis, MO 63125-5522
Senior Typist

1419
Mrs. Rebecca L. Schwartz
4798 Primm Street
St. Louis, MO 63116-3275
Weigher Operator

Line 10 (1½" top margin)

TO RACE THE WIND*

TS

TO RACE THE WIND is an autobiography by Harold Krents, who was the inspiration for the blind hero of the Broadway hit and the film <u>Butterflies Are Free</u>.

Born almost completely blind and becoming totally so by his eighth year, Harold Krents, encouraged by strong-willed parents, set for himself a headlong course through handicaps and discouragement of every known kind. This course brought him as many bruises and cruelties as blisses. He was and is an extraordinary person who never dodged difficulty. He never asked favors of fate. He never forgot how to laugh at himself and others. He never ceased to believe that all of existence is "a race straight forward into the darkness that waits there even for those who say they see."

By sheer courage, energy, and persistence, he became president of the student body of Scarsdale High School, a <u>cum laude</u> graduate of Harvard Law School, and a member of the bar of New York. Along the way, he played a lot of football--his friends dubbed him Cannonball Krents. He also wrote the music and lyrics of a number of songs, and he fell in love with a lovely sighted girl, Kit, who became his wife.

TO RACE THE WIND is a funny, touching, inspiring story of a young man who just happened to be blind.

Type a 1½" underline: 15 pica spaces; 18 elite spaces.

______________ SS

DS

*Published by G. P. Putnam's Sons.

42c ▶ 30 Learn to type a book report

full sheet;
60-space line;
DS (double spacing);
heading on Line 10

1. Type, line for line, a copy of the one-page book report illustrated above.

2. Proofread and mark your copy for correction. If time permits, begin typing the report from your marked copy.

251b-254b, continued

At the right is a portion of the Office Procedures Manual which includes form paragraphs used to reply to individuals who apply for a position with the Webster Manufacturing Co.

Letters which originate in the Administrative Division are typed in block style with open punctuation.

Job 6
Form letters

[LM pp. 55–62]

Reply to the applications of the individuals listed below using the paragraphs indicated to compose each letter. Obtain the complete name and address from the index cards typed in Job 3. Date the letters **October 17, 19--**; provide an appropriate salutation and complimentary close. The letters will be signed by **Mr. Mansfield as Assistant Director of Administration.** Make one carbon copy of each letter on plain paper.

Letter 1

To Applicant No. 1404
¶s 1.4, 2.2, 3.3

Letter 2

To Applicant No. 1410
¶s 1.1, 2.1, 3.1

Letter 3

To Applicant No. 1415
¶s 1.2, 2.3, 3.2

Letter 4

To Applicant No. 1417
¶s 1.3, 2.2, 3.2

Form Paragraphs for Replies to Job Applicants

1.1 Thank you for your recent letter in which you applied for a position as a/an (insert title of position). We appreciate your interest in the Webster Manufacturing Company.

1.2 Thank you for taking the time to complete our application form for a position as a/an (insert title of position).

1.3 We acknowledge, with thanks, your application form for a position as a/an (insert title of position). There is a possibility that we have a position for which you are qualified.

1.4 Several months ago, you applied for a position as a/an (insert title of position). At that time, we did not have an opening for which you were qualified. It is possible, however, that we shall have a vacancy in the very near future.

2.1 Will you please complete the enclosed application form and return it to us promptly. After we have had an opportunity to review your qualifications, we shall be able to determine whether you have the necessary prerequisites to fill the position.

2.2 Will you please call (insert your name) at 555-6200 (Extension 360) and arrange for a personal interview at a mutually convenient time so that we can discuss the position.

2.3 At this time, we do not have a position for which you are qualified. We shall keep your application on file for six months, however, and if the need arises during that time for an individual with your qualifications, we shall contact you.

3.1 Within ten days after we receive your completed application form, we shall let you know whether or not we have a position for which you are qualified.

3.2 Your interest in becoming a member of the Webster Manufacturing Company is appreciated.

3.3 If, for any reason, you are no longer interested in a position with the Webster Manufacturing Company, will you please call and let us know.

41c ▶ 14 Improve keystroking speed: guided writing

1. A 1′ writing on ¶ 1; determine *gwam*.
2. Add 4 *gwam* to set a new goal rate.
3. A 1′ writing on ¶ 1, trying to maintain your goal rate each ¼ minute.
4. Type ¶ 2 in the same way.
5. A 2′ writing on ¶ 1; if you complete the ¶ before time is called, start over.
6. A 3′ writing on ¶s 1–2 combined; determine *gwam*.

all letters used | LA | 1.4 si | 5.4 awl | 85% hfw |

	gwam 2′	3′
An excellent performance shows the true concern of the	5	4
performer for the task. It gives one a feeling of personal	11	8
triumph and prompts us as a matter of habit to do our best.	18	12
Really successful men and women take great delight in their	24	16
work and pursue it with a lot of dedication.	28	19
A factor common to all who succeed is the need to have	5	22
a good job recognized by others. If good work goes without	11	26
notice, the desire to excel may be reduced. Lucky, indeed,	18	30
are those who can study their own performance, evaluate its	24	34
quality, and do what must be done to improve.	28	37

gwam 2′ | 1 | 2 | 3 | 4 | 5 | 6 |
3′ | 1 | 2 | 3 | 4 |

41d ▶ 20 Type personal notes

half sheets, long side up; 60-space line; begin on Line 7 (1″ top margin)

1. Type line for line the personal note given at the right; center the street address on a separate line as shown.
2. Proofread, mark your copy for correction, and type the note from your marked copy.

November 6, 19--

QS (operate return 4 times)

Dear Mei-yu

DS

We are going to move to Clearwater, Florida, early next week.
Our new address will be

DS

2948 Bayview Drive

DS

where the Expanded ZIP Code is 33519-1026. Our new telephone
number will be (813) 271-4620.

DS

Plan to spend some time there with us during the holiday season. By then you'll want to get out of the "Frozen North,"
and I'll be glad to have you enjoy the sun and surf with us.

DS

Cordially

42

60-space line

42a ▶ 6 Conditioning practice

each line twice SS (slowly, then faster); DS between 2-line groups; if time permits, type each line again

alphabet 1 Judy Glaxon has been quick to try with full zeal to improve.

fig/sym 2 Didn't she say Invoice #9580 was for $376 (plus 4 1/2% tax)?

fluency 3 They may make their goals if they work with the usual vigor.

| 1 | 2 | 3 | 4 | 5 | 6 | 7 | 8 | 9 | 10 | 11 | 12 |

42b ▶ 14 Improve keystroking speed: guided writing

Retype 41c, above.
Goal: 2 *gwam* speed increase.

251b-254b, continued

Job 7
Interoffice memorandum

[LM p. 63]

At the right is a draft of a memorandum that Mr. Mansfield wishes to address to all supervisors in the company on October 30, 19—.

Type the memo in final form in the proper format. Select an appropriate subject. Make one carbon copy on plain paper.

To fill authorized *positions* ~~jobs~~, it is the policy of the Administrative Division to refer *qualified* applicants to supervisors for *a personal* interviews*,* prior to hiring. During these interviews, *all supervisors* ~~you~~ should remember that federal law forbids discrimination in hiring practices on the basis of race, color, religion, national origin, sex, or *(within limits)* age.

During *job* interviews, be *certain* ~~sure~~ that you ask the *applicant* ~~person~~ only the questions that *are clearly and* directly related to the *position* ~~job~~ to be filled. Do not ask about the *applicant's* ~~person's~~ marital status, living arrangements, the number and age of any *children* ~~dependents~~, or *financial status* ~~debts~~. It has been *determined* ~~decided~~ that these questions are not job related.

If you are not *certain* ~~sure~~ that a *specific* ~~given~~ question may be properly asked, check with this *office* ~~division~~ before asking it.

Job 8
Interview schedule
full sheet

From the worksheet at the right, type an interview schedule for Mr. Mansfield. In a main heading, indicate that this is a schedule of interviews; in a secondary heading, indicate that the schedule is for the week of November 3, 19—. Spell out the name of each position. Make two carbon copies.

Note: It is not necessary to include the ruled lines.

Date	Time	Applicant	Position
11/3	1:30	Oren F. Brubaker	Admin. Asst.
11/3	3:00	Louise A. Benedetti	Lab. Tech.
11/4	9:00	Alfred M. Conti	Junior Clerk
11/4	10:30	Alverna M. Schultz	Stenographer
11/4	2:00	Lucia L. Morales	Repro. Sup.
11/5	10:00	Yuan K. Cheng	Catalyst Op.
11/5	1:00	Susan A. Wetzel	Weigher Op.
11/5	3:00	Albert T. Monahan	Administrator
11/6	9:30	Mary Ann Kowalski	Sr. Typist
11/6	11:00	Rebecca L. Schwartz	Weigher Op.
11/7	8:30	Alex V. Molyneux	Lab. Tech.
11/7	10:00	Andrew C. Van Buren	Trans. Spec.

Line 7 (1" top margin)

November 5, 19--

Operate return 4 times
(3 blank line spaces)

Dear Aunt Joan

DS

You really surprised me by flying down for my birthday party. I couldn't believe it when you walked into the room carrying the lighted cake.

DS

The backgammon set you brought me is the "hit of the block." There's only one problem: "Curfew" is now an hour earlier--so the <u>adults</u> can play!

DS

Thank you for the gift. Thank you for being here. And thank you for making me seem "special" to my friends.

DS

Love

Chris

Personal note in block style (all lines begin at left margin)

40c ▶ 20
Learn to type personal notes

2 half sheets, long side up; 60-space line; type copy line for line

1. Starting on Line 7, type the personal note as shown in the model above.

2. Proofread, mark your copy for correction, and type the note from your marked copy.

41

60-space line

41a ▶ 6
Conditioning practice

each line twice SS (slowly, then faster); DS between 2-line groups; if time permits, type each line again

alphabet	1	Veda Lanzey was quick to jump for the box but lost her grip.
fig/sym	2	The new sample cover was made of Dura-Fiber PKG* 24# Bristol.
fluency	3	Eight of them did go to the social held by the big box firm.

| 1 | 2 | 3 | 4 | 5 | 6 | 7 | 8 | 9 | 10 | 11 | 12 |

41b ▶ 10
Learn to divide words

1. Use 60-space line. Clear all tab stops; then set new stops as indicated by the key beneath the columns of words.

2. Type the first word in Column 1 as shown; tab; then type the first word in Column 2; and so on.

started	vari-ous	what-ever	quali-fy-ing
longer	re-turned	pro-vided	be-gin-ning
wishes	pre-sented	tele-phone	nec-es-sary
promptly	poli-cies	tech-ni-cal	twenty-eighth

key | 8 | 6 | 10 | 6 | 11 | 6 | 13 |

Finance office

Learning goals

1. To improve your ability to type figures.

2. To refine production skill by typing typical financial office materials.

Machine adjustments

1. Line: 70 for drills; as necessary for problems.

2. Spacing: SS sentence drills with a DS between sentence groups; space problems as required.

255-258

255a-258a ▶ 5 Conditioning practice

each line twice SS (slowly, then faster); DS between 2-line groups; if time permits, retype selected lines

alphabet 1 Pam quickly began to explain the hazards we faced on the trip to Java.

figures 2 Please call 726-1982 between 9:30 a.m. and 4:15 p.m. prior to June 30.

fig/sym 3 Mann & Dalton offered a discount of $347 (10% and 2%) on Order 568941.

fluency 4 When it is time for the girls to go, she may take them to the airport.

| 1 | 2 | 3 | 4 | 5 | 6 | 7 | 8 | 9 | 10 | 11 | 12 | 13 | 14 |

255b-258b ▶ 45 Production typing

You have been hired as a junior typist in the Finance Division of Blaine-Derry Industries, Inc., 1901 Euclid Avenue, Cleveland, Ohio 44115-4735.

As the newest member of the staff, you will substitute for absent employees and type, when needed, in any of the offices, including the Tax and Audit Branch, Accounting and Payroll Branch, Cost and Budget Office, and the Administration Office.

Job 1
News release [LM p. 65]

Type the news release shown at the right. Type **FOR IMMEDIATE RELEASE** at the left margin and **For further information call:** starting at the center point of the page. After the last line of the final paragraph, DS and center ###. This indicates the end of the release and that nothing follows.

FOR IMMEDIATE RELEASE For further information call:
Bob Martin (216) 555-4300

TS

CLEVELAND, OH., March 3 -- Blaine-Derry Industries has announced outstanding revinues and earnings for the year which ended December 31. This is the 11th consecutive time that the company's profits have risen over the previous year. Net sales for the yaer rose 19% from $89,215,000 to $116,166,000. Net income for the year rose to $31,228,00 which can be compared with $26,544,000 for the prevuious year.

Blaine-Derry's board of directors announced a dividend of $1.40 per share. Karl T. Merrick, the firm's chairman, said, "our financial strength enabled us to declare a dividend and also to substantially increase capitol expenditures. The outlook looks good for a continuation of new records in both earnings and revenues."

Blaine-Derry is one of the nation's leading manufacturers of air craft and automobile parts.

unit 7 lessons 40-43

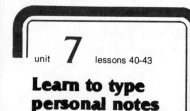

Learn to type personal notes and manuscripts

Learning goals

1. To learn to type personal notes on half sheets.

2. To learn to type book reports and article summaries.

3. To learn to divide words at line endings.

4. To learn to use the typewriter bell.

5. To improve keystroking speed and control.

Machine adjustments

1. Paper guide at *0*.

2. Ribbon control to type on top half of ribbon.

3. Margin sets: 60-space line (center − 30; center + 30 + 5) except as otherwise directed.

4. Line-space selector on *1* (SS) for drills; on *2* (DS) for ¶s; as directed for other tasks.

40

60-space line

40a ▶ 6 Conditioning practice

each line twice SS (slowly, then faster); DS between 2-line groups; if time permits, type each line again

alphabet 1 Dru Wolf can maximize skill by just improving her technique.

fig/sym 2 Type: #38 and (9%) and 15-lb. bag and 270 B&O at $46/share.

fluency 3 He may profit by good form and a firm wish to make the goal.

| 1 | 2 | 3 | 4 | 5 | 6 | 7 | 8 | 9 | 10 | 11 | 12 |

40b ▶ 24 Learn to divide words

60-space line

1. Study the word-division guides at the right.

2. Clear all tab stops; then set new stops as indicated by the key beneath the columns of words; for example, set the tab stop for second column 15 spaces (7 + 8) from left margin stop. Set line-space selector on **2** (DS).

3. Center and type the heading. Then TS; type the first word in Column 1 as shown; tab; type the first word in Column 2 as shown; and so on.

4. As time permits, identify the rule(s) that applies in the proper division of each word in each column.

Guides for dividing words

Divide a word at the end of a line only to help maintain a fairly even right margin. Avoid excessive word division. To indicate the division of a word, type a hyphen at the end of the line; type the rest of the word on the next line. The guides given here reflect current practice in dividing words.

1. Divide a word only between syllables (*pre-fer, pro-gram, em-ploy-ees, fi-nan-cial*). A word of one syllable, therefore, cannot be divided (*reached*).

2. Do not separate a one-letter syllable at the beginning of a word (*a*cross, *a*ware, *e*nough) or a one- or two-letter syllable at the end of a word (pri*or*, read*y*, fort*y*). Thus, most five-letter words should not be divided.

3. Usually, a word may be divided between double consonants (*writ-ten, sum-mer, din-ner*), including words such as *run-ning* in which the final consonant is doubled in adding the suffix *-ing*.

4. Divide after the double letters when adding a syllable to a word that ends in double letters (*express, express-ing; add, add-ing; will, will-ing*).

5. Divide before word endings *-able, -ible, -acle,* and *-ical* (*prob-able, convert-ible, mir-acle, cler-ical*) when the vowel *a* or *i* is a separate syllable. If a single-letter vowel syllable is not part of a word ending, divide after it (*sepa-rate, gradu-ate, evalu-ate*).

6. Divide only between the two words that make up a hyphenated word (*self-contained, well-developed*).

7. Do not divide a contraction (*didn't*) or a single group of figures (*$3,000,000*). Related groups of figures, however, may be separated, but no hyphen is used (*May 1, 1982*).

ACCEPTABLE WORD-DIVISION POINTS

TS

quickly	com-mon	ac-tions	prac-ti-cal
changes	great-est	prob-able	di-vis-ible
points	per-sons	sup-port	mir-acle
enough	ef-forts	get-ting	sepa-rate
boarded	in-crease	agree-ing	self-serve

key | 7 | 8 | 9 | 8 | 9 | 8 | 11 |

Enrichment material appears on LM p. 28.

255b-258b, continued

Job 2
Interoffice memos
[LM pp. 67–70]

1. From the computer printout below showing a portion of the personnel budget for the third quarter of this fiscal year, locate those divisions that, according to projections, will exceed their personnel budget.

2. Type the memorandum below from **Nora T. Frye, Budget Officer,** dated **October 16, 19–,** to each division chief who will exceed his or her budget. Compose an appropriate subject; make 1 cc on plain paper.

3. The chiefs of the divisions are:
Paul C. Wray, Engineering
Mark N. Cole, Technical
Ellen K. Taylor, Administration

PERSONNEL BUDGET AS OF THIRD QUARTER, CURRENT FISCAL YEAR

DIVISION	BUDGETED AMOUNT	EXPENDED TO DATE	PROJECTED TOTAL	OVER/UNDER
MARKETING	1,162,000	871,500	1,162,000	0
ENGINEERING	336,000	302,400	386,400	+ 50,400
FINANCE	252,000	189,000	251,000	- 1,000
TECHNICAL	342,000	340,000	420,600	+ 78,600
PURCHASING	504,000	378,000	504,000	0
MANUFACTURING	2,299,500	1,609,650	2,184,500	-115,000
PERSONNEL	342,000	246,240	331,740	- 10,260
ADMINISTRATION	216,000	205,200	270,000	+ 54,000

¶ For this fiscal year, a total of (insert budgeted amount) was budgeted for ~~personal~~ personnel expenses in your division. As of the ~~end~~ close of the third quarter, you have expended (insert expended to date), and at this rate, it is projected that your total personnel ~~costs~~ expenses for ~~this~~ the year will be (insert projected total) or (insert amount over) over your ~~authorized~~ budgeted amount.

In the absence of an ~~approved~~ authorized increase in your personnel budget, it will be necessary for you to (1) ~~decrease~~ reduce personnel costs during the ~~final~~ fourth quarter of this fiscal year and/or (2) transfer funds from other ~~areas~~ accounts to cover your ~~additional~~ increased personnel costs.

Will you please notify this office by ~~October 26~~ November 1 what action you plan to take to ~~remedy~~ correct this situation.

39c ▶ 14 Learn: " and *

" = quotation mark * = asterisk (star)

Quotation (")

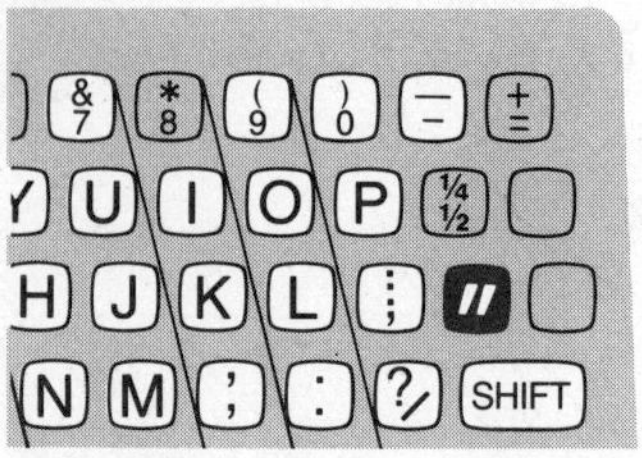

Electric

Type " (the shift of ') with the *right little finger*. Don't forget to shift *before* striking the " key.

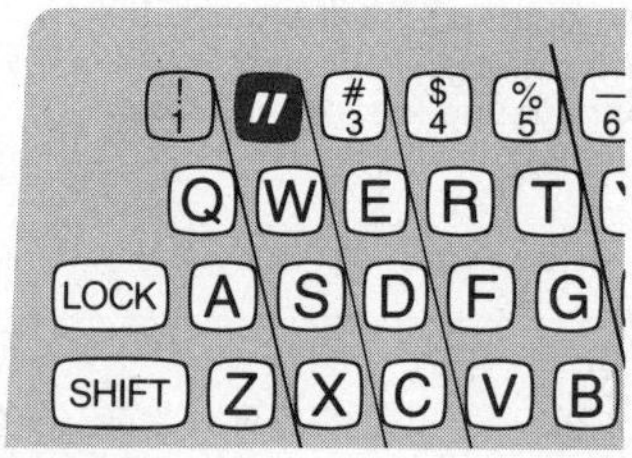

Manual

Type " (the shift of **2**) with the *left third finger*. Reach with the controlling finger. Hold other fingers over home keys.

Asterisk (*)

Electric

Type * (the shift of **8**) with the *right second finger*.

Manual

Type * (the shift of –) with the *right fourth (little) finger*.

Learning procedure

1. Locate key on appropriate chart above (electric or manual); study the reach–technique given with it.

2. Type the appropriate tryout drill (electric or manual) at the right.

3. Then type twice the two lines which emphasize the key (slowly, then faster).

" (quotation mark)

electric ▶ ' "; ' "; "; "; ' " I said, "Go!"
manual ▶ 2"s 2"s "s "s "2 I said, "Go!"

1 "To gain speed," she said, "think the word, not the letter."
2 Did Carlos type "lose" for "loose" and "chose" for "choose"?

* (asterisk)

electric ▶ 8*k 8*k *k *k 8* 8* *See p. 3.
manual ▶ –*; –*; *; *; –* –* *See p. 3.

3 You may use an * (asterisk) to indicate a source reference.*
4 All special gift items are indicated by an *; as 121*, 813*.

Enrichment (if time permits)

5 She said: "Use * to indicate a single footnote in a table."
6 "Its" is an adjective; "it's" is the contraction of "it is."

39d ▶ 15 Check/improve straight-copy typing skill

1. A 3′ writing on ¶s 1–2 combined; determine *gwam*.

2. A 1′ and a 2′ writing on each ¶; determine *gwam* on each writing.

3. If time permits, type another 3′ writing on ¶s 1–2 combined; determine *gwam*, circle errors.

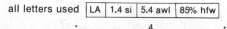

all letters used | LA | 1.4 si | 5.4 awl | 85% hfw |

	gwam 2′	3′
Often it has been said that everybody should learn how	5	4
to type. Although that may be stretching the truth, no one	11	8
was ever penalized for knowing how. A clerk or a secretary	17	12
must know how to type, of course; but typing can be quite a	23	16
help in private and professional communication as well.	29	19
Good typists are working in private and public offices	5	23
of every kind. They have a wide assortment of duties, too.	12	27
Not only do they have to prepare letters of all types; they	17	31
also compile and type reports, arrange and type tables, and	23	35
fill in many types of forms. They also do extra jobs.	29	39

gwam 2′ | 1 | 2 | 3 | 4 | 5 | 6
3′ | 1 | 2 | 3 | 4

Enrichment material for Unit 6 appears on LM pp. 24–27.

255b-258b, continued

Job 3
Payroll worksheet
[LM pp. 71–74]

Type an original and 1 cc of the Payroll Worksheet below.

PAYROLL WORKSHEET

Department: *Quality Control* Month of: *October, 19--*

Employee	Gross	FICA	Fed. Tax	State Tax	Local Tax	Net
Ray T. Ames	1,380	92.46	304.80	27.60	13.80	941.34
Joy M. Clark	1,900	127.30	399.20	38.00	19.00	1,316.50
Ken F. Edgar	1,620	108.54	264.80	32.40	16.20	1,098.06
Jerry N. Grier	2,000	134.00	391.60	40.00	20.00	1,414.40
Mary T. Jacobs	1,250	83.75	276.00	25.00	12.50	852.75
Henry C. Klein	930	62.31	144.00	18.60	9.30	695.79
Sean S. Martin	980	65.66	196.80	19.60	9.80	688.14
Helen K. Monroe	1,060	71.02	228.00	21.20	10.60	729.18
Carl W. Peters	2,100	140.70	411.60	42.00	21.00	1,484.70
Arlo S. Raub	1,490	99.83	279.60	29.80	14.90	1,065.87
Jean S. Sykes	1,850	123.95	349.20	37.00	18.50	1,321.35
Susan K. Tyler	1,060	71.02	189.60	21.20	10.60	767.58
Mark T. Warren	1,000	67.00	182.40	20.00	10.00	720.60
Lucy R. Yates	990	66.33	154.40	19.80	9.90	739.57

38c ▶ 8 Learn to "make" an exclamation mark (!)

at least once, untimed

If your typewriter has an exclamation mark key, the left little finger is used to operate it. To "make" the !:

Type ' (apostrophe); backspace and type a . (period).

The exclamation point (!) is used to express strong or sudden feeling: Go! Wow! Stop! Some people use the mark wrongly to imply that a preceding comment is intended to be funny: Ha! Ha! If the statement is funny, the reader will know without being told. The ! is used less frequently in business writing than in personal notes and letters. Even in the latter, though, the use of ! should be limited.

38d ▶ 22 Improve keystroking speed

1. A 1′ writing on each line; determine *gwam* on each writing.

2. Compare *gwam* on the 10 writings to identify the 3 slowest lines.

3. A 1′ writing on each of the 3 slowest lines to improve speed.

all letters/figures used

balanced-hand	1	Sign the work form for the six men to do the city dock work.
combination	2	Pamela saw a car go down the lane and swerve onto the grass.
3d row	3	Skill is sure to result if they just type at a steady speed.
3d/1st rows	4	Learn to make reaches to the shift keys with correct timing.
adjacent-key	5	Are you aware that their union has asked for a new contract?
1st row	6	Zane gave a cab card to each man and woman at my taxi stand.
outside-reach	7	Quin popped up to our prize pitcher in the top of the sixth.
direct-reach	8	Myra decided that curved fingers helped her to type numbers.
figure	9	Aida lived at 2740 Spruce; she moved to 3856 Elm on June 19.
fig/sym	10	He's sure Questions 36-40 are from Chapter 29 (pp. 481-507).

| 1 | 2 | 3 | 4 | 5 | 6 | 7 | 8 | 9 | 10 | 11 | 12 |

Enrichment material on figures and symbols appears on LM pp. 24–26.

39

60-space line

39a ▶ 6 Conditioning practice

each line twice SS (slowly, then faster); DS between 2-line groups; if time permits, type each line again

alphabet	1	Vi asked what prize antique she could buy for Jinx at Gumps.
symbol	2	Don't Sell Yourself Short! is a well-written book by Jo Kim.
fluency	3	The auditor is to aid the six antique firms with their work.

| 1 | 2 | 3 | 4 | 5 | 6 | 7 | 8 | 9 | 10 | 11 | 12 |

39b ▶ 15 Improve keystroking speed

Repeat Step 1 of 38d, above.
Goal: 2 *gwam* increase on each line.

255b-258b, continued

Job 4
Letter [LM p. 75]

Type the letter at the right in modified block style w/indented ¶s and mixed punctuation, dated **November 18, 19--**, to **Mr. J. P. Marston** of the firm **Marston, Finch, O'Conner, and Marks, Inc., 33 North La Salle Street, Chicago, IL 60602-3675.** Provide an appropriate salutation and complimentary close. The letter will be signed by **Thomas M. Reese**, who is **Vice President for Finance.** Make 2 carbon copies.

This *letter* will confirm the *telephone conversation* ~~telecon~~ of November 16 between Lorenzo L. Santini, my administrative *assistant* ~~aide~~, and Francis T. O'Conner of your office regarding a *proposed* bond issue.

To meet the *increasing* demand for air*craft* ~~plane~~ maintenance *tools and* equipment, we are planning to *enlarge* ~~increase~~ and update our *manufacturing facilities* ~~fabricating plant~~ in Akron. To do so, we are *contemplating* ~~thinking about~~ floating debenture bonds for $150,000 which will mature ten years from the date of issue. We are willing to *establish* ~~set up~~ a sinking fund to insure payment of these bonds at maturity in accordance with the *e*~~in~~closed schedule. This schedule is based on the *assumption* ~~idea~~ that ~~we can invest~~ funds *can be invested* at 6%, compounded annually.

If you are interested in *acting as the* ~~assuming the role of~~ investment banker in the issue of these bonds, I suggest we meet *in my office* at 1:30 p.m. on November 27 to discuss the matter. If you cannot meet at this time, please call Mr. Santini for another mutually agreeable time and date.

Job 5
Sinking fund schedule
full sheet

Type the table in reading position; DS the items. Use the title: **SINKING FUND SCHEDULE.** This schedule will accompany the letter in Job 4.

Year	Amount at Beginning	Interest at 6%	Annual Contribution	Total Increase	Amount at End
1			11,380.20	11,380.20	11,380.20
2	11,380.20	682.81	11,380.20	12,063.01	23,443.21
3	23,443.21	1,406.59	11,380.20	12,786.79	36,230.00
4	36,230.00	2,173.80	11,380.20	13,554.00	49,784.00
5	49,784.00	2,987.04	11,380.20	14,367.24	64,151.24
6	64,151.24	3,849.07	11,380.20	15,229.27	79,380.51
7	79,380.51	4,762.83	11,380.20	16,143.03	95,532.54
8	95,523.54	5,731.41	11,380.20	17,111.61	112,635.15
9	112,635.15	6,758.11	11,380.20	18,138.31	130,773.46
10	130,773.46	7,846.41	11,380.13	19,226.54	150,000.00

37d ▶ 15 Recall centering procedures

half sheet, long side up

1. Center the invitation vertically, each line horizontally.

2. Proofread your copy; mark the errors for correction using proofreader's marks (see p. 39 if necessary).

3. If time permits, type the invitation from your corrected copy.

YOU ARE INVITED
to become a member of
Future Business Leaders of America
October 27, 3:15 p.m.
Room 698, Student Activity Center
Membership Fee: $4.50

38

60-space line

38a ▶ 6 Conditioning practice

each line twice SS (slowly, then faster); DS between 2-line groups; if time permits, type each line again

alphabet	1	Dixie may pick Florine to judge the big show if Veloz quits.
fig/sym	2	I signed a 3-year note--$6,490 (at 12.5%)--with Ott & Cruze.
fluency	3	Did the bugle corps toot with the usual vigor for the queen?

| 1 | 2 | 3 | 4 | 5 | 6 | 7 | 8 | 9 | 10 | 11 | 12 |

38b ▶ 14 Learn: ' and _

' = apostrophe / _ = underline

Apostrophe (')

Electric
The ' is to the right of ; and is controlled by the *right little finger*.

Manual
Type ' (shift of **8**) with the *right second finger*. Reach with the controlling finger. Try to hold the other fingers over the home keys.

Underline (_)

Electric
Type _ (shift of the – key) with the *right little finger*. Reach with the finger without swinging the elbow out.

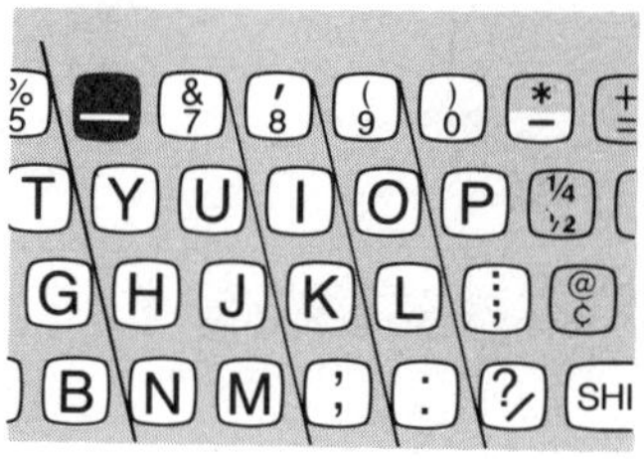

Manual
Type _ (shift of **6**) with the *right first finger*. Reach with the finger without letting the hand move forward.

Learning procedure

1. Locate key on appropriate chart above (electric or manual); study the reach-technique given with it.

2. Type the appropriate tryout drill (electric or manual) given at the right for it.

3. Then type twice the two lines which emphasize the key (slowly, then faster).

4. If time permits, type the enrichment lines twice.

' (apostrophe)

electric ▶ ';' ';' ';' ; ' ; 's I'm it's I've
manual 8'k 8'k 'k 'k 8's 8's I'm it's

1 Mrs. O'Fallon can't or won't pay for her son's trip to Troy.
2 I'll return the book if it's Alice's, Nancy's, or Kathryn's.

_ (underline)

electric ▶ -_; -_; _; _; _- _- Type Stop.
manual 6_j 6_j _j _j _6 _6 Type 6264.

3 Curve your fingers. Keep your wrists low, your hands quiet.
4 Use CAPS or underline for book titles--Word-Division Manual.

Enrichment (if time permits)

5 Curran & Sons published the book Echoes and Encores in 1982.
6 I use ' (apostrophe) to shorten phrases: I'd, it's, didn't.

255b-258b, continued

Job 6
Financial statement

Center, in reading position, the balance sheet at the right which is to be presented to the Board of Directors at their next meeting.

BLAINE-DERRY INDUSTRIES, INC.

Balance Sheet

Year Ended December 31, 19--

ASSETS

Cash	$12,317,000
Accounts receivable	25,755,000
Inventories	36,814,000
Prepaid expenses	750,000
Property, plant, and equipment, at cost	16,600,000
Total assets	$92,236,000

LIABILITIES AND SHAREHOLDERS' EQUITY

Liabilities	
Accounts payable	$12,494,000
Notes payable	5,200,000
Accrued interest	720,000
Total liabilities	$18,414,000
Shareholders' equity	
Capital investment	$50,000,000
Retained earnings	23,822,000
Total shareholders' equity	$73,822,000
Total liabilities and shareholders' equity	$92,236,000

Job 7
Financial statement

Center, in reading position, the consolidated income statement at the right in this special format for inclusion in the company's annual reports.

BLAINE-DERRY INDUSTRIES, INC.

Consolidated Statement of Income

Year Ended December 31, 19--

Net sales	$116,166,000
Less cost of sales	62,336,000
Gross sales	53,830,000
Less selling and other expenses	11,242,000
Income before taxes	42,588,000
Income taxes	11,766,000
Net income	$ 31,822,000
Dividend per share	$1.40

37

60-space line

37a ▶ 6 Conditioning practice

each line twice SS (slowly, then faster); DS between 2-line groups; if time permits, type each line again

alphabet 1 Vicki Dalb may win quite a just prize for her next pop song.
fig/sym 2 Of the 385, 250 (64.9%) typed over 47 words/min. on test #1.
fluency 3 Rick paid for both the visual aid and the sign for the firm.

| 1 | 2 | 3 | 4 | 5 | 6 | 7 | 8 | 9 | 10 | 11 | 12 |

37b ▶ 12 Learn: & and -

Use the standard plan for learning new key locations as given in 26b, page 44; type each set of lines twice.

& = ampersand (and)
– = hyphen
–– = dash

Space once before and after **&** used to join names.
No space precedes or follows – and –– used as punctuation.

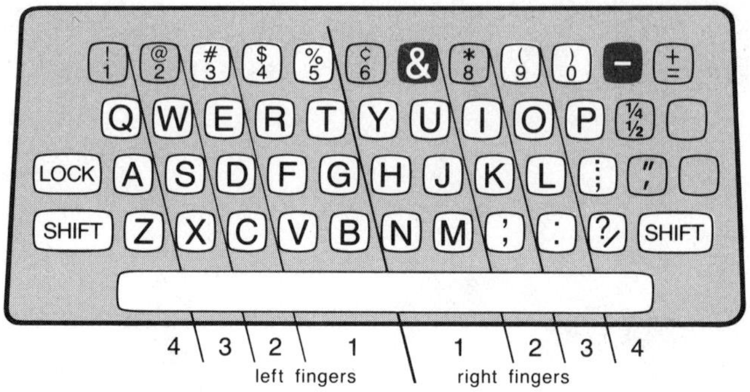

Reach technique for &

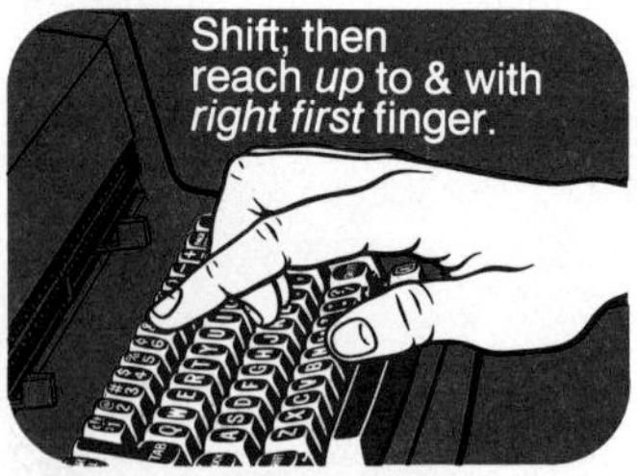

Shift; then reach *up* to & with *right first* finger.

& (ampersand)

1 7&j 7&j &j &j &7 &7 B&O CG&E James wrote to Swift & Company.
2 Brown & Jordan, Inc., has bought 250 shares of C&NW Railway.

Reach technique for –

Reach *up* to - with *right little* finger.

– (hyphen) –– (dash)

3 –;– –;– –; –; –– –– is 4–ply I use a 6–ply tire on my truck.
4 I used a 6–inch line––60 pica spaces––for the 5–page report.

Enrichment (if time permits)

5 Telfer & Van shipped us 4– and 6–ply tires of various sizes.
6 We use a 5–inch line––60 elite, 50 pica spaces––for letters.

37c ▶ 17 Develop skill on statistical copy

1. Two 1′ writings on each ¶; determine *gwam* on each.
2. Practice difficult words and figure/symbol combinations 2 or 3 times each.
3. Center the material vertically on a half sheet of paper: Center and type the heading **MOST-USED WORDS** above the material; then TS and type the ¶s DS.

all figures used

	gwam 1′	2′
The 50 most–used words account for 46% of the total of	11	5
all word uses in a study of 4,100 letters, memorandums, and	23	11
reports. The first 100 account for 53%; the first 500, 71%;	35	18
the first 1,000, 80%; and the first 2,000, just under 88%.	47	23
Of the first 7,027 most–used words (accounting for 97%	11	5
of all word uses), 209 are balanced–hand words (26% of all	23	11
uses) and 284 are one–hand words (14% of all uses). So you	35	17
see, practice on these words can help to improve your rate.	47	23

gwam 1′ | 1 | 2 | 3 | 4 | 5 | 6 | 7 | 8 | 9 | 10 | 11 | 12 |
2′ | 1 | 2 | 3 | 4 | 5 | 6 |

unit **52** lessons 259-264

Sales/purchasing office

Learning goals

1. To increase your knowledge of clerical typing tasks found in a sales office and a purchasing office.

2. To improve your skill in typing production materials.

Machine adjustments

1. Line: 70 for drills; as necessary for problems.

2. Spacing: SS sentence drills with a DS between sentence groups; space problems as required.

259-261

259a-261a ▶ 5 Conditioning practice

each line twice SS (slowly, then faster); DS between 2-line groups; if time permits, retype selected lines

alphabet 1 Executives may jeopardize a quick merger if they make the news public.

figures 2 Correct pages 3, 6, 7, 8, and 9; retype pages 46, 48, 73, 91, and 205.

fig/sym 3 On May 8, the price of Item #97631 will increase 5% (from $40 to $42).

fluency 4 The janitor kept the keys for the auto in the enamel box on the shelf.

| 1 | 2 | 3 | 4 | 5 | 6 | 7 | 8 | 9 | 10 | 11 | 12 | 13 | 14 |

259b-261b ▶ 45 Production typing

You have been employed as a senior typist and clerk by the Eastern Office Supply Corporation, wholesalers of office supplies and equipment, located at 200 Industrial Parkway West, Knoxville, TN 37921-6061. You will work in the office of Matthew E. DeYoung, who is the Sales Manager.

Job 1
Sales assignments

plain sheets

Make an original and two carbon copies of the sales assignments at the right. Center the material attractively on the page; use the heading:

SALES TERRITORIES AND GOALS FOR THE FISCAL YEAR ENDED DECEMBER 31, 19--

use next year's date.

Agent/District	Territory	Goal	Commission
Dominic C. Montella District A	Vermont Massachusetts Connecticut Rhode Island	$450,000	6.5%
Martin L. Polanski District B	New York Pennsylvania	$500,000	6.0%
Alice K. Watson District C	New Jersey Delaware Maryland Virginia	$420,000	7.0%
John P. Hamilton District D	North Carolina South Carolina Georgia	$300,000	7.5%
Mary C. Ellis District E	Florida Louisiana Mississippi Alabama	$420,000	7.0%
Lewis C. Tyler District F	Tennessee Kentucky Ohio	$425,000	7.0%
Douglas E. Marks District G	Michigan Indiana Illinois	$475,000	6.5%

36c ▶ 16 Learn: (%)

Use the standard plan for learning new key locations as given in 26b, page 44; type each set of lines twice.

(= left parenthesis
% = percent
) = right parenthesis

Do not space between ( ) and the copy they enclose; do not space between a figure and %.

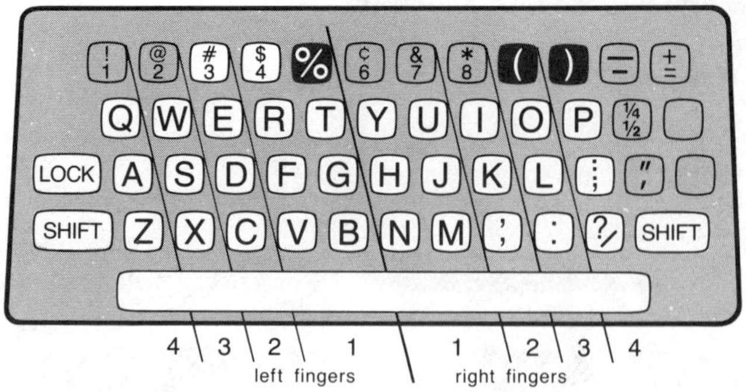

Reach technique for (

Shift; then reach *up* to (with *right third* finger.

Reach technique for %

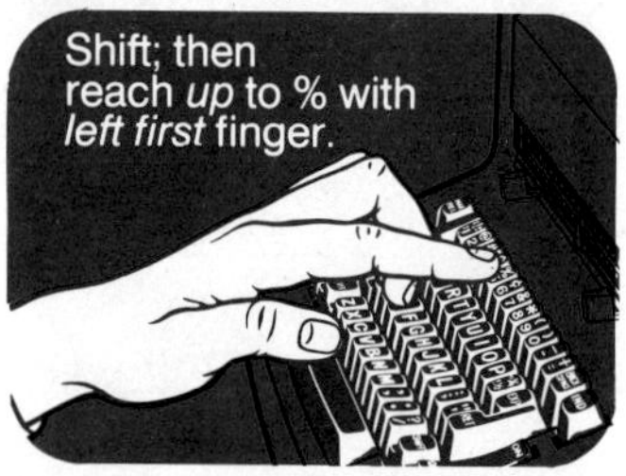

Shift; then reach *up* to % with *left first* finger.

Reach technique for)

Shift; then reach *up* to) with *right little* finger

((left parenthesis)

1 9(1 9(1 (1 (1 (9 (9 (2 (2 (19 To type (, shift and strike (.
2 As (is the shift of 9, use the same finger to type (and 9.

% (percent)

3 5%f 5%f %f %f 5% 5% 8% 8% 16% The discounts are 6%, 8%, 10%.
4 In 1979, 35% of our employees were women; now, over 45% are.

) (right parenthesis)

5 0); 0);););)0)0 p) p) up) To type), shift and strike).
6 As) is the shift of 0, use the same finger to type) and 0.

Enrichment (if time permits)

7 Speakers should (1) stand up, (2) speak up, and (3) shut up.
8 My savings account (#94783) draws annual interest at 5 1/2%.

36d ▶ 13 Develop skill on statistical copy

1. A 1′ writing on each ¶; determine *gwam* on each.

2. Practice difficult words and figure/symbol combinations 2 or 3 times each.

3. A 2′ writing on each ¶; determine *gwam* on each.

4. Center the material vertically on a half sheet of paper: Center and type the heading **FIGURE USAGE IN BUSINESS** above the material; then TS and type the ¶s DS.

all figures used	gwam 1′	2′
In a tabulation of figures found in 2,963 typed papers	11	5
prepared in 349 business firms, Grill learned that 41.4% of	23	11
all figure uses was accounted for by 0, 1, and 2. The next	35	17
highest percentage (27.9%) covered uses of 5, 3, and 4.	46	23
The figure least used was 8 (7.3% of all figure uses),	11	5
followed closely by 7 (7.4%) and 9 (7.5%). The digit 6, at	23	11
8.5%, led the last 4. These figures are important, though,	35	17
for even 0 accounted for only 15.4% of all digits used.	46	23

gwam 1′ | 1 | 2 | 3 | 4 | 5 | 6 | 7 | 8 | 9 | 10 | 11 | 12 |
2′ | 1 | 2 | 3 | 4 | 5 | 6 |

259b-261b, continued

Job 2
Memorandums

plain full sheets

1. Type twice the memo given at the right using a carbon pack of one original and three carbon copies each time for a total of eight copies. Leave a top margin of 1½" and side margins of 1". Use block style; correct errors as you type.

Note: DS after ¶1 in pica type; TS after ¶1 in elite type.

2. Use each copy as a form memo to each agent listed in Job 1. Fill in the blank spaces with the information given in the sales assignments in Job 1.

TO:

FROM: Matthew E. DeYoung, Sales Manager

SUBJECT: Sales Territories, Goals, and Commissions

DATE: November 20, 19--

TS

¶ Your sales territory for the ~~coming~~ next calendar year will include the states of

DS

¶ Your monthly goal, in net sales, has been set at

DS

¶ All commissions will be paid on the ~~last~~ final day of the month following the month of reported sales. Your commission will be the following percent of net sales in excess of your monthly sales goal:

Job 3
Index card file

[LM pp. 87–92]

1. Type an index card for each address at the right. On the third line from the top edge of the card, type the name of the company; triple space and type the complete name and address as shown in the list.

2. Alphabetize the cards *by company names*; then number the cards from 1 to 13 in the upper right-hand corner.

Hartford Office Supply Company
153 Farmington Avenue
Hartford, CT 06105-4498

Ms. Caroline T. Bradford, Chief Buyer
Lafayette Stationers, Inc.
445 Congress Street
Portland, ME 04101-3761

Mr. Lincoln S. Lyons, President
Capitol Office Equipment Company
106 West Allegan Street
Lansing, MI 48933-8067

Southern Office Supplies, Inc.
805 Broad Street
Augusta, GA 30902-4483

Mr. James C. Keonig, Buyer
Conway Industries, Inc.
201 Orange Avenue South
Orlando, FL 32801-6772

Jefferson Supply Company
2200 E. Glebe Road
Alexandria, VA 22305-5719

Mr. William C. Farnum, Vice President
First Pennsylvania Refiners, Inc.
1700 Market Street
Philadelphia, PA 19103-2030

Miss Elinor T. Calhoun, Director
Office of Supplies and Equipment
New York State
84 Holland Avenue
Albany, NY 12208-4008

Mr. Leon G. Martinez
Director of Purchasing
Overton Industries
65 Madison Avenue
Memphis, TN 38103-2146

Delaware Stationers, Inc.
918 Market Street
Wilmington, DE 19801-1467

Mrs. Beatrice T. White
Chief Purchasing Officer
Kentucky Enterprises, Inc.
251 East Liberty Street
Louisville, KY 40204-7364

Mrs. E. T. Grimes, Purchasing Agent
Davidson Manufacturing Company
202 S. College Street
Charlotte, NC 28202-3120

Valley Manufacturing Company
3501 Cherokee Road
Birmingham, AL 35223-1973

35c ▶ 8 Develop skill on statistical copy

1. A 1′ and a 2′ writing on the ¶; determine *gwam*.

2. Center the material vertically on a half sheet of paper: Center and type the heading **TYPING FIGURES/SYMBOLS** above the material; then TS and type the ¶ DS.

all figures used — gwam 2′

As you type figures such as 62, 30, 49, 58, or 71, try 5
to keep unused fingers near home row. When you shift for $ 11
and #, try to make the reaches without moving the hand down 17
for the shift or up for $ and #. Keep the hands quiet. 23

gwam 2′ | 1 | 2 | 3 | 4 | 5 | 6 |

35d ▶ 20 Improve keystroking skill: guided writing

1. A 1′ writing on ¶ 1; determine *gwam*.

2. Add 4 *gwam* to set a new goal rate.

3. Two 1′ writings on ¶ 1, trying to maintain your goal rate each ¼ minute.

4. Type ¶ 2 in the same way.

5. A 2′ unguided writing on each ¶. If you complete a ¶ before time is called, start typing that ¶ again.

6. A 3′ writing on ¶s 1–2 combined; determine *gwam*.

all letters used | LA | 1.4 si | 5.4 awl | 85% hfw | — gwam 2′ | 3′

Typewriter spacing is regular; that is, each letter of 5 | 4
the alphabet uses the same amount of space. Most type used 11 | 8
by printers, though, varies in space; that is, wide letters 17 | 12
take more space than narrow ones. Every line of typed copy 23 | 16
lines up at the left side but usually not at the right. 29 | 19

Printers can force lines of different lengths to align 5 | 23
at the right side by adjusting the space between words. As 11 | 27
you copy from print, then, do not expect every line to stop 17 | 31
at quite the same point. Many students and more than a few 23 | 35
teachers are puzzled by this peculiar quality of print. 29 | 39

gwam 2′ | 1 | 2 | 3 | 4 | 5 | 6 |
3′ | 1 | 2 | 3 | 4 |

36

60-space line

36a ▶ 6 Conditioning practice

each line twice SS (slowly, then faster); DS between 2-line groups; if time permits, type each line again

alphabet 1 Having pumped in six quick points, Jaye Wold froze the ball.
fig/sym 2 No space separates $ or / or # and figures: $59, 1/2, #360.
fluency 3 He is to pay for the eight pens she laid by the audit forms.

| 1 | 2 | 3 | 4 | 5 | 6 | 7 | 8 | 9 | 10 | 11 | 12 |

36b ▶ 15 Improve keystroking speed: guided writing

Repeat Steps 1–5 of 35d, above.
Goal: 2 *gwam* increase.

259b-261b, continued

Job 4
Price list

plain sheets

Make an original and 1 carbon copy of the price list at the right; use a top margin of 1″; center the material horizontally; DS the items. Keep the price list for use in typing some of the jobs which follow.

EASTERN OFFICE SUPPLY CORPORATION

Special Sale Prices, February, 19--

Stock Number	Item	Price
BI6930	Binder indexes, 5-tab, 8″ × 11 1/2″	$ .59 set*
CS7192	Carbon sets, 12# bond	14.95 per 1,000
EN2534	Envelopes, white, 6 1/2″ × 3 5/8″	32.75 per 1,000
EN2535	Envelopes, white, 9 1/2″ × 4 1/8″	34.80 per 1,000
IN5279	Index guides, alpha, letter size	4.90 set
IN5280	Index guides, numeric, letter size	4.90 set
FF5243	Manila file folders, 3-cut tab, legal size	6.50 box
FF5244	Manila file folders, 3-cut tab, letter size	5.50 box
PB5153	Paper, 20# bond, white, 8 1/2″ × 11″	3.90 ream
PB5154	Paper, 20# bond, white, 8 1/2″ × 13″	4.10 ream
PD4043	Paper, 20# duplicator, white, 8 1/2″ × 11″	3.20 ream
PD4044	Paper, 20# duplicator, white, 8 1/2″ × 13″	3.45 ream
PC2835	Paper clips, 1 1/4″ long	2.70 per 1,000
PC2836	Paper clips, 2″ long	5.90 per 1,000
PE8635	Pencils, No. 2, black	20.95 gross
PE8636	Pencils, red, w/erasers	32.50 gross
RB8345	Rubber bands, 1/16″ × 3″	3.25 lb.
RB7347	Rubber bands, 1/8″ × 3 1/2″	3.25 lb.
SA2384	Staples, 1/4″ leg	1.05 box
PD9301	Steno pad, 6″ × 9″	6.25 doz.
ST5012	Strapping tape, 3/4″ × 180′	2.75 roll
TT9340	Transparent tape, 1/2″ × 108′	.75 ea.

*Minimum order: 24 sets

Job 5
Sales letters

[LM pp. 93–100]

1. Type the letter at the right on executive-size stationery to Addressees **1, 3, 6,** and **13** of the address file typed in Job 3. Prepare the letter for **Mr. DeYoung's** signature.

2. Date the letter **January 12, 19--**. Use block style with open punctuation. Provide an appropriate salutation and complimentary close.

3. Include the name of the appropriate District Representative in the final paragraph of the letter. (Obtain the name of the representative who services the state of the addressee from Job 1.)

While the "cat's away," the mice don't always "play"! Take our Director of Marketing, Bob Rawlins, for example. While the "big boss," our President, Marvin Greene, is away, Bob has all of us busy planning our annual George Washington's birthday sale--not just a one-day sale but a sale that lasts the entire month of February.

During February ~~Furary~~, we reduce our inventories to the lowest level ~~point~~ possible so that when we take our annual physical inventory on March 1 we will save time and effort. To acheive this objective, we are willing to offer many of our most popular items at reduced prices as shown ~~indicated~~ on the enclosed special price list.

These special low prices are available only to our best customers ~~buyers~~ and only on orders recieved during the month of February. Don't miss this opportunity to save; send us your order today. Better still, call (800) 555-3500 and give your order to your District Representative, (give name).

unit **6** lessons 35-39

Learn to operate the symbol keyboard

Learning goals

1. To learn to type symbols by touch and with good techniques.

2. To improve skill in typing statistical copy.

3. To type straight copy at higher speeds and with improved control.

Machine adjustments

1. Paper guide at *0*.

2. Ribbon control to type on top half of ribbon.

3. Margin sets: 60-space line (center – 30; center + 30 + 5).

4. Line-space selector on *1* (SS) for drills; on *2* (DS) for ¶s; as directed for other tasks.

35

60-space line

35a ▶ 6 Conditioning practice

each line twice SS (slowly, then faster); DS between 2-line groups; if time permits, type each line again

alphabet 1 Five boys quickly mixed the prizes, baffling one wise judge.
figure 2 Review all the figures: 65, 74, 83, 92, 201, 299, 300, 640.
fluency 3 Pam is to go to the city hall to sign the land forms for us.

5-stroke words | 1 | 2 | 3 | 4 | 5 | 6 | 7 | 8 | 9 | 10 | 11 | 12 |

35b ▶ 16 Learn: $ /

Use the standard plan for learning new key locations as given in 26b, page 44; type each set of lines twice.

$ = dollar/dollars
/ = diagonal
= number/pounds

Do not space between a figure and **$**, **/**, or **#**.

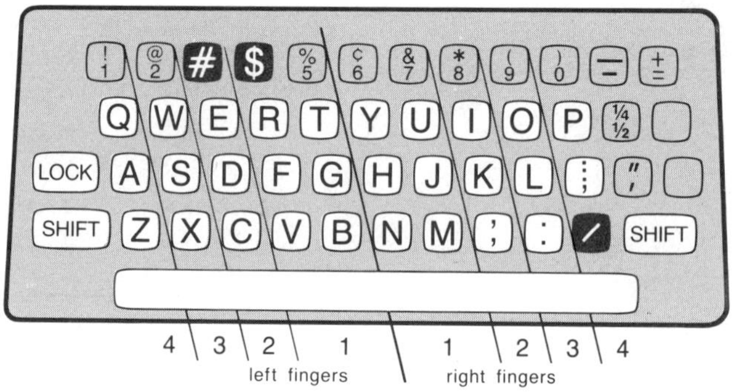

Reach technique for $

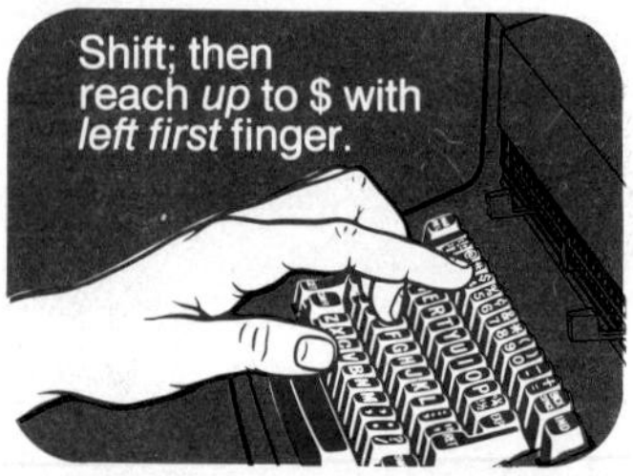

Shift; then reach *up* to $ with *left first* finger.

$ (dollar)

1 4$f 4$f $f $f $4 $4 $8 $8 $14 They will pay her $10; me, $8.
2 The $47 balance includes sales of $7.26, $15.80, and $23.94.

Reach technique for /

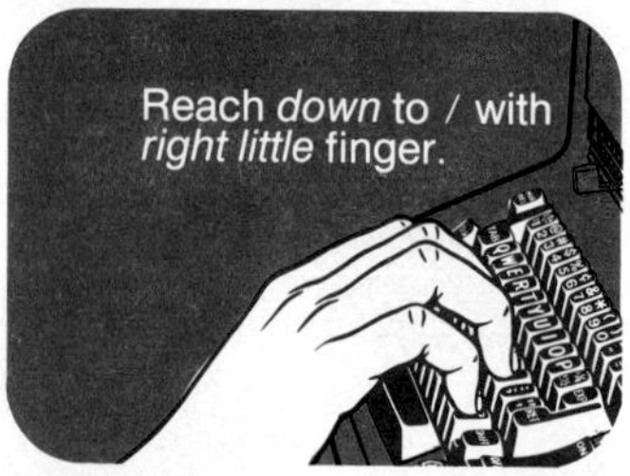

Reach *down* to / with *right little* finger.

/ (diagonal)

3 ?/; ?/; /; /; 1/3 1/12 and/or Did they type 1/4 and/or 1/12?
4 Space between a whole number and a fraction: 5 3/4, 16 2/3.

Reach technique for #

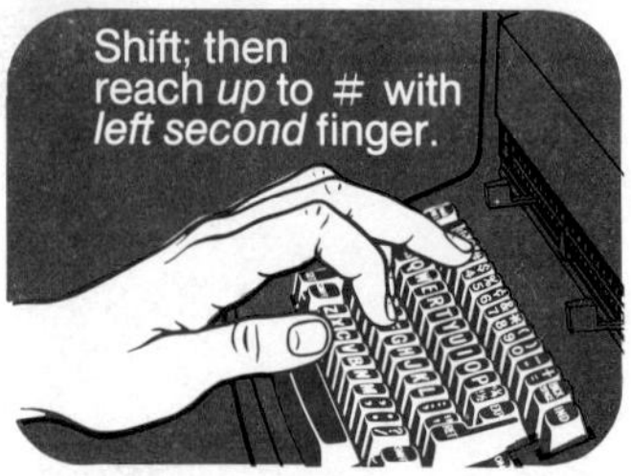

Shift; then reach *up* to # with *left second* finger.

(number/pounds)

5 3#d 3#d #d #d #3 #3 #6 #6 #15 Send 130# of #13; 30# of #139.
6 I shipped 150# of #130 seed on May 3; 130# of #31 on May 13.

Enrichment (if time permits)

7 I must shift to type $ and #, but not for /: $4, 3#, 4 7/8.
8 Order 100 reams of 20# paper at $8/ream; total cost is $800.

259b-261b, continued

Job 6
Invoices

[LM pp. 101–106]

1. Type invoices with 1 cc on plain paper for addressees **2, 5, 6, 9, 11,** and **12**, in the index card file prepared in Job 3. The items ordered are shown at the right.

2. Obtain the order numbers and carriers from the order register below. All terms are **2/10, n/30.** Use the shipping date as the date of the invoice.

3. Obtain the item names and prices from the price list prepared in Job 4. Compute the total cost of each item ordered; enter this in the total column, then determine and enter the total amount of each invoice.

Addressee 2

Quantity	Stock No.
5,000	EN2534
10 boxes	FF5243
100 reams	PB5153
500 reams	PD4043

Addressee 5

Quantity	Stock No.
30 sets	BI6930
6,000	PC2835
10 lbs.	RB8345
20 boxes	SA2384
10 rolls	ST5012

Addressee 6

Quantity	Stock No.
6,000	CS7192
5,000	EN2535
3,000	PC2836
10 gross	PE8635

Addressee 9

Quantity	Stock No.
50 boxes	FF5244
80 reams	PD4044
2 gross	PE8636
20 doz.	PD9301

Addressee 11

Quantity	Stock No.
20 sets	IN5279
50 boxes	FF5243
100 ea.	TT9340

Addressee 12

Quantity	Stock No.
100 reams	PB5153
50 reams	PB5154
10 lbs.	RB8345
80 boxes	SA2384
40 rolls	ST5012

ORDER REGISTER

	OUR ORDER	CUSTOMER'S ORDER	SHIPPING DATE	SHIPPED VIA (Carrier)
Conway Industries, Inc	F6317	8542A	March 9	Dixie Van Line
Delaware Stationers, Inc	F6318	T72914	March 15	R & L Freight
First Pa. Refiners, Inc	F6319	B5349	March 21	Southern Transit
Hartford Off. Sup. Co.	F6320	88-9654	March 17	Coastal Shipping Co.
Lafayette Stationers, Inc	F6321	JA-41695	March 31	King Trucking Co.
Overton Industries	F6322	071287	April 2	Tennessee Express Co.
Southern Off. Sup., Inc	F6323	11152-X	April 8	All-Cities Delivery
Valley Mfg. Co.	F6324	293847	April 13	Nay Bros. Vans, Inc

34c ▶ 10 Check/improve straight-copy skill

1. A 2′ writing on ¶s 1–3 combined; determine *gwam*; circle errors.

2. A 3′ writing on ¶s 1–3 combined; determine *gwam*; circle errors.

3. If time permits, type a 1′ guided writing on each ¶ for speed.

all letters used | LA | 1.4 si | 5.4 awl | 85% hfw |

	gwam 2′	3′
Since I am learning to center and type copy in message	5	4
form, typing is more fun. Of course I realize that without	11	8
good basic speed and control, typing a long letter or other	17	12
job would become very tedious work.	21	14
Therefore, I plan to boost my basic skill just as high	25	17
as possible even though one vital objective of practice now	31	21
is to learn to apply it. High skill and knowledge of style	37	25
are required to produce work of high quality.	42	28
A casual review of the personal and school papers that	47	32
I develop in longhand leads me to expect that basic symbols	53	36
as well as figures will have to be typed frequently. A job	59	40
in an office will certainly require skill in their use.	65	44

gwam 2′ | 1 | 2 | 3 | 4 | 5 | 6

3′ | 1 | 2 | 3 | 4

34d ▶ 25 Problem typing: centering announcements

2 half sheets (long side up)

Problem 1

Center the announcement vertically, each line horizontally. TS below the heading; DS between the other lines.

▶ Do not backspace for an odd or leftover letter, figure, or punctuation mark.

A HOLIDAY FANTASY

by the

Fine Arts Club

at

Playhouse in the Park

Friday, December 19, 7:30 p.m.

Problem 2

Center and type the announcement according to Problem 1 directions.

YOU ARE INVITED! ~~Judy~~ Judith Re And Yogi Mehte

in recital

Corbet auditorium

Saturday November 8, 2:30 p. m.

262a-264a ▶ 5 Conditioning practice

Use standard directions given in 259a-261a, p. 402.

alphabet	1	Governor Bamertz will quickly reject the new tax hike if it is passed.
figures	2	Tour 721 leaves May 14; Tour 965 on June 30; and Tour 863 on August 9.
fig/sym	3	In Shop 14-A, 1,340 units (25%) were rejected at a cost of $16,986.70.
fluency	4	I may go with them to the display in the city if they ask me to do so.
		| 1 | 2 | 3 | 4 | 5 | 6 | 7 | 8 | 9 | 10 | 11 | 12 | 13 | 14 |

262b-264b ▶ 45 Production typing

You have been hired as Chief of the Purchasing Section of the Administrative Services Division of Belmont Industries, 15 West 20th Street, Birmingham, AL 36201-2500. Your immediate supervisor is Sandra F. Goodman, Chief of the Administrative Services Division.

Job 1
Office reference file

1. Many clerical workers keep a file or notebook of instructions or steps to be followed when performing repetitive tasks similar to the material at the right.

2. Type the material at the right in unbound manuscript form. Use as a heading:

PROCEDURES FOR PURCHASING STATIONERY SUPPLIES

3. Keep the page for use in typing the Jobs which follow.

Stationery supplies will be reordered quarterly immediately following the quarterly ~~consolidated~~ inventory. To order stationery, ~~it will be necessary for you to~~ follow these steps:

1. Compare the quarterly inventory figures ~~amounts~~ with the inventory control records to identify ~~ascertain~~ those items that are at or below the reorder point.

2. Prepare a list of those supplies that are at or below the reorder point. ~~This list identifies those items to be ordered.~~

3. Compute ~~Determine~~ the amount of each item to be ordered by subtracting the amount on hand (inventory) from the optimum quantity ~~which you will find~~ indicated on the Inventory Control Record.

4. Prepare purchase orders for those items to be ordered from a standard contractor indicated on ~~as noted at the bottom of~~ the Inventory Control Record.

5. Prepare purchase requisitions for the Purchasing Division for those items for which there is no standard contractor.

6. For steps to be taken upon receipt of supplies, see "Procedures for Receipt ~~receiving~~ and Storage of Stationery ~~storing~~ Supplies."

33d ▶ 20 Problem typing: centering announcements

2 half sheets (long side up)

Problem 1

Center the announcement vertically, each line horizontally. TS below the heading; DS between the other lines.

▶ Do not backspace for an odd or leftover letter, figure, or punctuation mark.

JUNIOR ACHIEVEMENT CHAPTER

TS

announces

DS

Annual Awards Night and Banquet

DS

Convention Center

DS

Tuesday, February 15, 7 p.m.

Problem 2

Center and type the announcement according to Problem 1 directions.

HOLIDAY SALE

gifts for those special people

Unique Gifts in Gold, Silver, and Crystal

HOUSE OF GIFTS

Midtown Plaza, Level 2

December 3 through 9

34

60-space line

34a ▶ 6 Conditioning practice

each line twice SS (slowly, then faster); DS between 2-line groups; if time permits, type each line again

alphabet 1 Rozalyn has very quickly won a big chance from Jax Products.

figure 2 Long numbers may reduce the speed: 1,579, 2,485, and 5,630.

fluency 3 The city auditor may handle the penalty for the island firm.

| 1 | 2 | 3 | 4 | 5 | 6 | 7 | 8 | 9 | 10 | 11 | 12 |

34b ▶ 9 Develop skill on statistical script

1. A 1′ writing on the ¶; determine *gwam*.

2. A 2′ writing on the ¶; determine *gwam*.

3. Center the material vertically on a half sheet of paper: Center and type the heading **PAPER FACTS** above the material; then triple-space (TS) and type the ¶.

	gwam 1′	2′
Typing paper of standard size is 8.5 inches wide by 11	11	5
inches long. The maximum line length for such paper is 102	23	11
elite spaces or 85 pica spaces; it has a center point of 51	35	17
for elite type or 42 for pica. A full sheet has a total of	47	23
66 line spaces; a half sheet, 33. When used short side up,	59	29
the half sheet has a center point of 33 for elite or 27 for	71	35
pica and has a total of 51 line spaces.	79	39

262b-264b, continued

Job 2
Inventory control cards

[LM pp. 107–114]

Type as illustrated at the right an inventory control card for each item listed below. Arrange the cards in alphabetic order.

INVENTORY CONTROL RECORD

Item: Badges, I.D.

Location: Aisle F Sector 12

Optimum Quantity: 200

Reorder Point: 90

Standard Contract: None

ITEM	AISLE	SECTOR	OPTIMUM QUANTITY	REORDER POINT	STANDARD CONTRACT
Manila file folders, 3-cut tab, letter size	A	15	50 boxes	25 boxes	Eastern Office Supply Corp.
Manila file folders, 3-cut tab, legal size	A	15	30 boxes	15 boxes	Eastern Office Supply Corp.
Envelopes, white, 6 1/2″ × 3 5/8″	A	16	50,000	20,000	Eastern Office Supply Corp.
Envelopes, white, 9 1/2″ × 4 1/8″	A	16	70,000	30,000	Eastern Office Supply Corp.
Paper, 20# bond, white, 8 1/2″ × 11″	B	19	120 reams	55 reams	Eastern Office Supply Corp.
Paper, 20# bond, white, 8 1/2″ × 13″	B	20	40 reams	15 reams	Eastern Office Supply Corp.
Pencil sharpener, electric	C	7	12	6	A & D Manufacturing Co.
Steno pad, 6″ × 9″	C	8	15 doz.	7 doz.	Eastern Office Supply Corp.
Pencils, No. 2, black	D	1	8 gross	4 gross	Eastern Office Supply Corp.
Crayon pencil, black, mechanical	D	1	10 doz.	4 doz.	None
Erasers, typewriter, stick, w/brush	D	2	10 doz.	5 doz.	None
Pens, ball-point, blue ink	D	2	24 doz.	10 doz.	None
Scratch pads, 4″ × 6″, plain	E	8	2,000	900	None
Rulers, metal, 18″	E	19	20	10	None
Badges, I.D.	F	12	200	90	None
Binders, 3-ring, 11 1/2″ × 10 1/2″ × 2″, blue	F	14	50	25	None

33

60-space line

33a ▶ 6 Conditioning practice

each line twice SS (slowly, then faster); DS between 2-line groups; if time permits, type each line again

alphabet	1	Joe Vlassick was quizzed by Meg on one part of his tax form.
figure	2	Type these figures with quiet hands: 50, 128, 364, and 947.
fluency	3	Do rush the worn panels to the auto firm for them to enamel.

| 1 | 2 | 3 | 4 | 5 | 6 | 7 | 8 | 9 | 10 | 11 | 12 |

33b ▶ 9 Develop statistical typing skill

1. A 1′ writing on the ¶; determine *gwam*.

2. A 2′ writing on the ¶; determine *gwam*.

3. Center the material vertically on a half sheet of paper: Center and type the heading **EXPRESSING NUMBERS** above the material; then triple-space (TS) and type the ¶ DS.

all figures used — gwam 2′

Use figures in typing dimensions; for example, 128 ft. 5
9 in.; 73 cm; and 8.5 km. Use figures to state time, also: 12
4:10 p.m. Type dates in figures, too, as in March 6, 1992. 18
In addition, type in figures numbers preceded by nouns; for 24
instance: See Chapter 4, page 57, line 12. 28

gwam 2′ | 1 | 2 | 3 | 4 | 5 | 6 |

33c ▶ 15 Improve keystroking speed: guided writing

Type a 1′ writing on ¶1; determine *gwam*. Add 4 *gwam* to set a new goal rate; then type additional writings as follows:

1. Two 1′ guided writings on ¶1 at your new goal rate.

2. Two 1′ guided writings on ¶2 in the same way.

3. A 2′ writing on each ¶. If you complete a ¶ before time is called, start over.

4. A 3′ writing on ¶s 1–2 combined, without the guide; determine *gwam*.

Goals

1′: At least 21 *gwam*.
2′: At least 20 *gwam*.
3′: At least 19 *gwam*.

all letters used | LA | 1.4 si | 5.4 awl | 85% hfw |

Text	gwam 2′	3′
You are now able to type letters and figures by touch,	5	3
without gazing at your keyboard. You are also able to type	11	8
from copy that is presented in script and rough draft. You	17	12
are now learning to center copy on the page, a process that	23	16
is required in virtually all applied typing activities.	29	19
If you expect to continue to improve, put off the urge	5	23
to check the keys as you practice. Keeping the eyes on the	11	27
copy material eliminates time lost in trying to locate just	17	32
where you quit reading to start your checking. Look if you	23	35
get lost, of course; but make reduced looking the goal.	29	39

gwam 2′ | 1 | 2 | 3 | 4 | 5 | 6 |
3′ | 1 | 2 | 3 | 4 |

262b-264b, continued

Job 3
Inventory sheet
plain sheets

Make an original and 1 cc of the inventory sheet at the right. DS the items; leave a top margin of 1½" and 1" side margins. Do not type the lines.

Job 4
Order list
plain sheet

1. Compare the inventory sheet prepared in Job 3 above with the cards typed in Job 2 and prepare a list of items to be ordered. Leave a top margin of 1½" and 1" side margins. Use the heading: **STATIONERY ITEMS TO BE ORDERED** and three columns: **Item, Quantity,** and **Standard Contract.**

2. Refer to the "Procedures for Purchasing Stationery Supplies and Equipment" prepared in Job 1 for additional instructions.

INVENTORY OF STATIONERY SUPPLIES AND EQUIPMENT

January 31, 19--

Location	Item	Amount
A-15	Manila file folders, 3-cut tab, letter size	20 boxes
A-15	Manila file folders, 3-cut tab, legal size	10 boxes
A-16	Envelopes, white, 6 1/2" x 3 5/8"	10,000
A-16	Envelopes, white, 9 1/2" x 4 1/8"	30,000
B-19	Paper, 20# bond, white, 8 1/2" x 11"	50 reams
B-20	Paper, 20# bond, white, 8 1/2" x 13"	15 reams
C-7	Pencil sharpener, electric	10
C-8	Steno pad, 6" x 9"	5 doz.
D-1	Pencils, No. 2, black	3 gross
D-1	Crayon pencil, black, mechanical	5 doz.
D-2	Erasers, typewriter, stick, w/brush	4 doz.
D-2	Pens, ball-point, blue ink	9 doz.
E-8	Scratch pads, 4" x 6", plain	800
E-19	Rulers, metal, 18"	8
F-12	Badges, I.D.	50
F-14	Binders, 3-ring, 11 1/2" x 10 1/2" x 2", blue	20

Job 5
Purchase requisitions
[LM p. 115]

1. Using the order list prepared in Job 4, prepare **Purchase Requisitions Nos. 187 and 188** (3 items on each requisition) dated **February 16, 19—**, for those items that are *not* on a standard contract.

2. Request the items be delivered to you in **Room 102** of the **Administration Building** no later than **March 30.** The job number to which the items are to be charged is **Administrative Expenses.**

Job 6
Purchase orders
[LM p. 117]

1. Using the order list prepared in Job 4, prepare **Purchase Orders Nos. AD67543 and AD67544** (4 items on each order) dated **February 19, 19—**, for those items to be ordered from the Eastern Office Supply Corporation.

2. Obtain the stock number and price of each item from the list typed in Job 4, page 404.

3. All terms are **2/20, n/30**; items will be shipped by **Dixie Van Lines.**

4. In the "total" column, compute the total cost of each item ordered, and the total amount of each purchase order.

Center

SOPHOMORE CLASS OFFICERS
TS

Ellen Janacek, President
DS
Juan Lopez, Vice President
DS
Oma Tallchief, Secretary
DS
Dwight Huntington, Treasurer

Centered announcement

32c ▶ 30 Learn to center vertically (top to bottom)

2 half sheets (long side up)

1. Review the steps for horizontal centering on page 52.

2. Study the steps for vertical centering given at the right.

3. Center and type the model announcement shown above (entire problem centered vertically; each line centered horizontally).

4. Center and type the announcement shown at the right. TS below the heading; DS the other lines.

Vertical centering

1. Count the lines to be typed and the blank line spaces to be left between them (2 blank line spaces for triple spacing below main or secondary heading and 1 blank line space between double-spaced lines).

2. Subtract *lines needed* from 33 for a half sheet (or 66 for a full sheet).

3. Divide remainder by 2 to get top and bottom margins. If a fraction results, disregard it.

4. Space down from top edge of paper 1 space more than the number of lines to be left in top margin.

Lines available	33
Lines needed	− 10
	23 ÷ 2 = 11½

Start on Line 12.

ANNOUNCING
TS
Metropolitan Typewriting Contest
DS
Tuesday, November 29, 3 p.m.

Education Center, Room 140

Information: Ms. Edna Dahlman

PRIZES, AWARDS, CERTIFICATES

Enrichment problems appear on LM p. 23.

unit **53** lessons 265-268

Executive office

Learning goals

1. To improve your production skills by planning, organizing, and typing typical jobs in an executive office.

2. To improve your ability to plan and compose correspondence.

Machine adjustments

1. Line: 70 for drills; as necessary for problems.

2. Spacing: SS sentence drills with a DS between sentence groups; space problems as required.

265-268

265a-268a ▶ 5
Conditioning practice

each line twice SS (slowly, then faster); DS between 2-line groups; if time permits, retype selected lines

alphabet 1 Karl Bixby said he might weave the frieze in a rough jacquard pattern.

figures 2 On May 9, study Units 18, 20, and 35; on May 17, Units 24, 36, and 47.

fig/sym 3 Model #803 sells for $4, Model #651 for $7, and Model #863 for $29.75.

fluency 4 Six of the eight attorneys may claim custody of the special documents.

| 1 | 2 | 3 | 4 | 5 | 6 | 7 | 8 | 9 | 10 | 11 | 12 | 13 | 14 |

265b-268b ▶ 45
Production typing

You have been appointed as Administrative Secretary to Ms. Lenore C. Kelly, Marketing Vice President of Marvelon Cosmetics, Inc. The home office of Marvelon is located at 1515 Broadway, New York, NY 10036-7002.

Job 1
Directory

Type the directory of European offices of the Marvelon Company shown at the right on a full sheet. Center the material attractively on the page; provide an appropriate main heading. Keep the directory for use in the Jobs which follow.

City	Name/Address	Telephone
Amsterdam	Mr. T. C. Willem 40 Dam Amsterdam, Holland	20-43.32.22
Frankfurt	Frau Eva C. Holtz Mailaenderstr. 60 D-6000 FRANKFURT GERMANY, FED REP OF	06196/7878
London	Mr. Jon C. Wellington 18 Bedford Mews LONDON WC1R 4EJ England	01/722-7711
Madrid	Mr. Carlos T. Medina Princesa 29 Madrid 15, Spain	1/31.90.00
Munich	Herr Otto M. Koenig Leopoldstr. 200 D-8000 MUNICH GERMANY, FED REP OF	089/340971
Paris	Mlle. Claudette M. Marceau 71 Boulevard Victor F-78015 PARIS FRANCE	(1) 533 74 63
Rome	Mr. Luis P. Margiotti Via Aurelia Antica 415 I-64301 ROME ITALY	06-5872

31d ▶ 24 Learn to center horizontally (side to side)

2 half sheets (long side up)

1. Read the copy in the color block at the right.

2. Type the learning drills as directed below.

Learning drills

Drill 1. Starting on Line 14, center and type each line of Drill 1 on a separate line.

Drill 2. Starting on Line 13, center and type each line of Drill 2 in the same way.

To TS when machine is set for DS: DS, then turn the cylinder (platen) forward one space by hand.

Get ready to center

1. Insert paper with left edge at *0*.

2. Move left margin stop to *0*; move right margin stop to right end of scale.

3. Clear all tab stops; set a new stop at horizontal center of paper: elite, 51; pica, 42.

How to center

1. Tabulate to center of paper.

2. From center, backspace *once* for each *2* letters, spaces, figures, or punctuation marks in the line.

3. Do not backspace for an odd or leftover stroke at the end of the line.

4. Begin to type where backspacing ends.

Example

● center point

backspace ◀	1	1	1	1	1	1	1	1	1
	LE	AR	NI	NG	space T	O space	CE	NT	ER

Drill 1

LEARNING TO CENTER

TS

Horizontal Procedure

DS

Vertical Procedure

Drill 2

GUIDES TO TYPING SUCCESS

TS

Daily Work Goals

DS

Effort, Time, and Practice

DS

Finish What You Start

Enrichment problems appear on LM p. 23.

32

60-space line

32a ▶ 6 Conditioning practice

each line twice SS (slowly, then faster); DS between 2-line groups; if time permits, type each line again

alphabet 1 Janet will quickly explain what Dave Gibson made for prizes.

figure 2 Speed up easy pairs of figures: 11, 26, 27, 40, 83, and 95.

fluency 3 The firms may make a profit if they handle their work right.

| 1 | 2 | 3 | 4 | 5 | 6 | 7 | 8 | 9 | 10 | 11 | 12 |

32b ▶ 14 Improve technique: service keys

each set of lines twice SS (slowly, then faster); DS between sets of lines

Lines 1-3. Clear tab stops; beginning at left margin, set 2 new stops 25 spaces apart; return and begin Line 1.

Line 10: Type an incomplete word *exactly* as shown; then backspace and fill in missing letter **c**.

tabulator and return

1 to the —— tab ——→ if she —— tab ——→ he got
2 the form for them and they
3 she keeps big firms did visit

space bar

4 is on to in do is we it so if us and the did for she was six
5 to do | it is | if we | is on | if so | to us | and the | did six | she kept
6 If we are to do the work for the firm, shall we go at eight?

shift keys and lock

7 Lazaro has an Olivetti portable; Osami, an Olympia electric.
8 We drove through Florida, Georgia, and Alabama on that trip.
9 He uses the CENTURY 21 systems of typewriting and shorthand.

backspacer

10 a tion | for es | expe t | bla k | effe t | lo al | s hool | sour e | so ial

265b-268b, continued

Job 2
Partial text of speech

[LM p. 119]

On the 8″ × 5″ cards (or paper cut to 8″ × 5″ size), type the beginning of a speech Ms. Kelly is planning to give at a convention of beauticians. Use ½″ top, side, and bottom margins; DS.

The use of cosmetics is as old as mankind. The word cosmetics comes from the Greek kosmetikos which means "skilled in adornment." Historians report that the Egyptians used perfume and eye make up as far back as 5000 B.C. Several hundred years B.C., the Egyptians had become experts in cosmetics. They made up their eyebrows, eyes, lips, and fingertips and used perfumes.

When one hears the word "cosmetics," one almost immediately thinks of girls who "paint their faces" in order to make themselves prettier. Through the years, however, cosmetics have been used as much by men as by women. In Ancient Egypt and Rome, both sexes dyed thier hair, wore wigs, and applied make up. Shortly after the renaissance, both men and women of the nobility used makeup, and in England during the days of Elizabeth, both sexes of the court used powder and even wore beauty marks. In France during the Seventeenth Century, men wore ribbons, lace, wigs, and make up on their eyes and faces.

Today, the use of cosmetics is growing rapidly. Just before World War I, the sales of cosmetics in the United States was just under $40 million. By 1970, sales had risen to $4 billion and, during the 1980's, sales may exceed $5 billion. A key factor in this rise in the sale of dosmetics is the increasing use of cosmetics by men. Such products as perfumes, powders, facail masks, and skin moisturizers, once used almost entirely by women, are now being used by males in increasing amounts.

Some believe that the legendary beauty of Cleopatra was due in no small way to her skill in the use of cosmetics.

unit **5** lessons 31-34

Learn to center and arrange copy

Learning goals

1. To learn to center lines horizontally (side to side).

2. To learn to center copy vertically (top to bottom).

3. To improve keystroking speed on straight copy and on statistical copy.

Machine adjustments

1. Paper guide at *0*.

2. Ribbon control to type on top half of ribbon.

3. Margin sets: 60–space line (center − 30; center + 30 + 5).

4. Line–space selector on *1* (SS) for drills.

5. Line–space selector on *2* (DS) for paragraphs.

31

60-space line

31a ▶ 6 Conditioning practice

each line twice SS (slowly, then faster); DS between 2-line groups; if time permits, type each line again

alphabet	1	Jody Fox left my quiz show and gave back a prize he had won.
figure	2	What is the total of 15 and 17 and 28 and 39 and 40 and 206?
fluency	3	Keith may amend the six audit forms if it is right to do so.

5-stroke words | 1 | 2 | 3 | 4 | 5 | 6 | 7 | 8 | 9 | 10 | 11 | 12 |

31b ▶ 15 Check keystroking speed: skill comparison

1. A 1′ writing on each line; determine *gwam* on each writing.

2. Compare *gwam* to identify the 3 slowest lines.

3. A 1′ writing on each of the 3 slowest lines to improve speed.

balanced–hand	1	The key social work may end if they turn down the usual aid.
combination	2	At the start signal, work with great vigor to make the rate.
double–letter	3	Bess will be sorry if she cannot assist the class this fall.
adjacent–key	4	Louisa has opened her radio studio in the new western plaza.
one–hand	5	At best, I fear only a few union cases were ever acted upon.
direct–reach	6	Cecil carved this unique marble lynx for the county exhibit.
top–row	7	I type 37, 46, and 58 quickly, but I slow up for 23 and 190.

| 1 | 2 | 3 | 4 | 5 | 6 | 7 | 8 | 9 | 10 | 11 | 12 |

31c ▶ 5 Learn to use the backspacer

1. Read the copy in the block at the right to learn one use of the **backspacer (26).**

2. Type first incomplete word *exactly* as shown in the drill below the color block.

3. Backspace and fill in the missing letter **e**.

4. Type all other incomplete words in the drill in the same way.

Backspacer

To position the carriage or element to fill in an omitted letter, depress the **backspace key (26).** Locate the key on your typewriter.

Electric

Make a light, quick stroke with the little finger. Release the key quickly to avoid a double back–space. Hold the key down when you want repeat backspacing.

Manual

Straighten the little finger slightly and reach it to the backspace key with minimum hand motion. Depress the backspace key firmly; release it quickly.

1 ah ad| ar as| b gin| b low| chi f| cl an| d ath| d lay| fi ld| forc s

2 gre n| h art| h avy| hot l| lev l| m ans| mil s| mon y| nev r| oth rs

265b-268b, continued

Job 3
Travel schedule

In October, Ms. Kelly will visit some of the branch offices in Europe. Type her itinerary shown at the right centered on 8½" × 11" paper. Provide an appropriate heading; make 1 cc.

Sunday October 3	Leave Kennedy Airport 10 a.m.* for London on BA Flight 178
Monday October 4	Arrive Heathrow Airport 9:50 p.m. (Park Lane Hotel)
Tuesday October 5	Meet with Jon C. Wellington, Manager London Office
Wednesday October 6	Leave London 8 a.m. for Paris on BA Flight 304 Arrive Charles de Gaulle Airport 10 a.m. (George V Hotel)
Thursday October 7	Meet with Mlle. Claudette M. Marceau, Manager Paris Office
Friday October 8	Leave Paris 12:45 p.m. for Munich on Lufthansa Flight 310 Arrive Munich-Reim Airport 2:10 p.m. (Leopoldhaus Hotel)
Monday October 11	Meet with Herr Otto M. Koenig, Manager Munich Office
Tuesday October 12	Leave Munich 9:05 a.m. for Rome on Alitalia Flight 425 Arrive Leonardo Da Vinci Airport 10:30 a.m. (Excelsior Hotel)
Wednesday October 13	Meet Mr. Luis P. Margiotti, Manager Rome Office
Thursday October 14	Leave Rome 1:25 p.m. for New York City on TWA Flight 841 Arrive Kennedy Airport 4:30 p.m.

*All times given are local time

Job 4
Compose and type letters
[LM pp. 121–128]

1. Compose and type with one cc, a letter dated **August 21, 19—**, for your signature as **Administrative Secretary** to each manager of the branch offices Ms. Kelly will visit during her trip.

2. Tell each manager the date Ms. Kelly will meet with him/her and the date and time of her arrival.

3. Inform each manager that Ms. Kelly wishes to review the marketing operations of his/her office during the past year, to discuss any major problems, and to brief him/her on a new line of cosmetics for men to be marketed under the trade name, "Prince Michael."

4. Ask each manager to have someone meet Ms. Kelly at the airport and to arrange for her transportation to the airport upon her departure.

30c ▶ 15 Learn: 6 and figure 1

Follow the procedure given in 26b, p. 44, typing each reach-technique drill twice.

Using the figure "1"
When typing copy made up primarily of figures, it may be more efficient to type the figure "1" instead of to type the letter "l" for the figure.

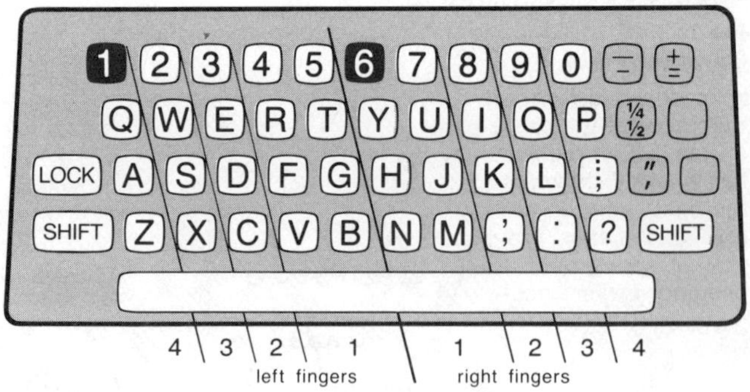

Reach technique for 6

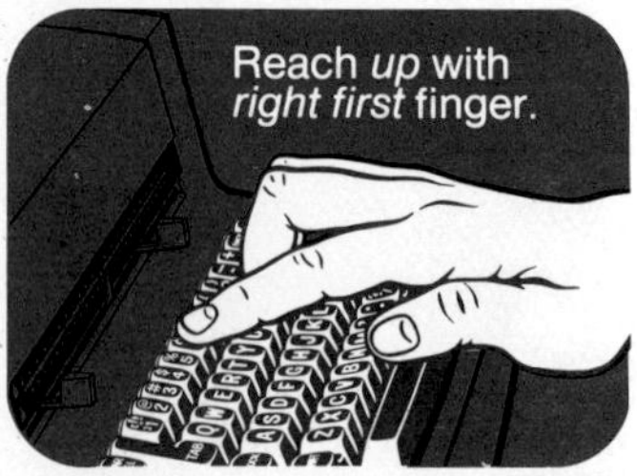

6 ▼

1 6j 6j 6 6 j6j j6j 16 16 61 61 Ship 6 copies of R66 on May 6.
2 We took Route 66 on November 6 and drove 666 miles to Tulsa.

Reach technique for 1

1 (one) ▼

3 la la l l ala ala 11 11 10 10 Take Route 1A1 instead of A1A.
4 We drove Route 101 for 111 miles, then Route 1 to Morro Bay.

all figures used

5 We planted 284 cedar, 375 elm, and 1,690 maple on Arbor Day.
6 Stock those lakes with 628 perch, 759 trout, and 1,340 bass.

30d ▶ 15 Check/improve keystroking speed

1. A 1′ writing on each ¶; determine *gwam* on each.
2. A 2′ writing on each ¶; if you finish a ¶ before time is called, start typing the ¶ again.
3. A 3′ writing on ¶s 1–2 combined; determine *gwam*.
4. If time permits, type additional 1′ writings on each of the 2 ¶s to improve speed.

all letters used | LA | 1.4 si | 5.4 awl | 85% hfw |

	gwam 2′	3′
All of you make an error now and then in performing an	5	3
act like driving a car, doing the high jump, or playing the	11	8
piano. Typing is no different. To err is human. The more	17	12
difficult the activity, the greater the opportunity to make	23	16
errors. Do not expect all your work to be correct now.	29	19
Do not infer from this, though, that the more mistakes	5	23
you make, the more human you are. A lot of your errors are	11	27
merely chance; why you make them is a real puzzle. Others,	17	32
however, are known to be due to lack of attention, improper	23	35
reading, and bad techniques. Try to reduce the latter.	29	39

gwam 2′ | 1 | 2 | 3 | 4 | 5 | 6 |
3′ | 1 | 2 | 3 | 4 |

Enrichment material for Unit 4 appears on LM pp. 21, 22.

265b-268b, continued

Job 5
Agenda for meeting

Center and type the agenda shown at the right in the reading position on 8½" × 11" paper. Justify the right margin; make 5 cc's. Use your name as the person who is to give the report of the previous meeting (Item 2 on the agenda).

Marvelon Cosmetics, Inc. (ALL CAPS)

Agenda for the (Monthly) Meeting of the Marketing Division

September ~~13~~ (14), 19--

1. ~~Call to Order~~ (Introductory Remarks) . . . . Lenore C. Kelly
2. Report of Prev~~ois~~(ious) Meeting . . . . (your name)
3. Reports of department cheifs
   - Storage and Inventory. . . . . Mark J. Hausmann
   - Advertiseing . . . . Lily C. Barnes
   - Sales . . . . Robert E. Polaskie
   - Research and ~~Development~~ (Engineering) . . . Helen T. Mancini
   - Transportation . . . . Michael L. Dauphine
4. Specail reports
   - "Prince Michael" Campiagn . . Lily C. Barnes
   - Development of (New) Beauty Marks . Helen T. Mancini
   - Plans for a far east office . Robert E. Polaskie
   - Visit to European ~~Branches~~ (Offices) . . Lenore C. Kelly
5. Open dis cussion. . . . . Lenore C. Kelly
6. ~~Adjournment . . . . Lenore C. Kelly~~

Job 6
Compose and type interoffice memorandums
[LM pp. 129–138]

1. Compose and type an interoffice memorandum from **Ms. Kelly** dated **August 28, 19—**, to *each* department chief listed on the agenda. Provide an appropriate subject line.

2. Notify the department chiefs that the monthly meeting will be held at **1 p.m. on September 14 in Conference Room B**. Ask each director to send Ms. Kelly a copy of the material he/she plans to present at the meeting by no later than **September 7**.

3. Make a carbon copy of the first memorandum *only*. On the bottom of this carbon, type **Memo also sent to:** then list the names of the other division chiefs to whom the memorandum is being sent.

29d ▶ 15 Improve skill on script, rough-draft, and statistical copy

1. Two 1′ writings on each ¶; determine *gwam* on each.

2. A 2′ writing on each ¶; determine *gwam* on each.

3. If time permits, compare the 2′ *gwam* on each ¶ and type the slowest ¶ again.

Recall

- close up
- delete
- insert
- insert comma
- insert period
- lc lowercase
- move right
- transpose

all letters used | LA | 1.4 si | 5.4 awl | 85% hfw

	gwam 1′	2′
A difference between the expert and a beginning typist	11	5
is that the former has all the act together, but the latter	23	11
is still trying to arrange the props. One works with quiet	35	17
control as the other works in jerks and pauses.	44	22
Like the peices for a *jigsaw* puzzle, ~~each of the~~ *every* movements in	11	5
typing ~~have to~~ *must* fit in to its specific place. *So* If you want to	23	11
get your typeing act together, ~~analyze~~ *study* how you type and find a	35	17
~~quicker~~ *better* way of fiting *all* the pieces to gether.	44	22
Numbers having only two digits typed by both hands, as	11	5
85, 49, or 27, may be easy to type. Longer ones typed with	23	11
one hand, as 170 or 352, often increase the difficulty. So	35	17
you see, numbers vary in difficulty just as words do.	46	23

30

60-space line

30a ▶ 6 Conditioning practice

each line twice SS (slowly, then faster); DS between 2-line groups; if time permits, type each line again

alphabet 1 Zip, can you have this quaint jug fixed for Ms. Kell by two?

figure 2 Take Delta 152 at 7:30 p.m.; pick up United 841 at 9:35 p.m.

fluency 3 The signs the six girls wish to hang may handle the problem.

| 1 | 2 | 3 | 4 | 5 | 6 | 7 | 8 | 9 | 10 | 11 | 12 |

30b ▶ 14 Learn to proofread your copy

1. Note the kinds of errors marked in the sample typed at right.

2. Proofread and mark for correction (using proofreader's marks, page 39) each error you make in a 1′ writing on ¶1 of 29d, above.

Goal: To learn the first step in finding and correcting your errors.

> Adifference betwen the expert and a be ginning typist
> is that the former all the act together, but thee latter
> is stell tring to arrange the propps. One works with queit
> control as theother works in jekks and pauses.

Line 1
1. Failure to space
2. Omitted letter
3. Faulty spacing

Line 2
1. Omitted word
2. Incorrect spacing
3. Added letter

Line 3
1. Misstroke
2. Omitted letter
3. Added letter
4. Transposition

Line 4
1. Failure to space
2. Strikeover, only one error counted per word

unit **54** lessons 269-271

Refine basic/ production skills

Learning goals

1. To increase your speed and accuracy on straight copy, rough-draft copy, and statistical copy.

2. To increase your speed in typing business letters, reports, and tables.

Machine adjustments

1. Line: 70 for all drills; as necessary for production problems.

2. Spacing: SS sentence drills with a DS between groups; DS timed writings; space problems as required.

269

269a ▶ 5 Conditioning practice

each line twice SS (slowly, then faster); if time permits, retype selected lines

alphabet 1 My objective was to standardize our freight and express rates quickly.

figures 2 My batting average in 1979 was .352; in 1980, .346; and in 1981, .407.

fig/sym 3 The minimum for Job #3612 (Technician) is $8,570; the maximum, $9,740.

fluency 4 The judicial panel may discuss the problems of formal civil authority.

| 1 | 2 | 3 | 4 | 5 | 6 | 7 | 8 | 9 | 10 | 11 | 12 | 13 | 14 |

269b ▶ 10 Skill-transfer typing

1. Type a 1′ writing on each ¶. Determine percent of transfer from ¶ 1 to ¶ 2 and from ¶ 1 to ¶ 3.

2. Type additional 1′ writings on ¶s 2 and 3 to increase percent of transfer as time permits.

all letters used | A | 1.5 si | 5.7 awl | 80% hfw |

gwam 1′

One of the major elements which led to the growth of the 11
civilized world was transportation. As the ability of people 24
to travel improved, trade and business began to expand. New 36
markets for merchandise led to more and better jobs for the 48
people. Our modern industrial complexes could not exist if 60
we did not have fast and efficient methods of travel. 71

The ~~utilization~~ use of the steam locomotive brought about ~~numerous~~ many 10
changes in the socail and ~~commercial~~ industrial life ~~in~~ of this ~~nation~~ country. The 23
rail roads ~~linked~~ united the ~~industry~~ factories of the North with the raw materails 36
and markets in the South and ~~led~~ paved the way ~~to~~ for the ~~opening~~ development ofthe 50
Western Territory. Much of the credit for the rapid ~~rise~~ growth of 63
our nation ~~rests with~~ belongs to the rail roads. 71

The advances in aviation have been quite remarkable. In 11
1930, the typical airplane could carry 20 passengers at a maxi- 24
mum speed of 300 miles an hour. By 1969, an airplane--the 36
747--could accommodate 500 passengers and travel at an amazing 48
rate of 640 miles an hour. The 747 is 213.3 feet long, 63.5 61
feet high, and has a wingspan of 195.7 feet--75.75 feet longer 73
than the first successful flight of 120 feet in 1903. 84

29

60-space line

29a ▶ 6
Conditioning practice

each line twice SS (slowly, then faster); DS between 2-line groups; if time permits, type each line again

alphabet 1 Vicky wants the quartz box for Pam, the jade ring for Belle.
figure 2 We had a work force of 345 in 1981; we may need 875 by 1987.
fluency 3 The right bid may entitle the girl to the handy ivory forks.

| 1 | 2 | 3 | 4 | 5 | 6 | 7 | 8 | 9 | 10 | 11 | 12 |

29b ▶ 15 Learn: 2 and 0 (zero)

Follow the procedure given in 26b, p. 44, typing each reach-technique drill twice.

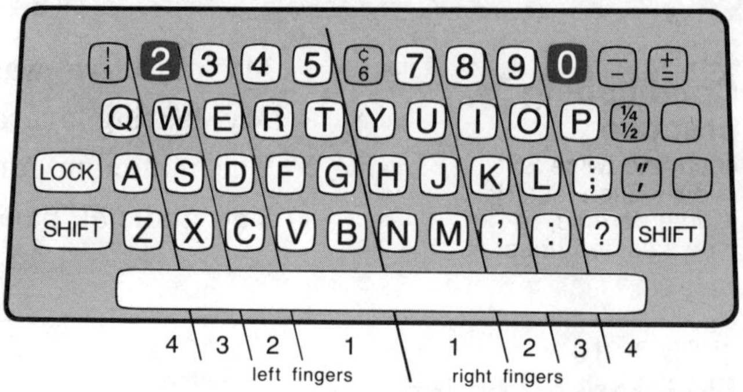

Reach technique for 2

2 ▼

1 2s 2s 2 2 s2s s2s 12 12 21 21 All 12 of them typed 22 w.a.m.
2 We had only 22 workers when our firm began on June 12, 1982.

Reach technique for 0

0 (zero) ▼

3 0; 0; 0 0 ;0; ;0; 10 10 01 01 We shipped Models 300 and 400.
4 Order 100 typing erasers, 80 tablets, and 50 reams of paper.

all figures learned

5 Type these numbers: 20, 37, 48, 59, 12, 72, 93, 85, and 40.
6 Our group sold 950 chili dogs, 487 sandwiches, and 312 pies.

29c ▶ 14 Improve keystroking technique: response patterns

1. Each line once from dictation; once from copy only.
2. If time permits, type a 1′ writing on Line 2, then on Line 4, then on Line 6; determine *gwam* on each.

word response
1 if they did | go with them | did he also | work for them | if she is
2 Did they make the right title forms for the eight big firms?

letter response
3 as you see | we are only | my tax case | as you save | are you aware
4 As you are aware, only we look upon him as a great pop star.

combination response
5 she is only | if the case | to the rate | go into the | were to save
6 They agreed to get the draft for the auditor when he starts.

figure
7 11 22 00 33 99 44 88 55 77 12 13 14 15 20 29 28 27 30 40 200
8 Try these figures as units: 20, 30, 40, 50, 92, 82, and 72.

| 1 | 2 | 3 | 4 | 5 | 6 | 7 | 8 | 9 | 10 | 11 | 12 |

269c ▶ 15
Refine basic skill: straight copy

Type two 5′ writings on the ¶s.

Goal: Higher speed and fewer errors on the second writing.

Compare scores on better writing with scores attained on 242c, page 380.

all letters used | A | 1.5 si | 5.7 awl | 80% hfw

gwam 1′ | 5′

There is no doubt that the invention of the typewriter completely 13 3
revolutionized the world of business. In the early days, the messages, 28 6
reports, and formal records of a company had to be written in ink by a 42 8
large number of clerks. This process took a great deal of time and 55 11
work, and the writing was so illegible at times that turmoil and even 69 14
lawsuits resulted. Today, messages, reports, and other vital records 83 17
can be produced quickly and legibly on the typewriter. 94 19

Before the invention of the typewriter, business was considered to 13 22
be a man's world. For this reason, almost all of the office jobs were 28 24
held by men. When the typewriter became a reality, schools began to 41 27
offer classes in typing to supply capable operators. Many women took 55 30
these classes and became expert in the use of the machine. Armed with 70 33
a needed skill, women were admitted to the business office. The type- 83 36
writer was the key that opened the doors of business to women. 96 38

Studies of employees who hold jobs as typists show that those who 13 41
succeed are effective in three major areas: typing, language arts, and 28 44
proofreading and correction. A person who is adept in these areas and 42 46
who has a positive attitude toward his or her job can progress from a 56 49
trainee to a supervisory job and to an executive position with consid- 70 52
erable ease. It is obvious, therefore, that learning to type well can 84 55
be the first rung in the ladder of success in the world of business. 97 57

gwam														
1′	1	2	3	4	5	6	7	8	9	10	11	12	13	14
5′		1					2					3		

269d ▶ 20
Refine production skill: letters

1. Type the letter in modified block style, mixed punctuation, to **Mrs. Alexis T. Fredericks,** who is the **Director of Marketing** for **Fidelity Office Supply Company, 1701 Exposition Avenue, Dallas, TX 75226-5070.** Date the letter **March 3, 19—.**

2. Use an appropriate salutation and complimentary close. Use your name in the closing lines as the **Purchasing Officer.** Correct errors as you type.

Goal: To produce a mailable letter in the time allowed.

words

(¶ 1) We appreciate your prompt attention to our order of February 17. The 14
entire shipment was received yesterday. (¶ 2) Unfortunately, there was an 28
error on the purchase order and invoice forms we ordered. As shown on the 43
enclosed copy of our purchase order, these forms were to be printed with our 58
corporate name and the address of our newest branch at 1700 Bradley Street. 74
The forms we received are printed with the address of our home office. 88
(¶ 3) Will you please send us purchase order and invoice forms with the correct 103
address printed on them as soon as possible. We will hold the incorrect forms in 119
our warehouse until you give us disposition instructions. 131

28c ▶ 15 Learn: 5 and 9

Follow the procedure given in 26b, p. 44, typing each reach-technique drill twice.

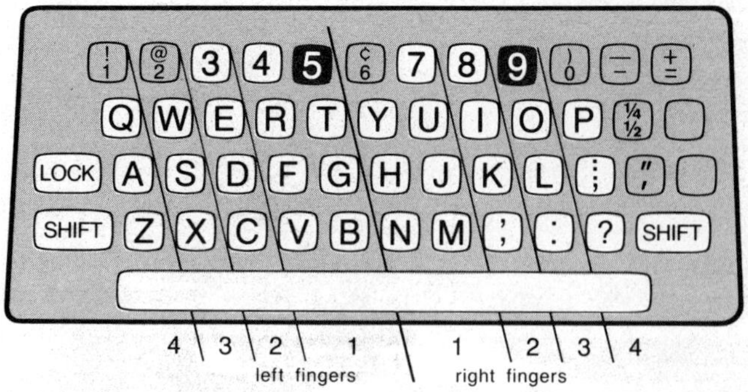

4 3 2 1
left fingers
1 2 3 4
right fingers

Reach technique for 5

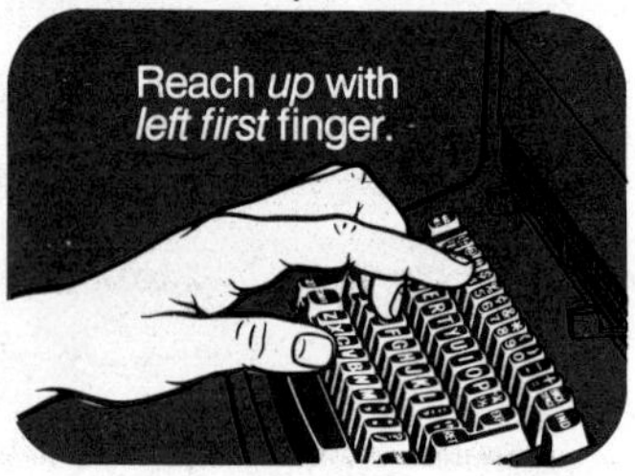

Reach *up* with *left first* finger.

Reach technique for 9

Reach *up* with *right third* finger.

5

1 5f 5f 5 5 f5f f5f 15 15 51 51 Local 1548 has 14,575 members.
2 My best golf scores were 85 on August 5 and 75 on August 15.

9

3 91 91 9 9 191 191 19 19 91 91 Lou was 19 on the 9th of July.
4 For the answer to Problem 49, see Unit 9, page 379, line 19.

all figures learned

5 Reach with your fingers to type 59, 95, 48, 84, 73, and 137.
6 Of 738 juniors, 544 take typing but only 194 take shorthand.

28d ▶ 15 Improve keystroking speed: guided sentences

1. A 1′ writing on each pair of lines with the 20″ call of the line ending.

Goal: To reach the end of each line just as each 20″ call is given. This means typing each line of the first pair at 15 *gwam*, of the second pair at 18 *gwam*, etc.

Technique cues

- curved, upright fingers
- *reach* with the fingers, not the hands
- eyes on textbook copy
- return and start each new line quickly

2. Two 1′ unguided writings on Line 13, then on Line 14; determine *gwam* on each.

		gwam 20″	15″
1	Veda has set a fast pace.	15	20
2	We typed 5 and 9 and 519.	15	20
3	She gave us the new gas quota.	18	24
4	Turn to text page 159, please.	18	24
5	Did you base the case on the facts?	21	28
6	Carla was born on October 13, 1975.	21	28
7	It is up to you to work with care, also.	24	32
8	The parade begins at 9:15 a.m. on May 9.	24	32
9	Did you forward the case to the state office?	27	36
10	If you can type 384, you can also type 1,597.	27	36
11	To get the right job is a chore for every student.	30	40
12	Over 75 percent of the group left on the 8:14 bus.	30	40
13	Joy has sent for a dozen pens and two boxes of pencils.	33	44
14	Al typed 95.4 percent of the figures right at 18 w.a.m.	33	44

| 1 | 2 | 3 | 4 | 5 | 6 | 7 | 8 | 9 | 10 | 11 |

270a ▶ 5 Conditioning practice

Use standard directions given in 269a, p. 413.

alphabet 1 Two biochemical experts have just finished analyzing the black liquid.
figures 2 The company printed 872,301 books in July and 839,564 books in August.
fig/sym 3 Sales in 1982 (based on final reports) rose $274,563 or 20% over 1981.
fluency 4 She can send all future payments on this loan to the bank in the city.

| 1 | 2 | 3 | 4 | 5 | 6 | 7 | 8 | 9 | 10 | 11 | 12 | 13 | 14 |

270b ▶ 10 Skill-transfer typing

Type the ¶s in 269b, page 413, as directed there.

270c ▶ 15 Refine basic skill: straight copy

Type two 5′ writings on the ¶s in 269c, page 414. Strive for higher speed.

270d ▶ 20 Refine production skill: reports

1. Type the material as a leftbound report. Correct errors as you type.

2. Type the footnote so there is a margin of approximately 1″ at the bottom of the page. The quote is from **page 70** of **CONSUMER ECONOMIC PROBLEMS, 9th ed.,** written by **Roman F. Warmke** and **Eugene D. Wyllie** and published by **South-Western Publishing Co., Cincinnati,** in **1977.**

Goal: To type an acceptable report in the time allowed.

words

THE AMERICAN SOCIETY--CAPITALISM IN A DEMOCRACY TS 10

"The American economy has given us the highest 19

level of living in the world, and it is still improv- 30

ing."[1] We earn better salaries, own better ~~houses~~ homes, buy 40

more ~~merchandise~~ goods and services, and have more ~~free~~ leisure time than any ~~of~~ other 54

~~the~~ people ~~in~~ on the ~~world~~ earth. 78

The ~~astounding~~ amazing success we have gained is ~~based~~ built on 87

the ~~fundamental~~ basic concept of ~~the~~ individaul liberty and eco- 97

nomic free dom in a capitalistic ~~setting~~ society. There is 107

~~enough~~ ample evidence to ~~uphold~~ confirm the beleif that an economic 118

system that is ~~established~~ based on Free Enter prize and the 125

profit motive, although far from perfect, will produce 138

greater ~~profits~~ benefits for our ~~nation~~ people than will any ~~of the~~ 147

other systems ~~which are~~ yet to be devised. 154

With less than ten percent of the world's population, we produce almost half of the world's goods.

footnote 189

27d ▶ 15 Learn: 3 and 7

Follow the procedure given in 26b, p. 44, typing each reach–technique drill twice.

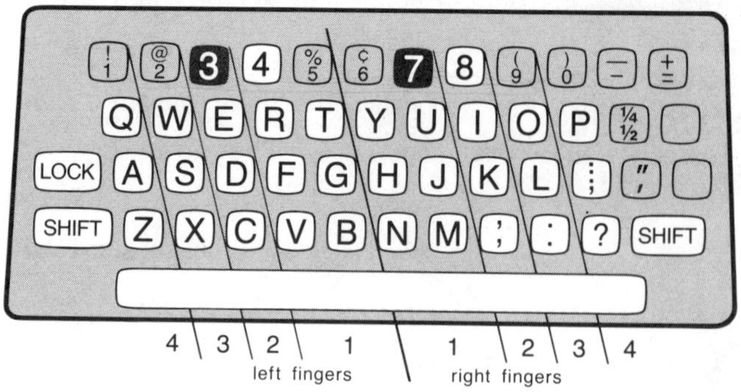

Reach technique for 3

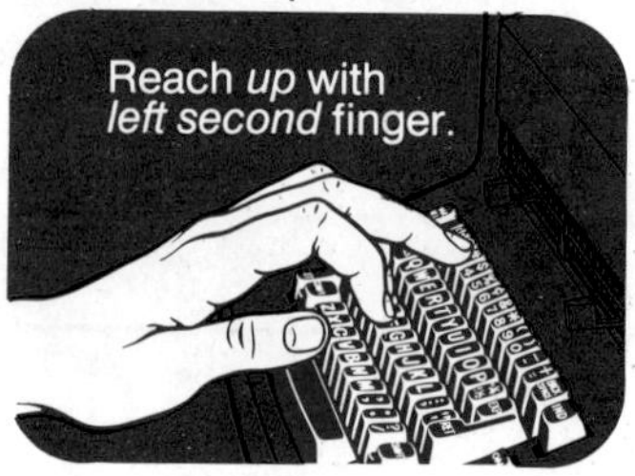

3

no space

1 3d 3d 3 3 d3d d3d 13 13 31 31 I typed 3 minutes at 33 w.a.m.
2 Sue missed only Problem 13; I missed Problems 3, 13, and 33.

Reach technique for 7

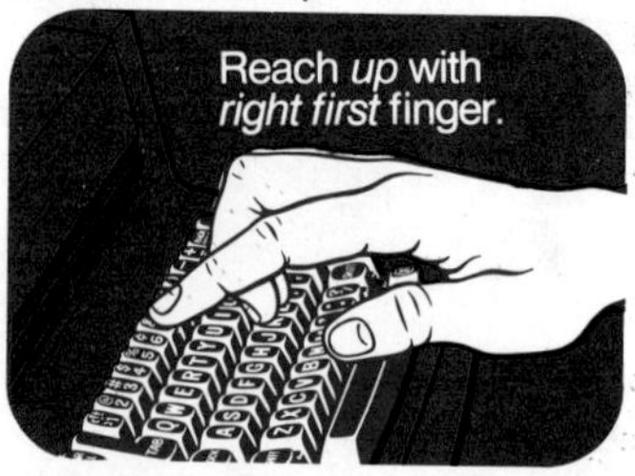

7

3 7j 7j 7 7 j7j j7j 17 17 71 71 I have read 7 of the 17 pages.
4 Tony will be 17 on Tuesday, October 7; he weighs 177 pounds.

all figures learned

5 I based my April 3 report on pages 374 to 383 of Chapter 17.
6 On October 17, 47 girls and 38 boys sold 487 boxes of candy.

28

60-space line

28a ▶ 6
Conditioning practice

each line twice SS (slowly, then faster); DS between 2-line groups; if time permits, type each line again

alphabet 1 Jerold quickly coaxed eight avid fans away from Buzz Parker.
figure 2 Type these figures: 1, 3, 8, 4, 7, 37, 48, 43, 78, and 137.
fluency 3 It is their wish to pay for land maps of eight island towns.

| 1 | 2 | 3 | 4 | 5 | 6 | 7 | 8 | 9 | 10 | 11 | 12 |

28b ▶ 14
Improve technique: service keys

1. Clear all tab stops.
2. Beginning at left margin, set two tab stops 25 spaces apart.
3. Type the drill once as shown.
4. If time permits, retype the drill at a faster pace.

space bar
1 us we do be am in is on an of go as it up or no me my so men
2 I am| if he| it was| as she| of his| to her| by him| if you| did own
3 I now know how to go from word to word with speed as I type.

shift keys and lock
4 Tomas Diaz has left for Tijuana; Aida Romero, for Vera Cruz.
5 Osami Kato of Japan won the finals from Gina Lanza of Italy.
6 She cited a quote from FAMILIAR QUOTATIONS by John Bartlett.

tabulator and return
7 to do —— tab ——→ he is —— tab ——→ if it
8 and the did pay she bid
9 with them they work both paid
10 busy panel worn signs such risks

271

271a ▶ 5 Conditioning practice

Use standard directions given in 269a, p. 413.

alphabet 1 They may be required to organize the complex work of the vast project.

figures 2 I drove 99 miles on May 6, 205 miles on May 7, and 314 miles on May 8.

fig/sym 3 The bill of lading for D & S should read "10,698#" rather than "986#."

fluency 4 If I help them fix the engine, the girls may go with us to the island.

| 1 | 2 | 3 | 4 | 5 | 6 | 7 | 8 | 9 | 10 | 11 | 12 | 13 | 14 |

271b ▶ 10 Refine basic skill: response patterns

1. Type the sentences DS at your highest rate.

2. Remove paper from typewriter and correct your errors in pencil. From your corrected copy, type a 1′ writing on each line with as few errors as possible.

Response patterns

word 1 She told me it is my job to plan for the party to be held in the city.

stroke 2 Concerned citizens quickly contacted numerous educational specialists.

combination 3 Construction of an interchange may facilitate the movement of traffic.

word 4 It is now time for both of us to go to the city to sign the six forms.

stroke 5 In my opinion, average state tax rates will decrease in several years.

combination 6 If you pay the full fare, she might be able to travel at a lower rate.

| 1 | 2 | 3 | 4 | 5 | 6 | 7 | 8 | 9 | 10 | 11 | 12 | 13 | 14 |

271c ▶ 15 Refine basic skill: straight copy

Type two 5′ writings on the ¶s in 269c, page 414. Try to maintain speed achieved on previous writings, but reduce errors.

271d ▶ 20 Refine production skill: tables

full sheet

Type the table in the reading position; DS the items; correct errors as you type.

Goal: To type an acceptable table in the time allowed.

A COMPARISON OF SOME METRIC AND TRADITIONAL UNITS OF MEASURE* (words 12)

Measure	Traditional	Metric	words
			23
Linear	1/4-inch wrench	6-mm (millimeters) wrench	32
Linear	9′ × 12′ rug	3 × 4 m (meter) rug	40
Distance	25 miles	40 km (kilometers)	48
Weight	9 oz. of nuts	250 g (grams) of nuts	56
Weight	4 1/2 lbs. of meat	2 kg (kilograms) of meat	67
Volume	16 gals. of gasoline	60 L (liters) of gasoline	77
Speed	50 MPH	80 km (kilometers) per hour	86
			89

____

Source: "What About Metric," National Bureau of Standards, 1974. 103

*Some comparisons are approximate. 109

26d ▶ 15 Improve keystroking speed: guided writing

Type a 1′ writing on ¶ 1; determine *gwam*. Add 4 *gwam* to set a new goal rate; then type additional writings as follows:

1. Two 1′ guided writings on ¶ 1 at your goal rate.
2. Two 1′ guided writings on ¶ 2 at your goal rate.
3. Two 2′ writings on ¶s 1–2 combined, without the guide; determine *gwam* on the better writing.
4. A 3′ unguided writing on ¶s 1–2 combined; determine *gwam*.

Goals
1′: At least 21 *gwam*.
2′: At least 19 *gwam*.
3′: At least 18 *gwam*.

all letters used

	gwam 2′	3′
You now know the basic techniques that are required in	5	3
building a high level of typing power. What you need to do	11	8
next is perfect your movements in terms of distance, speed,	17	12
and direction. With other fingers curved on home keys, the	23	16
one making a reach must move quickly to its target key.	29	19
A good way to improve speed is called mental practice.	6	23
When not at a machine, just pretend you have the fingers on	12	27
a keyboard. Then, as you mentally say words like also, if,	18	32
size, title, and city to yourself, quickly move the fingers	24	35
through the stroking motions. Doing so can add speed.	29	39

gwam 2′ | 1 | 2 | 3 | 4 | 5 | 6 |
3′ | 1 | 2 | 3 | 4 |

27

60-space line

27a ▶ 6 Conditioning practice

each line twice SS (slowly, then faster); DS between 2-line groups; if time permits, type each line again

alphabet 1 Jack Waven dozed off as he quietly prepped for his big exam.
figure 2 They typed 1 and 4 and 8 and 14 and 18 and 48 and 84 and 11.
fluency 3 Nana did sign the usual title forms for the eight box firms.

| 1 | 2 | 3 | 4 | 5 | 6 | 7 | 8 | 9 | 10 | 11 | 12 |

27b ▶ 14 Improve keystroking technique: response patterns

Lines 1-6: Once from dictation; then once from copy only.

word response
1 it is| or me| for us| is due| may go| did own| and the| pay them to
2 He is to pay them for the social work they did for the city.

letter response
3 as in| at no| be on| as you| on gas| you are| tax him| get my cards
4 As you are on my state tax case, get a few tax rates set up.

combination response
5 as she is| to see us| it was he| up to him| if you are| set it up
6 It was then up to him to pay the duty they set on the ivory.

Lines 7-9: 1′ writing on each line. Compare *gwam*.

word 7 The girls did their work then spent their pay for the chair.
letter 8 You acted on my tax case only after you saw my estate cards.
combination 9 You may chair my panel if you work on the tax audit for him.

| 1 | 2 | 3 | 4 | 5 | 6 | 7 | 8 | 9 | 10 | 11 | 12 |

27c ▶ 15 Improve keystroking speed: guided writing

Retype 26d, above.
Goal: 2 *gwam* increase.

unit **55** lessons 272-275

Apply for office employment

Learning and measurement goals

1. To demonstrate improvement in speed and accuracy in typing straight-copy material of average difficulty.
2. To type employment application papers in acceptable form.
3. To type at least two of five production problems in an acceptable manner.

Machine adjustments

1. Line: 70 for drills; as necessary for problems.
2. Spacing: SS sentence drills with a DS between sentence groups; DS timed writings; space problems as directed or necessary.

272-274

272a-274a ▶ 5 Conditioning practice

each line twice SS (slowly, then faster); DS between 2-line groups; if time permits, retype selected lines

alphabet 1 Judge Keys will question medical experts about the size of the groove.
figures 2 Flight 961 for Miami will arrive at Gate 7 at 3:58 and depart at 4:20.
fig/sym 3 He earned overtime pay of $24.70, $35.86, and $49--a total of $109.56.
fluency 4 If they wish us to do so, the men and I will do the repair work today.

| 1 | 2 | 3 | 4 | 5 | 6 | 7 | 8 | 9 | 10 | 11 | 12 | 13 | 14 |

272b-274b ▶ 8 Measure basic skill: straight copy

1. For each lesson, type a 5′ writing on all ¶s; determine *gwam* and circle errors.
2. Record the best of the three tests.

all letters used | A | 1.5 si | 5.6 awl | 80% hfw |

gwam 5′

When you apply for a job, there are three documents that you must 3 64
prepare or fill out--a personal data sheet, a letter of application, 5 67
and an application blank. The data sheet is a one-page summary of your 8 70
personal traits, skills, and abilities. Normally, it is divided into 11 73
five major sections--personal data, education, school activities, work 14 75
background, and references. The intent of the data sheet is to help 17 78
you gain an interview by arousing interest in you and what you can do. 19 81

The material in an application letter must be clear and concise. 22 84
Name the position for which you are applying and tell how you learned 25 86
that it was vacant. Mention your personal data sheet which you will 28 89
enclose and close by requesting an interview, stating the time you are 31 92
free. The appearance of your letter and your personal data sheet is 33 95
as critical as the data you provide. Take steps to insure that both 36 98
are free of errors in grammar, spelling, typing, spacing, and placement. 39 100

How you complete an application blank might reveal more about you 42 103
than you realize since it may test several of your abilities. If you 44 106
are required to print or complete the form in longhand, it might be a 47 109
test of your ability to produce documents neatly and legibly. If you 50 111
must type the form, it may be a check of your ability to produce neat 53 114
and error-free typewritten material. Further, it might be a test of 56 117
your ability to comprehend and follow directions and to express yourself 59 120
clearly and concisely in writing. Take care, therefore, to do your best. 61 123

gwam 5′ | 1 | 2 | 3 |

26a ▶ 6 Conditioning practice

each line twice SS (slowly, then faster); DS between 2-line groups; if time permits, type each line again

alphabet 1 Joey Knox led a big blitz which saved the play for my squad.
space bar 2 to do| of it| do so| it is| by the| is due| did go| she may| if they
fluency 3 Aldo may fix the bus panel for the city if the pay is right.

5-stroke words | 1 | 2 | 3 | 4 | 5 | 6 | 7 | 8 | 9 | 10 | 11 | 12 |

26b ▶ 15 Learn: 1, 4, and 8

For each new key

1. Find new key on the chart at right.
2. Find new key on keyboard.
3. Study appropriate reach illustration below.
4. Watch finger make reach to key and back to home row.
5. Type reach-technique drill twice (slowly, then faster).

Using the letter "l" as *1*

When typing "mixed" copy (copy composed of words and some figures), it is easier and faster to use the letter "l" for the figure *1*. *Do so until directed otherwise.*

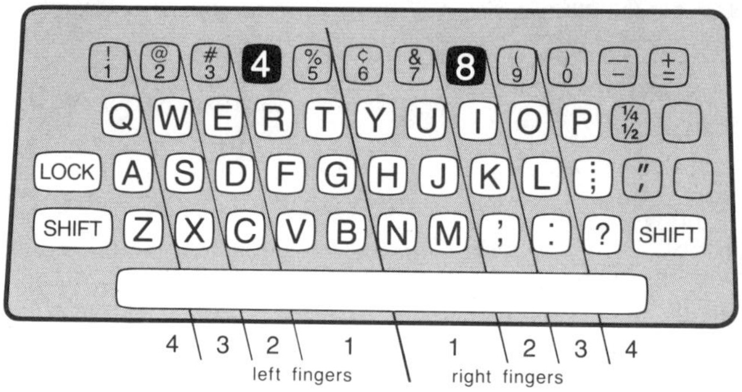

Reach technique for 4

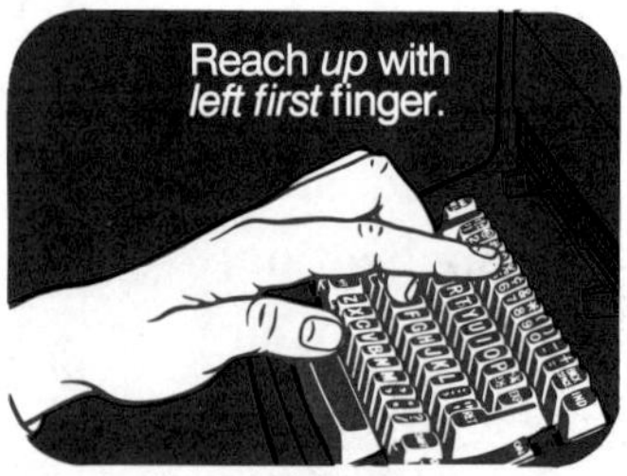

1 and 4 ▼

1 4f 4f 4 4 f4f f4f 14 14 41 41 He typed 1, 4, 14, 41, and 44.
2 Only 14 of the 144 boys got 41 of the 44 quiz answers right.

Reach technique for 8

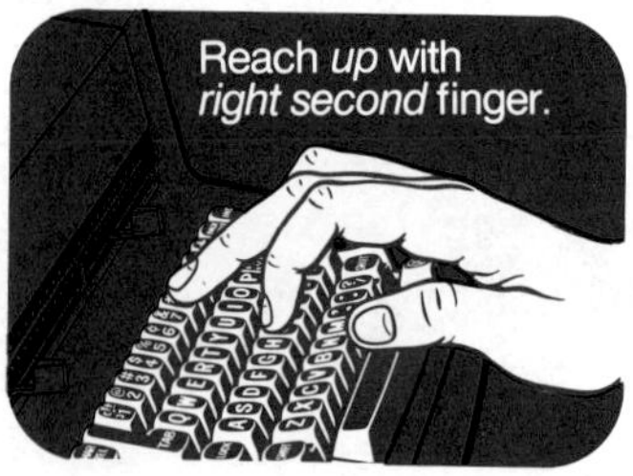

1 and 8 ▼

3 8k 8k 8 8 k8k k8k 18 18 81 81 She read 1, 8, 18, 81, and 88.
4 The test on the 18th will cover pages 11 to 18 and 81 to 88.

1, 4, and 8

5 Reach with the fingers to type 4 and 8 as well as 14 and 18.
6 Review Figures 44 and 48 on pages 414 and 418, respectively.

26c ▶ 14 Improve technique: keystroking

each pair of lines twice SS (slowly, then faster); DS between 4-line groups; if time permits, retype the lines that caused you to reduce your speed

Rows

home/3d 1 she quit| just try| they type| you should| please pay| we stopped
2 Olga said she tries to keep her eyes on all words she types.

home/1st 3 bad back| can land| hand ax| can call| small flag| all jazz bands
4 Max can call Zahn and Calla, and Alan can ask Javanna, also.

all rows 5 fit 484| lit 184| kit 884| rig 484| fill 481| lift 184| frill 4811
6 Just 18 of the girls and 14 of the boys passed all 48 tests.

| 1 | 2 | 3 | 4 | 5 | 6 | 7 | 8 | 9 | 10 | 11 | 12 |

272c ▶ 37
Prepare a personal data sheet

full sheet

Compose at the typewriter a data sheet similar to the one at the right, using your own personal data. Arrange the material attractively on the page. Include data under each of these major categories:

1. *Personal information*: age, place of birth, height and weight, etc.
2. *Education*: name of high school, major, and skills attained.
3. *School Activities*: Cocurricular activities in which you have participated and any honors you may have earned.
4. *Work Experience*: any work experience you have had, including part-time jobs of more than a few weeks.
5. *References*: three references other than relatives. State that you have permission to use the individuals as references.

After you have composed the data sheet, make corrections in pencil and retype the page in good form, correcting errors as you type.

INTRODUCING

Roberta J. Jefferson
8024 South Hermitage Avenue
Chicago, IL 60626-3107
(312) 555-4892

PERSONAL INFORMATION

Age:	18
Place of Birth:	Richmond, Virginia
Height and Weight:	5'8"; 120 pounds
Health:	Excellent

EDUCATION

High School:	Martin Luther King High School (Will receive diploma on June 15.)
Major:	Business Education
Skills Attained:	Typewriting straight-copy rate: 55 words a minute; transcribing machine rate: 46 words a minute
Office Machines:	Ten-key electronic calculator; mimeograph and direct-process duplicators; electronic typewriter

SCHOOL ACTIVITIES

Treasurer, Office Education Club for two years
Member of Future Business Leaders of America for three years
Reporter for The King's Voice, school newspaper, for two years
Member of the National Honor Society in senior year

WORK EXPERIENCE

Junior typist in the office of the Monroe Insurance Company for the past two summers. Typed and filed correspondence; answered the telephone; performed other general clerical duties.

Part-time secretary for the Guidance Counselor at Martin Luther King High School for the past two years which involved typing, filing, and keeping records of appointments and conferences.

REFERENCES (by permission)

Ms. Loretta C. Chesney, Guidance Counselor, Martin Luther King High School, 9500 South Michigan Avenue, Chicago, IL 60628-2934

Mrs. Rita S. Juarez, Assistant Director of Administration, Monroe Insurance Co., 175 West Jackson Street, Chicago, IL 60604-2874

Dr. T. Booker Hopkins, Pastor, First Baptist Church of Chicago, 9510 South Rhodes Avenue, Chicago, IL 60628-3233

phase **2** lessons 26-50

Learn the top row and basic applications

In the 25 lessons of this phase, you will:

1. Learn to type figures and basic symbols by touch and with good techniques.

2. Increase speed/control on straight copy, script, rough draft, and statistical copy.

3. Apply your basic skills in preparing simple personal and business papers.

Up to now most copy has been shown in typewriter type. In Phase 2 much of the copy is shown in printer's type. Continue to type it line for line as shown, unless otherwise directed.

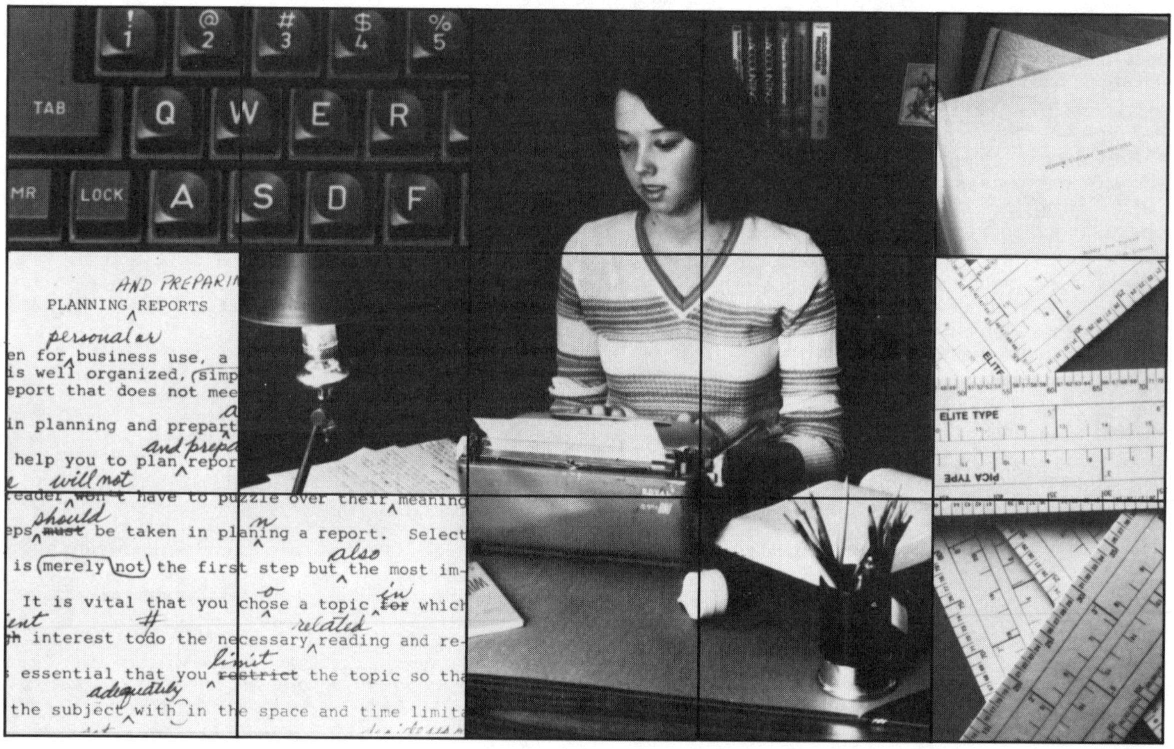

unit **4** lessons 26-30

Learn to operate the figure keyboard

Learning goals

1. To learn to type figures by touch and with good techniques.

2. To improve keystroking response patterns.

3. To improve keystroking speed and techniques.

4. To learn to proofread.

Machine adjustments

1. Paper guide at *0*.

2. Ribbon control to type on top half of ribbon.

3. Margin sets: 60–space line (center − 30; center + 30 + 5).

4. Line–space selector on *1* (SS) for drills.

5. Line–space selector on *2* (DS) for paragraphs.

273c ▶ 37
Prepare a letter of application

full sheet

Compose at the typewriter a letter of application similar to the one at the right for one of the following jobs which have been advertised in your local newspaper:

- Clerk-typist
- Correspondence Secretary
- Bookkeeping Machine Operator
- Data Processor

Use your home address for the return address, and use the letter style you prefer. Date the letter **May 5, 19—** and address it to **Mr. Elwood T. Barkley, Director of Human Resources, Continental Industries, Inc. 204 West Madison Street, your city, state, and ZIP Code.**

In the letter, tell Mr. Barkley:

1. You are replying to the advertisement in the newspaper.

2. When you will be available for work.

3. Your qualifications for the job, including your studies, work experience, and any special skills.

4. You are enclosing a personal data sheet.

Give any other information you believe will strengthen your application.

After you have composed the letter, make any corrections in pencil and retype the letter in good form, correcting errors as you type.

8024 South Hermitage Avenue
Chicago, IL 60626-3107
May 5, 19--

Mr. Elwood T. Barkley
Director of Human Resources
Continental Industries, Inc.
204 West Madison Street
Chicago, IL 60606-3313

Dear Mr. Barkley

Based on my education, experience, and ambition, I feel sure that I am qualified to fill the position of clerk-typist you have advertised in the Chicago Tribune. Please consider me an applicant for that position.

I will complete my studies at Martin Luther King High School on June 15 and will be available for work any time after that date. My general field of study has been business education. In addition to general courses such as English, mathematics, and social studies, my field of study included courses in business machines, correspondence, typewriting, office practice, and data processing. I have applied many of the skills learned in these courses in summer and part-time jobs during the past two years. The enclosed personal data sheet will give you more specific information about the skills I have attained and my work experience.

In addition to maintaining a B+ average in my studies in high school, I have been active in cocurricular activities. I have been a member of the National Honor Society and the Future Business Leaders of America. In addition, I have served as treasurer of the Office Education Club and as a reporter for the school newspaper.

May I come for an interview at a time that is convenient for you? I am free any afternoon after my classes end at 2:45 p.m. If you wish to call me, my telephone number is 555-4892.

Sincerely yours

Roberta J. Jefferson

Roberta J. Jefferson

Enclosure

25d ▶ 12 Check keystroking speed

1. A 1′ writing on each ¶; determine *gwam* on each.

2. Two 2′ writings on ¶s 1–2 combined; determine *gwam* on each writing.

3. One 3′ writing on ¶s 1–2 combined; determine *gwam*.

all letters used | E | 1.3 si | 5.2 awl | 90% hfw

	gwam 2′	3′
When you try to do better something that you	4	3
cannot do as well as you wish, you practice. You	9	6
do not just duplicate your actions; or if you do,	14	10
you do not improve. What you do repeat, instead,	19	13
is the general response but with some change.	24	16
So the next time you are asked to do a drill	28	19
again, try to do it in a better way. Think about	33	22
making quick, exact motions so that your mind can	38	26
tell the fingers what to do. Size up the problem	43	29
and learn better methods of increasing speed.	48	32

gwam 2′ | 1 | 2 | 3 | 4 | 5 |

3′ | 1 | 2 | 3 |

Enrichment material for Unit 3 appears below and on LM pp. 15, 16.

Enrichment activities

50-space line

On the basis of your speed check (25d, above), you may want to do additional practice to improve your keystroking technique and speed.

1. Type each line 3 times at increasing speeds to work out improved keystroking patterns.

2. Type the first line of each set as a 1′ writing; determine *gwam* on each.

3. Compare rates; then, type additional 1′ writings on the 3 slowest lines to improve your speed.

Technique cues

- curved, upright fingers
- hands quiet, wrists low and relaxed
- finger-reach stroking action
- quick down-in motion for spacing strokes

word response
1 Vi is to go with them to the quay by the big lake.
2 Dick is to make a visit to the eight island firms.
3 When she got such a profit, she paid for the land.

letter response
4 As you were on a tax case, we set up rates on gas.
5 You gave only a few facts in my case on oil taxes.
6 Test awards are based only upon faster base rates.

combination response
7 You may join their union only if you pay the fees.
8 The water in the city lake was bad for their fish.
9 We seated a panel of eight to decrease land waste.

double letters
10 Elly keeps her poodle in a kennel during the week.
11 Betty will see that the book display is a success.
12 Arruza knew that Eddie liked the books of puzzles.

adjacent keys
13 Eroica sang three pop ballads at my radio concert.
14 Art was there when the squids killed the porpoise.
15 Gregg washed three shirts, a skirt, and a sweater.

direct reaches
16 Jayne unlaced my ski shoes after I broke my ankle.
17 Marvin has many pieces of onyx and marble to sell.
18 Brig doubts that my vote can elect a new director.

| 1 | 2 | 3 | 4 | 5 | 6 | 7 | 8 | 9 | 10 |

274c ▶ 37 Complete an application blank

[LM p. 145]

1. Read carefully the headings and the questions on the application form.

2. Before typing the application form, type on a lined sheet of paper the information to be placed on each line of the form. Edit the material if necessary so that it will fit in the spaces provided. Abbreviations may be used to save space. Be sure each item of information is accurate.

3. Type the information neatly on the application form and sign the application in the space provided. Take extra care to insure that there are no typographical or other errors on the form.

APPLICATION FOR EMPLOYMENT — CONTINENTAL INDUSTRIES, INC.

AN EQUAL OPPORTUNITY EMPLOYER

PLEASE PRINT WITH BLACK INK OR USE TYPEWRITER

NAME (LAST, FIRST, MIDDLE INITIAL)	SOCIAL SECURITY NUMBER	CURRENT DATE
Jefferson, Roberta J.	242-07-4401	May 18, 1982

ADDRESS (NUMBER, STREET, CITY, STATE, ZIP CODE)	HOME PHONE NO.
8024 South Hermitage Avenue, Chicago, IL 60626-3107	(312) 555-4892

REACH PHONE NO.	U.S. CITIZEN?	DATE YOU CAN START
	X YES NO	June 18, 1982

ARE YOU EMPLOYED NOW?	IF SO, MAY WE INQUIRE OF YOUR PRESENT EMPLOYER?
No	

TYPE OF WORK DESIRED	REFERRED BY	SALARY DESIRED
Clerk-typist	Advertisement in Chicago Tribune	$ open

IF RELATED TO ANYONE IN OUR EMPLOY, STATE NAME AND POSITION: No one

	YES	NO	IF YES, EXPLAIN
DO YOU HAVE ANY PHYSICAL CONDITION THAT MAY PREVENT YOU FROM PERFORMING CERTAIN KINDS OF WORK?		X	
HAVE YOU EVER BEEN CONVICTED OF A FELONY?		X	

EDUCATION

EDUCATIONAL INSTITUTION	LOCATION (CITY, STATE)	DATES ATTENDED FROM MO.	FROM YR.	TO MO.	TO YR.	DIPLOMA, DEGREE, OR CREDITS EARNED	CLASS STANDING (CHK QUARTER) 1	2	3	4	MAJOR SUBJECTS STUDIED
COLLEGE											
HIGH SCHOOL Martin Luther King	Chicago, IL	9	79	6	82	Diploma	X				Business
GRADE SCHOOL											
OTHER											

LIST BELOW THE POSITIONS THAT YOU HAVE HELD (LAST POSITION FIRST)

1. NAME AND ADDRESS OF FIRM	DESCRIBE POSITION RESPONSIBILITIES
Martin Luther King High School 9500 South Michigan Avenue Chicago, IL 60628-2934	Typing; filing; keeping records of appointments and conferences
NAME OF SUPERVISOR: Ms. Loretta C. Chesney	
EMPLOYED (MO-YR) FROM: 9/80 - 6/82 TO:	REASON FOR LEAVING: Graduation from high school

2. NAME AND ADDRESS OF FIRM	DESCRIBE POSITION RESPONSIBILITIES
Monroe Insurance Company 175 West Jackson Street Chicago, IL 60604-2874	Typing; filing; telephoning; and other general clerical duties
NAME OF SUPERVISOR: Mrs. Rita S. Juarez	
EMPLOYED (MO-YR) FROM: Summer (June-Aug.) TO: 1980 and 1981	REASON FOR LEAVING: Part-time job

3. NAME AND ADDRESS OF FIRM	DESCRIBE POSITION RESPONSIBILITIES
NAME OF SUPERVISOR	
EMPLOYED (MO-YR) FROM: TO:	REASON FOR LEAVING

I UNDERSTAND THAT I SHALL NOT BECOME AN EMPLOYEE UNTIL I HAVE SIGNED AN EMPLOYMENT AGREEMENT WITH THE FINAL APPROVAL OF THE EMPLOYER AND THAT SUCH EMPLOYMENT WILL BE SUBJECT TO VERIFICATION OF PREVIOUS EMPLOYMENT, DATA PROVIDED IN THIS APPLICATION, ANY RELATED DOCUMENTS, OR RESUME. I KNOW THAT A REPORT MAY BE MADE THAT WILL INCLUDE INFORMATION CONCERNING ANY FACTOR THE EMPLOYER MIGHT FIND RELEVANT TO THE POSITION FOR WHICH I AM APPLYING, AND THAT I CAN MAKE A WRITTEN REQUEST FOR ADDITIONAL INFORMATION AS TO THE NATURE AND SCOPE OF THE REPORT IF ONE IS MADE.

Roberta J. Jefferson

SIGNATURE OF APPLICANT

24d ▶ 12 Check keystroking speed: skill comparison

1. A 1′ writing on each line; determine *gwam* on each writing.
2. Compare rates to identify the 3 slowest lines.
3. A 1′ writing on each of the 3 slowest lines to improve keystroking speed.

all letters used

balanced-hand	1	Pay them for the sign work they do if it is right.
combination	2	Vi read a theory on the state of art in the world.
double letters	3	Jenny is sorry she wasted her effort on that book.
adjacent-key	4	Vera did buy a top coin last night at an art sale.
one-hand	5	Zac gave only a few facts in my case on oil taxes.
direct reaches	6	Qyn found a gold nugget; it may bring a big price.

| 1 | 2 | 3 | 4 | 5 | 6 | 7 | 8 | 9 | 10 |

25

50-space line

25a ▶ 6 Conditioning practice

each line twice SS (slowly, then faster); DS between 2-line groups; if time permits, retype selected lines

alphabet	1	Jud aims next to play a quick game with Bev Fritz.
shift lock	2	Were those sports shows shown by NBC, CBS, or ABC?
fluency	3	Did they go by bus to visit six of the lake towns?

| 1 | 2 | 3 | 4 | 5 | 6 | 7 | 8 | 9 | 10 |

25b ▶ 12 Check keystroking speed: skill comparison

Retype 24d, above.
Goal: 2 *gwam* speed increase.

25c ▶ 20 Check typing techniques

each set of 3 lines twice SS; DS between 6-line groups

1. Clear all tab stops.
2. Set new tab stop 10 spaces to the right of center point.

Goals, line by line

1-3. Curved, upright fingers; low wrists; finger (not hand) action; quick, snap strokes
4-6. Down-in motion of right thumb; no pause before or after spacing stroke
7-9. Shift-type-release without moving hands downward or forward
10-12. Return quickly without long pauses before or after the return

Quick snap stroke

Down-and-in thumb motion

Shift, type, release

Quick return

all letters used

home	1	Jaka shall add half a glass as a lass adds a dash.
home/3d	2	It is a just law for us who work at the lake site.
home/1st	3	Zahn can have a van move his lynx back to the zoo.
	4	I am to get more pay if she is to go by the guide.
spacing	5	I will gladly pay any of the six to lay the brick.
	6	I know she said for us to stay on the beaten path.
	7	Most of us have to work: Miss, Mr., Mrs., and Ms.
shifting	8	Sue, Gib, and Vi went with Dr. Dye to St. Charles.
	9	Ask Mrs. Given to call Ms. Zelda Lamb on Thursday.
	10	——— tab ———→ Do not stop at
returning	11	the end of a line.——— tab ———→ Return quickly
	12	and start new line.

275

275a ▶ 5 Conditioning practice

Use standard directions given in 272a–274a, p. 417.

alphabet	1	Jed Lombard flew very quickly through hazy clouds en route to Phoenix.
figures	2	The new fund rose from 196 7/8 to 203 1/8 based on 45,600 shares sold.
fig/sym	3	The tax rate increased 7.6% in 1980, 12.5% in 1981, and 14.3% in 1982.
fluency	4	The men may not do the work if they do not receive their checks today.

| 1 | 2 | 3 | 4 | 5 | 6 | 7 | 8 | 9 | 10 | 11 | 12 | 13 | 14 |

275b ▶ 45 Measure production skill

1. Type the problems for 30′; correct errors as you type; compute *o–pram*.

2. Since only usable problems will count, proofread and correct each page before you remove it from the typewriter.

3. If you finish before time is called, retype Problem 5 as a leftbound report.

Problem 1
Letter [LM p. 149]

1. Type the letter in block style with open punctuation. Date the letter **June 7, 19—**; provide an appropriate salutation and complimentary close.

2. The letter will be signed by **Ms. C. Marian Freeman**, who is a **Personnel Specialist** in the **Human Resources Division.**

words

Letter to: Miss Theresa M. Moore, 1022 (S.)[sp] Maple (Ave.)[sp],
Oak Park, IL 60403-2800 [3 4] — opening lines 20
(¶1) The skills and abilities you ~~established~~ set forth in your personal 31
data sheet and letter of June 3 ~~reveal~~ indicate that you may 42
be qualified to fill a position as correspondence 52
secretary. This job demands ~~an individual~~ a person who 60
is a rapid and accurate typist and who is skilled 70
in the language arts, as shown on the enclosed job description. 83
(¶2) Would it be possible for you to come to our 92
office on June ~~12~~ 16 at 1 p.m. for an interview and 102
~~several tests.~~ testing? The interview will take approximately 112
(1)[sp] hour and the tests about (1½)[sp] hours. The tests 124
will consist of straight-copy timed writing and a test 135
on ~~representative~~ typical business ~~correspondence~~ documents. If we 143
find that you ~~meet the qualifications~~ are qualified for this position, 152
we would like you to start work on June 20. 161
(¶3) Will you please call Mr. David Grant of our 170
office (555-3210, Extension 210) and let him know if 180
~~this itinerary is~~ these arrangements are satisfactory to you. 190

closing lines 204

Problems 2 and 3 are on page 422.

23d ▶ 18 Improve keystroking speed: goal typing

Follow this practice plan:

1. A 1' writing on ¶1; determine *gwam*.

2. With your *gwam* as a base, select from the goals in the copy the first one to the right of your base rate.

3. Two 1' writings on ¶1, trying to reach or exceed your new goal rate. *As soon as you reach your new goal, try for the next higher goal rate.*

4. Type ¶2 in the same way.

Goals

- At least 18 *gwam*.
- At least 4 *gwam* increase over your base rate.

5. A 2' writing on ¶s 1–2 combined; determine *gwam*.

6. A 3' writing on ¶s 1–2 combined; determine *gwam*.

7. If time permits, type the 2 ¶s untimed; work for a steady pace (no pauses).

The paragraphs are marked with special signals to identify your practice goals.

Goals

| 1' | ▼ 18 | ■ 22 | ● 26 | ◆ 30 |

▼ acceptable
■ average
● good
◆ excellent

all letters used   gwam 2' | 3'

```
          .              4              .              8
    I am now learning to vary the typing rate to        4   3
       .             12          .              16    ▼
fit the ease of typing the words.  By learning to       9   6
    20              ■         24             ●      28
speed up the easy words, I can take time to break      14  10
    ◆               32           .             36        .
the longer words into parts for quick typing.          19  13
          .              4              .              8
    With more practice, I will be able to handle       23  16
       .             12          .              16    ▼
by word response some of the shorter words that I      28  19
    20              ■         24             ●      28
just now analyze and type letter by letter.  As I      33  22
    ◆               32           .             36        .
master this skill, I will become more expert.          38  25
```

gwam 2' | 1 | 2 | 3 | 4 | 5 |
     3' | 1 | 2 | 3 |

---

24   50-space line

24a ▶ 6 Conditioning practice

each line twice SS (slowly, then faster); DS between 2-line groups; if time permits, retype selected lines

alphabet 1 Gif Nixon will zip his mail to Dover by quick jet.

shift keys 2 Has Vic gone to Las Vegas? and Donna, to St. Paul?

fluency 3 The firm also owns the big sign by the town field.

| 1 | 2 | 3 | 4 | 5 | 6 | 7 | 8 | 9 | 10 |

24b ▶ 18 Improve keystroking speed: goal typing

Retype 23d, above.
Goal: 4 *gwam* speed increase.

24c ▶ 14 Improve skill transfer

1. A 1' writing on ¶1 of 23d, above; determine *gwam*.

2. Read ¶2 at the right to be sure you understand each rough-draft correction (Reference: 23b, p. 39).

3. A 1' writing on each ¶ at the right; determine *gwam*.

4. Type 3 additional 1' writings on the script ¶ and on the rough-draft ¶, trying to equal or exceed your straight-copy rate of Step 1.

gwam 1'

How well does your rate on script copy match   9
your rate on straight copy? The two rates should   19
now be within two or three words of each other.   29

Just how far below your speed on straight copy is   9
you rate on Rough Draft? These two rates should   19
now be within four to six words of each other.   29

275b, continued

Problem 2
Interoffice memorandum
[LM p. 151]
date the memo **June 16, 19—**

words

MEMO TO: C. Marian Freeman, Perso^n^nel Specialist 8

FROM: David Grant, Personnel Technic(ai)n 15

date 18

SUBJECT: Personnel data for Theresa M. Moore 25

(¶ 1) Attached is a completed personnel inter‿view ^form ~~blank~~ for 35

Theresa M. Moore, who has applied for a position as correspond- 48

^ence ~~ing~~ secretary. On a (5) sp -minute, straight-copy timed writing, 61

^Miss Moore achieved ~~the applicant attained~~ a score of 58 gross words a minute with 73

(4) sp errors. On the production ^test ~~exam~~, she finished four of the 85

five problems with all ^errors ~~of her mistakes~~ corrected neatly. 95

(¶ 2) Based on the interv(ei)w and her ^test ~~exam~~ scores, I recommend 106

that Miss Moore be ^offered ~~tendered~~ a job ~~at the earliest possible~~ 113

~~date~~ as a correspond^ence ~~ing~~ secretary. 119

closing lines 122

Problem 3
Table
full sheet; reading position; DS items

THE BIG BOOM IN CLERICAL POSITIONS 7

(Employment as of 1978 and Average Annual Openings to 1990) 19

Position	1978 Total *	Annual Openings	words
Bookkeepers	1,830,000	96,000	39
File clerks	273,000	16,500	44
Office machine operators	160,000	9,700	52
Receptionists	588,000	41,000	58
Secretaries/stenographers	3,684,000	305,000	67
Typists	1,044,000	59,000	72

(column heads: 33) 75

Source: *Occupational Outlook Quarterly*, Spring 1980. 92

* Estimated 94

Problems 4 and 5 are on page 423.

22d ▶ 16 Improve keystroking technique: response patterns

Lines 1-6: Each line once from dictation.

Lines 7-9: Two 1′ speed writings on each line; compare *gwam*.

Goals: To speed up on easy words and to type difficult ones with continuity.

word response	1	he she and own end air did but due man six may big
	2	did own | for six | the jam | but she | and may | an end cut
letter response	3	we you far him few oil get pin age poi act kin war
	4	see him | oil car | you set | few kin | bad pun | set my tax
combination response	5	on due oil big you own act sir pin cut ilk but age
	6	for him | due you | did zag | may set | and get | she saw me
word	7	Lana is due by six and may go to the city with us.
letter	8	I see you set my rate after you saw my data cards.
combination	9	They agree it is great for him to get such a wage.

| 1 | 2 | 3 | 4 | 5 | 6 | 7 | 8 | 9 | 10 |

23

50-space line

23a ▶ 6 Conditioning practice

each line twice SS (slowly, then faster); DS between 2-line groups; if time permits, retype selected lines

alphabet	1	Virgil Quin has packed twenty boxes of prize jams.
shift keys	2	Rosa and Juan are in Rio; Eiko and Huay, in Osaka.
fluency	3	To do the work right is the duty of the six of us.

| 1 | 2 | 3 | 4 | 5 | 6 | 7 | 8 | 9 | 10 |

23b ▶ 10 Learn to type from rough-draft copy

Copy that is corrected with pen or pencil is called *rough draft*. Some common marks that are used to correct copy are shown at the right. Study them before typing the rough-draft copy shown below, right.

Practice procedure

1. Type each ¶ once at an easy pace to learn to make corrections as you type.

2. Type the ¶s again at a faster rate to improve your speed on rough-draft copy.

Proofreader's marks

# add space	∧ insert	⊏ move left
Cap or ≡ capitalize	insert comma	⊐ move right
⁀ close up	⊙ insert period	¶ paragraph
delete	lc lowercase	tr or ∽ transpose

	gwam 1′	2′
~~Typed~~ copy that has ∧been corrected with pencil or	9	4
pen is called Rough Draft. I must learn to work	19	9
with the symbols writers use tomake changes⊙	28	14
¶ To forsee ~~the~~ changes made in the copy∧ I must	9	19
⊏ read ahead as I am typing. The ease of ~~my~~ the copy	19	24
⊐ depends up on just how ruogh the ∧rough draft is.	28	28

23c ▶ 16 Improve keystroking technique: response patterns

Retype 22d, above.

Goal: 4 *gwam* speed increase.

275b, continued

Problem 4
Purchase requisition
[LM p. 151]

words

DELIVER TO:	**David Grant, Personnel Tech.**	REQUISITION NO.	**479**	7
LOCATION:	**Room 102A**	DATE:	**June 27, 19--**	11
JOB NO.	**Administrative Overhead**	DATE REQUIRED:	**August 1, 19--**	19

QUANTITY	DESCRIPTION	
1,000	**Standard Employment Records (Form 162C)**	28
1,000	**Visible card files, 5″ × 8″**	35
500	**Interoffice memorandums, 8 1/2″ × 11″**	43

Problem 5
Unbound report
plain sheet
Add side headings as follows:
¶ 1: Correspondence Secretary
¶ 2: Administrative Secretary
Type the footnote so there is approximately a 1″ margin at the bottom of the page.

Word Processing--Where One Divided by Two Equals Two (center, All CAPS, TS) 11

Under the ~~system~~ concept of Word Processing (l.c. l.c.), the "secretary's job is 23
split into two jobs: that of word processor or correspondence 42
secretary. . . and that of the administrative secretary. . . ."[1] 62
side heading 71

The correspondance (e) secretary be comes a specialist in ~~provid-~~ 84
~~ing~~ producing typewritten ~~papers~~ documents of all ~~types~~ kinds. He or she prepares corre- 96
spondence, records, reports, forms, and similer (a) ~~material~~ matter by oper- 109
ating a typewriter or a ~~device~~ machine equipped with a typewriter-like 122
key board. The copy to be typed is recieved in the form of hand- 135
written notes, rough drafts, or transcri~~ption~~bing machine tapes. Final 148
copy may be stored on magnetic cards, tape, or floppy disks. 160
side heading 170

The Administrative Secretary (l.c. l.c.) executes all of the traditional 182
~~jobs~~ tasks of a secretary except for ~~the~~ typing. He or she reads and 195
routes incoming mail, schedules ~~meetings~~ appointments, answers the telephone, 208
greats (e) visitors, composes routine correspondence, and performs other duties 224
that ~~may~~ releive highly ~~payed~~ paid officials of clerical work and other 236
minor administrative ~~tasks~~ details. This new position may well be a ~~step~~ stepping 250
~~up~~ stone to ~~a~~ higher management ~~job~~ positions. 258
rule 262

[1]J. Marshall Hanna, Estelle L. Popham, and Rita Sloan Tilton, 274
Secretarial Procedures and Administration, 7th ed. (Cincinnati: 295
South-Western Publishing Co., 1978), p. 6. 304

21d ▶ 19 Improve keystroking speed: guided writing

Using the guided writing procedure given on p. 36:

1. A 1′ writing on ¶ 1; determine *gwam*. Add 2–4 words to set a new goal.

2. Two 1′ writings on ¶ 1 at your new goal rate, guided by ¼′ guide call.

3. Type ¶ 2 in the same way.

4. A 2′ writing on ¶ 1, then on ¶ 2. If you finish a ¶ before time is called, begin retyping it.

5. A 3′ writing on ¶s 1–2 combined; determine *gwam*.

gwam	¼′	½′	¾′	Time
16	4	8	12	16
20	5	10	15	20
24	6	12	18	24
28	7	14	21	28
32	8	16	24	32
36	9	18	27	36
40	10	20	30	40
44	11	22	33	44
48	12	24	36	48

all letters used

	gwam 2′	3′
If I am to build high skill, I must learn to	4	3
type without jerks or pauses. A very good way to	9	6
do this is to utilize guided writing as an aid in	14	10
pacing my efforts. If I can attain my speed goal	19	13
with each guide, I will soon build top skill.	24	16
I must also learn to read a bit ahead of the	4	19
typing to foresee the next letter sequences to be	9	22
typed. I have to fix my eyes on the words, but I	14	26
have to attend to the letters, too. If I read in	19	29
this way, I shall learn to type with fluency.	24	32

gwam 2′ | 1 | 2 | 3 | 4 | 5 |
3′ | 1 | 2 | 3 |

22

50-space line

22a ▶ 6 Conditioning practice

each line twice SS (slowly, then faster); DS between 2-line groups; if time permits, retype selected lines

alphabet 1 Aquela Javicz kept the new forms by the tax guide.

space bar 2 I am to|you and she|if he can pay|they are to play

fluency 3 Title to all of the lake land is held by the city.

| 1 | 2 | 3 | 4 | 5 | 6 | 7 | 8 | 9 | 10 |

22b ▶ 9 Type from handwritten copy (script)

1. Two 1′ writings on ¶ 1, then on ¶ 2; determine *gwam*.

Note. Words in partial line = strokes typed ÷ 5.

2. Type each ¶ once more untimed. Try to improve how you read and respond to the copy—and, thus, improve speed.

	gwam 1′
I must read with care when I type from script	9
copy. Every letter may not be exactly formed, but	19
I must type the word and the right letters in it.	29
I must also look ahead in the copy. Doing so	9
helps me to leave the right number of spaces after	19
a period, a comma, a colon, and other punctuation.	29

22c ▶ 19 Improve keystroking speed: guided writing

Retype 21d, above.
Goal: 4 *gwam* speed increase.

phase 12 lessons 276-300

Professional office simulations

Six units of simulated job tasks which provide meaningful experience in typing materials found in some professional offices are included in Phase 12. The offices represented are: a legal office, a medical office, an information processing office, a reprographic office, and a government office. Two additional units are included to build speed and accuracy in basic skill.

The activities in these 25 lessons will give you an opportunity to:

1. Increase your knowledge of the numerous typing tasks performed in business offices.

2. Apply—in realistic business situations—the basic knowledge, skills, and concepts you have learned previously.

3. Improve your ability to read and follow directions and to plan and organize your work effectively.

4. Increase your speed and accuracy in typing production materials.

5. Continue to build speed and control in basic skills.

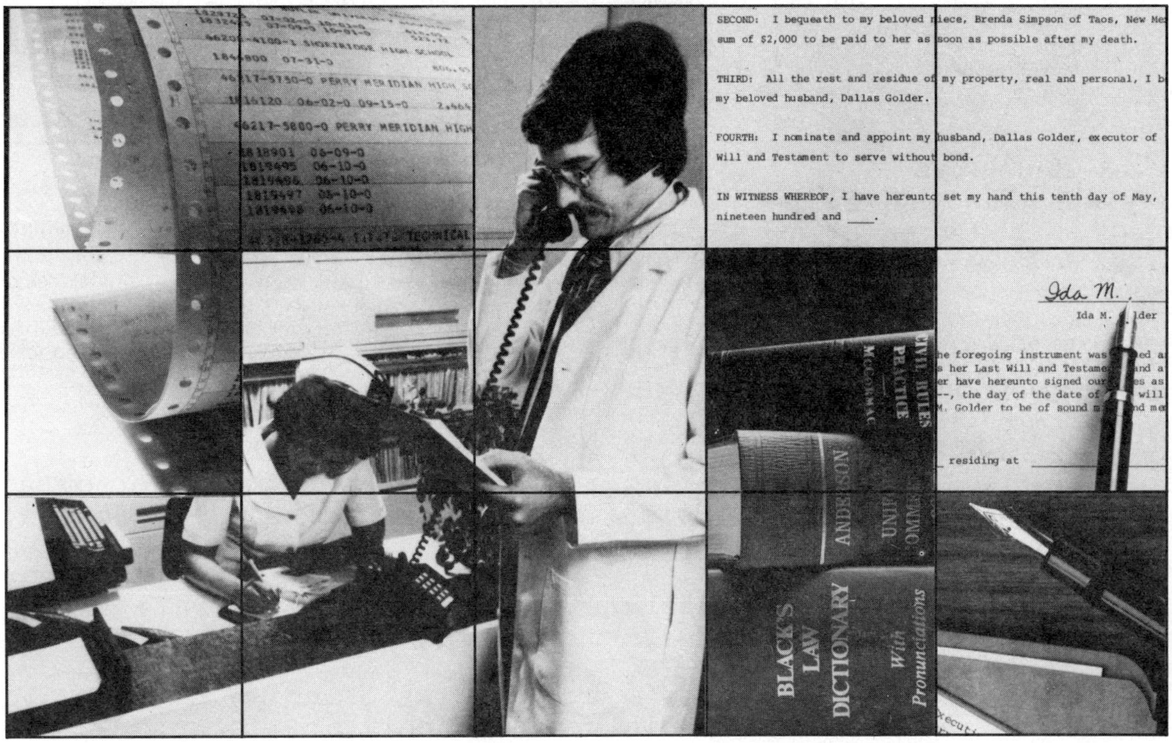

unit 56 lessons 276-278

Legal office

Learning goals

1. To increase your skill in planning, organizing, and typing a variety of realistic production materials.

2. To type in an acceptable form with all errors corrected a series of jobs found in a typical legal office.

Machine adjustments

1. Line: 70 for drills and timed writings; as required for production problems.

2. Spacing: SS sentence drills with a DS between sentence groups; space problems as required.

unit **3** lessons 21-25

Improve typing continuity/speed

Learning goals

1. To improve typing techniques.
2. To improve speed/continuity on sentence and paragraph copy.
3. To learn to type from handwritten and rough-draft copy.

Machine adjustments

1. Paper guide at *0*.
2. Ribbon control to type on top half of ribbon.
3. Margin sets: 50-space line (center − 25; center + 25 + 5).
4. Line-space selector on *1* (SS) for drills.
5. Line-space selector on *2* (DS) for paragraphs.

21

50-space line

21a ▶ 6 Conditioning practice

each line twice SS (slowly, then faster); DS between 2-line groups; if time permits, retype selected lines

alphabet	1	Jo Fox made five quick plays to win the big prize.
space bar	2	he may|she can|if any|is not|am to pay|if they may
fluency	3	He is to pay the man for the work and sign a form.
5-stroke words		| 1 | 2 | 3 | 4 | 5 | 6 | 7 | 8 | 9 | 10 |

21b ▶ 20 Improve keystroking technique: response patterns

1. Type Lines 1, 4, and 7 once from dictation.
2. Type Lines 1–9 twice at your own pace, trying to make the kind of response specified for each set of lines.
3. Type a 1′ writing on each of Lines 10–12; compare *gwam* on the 3 sentences.

Word response
Short, balanced-hand words (as in Lines 1–3) are so easy to type they can be typed as words. Think and type them at your top speed.

Letter response
Many one-hand words (as in Lines 4–6) are not so easy to type. Such words may be typed *letter by letter* with continuity (steadily, without pauses).

Combination response
Normal copy (as in Lines 7–9) includes both word- and letter-response sequences. *Use top speed for easy words, lower speed for more difficult ones.*

word response	1	us do if an so am go he to me or is of ah it by ox
	2	of us|if he|do so|it is|to us|or by|an ox|to do it
	3	He is to go to the town and to do the work for me.
letter response	4	at up as in we on be no ax oh ex my pi are you was
	5	as in|at no|be up|as my|be in|at my|we hum|see you
	6	As you saw up at my mill, my rate was up on water.
combination response	7	if on so as or we of no go at us my to be am up by
	8	is in|go on|if no|to be|is up|so as|is my|am up to
	9	If we are to be in the city, she may see him then.
word	10	I am to pay the six men if they do the work right.
letter	11	You set my tax only after I gave you my wage data.
combination	12	Daq may be paid extra if he works on my big barge.
		| 1 | 2 | 3 | 4 | 5 | 6 | 7 | 8 | 9 | 10 |

21c ▶ 5 Learn to type from handwritten copy (script)

1. Once at an easy pace to become familiar with typing from script.
2. Twice more at faster pace.

	gwam 1′
Copy that is written with a pencil or with a	9
pen is called script. I may be able to type this	19
kind of copy almost as fast as I type from print.	29

276-278

276a-278a ▶ 5 Conditioning practice

each line twice SS (slowly, then faster); DS between 2-line groups; if time permits, retype selected lines

alphabet 1 Jack Pew feared he might receive a zero on his quarterly biology exam.

figures 2 In Case 239401, cite the precedents on pages 58 and 76 of the Journal.

fig/sym 3 The law fees increased 7.6% in 1980, 12.5% in 1981, and 14.3% in 1982.

fluency 4 Can their attorney block the proxy sale of the land to the city today?

| 1 | 2 | 3 | 4 | 5 | 6 | 7 | 8 | 9 | 10 | 11 | 12 | 13 | 14 |

276b-278b ▶ 45 Production typing

You are a legal secretary in the offices of Donnelly, Everett, and Sloane, Attorneys-at-Law, at 927 Grand Avenue, Kansas City, MO 64106-8715. You work under the direction of Norma C. Sloane, who is your immediate supervisor. In addition, you have been licensed as a notary public and serve in that capacity for all members of the staff.

Job 1

Legal letters [LM pp. 155-158]

Mrs. Sloane has left a letter for you to type with this note: "Please type this letter to Ms. Dorothy E. Palmer, 6372 Wyandotte Street, Kansas City, MO 64113-7732 and to Mr. Elwood L. Tyson, 3907 Virginia Avenue, Kansas City, MO 64100-8715. Ask Ms. Palmer to come in on Friday morning, May 6, at 10:30 a.m. and Mr. Tyson to come in on Friday afternoon, May 6, at 2:30 p.m." Add an appropriate salutation and complimentary close.

Date the letter April 29; make one carbon copy of each letter. The signature block will be:

Mrs. Norma C. Sloane
Counselor-at-law

As counselors-at-law, this firm is representing Robert Dean Dawkins of 11902 Cherry Street, Kansas City, Missouri, in his efforts ~~attempt~~ to obtain workmen's compensation as a result of an injury sustained ~~which occured~~ on March 18 of this year on the premises of the Coronado Manufacturing Company ~~which is lo-~~ cated at 9500 Cambridge Avenue, Kansas City, Missouri.

As a witness to this incident, your testimony is very ~~quite~~ important ~~to~~ Mr. Dawkins' case. I ~~We~~ would appreciate ~~it,~~ ~~therefore, if you would meet~~ your meeting with me ~~us~~ on Friday ______, May 6, at ______ ~~in my office~~ so that we can discuss your ~~any~~ knowledge of the accident. At that time, I ~~we~~ will ask you to execute a deposition -- a sworn written statement setting forth ~~which will give~~ the circumstances of the accident as you perceived ~~know~~ them. This deposition will be included in a ~~a part of our~~ brief to be presented to the Missouri Workmen's Compensation Board.

If, for any reason, you are unable to ~~cannot~~ meet with me in my office at the time suggested ~~above~~, please call my legal secretary, (include your name), at 555-7400, extension 238, and arrange for another mutually convenient time.

Thank you for helping Mr. Dawkins in this very important matter.

20d ▶ 6 Check keystroking speed

1. Type a 1′ writing on ¶ 1, then on ¶ 2; note your *gwam* on each by using the dots and figures above the lines.

2. Type one 2′ writing on ¶s 1–2 combined; determine *gwam* by using the column at the right and the scale beneath the ¶s.

To determine 2′ *gwam*:

Add the figure at the right of the last complete line typed to the *gwam*–scale figure directly below the last word typed.

all letters used | E | 1.2 si | 4.7 awl | 95% hfw |

gwam 2′

```
                   ·         4         ·         8
¶ 1      I can now type each letter as I keep my eyes       4
       ·         12        ·         16        ·
     on the copy.  I can type with good form, also.  I      9
       20        ·         24        ·         28
     next need to learn how to improve each motion and     14
       ·         32        ·         36        ·
     to reduce the time between letters and words.         19
                   ·         4         ·         8
¶ 2      A step to which I must give attention in the      23
       ·         12        ·         16        ·
     days just ahead is reading.  The size of the word     28
       20        ·         24        ·         28
     can limit how I read.  I may focus on a short one     33
       ·         32        ·         36        ·
     quickly as a whole; a long one, part by part.         38

gwam 2′ |    1    |    2    |    3    |    4    |    5    |
```

20e ▶ 8 Improve keystroking speed: guided writing

Select a practice goal:

1. Type a 1′ writing on ¶1 of 20d, above; determine *gwam*.

2. Using the *gwam* as a base, add 4 *gwam* to determine your *goal* rate.

3. Choose from Column 1 of the table at the right the speed nearest your goal rate. At the right of that speed, note the ¼′ points in the copy you must reach to maintain your goal rate.

Quarter-minute checkpoints

gwam	¼′	½′	¾′	Time
16	4	8	12	16
20	5	10	15	20
24	6	12	18	24
28	7	14	21	28
32	8	16	24	32
36	9	18	27	36
40	10	20	30	40

4. Note from the word–count dots and figures above the lines in ¶1 the checkpoint for each quarter minute. [Checkpoints for 24 *gwam* are 6, 12, 18, and 24.]

Practice procedure

1. Type two 1′ writings on ¶ 1, above, at your goal rate guided by the quarter–minute calls (¼, ½, ¾, time).

Goal: To reach each of your checkpoints just as the guide is called.

2. Type ¶ 2, above, in the same way.

3. A 2′ writing on ¶s 1–2 combined, without the guides.

Speed level of practice

When the purpose of practice is to reach out into new speed areas, use the *speed* level. Take the brakes off your fingers and experiment with new stroking patterns and new speeds. Do this by:

1. Reading 2 or 3 letters ahead of your typing to foresee stroking patterns.

2. Getting the fingers ready for the combinations of letters to be typed.

3. Keeping your eyes on the copy in the book.

Enrichment activities (below, and on LM pp. 13, 14)

50-space line

On the basis of your technique check (19d, p. 35) and your speed check (20d, above), you may want to do additional practice to improve your performance.

To improve keyboard control, use 17c, p. 32
18b, p. 33
19b, p. 34
20b, p. 35

To improve keystroking speed, use 17d, p. 33
19c, p. 34
20e, above
Line 3 of 17b, p. 32
18a, p. 33
19a, p. 34
20a, p. 35

To improve machine parts control, use 19d, p. 35.

To improve return technique, practice the lines below.

```
It is up to us to try it.
Jane can also do this work.
Clyde will fix their gold urn.
Len is to work with us at eight.
May is to pay all six for the work.
```

276b-278b, continued

Job 2

Deposition [LM p. 159]

1. At the right is the deposition prepared for Ms. Palmer's signature. Prepare the same deposition for Mr. Tyson's signature, making the appropriate changes. Mr. Tyson has been an employee of the Coronado Manufacturing Company since June 17, 1970.

2. Before typing the deposition, study the directions for typing legal documents below:

TYPING LEGAL DOCUMENTS

1. DS legal documents on 8½" × 11", 13", or 14" paper.

2. Use a left margin of 1½" and a right margin of ½" on unruled paper; type within the ruled lines of legal paper.

3. Use a top margin of 2" and a bottom margin of 1" on all pages.

4. Indent paragraphs 10 spaces.

5. Number pages (except for the first page) ½" from the bottom of the page.

6. Proofread carefully to insure there are no errors. Avoid correcting figures, dates, names, and places. If they are corrected, the corrections must be initialed by all parties.

Note: The letters "ss." are the abbreviation for the Latin word *scilicet*, which means "namely." "L.S." is the abbreviation for the Latin phrase *locus sigilli* and is used in place of a seal.

DEPOSITION

STATE OF MISSOURI)
) ss.
County of Jackson)

Before me, the subscriber, a notary public for the County of Jackson, State of Missouri, personally appeared DOROTHY E. PALMER of Kansas City, Jackson County, Missouri, who being duly sworn deposes and says that

(1) she has been an employee of the Coronado Manufacturing Company at 9500 Cambridge Avenue, Kansas City, Missouri, since July 15, 1975.

(2) on March 18 of this year she witnessed an accident which befell Robert Dean Dawkins in Warehouse A of the Coronado Manufacturing Company.

(3) that the accident was caused by an oil slick on the warehouse floor deposited by faulty forklift equipment and through no fault of Robert Dean Dawkins.

______________________________(L.S.)
(student's name), Notary Public

My commission expires July 1, 1986.

19d ▶ 10 Check technique: machine parts

each pair of lines twice SS (slowly, then faster); DS between 4-line groups

Goals, line by line

1-2: down–in spacing motion

3-4: shift without pausing

5-6: release lock for typing lowercase letters

space bar	1	I knew it was my job to do my best in all my work.
	2	Try in the right way, and you can reach your goal.
shift keys	3	Jaye Garvey is to go to the dance with Paul Quinn.
	4	Flip Hahn said Jan Apel will go to Spain in March.
shift lock	5	Type in ALL CAPS items such as PTA, FBLA, and NFL.
	6	Type book titles in ALL CAPS: GONE WITH THE WIND.

20

50-space line

20a ▶ 6 Conditioning practice

each line twice SS (slowly, then faster); DS between 2-line groups; if time permits, retype selected lines

alphabet	1	Have my long quiz boxed when Jack stops by for it.
punctuation	2	Have we used these words: vote, view, five, gave?
easy sentence	3	He is to do social work for the city if they wish.

| 1 | 2 | 3 | 4 | 5 | 6 | 7 | 8 | 9 | 10 |

20b ▶ 20 Master letter reaches and sequences

1. Type the drill once as shown; type at an easy but steady pace.

Technique cues

- curved, upright fingers
- quick, snap keystrokes
- finger (not hand) motions
- down–in motion of right thumb when spacing
- quick return (no pause)

2. Type the drill again at a faster rate.

all letters used

r/e	1	are hers sure here term real over very share other
	2	The terms of her sale are there on the other side.
p/o	3	opt top pot bop copy port open poor stop upon drop
	4	The poet will opt for a top post in our port city.
a/s	5	ask has was gas say past last same cash axis basic
	6	Sam said the cash price for gas went up last week.
u/i	7	suit quiz ruin guide juice equip fruit built quick
	8	Our guide quips that she may give us a quick quiz.
w/e	9	we new owe few week news went knew were view power
	10	The news is that we may view a new film next week.
m/y	11	my may yam gym myth hymn cyme foamy myself symbols
	12	My need for gym drills is no myth to my gym coach.

| 1 | 2 | 3 | 4 | 5 | 6 | 7 | 8 | 9 | 10 |

20c ▶ 10 Check keystroking technique

type the drill twice

Technique cue: Keep the hands and arms quiet; let the *fingers* do the typing.

Rows

home/3d	1	for us | it was | the squid | we took | they are | jute rope
	2	Faye told us she took the file to the youth group.
home/1st	3	an ad; a van; can land; a mask; has flax; all can;
	4	Ann Lanz has a bad hand. Shall Nan sack all cash?
3d/1st	5	in it, we can, fix them, pay him, to quit, by size
	6	Vic can give you the vote count to prove my point.

| 1 | 2 | 3 | 4 | 5 | 6 | 7 | 8 | 9 | 10 |

276b-278b, continued

Job 3
Will [LM pp. 161]

You receive this note from Mrs. Sloane: "Mr. Lee Roy Barnes of Kansas City, Missouri, has asked us to prepare a will for him. His estate will go to his wife, Betty Karr Barnes or, should she not survive him, to his children, Karl Lee Barnes and Ray Mark Barnes. Mr. Barnes will be in my office on June 8 to sign the will. Prepare the will using a standard format as shown. Mr. Barnes has appointed our office the executor." If paper of acceptable size is available, prepare a backing sheet and type an endorsement as described and illustrated below.

LEGAL ENDORSEMENT

In some law offices, a description (called the *endorsement*) is typed on the outside cover of a backing sheet and prepared in a special way for storage in a safe deposit box or special filing cabinets.

Make a 1½" fold at the top of the backing sheet. Fold the backing sheet into equal thirds and type the endorsement in the middle third as shown in the illustration. Then, insert the typed document under the fold and staple it in place.

LAST WILL AND TESTAMENT OF (type full name; center over line of writing)

I, (type full name), a resident of the City of (type city), State of (type state), declare this to be my Last Will and Testament, and revoke all former Wills and Codicils.

FIRST, I direct that all my just debts be paid.

SECOND, I declare that I am married, and my wife's name is (type full name); I have (give number) child (or children) now living: (type full name/s).

THIRD, I give, devise, and bequeath all my property, real and personal and wherever situated, to my wife, (type full name). In the event my wife does not survive me, I leave my estate to my (son/daughter/children), (give name or names) (if more than one, continue) to be divided in equal shares.

FOURTH, I appoint as Executor of my Will the law firm of Donnelly, Everett, and Sloane of Kansas City, Missouri, to serve without bond.

This Will and Testament is subscribed by me on the (spell out date) day of (spell out month), 19—, at (type city and state).

TS

____________________________(L.S.)

DS

SIGNED, SEALED, PUBLISHED AND DECLARED by the above-named (type full name) to be his Last Will and Testament in the presence of us, and we, in his presence and the presence of each other, have hereunto subscribed our names as witnesses:

DS

____________________ ____________________

DS

____________________ ____________________

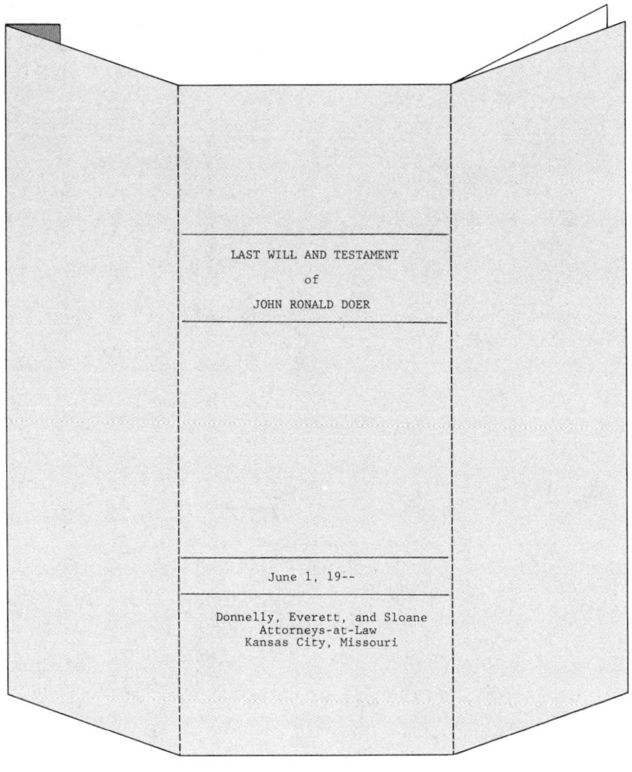

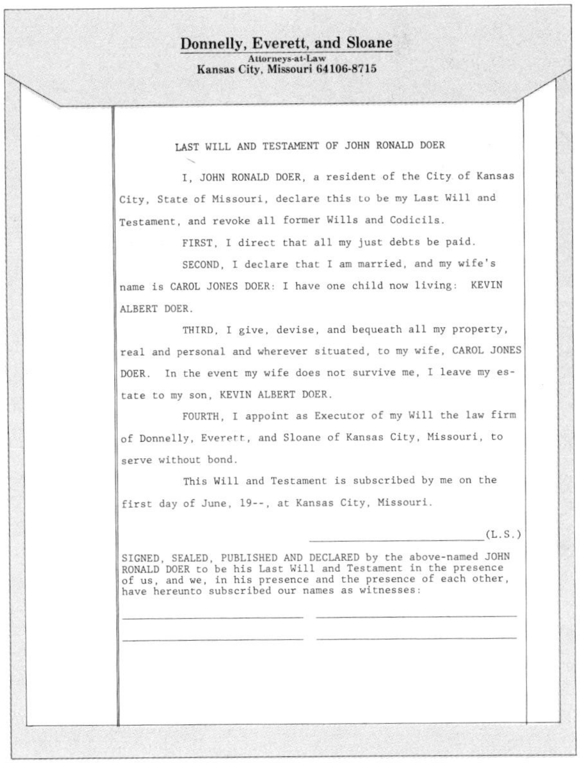
Donnelly, Everett, and Sloane
Attorneys-at-Law
Kansas City, Missouri 64106-8715

LAST WILL AND TESTAMENT OF JOHN RONALD DOER

I, JOHN RONALD DOER, a resident of the City of Kansas City, State of Missouri, declare this to be my Last Will and Testament, and revoke all former Wills and Codicils.

FIRST, I direct that all my just debts be paid.

SECOND, I declare that I am married, and my wife's name is CAROL JONES DOER: I have one child now living: KEVIN ALBERT DOER.

THIRD, I give, devise, and bequeath all my property, real and personal and wherever situated, to my wife, CAROL JONES DOER. In the event my wife does not survive me, I leave my estate to my son, KEVIN ALBERT DOER.

FOURTH, I appoint as Executor of my Will the law firm of Donnelly, Everett, and Sloane of Kansas City, Missouri, to serve without bond.

This Will and Testament is subscribed by me on the first day of June, 19--, at Kansas City, Missouri.

________________(L.S.)

SIGNED, SEALED, PUBLISHED AND DECLARED by the above-named JOHN RONALD DOER to be his Last Will and Testament in the presence of us, and we, in his presence and the presence of each other, have hereunto subscribed our names as witnesses:

18d ▶ 6 Improve keystroking continuity

1. Type the ¶ once at an easy but steady pace; give attention to good techniques and to keeping the carriage (element) moving.

2. Practice 2 or 3 times any words that caused you to hesitate.

3. Type the ¶ once more at a slightly faster pace.

all letters used | E | 1.2 si | 4.5 awl | 93% hfw |

	gwam 2′	
Now it is up to me to build a major skill to	4	23
prize. I can develop my speed if I will type the	9	28
copy in the right way. To reach the next goal, I	14	33
must move quickly from one letter to another.	19	38

gwam 2′ | 1 | 2 | 3 | 4 | 5 |

19

50-space line

19a ▶ 6 Conditioning practice

each line twice SS (slowly, then faster); DS between 2-line groups; if time permits, retype selected lines

alphabet 1 Hew amazed Jevan by escaping quickly from the box.
shift keys 2 Karen and Paul lost the first set to Ella and Sol.
easy sentence 3 I am to go to the dock, and he is to work with me.

| 1 | 2 | 3 | 4 | 5 | 6 | 7 | 8 | 9 | 10 |

19b ▶ 20 Master letter reaches and sequences

1. Type the drill once as shown; type at an easy but steady pace.

Technique cues

- curved, upright fingers
- quick, snap keystrokes
- finger (not hand) motions
- down-and-in motion of right thumb when spacing
- quick return (no pause)

2. Type the drill again at a faster rate.

all letters used

r/t
1 true part sort trip tried party trust forth expert
2 The party of forty set forth on a trip to Tripoli.

n/y
3 any many tiny sync funny rainy sunny penny anytime
4 Lyn says a smile turns a rainy day sunny for many.

o/i
5 oil soil loin foil lion coin toil join prior point
6 Eloise may join the oil firm; she has that option.

g/r
7 grid urge grin large gripe merge grown surge great
8 Quin urged the large firm to merge for new growth.

b/r
9 brow curb herb blurb bring derby brush brown brick
10 Herb did bring the brown brick to repair the curb.

r/v
11 river favor razor virus larva curve marvel service
12 Irv may marvel at the view we survey at the curve.

| 1 | 2 | 3 | 4 | 5 | 6 | 7 | 8 | 9 | 10 |

19c ▶ 14 Improve keystroking speed

1. Type a 1′ writing on the ¶ of 18d, above. Determine *gwam* using the color dots and figures above the lines.

2. Beginning where you stopped in the first writing, type a second 1′ writing. Determine *gwam*: Subtract your first *gwam* from the word count at the dot or figure nearest the last word typed in the second writing.

3. Type two more 1′ writings on the ¶ in the same way.

4. Type two 2′ writings on the ¶; determine *gwam* on each one.

Goal: To maintain your 1′ rate for 2 minutes.

To determine 2′ gwam:
Add the figure at the right of the last complete line typed to the *gwam*-scale figure directly below the last word typed.

276b-278b, continued

Job 4
Deed [LM p. 163]

Don Van, one of Mrs. Sloane's law clerks, left this deed for you to type.

Type the information in the blank spaces provided, using the variable line spacer to insure that the typewritten material is on the same lines as the printed material.

Note: Spell out the current year in the date.

This Indenture *MADE the* tenth *day of* July *in the year of our Lord one thousand nine hundred and* BETWEEN Byron J. and Anne C. Marks of Kansas City, Missouri,

of the first part, and Thomas C. and Mary L. Ryan of Kansas City, Missouri,

of the second part: **Witnesseth**, That the said parties of the first part, for and in consideration of the sum of sixty-two thousand dollars ($62,000.00) lawful money of the United States of America, to them in hand, paid by the said parties of the second part, at and before the sealing and delivery of these presents, the receipt whereof is hereby acknowledged, have granted, bargained, sold, remised, released and quit-claimed, and by these presents do grant, bargain, sell, remise, release and quit-claim, unto the said parties of the second part, and to their heirs and assigns forever, ALL that parcel of land described as Lot No. 119 in the Plan of Lots recorded in Jackson County in Deed Book Vol. 654, page 293, and known as 7110 Oak Street, Kansas City, Missouri.

Together with all and singular the tenements, hereditaments and appurtenances thereunto belonging, or in anywise appertaining, and the reversions, remainders, rents, issues and profits thereof; AND ALSO all the estate, right, title, interest, property, claim, and demand whatsoever, as well in law as in equity, of the said parties of the first part, of, in or to the above described premises, and every part and parcel thereof, with the appurtenances.

To have and to hold all and singular the above mentioned and described premises, together with the appurtenances, unto the said parties of the second part, their heirs and assigns forever.

In witness whereof, the said parties of the first part have hereunto set their hands and seals on the date and year written above.

SEALED AND DELIVERED
IN THE PRESENCE OF

____________________ (L.S.)

____________________ (L.S.)

17d ▶ 20 Improve keystroking speed

1. Two 30″ writings on Line 1, then on Line 2.

Goal: To reach the end of each line as "Return" is called (12 *gwam*).

2. Type the other pairs of lines in like manner. Each pair of lines must be typed 2 *gwam* faster than the preceding pair (12, 14, 16, etc.).

3. Type a 1′ writing on each of Lines 1, 3, 5, 7, and 9; determine *gwam* on each writing. Use the 5-stroke word scale to determine *gwam*.

all letters used	gwam 30″	20″	15″
1 Jan is to go to the city lake.	12	18	24
2 Cass did set a safe goal rate.	12	18	24
3 Rick is to fix a sign for the city.	14	21	28
4 Zaza may work at the big card firm.	14	21	28
5 Did the queen also visit the lake towns?	16	24	32
6 Did they ever get the test forms we saw?	16	24	32
7 The theme for the panel is world fuel profit.	18	27	36
8 Edward is eager to test the six antique cars.	18	27	36
9 Buzz works for the big map firm for the usual pay.	20	30	40
10 Jo kept a wage card on all of us at the milk firm.	20	30	40

5-stroke words | 1 | 2 | 3 | 4 | 5 | 6 | 7 | 8 | 9 | 10 |

18

50-space line

18a ▶ 6 Conditioning practice

each line twice SS (slowly, then faster); DS between 2-line groups; if time permits, retype selected lines

alphabet 1 By solving the tax quiz, Jud Mack won first prize.

space bar 2 if you|why it is|ask my son|for the arm|of the war

easy sentence 3 She is to go to the city by bus to sign the forms.

| 1 | 2 | 3 | 4 | 5 | 6 | 7 | 8 | 9 | 10 |

18b ▶ 20 Master letter reaches and sequences

1. Type the drill once as shown; type at an easy but steady pace.

Technique cues

- curved, upright fingers
- quick, snap keystrokes
- finger (not hand) motions
- down-and-in motion of right thumb when spacing
- quick return (no pause)

2. Type the drill again at a faster rate.

all letters used

a/z
1 zany jazz haze maze lazy daze hazy czar zeal amaze
2 The jazz band plays with zeal and zest at the zoo.

u/n
3 run unit fund until under bonus found sound annual
4 Our unit may not have its annual bonus until June.

e/c
5 ice once echo nice check since force expect record
6 Once we receive the pacer, you may expect a check.

f/t
7 oft gift lift soft left sift tuft loft fifty often
8 Faith left me fifty yards of soft lace for a gift.

a/q
9 aqua equal quota squad quake squawk equate acquire
10 My squad set a quarter quota to equal our request.

u/m
11 sum much dumb must mush human mutual summer volume
12 I must assume that sales volume is our mutual aim.

| 1 | 2 | 3 | 4 | 5 | 6 | 7 | 8 | 9 | 10 |

18c ▶ 18 Improve keystroking speed

Retype 17d, above.
Goal: 4 *gwam* speed increase.

unit **57** lessons 279-281

Medical office

Learning goals

1. To complete typical job tasks in a medical office in a satisfactory manner.

2. To improve your skill in typing production materials in a realistic setting.

Machine adjustments

1. Line: 70 for drills; as necessary for problems.

2. Spacing: SS sentence drills with a DS between sentence groups; space problems as required.

279-281

279a-281a ▶ 5 Conditioning practice

each line twice SS (slowly, then faster); DS between 2-line groups; if time permits, retype selected lines

alphabet 1 Wexford quietly criticized the vague remarks published in the journal.

figures 2 The Senate changed paragraphs 157.8 and 194.6 of SB 149320 on April 9.

fig/sym 3 On 6/15/82, Parker & Graves sold bonds at 7 3/4%, 9 1/2%, and 10 1/8%.

fluency 4 They may owe a big penalty if he does not pay the bill when it is due.

| 1 | 2 | 3 | 4 | 5 | 6 | 7 | 8 | 9 | 10 | 11 | 12 | 13 | 14 |

279b-281b ▶ 45 Production typing simulation

You are a medical typist in the Administrative Office of the Portland Pacific Medical Center located at 600 SW Park Avenue, Portland, Oregon 97205–3658. Your immediate superior is Miss Sylvia M. Hilty, who is Director of Administrative Services for the Center. Your job is to type correspondence, medical forms, and medical reports.

Job 1
Admissions form
[LM p. 165]
Type with 1 cc.

Portland Pacific Medical Center
600 SW Park Avenue
Portland, OR 97205-3658 (503) 555-9100

ADMISSIONS DATA

PATIENT NAME (LAST) Lewis, (FIRST) Timothy D. OCC. Accountant HOSPITAL NUMBER 1623-94
ADDRESS (IF DIFFERENT FROM SUBSCRIBER'S) EMP. City of Portland HOME PHONE 555-7807

SUBS. NAME Same
ADDRESS 17 NW Trail Ave. OCC.
CITY & STATE Portland, Oregon 97229-3825 EMP.

NEAREST REL. Lois A. Lewis
REL. TO PAT. wife
HOME PHONE 555-7807 WORK PHONE 555-9201
DRS ATT Dr. Mary D. Weir
REF Dr. Samuel Marek
ROOM NO. 812 RATE $190

BIRTH DATE	AGE	SEX	M.S.	RELIGION	HOW ADMITTED	DATE ADM.	TIME AM	PM	DATE DIS.	TIME AM	PM
3/19/55	27	M	M		Self	9/20/82	9:20				

COMMERCIAL	COMP.	INDIV.	GROUP	GROUP NO.	AGREEMENT NO.	MALE: SELF 1	HUS. 2	SON 3	FEMALE: SELF 4	WIFE 5	DAUG. 6
Stillcreek			X	8002-Z	A414062422	X					

ADMITTING DIAGNOSIS
Acute appendicitis

unit **2** lessons 17-20

Improve basic technique/speed

Learning goals

1. To master letter–key reaches.
2. To improve keystroking precision (direction/distance).
3. To improve technique/speed of spacing, shifting, returning carriage (element).
4. To increase keystroking speed on sentences/paragraphs.

Machine adjustments

1. Paper guide at *0*.
2. Ribbon control to type on top half of ribbon.
3. Margin sets: 50–space line (center − 25; center + 25 + 5).
4. Line–space selector on *1* (SS) for drills.
5. Line–space selector on *2* (DS) for paragraphs.

17

50-space line

17a ▶ 4 Recall

1. Get–ready–to–type procedure (see pages 4–5 if necessary).
2. Features of good typing position (see page 7).
3. Features of good hand and finger position (at right).
4. Motions to operate service keys (space bar, shift keys and lock, and the return).

Curved, upright fingers

Finger–action keystroking

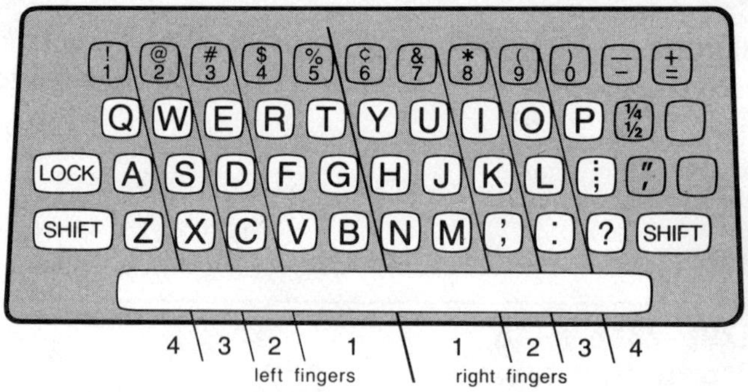

17b ▶ 6 Conditioning practice

each line twice SS (slowly, then faster); DS between 2-line groups; if time permits, retype selected lines

alphabet 1 Jay Peck has fixed a quaint fishbowl Ruiz gave me.

space bar 2 it is my | go to the | and to do | if she is | he may work

easy sentence 3 He or she is to go to the lake to do the map work.

5-stroke words | 1 | 2 | 3 | 4 | 5 | 6 | 7 | 8 | 9 | 10 |

17c ▶ 20 Master letter reaches and sequences

1. Type the drill once as shown; type at an easy but steady pace.

Technique cues

- curved, upright fingers
- quick, snap keystrokes
- finger (not hand) motions
- down–and–in motion of right thumb when spacing
- quick return (no pause)

2. Type the drill again at a faster rate.

all letters used

d/e
1 led made used side need wide heed idea guide delay
2 Ned said the guide used a slide film for her talk.

l/o
3 lox old lot told long hold loan whole local school
4 Lou told me that her local school loans old books.

j/u
5 jug juts just jute judge juice injure adjust jumbo
6 That judge just asked the jury for a just verdict.

s/w
7 was saw rows sows slow ways laws flaws shows swing
8 Wes said the first two rows saw flaws in the show.

k/i
9 kite bike knit like kind kick disk silk hike quick
10 A vivid blue silk kite jinked above the ski trail.

f/r
11 fire fore from first offer front favor wharf froze
12 Fran saw a fire leap from her boat onto the wharf.

5-stroke words | 1 | 2 | 3 | 4 | 5 | 6 | 7 | 8 | 9 | 10 |

279b-281b, continued

Job 2
Medical history worksheet [LM p. 167]

1. Timothy D. Lewis has been admitted to the hospital complaining of abdominal pains. Dr. Weir has examined him and completed his medical history worksheet.

2. Type the medical history worksheet, including the headings in the body of the report. Obtain any information not shown on the form from the Admissions Data typed in Job 1.

Portland Pacific Medical Center
MEDICAL HISTORY WORKSHEET

NAME: Timothy D. Lewis
ATTENDING PHYSICIAN:
DATE ADMITTED:
PATIENT NUMBER: 1623-94
CHIEF COMPLAINT: "Abdominal pains"
ROOM NUMBER:

PRESENT ILLNESS: The patient is complaining of abdominal pains which began early in the a.m. as a generalized pain and, after he vomited twice, the pain shifted to the right lower quadrant.

PAST MEDICAL HISTORY: Normal childhood diseases; T & A at age 6. At age 17, he was hospitalized for a fractured femur sustained while playing football. Patient had physical examination 4 months ago and was found to be in good health. No known allergies.

SOCIAL HISTORY: 27-year-old married male with 1 child; employed as an accountant for the City of Portland. Does not smoke or drink; jogs 3 miles a day.

FAMILY HISTORY: Patient's mother is living, age 62, and in good health. Father died in 1980 following a myocardial infarction. Patient has one brother, age 31, who is alive and well. Maternal aunt with diabetes. Patient denies any known tuberculosis, carcinoma, or arthritis in family.

REVIEW OF SYSTEMS: Head, Eyes, Ears, Nose, Throat-Unremarkable. Abdomen - Right lower quadrant tenderness.

ADMITTING DIAGNOSIS: Acute appendicitis.

Job 3
Report of operation
[LM pp. 169–172]

1. The final diagnosis for Timothy D. Lewis was acute appendicitis. Dr. Weir performed the appendectomy on 9/20/82 assisted by John C. Sanchez, M.D., and A. Charles Roan, R.N. A report of operation is on page 431.

2. Type the report of operation; SS the lines of the procedure. Obtain any information not given on the report from the Admissions Data typed in Job 1. Make 1 cc.

16b ▶ 25 Check typing techniques

each line once as shown; then retype as many lines as time permits

Goals, line by line

1-4. Do you return without pausing at the end of one line and at the beginning of the next line?

5-7. Do you shift-type-release quickly without moving your hands down?

8-10. Do you space between words without pausing before or after the spacing stroke?

11-13. Do you reach to the third and first rows of keys without moving your hands forward or downward?

14-16. Do you keep the carriage (or element) moving steadily, speeding up easy words and slowing down slightly for the harder ones?

Return

```
1 Try to type in the right
2 way as well as to strike the
3 right keys.  How you type may be
4 as vital as the copy typed just now.
```

Shift keys

```
left  5 Paul, Mario, and I may visit Mac and Janey in May.
right 6 Rosa Tovar and Guido Rossi now live in Fort Worth.
both  7 Did Mona Longi see Kiu Quan or Maria Bird in York?
```

Space bar

```
short words  8 he or she|it is for us|if she and he|so she did it
after y/n/m  9 am to pay|than a day|he may own it|any of them can
            10 I may go to the city to pay the firm for the sign.
```

Keystroking

```
home/3d  11 They took a quiet poll of the group for her today.
home/1st 12 Max lacks cash to back a small jazz band he plans.
3d/1st   13 Meg asked him when a vote on the issue might come.

balanced-     14 I am to fix it|he owns an auto|she lent me the map
and one-hand  15 she set the rate|you did tax work|the car title is
words         16 She gave them the form to get a title for the car.
5-stroke words | 1 | 2 | 3 | 4 | 5 | 6 | 7 | 8 | 9 | 10 |
```

16c ▶ 5 Check keystroking speed: sentences

two 1-minute (1′) writings on each sentence; determine *gwam* (total 5-stroke words typed)

```
alphabet      1 Glenda saw a quick red fox jump over the lazy cub.
easy sentence 2 He is to do all the field forms for the usual pay.
5-stroke words | 1 | 2 | 3 | 4 | 5 | 6 | 7 | 8 | 9 | 10 |
```

16d ▶ 12 Check keystroking speed: paragraphs

1. Type each paragraph (¶) once untimed for practice.

2. Type two 1-minute (1′) writings on each ¶; determine *gwam* (gross words a minute).

gwam = the nearest figure or dot above the last stroke typed

all letters used	easy	1.0 si	4.4 awl	95% hfw

```
     .   2   .   4   .   6   .   8   .
    Good form means to move with speed and quiet
 10  .  12   .  14   .  16   .  18   .
control.  My next step will be to size up the job
 20  .  22   .  24   .  26   .  28
and to do the work in the right way each day.

     .   2   .   4   .   6   .   8   .
    To reach my goal of top speed, I have to try
 10  .  12   .  14   .  16   .  18   .
to build good form.  I will try for the right key
 20  .  22   .  24   .  26   .  28
each time, but I must do so in the right way.
```

Enrichment material for Unit 1 appears on Laboratory Materials (LM) pages 1–8.

Portland Pacific Medical Center

600 SW Park Avenue
Portland, OR 97205-3658

REPORT OF OPERATION

PATIENT NUMBER: 1623-94 ROOM NUMBER:

NAME: Timothy D. Lewis

DATE OF OPERATION: 9/20/82

PREOPERATIVE DIAGNOSIS:

POSTOPERATIVE DIAGNOSIS: Appendicitis, acute

OPERATION:

SURGEON: Dr. Mary D. Weir ASSISTANTS: John C. Sanchez, M.D.
A. Charles Rodn, R.N.

PROCEDURE: Under general anesthesia, the abdomen was prepared and draped in a sterile manner. Incision was made over McBurney's point through the skin and subcutaneous tissue. Bleeding points were ligated with 3-0 Dexon. External oblique and internal oblique and transverse abdominal muscles were divided in the directions of their fibers. Peritoneum was picked up, edematous and stippled with evidence of inflammatory reaction, and opened. Abdominal fluid was cloudy, yellow, and the appendix was covered with exudate. Appendix was elevated, meso was clamped, divided, and ligated, as well as the base of the appendix, with 2-0 Dexon. Purse-string inversion of the stump was carried out with 2-0 chromic catgut suture. Hemostasis being satisfactory, the peritoneum was closed with a continuous 2-0 Dexon, fascia closed with interrupted 2-0 Dexon, and the skin closed with vertical mattress sutures of 4-0 Ethiflex. Patient withstood the procedure well and was returned to his room in good condition.

Job 4
Medical letter [LM p. 173]

Dr. Weir has requested that a letter be written to Mr. Lewis' family doctor, **Dr. Samuel Marek, 5001 North Greenley Avenue, Portland, Oregon 97217-3716** regarding the operation.

Miss Hilty tells you: "Compose and type a letter, dated September 24, to Dr. Marek for Dr. Weir's signature. Tell Dr. Marek that Mr. Lewis was admitted to the hospital on the morning of September 20 complaining of a generalized pain which shifted to the right lower quadrant. After tests confirmed the diagnosis of acute appendicitis, Mr. Lewis was taken to surgery where an appendectomy was performed. He was discharged on September 26, but is to return to Dr. Weir's office on September 30 for wound evaluation and suture removal." Enclose a copy of the Report of Operation.

15d ▶ 12 Learn: tabulator

To clear tab stops

1. Move carriage to extreme *left* (or element to extreme *right*).

2. Depress **tab clear (33)** and hold it down as you return carriage to extreme *right* (or element to ex–treme *left*) to remove all tab stops.

To set tab stops

Move the carriage (element) to the desired position; then depress the **tab set (25).** Repeat this procedure for each stop needed.

Tabulating technique

Electric (and some manual): Strike the **tab key (24)** [nearer little finger] or **bar** [right index finger]; release it and return the finger to home–key position at once.

Manual: Depress and hold down the **tabulator bar (24)** [right index finger] or **key** [nearer little finger] until the carriage stops.

Drill procedure

1. Clear all tab stops, as directed above.

2. Set a tab stop 5 spaces to the right of left margin stop.

3. Set the **line-space selector (5)** on "2" for DS (double spacing).

4. Type the paragraphs once DS as shown, indenting the first line of each paragraph.

```
Tab——►To indent the first line of a block of copy,
use the tab key or bar.
Tab——►On electrics, just strike the key or bar and
release it at once.
Tab——►On some manuals, though, you must strike and
hold down the key or bar.
```

16

50-space line

16a ▶ 8 Conditioning practice

each line twice SS (slowly, then faster); DS between 2-line groups; if time permits, retype selected lines

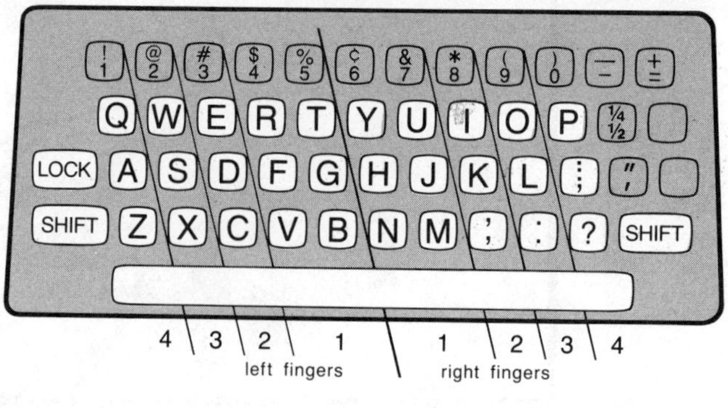


```
alphabet        1 Bix Glanz packed my bag with five quarts of juice.
v/LOCK          2 Have you seen the five games on KVOO TV this fall?
easy sentence   3 He may do all the work if he works with good form.
```

279b-281b, continued

Job 5
Doctor's service report
[LM p. 175]

Dr. Weir's administrative secretary has sent a Doctor's Service Report to be typed. This report is used to collect the doctor's fee from the insurance company.

Type the form using the information shown. Obtain any other information needed from other documents you have typed regarding Mr. Lewis' hospitalization. Be sure to include his address in Item 6.

Doctor's Service Report

STILLCREEK INSURANCE COMPANY
149 BAYBERRY DRIVE
SALEM, OR 97302-3620

FOR INSURANCE USE ONLY

(Items 4 and 5 may be obtained from subscriber's ID card.)

1. PATIENT'S NAME *(Last, First and Initial)* Lewis, Timothy D.
2. DATE OF BIRTH Mo. Day Yr.
3. SEX (1) M ___ (2) F ___
4. GROUP NUMBER
5. AGREEMENT NO. *(Including Alpha Prefix)*

6. APPLICANT-SUBSCRIBER'S NAME *(Last, First and Initial)* ADDRESS *(Including City, State and Zip Code)* Lewis, Timothy D.

7. RELATIONSHIP OF PATIENT TO APPLICANT-SUBSCRIBER (1) Self X (2) Spouse ___ (3) Dependent ___ (4) Other ___

8. WAS INJURY OR CONDITION RELATED TO: (1) PATIENT'S EMPLOYMENT ___ (2) NEITHER EMPLOYMENT NOR AUTO X (3) AUTO ACCIDENT ___ (4) BOTH EMPLOYMENT AND AUTO ___

9. DOES THIS PATIENT HAVE OTHER HEALTH INSURANCE? (1) Yes ___ (2) No X
MEDICARE PART B? (1) Yes ___ (2) No X

10. TYPE OF SERVICE (1) Medical ___ (2A) Diagnostic Surgical ___ (2B) Definitive Surgical X (3) Consultation ___ (4A) Diagnostic X-Ray ___ (4B) Professional Component ___ (5) Diagnostic Lab ___ (6) Radiation Therapy ___ (7) Anesthesia ___ (8) Assistant Surgeon ___ (9) Dental Services ___ (10) Maternity ___ (11) Diagnostic Medical ___ (12) Psychotherapy ___ (13) Other Describe ___

11A. DIAGNOSIS/SYMPTOMS *(If more than one, relate each by reference to line 1, 2, 3, etc. in Description of Services.)*

11B. DATE OF INJURY OR ONSET OF ILLNESS IF APPLICABLE/IF MATERNITY LMP Mo. Day Yr.

12A. DATES OF SERVICE Mo. Day Yr.	12B. PLACE CODE	12C. NO. OF SVCS	12D. PROCEDURE CODE	DESCRIPTION OF SERVICES - ITEMIZE *(If unusual or complicated describe in detail)*	12E. ITEMIZED CHARGES
(1) 9/20/82 - 9/26/82	1	1	16A	Diagnosis and surgery	$350
(2)					
(3)					
(4)					
(5)					

PLACE CODES: (1) IH-Inpatient Hospital (2) OH-Outpatient Hospital (3) OF-Office (4) HO-Home (5) IL-Independent Lab. (6) NH-Nursing Home (7) OP-Outpatient Psychiatric Facility (8) SN-Skilled Nursing Facility (9) SU-Short Procedure Unit (10) HC-Home Care Program (11) OL-Other Location (12) RS-Residential Substance Abuse Facility

13. HOME/OFFICE VISIT - IF PATIENT ABSENT FROM WORK DUE TO ABOVE CONDITION, PLEASE INDICATE
Last Day Worked MO./DAY/YR ___
Date Patient Returned to Work MO./DAY/YR ___
Did Condition Leave Patient Totally Disabled? Yes ___ No ___

14. FOR HOSPITAL CASES
Name of Hospital
Date Admitted MO./DAY/YR ___
Date Discharged MO./DAY/YR ___

16. HAS FEE BEEN PAID? (1) Yes ___ (2) No X

17. DID ANOTHER DOCTOR PARTICIPATE IN THIS CASE? (1) Yes X (2) No ___ If Yes, Complete Applicable Items Below
(1) Surgeon — Name of Operation — Date Mo. Day Yr.
(2) Consultant — Specialty
(3) Medical — Medical Diagnosis
(4) Other Anesthesiologist — Type of Service Anesthesiology 9/20/82

18. DOCTOR'S NAME, ADDRESS AND ZIP CODE
Mary D. Weir, M.D.

19. I CERTIFY THAT I AM LEGALLY QUALIFIED TO PERFORM THE REPORTED SERVICES AND THAT THEY WERE PERFORMED:
(1) A. ___ By Me Personally
(2) B. X By Me And My Associate in This Case, Dr. John Sanchez personally.
C. ___ Under My Supervision And in My Presence By A
___ (3) Resident ___ (4) Intern ___ (5) Registered Nurse ___ (6) Registered Nurse Anesthetist
(7) D. ___ Under My Supervision, But Not in My Presence By A
___ Resident ___ Intern ___ Registered Nurse ___ Registered Nurse Anesthetist
(No payment will be made for services listed in Section D)

I agree that I will accept as full payment the lesser of my charge as shown hereon; or the amount payable according to the applicable Fee Schedule Program (for under-income Subscribers) or Prevailing Fee Program.

20. SIGNED ___ DPM ___ DDS ___ DO ___ MD ___

21. TELEPHONE NUMBER *(Including Area Code)*

STILLCREEK INSURANCE USE ONLY

Eff. Date	Plan	Type	Cov.	Procedure	Vis-Tr	Action	Diag.	App. Amt.
BASIC				(1)				
DIAGNOSTIC				(2)				
AMT. OF ADJ.	Date	Clrk.	Control	(3)				
				(4)				
Explanation:				(5)				
Medical Director:								

7A-1 5/77

15b ▶ 12 Learn: v shift lock

each line twice SS (slowly, then faster); DS between 2-line groups; if time permits, type each line once more

Note

Depress the **shift lock (30)** and leave it down until the ALL–CAP combination has been typed. Operate the shift key to release the shift lock to return to regular capital–and–lowercase typing.

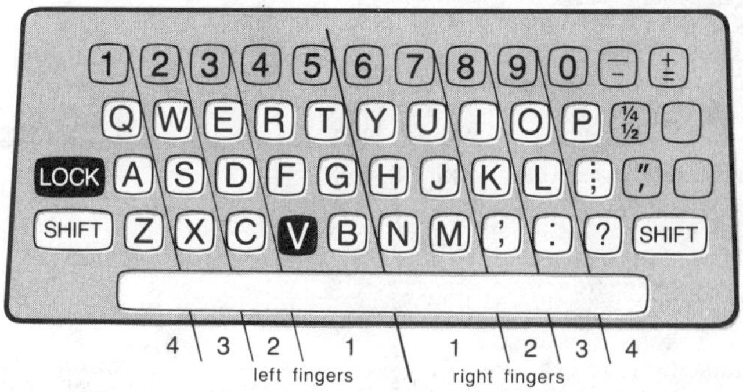

Abbreviations such as ERA, AMA, and TVA are typed solid (no internal spacing) and without periods.

Reach technique for v

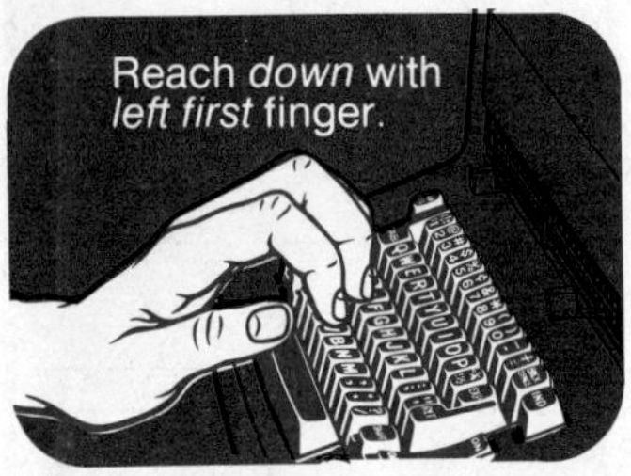

v ▼

1 v v v vf vf vf vie vie vie vim vim vim dives dives

2 vie vie vim vim view view five five vote vote have

3 vie for, vie for; has vim, has vim; a view, a view

Reach technique for shift lock

shift lock

4 Did he sit for the CPS? I know he has joined AMS.

5 It is on CBS, or on NBC. I may join NBEA and NEA.

6 Blanca said she heard them on two WLW radio shows.

15c ▶ 18 Improve keystroking technique

each line once as shown; if time permits, retype Lines 5-10

Goals, line by line

1-2. Quick, snap keystrokes; wrists low and relaxed.

3-4. Finger–reach action; keep hands and arms steady.

5-6. Fingers curved, upright over home keys.

7-8. Finger–reach action; minimum forward and downward movement of hands.

9-10. Steady carriage or element movement; no pauses.

Rows

home/3d 1 go say had fake just will stop quit post lose rude
home/1st 2 an van can lax man zag lab cab lack band jazz back

Fingers

1st/2d 3 gum vie kit cut fun vim but her jet bend very burn
3d/4th 4 lox pal was paw zap all zoo saw lap also slow opal

Adjacent-key reaches

5 we as oil are top say try art soil walk ruin leads
6 Luisa has a good view of the ruins from her porch.

Long (direct) reaches with same finger

7 my any deck many sync neck serve nerve under rumor
8 Glynn once more broke many records for gym events.

Alphabetic sentences

9 Buck Zahn will vex the judge if he quits my group.
10 Joy Wiz asked if Val Price gave me the quaint box.

unit **58** lessons 282-286

Information processing office

Learning goals

1. To increase your knowledge of the typing and clerical tasks performed by a correspondence secretary.

2. To improve your skill in completing production materials and applying language arts.

Machine adjustments

1. Line: 70 for drills; as necessary for problems.

2. Spacing: SS sentence drills with a DS between sentence groups; space problems as directed.

282-286

282a-286a ▶ 5 Conditioning practice

each line twice SS (slowly, then faster); DS between 2-line groups; if time permits, retype selected lines

alphabet 1 Jake Quigley ably expressed our fiscal views at the citizens' meeting.

figures 2 Paragraphs 10.9, 32.5, 64.7, and 86.5 of the bylaws must be rewritten.

fig/sym 3 Cut 2″ × 4″ lumber to these lengths: 4′6″, 5′8″, 3′1″, 7′9″, and 10″.

fluency 4 Is it time for the bus to take the sixty women downtown for the party?

| 1 | 2 | 3 | 4 | 5 | 6 | 7 | 8 | 9 | 10 | 11 | 12 | 13 | 14 |

282b-286b ▶ 45 Production typing

In the jobs of this simulation, all errors *may not* have been corrected. As you type, make any corrections necessary in spelling, grammar, punctuation, and keystroking.

You have been hired as a correspondence secretary in the Information Processing Center of Transcontinental Enterprises, Inc., in their main office at 4741 Connecticut Avenue, NW, Washington, DC 20008-7667.

The Information Processing Office is responsible for *data processing* (arranging information, primarily numbers, to provide useful data) and *word processing* (converting ideas into words in a typewritten form).

As a correspondence secretary, you will not be assigned to any one individual or office but will be assigned typing jobs of many kinds by the Correspondence Supervisor, Judy T. Bonaducci.

Job 1
Procedures manual

full sheet

1. Miss Bonaducci has given you a portion of the Center's Correspondence Procedures Manual, which she has revised. Study the material carefully before you type it, and follow the directions given when typing all jobs in this unit.

2. Type the material DS in final form as pages 2 and 3 of the Manual. Follow the directions given in the Manual for typing manuscripts.

Processing Correspondence

Documents to be *keyboarded* ~~typed~~ may be received from the author in several *different* forms: hand written, rough draft, recorded on tapes or disks, or dictated. The *first* draft of any document will be typed as *rapidly* ~~quickly~~ as possible in rough form. If you make an error, *backspace and strike the correct key.* ~~strike over it.~~

The first draft of a document will be *returned* ~~sent~~ to *the* originators who will proof read it, make any necessary changes, and return it to the information processing center. When *you receive the document,* ~~received~~ it will be your responsibility to proof read it *carefully* for correct gramar, punctuation, spelling and *typographical* ~~typing~~ errors. After making any corrections *necessary* ~~needed~~ in pencil, type the

(continued on p. 434)

14d ▶ 22 Improve keystroking technique

each line once as shown; if time permits, type Lines 3, 6, 9, and 12 once more

Goals, line by line

1-3. Finger–reach action; keep hands and arms steady.

4-6. Quick, snap keystrokes; fingers curved and upright over home keys.

Do not type the color dividers between phrases.

Rows

home/3d 1 Faye did quit the water polo squad to play squash.
home/1st 2 Max blows a sax in a jazz band six nights a month.
3d/1st 3 Can you be at the zoo by nine to fix a snake cage?

Fingers

1st/2d 4 he did buy much time in they met me it fig fit her
3d/4th 5 all saw|also was|a low pass|a zoo was|as a lax law
all 6 They know that she is the top skater in the plaza.

7-9. Reduce time between letters and words.

Balanced-hand words

7 city also name both paid wish form held make their
8 to the city|is due them|do the work|if she paid us
9 Chris may go with us to the town down by the lake.

10-12. Speed up easy words; type harder words at a slower but steady pace.

Balanced- and one-hand words

10 and you for him may set air bag may get but far to
11 to see|to set the|it was she|if you own|is set for
12 It is up to you to set the date to start the test.

5-stroke words | 1 | 2 | 3 | 4 | 5 | 6 | 7 | 8 | 9 | 10 |

15

50-space line

15a ▶ 8 Conditioning practice

each line twice SS (slowly, then faster); DS between 2-line groups; if time permits, retype selected lines

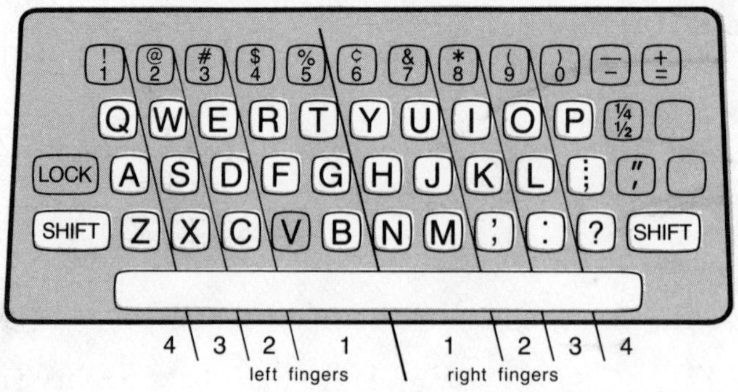

all letters learned 1 Jorgie plans to find that mosque by six with Zack.
space bar 2 of an if all is for to any and buy for may did own
b/?/q 3 Was it a squid Bobbi saw? Was it by the big quay?

282b-286b, continued

Job 1 (continued)

document neatly *in the proper form* ~~and correctly~~, all errors corrected. Since any copy~~s~~ *required* ~~needed~~ of a document will be made on a photo copy machine, no carbon copies are necessary.

All documents will be stored on Tapes or Disks. To insure *rapid* ~~quick~~ retrieval when needed, each document will be *coded* ~~marked~~ with the initials of the *originator* ~~author~~, the initials of the secretery, the number of the tape or disk, and the location of the document *on the tape or disk*. For example, the code "JB/dc 5.2" indicates that JB is the author, dc is *the* typist, and the document is stored in Location 2 of Disk or Tape 5. On letters, the code will replace the typist's initials; on all other documents, it will be placed a double space below the *final* ~~last~~ line.

Interoffice Memorandums and Letters

If a plus symbol (+) does not appear on your keyboard, a plus sign can be made as follows: strike diagonal; backspace once; strike hyphen (/-).

Inter office memorandums will be typed SS using a 6-inch line (15-87+, elite; 12-72+, pica) for all parts of the memorandum. Regardless of length, all letters will be typed in the block style with open punctuation using a 6-inch line *(15-87+, elite; 12-72+, pica)* with the date on Line 13. Since photo copies rather than carben copies are made, the abbreviation "pc" will be used in place of "cc" *for a copy notation*. Any speciel parts included in a letter or memorandum will be typed in accordance with the rules set forth in CENTURY 21 TYPEWRITING, third edition.

<u>Manuscripts</u>

All reports *, except special financial reports,* will be typed as unbound manuscripts using a six-inch line *(15-87+, elite; 12-72+, pica)* with one-inch top and bottom margins. The author will specify whether the report is to be single or double spaced. Any references cited will be typed as reference notes *with a bibliography at the end of the report*. Headings and any special features, such as side and paragraph headings, will be typed as shown in CENTURY 21 TYPEWRITING, third edition.

13c ▶ 20 Improve keystroking technique

each pair of lines twice SS (slowly, then faster); DS between 4-line groups; if time permits, retype Lines 2, 4, 6, and 8

Goals

- quick, snap keystrokes
- down reaches made with the *fingers* (not the hands)
- reach to shift keys without moving hands or arms

b/?/q
1 Bob quit the quiz show? Did you walk by the quay?
2 Was it a quid pro quo? Can they buy that big box?

m/z/y
3 So many prizes at my zany quiz show may amaze you.
4 The size of the team may add more zip to our play.

all letters learned
5 Jantz will fix my pool deck if the big rain quits.
6 Zampf did log quick trips by jet to the six towns.

easy sentences
7 Jen is to go by bus to the city to audit the firm.
8 He is to work with us if he is right for the work.

14

50-space line

This lesson has 3 basic goals:

1. To review all reaches you have learned.
2. To improve your space–bar, shift–key, and return techniques.
3. To improve your keystroking technique and speed.

Technique cues

1. Fingers curved and *upright*.
2. Hands and arms steady, wrists low and relaxed.
3. Finger–reach action, very little hand/arm movement.
4. Space, shift, and return without pausing before or after.

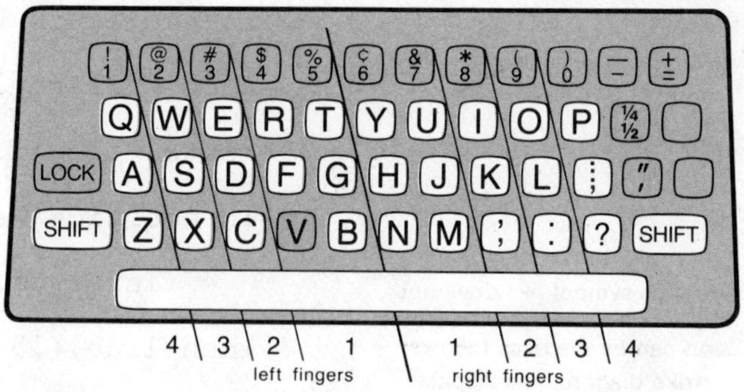

14a ▶ 8 Conditioning practice

each line twice SS (slowly, then faster); DS between 2-line groups; if time permits, retype selected lines

all letters learned
1 Marj had quickly kept a tab on wages of six zones.

shift keys
2 Maria Paso had a tea for Dr. and Mrs. Ruiz in Rio.

easy sentence
3 Kent paid the eight girls to aid us with the work.

14b ▶ 8 Improve space-bar technique

1. Once from dictation.
2. Once at your own pace.
3. Once more if time permits.

1 with they them than make when such then both their
2 he did| the end| to box| is due| or she| to buy| to work
3 Al is to go to the firm for the pay due the clerk.

14c ▶ 12 Improve return technique

1. Each 2–line sentence once as "Return" is called each 30 seconds (30").

Goal: To reach the end of each line just as the 30" guide ("Return") is called.

2. Repeat the drill.

	gwam 30"	20"
1 Do not pause at the end of the	12	18
2 line before making the return.	12	18
3 Instead, make the return as soon as	14	21
4 you type the last stroke in a line.	14	21
5 Make the return with quick motions; then	16	24
6 begin the new line with almost no pause.	16	24
7 Keeping your eyes on the copy as you make the	18	27
8 return will cut the waste time between lines.	18	27

TS

282b-286b, continued

Job 2
Draft of interoffice memo
plain full sheet

1. John C. Lopez, Supervisor of the **Information Processing Center**, wants this memo, dated **March 17**, to be addressed to **all correspondence secretaries**. Provide an appropriate subject. The memo will be stored on Location 12, Disk 8.

2. Type the memo DS in rough-draft form on plain paper. Note the time you begin and end the Job so that you can record the information on a daily log sheet [LM p. 179]. **Note:** If a log sheet is not available, record the information on a sheet of plain paper.

Job 3
Interoffice memo [LM p. 181]

1. Proofread the memo typed in Job 2 and make all necessary corrections in pencil.

2. Retype the memo in final form. Be sure to record the Job on your daily log sheet.

¶1 Each correspondence secretary will maintain a daily log sheet beginning on Monday, March 21. Print your name and the date in pencil or pen at the top of the form. For each job, record the time received, the storage location, the author's name and department, the type of document (letter, memo, report, form, or tabulation), the input form (hand written, rough draft, recorded, or dictated), the total lines typed, the time completed and the time required to do the job to the nearest minute. Count six lines for the opening and closing lines of a letter; three lines for the heading of a memo, report, or table; one line for each line in the body, regardless of length. ¶2 At the end of each day, compute the total lines typed and the total minutes required to do all jobs and give the form to your supervisor.

Job 4
Letter
plain full sheet

1. Jon C. Peters, Director of Sales, wants this letter sent to **Mrs. Alma C. Barnes, Supervisor** of Transcontinental's Southern Region at **170 Piedmont Avenue, NE Atlanta, GA 30303-2965** with a copy to **Eric T. Shea, Marketing VP**. Date the letter **April 2**; provide a salutation and complimentary close.

2. Type the letter in rough-draft form. It will be stored in Location 9 of Disk 17. Record the Job on your log sheet.

Job 5
Letter [LM p. 183]

1. Proofread the letter typed in Job 4 and make all necessary corrections in pencil.

2. Retype the letter in final form. Record the Job on your log sheet.

¶1 Their will be a special meeting of all regional supervisors in my office beginning at 9:30 a.m. on April 18. The major topics for discussion will be the affect of the currant credit restrictions on our marketing operations and our sales campagne for the next fisical year. A copy of the complete agenda is inclosed. ¶2 Please be prepared to present a detailed analisis of the effect of the credit restrictions on marketing operations in your region and to provide any ideas you may have for majer changes in our sales strategy. ¶3 A reservation has been made for you at the Jefferson Plaza Hotel on 2700 Virginia Avenue NW for the evenings of April 17 and 18. If you will notify Wally Brooks my Executive Assistant of the time of your arrival in Washington, he will have some one meet you at the air port.

13a ▶ 8 Conditioning practice

each line twice SS (slowly, then faster); DS between 2-line groups; if time permits, retype selected lines

all letters learned 1 Doug will pack sixty pints of prize jams for them.

space bar 2 me ox did men may got pay and for the she due them

1st row 3 Zahn sent them six sacks of flax, maize, and corn.

TS

13b ▶ 22 Learn: b ? (question) q

each line twice SS (slowly, then faster); DS between 2-line groups; if time permits, type each line once more

Goals

- curved, upright fingers
- quick, snap keystrokes
- hands and arms steady, almost motionless

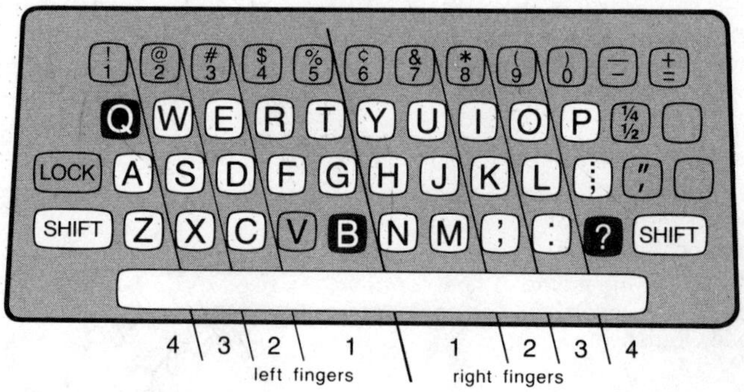

LOCK
SHIFT
SHIFT
4 3 2 1
left fingers
1 2 3 4
right fingers

Space twice after **?** at end of sentence, once after **?** *within* a sentence.

Reach technique for b

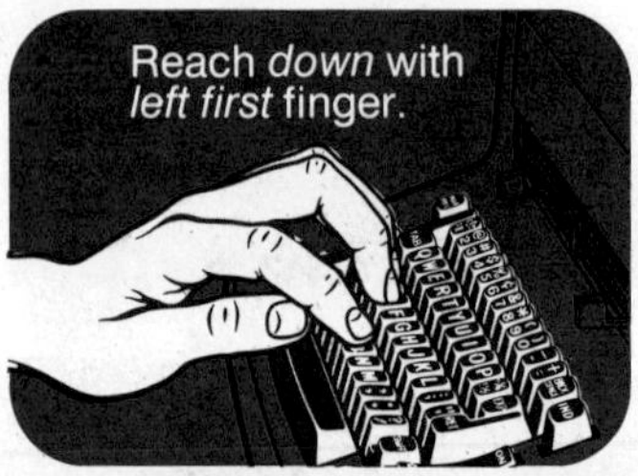

Reach *down* with *left first* finger.

Reach technique for ? (question)

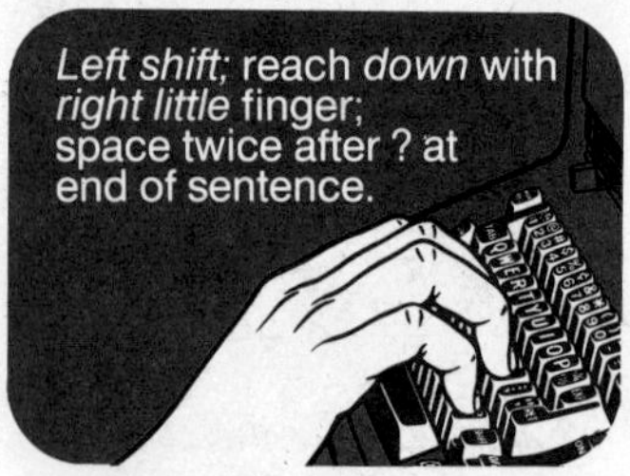

Left shift; reach *down* with *right little* finger; space twice after ? at end of sentence.

Reach technique for q

Reach *up* with *left little* finger.

b ▼

1 b b b bf bf bf by by by fib fib fib rib rib rib by

2 by by fib fib rib rib but but box box big big boys

3 by me, by me; too big, too big; buy it, buy it now

? (question) ▼

Space twice

? ? ? ?; ?; ?; Who? Who? Who is she? Was it he?

5 Are they here? Shall we go? Is it going to rain?

6 Can he type these words: zany? zone? maze? fuzzy?

Space once

q ▼

7 q q q qa qa qa quo quo quo quit quit quit is quite

8 quo quo quit quit quay quay quiz quiz quick quotes

9 a quiz, a quiz; to quit, to quit; pro quo, pro quo

TS

282b-286b, continued

Job 6
Computer program

1. Bruce E. Beaumont, a Systems Analyst, has submitted the BASIC program below to be typed.

2. Type the program on plain paper *exactly* as shown. Each individual block on the form is equal to one horizontal typewritten space.

3. Mr. Beaumont has given these special instructions: "Use a top margin of 1½"; a left margin of 1"; head the program TEST SCORING PROGRAM. Be sure all zeros are typed with a diagonal (Ø) so that the terminal or keypunch operator will not mistake them for the letter 'O'."

4. Proofread the program carefully to insure that it is spaced and punctuated exactly as shown. Since this program will be retrieved by name, a location code is not necessary. Note: On line 2500, print the less than/greater than symbols (< >) in pencil.

GENERAL PURPOSE CODING FORM

```
 1ØØØ DIM A(5Ø,5),K(5Ø),R(5Ø)
 11ØØ MAT A=ZRO
 12ØØ LET N=Ø
 13ØØ LET S=Ø
 14ØØ LET Q=Ø
 15ØØ READ L
 16ØØ MAT READ K
 17ØØ PRINT "RESULTS OF EXAMINATION"
 18ØØ PRINT "ID NO.","SCORE"
 2ØØØ READ U
 21ØØ MAT READ R
 22ØØ IF U=Ø THEN 4ØØØ
 23ØØ LET C=Ø
 24ØØ FOR I=1 TO L
 25ØØ    IF K(I)<>R(I) THEN 27ØØ
 26ØØ    LET C=C+1
 27ØØ    LET A(I,R(I))=A(I,R(I))+1
 28ØØ NEXT I
 29ØØ LET N=N+1
 3ØØØ LET S=S+1ØØ*C/L
 31ØØ LET Q=Q+(1ØØ*C/L)**2
 32ØØ PRINT U,1ØØ*C/L
 33ØØ GOTO 2ØØØ
 4ØØØ PRINT "N=";N,"MEAN=";S/N,"S.D.=";SQR(Q*N-S*S)/N
 41ØØ PRINT "QUEST.","A","B","C","D","E","% CORRECT"
 42ØØ FOR I=1 TO L
 43ØØ    PRINT I,A(I,1),A(I,2),A(I,3),A(I,4),A(I,5),1ØØ*A(I,K(I))/N
 44ØØ NEXT I
 45ØØ STOP
```

12b ▶ 22 Learn: m z : (colon)

each line twice SS (slowly, then faster); DS between 2-line groups; if time permits, type each line once more

Goals

- curved, upright fingers
- finger–reach action
- reach the *finger* (not the hand) down to **m** and **z**

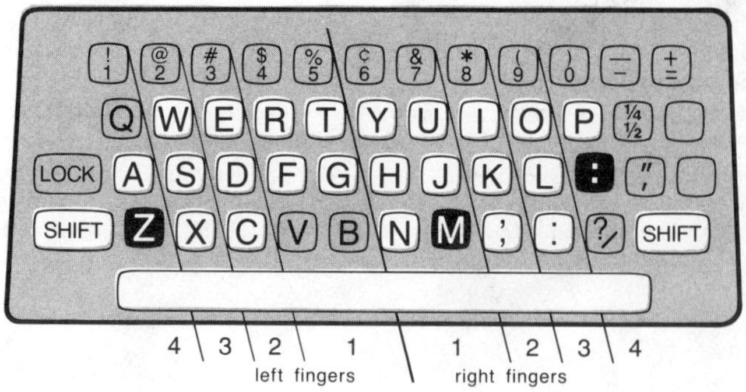

LOCK
SHIFT
SHIFT
4 3 2 1
left fingers
1 2 3 4
right fingers

Reach technique for m

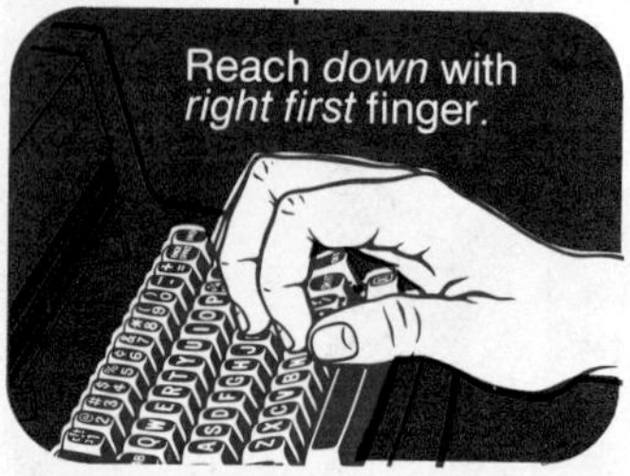

Reach *down* with *right first* finger.

Reach technique for z

Reach *down* with *left little* finger.

Reach technique for : (colon)

Left shift and strike ; key; space twice after : used as punctuation.

m ▼

1 m m m mj mj mj me me me am am am may may may makes
2 me me am am ham ham may may map map make make same
3 to me, to me; a ham, a ham; he may, he may; an amp

z ▼

4 z z z za za za zoo zoo zoo zap zap zap zooks zooks
5 zap zap zoo zoo zip zip zag zag oz. oz. zone zones
6 to zap, to zap; will zip, will zip; the zone prize

: (colon) ▼

7 : : : :; :; :; Dear Jo: Type: Shift and type a :
8 ;:; :p: To: Read: Date: Type: File: Reply to:
9 Elena: Dear Dr. Su: To wit: Follow these steps:

12c ▶ 20 Improve keystroking technique

each pair of lines twice SS (slowly, then faster); DS between 4-line groups; if time permits, retype selected lines

Goals

- quiet hands and arms
- wrists low and relaxed
- finger (not hand) action
- down–and–in spacing
- quick return, your eyes on textbook copy

reach review
1 nj ed ol za p: ws uj cd mj xs yj rf ,k gf .l tf hj
2 Janice Dux will type fast; Rick Maze met his goal.

m/z/:
3 Zelma, type these terms: zone, maze, zoom, maize.
4 Izzy read: To make the team, swim with more zest.

y/x/,
5 Tony saw a yak, a fox, four lynx, and six monkeys.
6 Roxy will play alto sax in the next of your shows.

all letters learned
7 Rip can go with Lex Zim to ski in just a few days.
8 Zoe Toll may win a gold cup for her six ski jumps.

5-stroke words | 1 | 2 | 3 | 4 | 5 | 6 | 7 | 8 | 9 | 10 |

282b-286b, continued

Job 7
Manuscript

2 full sheets

1. Mr. Beaumont has edited and resubmitted this manuscript which will accompany the program typed in Job 6.

2. Type the report in final form SS with a DS between paragraphs and enumerated items. As you type, correct any uncorrected errors. Record the Job on your log sheet.

Test Scoring Program User's Guide

A test scoring program has been prepared for use by the Personnel Division for [scoring] ~~grading~~ multiple-choice tests. The program is written in BASIC and may be invoked by the following [procedures:] ~~steps~~

1. Log [#] on to the system using your account, name, and password.

2. Type BASIC. This will [fetch] ~~call~~ the BASIC interpreter from the system's library.

3. Type LOAD TESTSCORE. This will load the test scoring program from the BASIC library of programs. When loading is [completed,] ~~finished~~ a caret prompt (>) will be issued.

4. Type ~~the~~ LIST 1ØØØ. BASIC will ~~then~~ print line 1ØØØ, [like so:] ~~as follows~~

```
1ØØØ DIM A(5Ø,5),K(5Ø),R(5Ø)
```

5. Retype line 1ØØØ, substituting [the number of] questions on the exam for each of the three "50"s. For example, if the exam has 10 questions, you would type: [DS]

```
1ØØØ DIM A(1Ø,5),K(1Ø),R(1Ø)
```

6. Now you must enter the exam's key. Do so by typing:

```
9ØØØ DATA N,A,A,A, . . .
```

7. Substitute the number of questions on the exam for "N" (be sure it matches the numbers you placed on line 1ØØØ). Each of the "A"s is [a correct] ~~the right~~ answer to a question, a number from 1 to 5 inclusive. Be sure to enter as many answers as there are questions or the program will not perform properly.

8. Each examinee's answers to the questions [are] ~~is~~ entered on lines following the exam key. Each line [begins] ~~starts~~ with 90XX DATA, where the "XX" is an ascending number starting with Ø1. Follow "DATA" with the examinee's ID number (up to 6 digits) and then the examinee's [responses] ~~answers~~ to the questions, separated by comas. [Again,] the answers [must] ~~should~~ be numbered from 1 through 5 and there must be

(continued on p. 438)

11d ▶ 22 Improve keystroking technique

each line once as shown; if time permits, type Lines 3, 6, 9, and 12 once more

Goals, line by line

1-3. Finger–reach action; keep hands and arms steady.

4-6. Quick, snap keystrokes; fingers curved and upright over home keys.

7-9. Reduce time between letters and words.

10-12. Speed up easy words; type harder words at a slower but steady pace.

Rows

home/3d 1 led pay got pod fig jot rod jog dug laws risk just
home/1st 2 an ax and can fan nag lax flax cash call lack hand
3d/1st 3 Carol is apt to win the gold cup in the next race.

Fingers

1st/2d 4 in cut fur den net yet gin dye dig run tin rug end
3d/4th 5 so wow pow pal lap low lax sop laws wasp soap pass
all 6 A judge will next read the laws to the open court.

Balanced-hand words

Do not type the color dividers between phrases.

7 an due own did and for the pay city than they such
8 it is due | to pay us | she is also | did go to the city
9 Keith did fix the city sign; the city paid for it.

Balanced- and one-hand words

10 if in is on it up an as he we us at or no if as he
11 if we did | up to you | if we aid | she saw us | is of age
12 They are to do the case work on the dates she set.

5-stroke words | 1 | 2 | 3 | 4 | 5 | 6 | 7 | 8 | 9 | 10 |

12

50-space line

12a ▶ 8 Conditioning practice

each line twice SS (slowly, then faster); DS between 2-line groups; if time permits, retype selected lines

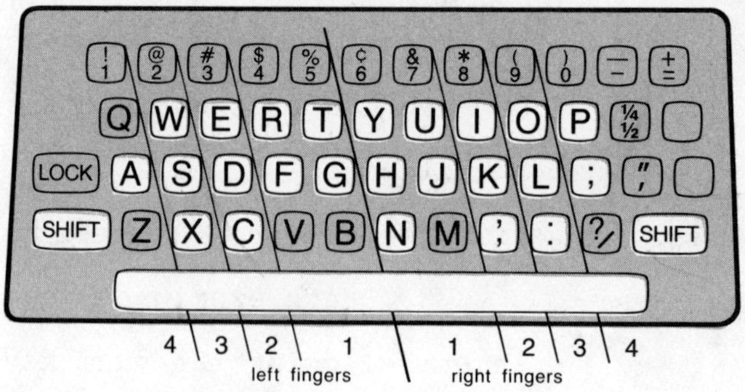

all letters learned 1 Jack has typed six lines using low finger strokes.
space bar 2 if to is do us so he or of an go it ah el pa ox ha
y/x/, 3 You can type such words as ax, ox, onyx, and lynx.

Space once after , used as punctuation.

282b-286b, continued

Job 7 (continued)

exactly the same number of responses as there are questions on the test. Example:

9Ø1Ø DATA 14523,1,3,2,4,3,3,2,4,4,3

If you make ~~an error~~ a mistake while entering a line, you may back space to correct it by striking the "DEL" or "RUB OUT" key on your terminal. If you ~~find~~ discover you made an error on a line after you hit the carriage return, simply retype the ~~complete~~ entire line to correct the error.

9. After you have entered all the students' examinations, enter 9998 DATA Ø,Ø,Ø,Ø, ... Type as many zeros as there are questions on the exam and then type one more. This signals the program that the last exam has been read. Follow this line by 9999 END. This makes the physical end of the program.

You are now ready to run the program. Type RUN. If ~~all~~ everything is in order~~s~~, the results will ~~appear~~ be typed on your terminal almost immediately.

Job 8
Tables

full sheet

1. This table was prepared on the computer for Delia G. Hope, Assistant Director of Personnel. Miss Hope has changed the identification numbers to the names of the examinees. Her special instructions are:

"Please type the table double-spaced in final form in two ways: first, type the table listing the examinees in alphabetical order; second, type the table with the scores of the examinees ranked from the highest to the lowest. Type both tables on the same page."

2. The tables will be stored in Location 17 of Disk 32.

RESULTS OF EXAMINATION

Name ~~ID NO.~~	S~~CORE~~ TS
David J. Stafford ~~62341~~	6Ø
Edward C. Moore ~~62342~~	82
Marie P. Gannon ~~62343~~	64
Margaret N. Sherwood ~~62344~~	98
Melissa M. Adams ~~62345~~	68
Francis Q. O'Brien ~~62346~~	7Ø
Joanna B. Langley ~~62347~~	86
Patricia R. Jones ~~62348~~	92
Byron J. Charles ~~62349~~	9Ø
Elizabeth S. Raeburn ~~6235Ø~~	74

10c ▶ 20 Improve keystroking technique

each pair of lines twice SS (slowly, then faster); DS between 4-line groups; if time permits, retype Lines 1-4

Goals

- quiet hands and arms
- wrists low and relaxed
- finger (not hand) motions
- down-and-in spacing

y/x/,
1 any flax, easy to fix, they will pay, has six oxen
2 Lex will try to fix the ax if you will pay for it.

u/c/p
3 putt to the cup, cut the price, paid you with cash
4 You can help us try to cut the cost per copy sent.

all letters learned
5 in cash, four or six, will pay you, asks the judge
6 A judge told her to pay for the six weeks in cash.

all letters learned
7 a high dock, they plan for six, just ask your wife
8 You know they can plan for just six to eight days.

11

50-space line

This lesson has 3 basic goals:

1. To review all reaches you have learned.

2. To improve your space-bar, shift-key, and return techniques.

3. To improve your keystroking technique and speed.

Spacing summary
Space once after **,** and **;** and once after **.** at end of an abbreviation or following an initial. Space twice after **.** at end of sentence. *Do not* space after any punctuation mark that ends a line.

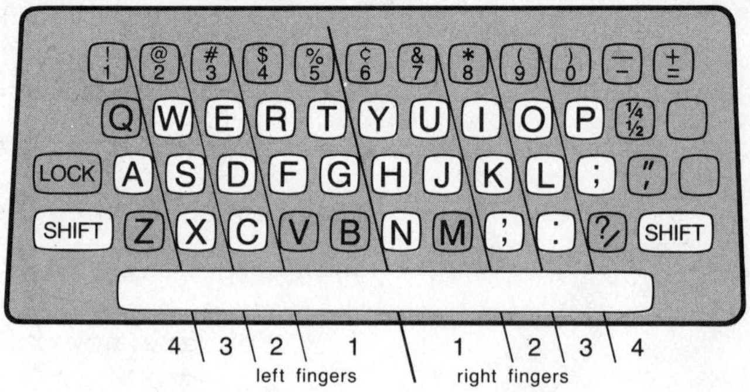

11a ▶ 8 Conditioning practice

each line twice SS (slowly, then faster); DS between 2-line groups; if time permits, retype selected lines

reach review 1 hj ed ol tf ik rf .l ws nj gf uj cd p; xs yj ,k .l

shift keys 2 Cory and Lara went with Jose and Rosa to San Juan.

all letters learned 3 Peggie has worked with us since the sixth of July.

11b ▶ 8 Improve space-bar technique

1. Once from dictation.
2. Once at your own pace.
3. Once more if time permits.

1 to an do if or it so is of us he go la for and the

2 it is | to do | is so | of us | or he | to go | to the | and she

3 He is to pay the girl for any work she did for us.

11c ▶ 12 Improve shift-key and return techniques

1. Each 2-line sentence once as "Return" is called each 30 seconds (30").

Goal: To reach the end of each line just as the 30" guide ("Return") is called.

2. Repeat the drill.

Note: *gwam* is gross words a minute typed if you reach the end of each line as the 30" guide is called.

	gwam 30"	20"
1 You know how to type now,	10	15
2 so keep up the good work.	10	15
3 Just pick a new goal each day;	12	18
4 use the right plan to gain it.	12	18
5 How you do the typing is what helps	14	21
6 you reach the daily goals you pick.	14	21
7 First, set a goal that is easy to reach;	16	24
8 next, try one that will push your skill.	16	24

unit **59** lessons 287-288

Refine basic skills

Learning goals

1. To refine and improve your basic typing techniques.

2. To increase your speed and improve your accuracy in typing script, rough-draft, and straight-copy material.

Machine adjustments

1. Line: 70 for drills.

2. Spacing: SS sentence drills with a DS between groups; DS timed writings.

287

287a ▶ 5 Conditioning practice

each line twice SS (slowly, then faster); DS between 2-line groups; if time permits, retype selected lines

alphabet 1 Josephine Wax quickly apologized for her rude behavior at the meeting.

figures 2 Items 5, 10, 18, and 24 on Form 9361 must be completed by February 17.

fig/sym 3 Model 380496 (AC/DC, 60 cycle, 110-120 volts) sells for $579, less 4%.

fluency 4 Did they go to the special party given for the eight foreign visitors?

| 1 | 2 | 3 | 4 | 5 | 6 | 7 | 8 | 9 | 10 | 11 | 12 | 13 | 14 |

287b ▶ 45 Refine basic skill: straight copy

1. Two 5′ writings on ¶s 1–3 combined. Determine *gwam* and circle errors; record better scores.

2. Two 1′ writings on each ¶ with a goal of increased speed.

3. Two 1′ writings on each ¶ with a goal of fewer errors.

4. Two 5′ writings on ¶s 1–3 combined. Determine *gwam* and circle errors; record better scores.

Goal: Increased speed and fewer errors in Step 4 when compared with scores recorded in Step 1.

all letters used | A | 1.5 si | 5.7 awl | 80% hfw

	gwam 1′	5′	
Reprographics is a fairly new term that is now used to cover a wide	14	3	60
range of reproduction processes. In a narrow sense, the term includes	28	6	63
only the job of making copies of all types of material. In a broad	41	8	66
sense, however, the term includes all the work necessary to reproduce	55	11	68
materials in some graphic form. As such, it includes planning and orga-	70	14	71
nizing the data to be reproduced as well as deciding the most effective	84	17	74
and efficient means of duplicating it.	92	18	76
There are a number of factors to be considered when you plan and	13	21	78
organize material for duplication. An important factor, of course, is	27	24	81
cost. The objective is to select a duplication process that will pro-	41	27	84
vide the lowest possible cost per copy. The appearance of the copy in	56	30	87
terms of clarity and eye appeal must be considered. Format, size, and	70	32	90
makeup of the copy are also of primary importance. Since the time avail-	84	35	93
able to do the job may affect quality and cost, time is a vital factor.	99	38	96
There are several kinds of duplicators that can be used to make	13	41	98
copies. The spirit duplicator is the least expensive way for runs of	27	44	101
several hundred copies and can produce copies in as many as five colors.	42	47	104
The mimeograph machine can produce thousands of copies in color at a	55	49	107
low cost. If cost is not a major factor, however, the offset duplicator	70	52	110
can produce copies of better quality. Xerographic or thermographic	84	55	112
machines can be used if just a few copies are needed quickly.	96	57	115

gwam 1′ | 1 | 2 | 3 | 4 | 5 | 6 | 7 | 8 | 9 | 10 | 11 | 12 | 13 | 14 |
5′ | 1 | 2 | 3 |

10

50-space line

10a ▶ 8 Conditioning practice

each line twice SS (slowly, then faster); DS between 2-line groups; if time permits, retype selected lines

all letters learned 1 Ponce has just gone to work for the new ski lodge.

c/p/w 2 Lew can pick a slow pace and work up to top speed.

t/u/g 3 Lt. Guffie sent us the gold urn as her guest gift.

TS

10b ▶ 22 Learn: y x , (comma)

1. Find new key on illustrated keyboard chart.
2. Locate new key on your typewriter keyboard.
3. Study reach-technique illustration for new key.
4. Watch finger make reach to new key a few times.
5. Type reach-technique drill twice (slowly, then faster).

Technique cues

- Fingers curved, upright.
- Reach with the *fingers* (not the hands).
- Keep the wrists low, hands and arms steady.
- *Curl* the finger to reach down for **,** and **x**.

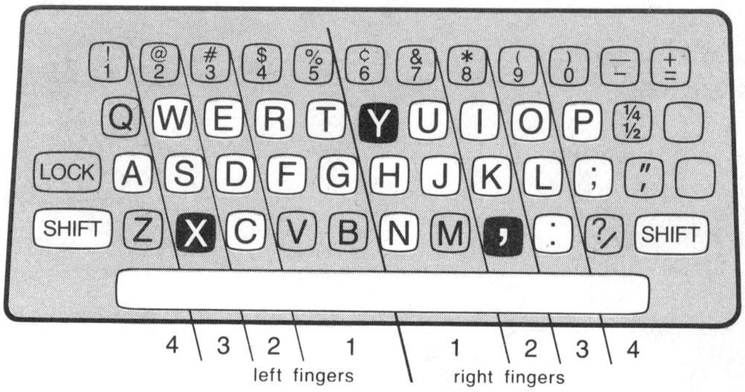

Reach technique for y

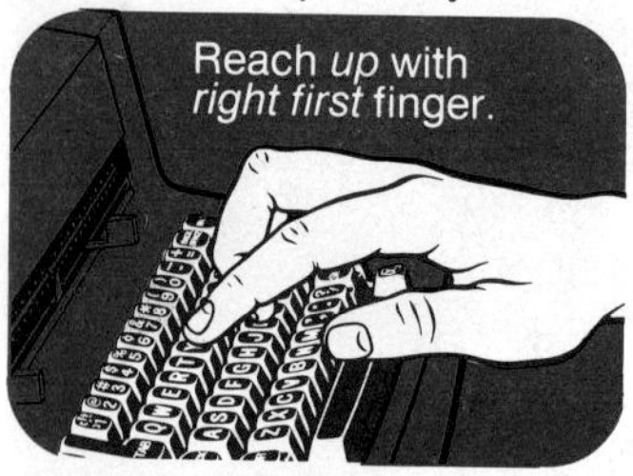

y ▼

1 y y y yj yj yj lay lay lay pay pay pay jay jay jay

2 lay lay pay pay yet yet yes yes you you play plays

3 you say; you say; can pay; can pay; a play; a play

Reach technique for x

x ▼

4 x x x xs xs xs ox ox ox six six six flax flax flax

5 ox ox ax ax fox fox six six fix fix flex flex flax

6 fix it; fix it; a hoax; a hoax; six oxen; six oxen

Reach technique for , (comma)

Reach *down* with *right second* finger; space once after , used as punctuation.

, (comma) ▼

7 , , , ,k ,k ,k kit, kit, He skis, jogs, and hikes.

8 a ski, a ski; to do, to do; to work, to work; wish

9 it is, it is; she is, she is; to us, to us; for us

TS

288a ▶ 5 Conditioning practice

Use standard directions given in 287a, p. 439.

alphabet	1	Hazel will bring many exotic foods like coq au vin to the June picnic.
figures	2	On May 31 he ordered 60 tables, 245 chairs, 72 lamps, and 98 cabinets.
fig/sym	3	They earned fees of $163.50, $179.28, and $349.62--a total of $692.40.
fluency	4	He may have a problem if both of them ask for a loan at the same time.

| 1 | 2 | 3 | 4 | 5 | 6 | 7 | 8 | 9 | 10 | 11 | 12 | 13 | 14 |

288b ▶ 15 Improve technique

1. Type the sentences DS at your highest rate.
2. Remove paper from the typewriter and correct errors in pencil. From your corrected copy, type a 1′ writing on each line.
Goal: as few errors as possible.

home row	1	Jeff said his dad can bake a cake; Gladys can also make a Jello salad.
third row	2	They were quoted an erroneous price for the typewriter four weeks ago.
bottom row	3	Max Mazzo can move a minimum of six ounces of cyanine in the zinc box.
adjacent keys	4	The clerk said the new typewriter was received in very poor condition.
long reaches	5	If the trustees agree, I might try to place my money in a growth fund.
double letters	6	All school committees will meet immediately after each weekly session.

| 1 | 2 | 3 | 4 | 5 | 6 | 7 | 8 | 9 | 10 | 11 | 12 | 13 | 14 |

288c ▶ 15 Skill comparison typing

1. Three 1′ writings on each ¶; compare *gwam*.
2. A 2′ writing on each ¶; compare *gwam*.
3. Additional 2′ writings on slower ¶ as time permits.

all letters used — ¶ 1: LA | 1.4 si | 5.4 awl | 85% hfw — ¶ 2: D | 2.0 si | 7.1 awl | 70% hfw

Text	gwam 1′	2′
The jobs done in an administrative office vary from com-	11	6
pany to company. A few of the more common jobs a clerk can	23	12
be expected to do are to type letters, reports, and forms;	35	17
file; use the telephone; process mail; and use office machines	48	24
of all kinds. A typist can expect to type a wide range of	59	30
work from simple labels to long, complex reports.	69	37
The administrative office has been called the nerve cen-	11	6
ter of an organization. The office performs functions that	23	12
are required for the smooth, efficient operation of a busi-	35	17
ness. Among the major functions assigned to an administrative	48	24
office are accounting, processing oral and written communi-	59	30
cations, managing records, and reproducing data.	69	34

288d ▶ 15 Refine basic skill: straight copy

Two 5′ writings on ¶s 1–3 combined of 287b, p. 439. Determine *gwam* and circle errors; record better scores. Compare scores with those achieved in Step 1, 287b, p. 439.

9b ▶ 22 Learn: u c p

each line twice SS (slowly, then faster); DS between 2-line groups; if time permits, type each line once more

Goals
- curved, upright fingers
- finger-action stroking
- down-and-in spacing motion
- quick return without pausing

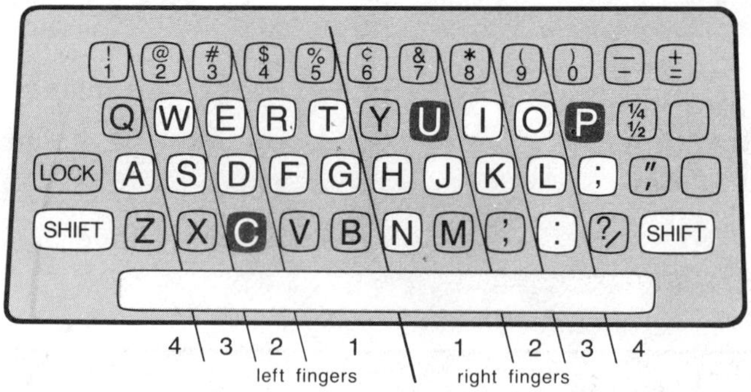

Reach technique for u

u ▼

1 u u u uj uj uj us us us due due due just just just

2 uj uj us us fur fur sue sue rug rug rust rust dusk

3 a fur; a fur; due us; due us; used rugs; used rugs

Reach technique for c

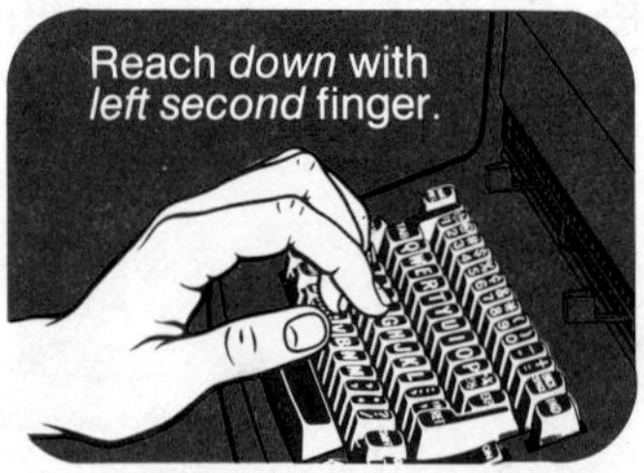

c ▼

4 c c c cd cd cd cod cod cod cow cow cow cot cot cot

5 cd cd cod cod cog cog cow cow lock lock dock docks

6 a cow; a cow; the lock; the lock; at cost; at cost

Reach technique for p

p ▼

7 p p p p; p; p; pa pa pa pen pen pen keep keep keep

8 p; p; pa pa pan pan apt apt nap nap kept kept keep

9 a pen; a pen; apt to keep; apt to keep; kept a pen

TS

9c ▶ 20 Improve keystroking technique

each pair of lines twice SS (slowly, then faster); DS between 4-line groups; if time permits, retype selected lines

Goals
- quiet hands and arms
- wrists low and relaxed
- finger (not hand) action
- down-and-in spacing
- quick return, your eyes on textbook copy

home/3d
1 p; ws uj ed ol rf ik tf hj gr pa us up jut ape dug
2 is due us; apt to sue; is up to us; to keep it up;

home/1st
3 .l cd nj and fan can jack call hack hand lack sand
4 a cash call; and a fan; can call a hack; lack cash

u/c/p
5 Lu had a cup of pea soup; Ric chose a plate lunch.
6 Curtis put on speed to cop the cup for top runner.

all letters learned
7 Our goal is to take the finals the first of April.
8 Juan said that all of us can pick the right words.

unit **60** lessons 289-291

Reprographics office

Learning goals

1. To increase your knowledge of the art of reprographics.

2. To familiarize you with three common methods of copy reproduction used in business.

3. To learn how to type materials that are to be reproduced by spirit duplication, stencil duplication, and photo or thermal copiers.

Machine adjustments

1. Line: 70 for all drills; as necessary for problems.

2. Spacing: SS sentence drills with a DS between sentence groups; space problems as directed or necessary.

289-291

289a-291a ▶ 5 Conditioning practice

each line twice SS (slowly, then faster); DS between 2-line groups; if time permits, retype selected lines

alphabet 1 Page was amazed by the extra large quantity of junk mail she received.

figures 2 They will meet on June 9, 13, 17, and 20 and on July 5, 6, 14, and 18.

fig/sym 3 Last year the rate jumped from 10 3/4% to 15 1/2% and then to 17 1/4%.

fluency 4 If they pay the big penalty, they may not make a profit in the future.

| 1 | 2 | 3 | 4 | 5 | 6 | 7 | 8 | 9 | 10 | 11 | 12 | 13 | 14 |

289b-291b ▶ 45 Production typing simulation

You have been hired as a general typist by Dupli-Matic, Inc., 4110 Fifth Avenue, Pittsburgh, PA 15213-8219, a company that offers a wide variety of reprographic services. Your supervisor is Lisa J. LeBarron, who is the Office Manager.

Note: For a general discussion of Reprographics, review 287b, page 439.

Job 1
Standard office operating procedures

3 full sheets

Ms. LeBarron has given you the first draft of a portion of the Standard Office Operating Procedures (SOP) for the Reprographics Center.

Type the material as a leftbound manuscript. Study the material carefully as you type it and make any corrections in spelling, grammar, punctuation, and typing that may be necessary.

REPROGRAPHIC PROCESSES *TS*

All material *received* ~~submitted~~ for reproduction will be duplicated in the manner *specified* ~~designated~~ by the *person* ~~one~~ who submit*ted it.* ~~s the material.~~ If no method of duplication is *specified* ~~indicated~~, the process that will provide *the* lowest cost per copy will be selected, unless quality and time are of greater importance. The reprographic processes we have available include:

TS

<u>Photo or Thermal Processes</u>

These *direct* copiers are cost affective when only 1 to 10 copies are *needed* ~~required~~. A few of *these machines* ~~them~~ will *produce* ~~make~~ copies in colors; most of them, however, will *produce* ~~make~~ only copies in black and white. No special ribbon *or preparation* is required for most *direct* ~~of these~~ copiers. *Always* ~~Keep~~ *keep* in mind, *however* ~~though~~, that these *machines* ~~copier~~s produce an <u>exact</u> copy and that any errors on the original will appeer on the copies.

(continued on page 442)

8d ▶ 8 Improve shift-key technique

each line once as shown; then repeat each line

Goal: To use each of the shift keys without wasting time or motion.

Shifting cues

1. Depress the shift key.
2. Strike the letter key.
3. Release shift key quickly.

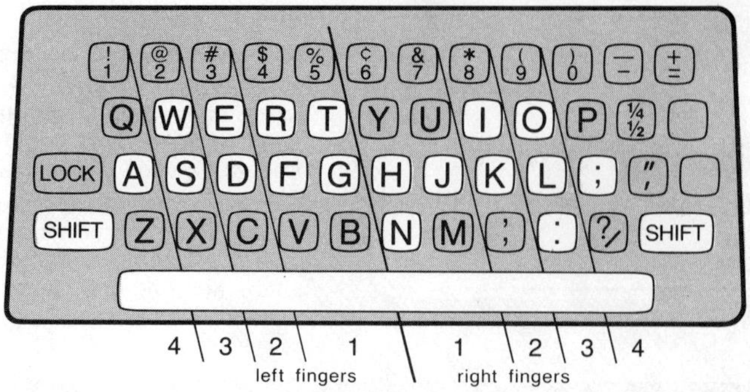

left 1 Jason Hall left the file on the desk for Lana Han.
right 2 Todd and Rona went to the lake with Foss and Tina.
both 3 Nestor Salas and Iris Rios are now in Los Angeles.

TS

8e ▶ 16 Improve keystroking technique

each line once as shown; if time permits, retype Lines 5 through 10

Goals, line by line

1-2. Finger–reach action; hands and arms steady.

3-4. Fingers curved and upright over home keys; wrists low and relaxed.

5-6. Reduce time between letters and words.

7-8. Steady, even pace (no pauses).

9-10. Speed up easy words; type harder words at a slower but steady pace.

Rows

home/3d 1 go old led ski rows loft fold jade golf skid eight
home/1st 2 an and nag fan land hand sand gang sank dank flank

Fingers

1st/2d 3 if it he in id did fir eke fig die gin jet net tie
3d/4th 4 so la as all sow low also laws slow loss slaw wall

Balanced-hand words

5 a of to is it or if an do so he go she the and for
6 He or she is to go to town to work with the girls.

One-hand words

7 a on as in at no we oh was nil are oil see ink gas
8 I see we read at a fast rate in a test on estates.

Do not type the color dividers between phrases.

Balanced- and one-hand words

9 as it is | are to go | is to see | is in the | for she was
10 Jane got the oil at the rate he set on the eighth.

TS

9

50-space line

9a ▶ 8 Conditioning practice

each line twice SS (slowly, then faster); DS between 2-line groups; if time permits, retype selected lines

all letters learned 1 Karl has gone for a flight in a jet with a friend.
space bar 2 She is to do the work; she owns all the lake land.
shift keys 3 Dodi and Jan are to see Gil and Elka in New Delhi.

TS

Job 1, continued

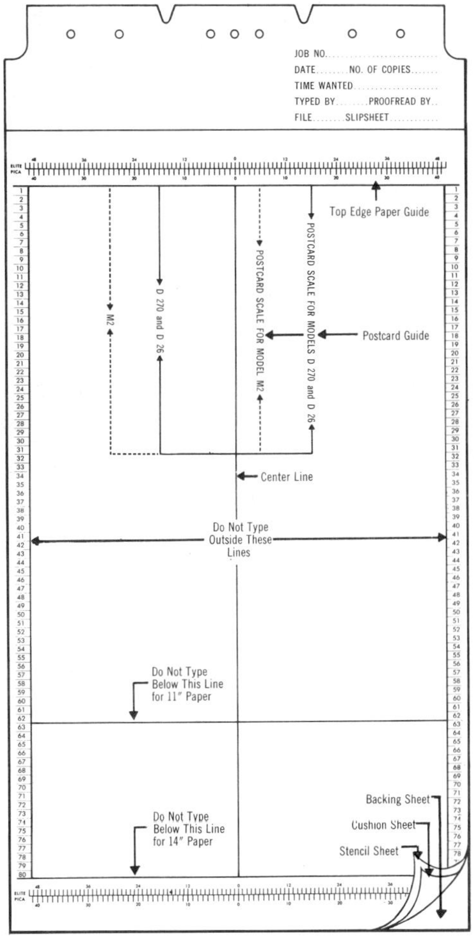

Stencil Duplication Process

Thousands of copies of material canbe *(#)* *re*produced in a ~~very~~ short time, *by* ~~using~~ the stencil duplication process. A stencil consists of three parts: the stencil sheet, the backing sheet, and the cushion sheet. When a typewriter key strikes the stencil sheet, it "cuts" an impression in the shape of the *type* ~~key~~. The cushion sheet is placed between the stencil and the backing sheet to absorb the impact of the keys. A film sheet may be *placed* ~~put~~ over the stenil *(c)* sheet if *darker* ~~blacker~~ print is desired. This film *also* protects the stencil sheet *from* ~~for~~ letter cut out when the type face is *extremely* ~~quite~~ sharp.

Before typing the stencil, type a model *copy* of the material to be reproduced. Be sure the copy will fit within the borders *printed* ~~indicated~~ on the stencil. The scales at the top and sides of the stencil will help you *position* ~~place~~ the copy on the stencil *correctly* ~~properly~~.

Insert the stencil assembly into the typewriter and align it exactly as you would a *sheet* ~~piece~~ of paper. Use a firm uniform touch as you type. If you make *an error* ~~a mistake~~, correct it with correction fluid. If there is a film over the stencil, it must be *detached* ~~removed~~ until you resume typing. Use a glass burnisher or a smooth paper clip to rub the surface of the error on *the* stencil sheet. Place a pencil between the stencil sheet and the cushion sheet and apply a *light* coating of the *correction* fluid over the error. Let it dry and then make the correction*, using a light touch.*

(continued on page 443)

7c ▶ 20 Improve keystroking technique

each pair of lines twice SS (slowly, then faster); DS between 4-line groups; if time permits, type each line once more

all keystrokes learned are used

reach review
1 ed ol rf ik ws hj gf nj tf; Jae Flo Lt. J. W. Kahn
2 Jeff said that he rowed for the shore of the lake.

g/n
3 go go no no jog jog gin gin ago ago long long gong
4 go on; go on; sign in; sign in; long ago; long ago

all letters learned
5 Gigi saw the skier go into the Golan Hotel at one.
6 She and Jean are to go into the town for the show.

all letters learned
7 Alfie and he are to work on the ski tow this week.
8 Janis and Angie are going to San Diego for a week.

8

50-space line

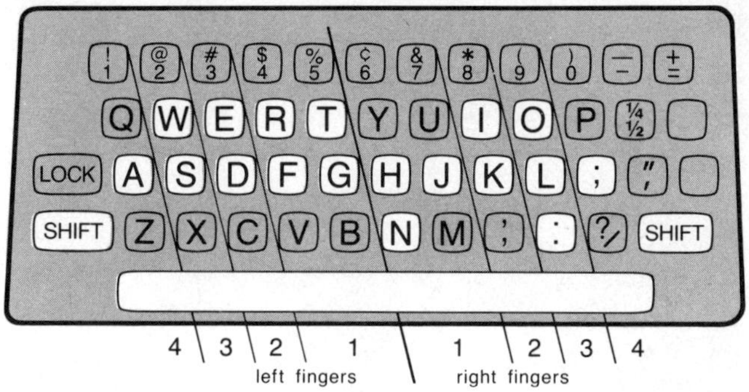

8a ▶ 8 Conditioning practice

each line twice SS (slowly, then faster); DS between 2-line groups; if time permits, retype selected lines

home row
1 has half; ask a lass; had a glass; had a jak salad

3d row
2 is to jog; do the work; a good wok; he is too slow

all letters learned
3 Gig has a list. Jane was there. I asked for her.

TS

8b ▶ 8 Improve space-bar technique

1. Once from dictation.
2. Once at your own pace.
3. Once more if time permits.

1 is to if do of go an so or he it ha if ah it is to
2 of off too and got she for dog fit wok fig toe jak
3 land work held fish goal jell wish hand with field

TS

8c ▶ 10 Improve return technique

each line once SS on a separate line; repeat the drill if time permits

Goals

1. To make the return quickly.
2. To return without pausing at the end of one line or at beginning of next line.

1 Doris took the right file
2 with her to the new site.

3 Jason said he saw the new desk
4 he wants when he goes to work.

5 Gina will take the first train into
6 town to see the new dog show there.

7 Hestor will ask her to talk with all the
8 workers who are here for the first week.

TS

289b-291b, continued

Job 1, continued

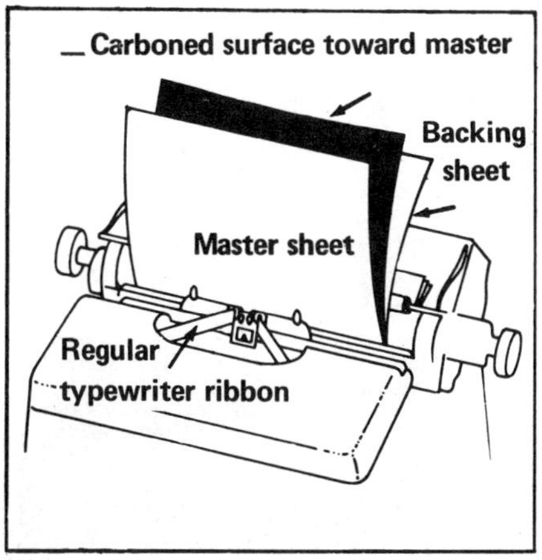

Spirit Duplication Process

The spir[i]t duplication process is used when from 11 to 150 low-cost copies of material are [required] ~~needed~~. The [master] spirit set consists of two parts: the master [sheet] ~~set~~ and a sheet of spe~~ail~~[cial] carbon paper that can [be] used once only. A back[ing] sheet may [also] be used to improve the [consistency] ~~uniformity~~ of the type. If a [specially] ~~specifically~~ prepared master set is not available, simply place the [special] carbon paper between the master [sheet] and the backing [sheet] with the [glossy] ~~shiny~~ side toward you. When you type, the carbon will be on the back of the master [sheet]. To prepare a spirit master, proceed as [follows] ~~below~~:

1. Prepare a model [copy] of the material [sp] to be typed. [DS] Leave a margin of at least 1/2 inch at the top.
2. Clean the type and use a light-weight ribbon to avoid "fuzzy" type and filled-in characters. Use a firm, even stroke on a non electric machine. On electric typewriters, a lower setting on the impression control lever usually [DS] provides better copies.
3. If you make an error, scrape off the uncorrect letter or word on the reverse side of the master sheet with a razor blade or knife. Tear off an unused portion of the carbon at the top and slip it under the part to be retyped with the glossy side toward you. Type over the incorrect letter or word. Remove the piece of carbon as soon as you have corrected the error.

Job 2
Model copy for stencil duplication

plain full sheet

1. Type a model copy of the letter at the right for stencil duplication. Since there will be no inside address, leave 3 blank line spaces between the date and the salutation. Position the letter attractively on the page.

2. List and indent the asterisked items 5 spaces from both margins; SS each 2-line item; DS between items.

3. If facilities and time permit, type a mimeograph stencil and reproduce 10 copies on plain paper.

August 2, 19-- Dear Customer (¶ 1) In these days of constantly rising prices, it is rare indeed to find price reductions. Yet, Dynamics Universal has reduced prices on 50 of its best-selling items. The supplemental price list enclosed reflects savings of 10 percent or more on lots of 500 to 1,000 units. These are all first-quality items, not seconds. Check our regular catalog for more details about each item. (¶ 2) Keep in mind that, as leaders in the field, Dynamics Universal gives you more than quality merchandise. Here are five good reasons we can provide you with quick, efficient service to save you time and money: ** Computerized order processing and inventory control. ** Coast-to-coast delivery from our 30 storage facilities. ** Over $10,000,000 inventory of more than 250,000 items. ** Same day shipment on 90% of all orders. ** Special components produced quickly in our ultramodern factory. (¶ 3) Act now! These price reductions are in effect only until September 30. Write, wire, or phone us for any additional information you desire. Sincerely Ms. Linda M. Cadwallader Sales Manager

7a ▶ 8 Conditioning practice

each line twice SS (slowly, then faster); DS between 2-line groups; if time permits, retype selected lines

all letters learned are used

home row 1 a lass had a jak; a fall fad; ask a lad; has a jak

e/o/i/t 2 he is to see it; she has told; this is the old oak

left shift and r/./w 3 Kae left at two. Jae rode for her. Jeff did row.

TS

7b ▶ 22 Learn: n g right shift

1. Find new key on illustrated keyboard chart.
2. Locate new key on your typewriter keyboard.
3. Study reach-technique illustration for new key.
4. Watch finger make reach to new key a few times.
5. Type reach-technique drill twice (slowly, then faster).

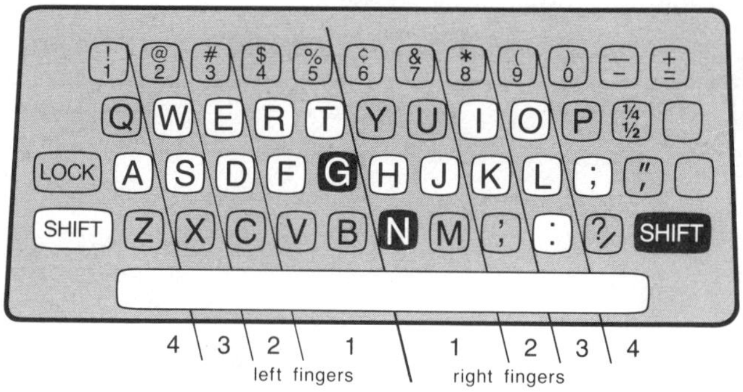

Reach technique for n

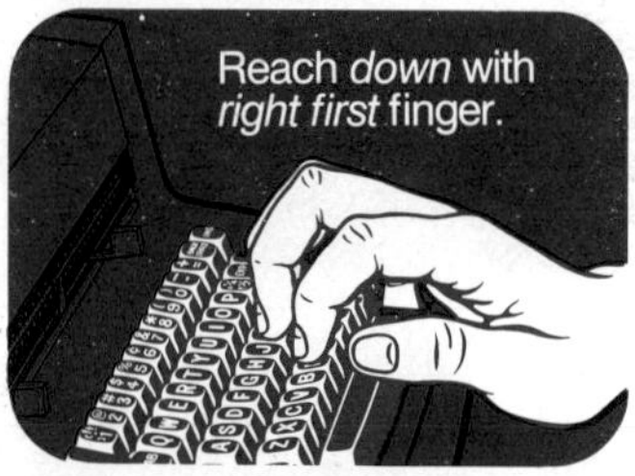

n ▼

1 n n n nj nj nj an an an and and and land land land

2 an an and and land land end end lend lend in in on

3 an end; an end; on hand; on hand; one win; one win

Reach technique for g

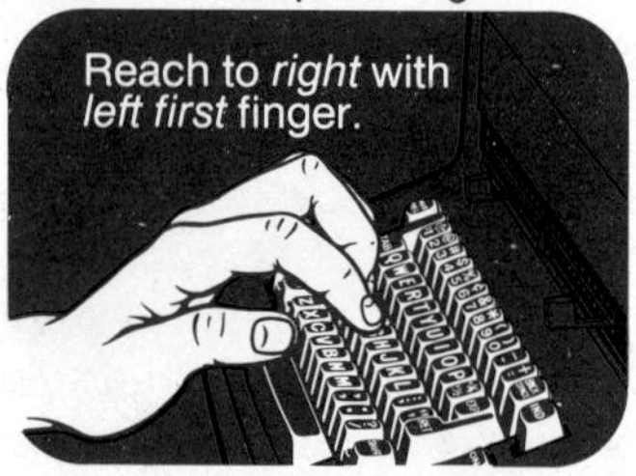

g ▼

4 g g g gf gf gf go go go got got got flag flag flag

5 go go got got fog fog dog dog dig dig rig rig good

6 to go; to go; or fog; or fog; rig it; rig it; good

Control of right shift key

right shift ▼

7 A; A; Al Al Ali Ali Eli Eli Flo Flo Sol Sol Al Ali

8 Al is to see Flo Towle. Sol works for Elsa Rolfs.

9 Si and Dot are here; Tod and Ali are at Salt Fork.

TS

289b-291b, continued

Job 3
Model copy for spirit duplication

full sheet

1. Type a model copy of the material at the right for spirit duplication.

2. Set margins for a 65-space line and a one-inch top margin. For the example at the bottom of the page, use a 31-space line.

JUSTIFYING THE RIGHT MARGIN

Bulletins published by business firms and newspapers published by schools are often typed in columns with the right margin even (justified). Except for the last line of the paragraph, the words in each line are spaced so that the right margin will be even and give the appearance of a printed page.

To justify the right margin of material in columns, select a specific line length (30 to 40 spaces when typing two columns) and then type a work copy. Use the diagonal (/) at the end of each line to show the number of additional spaces needed. If it is necessary to reduce the number of spaces in a line, type the number to be reduced to the right of the line. After you have completed the work copy, type the copy in final form, adding and reducing spaces as needed. An example of this procedure is shown at the bottom of the page.

To <u>add</u> spaces to a line:

1. Space three times after a period, question mark, exclamation point, or colon.

2. Space twice after a comma or semicolon.

3. Space twice between selected words or phrases.

To <u>reduce</u> the number of spaces in a line:

1. Space once after a period, question mark, exclamation point, or colon.

2. "Squeeze" commas or semicolons.

3. "Squeeze" words. If possible, choose two- or three-letter words to be "squeezed."

To justify the right margin of material typed in columns, it may be necessary to divide a word at other than the preferred division point. However, always divide a word between syllables.

```
     Record sales in a year of/
consolidation! That statement/
best describes the Arvin Company-1
during the past year as earnings-1
rose to a record $33.6 million.
Credit for this record must go/
to our employees, management,//
and our customers.
```

```
     Record sales  in a year of
consolidation!  That statement
best describes the Arvin Company
during the past year as earnings
rose to a record $33.6 million.
Credit for this record  must go
to  our employees,  management,
and our customers.
```

6b ▶ 22 Learn: r . (period) w

each line twice SS (slowly, then faster); DS between 2-line groups; if time permits, retype selected lines

Follow *Standard Plan for Learning New Keys,* page 12.

Keystroking cue: Keep your fingers curved and upright (not slanting); move your fingers, *not* your hands.

Spacing cue: Space once after . following an initial or at the end of an abbreviation; twice at end of sentence.

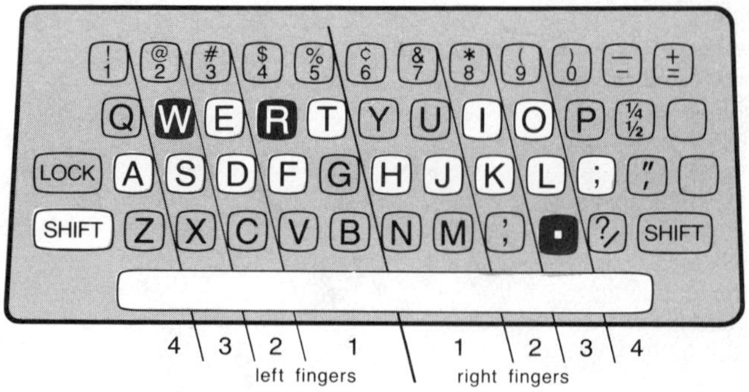

Reach technique for r

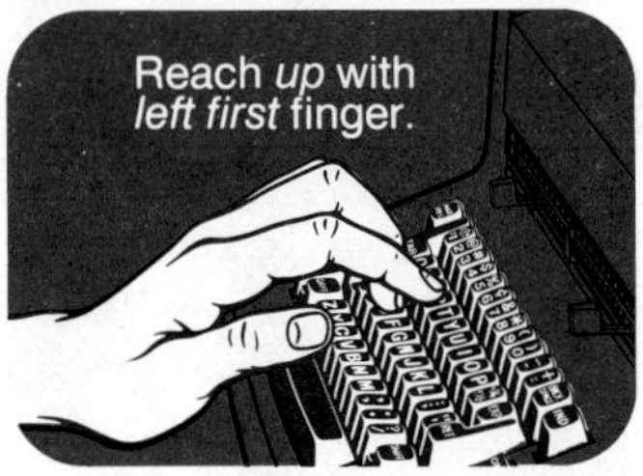

r

1 r r r rf rf rf or or or for for for risk risk risk

2 rf rf or or rid rid rod rod for for jerk jerk ride

3 a jar; a jar; for her; for her; she rode; she rode

Reach technique for . (period)

Reach *down* with *right third* finger; space twice after . at end of sentence.

. (period)

4 . . . .l .l .l ed. ed. ed. I do. He did. Jae is.

5 He is to do it. Hi has the list. I shall see it.

6 Lt. Hoffa sold the skiff. J. O. Hakes lost a ski.

Reach technique for w

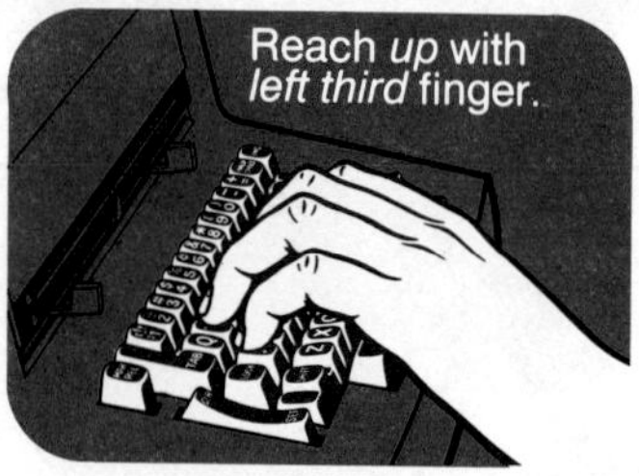

w

7 w w w ws ws ws ow ow ow wow wow wow wish wish wish

8 ws ws ow ow low low wit wit how how with with slow

9 we owe; we owe; low wok; low wok; we wish; we wish

TS

6c ▶ 20 Improve keystroking technique

each pair of lines twice SS (slowly, then faster); DS between 4-line groups

Goals

- quick, snap keystrokes
- down–and–in spacing motion
- return without pausing

home row
1 ask ask had had has has half half dash dash salads
2 a half; a salad; has a kaha; add a dash; had a jak

reach review
3 tow tow his his let let her her work work rid ride
4 is to; did it; will do; to joke; for her; the work

left shift and r/w/.
5 Jake wrote wk. for week. Lisa wrote ft. for feet.
6 O. L. Lowe has worked for Lt. Jarow for two weeks.

all reaches learned
7 Jeri said she saw their show; her dad also saw it.
8 He will do this work free if we ask that he do so.

289b-291b, continued

Job 4
Justifying the right margin

full sheet

1. Set a left margin of ½″. Type the material at the right SS with a DS between ¶s in a column of 36 spaces as a work copy. As a heading, center **DIRECT COPIERS** over the line of writing, 1″ from the top edge.

2. Reset left margin 4 spaces to the right of center of the page. Type the final copy, justifying the right margin.

There are a number of direct copy machines available that will copy typewritten or printed material from an original copy. These machines operate on a principle of xerography (light) or thermography (heat) to transfer the material from the original to special copy paper or plain paper.

Direct copy machines are especially useful in making additional copies of documents such as customers' orders and bills of lading as well as making copies of correspondence and reports. Considerable time is saved by making copies from the original, and the danger of errors which may be made when the material is retyped is eliminated.

When you type materials that will be reproduced on a direct copier, be sure the type is clean and the ribbon will produce dark print. If you make an error, eliminate it completely by erasing or using lift-off tape. If you use correction tape which merely covers up the error, it is possible the original error may show through on the copy, especially if a thermal copier is used.

Although some copiers have been designed to reproduce more than 100 copies per minute, their use as duplicators has been restricted to a great extent by the cost. If only a few copies are required, however, time and labor may be saved by using a direct copy machine. This procedure eliminates the necessity for making carbon copies and frees the typist from the tedious task of correcting errors on multiple carbon copies.

5e ▶ 10 Improve shift-key and return technique

each line once SS on a separate line; repeat the drill if time permits

Goals

1. To shift without moving the hand down.

2. To return without pausing at the end of one line or at beginning of next line.

Left shift

Electric return

Manual return

all letters learned are used

```
 1 Jake has a list
 2 of all the oak;

 3 Lisa is to ask if he
 4 is to sell the jade;

 5 Hal said that he left the
 6 old file at the ski lake;

 7 Ila asked to see the odd flask
 8 that he had to sell last fall;

 9 Joel said that he did file the test
10 list she said she left at his desk;
```

6

50-space line

In this lesson and the remaining lessons in this unit, the time for the Conditioning Practice is changed to 8 minutes. In this time you are to make machine adjustments, get ready to type, and type the 3 lines of the Conditioning Practice as directed.

Daily get-ready-to-type

1. Arrange work area.

2. Insert paper (straighten if necessary).

3. Adjust paper guide.

4. Set line-space selector on "1" for single spacing.

5. Set ribbon control on black (to type on top half of ribbon).

6. Set left margin stop (center of paper – 25 spaces).

7. Move right margin stop to right end of scale.

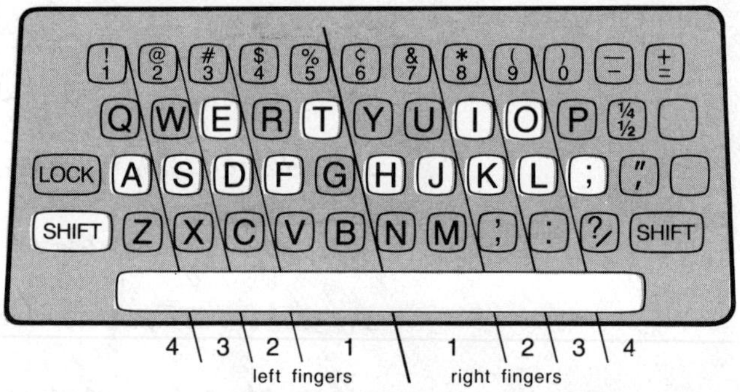

6a ▶ 8 Conditioning practice

each line twice SS (slowly, then faster); DS between 2-line groups; if time permits, retype selected lines

Technique cues

- curved, upright fingers
- wrists low, relaxed
- down-and-in motion of right thumb to space
- quick shift-type-release movements when shifting
- quick return without pausing before or after

Curved, upright fingers

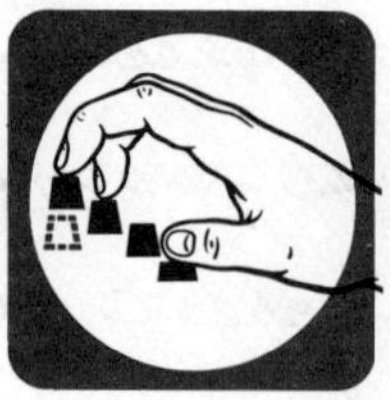
Finger-action keystroking

Down-and-in-thumb motion

all letters learned used in each line

```
1 tf ft ik ki ed de ol lo fl lf sk ks ja aj ha ah hj

2 el el so so it it off off; aid aid jak jak she she

3 Jeff said that Keith had left to hike at Oak Lake;
```

TS

289b-291b, continued

Job 5
Model copy of program

full sheets

Prepare a model copy of a 4-page program for a front-and-back stencil duplication, similar to the one at the right, based on the following information:

Page 1: The Fort LeBoeuf High School Future Business Leaders of America will hold their annual spring banquet on April 26, 19—, beginning at 8:30 p.m., at the Park Sheraton Motel.

Page 2: The dinner menu will consist of fresh fruitcup; boneless breast of capon on hickory slice with sauce Eugene; baked potato with sour cream; tossed salad with house dressing; rolls and butter; coffee, tea, or milk; and chocolate parfait with mint sauce.

Page 3: The program will include a welcome by Michelle Wheatley, President; an invocation by Antonio Tores; the introduction of the guest speaker by Raymond Olivier, the program chairperson; a speech by Carl W. Jackson, President of the Teen Sportswear, Inc.; the presentation of awards by Bonda Dahlin, Advisor. Entertainment will be provided by The Magic World of Dennis Perkins; dancing will be to the music of Robert Maize and the Ears of Corn.

Page 4: The officers of the Fort LeBoeuf High School Future Business Leaders of America are: Michelle Wheatley, President; Raymond Olivier, Vice-President; Antonio Tores, Secretary; Lisa Anthony, Treasurer; and Nicole Sutton, Historian. The advisor is Bonda Dahlin. The officers of the club wish to thank all of those who helped make this a successful year and to express their appreciation and thanks.

Typing Spread Headings

1. Backspace from center once for each letter, character, and space *except the last letter or character* in the heading. Start typing where the backspacing ends.

2. When typing a spread heading, space once after each letter or character and three times between words.

Moon Area High School

BUSINESS EDUCATION CLUB

O F F I C E R S

Maria Sanchez . . . . President

Jessica Harper . . . . Vice-President

Carl Jackson . . . . Secretary

Christine Pavlov . . . . Treasurer

Advisor: Nancy Davidson

!!!!!!!!!

The Officers of the Moon Area High School Business Education Club wish to congratulate those students who were honored this evening

Mary Helen Allen

Joyce T. David

Frederick W. McCormich

Alica M. Showalter

Susanne K. Weston

fold line

page 4

Moon Area High School

BUSINESS EDUCATION CLUB

ANNUAL AWARDS BANQUET

May 4, 19--

6:30 p.m.

Algonquin Hotel

Pittsburgh, Pennsylvania

page 1

B A N Q U E T   M E N U

Tomato Juice

London Broil Au Jus

Mashed Potatoes with Gravy

Buttered Corn

Rolls and Butter

Coffee or Iced Tea

Raspberry Supreme

Assorted Mints

fold line

page 2

P R O G R A M

Greetings and Introduction of Guests . . . Maria Sanchez

Announcements . . . . Joseph Daniels, Secretary

Introduction of Guest Speaker . . . . . . Jessica Harper, Vice-President

GUEST SPEAKER:

"The Office of the Future"

William C. Markham
Director of Business Education
Commonwealth of Pennsylvania

Presentation of Awards . . . Nancy Davidson, Advisor

E N T E R T A I N M E N T

The Rose Tree Chorus

D A N C I N G

The Heavenly Hash Combo

page 3

5

50-space line

5a ▶ 5 Recall

1. Recall the steps in getting ready to type (see pages 4–5 if necessary). Take these standard steps daily.

2. Review the features of correct typing position, page 7. Correct typing position helps you to gain keystroking control.

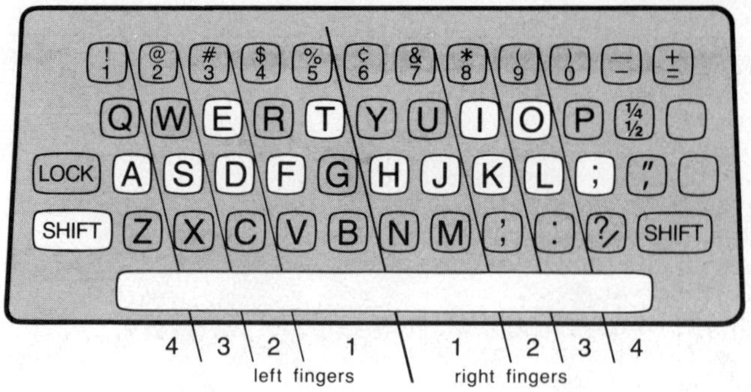

5b ▶ 7 Conditioning practice

each line twice SS (slowly, then faster); DS between 2-line groups; if time permits, type each line again

home row 1 hj ds lk af aj lf sa fl sk da sl fa ja ak ka la fa

3d row 2 ed ol tf ik led led old old kid kid ode ode it its

all letters learned 3 as a kid; has to sit; had a jak; if all the oak is

TS

5c ▶ 14 Improve keystroking technique

1. Each pair of lines twice SS (slowly, then faster); DS between 4-line groups.

2. If time permits, type all 8 lines once more.

Goals

- curved, upright fingers
- quick, snap keystrokes
- finger-reach action

home row
1 as lad has had ask jaks lash sash fall flash flask
2 as all jaks; all oak had; ask a lass; half a flask

3d row
3 of off to too it fit tie jade folk doll diet filed
4 off the; old jade; he filed it; she ate half of it

all letters learned
5 she is to ski at the lake; that jade fish is sold;
6 Jae said the sash is silk; Ike is to file the list

all letters learned
7 he is to hike to the lake; she did that as a joke;
8 Ola left this silk sash; Jeff said he had the kite

TS

5d ▶ 14 Improve space-bar technique

1. Each pair of lines twice SS (slowly, then faster); DS between 4-line groups.

2. If time permits, type all 8 lines once more.

Goals

- right thumb on or close to space bar
- quick down-and-in motion of right thumb
- no pause before or after spacing stroke

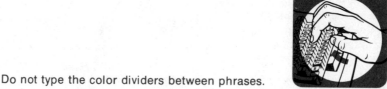

Down-and-in thumb motion

Do not type the color dividers between phrases.

1 a is is it it so so if if to to ah ah of of do doe
2 it is|it is|do so|do so|of it|of it|to do|is to do

3 ha ha as as do do he he so so la la ti ti at at id
4 the id|the id|as is|as is|ah so|ah so|if he|if she

5 the the sit sit off off let let odd odd fall falls
6 to let|to let|he did|he did|if she has|if she does

7 Kae has said that she is to sell all the old jade;
8 Hal has said he also sold off all the aloe he had;

TS

unit **61** lessons 292-294

Government office

Learning goals

1. To learn how to type U.S. Government correspondence and other materials in proper form.

2. To improve your skill in producing acceptable production materials.

Machine adjustments

1. Line: 70 for all drills; as necessary for problems.

2. Spacing: SS sentence drills with a DS between sentence groups; space problems as directed or necessary.

292-294

292a-294a ▶ 5
Conditioning practice

each line twice SS (slowly, then faster); DS between 2-line groups; if time permits, retype selected lines

alphabet 1 Experts will solve the budget dilemma in June if we economize quickly.

figures 2 The company's labor force grew from 90,467 in 1975 to 152,836 in 1980.

fig/sym 3 The winning pole vault was 17′ 3″; high jump, 6′ 9″; triple jump, 54′ 6″.

fluency 4 Did she pay the men for the fine work they did on the lights downtown?

| 1 | 2 | 3 | 4 | 5 | 6 | 7 | 8 | 9 | 10 | 11 | 12 | 13 | 14 |

292b-294b ▶ 45
Production typing simulation

You have been hired as a clerk-typist (GS-2) in the Administrative Division of the Human Resources Agency of the Federal Government located at 1402 Pennsylvania Avenue NW, Washington, DC 20004-1156. Under the supervision of John D. Hobson, Assistant Director, you will perform general typing and clerical work, including answering telephones, handling mail, and typing or processing forms and letters. All correspondence will be signed by Ms. Vonda T. Brooks, Director of Administration.

Job 1
Form letters [LM pp. 187–198]

The form letter shown at the right is used when individuals apply directly to the Agency for a job. Type the letter, with two carbon copies, dated April 24, 19—, to

Ms. Mary Ann Tyler
4655 King Street
Alexandria, VA 22302-4426

and to

Mr. Gregory T. Perry
5620 Fishers Lane
Rockville, MD 20852-5513

Provide an appropriate subject line.

The symbol for the originating office is HURA; the dictator is John D. Hobson. Add your initials and the date to the identification data at the close of the letter. Remember, this information is typed on the carbon copies only.

Note: See page 297 for the format of an informal government letter. All letters will be mailed in window envelopes.

Form Letter 118-A

Thank you, (title and last name of individual), for your recent letter in which you applied for a position as a clerk-typist. We appreciate your interest in the Human Resources Agency.

All General Service positions within this Agency are filled through the Civil Service Commission. To qualify for a position as a clerk-typist (GS-2), you must

a. Pass a written test covering verbal abilities and clerical aptitudes.

b. Have had six months of clerical or office experience; or be a high school graduate; or have passed a GED test.

c. Be able to type a minimum of 40 words a minute. Your typing skills may be gained through schooling, employment, or otherwise. When you complete your application, be sure to show your current speed and how you got your typing skills. Your claimed proficiency may be evaluated at the time of appointment and, if you are unable to meet the proficiency requirements at that time, you will not be appointed.

If you feel that you have the qualifications for appointment as a clerk-typist, please contact the nearest office of the Civil Service Commission (listed under "U.S. Government" in the telephone directory) for information regarding current vacancies. That office can also provide you with all necessary application forms and any additional information you may like to have.

4c ▶ 20 Learn: t i left shift key

each line twice SS (slowly, then faster); DS between 2-line groups; if time permits, type each line once more

Follow *Standard Plan for Learning New Keys*, page 12.

Goals

- curved, upright fingers
- finger-action stroking
- quick return, your eyes on textbook copy

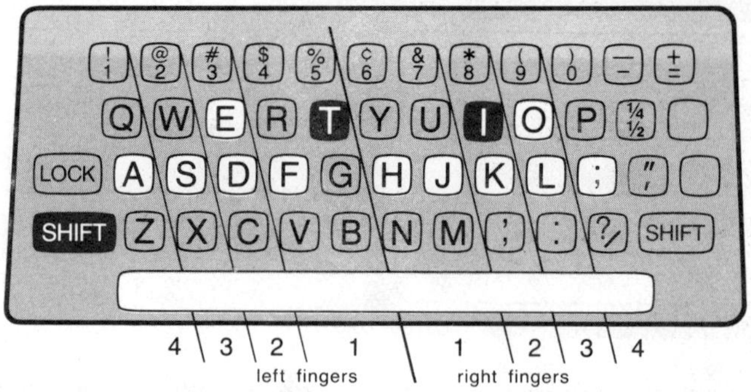

Reach technique for t

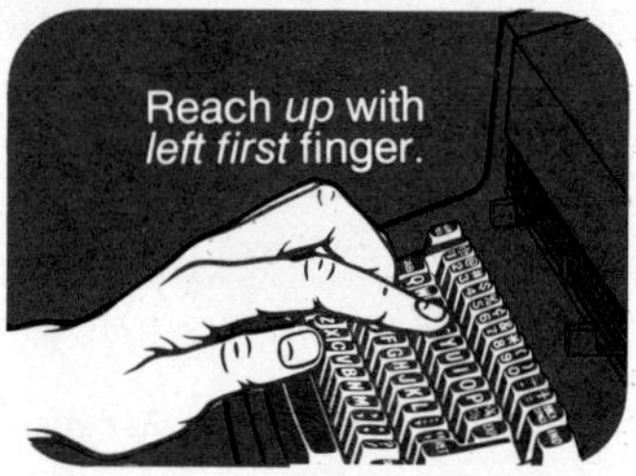

Reach *up* with *left first* finger.

t ▼

1 t t t tf tf tf to to to toe toe toe soft soft soft

2 to to at at dot dot lot lot jet jet take take talk

3 a lot; a lot; off the; off the; the jet; the jets;

Reach technique for i

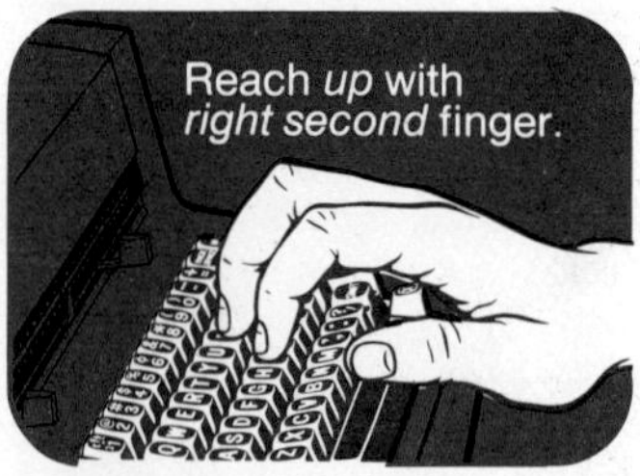

Reach *up* with *right second* finger.

i ▼

4 i i i ik ik ik if if if did did did said said said

5 ik ik is is aid aid die die lid lid idle idle file

6 he did; he did; did she; did she; is idle; is idle

Control of left shift key

Reach *down* with *left little* finger; shift, type, release.

left shift key ▼

7 La La La Ka Ka Ka Ja Ja Ja Hal Hal Hal Kae Kae Kae

8 Kae Hakes has jade; Jake Oakes led; Hal Lake fell;

9 Jae led Kae all fall; Jesse sold Jeff a jade fish;

TS

4d ▶ 18 Improve keystroking technique

each pair of lines twice SS (slowly, then faster); DS between 4-line groups; if time permits, retype selected lines

Goals

- curved, upright fingers
- finger-action stroking
- down-and-in spacing
- quick return, your eyes on textbook copy

home keys
1 fj fk fl dj dk dl sj sk sl aj ak al jd sk fl la ld
2 a jak; a fad; a lad; a lass; a fall ad; a sad fall

h/e/o
3 hj hj ed ed ol ol old old led led jell jello hello
4 old joke; she led; he sold; half off; half off the

t/i
5 if if it it fit fit sit sit hit hit this this that
left shift
6 Hal is tall; Jae is to see Kae; Jo left this list;

all letters learned
7 Hal said it is this jet he is to take to Oak Lake;
8 Heidi did aid Jae at the lake fish sale this fall;

292b-294b, continued

Job 2
Government report
(4 full sheets)

Type the report at the right with 3 ccs.

Note: Government reports are usually typed SS with 1-inch margins on all four sides. The title of the report, typed in ALL CAPS, is centered 1 inch from the top of the page. If there is a subtitle, it is centered a DS below the main title, followed by a DS. Side headings, if used, are preceded and followed by a DS. Although practices vary somewhat among the various government agencies, the report at the right, when typed, will illustrate the *general style* used in preparing government reports.

ALL CAPS {Affirmative Action to Employ Handicapped People

Fact Sheet

Every employer doing business with the federal government under a contract for more than $2,500 must take "affirmative action" to hire handicapped people. Affirmative action also applies to job assignments, promotions, training, transfers, accessibility, working conditions, terminations, ~~etc.~~ and the like.

Definitions

A handicapped person is anyone who (1) has a physical or ~~brain~~ mental impairment which substantially limits one or more of his, or her major life activities; (2) has a record of such impairment; or (3) is regarded as having such an impairment.

Substantially limits describes the ~~limit~~ degree to which the disability affects employability. A handicapped worker having a hard time getting a job or getting ahead on the job because of a disability would be considered "substantially limited."

Major life activities include communication, ambulation, self-care, socialization, education, vocational training, transportation, housing, and employment. The ~~major~~ main emphasis is on those life activities that affect employment.

Qualified. A person must be qualified to perform a particular job--with reasonable accommodation to his ~~disability.~~ or her handicap.

Government contracts included

Contracts over $2,500 for supplies or services or for the use of real or personal property, including construction, are included. Sub contracts are also included. "Services" include such things as utility, construction, transportation, research, and insurance. Construction means not only the erection of buildings but their repair, alteration, extension, and demolition. Highways are not included.

Notice to ~~Handicapped~~ Job Applicants

Job applicants will be given a notice which reads substantially as follows: "If you have a handicap and would like to be considered under the affirmative action program, please tell us. This information is voluntary and will be kept confidential except that (1) supervisors and managers may be informed regarding work restrictions or accommodations, and (2) first aid people will be informed regarding possible emergency treatment." The notice will also ask the handicapped person about any special skills or methods he or she has worked out to assist in performing the job satisfactorily as well as any special adaptations he or she may need due to the handicap.

3d ▶ Improve keystroking technique

each pair of lines twice SS (slowly, then faster); DS between 4-line groups; if time permits, retype the drill

Do not type line identifications.

home-key letters	1	aj ja ak ka al la lf fl ld dl ls sl la al ak ka ja
	2	jak jak ask ask lad lad all all lass lass all fall
h/e/o	3	he he she she foe foe hoe hoe shoe shoe joke jokes
	4	she jokes; he sold; shoe sale; odd hoes; old foes;
all letters learned	5	she has oak; he has sold; a hoe sale; load of jade
	6	he has half; she does lead; he had led; old jokes;
all letters learned	7	old oak keel; a shelf of jade; she had a shoe sale
	8	a shelf of jell; has old jade; he held a fall sale

4

50-space line

Time schedule

A time schedule for the parts of this lesson and lessons that follow is given as a guide for your minimum practice. The figure following the triangle in the lesson part heading indicates the number of minutes suggested for the activity. If time permits, however, retype selected lines from the various drills of the lessons.

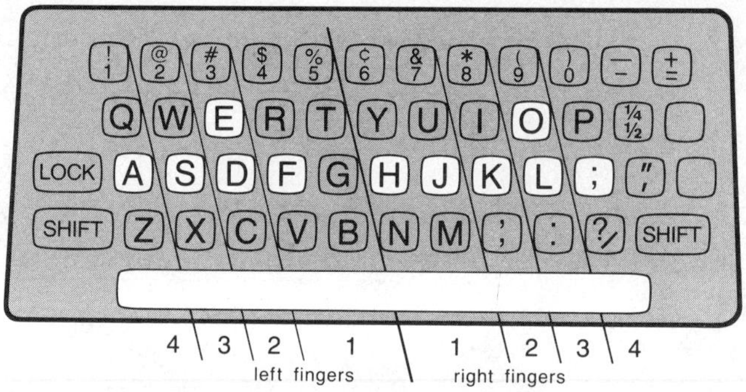

4a ▶ 5 Get ready to type

Follow steps on pages 4-5.

4b ▶ 7 Conditioning practice

each line twice SS; DS between 2-line groups

Goals

First time: Slow, easy pace, but strike and release each key quickly.

Second time: Faster pace; move from key to key quickly; keep carriage (element) moving.

Technique cues

1. Keep fingers upright and well curved.

2. Try to make each key reach without moving hand or other fingers forward or downward.

home row	1	had had has has ask ask; jak jak add add half half
h/e/o	2	he he of of do do so so; she she hoe hoe joke joke
all letters learned	3	he sells kale; she sold jade; as a joke; half of a

TS

292b-294b, continued

Job 3
Government letter
[LM pp. 199–206]

1. Type the letter shown at the right, written by **John D. Hobson** for Ms. Brooks' signature, to:

Mr. Carmen T. Ramos
Director of Personnel
Dorman Steel, Inc.
1917 Morris Avenue
Birmingham, AL 35203-4976

Date the letter **May 14, 19—**; provide an appropriate subject line; make 3 ccs.

2. Enclose a copy of the report you typed in Job 2. Under the enclosure notation in the closing lines, give the title of the enclosure. Be sure to place the identifying data on the carbon copies.

In your letter of May 6, you asked about the ~~steps which~~ procedures ~~should~~ must be ~~taken~~ followed by a handicapped person who ~~believes~~ feels that he or she is a ~~may be the~~ victim of discrimination. In general, the following steps must be taken:

a. The person, or someone authorized as a representative, must file a written complaint with the Office of the Federal Contract Compliance of the (Depart.) sp of Labor.

b. If the company has an ~~interval~~ internal review ~~program~~ procedure, the complaint must first follow those procedures. ~~be considered under this program.~~

c. If the company does not have an ~~interval~~ internal review procedure, the (Depart.) sp of Labor will ~~makes~~ make a thorough investigation.

d. If the (Depart.) sp of Labor investigation ~~reveals~~ shows no violation, the handicapped ~~individual~~ person can ask for a review of the case.

e. If the investigation reveals a violation, efforts will be made ~~to have~~ encourage the contractor to comply. If he or she ~~does~~ does not comply, he or she will be given an opportunity for a hearing of the case.

f. If the decision goes against the contractor, sanctions can be imposed by the (Depart.) sp of Labor, including the ~~closing~~ termination of the government contract.

Enclosed ~~you will find~~ is a fact sheet which ~~includes~~ provides additional ~~data~~ information regarding the government's ~~aggressive~~ affirmative action program ~~designed~~ to employ ~~more~~ handicapped people.

3a ▶ Get ready to type

Follow steps on pages 4-5.

1. Arrange work area.
2. Insert paper.
3. Adjust paper guide, if necessary.
4. Set line-space selector on "1".
5. Set ribbon control to type on top half of ribbon.
6. Set margin stops.

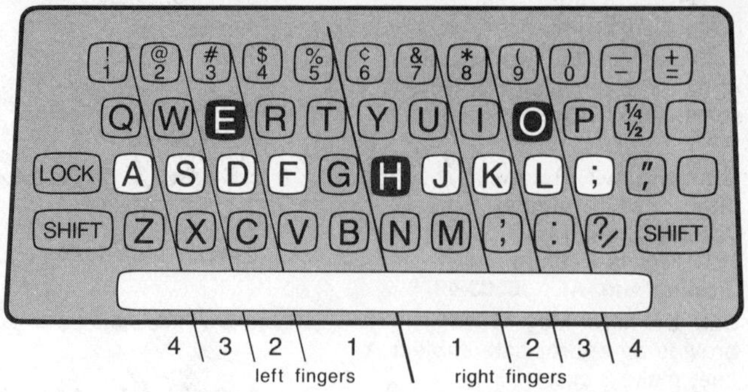
LOCK
SHIFT
SHIFT
4 3 2 1
left fingers
1 2 3 4
right fingers

3b ▶ Conditioning practice

each line twice SS
(once slowly, then faster);
DS between 2-line groups

Goals

- recall home-key locations
- quick, sharp keystroking
- down-and-in spacing
- return without pausing

all letters learned

1 al ks ja fl ds lk fa ll sk as sl da lf sa ff aj ss

2 ad ad as as jak jak fad fad all all fall fall lass

3 ask dad; ask dad; flak falls; flak falls; as a jak

Triple-space (TS) between lesson parts.

3c ▶ Learn: h e o

For each key to be learned in this lesson and lessons that follow, use the Standard Plan at the right.

Standard Plan for Learning New Keys

1. Find new key on keyboard chart (above).
2. *Look* at your typewriter keyboard; find new key on it.
3. Study reach-technique drawing at left below; read the printed instruction.
4. Identify finger used for new key.
5. Curve your fingers; place them in home-key position.
6. *Watch* your finger as you reach it to new key and back to home position a few times (keep it curved).
7. Type twice each of the 3 lines at the right of the reach-technique drawing:
   slowly, to learn the new reach;
   faster, to get a quick, snap stroke.
8. If time permits, type each line again.

Reach technique for h

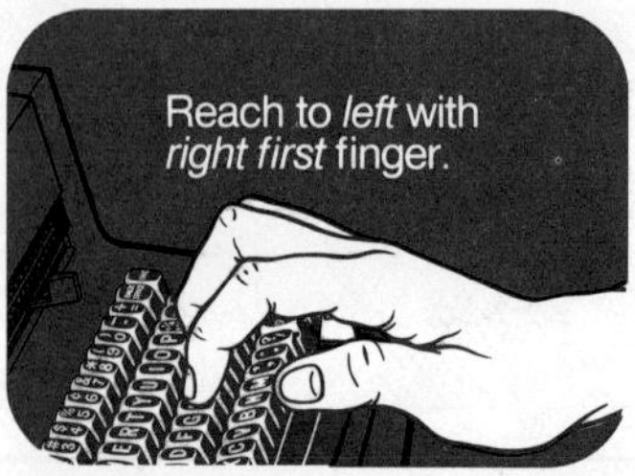
Reach to *left* with *right first* finger.

h ▼

1 h h h hj hj hj ah ah ah ha ha ha had had had hj hj

2 ah ah ha ha has has had had ash ash dash dash half

3 ah ha; has had; has had; a hall; a hall; had half;

Reach technique for e

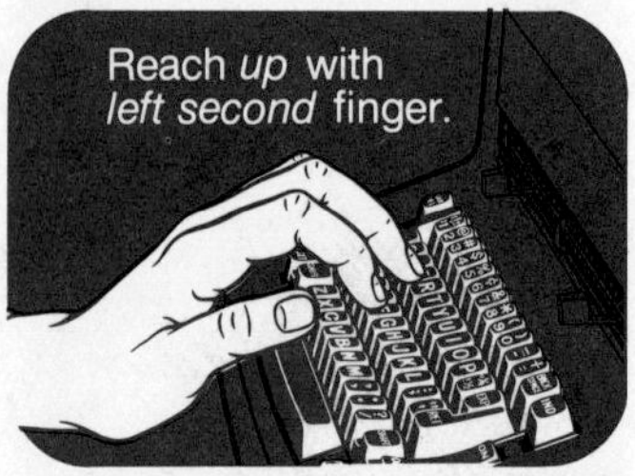
Reach *up* with *left second* finger.

e ▼

4 e e e ed ed ed el el el led led led fled fled fled

5 ed ed led led fled fled lake lake jell jell a sale

6 a leek; a leek; jade sale; jade sale; a jade sale;

Reach technique for o

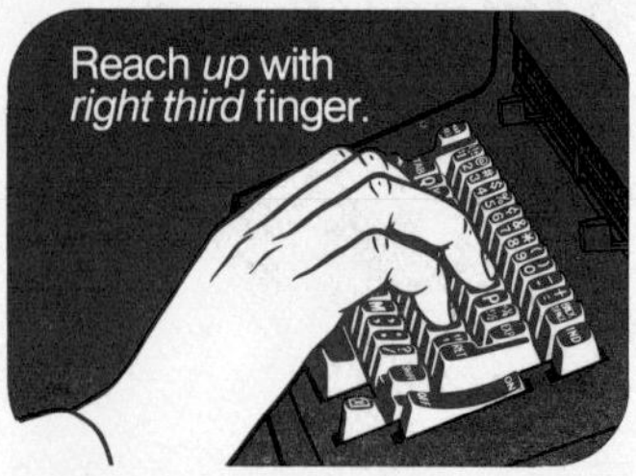
Reach *up* with *right third* finger.

o ▼

7 o o o ol ol ol do do do sod sod sod sold sold sold

8 ol ol do do odd odd oak oak old old sold sold fold

9 do so; do so; of old; of old; a loss of; a loss of

292b-294b, continued

Job 4
Message reply form
[LM pp. 207–212]

1. Type the message shown below; make 2 ccs.

2. On plain paper, compose a reply, dated May 20, 19—, to be signed by Ms. Brooks. Tell Ms. Ray that a copy of a fact sheet which provides general information regarding the government's affirmative action program to employ handicapped people is attached and that, for more detailed information, she should requisition a copy of the Rehabilitation Act of 1973, as amended. In addition, tell Ms. Ray that if visitors request detailed information she may refer them to your office. In addition, all correspondence on this subject should be sent to your office for reply.

3. Edit your reply and then type it in final form in the reply section of the message reply form.

MESSAGE REPLY MEMO

HUMAN RESOURCES AGENCY

WASHINGTON, DC 20004-1156

MESSAGE

TO Vonda J. Brooks
Director of Administration
Room 201

DATE May 16, 19--

SUBJECT Handicapped Employment

We have received several letters and visitors requesting information about the government's program to employ handicapped people.
Will you please provide us with any background material available on this subject.

SIGNED Georgia A. Ray, Receptionist

REPLY

DATE

2d ▶ Type home-row letters, words, and phrases

once as shown DS; then at a slightly faster pace

Curved, upright fingers

Finger–action stroking

Spacing technique

Electric return

```
 1 fj fj a; a; fdsa jkl; fdsa jkl; asdf ;lkj a;sldkfj
 2 jf jf kd kd ls ls ;a ;a fj fj dk dk sl sl a; a; fj
 3 ff jj dd kk ss ll aa ;; fj dk sl a; fj dk sl a; fj

 4 a a ad ad as as lad lad all all ask ask fall falls
 5 as as jak jak ads ads lass lass fall fall add adds
 6 ad ad sad sad fad fad all all fall fall as as asks

 7 a jak; a jak; a sad lass; a sad lass; all add ads;
 8 a fad; a fad; as a lad; as a lad; all ads; all ads
 9 as a fad; as a fad; as all ask dad; as all ask dad

10 all ads add; all ads add; asks a lass; asks a lass
11 a sad fall; a sad fall; adds a flask; adds a flask
12 as fall ads; as fall ads; a jak falls; a jak falls
```

2e ▶ End of lesson

1. Raise **paper bail (11)** or pull it toward you. Pull **paper release lever (18)** toward you.

2. Remove paper with your left hand. Push paper release lever back to its normal position.

3. On movable carriage type–writers, depress **right carriage release (19)**; hold **right platen knob (20)** firmly and center the carriage.

4. Turn *electrics* **off.**

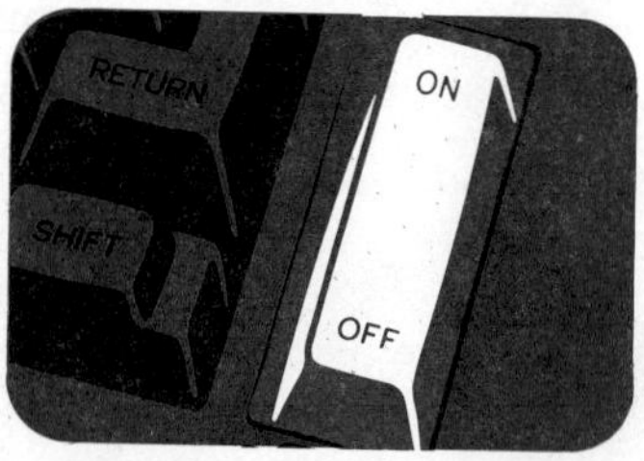

unit 62 lessons 295-300

Measure basic/production skills

Measurement goals

1. To type straight-copy material for 5′ at your highest rate with as few errors as possible.

2. To type correspondence for 30′ at your highest production rate as measured by *o-pram*.

3. To type reports for 30′ at your highest production rate as measured by *o-pram*.

4. To type forms and tables for 30′ at your highest production rate as measured by *o-pram*.

Machine adjustments

1. Line: 70 for drills; as necessary for problems.

2. Spacing: SS sentence drills with a DS between sentence groups; DS timed writings; space problems as directed or necessary.

295

295a ▶ 5 Conditioning practice

each line twice SS (slowly, then faster); DS between 2-line groups; if time permits, retype selected lines

alphabet 1 Her unique policy covers six big hazards most workers face on the job.

figures 2 We produced 984 units on May 2; 2,695 on June 11, and 3,087 on July 2.

fig/sym 3 The balance ($285.93) was paid by Blok & Kane on July 7 by Check 1460.

fluency 4 This proviso in the amendment might entitle the girls to a big profit.

| 1 | 2 | 3 | 4 | 5 | 6 | 7 | 8 | 9 | 10 | 11 | 12 | 13 | 14 |

295b ▶ 10 Premeasurement drill: basic skill

1. Three 1′ writings on ¶ 1; determine *gwam*. Note highest speed typed.

2. Three 1′ writings on ¶ 2; determine *gwam*. Note highest speed typed.

3. Additional 1′ writings on ¶ 2 as time permits.

Goal: To equal or exceed on ¶ 2 the highest speed typed on ¶ 1.

¶ 1 — all letters used | E | 1.3 si | 5.2 awl | 90% hfw |

¶ 2 — | HA | 1.7 si | 6.0 awl | 70% hfw |

	gwam 1′	2′
Music is one of the oldest forms of art in the world. There is no	13	7
record of any group of people who did not have some kind of music. No	28	14
one knows when, where, or how music began. It is likely that people	41	21
made music with their voices before they built instruments of wood to	55	28
provide a basic beat or rhythm. When pipes of clay or other material	69	35
were made to add changes in pitch, real music began. Many of these	83	42
simple means of making music have been found which are known to be more	97	49
than three thousand years old.	103	52
In our modern civilization we are surrounded by music of all kinds,	14	7
extending from symphonic works to "rock" in its numerous forms. Busi-	28	14
ness has discovered that music has a favorable effect upon employees and	42	21
their productivity. Companies that have introduced music into the work-	57	28
place believe that it reduces the midmorning and midafternoon slumps in	71	36
productivity. Retailers play quiet music in their stores for customers	85	43
to enjoy and to place them in a mood to buy. Whether we realize it or	100	50
not, music has a profound effect upon our everyday lives.	111	56

gwam 1′ | 1 | 2 | 3 | 4 | 5 | 6 | 7 | 8 | 9 | 10 | 11 | 12 | 13 | 14 |
2′ | 1 | 2 | 3 | 4 | 5 | 6 | 7 |

2a ▶ Get ready to type

Refer to pages 4-5 if necessary.

1. Arrange work area.

2. Insert paper (straighten if necessary).

3. Adjust paper guide.

4. Set line-space selector on "1" for single spacing.

5. Set ribbon control (to type on top half of ribbon).

6. Set left margin stop (center of paper – 25 spaces):
elite, 51 – 25 = 26
pica, 42 – 25 = 17

7. Move right margin stop to right end of scale.

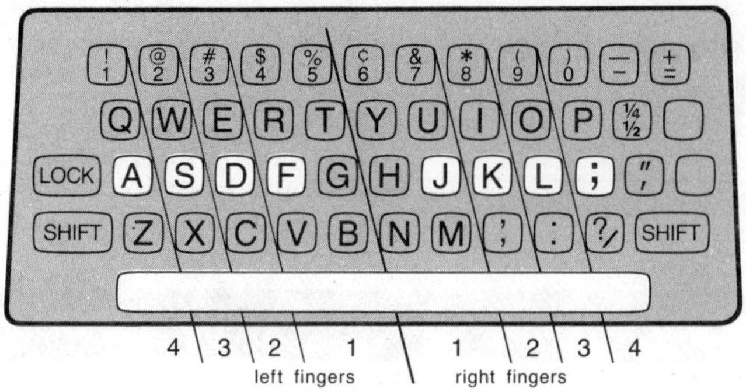

2b ▶ Review keystroking, spacing, and carriage (element) return

Keystroke

Curve fingers of your left hand and place them over **a s d f**
Curve fingers of your right hand and place them over **j k l ;**
Strike each key with a quick, snap stroke; release key quickly.

Space

To space after letters, words, and punctuation marks, strike the space bar with a quick down–and–in motion of the right thumb. Do not pause before or after spacing stroke.

Return

Electric: Reach the little finger to return key, strike the key, and release it quickly.

Manual: Reach to lever and return the carriage with a quick flick–of–the–hand motion.

Note: If you are typing on an electric machine, strike each key with a light tap with the tip of the finger; otherwise, keystroking technique is the same as for a manual typewriter.

type the lines once as shown

Space once

```
1 ff jj ff jj dd kk dd kk ss ll ss ll aa ;; aa ;; a;
                                                  DS
2 f ff j jj d dd k kk s ss l ll a aa ; ;; fj dk sl a
```

Return 3 times to triple–space (TS)

2c ▶ Improve home-key stroking

1. Type Line 1 twice single–spaced (SS); then double–space (DS).

2. Type Line 2, then Line 3, then Line 4, in the same way.

3. Check your typed copy with the model. Do you have 4 pairs of single–spaced lines with double spacing between the 2–line groups? If time permits, retype the drill.

Goals

- curved, upright fingers
- quick, snap keystrokes
- down–and–in spacing

```
1 a al ak aj s sl sk sj d dl dk dj f fl fk fj a; dk;
                                                  DS
2 j ja js jd jf k ka ks kd kf l la ls ld lf ; ;a ad;
                                                  DS
3 ; a ;a l s ls k d kd j f jf a; sl dk fj dk sl a; a
                                                  DS
4 as sa al la ak ka aj ja af fa sk ks fl lf ad da ja
                                                  TS
```

```
a al ak aj s sl sk sj d dl dk dj f fl fk fj a; dk;
a al ak aj s sl sk sj d dl dk dj f fl fk fj a; dk;

j ja js jd jf k ka ks kd kf l la ls ld lf ; ;a ad;
j ja js jd jf k ka ks kd kf l la ls ld lf ; ;a ad;

; a ;a l s ls k d kd j f jf a; sl dk fj dk sl a; a
; a ;a l s ls k d kd j f jf a; sl dk fj dk sl a; a

as sa al la ak ka aj ja af fa sk ks fl lf ad da ja
as sa al la ak ka aj ja af fa sk ks fl lf ad da ja
```

295c ▶ 15
Measure basic skill: straight copy

1. Two 5′ writings on ¶s 1–3 combined.

2. Determine *gwam* and errors on better writing. Compare with scores achieved on 226b, page 358.

all letters used | A | 1.5 si | 5.7 awl | 80% hfw |

	gwam 1′	5′
One of the most difficult periods in the lives of most individuals	13	3
is the first several months on a job. As the "new kid on the block,"	27	5
you will find yourself in a new and different environment, usually among	42	8
many strangers. Worst of all, you are not quite certain what to do and	56	11
how to do it. Even though you may have the appropriate skills to com-	70	14
plete your assigned tasks, you must first learn the specific policies	84	17
and operating procedures that are essential to the efficient completion	99	20
of your duties.	102	21
Most business firms realize that there must be a period of adjust-	13	23
ment or orientation for a new employee. To make it easier for the new	27	26
employee, many firms have formal programs to introduce the employee to	42	29
his or her work and fellow employees. These programs may include classes	56	32
on the policies and procedures that must be followed. Some companies	70	34
also use the "buddy system," under which each new employee is assigned	85	37
to a worker with experience who takes care of the new employee and ac-	99	40
quaints him or her with the duties of the job.	108	42
You can contribute a great deal to your satisfactory adjustment to	13	45
a new job. Pay careful attention to all instructions given you. It is	28	47
a good idea to carry a notebook with you for important notes that you	42	50
can review at your leisure. Listen carefully, but do not hesitate to	56	53
ask your trainer or supervisor for clarification of any particular as-	70	56
pect you do not comprehend. Be friendly with the other employees and	84	59
they will do their utmost to assist you in adjusting to your new envi-	98	61
ronment.	99	62

gwam 1′ | 1 | 2 | 3 | 4 | 5 | 6 | 7 | 8 | 9 | 10 | 11 | 12 | 13 | 14 |
5′ | 1 | 2 | 3 |

295d ▶ 20
Premeasurement drill: letters

average-length letter; plain full sheet

1. Type the letter in modified block style, mixed punctuation, to **Mr. Arthur C. Robins, 1101 Crabtree Boulevard, Raleigh, NC 27610-3500.** Date the letter **May 3, 19--.**

2. Use an appropriate salutation and complimentary close. Use your name in the closing lines as the District Manager.

Goal: To produce a mailable letter in the time allowed.

(¶ 1) Your inquiry regarding your Policy #542196A addressed to our national headquarters in Omaha, Nebraska, has been referred to this office for reply. (¶ 2) Your policy was established in March of 1965 as a Tax Sheltered Annuity under Section 501 of the Internal Revenue Code. Under the provisions of the Code, all payments made into the annuity and any interest accumulated is tax free until the date of your retirement, which can occur no earlier than age 59. (¶ 3) You can withdraw all or part of the money you have invested in this annuity prior to age 59; however, if you do so, these funds will be fully taxable in the year of withdrawal. (¶ 4) If you would like any further information regarding your policy, please write me or call me at 555-4301, Extension 91.

1g ▶ Type home-key letters

Type the lines once as shown, leaving one blank line space between lines (DS). With the **line-space selector (5)** set on "1," operate the return lever or key twice at the end of the line to double-space.

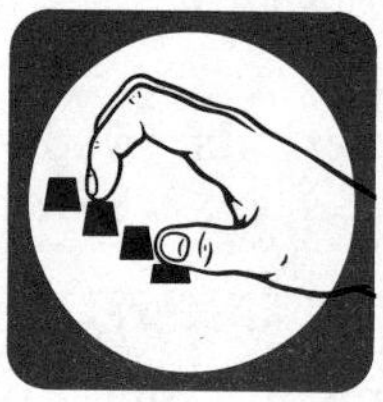

Correct finger curvature

Correct finger alignment

Do not type the line numbers.

```
1 jj jj ff ff kk kk dd dd ll ll ss ss ;; ;; aa aa ;;
                                                  DS
2 f ff j jj d dd k kk s ss l ll a aa ; ;; fj dk sl a
                                                  DS
3 f j fj d k dk s l sl a ; a; fj dk sl a; fj dk sl a
                                                  DS
4 fl lf da ad aj ja lk kl fa af ld dl sl ls al la ks
```

Return 3 times to triple-space (TS)

1h ▶ Type words and phrases

Type the lines once as shown (DS). If time permits, retype them.

Space with right thumb

Use down-and-in motion

Spacing cue: Space once after words and after **;** used as punctuation. At the end of the line, however, return without striking the space bar.

```
1 a a as as ask ask a a ad ad lad lad all all ad ads
                                                  DS
2 sad sad all all fad fad lass lass fall fall ad ads
                                                  DS
3 a jak; a jak; ask dad; ask dad; as all; as all ads
                                                  DS
4 a fall ad; a fall ad; as a fad; as a fad; all ads;
                                                  DS
5 all lads fall; all lads fall; as a lass; as a lass
```

Return 3 times to triple-space (TS)

1i ▶ End of lesson

1. Raise **paper bail (11)** or pull it toward you. Pull **paper release lever (18)** toward you.

2. Remove paper with your left hand. Push paper release lever back to its normal position.

3. On movable carriage typewriters, depress **right carriage release (19)**; hold **right platen knob (20)** firmly and center the carriage.

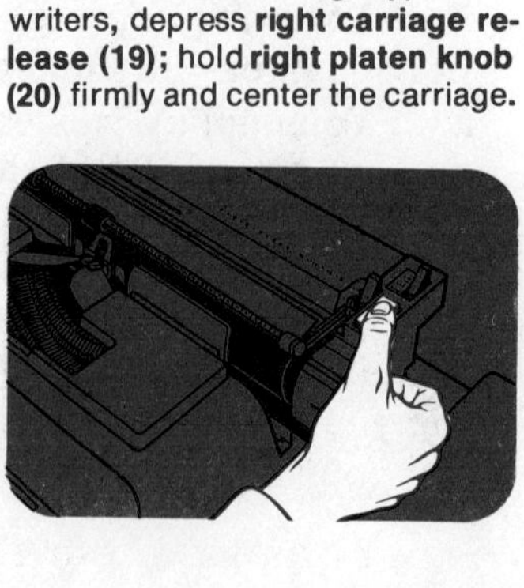

4. Turn *electrics* **off.**

296

296a ▶ 5 Conditioning practice

Use standard directions given in 295a, page 451.

alphabet 1 Their quick behavior thwarted six crafty men from seizing a jet plane.

figures 2 My account number was changed from 1594023-7 to 2687459-1 on March 30.

fig/sym 3 The premium on Policy #87234, due March 27, is $190.96 (34.1% × $560).

fluency 4 Dick may fix the turn signals on the antique auto for a busy neighbor.

| 1 | 2 | 3 | 4 | 5 | 6 | 7 | 8 | 9 | 10 | 11 | 12 | 13 | 14 |

296b ▶ 10 Premeasurement drill: basic skill

Type two 2′ writings on each ¶ of 295b, page 451. **Goal:** As few errors as possible.

296c ▶ 15 Measure basic skill: straight copy

Type two 5′ writings on the ¶s in 295c, page 452, as directed there.

296d ▶ 20 Premeasurement drill: report

full sheet

1. Type the material at the right as a leftbound report. Correct errors as you type.

2. Use as title: **IS OFFICE AUTOMATION A THREAT TO CLERICAL JOBS?** Add a proper footnote 1″ from the bottom of the page. The quote is from an article written by **Thomas Nardone** entitled, **"The Job Outlook in Brief,"** in the **Occupational Outlook Quarterly (Spring 1980), p. 8.**

Goal: To type an acceptable report in the time allowed.

In ~~a number of~~ many large organizations ~~firms~~, the "office of the future" is here today. Electr~~ic~~onic type writers with editing capabilities can be programmed ~~utilized~~ to prepare ~~complete~~, file, store, and retreive documents quickly and efficiently. Errors can be automatically corrected and, without reetyping an entire ~~a complete~~ document, you can add or delete words, snetences, and even whole paragraphs.

Will office automation drastically ~~actually~~ reduce the need for typists in the future? According to the Bruеau of Labor Statistics, Clerical Workers will be the largest and fastest growing white-collar group ~~body~~ for the next two decades ~~twenty years~~. By 1990, the Bureau estimates there will be 21,700,000 clerical workers in the labor ~~work~~ force and "Demand (will be) particulerly strong for typists who ~~and~~ can handel a variety of office duties and operate word processing equipment."[1]

1d ▶ Learn to strike keys and space bar

Study the keystroking and spacing illustrations; then type the drill given below as directed there.

Strike the key with a quick, sharp finger stroke; snap the finger slightly toward the palm of the hand as the keystroke is made.

If you are typing on an electric machine, strike each key with a light tap with the tip of the finger; otherwise, keystroking technique is the same as for a manual typewriter.

Strike the space bar with the right thumb; use a quick down-and-in motion (toward palm). Avoid pauses before or after spacing.

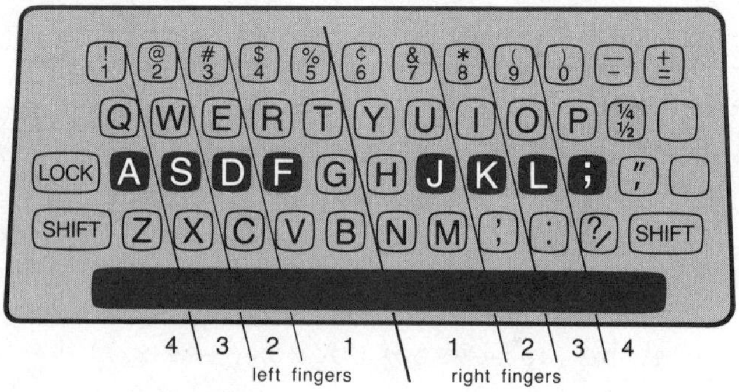

Space once

Type **ff** (space) **jj** (space) twice as shown: 1 `ff jj ff jj`

On same line, type **dd** (space) **kk** (space) twice: 2 `dd kk dd kk`

On same line, type **ss** (space) **ll** (space) twice: 3 `ss ll ss ll`

On same line, type **aa** (space) **;;** (space) twice: 4 `aa ;; aa ;;`

1e ▶ Return the carriage (or element carrier)

The **return key (34)** on an electric typewriter or the **return lever (1)** on a manual one is used to space the paper up and to return the carriage or element to the beginning of the new line.

1. Study the illustrations at the right; then make the return 3 times (triple-space) at the end of your typed line.

2. To see how your typed line should look, check **1f** below.

Electric return

Reach with the little finger of the right hand to the return key, tap the key, and return the finger quickly to its typing position.

Manual return

Move left hand, fingers bracing one another, to carriage return lever; move lever inward to take up the slack; then return the carriage with a quick inward flick-of-the-hand motion. Drop the hand quickly to typing position without letting it follow carriage across.

1f ▶ Check your typing

Your typed line should look like the line at the right. The **printing point indicator (13)** of your typewriter should be under the first **f**.

```
ff jj ff jj dd kk dd kk ss ll ss ll aa ;; aa ;;
```

Return 3 times to triple-space (TS)

297

297a ▶ 5 Conditioning practice

Use standard directions given in 295a, page 451.

alphabet 1 Jan Blake hired an executive who specializes in quality manufacturing.

figures 2 Public Law 35754, which was passed in 1980, applies in only 26 states.

fig/sym 3 Reduce Item 78 by 30%; Item 84, 25%; Item 196, 15%; and Item 367, 10%.

fluency 4 The amendment may name a panel to study the problem of the dual forms.

| 1 | 2 | 3 | 4 | 5 | 6 | 7 | 8 | 9 | 10 | 11 | 12 | 13 | 14 |

297b ▶ 10 Premeasurement drills: basic skill

1. Type the sentences at the right DS at your highest rate of speed.

2. Remove the paper from the typewriter and correct your errors in pencil. From your corrected copy, type a 1′ writing on each line with as few errors as possible.

long words 1 Deliberate misrepresentation caused administrators irreparable damage.

short words 2 She may take over his job when he goes to the main office in the city.

combination 3 Did the bookkeeper check my calculations in the six financial reports?

left hand 4 Eager stewardesses began serving preferred passengers extra beverages.

right hand 5 In my opinion, Jon will join Kim and buy my pink nylon kimono for Joy.

balanced hand 6 If they go to the city with us, he may go downtown with the eight men.

| 1 | 2 | 3 | 4 | 5 | 6 | 7 | 8 | 9 | 10 | 11 | 12 | 13 | 14 |

297c ▶ 15 Measure basic skill: straight copy

Type two 5′ writings on the ¶s in 295c, page 452, as directed there.

297d ▶ 20 Premeasurement drill: table

full sheet

Type the table in reading position; DS items; correct errors as you type.

Goal: To type an acceptable table in the time allowed.

PRINCESS ALICIA WOMEN'S FASHIONS, INC.

Top Sales Representatives of the Year

Name	Region	Dollar Sales*
Denise L. Cooper	Northeastern	$1,498,500
Roger C. Bryant	Northwestern	1,264,800
Frank L. Greenfield	Central	1,107,600
Margo G. Columbo	Southeastern	1,245,300
Michael T. Brennan	Southwestern	1,008,400

Source: Annual Report to the Stockholders, 19--.

* For the 12-month period ended October 31, 19--.

1a ▶ Get ready to type

1. Study the *Know-your-typewriter* information on pages 1-3.
2. Take each step in the *Daily get-ready-to-type* procedure on pages 4-5.

1b ▶ Take typing position

1. Study the illustrations of correct typing position shown below.

2. Observe each of the listed points as you position yourself at your typewriter.

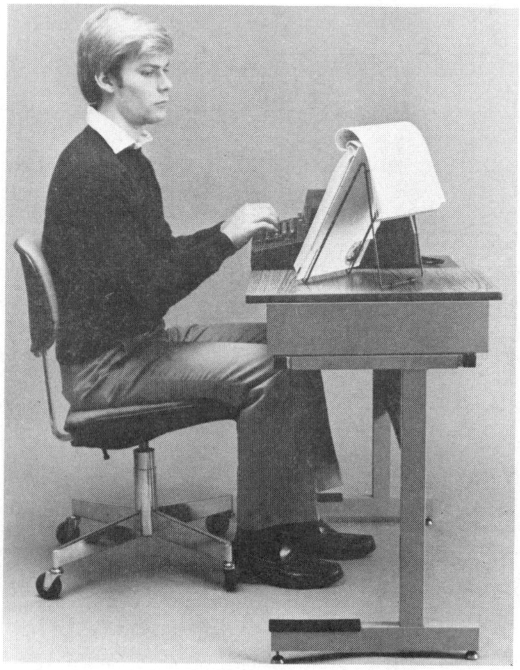

eyes on copy

fingers curved and upright; wrists low

forearms parallel to slant of keyboard

sit back in chair; body erect

textbook at right of machine; top raised for easy reading

table free of unneeded books

feet on floor for balance

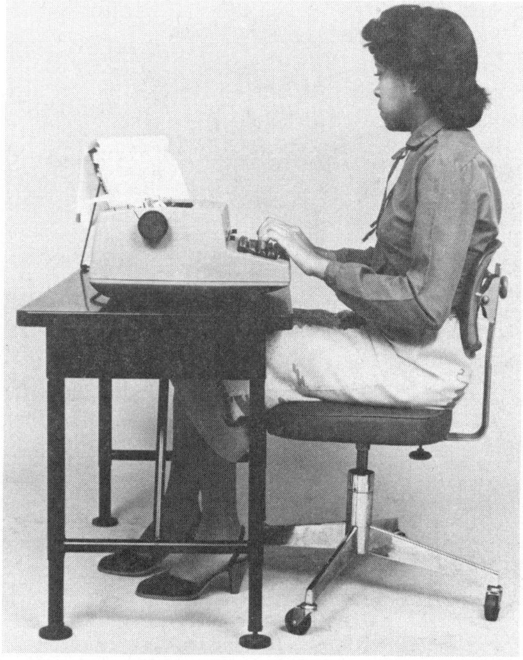

1c ▶ Place your fingers in home-key position

1. Locate on the chart **a s d f** (home keys for left hand) and **j k l ;** (home keys for right hand).

2. Locate the home keys on your typewriter. Place fingers of your left hand on **a s d f** and of your right hand on **j k l ;** *with your fingers well curved and upright (not slanting).*

3. Remove your fingers from the keyboard; then place them in home–key position again, curving and holding them *lightly* on the keys.

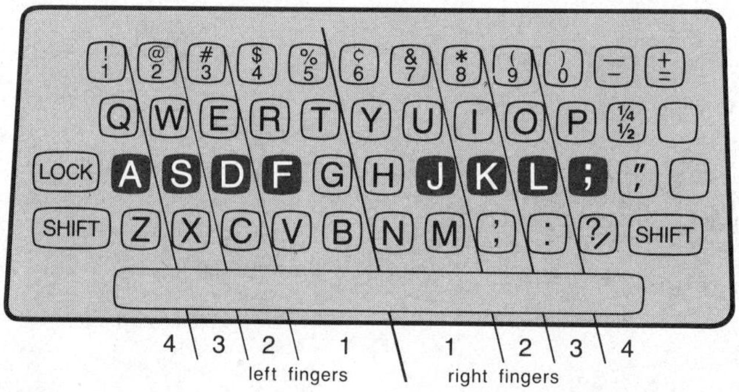

Fingers curved

Fingers upright

298-300

298a-300a ▶ 5
Conditioning practice

Use standard directions given in 295a, p. 451.

alphabet 1 **Jeff Grayson zoomed quickly down the wide boulevard to the expressway.**

figures 2 **Models 28651, 39472, 40753, and 61980 will be discontinued on April 2.**

fig/sym 3 **Ray & Sons reduced the price of Item #452897 by 10% (from $70 to $63).**

fluency 4 **When he finds the keys for the auto, they may go to the lake and fish.**

| 1 | 2 | 3 | 4 | 5 | 6 | 7 | 8 | 9 | 10 | 11 | 12 | 13 | 14 |

298b ▶ 45
Measure production skill: correspondence

1. Type the problems at the right and on page 456 for 30′; correct errors as you type. If you finish all problems before time is called, start over.

2. After time is called, go over each page carefully and circle any errors you did not correct. Compute *o-pram* (Office Production Rate a Minute). Compare score with that attained on 227b, page 361.

Problem 1
Average-length letter
plain full sheet

1. Type the letter in block style, open punctuation, to **Miss Eileen T. Roberts, Executive Vice President** of the **Wabash Manufacturing Company, 131 North Main Street, Dayton, OH 45402-3030.** Date the letter **May 22, 19--.**

2. Use an appropriate salutation and complimentary close. The letter will be signed by **Ms. Cynthia T. Storm, President** of **Information Technologies, Inc.** Use the company name in the closing lines.

words

opening lines 30

[The [information] ~~data~~ gathered during our in-depth analys[i]~~e~~s of your 43
administrative operations has been (analyzed) (thoroughly) ,and 55
we are prepared to present a [detailed] report of our findings in the 68
~~very~~ near future. 71

[An [significant] ~~important~~ part of our report will be a [recommendation] ~~suggestion~~ 83
that your information processing system be completely auto- 94
mated through the use of electronic office equipment. This 106
will represent a [drastic] ~~major~~ change in your [administrative] ~~methods of~~ operations. 120

[We have [found] ~~discovered~~ that most executives [require] ~~need~~ some back- 131
ground material before they are [able] ~~in a position~~ to appreciate 141
the advantages of office automation. ~~It is~~ for [For] this reason, 152
~~that~~ we have developed a special [two-hour] orientation program which 164
includes [the steps involved in] ~~a broad outline of~~ planning, [and] organizing ~~, implementing,~~ 175
~~and controlling the~~ [an] automated office. 188

[I have asked Mr. Thomas C. Shea, our Director of Manage- 199
ment Development, to [call] ~~get in touch with~~ you so that you can 208
arrange a schedule for the presentation of this [orientation] ~~special~~ pro- 221
gram to your executives. 226

(as described in the enclosed pamphlet.)

closing lines 244

Problems 2, 3, and 4 are on page 456.

phase 1 lessons 1-25

Learn to typewrite

You can learn to type—just as millions of other students have. How quickly you learn, though, depends on you: your interest, your effort, and your ability to follow directions closely.

To get the best results in typing, you must read, listen, observe, and practice with a purpose. Make *improvement* your goal each time you practice.

Before you can use the typewriter to type personal and business papers, you must become skilled in operating the letter keys and other operative parts.

The 25 lessons of Phase 1 are designed to help you learn:

1. To operate the letter keys by touch (without looking).

2. To use the basic parts of your typewriter with skill: space bar, shift keys, the return, and the tabulator.

3. To type words, sentences, and paragraphs without time-wasting pauses and with good keystroking techniques.

4. To type from typed, handwritten, and rough-draft copy.

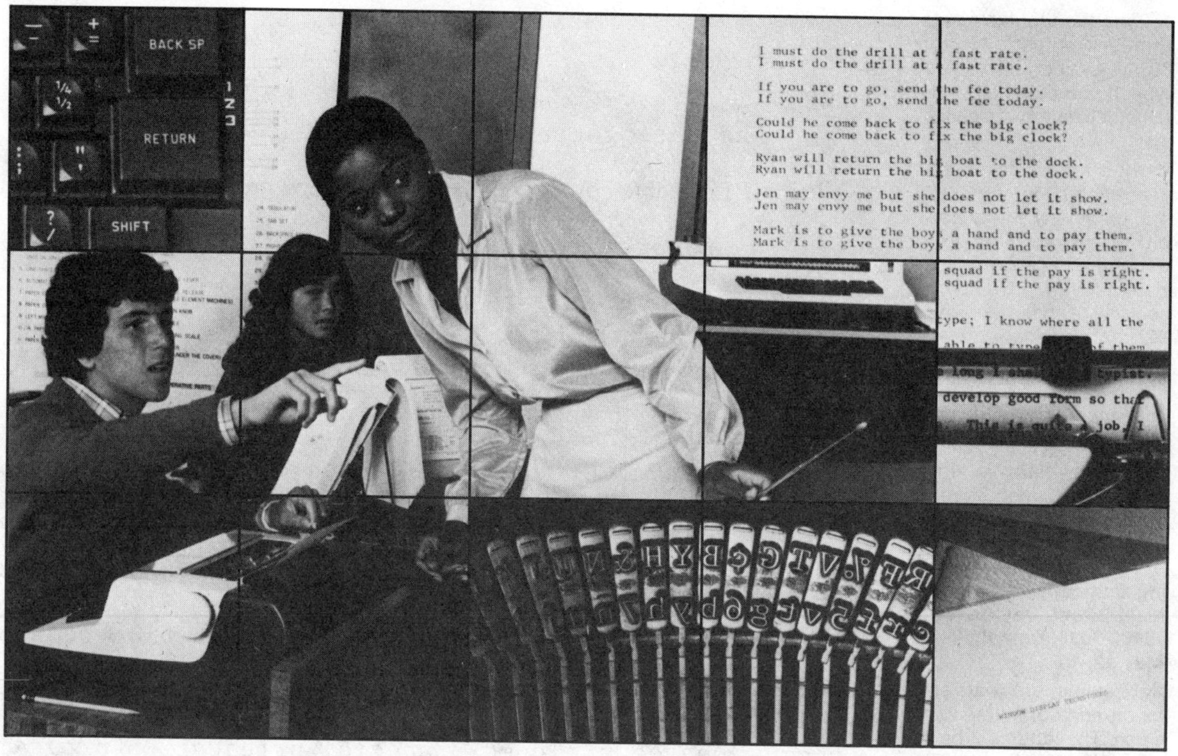

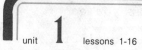

unit 1 lessons 1-16

Learn to operate the letter keyboard

Learning goals

1. To learn to operate letter keys by touch.

2. To learn to operate basic service keys (space bar, return, shift keys) by touch.

3. To learn to type sentences and paragraphs.

Machine adjustments

1. Paper guide at *0*.

2. Ribbon control to type on top half of ribbon.

3. Margin sets: left (center – 25); right (move to right end of scale).

4. Line-space selector on *1* to single-space (SS) drills.

5. Line-space selector on *2* to double-space (DS) paragraphs.

298b, continued

Problem 2
Interoffice memorandum
[LM p. 217]

Type the memorandum to **Thomas C. Shea, Director of Management Development.** The memo is from **Kevin L. Orlando,** who is the **Administrative Assistant** to Ms. Storm. Date the memo **May 22, 19—; Subject: Office Automation Orientation Program.**

words

opening lines 29

Enclosed for your information and necessary action is a 40
copy of a letter ~~Miss~~ Ms. Storm ~~wrote~~ has written to Miss Roberts, ~~who is~~ 51
Executive Vice President of the Wabash Manufacturing Co. (sp) 64
Please arrange with Miss Roberts ~~or her appointed~~ 71
~~representative~~ to present our ~~special~~ two-hour orientation program 79
on office automation to all ~~administrators~~ executives of the 89
Wabash Manufacturing Company at mutually agreeable 99
times. As soon as you have a firm schedule, please 109
send a copy to ~~Ms. Storm~~ this office. 115
If her schedule permits, Ms. Storm will introduce ~~all~~ each 126
two-hour sessions. If ~~it is~~ not ~~possible for her to do this~~, 131
I will represent her at all of the sessions. 140

closing lines 143

Problem 3
Average-length letter
plain full sheet

1. Type the letter in modified block style, mixed punctuation, to **Mr. Joseph C. Taborski, Director of Administration, Gateway Industries, Inc., 560 Forbes Avenue, Pittsburgh, PA 15219-6066.** Date the letter **May 28.**

2. Use an appropriate salutation and complimentary close. **Subject: Word Processing Survey.** The letter will be signed by **Thomas M. Gallo, Chief** of the **Systems Analysis Branch.**

Problem 4
plain full sheet

1. Type the letter in Problem 3 in modified block with indented ¶s, mixed punctuation, to **Ms. M. J. Burns, President** of **Burns-Roth, Inc., 901 Mack Road, Detroit, MI 48207-3756.** Indent the subject line 5 spaces.

2. Date the letter **June 1** in response to Ms. Burns' inquiry of May 26. Use Ms. Burns' name in the first and third ¶s. Send the letter by **CERTIFIED MAIL.**

opening lines 37

The answer to your ~~query~~ inquiry of May 24 regarding the estab- 48
lishment of a word processing center is ~~a difficult~~ not an easy one, Mr. 61
Taborski. A ~~thorough~~ complete study and analysis of your operations 73
must be undertaken before we can ~~ascertain~~ determine if word process- 84
ing will pay off for you. 90

If you would like us to make a preliminary survey of your paper 103
problems, we can do so quickly and ~~efficiently~~ inexpensively. This survey 115
will provide a basis for determ(in)ing whether it is ~~possible~~ feasible 127
and cost effective to consider ~~setting up~~ establishing word processing in 139
your organization. 143

Please call me at 555-6300, Mr. Taborski, and we will arrange to have 157
one of our expert teams complete the survey of your administrative proce- 172
dures. 173

closing lines 186

5 Set line-space selector

Set **line-space selector (5)** on "1" to single-space (SS) the lines you are to type in Phase 1 lessons.

When so directed, set on "2" to double-space (DS) or on "3" to triple-space (TS).

Single-spaced (SS) copy has no blank line space between lines; double-spaced (DS) copy has 1 blank line space between lines; triple-spaced (TS) copy has 2 blank line spaces between lines.

```
1 Lines 1 and 2 are single-spaced (SS).
2 A double space (DS) separates Lines 2 and 4.
3             1 blank line space
4 A triple space (TS) separates Lines 4 and 7.
5
6             2 blank line spaces
7 Set the selector on "1" for single spacing.
```

6 Plan and set margin stops

Study the following information, then set margin stops for a 50-space line as directed on page 3 for your typewriter.

Typewriters have at least one **line-of-writing scale (22)** that reads from 0 to *at least* 110 for machines with *elite* type, from 0 to *at least* 90 for machines with *pica* type.

The spaces on the line-of-writing scale are matched to the spacing of the letters on the typewriter—elite or pica, as shown above right.

When 8½- by 11-inch paper is inserted into the typewriter (short side up) with left edge of paper at 0 on the line-of-writing scale, the exact center point is 51 for elite, 42½ for pica machines. Use 51 for elite, 42 for pica center.

To have typed material centered horizontally, set left and right margin stops the same number of spaces from center point of paper (51, elite center; 42 pica center).

A warning bell on the typewriter rings 6 to 11 or more spaces before the right margin stop is reached, so add 3 to 7 spaces (usually 5) before setting right margin stop.

The diagrams at right indicate margin stop settings for 50-, 60-, and 70-space lines, assuming the paper is inserted with the left edge at 0 on the line-of-writing scale and that 5 spaces are added to right margin for ringing of the bell.

```
You can type 12 elite characters in a horizontal inch. (2.54 centimeters)
You can type 10 pica characters in a horizontal inch.
```

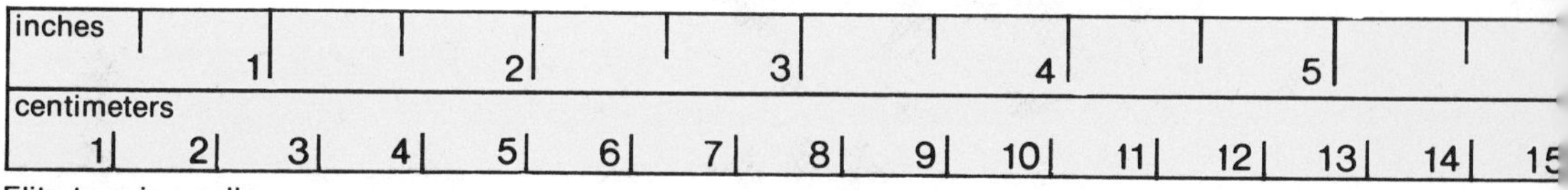

Elite type is smaller than pica type. As a result, there are 12 elite spaces but only 10 pica spaces to an inch.

Elite center

Pica center

Elite

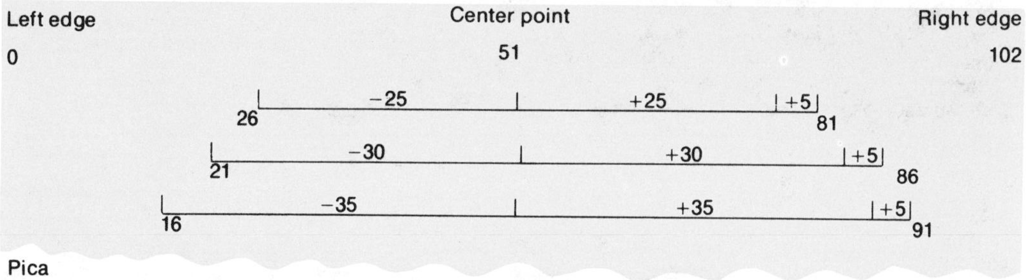

Pica

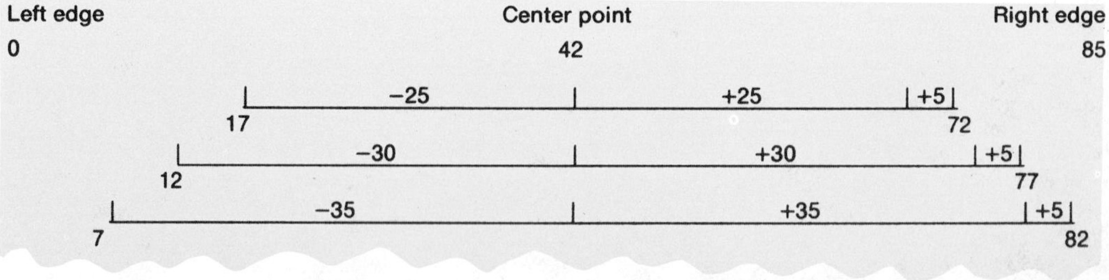

299b ▶ 45
Measure production skill: reports

1. Type the problems at the right, on page 458, and at the top of page 459 for 30′; correct errors as you type. If you finish before time is called, start over.

2. After time is called, go over each page carefully and circle any errors you did not correct. Compute *o-pram*. Compare score with that attained on 228b, page 363.

Problem 1
Unbound report with side headings and footnote
2 full sheets

Use as a main heading: **EVALUATING EMPLOYEE PERFORMANCE;** as a secondary heading: **Criteria of a Formal Employee Evaluation Program.** The quote is from **Herbert J. Chruden and Arthur W. Sherman, Jr., Personnel Management, 6th ed. (Cincinnati: South-Western Publishing Co., 1980), p. 228.** Type the footnote so that it will be 1" from the bottom of the page.

words
headings 16

There should be no ~~question~~ debate about whether or not to ~~rate~~ evaluate 28
employees on their job performances. As Chruden and Sherman say, "Performance evaluation 46
occurs whether or not there is a formal evaluation program. . . . 59
Superiors are constantly observing the manner in which subordi- 72
nates carry out their assignments and forming impressions as to 85
their relative worth to the organization."[1] The only problem to 98
be resolved is the specific kind of evaluation program to be adopted by an organization. 116

In establishing a formal evaluation program, there are certain 128
general criteria that should be ~~applied~~ followed: 137

The Rater and the Ratee 146

The purpose of the program must be clearly established, 157
thoroughly understood, and fully accepted by ~~all~~ the raters and the ratees. Raters must 174
be taught how to do a good job of making accurate ratings, and at least 189
two raters should ~~rate~~ evaluate an ~~individual~~ employee. 197

The Rating Form 203

The form should be so constructed that ratings can be made 215
easily and ~~quickly~~ with a minimum of time. All instructions must be written so that 230
they are easy to understand and free from ambiguity. Every effort must be made to minimize the "halo effect." 253

Only those traits should be ~~found~~ included on a rating form that 265
cannot be measured by objective means. Further, each trait must 278
be defined in terms that leave nothing to the ~~individual~~ personal interpre- 290
tation of the rater. The degrees of excellence for each trait 303
must be defined carefully so that raters will apply them uniformly 316
to all ratees. Such terms as "average," "good," and "poor" ~~etc.,~~ 328
must be avoided since they are ~~open~~ subject to interpretation by each 341
~~individual~~ rater. 343
footnote 373

Problem 2 is on page 458.

❶ Arrange work area

Begin each lesson by arranging your desk or table as shown.

- Typing paper at left of typewriter
- Front frame of typewriter even with front edge of desk.
- Book at right of typewriter; raise top for easy reading.
- Rest of desk clear of unneeded books and other materials.

❷ Adjust paper guide

Move **paper guide (7)** left or right so that it lines up with 0 (zero) on the **paper-bail scale (11)** or the **line-of-writing** or **margin scale (22).**

❸ Adjust ribbon control

Set **ribbon control (31)** to type on top half of ribbon. The ribbon control on some electrics is under the cover (lid).

❹ Insert typing paper

Take a sheet of paper in your left hand and follow the directions and illustrations below.

1. Pull **paper bail (11)** forward (or up on some machines).

2. Place paper against paper guide, behind the **platen (17).**

3. Turn paper into machine, using **right platen knob (20)** or **index key.**

4. Stop when paper is about 1½ inches above **aligning scale (21).**

5. To straighten paper, pull **paper release lever (18)** toward you.

6. Straighten paper, then push paper release lever back.

7. Push paper bail back so that it holds paper against platen.

8. Slide **paper bail rolls (10/14)** into position, dividing paper into thirds.

299b, continued

Problem 2
Leftbound report with indented quotation and footnote
full sheet

1. Use as a heading: **THE "HALO EFFECT" IN RATING EMPLOYEES;** SS and indent the quotation 5 spaces from side margins.

2. The quote is from **B. Lewis Keeling, Norman F. Kallaus, and John J. W. Neunder, <u>Administrative Office Management</u>, 7th ed. (Cincinnati: South-Western Publishing Co., 1978), p. 702.** Type the footnote so that it will be 1" from the bottom of the page.

Problem 3 is on page 459.

words
heading 8

Forms used by employers to rate employees usually include 19
a number of characteristics or factors that are considered 31
essential to success on the job. Among these characteristics 43
may be such traits as dependability, appearance, initiative, 56
and personality. These factors are usually measured on a 67
scale ranging in degree from "low" to "high." 77

The "halo effect" is the tendency of a rater to rate a 88
person "high" on <u>all</u> factors because that person is out- 99
standing in one characteristic. An employee, for example, 111
may have a pleasing personality that impresses the rater 122
and colors his or her judgment in rating all other factors. 134
The opposite may be true, of course, and a person may be 146
rated "low" overall because of one poor trait. In this case, 158
the influence on the rater might be called the "pitchfork 170
effect." 171

Under some rating systems, an effort is made to offset 182
the "halo" and "pitchfork" effects by requiring raters to 194
justify, in writing, ratings which are consistently high or 206
consistently low. Keeling, Kallaus, and Neunder suggest that: 219

To provide for a less biased evaluation by the rater, 229
it is suggested that the form be arranged so that, for some 241
factors, the highest rating degree appears first, and, for 253
others, the highest rating degree appears last. Alternating 265
. . . the order of the degrees requires the evaluator to 277
make an individual appraisal of each employee.[1] 286

footnote 329

Margin stops

Type A

Push-button set

Adler, Olympia, Remington, Royal 700/870 manuals, Smith–Corona

1. Press down on the left margin set button.

2. Slide it to desired position on the line–of–writing (margin) scale.

3. Release the margin set button.

4. Using the right margin set button, set the right margin stop in the same way.

Type B

Push-lever set

Single element typewriters, such as Adler, Olivetti, Remington Rand, Royal, Selectric

1. Push in on the left margin set lever.

2. Slide it to desired position on the line–of–writing (margin) scale.

3. Release the margin set lever.

4. Using the right margin set lever, set the right margin stop in the same way.

Type C

Magic margin set

Royal 470/560/970

1. Pull left magic margin lever forward.

2. Move carriage to desired position on the line–of–writing (margin) scale.

3. Release the left margin lever.

4. Using the right magic margin lever, set the right margin stop in the same way.

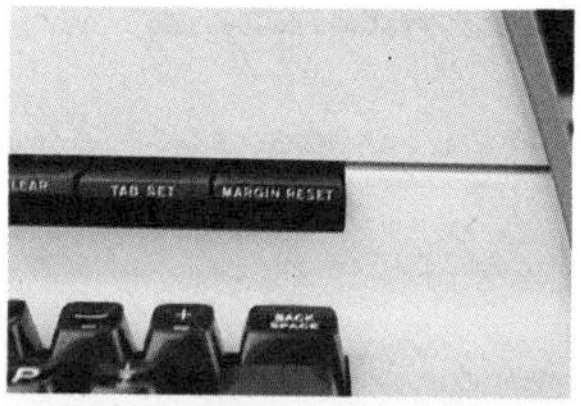

Type D

Key set

IBM typebar, Olivetti electric

1. Move carriage to the left margin stop by depressing the return key.

2. Depress and hold down the margin set (IBM reset) key as you move carriage to desired left margin stop position.

3. Release the margin set (IBM reset) key.

4. Move carriage to the right margin stop.

5. Depress and hold down the margin set (IBM reset) key as you move carriage to desired right margin stop position.

6. Release the margin set (IBM reset) key.

Type E

Lever-arrow set

Olivetti manual

If margin stop is to be moved inward:

1. Move carriage to desired position.

2. Pull appropriate margin lever forward.

If margin stop is to be moved outward:

1. Move carriage to existing margin stop.

2. Move appropriate margin lever forward and hold it in the forward position.

3. Depress carriage release button and move the carriage to desired position.

4. Release margin lever.

Tabulator stops

To clear tab stops

1. Move carriage to extreme *left* (or carrier to extreme *right*).

2. Depress **tab clear (33)** and hold it down as you return carriage to extreme right (or carrier to extreme left) to remove all tab stops.

To set tab stops

Move the carriage (carrier) to the desired position; then depress the **tab set (25).** Repeat this procedure for each stop needed.

Tabulating technique

Electric (and some manuals): Tap lightly the **tab key (24)** [nearer little finger] or **bar** [index finger]; return the finger to home–key position at once.

Manual: Depress and hold down the **tabulator bar (24)** [right index finger] or **key** [nearer little finger] until the carriage has stopped.

General information for setting margin and tabulator stops is given here. If you have the manufacturer's booklet for your typewriter, however, use it; the procedure for your particular model may be slightly different.

299b, continued

Problem 3
Financial report
full sheet
Type the report as a topbound manuscript. DS and indent the financial highlights 5 spaces from side margins.

words

INFORMATION TECHNOLOGIES, INC. 6

Financial Highlights for Fiscal Year Ended June 30, 19-- 18

This fiscal year was the fifth consecutive year of record- 29
breaking operations. The following financial highlights vividly 42
illustrate the success we achieved: 50

		words
Revenues	$295,399,433	63
Net Income	$ 26,585,950	77
Net Income as a Percent of Revenues	9%	90
Earnings Per Share	$1.95	103
Dividends Paid Per Share	$ .51	116
Shareholders' Equity	$150,000,000	129
Percent of Return on Shareholders' Equity	17.7%	142

300b ▶ 45
Measure production skill: forms and tables

1. Type the problems at the right and on page 460 for 30′; correct errors as you type.
2. After time is called, go over each page carefully and circle any errors you did not correct. Compute *o-pram*. Compare score with that attained on 229b, page 365.

Problem 1
Purchase order
[LM p. 219]

PURCHASE ORDER NO. 7032B 1

TO: Capital Equipment, Inc. — DATE July 26, 19-- 9
52 West Broad Street 13
Columbus, OH 43215-9084 — TERMS Net 19

SHIP VIA COHO Van Lines 22

QUANTITY	CAT. NO.	DESCRIPTION	PRICE	TOTAL	
6	161-072	Desks, executive, 60″ × 30″	227.00	1,362.00	33
6	161-412	Chairs, executive, swivel	181.50	1,089.00	43
6	248-305	Bookcases, 31″ × 36″ × 12″	73.85	443.10	53
12	053-972	File cabinets, 4-drawer, legal	145.80	1,749.60	65
36	474-280	Waste containers, steel, 18″ ×			73
		38 1/2″, walnut	131.75	4,743.00	81
				9,386.70	83

Problem 2
Invoice [LM p. 219]

DATE August 23, 19-- 3

SOLD TO: Gateway Industries, Inc. 8
560 Forbes Avenue — OUR ORDER NO. 522631 13
Pittsburgh, PA 15219-6066 18
CUST. ORDER NO. 7829M 20

TERMS: Net — SHIPPED VIA Special Messenger 24

QUANTITY	DESCRIPTION	UNIT PRICE	TOTAL	
200	Booklets, "Do You Need Word Processing?"	3.75	750.00	36
50	Reports, "Preliminary Survey"	60.00	3,000.00	45
125	Studies, "Productive Employee Evaluation"	29.00	3,625.00	57
12	Studies, "The Feasibility of Automating			67
	Administrative Procedures"	420.00	5,040.00	77
			12,415.00	79

Problems 3, 4, and 5 are on page 460.

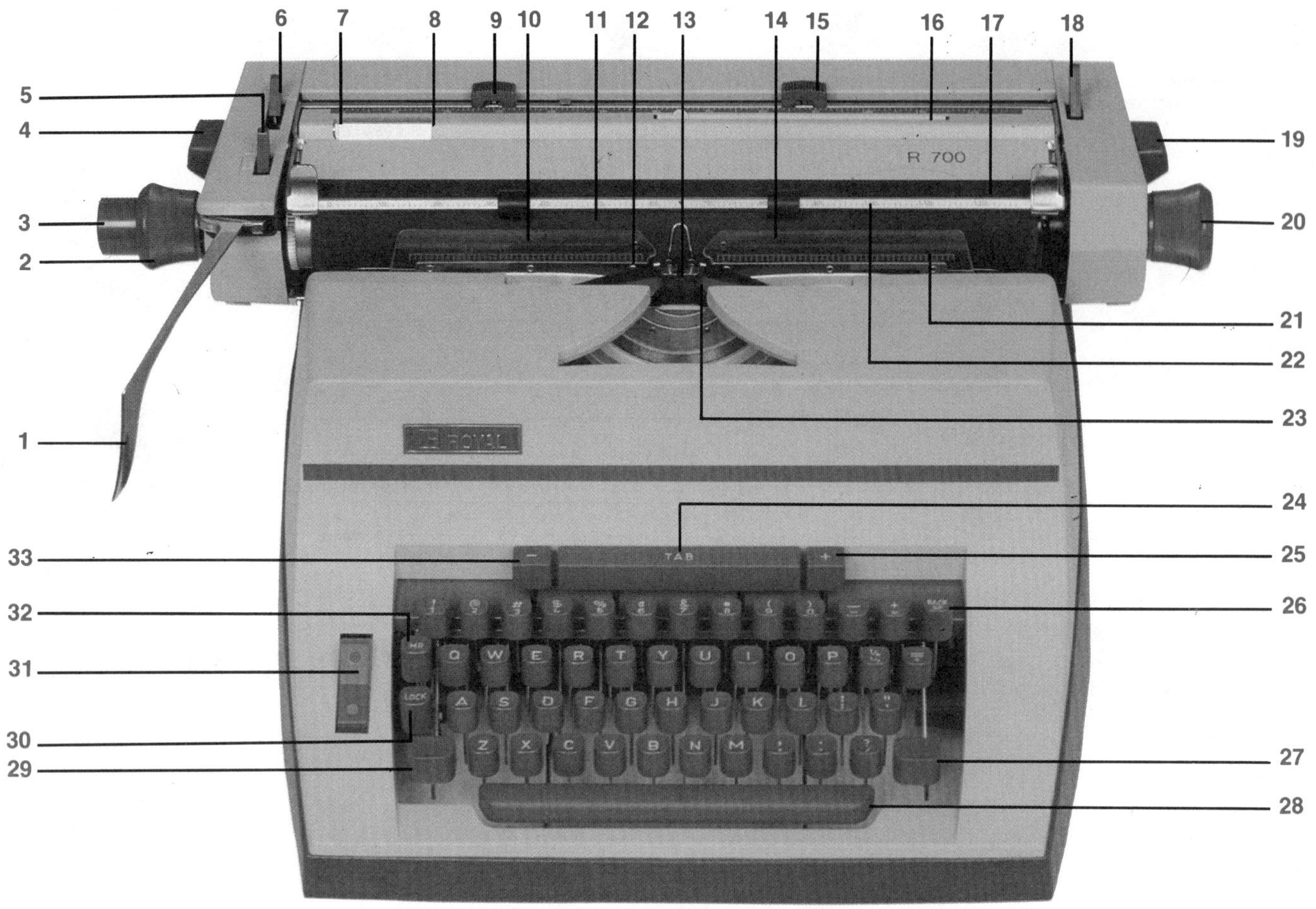

The diagram above shows the parts of a manual (nonelectric) typewriter; the diagram on page 1 shows the parts of an electric typewriter.

Since all typewriters have similar parts, you will probably be able to locate the parts on your typewriter from one of these diagrams. However, use the instructional booklet that comes with your machine if you have it, as it will identify the exact location of each operative part.

1 Carriage return lever: used to return carriage to left margin and to move paper up

2 Left platen knob: used to push carriage to the right

3 Variable line spacer: used to change writing line setting permanently

4 Left carriage release: used to release carriage so it moves freely to left or right

5 Line-space selector: used to move paper up 1, 2, or 3 lines for single, double, or triple spacing

6 Automatic line finder: used to change line spacing temporarily, then refind the line

7 Paper guide: used as a permanent guide for inserting paper

8 Paper guide scale: used to set paper guide at desired position

9 Left margin set: used to set left margin stop

10/14 Paper bail rolls: used to hold paper against platen

11 Paper bail: used to hold paper against platen

12 Card/envelope holders: used to hold cards, labels, and envelopes against platen

13 Printing point indicator: used to position carriage at desired point

14 (See 10)

15 Right margin set: used to set right margin stop

16 Paper table: supports paper when it is in typewriter

17 Platen (cylinder): provides a hard surface against which typebars strike

18 Paper release lever: used to allow paper to be removed or aligned

19 Right carriage release: used to release carriage so it moves freely to left or right

20 Right platen knob: used to turn platen as paper is being inserted

21 Aligning scale: used to align copy that has been reinserted

22 Line-of-writing (margin) scale: used when setting margin and tab stops and in horizontal centering

23 Ribbon carrier: positions and controls ribbon

24 Tabulator: used to move carriage to tab stops that have been set

25 Tab set: used to set tabulator stops

26 Backspace key: used to move printing point to left, one space at a time

27 Right shift key: used to type capitals of letter keys controlled by left hand

28 Space bar: used to move printing point to right, one space at a time

29 Left shift key: used to type capitals of letter keys controlled by right hand

30 Shift lock: used to lock shift mechanism so that all letters are capped

31 Ribbon control: used to select ribbon typing position

32 Margin release key: used to move carriage beyond margin stops

33 Tab clear: used to clear tabulator stops

300b, continued

words

Problem 3
Table
full sheet; reading position; DS items

INFORMATION TECHNOLOGIES, INC. 6

Correspondence Center 11

Summary of Production for Week Ended September 6, 19-- 22

Number	Name	Total Lines	Total Minutes	words
				36
151-01-3521	Susanne Bertrum	4,915	2,240	44
235-06-9905	Martin Bierman	4,750	2,102	52
247-03-1021	Larry Ciccone	4,326	2,080	60
266-07-4932	Lydia Parkinson	4,810	2,248	68
275-04-6713	Mildred Robinson	4,528	2,119	76
290-01-4433	Dean Marks	4,215	1,973	83
301-04-5802	Mary Bethune	4,729	2,200	90
362-05-7091	Cynthia Zimmerman	4,973	2,313	99
570-02-4681	James Taylor	4,770	2,178	106
665-03-5518	Theresa Marziotti	4,095	2,037	115
690-08-2141	William Deemer	4,651	2,194	122
695-08-9456	Gloria Thompson	4,428	2,109	130

Problem 4
Table
full sheet; reading position

Problem 5
Retype Problem 3; SS columnar items.

THE JOB OUTLOOK FOR SELECTED CLERICAL OCCUPATIONS 10

Occupation	Average Annual Openings 1978-1990	Employment Prospects	words
			18, 32
Bookkeeping workers	96,000	Employment expected to grow more slowly than average due to increasing use of bookkeeping machines and computers.	41, 47, 51, 56, 61
Office machine operators	9,700	Employment is expected to grow about as fast as average.	68, 74, 78
Secretaries and stenographers	305,000	Skilled persons seeking secretarial positions should find numerous opportunities.	89, 96, 102, 105
Typists	59,000	Good opportunities expected as business expansion increases the amount of paperwork and replacement needs remain high.	112, 118, 123, 128, 133

137

Source: Thomas Nardone, "The Job Outlook in Brief," Occupational Outlook Quarterly (Spring 1980), pp. 6-21. 150 165

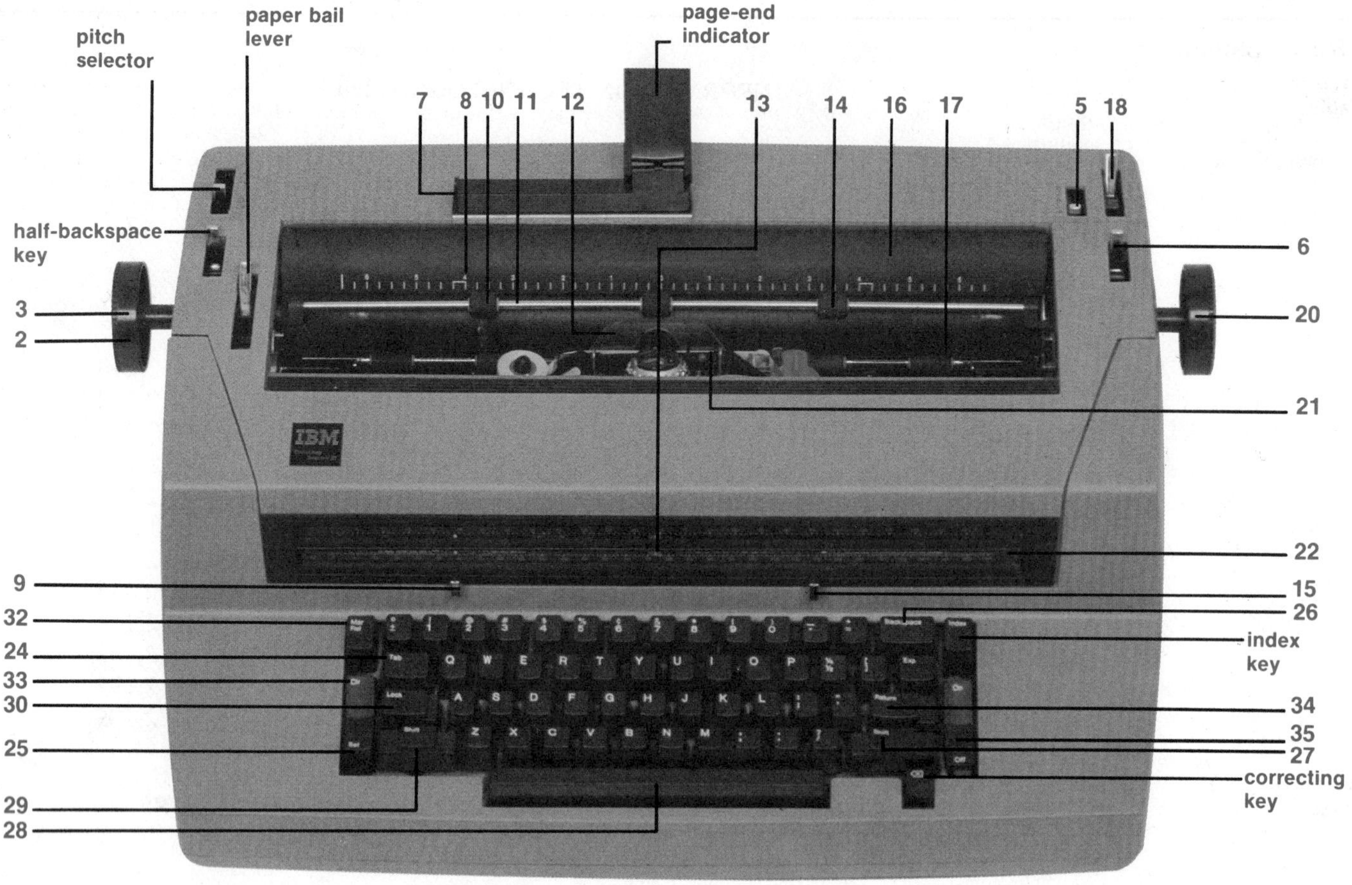

The diagram above shows the parts of an electric typewriter; the diagram on page 2 shows the parts of a manual (nonelectric) typewriter.

Since all typewriters have similar parts, you will probably be able to locate the parts on your typewriter from one of these diagrams. However, use the instructional booklet that comes with your machine if you have it, as it will identify the exact location of each operative part.

1 Carriage return lever (not on electric)

2 Left platen knob: used to push carriage to right (except on single element typewriters—Adler, Olivetti, Olympia, Royal, Selectric, and Remington Rand)

3 Variable line spacer: used to change writing line setting permanently

4 Left carriage release: used to release carriage so it moves freely to left or right (except on single element typewriters)

5 Line–space selector: used to move paper up 1, 2, or 3 lines for single, double, or triple spacing

6 Automatic line finder: used to change line spacing temporarily, then refind the line

7 Paper guide: used as a permanent guide for inserting paper

8 Paper guide scale: used to set paper guide at desired position

9 Left margin set: used to set left margin stop

10/14 Paper bail rolls: used to hold paper against platen

11 Paper bail: used to hold paper against platen

12 Card/envelope holders: used to hold cards, labels, and envelopes against platen

13 Printing point indicator: used to position carriage (or element carrier) at desired point

14 (See 10)

15 Right margin set: used to set right margin stop

16 Paper table: supports paper when it is in typewriter

17 Platen (cylinder): provides a hard surface against which type element or bars strike

18 Paper release lever: used to allow paper to be removed or aligned

19 Right carriage release: used to release carriage so it moves freely to left or right (except on single element typewriters)

20 Right platen knob: used to turn platen as paper is being inserted

21 Aligning scale: used to align copy that has been reinserted

22 Line–of–writing (margin) scale: used when setting margin and tab stops and in horizontal centering

23 Ribbon carrier: positions and controls ribbon at printing point (not shown—under the cover)

24 Tabulator: used to move carriage (carrier) to tab stops

25 Tab set: used to set tabulator stops

26 Backspace key: used to move printing point to left, one space at a time

27 Right shift key: used to type capitals of letter keys controlled by left hand

28 Space bar: used to move printing point to right, one space at a time

29 Left shift key: used to type capitals of letter keys controlled by right hand

30 Shift lock: used to lock shift mechanism so that all letters are capped

31 Ribbon control: used to select ribbon typing position (not shown—under cover)

32 Margin release key: used to move carriage (carrier) beyond margin stops

33 Tab clear: used to clear tab stops

34 Carriage return key: used to return carriage to left margin and to move paper up

35 ON/OFF control: used to turn electric typewriters on or off

Know your typewriter; electric